HIGH STAKES

Where the Cold War started? The German V2 was the first high speed
ballistic missile capable of carrying a heavy warhead and against which
there was no defence.
(Courtesy Deutsches Museum, München. Image BN_38439)

This book is dedicated to all airmen and airwomen
of the British armed services who gave their lives,
or suffered privations, through the many operations described within.

HIGH STAKES

Britain's Air Arms in Action 1945–1990

by
Vic Flintham

Pen & Sword
AVIATION

First published in Great Britain in 2009 by
Pen & Sword Aviation
an imprint of
Pen & Sword Books Ltd
47 Church Street
Barnsley
South Yorkshire
S70 2AS

ISBN 978 1 84415 815 7

A CIP catalogue record for this book is
available from the British Library

Typeset in Sabon by
Phoenix Typesetting, Auldgirth, Dumfriesshire

Printed and bound in Thailand by
Kyodo Nation Printing Services Co., Ltd

Pen & Sword Books Ltd incorporates the Imprints of Pen & Sword Aviation, Pen & Sword Maritime,
Pen & Sword Military, Wharncliffe Local History,
Pen & Sword Select, Pen & Sword Military Classics and Leo Cooper.

For a complete list of Pen & Sword titles please contact
PEN & SWORD BOOKS LIMITED
47 Church Street, Barnsley, South Yorkshire, S70 2AS, England
E-mail: enquiries@pen-and-sword.co.uk
Website: www.pen-and-sword.co.uk

Contents

Acknowledgements

Preparation of this book has been a largely solitary exercise, drawing on my own research and a number of reliable published sources. However, the following have helped with answers to queries or have helped with photographs: Kev Darling, Mike Draper, Peter Green, Bill Hartree, Lee Howard and Graham Pitchfork. My editor, Peter Coles, has been his usual professional self, and I have no doubt that he will turn my text into a book of quality, at least in terms of presentation – content is my responsibility alone! Special thanks also go to my writing chum Andy Thomas, always happy to point me towards contacts and generous to a fault in the supply of photographs where I have gaps.

In the 1950s the artist Russell Flint was asked how he could justify the £800 price tag on one of his landscapes. 'How long did it take you to paint?' enquired the American lady potential buyer. 'A lifetime' was the instant response. It has sometimes felt that the present volume has taken a lifetime in the accumulation of data and the sifting of facts. My interest in aviation and flying has cut into family life over many years, and therefore I should like to acknowledge the support and patience of my family and friends and the singular debt I owe them, especially my mother, my wife Christine who drew the maps and our children, Gael and Neil.

Vic Flintham
Braughing
March 2008

Preface

For many years I have been persuaded to write an update of my first book, *Air Wars and Aircraft*, published in 1988. However, that book took me many years of preparation and writing, and since then much has come to light and many more conflicts have erupted. I now believe that a comprehensive volume on all post-war wars involving aircraft is beyond the capacity of one author.

However, I have kept careful records of actions involving British military aircraft and units, and felt that a thorough description of actions through the post-war years 1945 to 1990, embracing the Cold War, was feasible. My publisher agreed. In parts the present book is an update of the first, with new information, more precise dates and some amendments. There are, however, new chapters, including those on the nuclear deterrent and humanitarian aid, at which the British armed services are singularly good.

Although it was an apparently passive and reactive function, I decided to include the nuclear deterrent because it was operational, and as far as anyone can tell, it worked. Certainly, having lived through the Cold War, I felt happier having the V-force, although my researches suggest that it was barely independent.

On the strength of the first book I undertook a short-term but well-paid research contract which enabled me to learn to fly. At the time of writing I have accumulated several hundred hours in the relatively tame and at least forecastable climate of northern Europe, and this has given me great respect for the many unsung crews of aircraft supplying aid or evacuation throughout the world. This is often in the most trying conditions, requiring fine flying skills and expert navigation. This work is as operational in today's society as any amount of bombing.

In general I have concentrated on the involvement of British air arms, but have included reference to both allied and enemy air arms as appropriate. Thus in respect of the Netherlands East Indies I have included the handful of Dutch units involved at the time, but in respect of Korea I have confined the listings to British units. (For those wanting full listings of all foreign units for actions to 1988, my first book remains easy to find in its US edition.)

In constructing the book I have tried to work the chapters broadly chronologically, grouping similar actions. I have tried to describe operations in a political context and have concentrated on actions rather than personalities. The reasons for this are twofold. First, I had space considerations, and had I mentioned any one personality, it would have been invidious not to have mentioned them all. The exceptions to the rule are the main political players. The second reason is that personal exploits are widely covered elsewhere. There is a third, rather feeble reason, but one that will increasingly inhibit authors, and that is the risk of litigation through inadvertent or implied defamation.

With places, as opposed to people, I have included all relevant references. In respect of place names, because these are usually anglicised versions of spoken names I have tried to use contemporaneous spellings throughout. While this should appeal to those who were there, it can make it difficult to locate them on current maps, typically in Arabia. The trick here is to say the name and then read aloud from a current map anything that might sound similar. It works!

This book is essentially a collation. I have undertaken much basic research on my own account, but have also drawn heavily on the work of a number of British writer/researchers, whose thoroughness and reliability are second to none. Where there are gaps, I have been prepared to draw on less reliable reports, clearly indicated as such. I have also been prepared to speculate based on my knowledge of politics and the way things work.

I should say at this juncture that I am not a conspiracy theorist; in my experience, nine out of ten cock-ups are just that. There are a few areas of high sensitivity and I have trodden a careful line between describing what is clearly in the public interest and keeping secret that which would be helpful to our enemies. Some of what is written elsewhere about certain sensitive current activities is either misinformation or disinformation, and I am not prepared either to repeat it or to speculate on my own account.

In writing I have tried to be non-partisan. The work is about all British air arms, not just the RAF. I have tried to remain domestically apolitical and also non-judgemental about those with whom and against whom we fought.

I have even tried to be objective in relation to the United States of America, although as the years go by and the more I research, the less I am inclined to feel comfortable with the so-called 'special relationship', which is so demonstrably one-sided.

Indeed, I started writing this book believing that it would be about Britain and the air arms of her military services. As work progressed, it became clear that the story was inevitably as much to do with Anglo-American relations at every level. To say that these relationships are complex is an understatement. The intelligence agencies seem often to work outside the direction of government, while liaison between each of the armed services of the two countries appears often to work better than national relationships between the services.

Despite many years of searching I have still to find the legal basis for US bases in the United Kingdom, and the freedom with which they may be used. The attack on Libya from East Anglia and the Cotswolds in 1986 may or may not have required permission from the UK Government.

One thing that my research has led me to appreciate is the surprise factor in so many conflicts. Looking to the future I shall not be surprised to see Europe and China at war with the United States within thirty years as oil reserves begin to run out.

At the time of writing, morale in the services has probably never been lower since the Battle of Hastings. Battalions are reduced in size, and depleted in respect of equipment, and even trials units are now given RAF squadron numbers in a deceit which fools no one. There is a limited manufacturing and design base, and arguably the Eurofighter Typhoon is not the aircraft needed for the sort of warfare for which the country needs to prepare. Further, getting into bed with the United States in respect of the Joint Strike Fighter will turn into a folly of enormous proportions if post-war history is anything to go by.

For the future, Britain is probably best advised to secure simple and reliable combat aircraft, portable support like radars and communications equipment, a good balance of modern transports and refuellers, intelligence collectors and disseminators, and aircraft carriers plus the aircraft to use from them. (The effective role of carriers is a recurring theme in the conflicts described.) Collaboration with Europe is probably more promising than across the Atlantic. Concentration on special forces and intelligence may be more fruitful than expensive white elephants, and for the future could be one of several unique contributions to legitimate collaborative ventures.

Prologue

The defining moment of the twentieth century was 08.15.11 hrs on Monday 6 August 1945. At that time Colonel Paul Tibbets, commander of the USAAF's 509th Composite Group, released the *Little Boy* atomic bomb, armed with uranium 235, over Hiroshima in southern Japan. He had taken off from Tinian Island in B-29 44-86292/82 *Enola Gay* of 393 Composite Squadron at 02.45 preceded by three weather reconnaissance aircraft, and there had been no recall. The 12.5-kiloton weapon, released at 31,600 feet, exploded at 1,850 feet over the city fifty-one seconds later, killing an estimated 70,000 people instantly and injuring a further 70,000.

At the Potsdam conference on 26 July the Allies had called for Japanese surrender against the threat of '. . . prompt and utter destruction'. Joseph Stalin, the Soviet leader, was advised by American President Harry Truman simply that the Americans '... had a new weapon of special destructive force'. Through spies engaged in the development of the atomic bomb, especially Klaus Fuchs, Stalin was already well aware by July 1945 that the Americans had constructed the new weapon, and probably that by then the first had been tested. What Stalin would not have known – and could probably not have imagined – was that the order to use an atomic bomb against Japan had been given by Truman the previous day.

At that time the Soviet Union enjoyed a non-aggression pact with Japan, and it was known by the Western Allies that Japan was seeking help with securing peace through channels with Moscow. It seems, therefore, that the Japanese Government might have had some idea of a potential attack and the broad nature of that attack. It could be argued that it would be ready with a response.

The immediate devastation was such that news of what had occurred at Hiroshima was slow to reach Tokyo, just 430 miles away. Total power failure and the loss of all forms of communication other than personal attendance, coupled with lack of Japanese experience of the weapon, meant that two days later there was still limited appreciation of the disaster. The Americans had tested the first bomb, codenamed *Trinity*, at Alamogordo Air Base, New Mexico, on 16 July 1945, just three weeks earlier. It seems difficult to believe that they would not have appreciated the confusion of the aftermath.

If the Japanese had ignored or overlooked the signals of impending atomic disaster prior to the Hiroshima attack, they should have been under no illusions in the immediate aftermath. Late on 6 August, in a press statement, President Truman announced that the destruction of Hiroshima had been the result of an atomic bomb, and he gave broad details of the background to development.

Without giving time for a considered Japanese response to the attack on Hiroshima, a second weapon, this time a plutonium implosion bomb, *Fat Man*, was dropped on Nagasaki. The pilot was Major Charles W. Sweeney, who had flown one of the accompanying B-29s on the Hiroshima raid, flying B-29 44-27297/77 *Bockscar*, again from Tinian in the Marianas. The 22-kiloton weapon created a greater impact than that at Hiroshima but with less follow-through firestorm. This time the death toll was 36,000, with 40,000 injured; Nagasaki had a lower population density in the area where the bomb fell.

There has been continuing controversy about the scale of destruction, both in terms of deaths and injuries at the time and in respect of post-war deaths through exposure to radiation. The figures given here are conservative approximations. For the purpose of this narrative the exact numbers are irrelevant: the scale of destruction was overwhelming. The two nuclear raids caused 3% of deaths through strategic bombing of Japan in just a year. In a conventional firebomb raid on Tokyo on 9 March 1945, for instance, an estimated 83,000 were killed and 102,000 injured.

Since the Japanese had stoically endured great loss of life and destruction through conventional bombing, it must be assumed that the Hiroshima bomb was intended to force an early conclusion to the war while giving the Japanese the opportunity of saving face. If that is so, it is difficult to see why a second weapon was dropped so quickly after the first; unless, of course, the intention was to make broader statements, especially to the Soviet Union.

The targets for the nuclear attacks had been carefully chosen by a target committee set up in April 1945. Tokyo was ruled out because of the risk of inciting the Japanese to even greater commitment to defence if the Emperor were to be killed or injured. The ancient capital Kyoto was ruled out through concern for its historical importance and the risk of deep-seated post-war anti-American feeling. Other possible targets were dismissed because of the need to test the new weapons on areas hitherto relatively untouched in order to be able to assess the full extent of the damage, which could only be extrapolated from the *Trinity* test.

The targets eventually selected were Hiroshima, Kokura, Nagasaki and Niigata, in that order of priority, although the last was removed from the list because of the distance involved. Kokura was the intended second target, but in the event it was obscured by cloud, leaving Nagasaki as the back-up. This was less satisfactory for the scientists, who wanted to observe the full effects of the plutonium weapon, since Nagasaki was already partially damaged through five previous conventional bombing raids.

The Japanese accepted surrender terms on 10 August, subject to the future status of the Emperor Hirohito, and the war came to an end on 15 August 1945. On 14 August, in order to maintain pressure, there were further extensive conventional bombing raids, and it has been suggested that if a third nuclear bomb had been available it would have been used. The Soviet Union abrogated the non-aggression pact with Japan on 9 August and entered the war in the East at the eleventh hour. They quickly invaded Manchuria and by the end of the war also occupied North Korea.

The full significance of the events of 6 August 1945 are that a nation at war developed and produced a weapon of hitherto unthinkable destructive power *and* demonstrated that it had the will to use it. Three days later the second attack reinforced American determination.

There are two essential prerequisites of all negotiation. The first is that either party must be in a position to apply sanctions if the outcome to negotiations is not to their liking. The second, often overlooked, prerequisite is that each party must perceive that the other has the will to apply those sanctions. With the Hiroshima bomb the United States demonstrated beyond doubt the scale of its sanction and its will to apply it. The importance of the event in shaping relations between America and the Soviet Union in subsequent years cannot be understated – indeed, before Potsdam and the *Trinity* test, President Truman had said of the Soviet Union, 'If the bomb explodes I'll certainly have a hammer on those boys.'

The question remains why the United States dropped not just one, but two, nuclear weapons on Japan. It is not easy to say with confidence precisely how many objectives dropping the first bomb was intended to achieve, but there were certainly more than one.

The Americans were becoming increasingly concerned about the cost in human terms of a war against a fanatical enemy who culturally could not accept defeat. An island-hopping campaign leading eventually to occupation of the homeland would have led to horrendous casualties. The battle for Okinawa, for example, was the most costly of the war; on 6 April 1945 alone some 350 suicide bombers were launched from Kyushu against the US Fleet. During the battle thirty-eight vessels were sunk and 368 damaged. The ground battle was equally murderous, with 20,195 Americans killed and 55,162 wounded. Applied pressure on the Japanese homeland coupled with the grounds for an acceptable and face-saving surrender seemed the only way forward.

The war was expensive in economic terms. The Allies were tired after, for the British and Commonwealth forces, six continuous years of fighting on multiple fronts and with extended supply lines. Britain was bankrupt, the industries of much of Europe and the Far East had been comprehensively destroyed by bombing, and with the war in Europe ended the Americans were tired and there were home demands for a quick end to the war.

Early conclusion to the war in the East would have pre-empted Soviet involvement in any settlement. In the event the Soviet Union managed to scrape into the war with Japan several days before the inevitable surrender, and in the process secured important footholds.

A separate reason for dropping the bomb was to impress on the Soviet Union American will. The potential for future conflict between the Western Allies and the Soviet Union was already clear. President Truman had alluded to the atom bomb at Potsdam unaware that Stalin already knew much more through spies, but it was essential to give a lesson in the application of power to whoever might be interested in learning.

The bomb had been developed within a huge research and development budget estimated at $2 billion from 1941. It could have been felt that one test was insufficient return on the investment and that since a further two bombs had been constructed they ought to be used.

Although it had been tested in one form, the bomb could be tested in all its variations. There was every justification for making the tests in an operational setting if they could achieve wider objectives. It seems that a majority of scientists favoured use of the bomb in support of war goals in the Far East, even though those goals were different from those for which the bomb had originally been developed. Careful selection of target sites which had been preserved from conventional bombing and where the surrounding hills acted to focus the blast effect confirms the test status of the Hiroshima and Nagasaki bombs.

What was to become the Manhattan Project within which the atomic bomb had been developed was started in 1941, employing a number of European and North American scientists and based in the United States. The sole purpose of tackling the vast problems involved was to ensure that the Allies maintained a lead over potential German development. In other words, from the outset the bomb would have been intended primarily as a deterrent. Given the geography of Europe it is difficult to imagine that Britain and the occupied Allies would have agreed to a weapon of fearsome but unknown potential being used over Germany.

It has been argued that President Truman was not fully aware of the destructive power of the weapon, perhaps seeing it as simply a big brother to the British 22,000 lb Grand Slam Torpex bomb. Up to the *Trinity* test no one could be confident about the behaviour of the bomb, and that test took place after Truman had set sail for Europe and Potsdam. The project was under military control, and if the generals were minded to use the bomb it would not have been in their interest to have stressed its force and residual problems like radioactive fallout. Truman, after all, had only assumed the presidential mantle on 12 April 1945 on the death of Roosevelt, whose vice-president he had been. The atom bomb would have been only one of many dilemmas confronting the new President.

Finally, there *may* have been an inevitability about the use of the bomb: it was used simply because it *could* be used. Put another way, there was a momentum leading to the ultimate test.

As to the moral issues which might have affected the decision, any American perspective would have encouraged rather than discouraged use of the atomic bomb against the Japanese. The latter were not signatories to the Geneva Accord and had an appalling record of torture and killing prisoners of war. It appears from the evidence that as a nation the United States saw non-Caucasians as inferior – their own armed services were segregated throughout the war, and in the nineteenth century they had butchered many native American Indians. In Europe the Allies were inured to the idea of indiscriminate bombing of civilians, as Rotterdam, then Hamburg, then London (V-weapon attacks), then Dresden had been subject to aerial bombardment.

The second bomb may have been dropped to put greater pressure on the Japanese, to prevent further Soviet territorial gains before the war's end or to test the plutonium weapon. Although the Allies had called for *unconditional* Japanese surrender, in the event one condition was agreed – sovereignty of the Emperor was retained. There is every probability that this outcome could have been secured through negotiation in May 1945.

The scene was finally set for post-war world relations between the Superpowers. The Cold-War was beginning, and over the next two or three years both major players changed the world map as they imposed their influence and will on others through a range of devices, more or less democratically.

At the end of the war the Western Allies had large fleets of strategic bombers, whereas the Soviet Union, Japan and Germany had essentially tactical or defensive aircraft. However, the last-named had a weapon of greater significance for the future and one which was to be secured – with the supporting expertise and technology – by both Superpowers. This was the A-4 ballistic missile.

From early civil beginnings on rocket research in the 1920s, Germany was ready to launch the first A-4 ballistic missile, popularly known as the V-2 (*Vergeltungs-Waffe 2*, or Revenge Weapon 2), by 1942. The first successful launch was from Peenemunde on 16 August of that year, and full-scale production was ordered for use against London. By the time the missile was ready for operational use the Allies had invaded continental Europe and the type was used from mobile launch sites in the Netherlands.

The first operational firing of the A-4 was at 08.30 hrs on 8 September 1944. Two rockets were fired from the Hague in the Netherlands against Paris by the experimental and demonstration unit *Lehr und Versuchs Batterie* 444. Later on the same day the first of 1,115 V-2s to reach England between then and 27 March 1945 was fired against London. A total of 1,712 was successfully fired against Antwerp, which was the main Allied port installation supplying the occupying armies. Of an order for 12,000 missiles, in excess of 6,500 V-2s were produced at the rate of 600 a month at Nordhausen. Unit cost was £12,000.

The A-4 was probably the most important vehicle of war to be developed and used operationally during the twentieth century. By 1944 the United Kingdom was protected by the most comprehensive and sophisticated air defence system possible. Radar, interceptor fighters, anti-aircraft artillery, balloon barrages, searchlights and the Observer Corps worked in concert to prevent assault from the air; so effective was the defence that in the so-called 'baby blitz' of early 1944, Operation *Steinbock*, 71% of the German air fleet of 524 bombers had been destroyed. In June 1944 Germany began an assault on the south-east of England by the unguided pulse-jet-powered 400 mph Fi-103 V-1, the precursor of the cruise missile, otherwise known as the flying-bomb, or 'doodlebug', and code-named *Diver*. Between June 1944 and March 1945 the total number of V-1 launches plotted (including failures) was 9,251, of which the defences accounted for 4,261.

British defences were powerless against a ballistic missile which travelled at 3,600 mph, reaching 60 miles at its apogee. The V-2, referred to in Britain by the code *Big Ben*, defied interception; and although attempts were made to attack mobile launch sites, they failed.

Results of the Allied counter-offensive were poor. In England alone, 2,754 civilians were killed by V-2 rockets, with a further 6,523 injured. Several hundred remain missing to this day. By 7 March 1945 the Germans reported fifty-one rocket troops killed and 117 wounded, and fifty-eight lorries, eleven oxygen trucks and forty-eight missiles damaged in the Netherlands. The cost was high, with typically 933 sorties flown by Fighter Command fighter-bombers in February dropping 192 tons of bombs and expending thousands of rounds of cannon shells.

The victorious Allies were generally not slow to take full advantage of the weapons, research and scientific personnel which fell into their hands. The Americans had removed a hundred complete missiles from the Nordhausen factory for shipping to the US, and the British recovered a considerable number of unassembled rockets.

However, the post-war British Government was not prepared to engage in rocket research with a former enemy. The Americans, on the other hand, had no such qualms about working with German scientists, and their first A-4 firing was in March 1946 at the White Sands range in New Mexico. In contrast, the Russians had fewer 'liberated' scientists available on a voluntary basis, and the first launch of their A-4, designated R-1, was on 18 October 1948 at Kapustin Yar.

Thus, by the end of the war, one of the Allies had developed, tested and used operationally a new weapon of remarkable and terrifying potential. Concurrently, one of the Axis partners had developed, tested and used operationally a means of delivering a warhead which was impervious to any known or perceived means of defence. The Americans had a lead, but not to the extent that they imagined.

British Military Air Power and the Cold War, 1945–90

The period from the end of the Second World War to the break-up of the Soviet Union saw the development of weapons of appalling destructive power. It also witnessed widespread conflict, proxy wars and sabre-rattling between the Superpowers, with each intent on extending its spheres of influence and thus denying power to the other. The culmination of this posturing brought the world very close to a third world war in 1962, but the withdrawal from confrontation led to a reduction in tension, and in the writer's view marked a turning point in the Cold War. From now on, there was the very real prospect of a balance of power and relative security.

The Second World War ended with much of the so-called developed world, apart from the United States, physically or economically in ruins, but with some nations having access to weapons of unprecedented destructive power and effectiveness. From 1945 the future outline shape of Europe and much of the Far East had been determined by negotiation between the potential victors, and for several years after the war boundaries and alliances were consolidated, until by the late 1940s most borders and spheres of influence were set for the foreseeable future.

During the war key representatives of the three major Powers, the United States, Great Britain and the Soviet Union, plus other influential leaders, had met to discuss the prosecution of the war against Germany and Japan. Implicit in a number of early discussions were agreements which would affect the post-war world, while later conferences increasingly turned their attention explicitly to such matters. Through many of these meetings the key actors were Franklin Roosevelt, President of the United States, Winston Churchill, Prime Minister of the United Kingdom and Josef Stalin, leader of the Union of Soviet Socialist Republics.

The first bipartite conference which established lease-lend provision for the Soviet Union from the UK was held in Moscow in September and October 1941. A second Moscow conference was held in August 1942 between Churchill and Stalin, at which it was agreed that a second front would be opened in the West. The first of the intended 'Big Three' conferences was at Casablanca in January 1943, although in the event Stalin declined the offer to attend. At this meeting the broad steps to victory were agreed, including the requirement on Germany of unconditional surrender.

The next meeting was the first Quebec Conference of August 1943 between Roosevelt, Churchill and Mackenzie, the Prime Minister of Canada, which authorised the Allied invasion of France and in terms of post-war matters addressed the future arrangements for producing the atom bomb and the short-term future of Palestine. In October 1943 a further Moscow conference of Allied foreign ministers agreed on a post-war conference to establish a formal United Nations Organization.

The first actual 'Big Three' meeting was at Teheran in late November 1943 to discuss *inter alia* the road to victory over the Third Reich. In terms of post-war influence, Yugoslavia, Turkey, Bulgaria and Iran were discussed.

EUROPE DIVIDED

A second Quebec conference followed in September 1944, again between Roosevelt and Churchill, at which the US/British stance on the partition and future of Germany was agreed in principle. Churchill and Stalin, with senior US representatives, then met in Moscow in October 1944, where they talked about the timing of Soviet entry into the war with Japan and the division of eastern Europe post-war. On a scrap of paper Churchill and Stalin noted the following balance of British/Soviet influence:

Greece	90/10
Romania	10/90
Yugoslavia	50/50
Hungary	50/50
Bulgaria	25/75

The penultimate conference was at Yalta in February 1945, which addressed a number of issues affecting post-war relations. It determined new borders for Poland (which had the effect of shifting the country to the West) and Yugoslavia, and agreed on the partition of Germany. Also discussed, but inconclusively, were Soviet naval access to the Mediterranean via the Dardanelles, the border between Italy and Yugoslavia, and Allied withdrawal from Iran. In the Far East the transfer of northern Japanese Islands to the Soviet Union and support to China were agreed as conditions for the USSR to enter the war against Japan, and Korea was to be divided laterally on the 38th parallel, with Soviet influence to the north and American to the south.

The agreements were consolidated at the final conference at Potsdam in July 1945. Roosevelt had died and been succeeded by Harry Truman, while halfway through the conference Churchill was replaced by Britain's new Labour Prime Minister, Clement Attlee. The Western European nations were to retain national independence; Greece was to remain in the British sphere of influence, while Albania, Romania and Bulgaria were to come under Soviet domination. The boundaries of the central European nations were the subject of dispute until 1947, by which time Poland, Czechoslovakia, Hungary and East Germany were also subject to Soviet influence. Austria and Yugoslavia were able to retain a degree of neutrality.

After six years of war, Europe in 1945 was in turmoil. There was considerable domestic pressure for the return of US personnel home, and within months of the war's end a considerable percentage of forces had departed from Europe. However, even before the war against Germany had ended on 8 May 1945, Greece was struck by civil war, in which British forces, including RAF units, were initially involved.

THE MIDDLE AND FAR EAST

In the Middle East the British retained their mandate over a troubled Palestine and kept their influence and military bases in Iraq. The United States had commercial oil interests in Saudi Arabia; the British in Kuwait and Iran. The French had effectively been relieved of their pre-war responsibilities in Lebanon and Syria. Slightly further afield Italy had lost her north and east African colonies, although otherwise in immediate post-war Africa things were somewhat more ordered.

In India and the Far East the European empires were also showing signs of disintegration. When the Second World War came to an end there were numerous Communist or Nationalist groups which had taken to arms on behalf of the Allies to fight the Japanese during the latter's occupation of the region. These groups then turned their attention either to the spread of Communism or to independence from colonial rule. Throughout the area the United States made little effort to help the colonial Powers to defeat the new threat, being determined to support the dismantling of the European empires.

The British were initially involved in fighting in the Netherlands East Indies in an effort to stabilise the country, primarily to enable the orderly repatriation of Allied prisoners-of-war and internees. The British also occupied Indo-China before handing control to the French. There were early signs of unrest in Malaya, and it was clear that India would secure independence and partition. US Marines were in southern and eastern China, where they initially supported the Nationalist forces in the civil war.

THE UNITED STATES AND RUSSIA

Germany surrendered on 7 May 1945, and Japan on 15 August the same year, but it quickly became clear that in the aftermath of war there would be no peace. Not only were Britain, France and the Netherlands engaged in conflicts in the Balkans, the Middle East and the Far East, but the two emerging Superpowers – the United States and the Soviet Union – were jockeying for political position while dismantling the geographical and physical assets of the conquered.

The two incompatible philosophies – Capitalism and Communism – had been prepared to collaborate from 1941 to defeat Germany. With victory in Europe, though, only the most short-sighted optimist could have believed that the wartime accommodation would have somehow been sustained for very long.

On 3 February 1946 the US State Department asked George F. Kennan, its Moscow *Chargé d'Affaires*, for a fast summary of the Soviet Union's stance. He responded on 22 February with an 8,000-word cable, now famous as the 'long telegram', which described how the USSR viewed the world, with recommendations for how the US should respond. The observations were remarkable, and although subject to subsequent criticism, they need to be seen in the light of the evidence available at the time. While it is presumptuous to summarise Kennan's assessment, an appreciation of the key features is critical to an understanding of how East–West relations developed over the succeeding fifty years.

Basic Soviet outlook
The USSR saw itself as living within a Capitalist encirclement. Capitalist states would enjoy internal conflicts which would generate wars. These wars could spill over, but also present an opportunity for Communist expansion. Socialism was seen as a major threat to Communism.

The Soviet strategy
Simple: advance Soviet strength; reduce Capitalist strength and influence; exploit differences between Capitalist Powers.

The Soviet 'how'
The USSR would pursue its broad strategy in relation to the West at two levels – the official plane and the 'subterranean' plane.

At the official plane there would be an intensive military build-up coupled with great displays of strength, while retaining total secrecy, both to hide weaknesses and to keep opponents mystified. Every effort would be made to extend territorial grip. The USSR would use international bodies like the UNO cynically, solely to further its own interests. Colonial or dependent peoples would be helped to rid themselves of Western Power and influence. The USSR would align with countries demonstrably in opposition to Western Powers, especially in the Middle East.

At the unofficial level full support would be given to the inner cores of the Communist parties in the West. Front organizations would work to undermine the host country while promulgating Soviet ideals. International organizations would also serve to lobby more widely, and vehicles like the Russian Orthodox Church and Pan-Slav movements would also be utilized.

Soviet objectives
In the West disrupt national self-confidence; hamstring national defence; increase social unrest; encourage resolution of dissatisfaction through violent unrest; set factions against one another. Authority of Western Powers to be weakened in colonies; liberal opinion marshalled to free colonies; colonial resentment to be fostered; Soviet puppets to be prepared to take over on independence. With independent countries which stand in the way of Soviet objectives, remove at all costs. Create division between US and UK. Infiltrate and penetrate organs of government everywhere.

Deductions from a US perspective
No possible USSR long-term coexistence with US. USSR has vast, flexible and skilful resources for exertion of force. The US response should be a similar outlay in planning effort. USSR not adventuristic; impervious to logic of reason but highly sensitive to the logic of force and therefore easily withdraws.

USSR is far weaker than West, therefore West must remain united. Future of Communism not assured. Soviet propaganda crude and thus easy to counter with planning. US must invest in intelligence. Public must be educated; little to lose by any course of action in that US has no stake in USSR. US to remain healthy. Europe to be supported in meeting security needs and given guidance.

Although he does not use the word, Kennan describes a paranoid government seeing threats from every quarter, but especially from Capitalism. The road to true socialism enjoyed numerous diversions which resulted in gross inefficiencies. In turn this led to the Soviet leaders closing their society to deny Western access to the true picture and Soviet citizens access to Western materialism. Paranoia on the one hand, resulting in a secretive and closed society, without even the benefit of cultural contact, was met by a desperate need to penetrate the secrecy and 'counter-paranoia' on the other.

Kennan also describes a leadership seeing and believing only what it wanted to and which fitted its view of the outside world. Such was the fear of Stalin and his immediate coterie that few if any would give true intelligence analyses if they did not confirm preconceived beliefs. This was to have a serious long-term effect in respect of communications between East and West at head-of-state level.

DIMENSIONS OF CONFLICT

The position of the United Kingdom was far from straightforward. Clearly she was a Western Power allied to the United States, and part of the North Atlantic Treaty Organization, but she was also at odds with the former in maintaining an empire. The UK and US also had competing oil interests in the Middle East.

The United Kingdom's engagement in war from 1945 was thus a strange mix, ranging from homeland security, through insular actions within the colonies or protectorates to preserve empire, to playing a major part in confronting the Soviet Union. The types of active involvement of the Royal Air Force, the Fleet Air Arm and the Army Air Corps (and its predecessor) between 1945 and 1990 include the following, with examples:

Maintaining local stability
  Greece, Netherlands East Indies
Maintaining empire
  Malaya, Kenya
Defending empire
  Borneo, Falklands
Defending interests
  Suez, Kuwait
Homeland security
  Northern Ireland, air defence
Confrontation
  Berlin airlift, Korea
Covert action
  Albania, strategic reconnaissance
Humanitarian and peacekeeping
  Jordan, Cyprus
Development of deterrent
  Bombs, bombers, missiles

At the end of the Second World War Britain had large, mainly conscript, armed services and had the capacity to fight alone on several fronts simultaneously. As equipment became more complex to operate and with economic pressure for manpower, National Service ended from 1958. Over succeeding years Britain parted company with her empire but tried to maintain a seat on the world political stage through building and deploying independent nuclear weapons.

Many of the actions described in this book were collaborative, and the Falklands War probably represented the last occasion on which the United Kingdom could act independently. By the end of the Cold War in 1990 she could probably contain the smallest of insurrections, but from that time most actions have been in concert with a range of allies, under the auspices of loose and informal coalitions, the United Nations, NATO and the European Union.

To put the United Kingdom's post-war actions in context there are brief introductions to the wider scene in each chapter. Further, there are orders of battle for operational units involved. Most types of operational aircraft are described through the text, and Appendix A indicates where to find them. Performance data for operational aircraft need to be handled with care. Each data item is independent and usually indicates a maximum in 'normal' conditions. Range is shown for aircraft with minimum load (other than fuel), and climate and altitude greatly affect performance. In practice most figures for range and/or passengers/freight load and/or weapons may be halved. Appendix B is a list of all operations and exercises, and there are chapter-specific and general bibliographies.

Throughout there are maps to illustrate the actions described, and the photographs have been selected as much to illustrate the variety of types used as the actions within which they were deployed.

And finally – the most widely used and most robust aircraft covered in these chapters? The Avro Shackleton.

CHAPTER ONE

The Immediate Post-War 'Colonial' Conflicts

At the end of the Second World War Britain found herself with her military forces dispersed across the face of the world. They were immediately to become involved in further conflict in three distinct ways.

First, Britain was either given, or assumed, responsibility for establishing order and handing occupied countries back to properly constituted and functioning civil governments. In this way she became involved in maintaining order in Greece, French Indo-China and the Netherlands East Indies.

Second, order had to be restored in a number of British colonies or mandated territories, where the end of the war gave Nationalists opportunities to press for independence, sensing that a tired and nearly bankrupt Britain would not have the resolve or resources to fight. Thus Jews in Palestine fought hard to secure an independent Jewish state. Beyond that nasty conflict there were no *immediate* post-war independence struggles, but they were not long in coming.

The third type of conflict – intervening in tribal or local territorial disputes – was familiar and almost a resumption of business as usual. The RAF applied or supported air control in Aden, Somaliland and the North-West Frontier of India.

Sustaining these operations was not made easier by conscripted men expecting early demobilisation on the cessation of hostilities. Morale was poor in some areas, and this was particularly the case in the Far East, where there was a state of near-mutiny within elements of the RAF in India.

Notwithstanding the trials and tribulations, British armed services acquitted themselves well in trying circumstances, often appearing to be fighting someone else's war.

1.1   THE GREEK CIVIL WAR, 1944–9

BACKGROUND

Prior to German occupation in 1941 Greece had been led by a right-wing military dictatorship underpinning the monarchy. The British sent an expeditionary force in February 1941 in an attempt to contain an inevitable and planned German invasion through Yugoslavia. In the event the British were forced to withdraw, and through more than three years of occupation the Communists formed the backbone of the resistance. Britain was keen to see Greece as an important client state, and supported the resistance from bases in Egypt.

BRITISH INVOLVEMENT

Greece was first reoccupied by British troops on 17 September 1944, and by the 23rd of that month Araxos airfield had been captured, while Athens and the surrounding airfields were retaken by mid-October after a para-drop on

Megara airfield. The first RAF fighter units to be based in Greece were 6 Sqn with Hurricanes and 32 Sqn with the Spitfire Mk Vc, both at Araxos. While the Hurricanes soon left for Palestine via Italy, the Spitfires moved on to Kalamaki after just a month.

Initially the British were welcomed, and Dakotas of 216 Sqn were soon ferrying in supplies from Egypt as Spitfires of 32 and 94 Sqns, Beaufighters of 108 Sqn and Wellingtons of 221 Sqn, all under the aegis of 337 Wing RAF, flew into Kalamaki airfield (renamed Hassani from 1 December 1944), outside Athens. In November they were joined by two more Wellington squadrons, 38 and 13 (Greek), and the two Greek Spitfire squadrons, 335 and 336. The latter units were retained in a training role only, until May 1945. With northern Greece liberated, 32 Sqn moved north to Sedes in November.

The Communist-based National Liberation Front (EAM) and National Popular Liberation Army (ELAS) had been offered a limited role in the post-war government, but dissatisfaction with this arrangement resulted in demonstrations in Athens, and at one banned meeting on 2 December British troops opened fire and ten or eleven demonstrators were killed. Two days later police stations were attacked and RAF units at Hassani began flying attack sorties against ELAS and EAM targets, mainly in the Athens area.

On 8 December Spitfires of 73 Sqn were detached to Hassani from Italy, and together with 94 Sqn aircraft strafed soft targets, while the Beaufighters of 108 Sqn attacked buildings with 25 lb bombs. Bombing was of limited value, however, and from 15 December a flight of six rocket-equipped Beaufighters of 39 Sqn was attached to 108

Formal inspection of 336 Squadron, Royal Hellenic Air Force at Hassani 0n 22 November 1944 by the Greek Prime Minister M A Papandreou, accompanied by the AOC RAF Greece, Air Commodore G W Tuttle. Nearest to the camera is Spitfire V ER194/N. 13 Sqn with Baltimores was also on parade *(Crown copyright)*

Sqn until 18 January 1945. These aircraft were highly successful, and in just two weeks 39 Sqn flew sorties against 105 targets as follows: two radio stations; seven guns; nineteen HQs; fifty-five buildings; ten ammunition and fuel dumps; and twelve transit. The host unit flew 244 day and twenty-one night operational sorties in December.

The Wellingtons of 221 Sqn were involved in supplying 32 Sqn at Sedes, dropping flares in support of night attacks, and leaflet raids. On two nights the Wellingtons bombed targets with 250 lb and 500 lb bombs, all with delayed fuses. Although it had been decided to prohibit the operational use of the Greek fighter squadrons, 13 Sqn HAF (Hellenic Air Force) assisted with the leaflet-dropping task. The hard-worked Dakotas of 216 Sqn were supplemented by 44 Sqn SAAF from December to March 1945.

On 19 December AHQ Greece at Kifisia was attacked by ELAS troops, and despite a spirited defence by 2933 Sqn RAF Regt was overrun the next day. Many British prisoners were taken and marched north, being supplied by air by 221 Sqn. By 7 January Athens was again in British control, with ELAS irregulars fleeing north. A cease-fire was announced on 11 January and confirmed in the Varkiza agreement on 12 February.

Throughout this period photo-reconnaissance was provided by Spitfires detached from 680 Sqn in Egypt and based at Hassani. A further support role was that of mine clearance, which was initially conducted by 624 Sqn Walrus amphibians, and when that unit disbanded the work was continued by 1702 NAS with the Sea Otter.

Unkept promises led to continuing fighting through 1945, but all RAF fighter units, which were of limited operational value, were withdrawn by early summer. Their roles were assumed by 335 and 336 Greek Squadrons. Three light-bomber squadrons, 13, 18 and 55 – all of 252 Wing RAF – were flown into Hassani from Italy in September 1945. Nos 13 and 18 Sqns were disbanded in the spring of 1946, while 55 Sqn converted to the Mosquito XXVI in the summer and remained as the last RAF unit until December 1946.

Armourers are overseen by Gp Capt M G F Pedley DFC, OC 337 Wing, as they prepare 250 lb bombs for the Spitfires of 336 Sqn. The whole scene seems rather casual with all three officers smoking! *(Crown copyright)*

British Army units were committed in support of the Greek National Army, and early in 1945 a British Military Mission formed with *c*.1,300 personnel. In mid-1946 the Greek RAF squadrons formally transferred to the Royal Hellenic Air Force (RHAF), and by the end of the year all RAF units had gone. With Greek Communist Party (KKE) support, the Greek Democratic Army (DSE) was formed, initially with 11,000 men, which soon controlled much of rural Greece.

SEQUEL

At this time Britain had widespread military commitments across the world, but the USA and Britain were keen to maintain Western control of Greece as agreed with Stalin. The US began an aid programme in 1947, but British advisers and ground forces remained until 1952, not directly confronting the DSE, but operating in a support and training role. It is also believed that Mosquitoes of 13 Sqn RAF helped occasionally with photo-reconnaissance.

The Greeks conducted their first major military operation in April 1947, and continued on the offensive until, with guerrilla resistance finished, a ceasefire was declared from 16 October 1949. By then the SB2C-5 Helldiver supplemented the Spitfires in the three fighter units. The civil war cost the Government forces 12,777 dead and 37,732 wounded, the ELAS/DSE losing an estimated 38,000 dead and 40,000 wounded; 4,289 civilians were executed by anti-Government forces.

Spitfire IX MJ238/X of 73 Sqn at Hassani. The aircraft displays the pre-war fuselage markings which had been applied throughout the war in place of unit codes. *(Crown copyright)*

SUPERMARINE SPITFIRE

The Spitfire must surely be the best known of the RAF's fighters of the Second World War, but later versions were in service with the RAF until 1959. The Spitfire was designed by R.J. Mitchell to specification F.37/34 for an eight-gun fighter with a speed of not less than 275 mph. The prototype was built in a remarkably short time and first flew on 5 March 1936. The type entered squadron service with 19 Squadron from August 1938, and its Merlin II or III engine conferred a top speed of 362 mph. This brief reference to the initial version is given solely to put the later variants which served after the war into some context. In its Mark IX, XIV and XVI forms the Spitfire was the primary day-fighter post-war, yet to be eclipsed by the new jet types.

The Type 359 **Mark VIII** preceded the Mark IX on the drawing board but entered service later. The Mark VIII was the medium/low-altitude version of the Mark VII with Merlin 61 engine and retractable tailwheel, but without pressurization; a total of 1,658 were built. Armament fit now included provision for one 500 lb and two 250 lb bombs, and top speed was 408 mph compared to 357 mph for the Mark V. All aircraft of this version were fitted with unobtrusive tropical filters in production, and by 1946 the Mark VIII equipped units in the Middle and Far East only. The last RAF Mark VIII departed 253 Sqn in December 1947.

Fighter units equipped – 20, 92, 136, 152, 155, 253

The Type 361 **Mark IX** was moved swiftly into production to meet the threat of the Fw 190. Whereas the lineage of the Mark VIII was through the VI and VII, the Mark IX was an upgraded Mark V, many of which were production-line or retrospective conversions of the Mark V to the later specification. Engine and performance were similar to those of the Mark VIII, although the tailwheel was fixed.

The Mark IX came in three forms in respect of altitude: the LF with clipped wings, the standard-span medium-altitude fighter, and the HF with standard wingspan but the Merlin 70 engine. By now the eight-machine-gun armament had been superseded by combinations of machine-gun and cannon or cannon alone. Variants of the Mark IX were fitted with the B, C and E wing, the latter accommodating two 20 mm cannon and two .5-calibre machine-guns. Some later models had the broad-chord rudder, cut-down rear fuselage and teardrop canopy. A total of 5,665 of this popular version of the Spitfire were built from new, and its final operational service with the RAF was with 73 Sqn, whose last aircraft were withdrawn in May 1948.

Fighter units equipped – 32, 43, 72, 73, 87, 111, 129, 130, 164, 165, 208, 225, 234

The Type 379 **Mark XIV** was the second of the Griffon-engined Spitfires. For some time it had been intended to fit the more powerful engine, and the prototype, built to specification F.4/40, first flew in 1941. The variant was essentially the Mark VIII with the Griffon 65 or 67, with the camshaft and supercharger gear moved forward in order to keep overall length broadly the same as in the Merlin-engined versions. Notwithstanding the modification to the engine, the Mark XIV was longer than the Mark IX by 1½ ft. The five-blade airscrew had a larger spinner, and the added length was compensated for by a larger fin and rudder. The fuselage contours changed on the nose with fairings on either side to accommodate the cylinder blocks.

As with later models of the Mark IX, for better all-round vision the rear fuselage was cut down and a teardrop canopy fitted, albeit at the expense of slight deterioration in directional stability. Some aircraft had the clipped wing for low-altitude work, including a number of the FR variant which were equipped with an obliquely mounted F.24 camera. Apart from the four 20 mm Hispano cannon there was provision for one 500 lb bomb or Mark IX rocket projectiles.

Beaufighter XI of the MEAF over Malta. With cannon and rocket armament aircraft from 108 Sqn were in action throughout the winter of 1944-45. *(Crown copyright)*

USAAF C-47s drop British paratroops on Hassani October 1944. Athens and Piraeus were occupied by the 14th with little resistance. *(Crown copyright)*

Fighter/FR units equipped – 2, 11, 16, 17, 20, 26, 28, 41, 132, 411, 412, 416, 443, 451, 600, 602, 607, 610, 611, 612, 613

The **Mark XVI** Type 380 was the next Spitfire variant; the Mark XV was a Seafire. This final Merlin version of the Spitfire was similar in all essential features to the Mark IX but fitted with a US-built Packard Merlin 266. At one stage the production line was delivering both marks depending on which engine was to hand. Like some late-model Mark IXs, some XVIs had the cut-down rear fuselage and rear-view canopy. The last Merlin-engined Spitfire XVIs in RAF front-line service were withdrawn from 63 Sqn in May 1948, but the type continued in service with the RAuxAF until June 1951 (612 Sqn), and well into the mid-fifties with second-line or training units.

Fighter units equipped – 19, 63, 65, 126, 164, 302, 308, 317, 349, 350, 443, 501, 601, 603, 604, 609, 612, 614

The Type 394 **Mark XVIII** was the next Spitfire variant; it was a XIV but with a new wing with increased fuel capacity. All had clear-view canopies, and 300 were built, of which 200 were fighter-reconnaissance variants fitted with one oblique and two vertical F.24 cameras. Production was barely under way before the war ended. In the Far

East, with 60 Sqn, the FR.18 flew the last RAF Spitfire fighter sortie on 1 January 1951 with an attack on a terrorist hideout in Johore.

Fighter units equipped – 11, 28, 32, 60, 81, 208

The **Mark XIX** is described in Chapter 4, Section 5. The **Type F Mark 21** introduced a new strengthened wing of subtly different planform, with the span increased by one inch. The original fuselage profile and canopy was retained and armament fixed at four 20 mm cannon. Powerplant was the Griffon 61 or 64, although some later aircraft were fitted with the Mark 85 driving contra-rotating propellers. Late-production aircraft were also fitted with a 24-volt electrical system. The undercarriage was strengthened to cope with a greater all-up weight. The F.21 entered service just as the war in Europe was ending.

Fighter units equipped – 1, 41, 91, 122, 600, 602, 615

The **F Mark 22** Type 356 was similar to the F.21 but with a cut-down rear fuselage and teardrop canopy. Some later models were fitted with a larger fin and rudder, similar to that fitted to the Spiteful; as with the F.21, some were fitted with the Griffon 85 driving contra-rotating propellers. A total of 278 was built compared with 122 of the preceding version.

Fighter units equipped – 73, 500, 502, 504, 600, 602, 603, 607, 608, 610, 611, 613, 614, 615

Dakotas of 216 Sqn flew regular supply runs to Athens from their base at Cairo West. Of note is the post-war application of roundel and fin flash on GH-P, which also has a different code lettering style. *(Crown copyright)*

The Hurricane was still very much in front-line use in the Balkans at the war's end. In these two photos Mk IV aircraft of 6 Sqn are refuelled at Araxos. Each aircraft is fitted with four 3 in rockets and one 44 gallon drop tank; which wing took which seemed not to matter. 6 Sqn soon moved on to Palestine, being replaced by the Spitfires of 94 Sqn. *(Crown copyright)*

(Above) The Douglas Boston was used extensively in the Middle East and illustrated are three Mk V aircraft of 13 Sqn. The squadron operated from September 1945 to April 1946 from Hassani in support of ground forces. *(Crown copyright)*

Wellington XIII MF263 of 221 Sqn – normally operating in the anti-shipping role – is seen being loaded with newspapers in the winter of 1945. The unit was initially committed to bombing but was later heavily involved in Red Cross flights and keeping isolated villages supplied with clothes and newspapers. Aircraft of 221 Sqn also supplied the column of British prisoners marched north from Kifisia in December 1944. *(Crown copyright)*

The Type 356 **F Mark 24** was the definitive Spitfire. Powered by the Griffon 61 driving a five-blade airscrew, it carried extra fuel tanks in the fuselage and had the enlarged elliptical fin and rudder of the Spiteful. Twenty-seven F.22s were partially converted, while fifty-four new-build aircraft were fitted with four Hispano Mk V 20 mm cannon and zero-length underwing rocket launchers. The F.24 served only with 80 Sqn, which exchanged it for the Hornet in December 1951.

Fighter unit equipped – 80

The Greek Civil War, 1944–9

Unit	Aircraft (code)	Base	From	To
RAF				
6 Sqn	Hurricane IV (JV)	Araxos	10.44	11.44
32 Sqn	Spitfire Vc (GZ)	Araxos	24.9.44	17.10.44
		Hassani[1]	17.10.44	13.11.44
		Sedes	13.11.44	25.2.45
94 Sqn	Spitfire Vb/Vc (GO)	Hassani	17.10.44	14.2.45
	Spitfire VIII, IX (GO)	Sedes	14.2.45	30.4.45
73 Sqn	Spitfire Lf.IX	Hassani	8.12.44	28.1.45
108 Sqn	Beaufighter VIf/VIII	Araxos	13.10.44	25.10.44
		Hassani	25.10.44	28.2.45
39 Sqn det	Beaufighter VIf	Hassani	15.12.44	18.1.45
252 Sqn	Beaufighter X	Hassani	18.2.45	28.8.45
		Araxos	28.8.45	1.12.46
221 Sqn	Wellington XIII	Hassani	24.10.44	8.4.45
38 Sqn	Wellington XIII	Hassani	11.44	13.12.44
13 Sqn	Boston V		12.9.45	19.4.46
18 Sqn	Boston V	Hassani	14.9.45	31.3.46
55 Sqn	Boston V	Hassani	20.9.45	7.46
	Mosquito XXVI	Hassani	7.46	1.12.46
680 Sqn det	Spitfire XI, Mosquito IX	Hassani	28.12.44	2.45
216 Sqn det	Dakota IV (GH)	Cairo	10.44	3.46
624 Sqn det	Walrus I	Hassani	2.45	9.7.45
		Sedes	30.4.45	30.11.45
FAA				
1702 NAS det	Sea Otter I (O2A)	Hassani	27.10.45	27.4.46
		Araxos	17.4.46	27.4.46
SAAF				
40 Sqn[2]			09.12.44	25.1.45
44 Sqn	Dakota IV	Cairo	12.44	3.45
RHAF (initially under RAF control)				
13 Sqn	Baltimore IV			
	Wellington XIII	Hassani	1.11.44	31.10.46[3]
335 Sqn	Spitfire Vb, Vc (XT)	Hassani[4]	10.11.44	12.5.45
		Sedes	12.5.45	31.7.46[3]
336 Sqn	Spitfire Vb, IX (ZP)	Hassani	9.11.44	16.5.45
		Sedes	16.5.45	30.6.46[3]

NOTES
1   Originally Kalamaki to 30.11.44
2   Pilots only to 73 Sqn
3   To Greek Air Force control
4   Training only

1.2   Indo-China and Siam, 1945–1946

Background

Indo-China comprised the five French colonies or protectorates of Tonkin, Annam and Cochin-China (now Vietnam), Laos and Cambodia. During the Second World War it was occupied by the Japanese, but until March 1945 the Vichy French colonial government was allowed to continue to administer the territory. By then France had been liberated and a new French Government installed, after which British, American and French agents were infiltrated into Indo-China to support Nationalists against the Japanese. The Viet Nam Doc Lap Dong Minh Hoi, abbreviated to Viet Minh, had been founded in China in May 1941 to link Nationalist movements. Its post-war aim was to achieve independence for Vietnam, and its leader was the Communist Nguyen Ai Quoc (Nguyen the Patriot), better known as Ho Chi Minh (He Who Enlightens). Vo Nguyen Giap was appointed to form guerrilla bands around Cao Bang, but there were few operations during the war.

On 9 March 1945 the Emperor Bao Dai, on the instructions of the Japanese, proclaimed the independence of Vietnam, and the French were disarmed and interned. There followed four months of sporadic fighting. At the Potsdam conference in July 1945 it was agreed that China would accept the Japanese surrender north of the 16th Parallel, while the British were to occupy the south. It was understood that the country would eventually be handed over to the French, although the Americans were keen to see the disbandment of the British, Dutch and French empires, especially in Asia.

To the west of Indo-China is Siam, which as an independent kingdom had maintained a functioning civil government throughout the Japanese occupation.

Calm and chaos

The war in the Far East ended suddenly in mid-August following the dropping of the atomic bombs at Hiroshima and Nagasaki, but the Supreme Allied Commander, General MacArthur, was slow to accept the surrender of the Japanese.

In the intervening period, Giap ensured that the Viet Minh filled a vacuum, and it quickly established control around Hanoi and Saigon, and on 2 September, as the surrender was accepted, Ho Chi Minh declared the independence of Vietnam as a republic; in the north, the Chinese began disarming the Japanese, transferring many of their weapons to the Viet Minh.

On 11 September Dakotas of 62 Sqn brought the first troops of the 80th Brigade, 20th Indian Division, to Saigon, and the following day 150 French troops arrived in C-47s of the *Escadrille de Marche d'Extrême-Orient* (EMEO). The British then, in effect, allowed the French to deal with the Viet Minh while themselves disarming the Japanese. Rioting around Saigon made it clear that the Viet Minh could not control a number of Nationalist groups, and there was soon serious fighting around the capital. After a fragile truce fighting again broke out, and on 13 October Tan Son Nhut airfield came under heavy attack.

The British were now required to use the Japanese to assist in containing the Viet Minh. 273 Sqn RAF, equipped with Spitfire VIIIs, had flown into Tan Son Nhut on 19 September, and the aircraft were now involved in armed reconnaissance flights in the south. By the date of the attack on the airfield, 267 Sqn with Dakotas and a flight of Mosquito PR.34s of 684 Sqn were also present, together with a unique outfit called the Gremlin Task Force. This was a unit of Japanese pilots under British command formed to fly and maintain Japanese transport aircraft in support of British and French forces, and by the end of January 1946, when the unit was disbanded, it had flown over 2,000 sorties. AHQ French Indo-China was formed on 1 October 1945 under the auspices of AHQ Burma; it was disbanded just four months later on 15 February 1946.

French aircraft were also operational from October: the *9e Division d'Infanterie Coloniale* (DIC) brought several L-4Bs to Saigon, and *Groupe de Chasse* (GC) *I/7* flew some captured Ki-43 fighters for a short time from Phnom Penh. In France, the *Aéronavale* had established the *Groupement Aéronavale Indochine* (GANI) on 24 August, the first unit of which, 8F, equipped with the PBY-5 Catalina flying-boat, began arriving at Saigon on 27 October. Already operating in the theatre was 8S, which had formed during September at Cat Lai on locally available aircraft, including captured Japanese types.

Spitfire XIV RN218/MS-F of 273 Sqn flying out of Saigon. On 11 December 1945 the squadron flew offensive sorties in support of French troops against Viet Minh guerrillas at Ban Me Thuot. *(via A S Thomas)*

Two further brigades of the 20th Division were flown into Saigon, and through November there was continuing fighting. The targets were mainly French troops or settlers, and on 11 December the Spitfires of 273 Sqn fired their guns in anger against Viet Minh guerrillas surrounding a French force at Ban Me Thuot. Leaflets were dropped in advance. Two days later the first *Armée de l'Air* (AdlA) fighter unit proper, GC II/7, was formed at Tan Son Nhut with Spitfire VIII fighters borrowed from the RAF, pending delivery of Spitfire IXs, which arrived in January. Gradually, control of Saigon was handed over to the French, and the last British troops left on 30 March 1946. 273 Sqn was disbanded on 31 January, and the 267 Sqn element returned to Burma; the Mosquito detachment had completed its mapping task on 12 January. During the phase of British occupation, forty Allied troops were killed, against 2,700 Viet Minh dead. The RAF retained a staging post, supported by 2963 Sqn RAF Regiment, until the end of March.

British involvement resulted in a relatively orderly transfer of power to France in the south, but in the north it was another matter. During March the French entered the north, having formally recognized the Republic of Vietnam. AdlA strength now stood at thirty Spitfires (GC 7), twenty-three C-47s (CMTEO) and eighteen AAC.ls (GT I/34). By the end of the month Haiphong and Hanoi were occupied. The C-47s of what was now the *Groupe de Marche de Transport d'Extrême-Orient* (GMTEO) had flown 4,000 hrs and had dropped fifteen tons of 50 kg and 100 kg bombs, while Spitfires of GC I/7 and GC II/7 had flown 600 sorties, dropping twenty-eight tons of bombs and firing 150,000 rounds of ammunition.

In contrast, the situation in Siam was straightforward and no British troops were deployed. However, 909 Wing was established at Don Muang airport with a squadron of Spitfires, one of Mosquito fighter-bombers and detachments of 681 Sqn photo-reconnaissance Spitfires and 684 Sqn Mosquitoes. The airfield was defended by 2945 Sqn RAF Regiment. The main task was supervising the repatriation of prisoners of war, which was conducted by Dakotas of 62, 194 and 267 Sqns, all of 345 Wing at Mingaladon, Burma. AHQ Siam was formally established on 1 October 1945, and with most operational units having left in January 1946, the AHQ disbanded in April.

SEQUEL

During the summer of 1946, talks were held in France to try to settle the future of Indo-China amicably, and there was agreement in principle to the autonomy of Laos and Cambodia within a federation, itself within the French Union. Ho Chi Minh accepted, but he was unable to effect compliance. Isolated fighting had occurred in Laos in September when paratroopers were dropped at Luang Prabang, and the next paratroop action was on 25 November when four hundred men were dropped north of Haiphong to recapture the airfield at Cat Bi and contain Viet Minh forces after serious fighting had broken out. Three days later, with no let-up in sight, the French commander gave a two-hour ultimatum to the Viet Minh to stop fighting. When they refused, the sloop *Savorgnan de Brazza*, standing off the port, opened fire on the Indo-Chinese suburbs of the city, reportedly killing over 6,000 during the course of an intensive bombardment.

The situation deteriorated and resulted in eventual defeat for the French in Indo-China at the battle of Dien Bien Phu in 1954, when 2,293 French soldiers were killed and over twice that number seriously injured. The United States was heavily involved behind the scenes, having decided to support the French in spring 1950. This aid critically involved the provision of air transport, through a Military Assistance Advisory Group (MAAG). By the end of the war the Americans were meeting 80% of the cost, much of it in aircraft. A formal ceasefire came into effect in July 1954, recognising two Vietnams, and the French began their withdrawal from the north while the Viet Minh purportedly did the same in the south.

There was a further brief British involvement in the area when aircraft from HMS *Warrior* were engaged in covering the evacuation from Haiphong in 1954.

The United States continued to support the South Vietnam government, which suffered increasing insurgency from North Vietnamese-backed Viet Cong guerillas. Despite such close involvement in the latter years of French rule, in which a professional standing army was defeated by peasants, and despite the lessons of the Korean war, the US allowed itself to be sucked into a new war. American troops arrived in 1965 (there were already 23,000 servicemen in 'advisory' roles in the country), and this number rose to a peak of 536,100 in 1968. The war was formally ended in 1973 with US disengagement, but fighting between the North and South dragged on until 1975 at which time the remaining US 'advisors' made a widely televised and ignominious departure from the American embassy.

The cost to the United States was around 56,000 dead and 300,000 wounded, while South Vietnam lost around 184,000 dead and the Viet Cong and North Vietnam some 900,000. North and South Vietnam are now united and at peace with the world.

Indo-China and Siam, 1945–1946

Unit	Aircraft (code)	Base	From	To
Indo-China				
RAF AHQ French Indo-China				
273 Sqn	Spitfire VIII (HH)	Tan Son Nhut	19.9.45	1.46
	Spitfire XIV (MS)	Tan Son Nhut	11.45	31.1.46
684 Sqn det	Mosquito XXXIV	Tan Son Nhut	12.10.45	12.1.46
Gremlin Task Force	Ki-21 *Sally*, Ki-36 *Ida*, Ki-48 *Lily*, Ki-54 *Hickory*, Ki-46 *Dinah*, Ki-57 *Topsy*, Ki-67 *Peggy*, L2D2 *Tabby*, Ki-79	Tan Son Nhut	10.45	31.1.46
French Air Force				
9 DIC	L-4B, MS.500	Tan Son Nhut	9.45	
1 GAOA	MS.500	Tan Son Nhut	2.46	

THE IMMEDIATE POST-WAR 'COLONIAL' CONFLICTS

Unit	Aircraft (code)	Base	From	To
GC I/7	Ki-43 *Oscar*, Spitfire VIII	Tan Son Nhut	26.1..45	
GC II/7	Ki-43 *Oscar*, Spitfire VIII, IX	Tan Son Nhut	13.12.45	
EMEO/ GMTEO	C-47B	Tan Son Nhut, Gia Lam	1.45	
SAL 99[1]	Ki-36 *Ida*, Ki-46 *Dinah*, Ki-51 *Sonia*, Ki-54 *Hickory*	Tan Son Nhut	12.45	3.46
ELA 52	NC701, MS.500	Tan Son Nhut	3.46	
GT I/34	Ju 52/3M, Ki-21 *Sally*, L2D2 *Tabby*	Tan Son Nhut, Bien Hoa, Nha Trang	2.46	
French Navy				
8S	Loire 130, MS500, Aichi E13A1 *Jake* A6M2-N *Rufe*, JRF-5, PBY-5A	Cat Lai, Can Tho, Cat Bi, Pleiku, Nha Trang	9.45	
BM1/SLI	C-47, MS.500, AAC.1, L-19 Loire 130,	Tan Son Nhut	10.45	
8F	PBY-5A, PB4Y-2	Tan Son Nhut, Cat Lai, Cat Bi, Tourane	27.10.45	
Siam				
RAF AHQ Siam				
273 Sqn	Spitfire VIII (HH)	Don Muang	11.9.45	19.9.45
20 Sqn	Spitfire VIII (HN)	Don Muang	28.9.45	11.45
	Spitfire XIV (HN)	Don Muang	11.45	27.1.46
211 Sqn	Mosquito VI	Don Muang	27.11.45	15.3.46
681 Sqn det	Spitfire XIX	Don Muang	10.1.46	3.46
684 Sqn det	Mosquito XXXIV	Don Muang	20.1.46	3.46
RAF AHQ Burma (supported POW repatriation Siam and Indo-China)				
342 Wing				
62 Sqn	Dakota	Mingaladon	18.9.45	15.3.46
194 Sqn	Dakota	Mingaladon	21.8.45	15.2.46
267 Sqn	Dakota	Mingaladon	30.8.45	21.7.46
North Vietnam evacuation 1954				
Fleet Air Arm				
811 NAS	Sea Fury FB.11	HMS *Warrior*	6.54	7.54
825 NAS	Firefly AS.5	HMS *Warrior*	6.54	7.54

Note
1 Became ELA 52

1.3   NETHERLANDS EAST INDIES, 1945–6

BACKGROUND

The Dutch had colonized the East Indies from the seventeenth century, but when Japan entered the war in December 1941 the territory was invaded and occupied. For the Japanese the East Indies were vital for strategic and economic reasons, especially in relation to oil.

In April 1945 the Australian 9th Division landed at Tarakan in Borneo to begin the process of retaking the Netherlands East Indies from the Japanese. As the Japanese Empire collapsed, Field Marshal Hisaichi Terauchi promised the Indonesians independence, but on 14 August the Japanese surrendered. Significantly, the whole of the Indies was placed under South-East Asia Command (SEAC), a British area of operations. On the 16th, the leading Nationalist, Achmed Soekarno, was advised by the Japanese that as they were now agents of the Allies there could be no independence from Dutch colonial rule.

ACTION

Also on 16 August the Recovery of Allied Prisoners-of-War and Internees (RAPWI) programme was established, and in September 28 Sqn with the Spitfire XIV was dispatched to Medan, Sumatra, to cover the evacuation of Allied detainees. On the 17th, Soekarno declared independence, and it was anticipated that Nationalists would attempt to disrupt the evacuation.

During September, Air Headquarters Netherlands East Indies (AHQNEI) was formed from HQ 221 Group RAF in Burma; 904 Wing, comprising 60 and 81 Sqns, both equipped with the Thunderbolt II, was the air component. On 15 September, HMS *Cumberland* docked at Tandjoeng with a RAPWI control unit that linked up with a reconnaissance group which had been parachuted into Batavia (Djakarta) on the 8th; later in the month, 23 Division arrived at Batavia. Meanwhile A Flt 656 Sqn became operational at Soerabaya, and on the 31st a flight of Mosquito FB.6s of 110 Sqn arrived at Kemajoram, Batavia, from Seletar to provide cover pending the arrival of 904 Wing.

The task of the British was to return the Japanese and repatriate APWI before handing the NEI over to civilian control. The British made it clear that they recognized the new Republic, which the growing number of Dutch troops and rearmed internees found unsatisfactory, especially since the Republicans had aided the Japanese during their occupation. The first sign of trouble came on 10 October, when a British patrol was ambushed. From then on there were regular clashes, as the Indonesians did not trust the British to support their claim against another colonial Power.

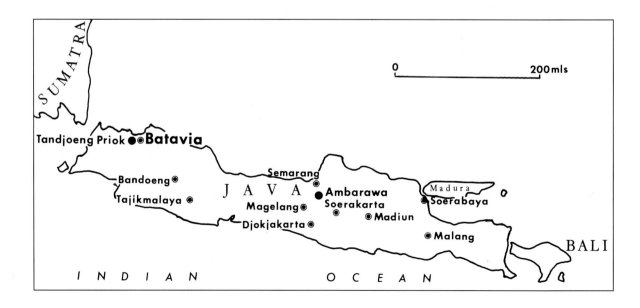

Mosquito VI of 110 Sqn being serviced by aircraftmen of 3210 Servicing Commando Unit at Kemajoram in October 1945. For several months the Mosquitos flew close support sorties to protect convoys. In aluminium finish the anonymous aircraft is named *Diana*. *(Crown copyright)*

On 17 October, 904 Wing, including two squadrons of the RAF Regiment, landed at Batavia and immediately set about preparing Kemajoram to support operations. On the 19th, both Thunderbolt squadrons were operational and within hours were in action. SEAC forces had landed at Semarang and worked south to free APWI. A company of 3/10 Gurkhas was cut off and required air support and resupply by Dakotas of 31 Sqn.

By the 24th, British bridgeheads were established at Batavia, Semarang and Soerabaya, and on the 25th the Thunderbolts made round trips of 900 miles to cover the landing of 49 Brigade at Soerabaya. There was heavy fighting, and six Thunderbolts of 60 Sqn were detached to Soerabaya to provide immediate support to ground forces. The Republicans were strongest in the east and were well armed from Japanese stocks. They had also captured a number of assorted Japanese aircraft in the vicinity of Soerabaya and Djokjakarta, and first flew one, a Yokosuka K5YI trainer, on 27 October from Tajikmalaya; later, numbers of these aircraft were flown against Dutch forces.

The fighting around Soerabaya continued, despite the fact that Soekarno was flown in by the British to calm the local population. On the 30th, Brigadier A.W.S. Mallaby was killed while attempting to negotiate a ceasefire, after which fighting spread to the west around Batavia. There was now considerable difficulty in repatriating the prisoners of war. No. 31 Sqn, now based at Kemajoram, was stretched supplying RAPWI teams after several road convoys and trains had been ambushed, but during November 10,000 internees were freed, many lifted out by air.

On 9 November, two brigades of 5 Indian Division arrived at Soerabaya to reinforce 49 Brigade, which was confined to the dock area. Mosquitoes of 84 and 110 Sqns from Seletar were busy on leaflet-dropping sorties, exhorting the Republicans to lay down their arms. The following day eight Thunderbolts of 60 Sqn and two Mosquitoes of 110 Sqn were detached to Soerabaya, where they attacked buildings; ten direct hits were confirmed.

Posed photo of armourers of 47 Sqn fitting 60 lb rockets under the wing of a 47 Sqn Mosquito VI. Immediately behind is RF942/KU-H minus rocket rails. *(Crown copyright)*

The aircraft continued bombing sorties for several days, and it was decided to strengthen 904 Wing by sending more aircraft to Batavia. Elements of 47, 84 and 110 Sqns, all with Mosquito FB.6s, were available for close support, the 47 Sqn aircraft being equipped to fire rockets; in addition, Spitfire PR. 19s of 681 Sqn for photo-reconnaissance and Beaufighter Xs for rescue support were detached. For some time the Semarang–Magelang road had been closed, and on 20 November Indonesian positions were bombed in an attempt to reopen it. Three days later Dakota III KG520 crash-landed five miles south-east of Kemajoram; tragically, twenty-one sepoys and the crew of five were killed on the ground by terrorists. The same day Thunderbolt II KJ226 of 81 Sqn crashed into the sea on a strafing run against a gun-running ship off Djokjakarta.

On the 24th, radio stations at Soerakarta and Djokjakarta were bombed and destroyed by 47 Sqn after Beaufighters of 27 Sqn had dropped warning leaflets. By the end of November the first Dutch unit, 321 Sqn Marine Luchtvaart Dienst (MLD), equipped with Catalinas and Liberators, was also based at Kemajoram, which was by now becoming overcrowded.

As the flow of freed APWI increased, Sunderland flying-boats of 230 Sqn began repatriation flights to Malaya from Batavia. Operating conditions at Kemajoram were appalling, the short runways breaking up through use and floods, and to ease congestion and spread support the balance of 60 Sqn went to Soerabaya on 1 December. Maintenance was very difficult, and 390 MU at Seletar acquired three Dakotas to fly spares throughout the theatre.

No. 31 Sqn was now delivering 425 tons a week in Java, and the importance of air transport was underlined when a road convoy was ambushed at Soekaboemi on the 9th. Despite heavy fighter escort, there were numerous casualties, including two RAF controllers. In the new year the fighting diminished, but the convoy and train escort work was maintained.

In January 1946 the RAF organization changed. Soerabaya was brought into full use with 60 Sqn and detach-

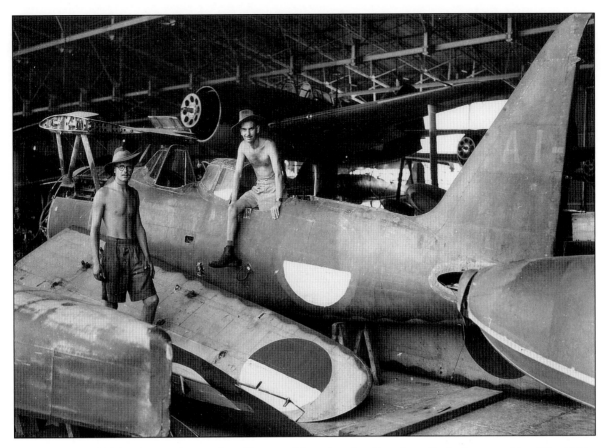

Ground crew of 81 Sqn inspect the remains of Japanese Navy aircraft at Sourabaya. In the foreground is a Mitsubishi F1M (*Pete*) observation seaplane while three Kawanishi N1K1 Kyofu (*Rex*) floatplane fighters are in the background. The Japanese Hinomaru national marking of a red circle has been partially overpainted in white by Indonesian nationalists to reflect their colours. *(Crown copyright)*

ments of 47 and 656 Sqns. Also at the station were the Catalinas of 321 Sqn MLD, the Liberators having been returned to the United States. No. 904 Wing at Kemajoram comprised 81 and 84 Sqns plus a detachment of 110 Sqn and the Dakotas of 31 Sqn. 27 Sqn returned to Malaya to disband, but on the 15th, 18 NEI Sqn RAAF was transferred back to the Royal Dutch Indies Army – Army Aviation (KNIL-ML); equipped with the B-25, this unit was the first to be based at Tjililitan.

The 681 Sqn detachment returned to Malaya, but its duties were taken over by Mosquito PR.34s of 684 Sqn based at Seletar. To cover RAPWI work in Sumatra, 155 Sqn with the Spitfire FRXIV replaced the 28 Sqn detachment at Medan, where it was supported by aircraft of 152 Sqn operating out of Tengah. From March, as the Dutch gradually trickled back, the situation deteriorated and convoy escorts were stepped up, especially from Bandoeng.

Around Soerabaya the position was improved, and Dutch forces replaced British. No. 120 Sqn ML replaced 60 Sqn, which returned to Kemajoram, from where both 47 and 84 Sqns had departed for Malaya by April. Local negotiations brought about the recognition of an Indonesian Republic with authority in Java and Sumatra, while the Dutch, who had reoccupied the remaining major islands, would share the task of helping to bring the remainder of the East Indies into a federation. In the Netherlands, however, the more formal talks broke down.

As the Dutch assumed greater control and their air units began to replace RAF squadrons, the Indonesians also formed an embryo air force. On 9 April the Aviation Division of the People's Security Force was formed, with about fifty ex-Japanese aircraft in flying condition. The Nationalists effectively controlled large areas of Sumatra and Java, and their main stronghold was at Djokjakarta.

Dakota KNIV KN677/U of 31 Sqn. This unit handled all in-theatre transport for a year handling repatriation of prisoners of war in addition to supplies between bases, especially when road convoys were vulnerable to attack.
(Crown copyright)

During May 1946 one of a flight of six Ki-9 trainers *en route* from Sumatra to Djokjakarta crashed, killing the pilot – the first Indonesian Air Division casualty. On 20 May two Dakotas of 31 Sqn landed at Solo airfield, Soerakarta, to begin the final evacuation of 10,000 APWI. In June, 81 Sqn disbanded, leaving just 60 Sqn in Java and 155 Sqn in Sumatra; in July, the Dutch assumed control of affairs in the NEI and there was a flare-up of anti-British feeling.

The two RAF Regiment squadrons, 2962 at Kemajoram and 2739 at Medan, were fully committed to defending the bases from attack. By the end of August, only 60 and 31 Sqns RAF remained in the NEI, with the Austers of 656 Sqn. From September 1945 the British had lost 556 dead (507 of whom were Indian troops) and 1,393 (1,259) wounded. The Dutch formally assumed responsibility for air support on 19 September, and by the end of 1946 had three fighter and three light-bomber units in-theatre.

During September, 31 Sqn disbanded at Kemajoram. In one year and six days, its Dakotas had flown over 11,000 sorties, carrying 127,800 passengers (many repatriated APWI) and 26,000 tons of freight, and two aircraft with their crews had been lost in crashes. After completing 843 sorties in 719 operational hours, 656 Sqn returned to Malaya in November, and on the 28th 904 Wing and AHQNEI were disbanded; the Thunderbolts of 60 Sqn were broken up as the unit left for Singapore to re-equip. The last British troops left NEI at the end of November. During the brief campaign the RAF flew some 19,533 sorties.

SEQUEL

By the end of 1946 agreement appeared to have been reached on the future of Indonesia as a group of federal united states with Dutch allegiance. A ceasefire agreement had been reached, but through early 1947 there were numerous breaches. There were, moreover, many misunderstandings on both sides about the exact nature and authority of

Thunderbolts of 60 and 81 Sqns provided support to ground forces and convoy protection. Here, in another posed photograph, a Mk II of 81 Sqn is refuelled at Kemajoram. The long-range underwing tanks are noteworthy.
(Crown copyright)

the new Republic, which the Dutch attempted to control from enclaves around Batavia and Soerabaya in Java and Medan, Padang and Palembang in Sumatra.

The Dutch fought a rearguard action to retain control but bowed to the inevitable, and the United States of Indonesia was formed on 27 December 1949. However, the new republic suffered internal rebellion through the 1950s, during which the American Central Intelligence Agency (CIA) gave covert support to an attempt to break Sumatra from Indonesia in 1957.

There was further trouble in 1962 when Indonesia laid claim to Dutch New Guinea (West Irian), and that conflict was resolved peacefully with the territory handed over to Indonesia. There has been continuing and sporadic fighting over East Timor, which Indonesia invaded and secured in 1975. Finally, in 1962 Indonesia presumed to extend her empire by absorbing Borneo, and this confrontation is addressed in Chapter 7, Section 2.

REPUBLIC THUNDERBOLT

The heavy Thunderbolt single-engined fighter was taken into RAF service to supplement the limited number of fighters in the Far East, where, apart from an operational training unit in the Middle East, it served exclusively. The **Mark I** was equivalent to the USAAF P-47B or early -D models and was no longer in service by 1946.

Featuring a teardrop canopy and R-2800-59 Double Wasp engine, the **Mark II** was equivalent to the American P-47D-25. It joined 146 and 261 Sqns in India in September 1944. The armament comprised eight .50 in. guns in the wings and provision for the carriage of two 1,000 lb bombs. After service in support of British troops in the Netherlands East Indies the Thunderbolt was withdrawn from service in December 1946.

Fighter units equipped – 5, 30, 42, 60, 79, 81, 131, 258

Netherlands East Indies, 1945–6

Unit	Aircraft (code)	Base	From	To
RAF				
28 Sqn	Spitfire XIV	Medan	9.45	9.45
60 Sqn	Thunderbolt II (MU)	Kemajoram	21.10.45	1.12.45
		Soerabaya	1.12.45	12.5.46
		Kemajoram, Medan det	12.5.46	2.12.46
81 Sqn	Thunderbolt II (FL)	Kemajoram	21.10.45	30.6.46
110 Sqn det	Mosquito VI	Kemajoram	31.9.45	27.2.46
84 Sqn det	Mosquito VI (PY)	Kemajoram Soerabaya	20.10.45	16.1.46
		Kemajoram	16.1.46	21.5.46
47 Sqn	Mosquito VI (KU)	Kemajoram	15.11.45	21.3.46
27 Sqn	Beaufighter X	Kemajoram	15.11.45	1.2.46
681 Sqn det	Spitfire XIX	Kemajoram	15.11.45	28.5.46
684 Sqn det	Mosquito XXXIV	Seletar	20.1.46	1.9.46
31 Sqn	Dakota IV (5D?)	Kemajoram	30.10.45	30.9.46
230 Sqn	Sunderland V (4X)	Batavia	1.12.45	15.4.46
656 Sqn A Flt	Auster V	Batavia, Soerabaya	14.11.45	28.11.46
656 Sqn B Flt	Auster V	Semarang	15.1.46	28.11.46
656 Sqn C Flt	Auster V	Bandoeng	15.1.46	28.11.46

Armed with two 250 lb bombs apiece Thunderbolts of 60 and 81 Sqns taxi out at Kemajoram for a strike against 'extremists' at Tjibadak. In the background is KL187/MU-M of 60 Sqn undergoing maintenance; also visible in the original print are Dakotas of 31 Sqn and B-25s and PBYs of the Dutch services. *(Crown copyright)*

Sunderland flying boats of 230 Sqn were operational for four months from December 1945, maintaining a watch on shipping and repatriating prisoners of war. *(Crown copyright)*

Unit	Aircraft (code)	Base	From	To
155 Sqn	Spitfire XIV (	Medan	4.2.46	31.8.46
152 Sqn	Spitfire XIV (UM)	Tengah	1.46	18.6.46
Netherlands East Indies Air Force				
18 Sqn	B-25D, J	Tjililitan	15.1.46	
120 Sqn	P-40N	Semarang	6.4.46	
121 Sqn	P-51D	Tjililitan	1.5.46	
17 Sqn	L-4J	Medan, Palembang	10.7.46	
Netherlands Navy				
312 Sqn	PBY-5A	Kemajoram	11.45	
860 Sqn	Firefly I	HrMs *Karel Doorman*	6.46	

Indonesian Nationalists

From September 1945 Indonesian Nationalists used salvaged Japanese types, including the Ki-9 *Spruce*, Ki-21 *Jane*, Ki-36 *Ida*, Ki-43 *Oscar*, Ki-46 *Dinah*, Ki-51 *Sonia*, Ki-61 *Tony*, K6K5 *Mavis* and K5Y1 *Willow*. They were flown mainly from Klutan, Malang and Soerabaya.

1.4　PALESTINE, 1945–8

BACKGROUND

After conquering Palestine from Turkey in the First World War, Britain was granted a League of Nations mandate in 1920. The British Government supported the establishment of a Jewish state in principle, to the concern of Arabs, who had understood that for their support in the war they would also secure an established state. In 1917, the British cabinet approved a statement to British Zionists which in the form of the Balfour Declaration, read

> His Majesty's Government view with favour the establishment in Palestine of a national home for the Jewish people, and will use their best endeavours to facilitate the achievement of this object, it being clearly understood that nothing shall be done which may prejudice the civil and religious rights of existing non-Jewish communities in Palestine, or the rights and political status enjoyed by Jews in any other country.

As the Jewish population rose from 4,000 in 1931 to 62,000 in 1935, with no sign of developments, illegal Jewish militia organizations were established. In 1936 serious fighting broke out, but the Second World War led to a temporary cessation of violence. During the war Britain based troops in Palestine and began an extensive airfield construction programme.

In general the Jews co-operated with the British, some serving with distinction. As the war drew to a close and many stateless and homeless Jews fled to Palestine from the concentration camps, impatience with the administration led to a resumption of fighting.

Most Jews in Palestine lived in settlements, and it was here that the Yishuv movement spawned the Irgun Haganah. Within, or deriving from, Haganah were the Chish, Rekhesh, Palmach and Aliyah Bet movements. All of these organizations benefited from having worked with the British, and in general were committed to the protection of Jews actually or potentially in Palestine. There were those who wanted to see a more proactive stance taken, and these extremists formed the Irgun Zvai Leumi (IZL) and Lohamei Herut Israel (LHI).

THE JEWISH OFFENSIVE

LHI opened the post-war offensive with the assassination of the British Minister of State, Lord Moyne, in Cairo in April 1945. 6 Sqn RAF, with Hurricane IVs, and recently operational at the outset of the Greek civil war, was moved to Meggido, and 208 Sqn, with Spitfire IXs, joined 32 Sqn (Spitfire Vc) at Ramat David. From August two Liberator units were moved to Ein Shemer for maritime reconnaissance, but in October they departed, to be replaced by 37 Sqn at Aqir.

As British attitudes to illegal immigration hardened, Irgun and LHI agreed with Haganah to work in concert as the Tenuat Humeri (TH). A bombing campaign now began, concentrating initially on the railway system. As 32

Sqn moved south to Petah Tiqva it was replaced at Ramat David by the Mustangs of 213 Sqn, while 6 Sqn converted to the Spitfire IX. By November, there was in addition 644 Sqn with Halifaxes, a detachment of Dakotas of 78 Sqn at Aqir, Warwick GR.5s of 621 Sqn for anti-immigration patrols and, of great value in an anti-terrorist campaign, a flight of Austers of 651 Sqn. Survey work in the Eastern Mediterranean was conducted by detached Mosquitoes of 680 Sqn at Aqir.

At January 1946 there were 80,000 British troops in Palestine, and they were to be the target of the next offensive: on 22 January the RAF base at Aqir was raided and arms stolen. On 20 February the RAF radar station on Mount Carmel was attacked and damaged, and five days later seven Spitfires of 208 Sqn were destroyed in a raid on Petah Tiqva. The same day no fewer than eleven Halifax transports of 644 Sqn were destroyed or damaged beyond repair, while two Ansons were destroyed in an attack at Haifa. As incidents increased the security forces occupied the Jewish Agency offices on 29 June and swept the settlements: some 2,700 arrests were made.

Within a month, Irgun retaliated by blowing up the King David Hotel in Jerusalem, and ninety-one people, mostly associated with the security forces, were killed. In September the 6th Airborne Division occupied Tel Aviv and RAF fighters flew constant armed reconnaissance patrols, reporting on traffic and curfew violations. At the end of 1946 the RAF transport force had increased and 38 Sqn had succeeded 620 and 621 Sqns in the anti-smuggling and immigration patrol role, flying what were originally designated *Sunburn* sorties. The operational code changed to *Bobcat* in September 1946. 6 and 213 Sqns had meanwhile moved to Cyprus to re-equip with the Tempest F.6, while 32 and 208 Sqns had re-equipped with the Spitfire FR.18.

Military strength had increased to 100,000 men, but this did nothing to stem the flow of extremist activities. As the situation worsened, women and children plus some male civilians were evacuated to Egypt by Halifax transports of 113 Sqn or by train in Operation *Polly* on 5 February 1947. This was to minimize the potential for hostage-taking. At the end of March an oil refinery at Haifa was blown up, and in May Irgun organized a breakout from Acre prison in which 271 escaped. Some of the organizers were caught and hanged, and on 30 July two British Intelligence Corps sergeants were hanged at Natanya in retaliation.

This event, together with the turning back of the refugee ship *Exodus*, focused world opinion, and on 29 November the UN voted 33–13 in favour of the partition of Palestine west of the Jordan. As Britain prepared to withdraw, there was no let-up in the watch on illegal immigration and arms smuggling. In mid-September 1947 Lancasters of 203 Sqn were detached to Ein Shemer to supplement those of 37 Sqn which had formed in mid-month.

On 15 November Lancasters spotted the steamer *Elia*, which, when intercepted and boarded by the destroyer HMS *Venus*, was found to have 800 illegal immigrants on board. In another interception on 22 December by Lancasters of 37 Sqn, 850 immigrants were caught on a small vessel off the coast. Throughout this period the air group of HMS *Triumph* comprising 800 and 827 NASs were also active in the eastern Mediterranean. By May 1948 forty-seven ships carrying more than 65,000 illegal immigrants were identified and stopped by Royal Navy ships, most of the wretched passengers being interned on Cyprus.

Civil war

In the autumn of 1947 the Jews created Shin Aleph, the air arm of Haganah. Initially equipped with flying-club aircraft, it acquired eight Taylorcrafts in July, while a further eighteen Auster AOP.5s were built from twenty-five airframes surreptitiously bought from the RAF as scrap, many of the aircraft being given identical registrations to conceal their numbers from the British. During April the fledgling air force, soon to become the Chel Ha'avir, lost several aircraft to ground fire, including Tiger Moths VQ-PAT and -PAU.

The aircraft operated from Sde Dov in support of Jewish groups in Palestine, flying liaison, reconnaissance and supply sorties. By now civil war had broken out between Jew and Palestinian Arab, and the British were obliged to intervene in an often vain attempt to maintain order. The Jews organized the supply of arms from a number of sources: on 31 March, for example, an American-registered DC-4 delivered a consignment from Prague to Beit Daras, although further shipments were stopped by US intervention.

Early in 1948 the RAF suffered several attacks by REAF fighters in the El Arish area, which was a restricted area. The victims were communications aircraft which had strayed off course. During this period the Austers of 651 Sqn, which by now was operating in flights, were heavily involved in liaison and low-level reconnaissance, and were often fired on as they directed army units to various acts of lawlessness.

The Spitfires of 32 and 208 Sqns were kept busy, and in April 1948 they supported an attack by the Life Guards and 4/7 Dragoon Guards on Jewish headquarters in the Gold Star brewery in Jaffa. The city was occupied by Arabs but surrounded by Jewish militia who were frustrating British attempts to evacuate through the port. The extent of fighting in the last few months of the mandate can be gauged from Jewish deaths alone, which numbered around 1,200 between January and May 1948.

On 15 May 1948 the State of Israel was declared, and the emergent nation was immediately attacked and invaded by all neighbouring Arab states. For some months leading up to independence, Jewish road convoys from the coast to settlements had been attacked by Arab Nationalists, and on 9 April the Jews retaliated. A joint LHI/Irgun force attacked the village of Deir Yassan, astride the Tel Aviv–Jerusalem road, killing 254 Arabs, including many women and children. As a result five Tempests of 249 Sqn were detached from Habbaniyah to Ramat David, from where they undertook armed recce sorties for several weeks.

A number of British units remained in the country for a few weeks, and at dawn on 22 May Spitfire IXs of 2 Sqn Royal Egyptian Air Force (REAF) attacked Ramat David airfield, then occupied by 32 and 208 Sqns. Two Spitfire FR.18s of 32 Sqn, including TZ232, were destroyed, and in another attack two hours later seven aircraft of 208 Sqn and a visiting Dakota of 204 Sqn were damaged. This time the RAF was prepared, and two REAF Spitfires were shot down by 208 Sqn, with a further two aircraft destroyed by RAF Regiment anti-aircraft fire. This was the only occasion between the end of the war and the present time when RAF pilots were to claim victory in air–air combat. The following day the RAF left Ramat David, keeping 1909 Flt of 651 Sqn at Haifa until 18 June, when it departed for Amman. Policing Palestine from 1945 to independence cost the British security services 223 dead and 478 injured.

SEQUEL

Egypt, Jordan, Iraq, Syria and Lebanon attacked Israel from 14 May on the ground and with air support. Initially the Israeli Defence Force (IDF/AF) had only light aircraft with some minimal bombing capability, but over some months managed to hold the Arabs at bay while securing more formidable aircraft in the form of Avia S.199, P-51 and Spitfires plus three B-17 bombers.

The RAF maintained a watch on affairs from bases in Egypt, and on 20 November 1948 Mosquito PR.34 VL620 of 13 Sqn from Fayid was shot down by an Israeli P-51 off the coast, with the loss of the two crew. Then on 7 January 1949 four Spitfire XVIIIs of 208 Sqn were conducting an armed reconnaissance along the border when one aircraft was brought down by AA fire. The remainder were bounced by IDF/AF Spitfires of 101 Sqn and all three shot down with the loss of one pilot and the capture of two others. Later in the day Tempest FB.6 NX207, one of seventeen from 6 and 213 Sqns sent to search the area, was also shot down by a patrolling Israeli Spitfire, with the loss of the pilot.

At the end of January the British Government formally recognized the State of Israel, which over succeeding months concluded armistices with her neighbours, apart from Iraq.

THE AUSTER

The Auster is unusual in that the manufacturer in due course adopted the type name of the first version in military service, and the name was then used as the type name through numerous marks which included completely new designs (*Auster* is the South Wind.) Taylorcraft Aeroplanes (England) was formed to produce the American Taylorcraft light-aircraft design under licence.

The early marks I, II, III and IV were out of front-line service by the end of the war. The Type J **Mark V** was a high-winged, two-seat monoplane powered by a Lycoming O-290 engine. It incorporated several improvements on the Mk IV, notably an elevator trim tab and blind-flying panel.

Air Observation units equipped – 652, 653, 654, 656, 657, 658, 659, 660, 661, 662, 663, 664; 1901, 1902, 1903, 1904, 1906, 1907, 1908, 1909, 1910, 1911, 1914, 1951, 1952, 1953, 1954, 1956, 1957, 1958, 1960, 1961, 1963, 1964, 1965, 1966, 1967, 1968, 1969, 1970 Flts

Initially two Liberator squadrons were sent to Ein Shemer for maritime reconnaissance but as lend-lease came to an end they were replaced by the Lancasters of 38 Sqn from July 1946. Mk III SW336/V was delivered after the end of the war and remained in service until 1956. *(38 Sqn records)*

The Type **K AOP Mark 6** was a further development of the Taylorcraft, the prototype of which, TJ707, flew on 1 May 1945. It had a completely different nose again, this time housing the Gipsy Major 7 engine of 145 hp with an electric self-starter. Fuel load was increased, the blind-flying panel was replaced, and the undercarriage lengthened. The most significant change was the addition of auxiliary flaps which reduced the take-off and landing run. The type entered service with 657 Sqn in June 1946.

Air Observation units equipped – 651, 652, 653, 654, 656, 657, 661, 662, 663, 664, 666; 1340, 1900, 1901, 1902, 1903, 1904, 1905, 1908, 1909, 1910, 1912, 1913, 1915, 1954, 1958, 1961, 1966, 1967 Flts; 8, 10, 12, 15 Army Flts

The **AOP Mark 9** Type B5 was the final operational fixed-wing recce aircraft flown by the Army. The type was unusual in not being developed from a civil design and it incorporated a number of improvements on the Mk 6, including better instrumentation. It was relatively light, although the hydraulic flaps were slower to respond than the manual ones of the earlier types. The prototype, WZ662, flew on 19 March 1954 and it entered service operationally with 656 Sqn in Malaya.

Air Observation units equipped – 651, 652, 653, 654, 656, 657; 1900, 1901, 1902, 1903, 1906, 1907, 1911, 1912, 1914 Flts; 2, 3, 5, 6, 7, 8, 10, 11, 12, 13, 14, 16, 18, 20, 21 Army Flts; 1/10 GR, LG, 14/20 H, 5 IDG, QDG, QRIH, RA, 3 RGJ, 4 RTR Air Plats; 1 Comm Div LL, 2 Wing Av, 2 Div Av Sections

Palestine, 1945–8

Unit	Aircraft (code)	Base	From	To
RAF				
6 Sqn	Hurricane IV (JV)	Meggido	13.7.45	3.9.45
		Petah Tiqva	3.9.45	28.9.45
	Spitfire IX (JV)	Ramat David	28.9.45	2.6.46
		Ein Shemer	2.6.46	3.10.46
		Nicosia	3.10.46	
32 Sqn	Spitfire Vc (GZ)	Ramat David	25.2.45	27.9.45
	Spitfire IX (GZ)	Petah Tiqva	27.9.45	15.3.46
		Aqir	15.3.46	6.6.46
		Ramat David	6.6.46	3.10.46
	Spitfire FR.18 (GZ)	Ein Shemer	3.10.46	25.3.48
		Nicosia	25.3.48	
208 Sqn	Spitfire IX, VIII (RG)	Ramat David	5.7.45	13.8.45
		Petah Tiqva	13.8.45	12.3.46
		Aqir	12.3.46	6.6.46
	Spitfire FR.18 (RG)	Ein Shemer	6.6.46	26.3.48
		Nicosia	26.3.48	
213 Sqn	Mustang IV (AK)	Ramat David	13.9.45	25.9.46
		Nicosia	25.9.46	
249 Sqn det	Tempest F.6	Ramat David	14.4.48	17.5.48
37 Sqn	Liberator VI	Aqir	16.10.45	12.12.45
	Lancaster ASR.3	Ein Shemer	14.9.47	31.3.48

Fine photo of Griffon-engined Spitfire FR.18 TP330/GZ-G of 32 Sqn. Together with aircraft of 208 Sqn the Spitfires flew border patrols and were available for support of ground forces. *(Author's collection)*

Unit	Aircraft (code)	Base	From	To
178 Sqn	Liberator VI	Ein Shemer	25.8.45	5.11.45
214 Sqn	Liberator VIII	Ein Shemer	24.8.45	7.11.45
621 Sqn	Warwick V	Aqir	20.4.46	6.6.46
	Lancaster ASR.3	Ein Shemer	6.6.46	1.9.46
18 Sqn[1]	Lancaster ASR.3	Ein Shemer	1.9.46	15.9.46
38 Sqn	Lancaster ASR.3 (RL)	Ein Shemer	7.46	31.3.48
203 Sqn det	Lancaster GR.3 (CJ)	Ein Shemer	10.47	12.47
644 Sqn	Halifax VII, IX	Qastina	1.12.45	1.9.46
620 Sqn	Halifax VII, Dakota	Aqir	14.6.46	1.9.46
113 Sqn[2]	Halifax VII, IX, Dakota	Aqir	1.9.46	1.4.47
680 Sqn	Mosquito XVI	Aqir (det)	2.45	9.7.46
	Mosquito PR.34	Ein Shemer	9.7.46	1.9.46
13 Sqn[3]	Mosquito PR.34	Ein Shemer	1.9.46	14.12.46
651 Sqn[4]	Auster AOP.5	Ramleh	2.2.46	10.7.46
		Petah Tiqva	10.7.46	1.7.47
1908 Flt	Auster AOP.6	Petah Tiqva	31.12.46	1.7.47
		Qastina	1.7.47	11.2.48
		Petah Tiqva	11.2.48	28.4.48
1909 Flt	Auster AOP.6	Ramat David	31.12.46	25.3.48
		Haifa	25.3.48	18.6.48
1910 Flt	Auster AOP.6	Qastina	24.7.47	11.2.48
		Petah Tiqva	11.2.48	28.4.48
512 Sqn	Dakota	Qastina	8.10.45	24.10.45
78 Sqn	Dakota C4 (EY)	Det Aqir	20.9.45	19.9.46
		Kabrit	19.9.46	
216 Sqn	Dakota C4 (GH)	Fayid	5.9.46	14.2.47
		Kabrit	14.2.47	
215 Sqn	Dakota C4	Kabrit	1.8.47	31.10.47
		Aqir	31.10.47	23.11.47
		Kabrit	23.11.47	1.5.48
204 Sqn	Dakota C4	Kabrit	1.8.47	
114 Sqn	Dakota C4	Kabrit	1.8.47	
FAA				
800 NAS	Seafire XVII	HMS *Triumph*	6.47	30.5.48
827 NAS	Firefly FR.1	HMS *Triumph*	6.47	30.5.48
REAF				
1 Sqn	Spitfire IX	El Hama	15.5.48	
2 Sqn	Spitfire V, IX	El Arish	15.5.48	
3 Sqn	Anson, Magister	El Arish	15.5.48	
4 Sqn	Anson, C-46	El Arish	15.5.48	
6 Sqn	Spitfire V	El Arish	15.5.48	
7 Sqn	Dakota, C-46	El Arish	15.5.48	

Spitfire FR.18s of 32 Sqn at Ein Shemer airfield in 1948. Nearest is TZ214/GZ-J. Two aircraft were lost at Ramat David in an airfield attack by REAF Spitfire IXs on 22 May, but the loss was quickly avenged by 208 Sqn which shot down two Egyptian aircraft involved in a follow-up raid. *(Crown copyright)*

Unit	Aircraft (code)	Base	From	To
IDF				
Tel Aviv Flt	Rapide, Autocrat, Bonanza	Sde Dov	12.47	
Negev Flt	Taylorcraft J-2	Beit Daras	3.48	
Judea Flt	Auster V	Yavneel	4.48	
101 Sqn	S.199	Herzliya	5.48	
13 Sqn	C-46, C-47	Ekron	17.5.48	

NOTES
1　Re-formed from 621 Sqn; became B Flt 38 Sqn
2　Re-formed from 620 Sqn
3　Re-formed from 680 Sqn
4　Renumbered as 1908 to 1910 Flights from 31 December 1946

1.5　SOUTHERN ARABIA, 1945–50

BACKGROUND

Southern Arabia from the Red Sea to Dhofar was subject to British influence from 1839, with Aden becoming a Crown Colony in 1937. In the hinterland there were constant inter-tribal conflicts, and after the success of air

Lincoln bombers of three squadrons were deployed to Aden in October 1947 to give support to the light bombers of the local 8 Sqn. Here RF440/NF-X is seen at Wyton before the deployment; the aircraft was destroyed in an overshoot accident at Shallufa. *(Author's collection)*

control in Iraq the process was extended to the Aden Protectorates in 1927 with the posting of 8 Sqn. Problems were thus dealt with by a combination of air policing and expeditions of ground forces, including the Aden Protectorate Levies (APL).

Although a singularly unpleasant environment, Aden was an important British base because of its location both on the route to India and between East Africa and the Gulf, both spheres of British influence.

ACTION

During the Second World War little attention was paid to tribal disputes, but in May 1945 RAF armoured cars supported by Mosquitos of 114 Sqn dealt with hostilities within the Subeihi tribe. In 1946 there were further demonstrations of force after the Dathina tribe ambushed the local assistant political officer. In September 114 Sqn was renumbered 8 Sqn, and the following year Sheikh Othman airfield was placed on a care and maintenance basis as Khormaksar was developed.

In early February 1947 a dissident fort on Jebel Jihaf was attacked by a force of RAF armoured cars and APL, and rocketed by 8 Sqn Mosquitoes. In April, as 8 Sqn was converting to the Tempest F.6, a mixed flight of both types attacked the village of Al Husein after the political agent had been killed collecting fines. Some sixty miles to the north of Aden, situated on the important Dhala road, the ancient trade route into the Yemen, is Thumier. The local Quteibi tribe had long practised the extraction of tolls for safe passage, but a series of lootings in 1947 led to complaints and demands for retaliation.

Over the years various local leaders had sought British protection through formal agreement, and positive action in upholding the law was essential. Thumier was attacked by air in October and the village substantially destroyed. Tempests of 8 Sqn were supported by Lincoln bombers of 101 Sqn on a *Sunray* exercise: 66.7 tons of bombs and

247 rockets were expended, but advance notice was, as usual, given by leaflets dropped by Anson communications aircraft.

Action against dissident tribes continued through 1948: at Wadi Mirria, sixteen forts of the Mansuri tribe were attacked over three days, 468 60 lb rockets being fired and resulting in the destruction of eleven of the forts. In 1949 8 Sqn re-equipped with the Brigand B.1 light bomber, which it used to attack forts at Naqd Marqad in August and in the Wadi Hatib two years later.

SEQUEL

From 1948 there was relative calm for two years, but tribal disputes and insurgency increased, resulting eventually in British departure in 1967. This period is covered in Chapter 5, Section 1.

DE HAVILLAND MOSQUITO (BOMBER VARIANTS)

The DH 98 Mosquito was remarkable in terms of both performance and construction. It was designed as a private venture in 1938 and constructed mainly of wood. As a bomber it was to be unarmed, and when it entered service in 1941 it was (and remained to 1944) the fastest aircraft operated by the RAF. In its bomber and reconnaissance forms it flew with no defensive armament. On 1 March 1940 Specification B.1/40 was issued to cover development of the bomber variant, while Specification F.21/40 covered the simultaneous development of the design as a fighter. The Mark I prototype W4050 flew on 25 November 1940 from Hatfield.

The **FB Mark VI** was developed from the NF Mk II, but with provision for four 250 lb bombs (Series 1) in addition to the eight-gun armament or four 500 lb bombs (Series 2). Alternatively extra fuel could be carried. Series 2 aircraft also featured twin Merlin 25 engines. The prototype first flew on 1 June 1942. The first unit equipped with the FB Mk VI was 418 Sqn from May 1943, and the variant remained in service as the light-bomber mainstay in occupied Germany until 1950.

Fighter bomber units equipped – 4, 8, 11, 14, 18, 21, 36, 39, 45, 47, 69, 82, 84, 107, 110, 114, 211, 248, 268, 305

The **B Mark XVI** was a pressurized high-altitude bomber version of the PR Mk IX. The armament was confined to one 4,000 lb bomb or six 500 lb bombs in a bulged bomb-bay, in addition to two 100 gal drop-tanks. Four hundred were built, and it remained in widespread service for some time after 1946.

Bomber units equipped – 14, 69, 98, 105, 109, 114, 128, 139, 180, 256

The **B Mark 25** was a Canadian variant of the B Mk XX with Merlin 225 engines delivering 1,620 hp. Of the 400 built, the majority were delivered to the RAF.

Bomber units equipped – 139, 502

The **FB Mark 26** was similar to the FB Mk 21, but with the Packard Merlin 225 engine. Most of the 337 built were used by the RAF in the Middle East.

Fighter-bomber units equipped – 55, 249

The last bomber variant was the **B Mark 35**, an improved B Mk XVI with the Merlin 113/114. A total of 276 was built, mostly post war, and it entered service in 1946.

Bomber units equipped – 14, 98, 109, 139

84 Sqn Brigand B.1 RH818 taxies in at Mogadishu after a demonstration flight. The Brigand was used only in the Middle and Far East and suffered from high attrition. *(84 Sqn records)*

Southern Arabia, 1945–50

Unit	Aircraft (code)	Base	From	To
RAF				
114 Sqn[1]	Mosquito FB.6 (RT)	Khormaksar	5.45	1.9.46
8 Sqn	Mosquito FB.6 (RT)	Khormaksar	1.9.46	3.47
	Tempest F.6	Khormaksar	3.47	12.49
	Brigand B.1	Khormaksar	6.49	1.53
101 Sqn det	Lincoln B.2 (SR)	Khormaksar	10.47	11.47
138 Sqn det	Lincoln B.2 (NF)	Khormaksar	11.47	11.47
57 Sqn det	Lincoln B.2 (DX)	Khormaksar	10.47	11.47

NOTE
1   became 8 Sqn 1.9.46

1.6   SOMALILAND, 1947–50

BACKGROUND

Situated on the Horn of Africa, what is now the Somali Republic was once two colonies: the northern part, on the Gulf of Aden, was British Somaliland, while the eastern part, facing the Indian Ocean, was Somalia Italiana. The Italian territory was occupied by the British from 1941, and after the war there were tribal revolts, mainly on the part of the Shifta and revolving around land disputed with Ethiopia in the Ogaden.

ACTION

During the spring of 1947 Mosquito FB.6s of 8 Sqn were to be seen at Hargeisa showing the flag, and in January 1948 Tempests of 6 Sqn were detached to Mogadishu to fly demonstration sorties. From time to time they were

Brigands of 84 Sqn in flight including RH817/A and RH815/E. *(84 Sqn records)*

Tempest F.6s of 8 Sqn at Hargeisa in 1948. NX169/C is in natural metal finish. At 435 mph the tropicalised F.6 was fast and with drop tanks had a very good radius of action. *(via A S Thomas)*

Between January and April 1952 Lancasters of 683 Sqn were detached to Hargeisa for a major survey. PR.1 RA626 is here seen at Shallufa in 1952: the mother and child casually strolling past the nose suggest that the aircraft is very much at rest! *(Author's collection)*

supplemented by aircraft of 8 Sqn from Aden which flew into Hargeisa when there was unrest, for example, in nearby Jijiga at the end of March 1948.

There was increased activity in June 1948 when it was announced that the disputed Ogaden territory was to be transferred to Ethiopia. The Somali Youth League (SYL) fomented unrest, and the RAF sent 213 Sqn to Mogadishu; again, demonstration flights were often sufficient to stabilize the situation. On 23 September 1948 the last British troops left the Ogaden, and in October 213 Sqn returned to Deversoir. Tempests and then Brigands of 8 Sqn were flown to Mogadishu throughout 1949 as the local situation demanded, until in February 1950 84 Sqn sent a detachment of Brigands from Habbaniyah to coincide with the handing back of Somalia Italiana to Italian administration.

In British Somaliland the RAF retained facilities at Hargeisa, but with no aircraft permanently based; an RAF officer commanded the contingent of native scouts, and any potential local disturbances would have been contained through air policing.

SEQUEL

On 1 July 1960 British Somaliland and the Italian Trust Territories achieved independence as the Somali Democratic Republic. The Shifta laid claim to various lands in Kenya and especially Ethiopia, and there has been serious intermittent fighting since, with great loss of life and hardship.

HAWKER TEMPEST

The Tempest was a natural development of the Typhoon built to specification F.10/41 and originally named Typhoon Mark II. The main differences were in the wing, which was to a new elliptical plan and much thinner, and the fuselage, which was longer to accommodate the fuel no longer carried in wing tanks. A dorsal fillet was also incorporated. Because of problems with the early Sabre engines, prototypes were ordered to be fitted with a variety of engines – Mark I Sabre IV, Mark II Centaurus IV, Mark III Griffon IIB, Mark IV Griffon 61 and Mark V Sabre II.

In the event the Mark V flew first, followed by the Mark I on 24 February 1943, but due to problems with the Sabre IV this version was abandoned. The Marks III and IV were never flown due to a shortage of Griffons, while the Mark II was last on the scene.

The **Mark II** first flew on 28 June 1943, powered by the Centaurus V, but engine teething troubles resulted in delayed introduction into service. The Tempest was armed with four 20 mm cannon and it could carry two 500 lb or 1,000 lb bombs under the wings, or eight rocket projectiles. The fighter was optimised for the war in the Far East, with long-range and heavy armament. The prototype flew on 28 June 1943 but it did not enter service (with 183 Sqn) until June 1945.

Fighter units equipped – 5, 16, 20, 26, 30, 33, 54, 152, 247

The **Mark V** was the first variant to fly. Unlike the later radial-engined Mark II, the Mark V shared the distinctive deep-chin radiator of the Typhoon. In other respects it was similar to the Mark II but was 5 knots slower. The prototype flew on 2 September 1942, and the first squadron equipped with the type was 486. Post war the Mark V served in Europe, while the Mark II was used additionally in the Far East.

Fighter units equipped – 3, 16, 26, 33, 41, 56, 80, 174

The **Mark VI** was a tropicalized version similar in most respects to the Mark V. However, it was powered by the Sabre V and had the air intakes moved from the radiator to the wing. The version served exclusively in the Middle East and India (one squadron), joining 6 and 249 Sqns concurrently in December 1946.

Fighter units equipped – 6, 8, 39, 213, 249

Somaliland, 1947–50

Unit	Aircraft (code)	Base	From	To
RAF				
8 Sqn det	Mosquito FB.6 RT)	Mogadishu	3.47	5.47
	Tempest F.6	Hargeisa	3.48	3.48
	Brigand B.1	Mogadishu	9.49	12.49
			2.50	3.50
6 Sqn	Tempest F.6 (JV)	Mogadishu	26.11.47	5.5.48
213 Sqn	Tempest F.6 (AK)	Mogadishu	17.8.48	2.10.48
			9.49	12.49
84 Sqn det	Brigand B.1	Mogadishu	2.50	3.50
683 Sqn	Lancaster GR.1	Hargeisa	1.52	4.52

1.7   NORTH-WEST FRONTIER OF PAKISTAN, 1947

While newly partitioned Pakistan and India were fighting over Kashmir, tribes on the North-West frontier with Afghanistan were encouraged to revolt by the Faqir of Ipi. The newly created Royal Pakistani Air Force (RPAF) now had to assume the policing role previously managed for so many years by the RAF.

In December 1947 the Tempest II fighters of 5 Sqn were moved up to Peshawar, and they were soon in action in the Khyber Pass area, flying forty-seven offensive sorties in the month in support of ground troops. The Dakotas of 6 Sqn were meanwhile busy airlifting troops based at Razmak from Miranshah to Peshawar. The aircraft are believed to have been supplemented by Dakotas from 10 and 31 Sqns RAF, which had remained at Mauripur and Chaklala after partition.

SEQUEL

Fighting continued into 1948, and in June it was the turn of 9 Sqn to fly its Tempests up to Peshawar. The squadron flew in support of a unit of Tochi Scouts who became involved in fierce fighting at Isha, just south of the Pass, flying 119 sorties in three days. From the summer the fighting diminished considerably, but continuing skirmishes obliged the RPAF to maintain a squadron of piston-engined fighters in the area for some years. The fighter squadrons exchanged their Tempests for the Sea Fury FB.60 from 1950.

North-West Frontier of Pakistan, 1947

Unit	Aircraft (code)	Base	From	To
RAF				
10 Sqn	Dakota (ZA)	Mauripur	5.6.46	15.12.47
31 Sqn	Dakota (5D?)	Mauripur, Palam	1.11.46	15.12.47
RPAF				
5 Sqn	Tempest II	Peshawar	15.8.47	
9 Sqn	Tempest II	Peshawar	15.8.47	
6 Sqn	Dakota	Mauripur	15.8.47	
1 AOP Flt	Auster V, VI	Peshawar	15.8.47	

RAF Dakotas helped the nascent Pakistan Air Force in its attempts to control revolt around the Khyber Pass. Illustrated is a well-worn but anonymous aircraft of 31 Sqn code US on the nose. *(via A S Thomas)*

Confrontation (1) – Ideological

As relations soured between the West and the Soviet Union from 1946, it was perhaps inevitable that there would be confrontation and tests of resolve. In these confrontations, Britain was usually a junior partner to the United States.

The first such situations were in the Middle East, where the Soviet Union made threats towards Turkey and refused to withdraw from Iran. In each case, after a combination of a display of force and diplomacy, the USSR backed down.

Much more serious was the (illegal) closure of land routes into Berlin in 1948. The US/British response was to determine to supply the city by air. This was costly and barely maintained the city at subsistence levels, but it demonstrated the Western Powers' resolve. After fifteen months the Soviets backed down, by which time the North Atlantic Treaty Organization (NATO) was formed. The alliance initially comprised ten western European nations plus Canada and the USA, but at the time of writing it embraces a number of former Warsaw Pact countries, including Poland, the Baltic states, Hungary, Bulgaria, Romania and the Czech Republic.

From the end of the war the United Kingdom and United States embarked on a far-ranging series of covert operations in countries falling subject to the USSR. For the enthusiasts of this form of confrontation there was the hope of revolt; for the pragmatists there was the opportunity for intelligence, plus the prospect of destabilisation and tying down security forces.

While the covert infiltration of agents and agitators was small scale, the United Nations 'police action' in Korea was a very big war indeed, costing hundreds of thousands of lives. The USA, British Commonwealth and various smaller nations fought the North Koreans, who were explicitly supported by Chinese People's Army 'volunteers', and behind them – and very secretly so – Soviet pilots and 'advisers'. (The Korean War seems to be one of euphemisms!) It was a long-drawn-out affair and one which many observers felt would lead to global engagement with nuclear weapons, but although the country continues to be divided fifty years on it remained a regional conflict in which new weapons and tactics were tested.

Closely related to the Korean War was Hong Kong, which was as essential as a port and staging-post as it was for spying on the new Communist China. While the Chinese could have walked in with impunity at any time, Britain maintained sufficient forces to contain local riots.

A new military alliance was confirmed in May 1955 with the formation of the Warsaw Pact, designed to tie the eastern European Communist states. East Germany joined in 1956, and it was to be here that the next major confrontation occurred. The Russians decided in 1961 to divide Berlin physically in order both to provoke and to stem the flow of refugees to the West. This was to be a trial of strength for newly elected President John F. Kennedy, who countered Soviet aggression tank for tank, aeroplane for aeroplane. The situation was defused by spring 1962, but another, more serious encounter was brewing much nearer to home for the United States.

The CIA accumulated evidence that the Soviet Union was basing offensive missiles on Cuba. The Cuban Missile Crisis, which came to a head in October 1962, brought the world as close to nuclear war as any post-war confrontation. The USAF strategic bombing force was placed on the highest alert and deployed to war bases, but in the UK, although the bomber force was brought to readiness it was not dispersed to forward operating bases. In the end Premier Khruschev was forced to back down, securing small concessions to save face.

It was generally the United States which took the prominent role in confrontation with the Soviet Union and China, with Britain taking very much a supporting position, or in many instances – beyond the scope of this book – not becoming involved at all. Only in the covert Cold War against Russia through the Eastern Bloc countries, and in Hong Kong, did the United Kingdom take a leading role. The confrontations described were costly and at times came worryingly close to global nuclear war. The actions described did serve a purpose in demonstrating resolve, in containing the spread of Communism, in destabilising the Soviet Union and its client states, and in gathering much-needed intelligence.

2.1   IRAN AND TURKEY, 1946

BACKGROUND

From 1941 it was essential to maintain as many supply routes as possible between the West and the Soviet Union. Since Turkey was neutral until the closing days of the Second World War, the Dardanelles route to the Soviet Union was closed to the Western Allies. With the sea route barred, the Allies were required to occupy Iran and to build roads to get supplies through. In 1942 Britain and the Soviet Union had placed troops in Iran both to keep Germany at bay and also to protect the supply line. It was agreed that Allied troops would withdraw within six months of the end of the war.

TENSION

The Soviet Union decided to apply pressure for access to the Dardanelles in 1946, while at the same time refusing to remove troops from the important oilfield areas in the north of Iran. Indeed, the Soviet Union had been supporting a separatist movement in Azerbaijan. In support of the alleged troubles the Russians had moved several fighter units to Tabriz, while Iranian Hurricanes flew armed reconnaissance sorties. British involvement extended to reconnaissance sorties flown by Mosquitoes of 680 Sqn reportedly detached to Habbaniyah.

In the eastern Mediterranean the Soviet Union demanded rights of passage through the Straits and a naval base

When the Soviet Government refused to withdraw forces from northern Iraq in 1946 the situation was carefully monitored by RAF Mosquitoes, probably operating from Habbaniya. MM347/N is a PR XVI of 680 Sqn.
(via A S Thomas)

in the Dardanelles, plus return of territories in eastern Turkey. The Turks refused, and in support the United States sent the battleship USS *Missouri* (BB-63) in the spring of 1946, followed by the carrier USS *Franklin D Roosevelt* (CVB-42) in the late summer. The Royal Navy carrier HMS *Ocean* was also deployed to the area.

These two related confrontations were the first of the Cold War during which the West stood firm behind allies. In due course both issues were resolved through diplomacy.

SEQUEL

With Britain having to reduce her financial commitments in the immediate post-war years the United States gave support to Turkey, which became a member of NATO in 1952.

The United States also attempted to ensure that Iran remained on-side, backing a coup in 1953 against the Nationalist Prime Minister Dr Mohammad Mossadegh which resulted in the reign of the Shah until he was deposed in 1979. Since then Iran has been involved in a costly war with Iraq, and at the time of writing appears to be moderating its position.

Iran and Turkey, 1946

Unit	Aircraft (code)	Base	From	To
RAF				
680 Sqn	Mosquito XVI	Habbaniya	2.45	1.9.46
FAA				
805 NAS	Firefly I	HMS *Ocean*	7.46	6.48
816 NAS	Firefly I	HMS *Ocean*	7.46	6.48
1702 NAS det	Sea Otter I	HMS *Ocean*	7.46	6.48
USN CVBG-75				
VF-75	F4U-4	USS *Franklin D. Roosevelt*	6.8.46	4.10.46
VBF-75	F4U-4	USS *FDR*	6.8.46	4.10.46
VB-75	SB2C-5	USS *FDR*	6.8.46	4.10.46
VT-75	SB2C-5	USS *FDR*	6.8.46	4.10.46

2.2   THE BERLIN AIRLIFT, 1948–9

BACKGROUND

At the end of the Second World War, Germany was occupied by France, Great Britain, the Soviet Union and the United States. The division of Germany into zones resulted in serious problems for the Western Allies, given that the Western zones were the heart of industrial capacity, while the Eastern, Soviet, zone was primarily agricultural. The Russians retained foodstocks, and one result of this was bread rationing in the UK to ensure that grain was available in Germany; bread had not been rationed throughout the war!

Berlin, the German capital, was in the Soviet-controlled Eastern zone but was also occupied by the four Powers. With Russian influence extending throughout eastern Europe, Stalin felt that Berlin should be unified within the Soviet sphere of influence.

Access to the city from the Western zones was by three rail routes, one major and two lesser roads and by air, all carefully monitored by the Russians. On 31 March 1948, it was announced that all road traffic would be subject to inspection. The next day a US military train carrying 300 personnel was stopped and documentation sought and inspected. The Americans immediately started flying in all military supplies to Berlin, and in eleven days moved 327 tons. In June, the Western occupying Powers announced their intention to create a single West German state.

BLOCKADE

On 15 June all rail traffic into Berlin was stopped, and on the 19th the British Air Forces of Occupation's (BAFO) planned Operation *Knicker* was issued. This provided for the resupply of the British Berlin garrison by air. All rail and road passenger and freight traffic was formally cut from 06.00 hrs on 24 June, and the following day the Russians announced that they would not provide food for the 2.25 million people living in the western parts of Berlin.

RAF Dakotas began flying into Germany from the UK, beginning with 30 Sqn from Oakington, and the USAF made immediate arrangements to begin pulling in C-54 Skymasters to supplement the 105 C-47s of 60 and 61 Troop Carrier Groups (TCG). The decision to maintain the city, for an indefinite period and relying solely on air supply, had been taken.

The airlift began formally on 26 June 1948: the task was to transport a minimum of 4,500 tons of essential materials daily. Operation *Knicker* was ordered on 28 June, and RAF Dakotas of 38 and 46 Groups flew in 44 tons in the first twenty-four hours of operations. Two days later, as Yorks of 47 Group joined the Dakotas in Germany, the exercise was updated to Operation *Carter Paterson*; in July the British part in the airlift was renamed Operation *Plainfare*, while the US part was named Operation *Vittles*.

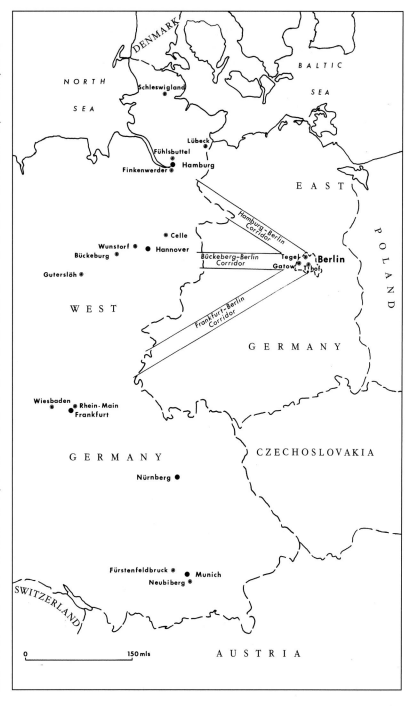

On 5 July Sunderland flying-boats of 201 and 230 Sqns from Calshot began flying in salt, and the first York sortie was flown to Gatow on the 10th. The West German airfields in closest proximity to Berlin were in the British zone: Schleswigland in the north, Fühlsbuttel outside Hamburg, Lübeck on the border, Fassberg and Celle north of Hannover, and Wunstorf and Buckeburg to the west of Hannover. The Sunderlands used a stretch of the Elbe east of Hamburg at Finkenwerder.

Much farther away, near Frankfurt in the US zone, were Rhein-Main and Wiesbaden. In Berlin there was Gatow (British sector) and Tempelhof (American sector), the Sunderlands alighting on Havel See, which conveniently backed on to Gatow. In August construction of a third airfield began at Tegel, in the French sector, and it was operating from 7 December 1948.

The aircraft flying into Berlin used one of two air corridors, twenty miles wide and 10,000 feet high, from Hamburg and Frankfurt, and returned via a third towards Hannover or at low level using the Hamburg corridor. The northern and central routes were over flat country, but the longer southern route lay over mountains. Timing was critical, and aircraft were required to report at beacons at Wedding for Tempelhof and Frohnau for Gatow and Tegel within thirty seconds of scheduled time. Flights often arrived at the rate of one every four minutes.

Initially the RAF Dakotas had been based at Wunstorf, but the Yorks' arrival resulted in overcrowding. The Dakotas transferred to Fassberg on 19 July. By now some transports had been buzzed by Soviet fighters, and with only one Fighter Group (FG) in Europe (the 86th, equipped with the F-51D), the US deployed the 56th FG with the F-80A to Furstenfeldbruck. A second FG, the 36th, brought its F-80 Shooting Stars to Europe by sea, and in August it replaced the 56th at Furstenfeldbruck.

The RAF maintained one Tempest Wing at Gütersloh, and 80 Sqn joined it there on 14 July, having spent three weeks at Gatow. The US moved one B-29 Group from the States to West Germany and a further three to East Anglia; these latter moves were intended to convince the Russians that the West regarded the situation seriously. The Bomb Groups (BG) were rotated every ninety days from the USA. In addition, the four Germany-based Mosquito light-bomber squadrons were placed on alert, as were the Mosquitoes, Lancasters and Lincolns (a total of seven wings) of RAF Bomber Command in the UK.

Later in the month, on the 27th, the first British civil charter flight was made when a Lancastrian of Flight Refuelling Ltd transported a load of M/T fuel. Liquid fuels were to provide much of the work for the charter companies flying mainly from Wunstorf and, latterly, Schleswigland.

The C-54 was now replacing the USAF C-47 in large numbers, being brought in from Panama, Hawaii, Alaska, the Aleutians, Guam and TAC. Overcrowding at the two US bases became a problem, and from 22 August some fifty C-54s moved into Fassberg, forcing the RAF Dakotas to move again, this time to Lübeck. By the end of September all USAF C-47s had been withdrawn, and on the RAF side Australian, New Zealand and South African crews joined the effort.

A joint Anglo-American organization was established as the Combined Air Lift Task Force (CALTF) on 15 October to ease the difficult scheduling and co-ordinating problems being encountered. The commander of CALTF was the experienced Gen. William H. Tunner, who had earlier organized the massive airlift in South-East Asia from Assam over the 'Hump' to China. His resources were further enhanced from 11 November with the first RAF Hastings sortie from Schleswigland. Two days earlier two USN R5D units had also begun operations, attached to existing TCCs.

By now the US had phased out the C-47 and operated the C-54 or R5D in five transport groups. From Rhein-Main, 60 TCG had moved to Wiesbaden to make room for 513 TCG; also at Wiesbaden was 317 TCG, which moved to Celle on 16 December, while 313 TCG was at Fassberg. The newer TCGs were formed from squadrons that had arrived from across the world in the summer. The extra resources more than compensated for the withdrawal of the Sunderlands from 14 December through concerns that the Havel See would ice over (the winter of 1948/9 was particularly vicious). Apart from the C-47 and C-54, the USAF also used five C-82s from September 1948, and a sole C-74 and a C-97 towards the end of the operation.

The airlift continued through the winter with little sign of relief, but in March 1949 the Soviet delegate to the UN hinted that the blockade could be lifted. By 4 May the four Powers had reached agreement, and free access was enabled from 00.01 hrs on 12 May. The airlift did not end, however, as stocks were built up.

From July, units began to return to other commitments, and on 1 September CALTF was disbanded. The airlift officially finished with a USAF flight on 30 September after 462 days. The last civilian flight had been on 16 August, the last RAF flight on 23 September.

After a precarious start the airlift ran smoothly, thanks to superb organization and commitment. Aircraft and aircrews were to some extent pooled, and because of the demands on flying time completely new maintenance arrangements were made. Despite the intensity of flying and the pressure on aircraft and their crews, accidents were relatively few. The US lost four C-47s, six C-54s and one R5D, with a total of 27 killed. The RAF lost three Dakotas, one York and a Hastings, with a loss of life of eighteen plus seven German passengers. Three civilian Haltons and a York were lost, together with ten aircrew.

After the war many surplus Dakotas were bought by emergent civil airlines, often established by ex-RAF personnel. Many of these were used on the Berlin airlift. Seen at Fülsbuttel are aircraft of Kearsley Airways and Air Transport.
(Crown copyright)

During the airlift 2,325,800 short tons (2,000 lb) of supplies were delivered in 277,804 flights committing a total of 57,000 personnel. This averaged 5,560 tons a day, or one ton per Berliner over the period. The total included 1,586,539 tons of coal and 538,016 tons of food. Wet fuel made up most of the remainder and was generally handled by civilian contractors at a contract rate of £98 per hour. The RAF also handled backloading, which included the 'export' of 7,530 tons of mail, 6,800 tons of freight, 5,000 tons of manufactured goods and 35,600 people. The overall balance of activity of the three contributors was as follows:

	USAF/USN	RAF	Civilian
Tonnage	1,783,572	394,509	147,727
Sorties	189,963	65,857	21,984
No. of aircraft	441	147	104
Accidents (fatal)	11	7	6
Lives lost (total)	28	30	10

The United States managed 76.7% of the tonnage, the RAF 17% and the civilian aircraft 6.3%. But this was not the whole picture, since the RAF also brought in awkward freight loads and brought out people and 34,240 tons of manufactured goods for export.

Finally, mention should be made of the units working in the background to support the airlift. The RAF operated a maintenance function at RAF Honington where all major servicing of Dakotas was carried out. The Transport Command Major Servicing Unit operated a 'Plumber' flight of six Dakotas supplying parts to bases in Germany. A similar function was carried out at RAF Burtonwood, Lancashire, for the USAF aircraft. The USAF also operated 18 Weather Squadron from Rhein-Main to provide critical meteorological support.

SEQUEL

Berlin is, for the Western Powers, a symbolic but tangible illustration of their determination to stand firm against the perceived threat of Communist expansion in Europe. The organization of the airlift, bearing in mind the relatively small individual loads carried, was a major achievement, and it was clear that air supply could have kept the city sustained, if not thriving, indefinitely.

AVRO YORK

The Avro Type 585 York was first flown in July 1942, but it was not in significant RAF service during the war. Due in large part to American constraints on British development and production of transport aircraft, as just one condition of Lend-Lease, the type was based on the Lancaster, utilising the bomber's wings, undercarriage and engines but with a new, box-section fuselage and tail unit. It was built to Specification C.1/42 to carry twenty-four passengers or 6,400 lb of freight.

The basic York **C Mark I** was powered by four Merlin T.24 engines that gave it a top speed of 298 mph at 21,000 ft. It served with ten squadrons, and played a significant part in the Berlin Airlift, being replaced by the Hastings in due course. The York was fitted either as a freighter or passenger transport or in a combined form; it was finally withdrawn from service in 1957.

Transport units equipped – 24, 40, 48, 51, 59, 99, 206, 242, 246, 511; 1310, 1359 Flts

Dakota KN369/49 of the Waterbeach wing is refuelled at Lübeck. The Dakotas, C-47s and DC-3s were supplemented by the more capacious York, C-54 and Haltons and Lancastrians in RAF, USAF and civilian service respectively.
(Crown copyright)

The Berlin Airlift, 1948–9

Airlift

Unit	Aircraft (code)	Base	From	Home base
RAF				
38 Group				
30 Sqn	Dakota (JN)	see below*	25.6.48	Oakington
46 Sqn	Dakota (XK)	see below*	28.6.48	Oakington
18 Sqn	Dakota	see below*	28.6.48	Waterbeach
27 Sqn	Dakota	see below*	7.48	Oakington
53 Sqn	Dakota (PU)	see below*	7.48	Waterbeach
77 Sqn	Dakota (YS)	see below*	7.48	Waterbeach
240 OCU	Dakota (NU)	see below*	7.48	Waterbeach
62 Sqn	Dakota	see below*	21.7.48	Waterbeach
238 Sqn[1]	Dakota	see below*	7.48	Oakington
10 Sqn[2]	Dakota	Lübeck	4.10.48	Oakington
24 Sqn	Dakota	Lübeck	22.8.48	Bassingbourn

Aircraft of these units were deployed during June or July, first to Wunstorf, then to Fassberg from 19 July 1948, and finally to Lübeck from 22 August 1948. From here they returned to the UK from June to September 1949.

Notes – [1] to 10 Sqn [2] ex-238 Sqn

Unit	Aircraft (code)	Base	From	Home base
47 Group				
24 Sqn	York C.1	Wunstorf	9.48	Bassingbourn
40 Sqn	York C.1	Wunstorf	19.7.48	Abingdon
51 Sqn	York C.1 (MH)	Wunstorf	19.7.48	Bassingbourn
59 Sqn	York C.1 (BY)	Wunstorf	19.7.48	Abingdon
99 Sqn	York C.1 (A)	Wunstorf	19.7.48	Lyneham
242 Sqn	York C.1 (KY)	Wunstorf	19.7.48	Abingdon
511 Sqn	York C.1	Wunstorf	19.7.48	Lyneham
241 OCU	York C.1 (YY)	Wunstorf	9.48	Lyneham
206 Sqn	York C.1	Wunstorf	11.48	Lyneham
47 Sqn	Hastings C.1	Schleswigland	1.11.48	Dishforth
297 Sqn	Hastings C.1	Schleswigland	28.11.48	Dishforth

Unit	Aircraft (code)	Base	From	Home base
19 Group				
201 Sqn	Sunderland GR.5 (NS)	Finkenwerder	5.7.48	Calshot
230 Sqn	Sunderland GR.5 (4X)	Finkenwerder	5.7.48	Calshot

The Sunderlands returned to the UK on 14 December 1948 with the onset of winter and the potential for ice on the Havel See

Unit	Aircraft (code)	Base	From	Home base
Plumber Flt	Dakota	Honington	10.48	Honington
USAF				
60 TCG*				
10 TCS	C-47, C-54	Rhein-Main	6.48	Rhein-Main
12 TCS	C-47, C-54	Rhein-Main	6.48	Rhein-Main
333 TCS	C-47, C-54	Rhein-Main	6.48	Rhein-Main
62 TCG	C-82A (5 a/c)	Rhein-Main	16.9.48	Bergstrom AFB
1601 ATG	C-74 (1 a/c)	Kaufbeuren	17.8.48	Brookley AFB

* From 16 December 1948 the 60th TCG moved to Wiesbaden

61 TCG

14 TCS	C-47, C-54	Rhein-Main	26.6.48	Rhein-Main
15 TCS	C-47, C-54	Rhein-Main	26.6.48	Rhein-Main
53 TCS	C-47, C-54	Rhein-Main	26.6.48	Rhein-Main
VR-8	R5D	Rhein-Main	9.11.48	Honolulu

513 TCG

330 TCS	C-47, C-54	Rhein-Main	7.48	*see* note below
331 TCS	C-47, C-54	Rhein-Main	7.48	*see* note below
332 TCS	C-47	Rhein-Main	7.48	*see* note below
VR-6	R5D	Rhein-Main	9.11.48	Guam

317 TCG*

39 TCS	C-54	Wiesbaden	8.48
40 TCS	C-54	Wiesbaden	8.48
41 TCS	C-54	Wiesbaden	8.48

* From 16 December 1948 the 317th TCG moved to Celle

313 TCG

11 TCS	C-54	Fassberg	21.8.48	
29 TCS	C-54	Fassberg	21.8.48	
47 TCS	C-54	Fassberg	21.8.48	
48 TCS	C-54	Fassberg	21.8.48	Bergstrom AFB

All USAF C-47s had been withdrawn by the end of September 1948 to be replaced by the C-54. C-54 aircraft for 513 TCG were provided by 19 TCS (Hickam AFB), 20 TCS (Panama) and 54 TCS (Anchorage)

18 WS	WB-29A	Rhein-Main	00.6.48

British civil operators

Operator	Type	Usual base	Sorties
Air Contractors	Dakota	Fühlsbuttel	386
Airflight	Tudor, Lincoln	Wunstorf	967
Airwork	Bristol Freighter	Fühlsbuttel	74
Air Transport(CI)	Dakota	Fühlsbuttel	205
Aquila Airways	Hythe	Finkenwerder	265
BAAS	Halton	Fühlsbuttel, Schleswigland	661
British Nederland AS	Dakota	Fühlsbuttel	76
BSAA	Tudor 2/V	Wunstorf	2,562
BOAC	Dakota	Fühlsbuttel	81
Bond Air Services	Halton	Fühlsbuttel	2,577
Ciros Aviation	Dakota	Fühlsbuttel	328
Eagle Aviation	Halton	Fühlsbuttel	1,054
Flight Refuelling	Lancastrian	Wunstorf, Schleswigland	4,438
Hornton Airways	Dakota	Fühlsbuttel	108
Kearsley Airways	Dakota	Fühlsbuttel	246
Lancashire Aircraft Corp.	Halton	Schleswigland	2,760
Scottish Airlines	Dakota, Liberator	Wunstorf	497

Operator	Type	Usual base	Sorties
Silver City Airways	Bristol Freighter	Fühlsbuttel	213
Sivewright Airways	Dakota	Fühlsbuttel	32
Skyflight	Halton	Fühlsbuttel	40
Skyways	York. Lancastrian	Wunstorf, Schleswigland	2,749
Transworld Charter	Viking	Wunstorf	118
Trent Valley Aviation	Dakota	Fühlsbuttel	186
World Air Freight	Halton	Fühlsbuttel	526
Westminster Airways	Dakota, Halton	Fühlsbuttel, Schleswigland	772

Air defence in Germany

Unit	Aircraft (code)	Base	From	To
RAF				
3 Sqn	Vampire F.1 (J5)	Gütersloh[1]	25.6.48	9.8.48
80 Sqn	Spitfire F.24 (W2)	Wunstorf	5.6.48	22.6.48
		Gatow	22.6.48	14.7.48
		Gütersloh[2]	14.7.48	2.7.49
135 Wing				
16 Sqn	Tempest F.2 (EG)	Gütersloh[3]	2.2.48	12.48
	Vampire FB.5 (EG)	Gütersloh	12.48	
26 Sqn	Tempest F.2 (XC)	Gütersloh[4]	6.3.48	4.49
	Vampire FB.5 (XC)	Gütersloh	4.49	
33 Sqn	Tempest F.2 (5R)	Gütersloh	5.6.48	2.7.49

Notes – [1] to Lübeck 9.8.48 to 4.9.48. [2] to Lübeck 22.7.48 to 24.8.48. [3] to Lübeck 14.7.48 to 7.8.48. [4] to Lübeck 7.6.48 to 5.7.48

York AJ of 99 Sqn being loaded by Coles crane at Wunstorf. RAF Yorks completed over 29,000 sorties typically with eight ton loads. *(Crown copyright)*

USAF

86th Fighter Group

| 525, 526, 527 FS | F-47D | Neubiberg | 1.7.48 | |

56th Fighter Group[1]

| 13, 61, 62, 63 FS | F-80A | Fürstenfeldbruck | 21.7.48 | 31.8.48 |

36th Fighter Group

| 22, 23, 53 FS | F-80A, B | Fürstenfeldbruck | 13.8.48 | |

Notes – [1] From Selfridge Field pending arrival of newly formed 36th FG

Strategic bombers – mainly UK based

Unit (code)	Aircraft	Base
RAF		
1 Group		
105, 139 (XD) Sqns	Mosquito B.16, 35	Coningsby
9 (WS), 12 (PH), 101 (SR), 617 (KC) Sqns	Lincoln B.2	Binbrook
50 (VN), 57 (DX), 61 (QR) Sqns	Lincoln B.2	Waddington
83 (OL), 97 (OF), 100 (HW) Sqns	Lincoln B.2	Hemswell
3 Group		
7 (MG), 49 (EA), 148 (AU), 214 (QN) Sqns	Lancaster B.1, 3	Upwood
35 (TL), 115 (KO), 149 (OJ), 207 (EM) Sqns	Lancaster B.1, 3	Stradishall
15 (LS), 44 (KM), 90 (WP), 138 (NF) Sqns	Lincoln B.2	Wyton

Unit	Aircraft	Base	From	To
USAF TDY				
301 BG ex-Smoky Hill AFB				
32, 352, 353 BS	B-29A	Fürstenfeldbruck	6.48	8.48
28 BG ex-Rapid City AFB				
77, 717, 718 BS	B-29A	Scampton	17.7.48	10.48
307 BG ex-MacDill AFB				
370, 371, 372 BS	B-29A	Marham	18.7.48	11.48
2 BG ex-Hunter AFB				
20, 49, 96 BS	B-29A	Lakenheath	8.8.48	13.11.48
301 BG ex-Smoky Hill AFB				
32, 352, 353 BS	B-29A	Scampton	10.48	1.49
22 BG ex-Smoky Hill AFB				
2, 19, 33 BS	B-29A	Lakenheath	17.11.48	15.2.49

This Avro Tudor G-AHNI of British South American Airways is here being loaded with heavy boxed freight at Wunstorf. The BSAA fleet flew over 2,500 sorties during the airlift. *(Crown copyright)*

97 BG ex-Biggs AFB

340 BS	B-29A	Marham	20.11.48	15.2.49
341, 342 BS	B-29A	Waddington	20.11.48	15.2.49

92 BW ex-Spokane AFB

325, 326, 327 BS	B-29A	Sculthorpe	7.2.49	5.49

307 BW ex-MacDill AFB

370 BS	B-29A	Marham	15.2.49	5.49
371, 372 BS	B-29A	Lakenheath	15.2.49	5.49

2.3   ALBANIA, UKRAINE, POLAND AND THE BALTIC STATES, 1949–54

BACKGROUND

At the end of the Second World War the British Special Operations Executive (SOE) and American Office of Strategic Services (OSS) were largely disbanded on the basis that there would longer be a need for special, or covert, operations. However, as the Soviet Union tightened its grip on eastern Europe, some limited action was permitted where it appeared that there was some genuine expectation of revolution from within. At least four areas chosen for insertion of agents were Albania, Ukraine, Poland and the Baltic states.

LOST CAUSES

To the British Albania was an obvious place in which to foment unrest. It was known that Albania was providing arms to the Greek Communists, probably on behalf of the Soviet Union. Second, Albania was geographically isolated from the USSR. Third, it was discovered that the Soviet Union had reached agreement to build a submarine base at Valdona. Fourth, there was a continuing case in the International Court over the Corfu Channel Incident of 1946.

On 14 May 1946 HMS *Orion* and HMS *Superb* had been fired on by Albanian shore batteries while asserting the right to sail in international waters between Corfu and Albania. On 22 October 1946 a naval convoy comprising the cruisers HMS *Mauritius* and HMS *Leander* and destroyers HMS *Saumarez* and HMS *Volage* sailed the Corfu Channel further to assert the right. *Saumarez* hit a mine in a freshly laid minefield and suffered considerable damage, with thirty-one dead and many wounded. HMS *Volage* made to take the stricken ship in tow and was herself damaged by a second mine, with the loss of thirteen of her crew. Among vessels in support was HMS *Ocean* with two Firefly squadrons embarked. The UK froze Albanian assets and sought compensation.

The Secret Intelligence Service decided to run Albanian dissidents into the country in Operation *Valuable*. Some 200 Albanians were recruited from displaced persons' camps and trained on Malta before being sent by boat or overland from Greece from October 1949, although there had been some probing expeditions earlier. Landing places were selected from examination of reconnaissance photos taken by Mosquitoes of 13 Sqn.

Unfortunately, most groups inserted were soon compromised, although some stragglers returned through Greece or Yugoslavia. From 1950 the CIA picked up the reins and trained a larger group as Company 2000 near Munich, members of which were parachuted into Albania via Greece, probably Crete. The pilots involved were reported to be ex-RAF Polish aircrew. The exercise was abandoned in 1954, but not before at least one group was turned by the Albanian Secret Police to encourage the Americans to continue to send agents and equipment.

It would seem that the British did not expect to secure revolution, but rather to destabilize the Albanian Government and to gain intelligence. In the Ukraine, though, there was a limited hope of a popular uprising, given the history of Ukraine's acceptance of German occupation, and indeed support for Germany in the Second World

Mosquito PR.34 VL619 of 13 Sqn, seen here in cerulean blue finish. For some years after the war the PR Mosquito was largely immune from interception and the aircraft were involved in covert identification and mapping of possible landing sites in Albania. (*Author's collection*)

War. Many guerillas had taken to the hills, and there were many émigrés willing to make contact and support unrest. Agents were also trained in Malta and dropped from Dakotas flying from there or from Crete in Operations *Project* I, II, III and IV.

The aircraft used routes reconnoitered by ELINT aircraft and known to be free of radar cover. (The author has failed to identify which, if any, RAF unit was involved. It is just possible that civil aircraft were used under contract at a time when many ex-RAF pilots were operating shoestring 'airlines' and would have been pleased of work, however risky.) As in Albania, there was a significant CIA complementary action. In reality there was little chance of doing more than irritate Premier Stalin.

Another area seen ripe for intelligence gathering was the Baltic States, where SIS had excellent contacts and agents from the wartime period. No details appear to have been published of agent dropping. Finally, Poland was also seen as susceptible to incursion, and numerous agents were dropped for some years after the war in predominantly American operations.

The USA used the 582nd Air Resupply Group to infiltrate and extricate agents in eastern Europe. In addition a major CIA signals station was established in the UK in 1954 under RAF cover, probably at RAF Croughton.

SEQUEL

Soviet Premier Josef Stalin maintained a ruthless grip across the Soviet Bloc, which made it almost impossible for agents, guerillas or insurgents to operate. There was little chance of any revolt but every chance of securing much-needed intelligence. Further, the various émigré factions exaggerated their support and intelligence and were also both penetrated and lax in terms of security. However, the efforts, although costly, did have some useful by-products. In an operation outside the scope of this book, the CIA tainted numerous Eastern Bloc politicians with alleged contact with spies and agents, resulting in a very large number of 'innocent' Communists being arrested and imprisoned or executed.

In 1991 the Ukraine left the Soviet Union in the wake of the Chernobyl nuclear reactor disaster, prompting its demise.

Albania, Ukraine, Poland and the Baltic States, 1949–54

Unit	Aircraft	Base
FAA (October 1946)		
805 NAS	Firefly FR.1	HMS *Ocean*
816 NAS	Firefly FR.1, NF.1	HMS *Ocean*
RAF (1949–51)		
13 Sqn	Mosquito PR.34	Kabrit
?	Dakota	? Egypt
USAF (1949–57)		
433 TCW	C-119C	Rhein-Main
582 ARG	C-47, C-119C,	
	B-29A, SA-16A	Wiesbaden, RAF Molesworth

2.4   KOREA, 1950–53

The Korean War was the second major confrontation between Communism and the West, after the Berlin Airlift, and it was the first to embrace all-out war. The British committed considerable ground forces, but in the air were primarily represented by the Fleet Air Arm. At this time the RAF was committed to building a bomber force and its associated defence, and was also fighting in Malaya and South Arabia, while retaining a considerable presence in the Middle East, notably in Egypt. Further, Korea was unknown to the British and was outside Far East Command. Britain thus played an important, but relatively limited, part, which is described after the flow of the war is related in broad terms.

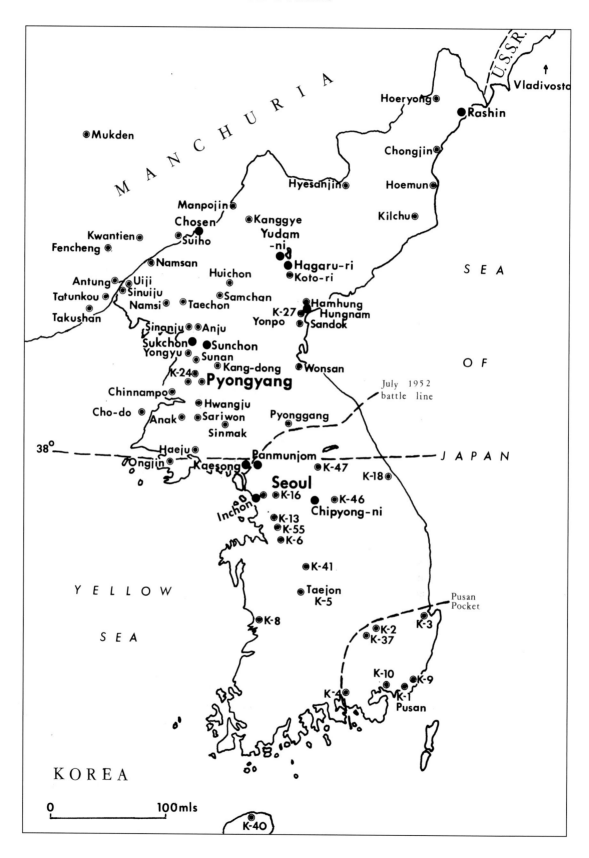

That the war was a confrontation between the West and the Soviet Union is without doubt. The Soviet Union had aided the People's Republic of China in respect of air defence since February 1949, when the PRC had requested help with air cover against Nationalist Chinese raids from Taiwan. From November 1950 the 64th Fighter Aviation Corps was formed in Manchuria to defend airfields, bridges and power stations supplying North Korea, freeing the Chinese and North Koreans to pursue the ground war. Initially Soviet advisers were required to remain north of the 38th Parallel, but from September 1951 they remained clear of the country altogether. The MiG-15s were painted in Chinese markings, and aircrews wore Chinese uniforms, speaking in limited Korean on air. At its peak the Soviet Air Corps comprised over 300 fighters, nearly all MiG-15s. In addition the North Korean Air Force and Chinese Volunteer Air Divisions fielded a further hundred MiGs by 1951.

BACKGROUND

At the end of the Second World War, the Japanese occupied Korea. The Soviet Union was given responsibility for disarming the Japanese north of the 38th Parallel, while the United States had a similar task in the south. It was then assumed that the two Koreas would unify, but this did not happen. Instead, a Communist regime developed in the north, and Kim Il Sung was proclaimed President of the Democratic People's Republic of Korea in September 1948, just three months before the Russians departed; in the south, Dr Syngman Rhee became President at the same time.

For the next two years there were incidents across the parallel, but the Americans, who retained an advisory group in the south, underestimated the military strength of the north and the degree of anti-Rhee feeling in the south, where no progress was being made to rebuilding and reform.

THE WAR OVERALL

Without warning, the North Koreans invaded the south at 04.00 hrs on 25 June 1950, quickly reaching Kaesong. The United Nations met, and in the absence of the Soviet Union adopted a resolution calling for the withdrawal of North Korean forces. Two days later, as the US agreed to give support to South Korea, the UN called on member nations to give aid in repelling the invasion. That day USAF B-29s bombed targets on the Han river outside Seoul, but this did not prevent the capital falling on the 29th.

The North Korean People's Army (NKPA) pushed south relentlessly. The first US troops of the 24th Infantry Division had landed at Pusan on 1 July, and when they met the NKPA on the 4th at Osan the leading elements were routed. By 2 August the Americans, now forced back to the Naktong river, had reinforced the initial division with three more and the First Marines Brigade. They now held a perimeter roughly forty miles around Pusan, and as the British 27th Brigade arrived from Hong Kong, plans were already in hand for relieving the position.

It was decided to mount an invasion way behind enemy lines at Inchon, the gateway to Seoul. Involving no fewer than 230 allied ships and risking high tides, the invasion was successful, and by the 26th X Corps led by the Marines had retaken Seoul; at the same time UN forces broke out of the Pusan pocket.

Whereas it was the UN intention to stabilise the borders at the 38th Parallel, the Supreme UN Commander, General MacArthur, thought otherwise, and South Korean Republic of Korea (ROK) troops crossed the parallel on 1 October, followed a week later by US forces. UN troops now advanced at a very fast rate: on the 19th Pyongyang fell as the 187th Regimental Combat Team was parachuted into positions north of the city to cut supply lines and escape routes, and on 25 October the ROK 6th Division reached Chosan on the Yalu river, where they were suddenly confronted by counter-attacking Chinese troops of the Chinese People's Volunteer Army (CPVA).

The entry of the Chinese into the war came as a total surprise, and within days the UN forces were forced to

The RAF commitment to Korea was necessarily limited given commitments in Malaya and in Europe. However, Sunderlands of the flying boat wing at Singapore (88, 205 and 209 Sqns) were detached to Iwakuni in Japan and operated under the control of Fleet Air Wing 6 in the maritime reconnaissance role. They also flew supplies and mail into and from Hong Kong. *(via A S Thomas)*

retreat. The next surprise for the UN came on 1 November, when for the first time Chinese MiG-15 fighters appeared over North Korea; the first major air battle followed on the 8th. After a lull in the fighting as diplomatic moves were made, MacArthur launched an offensive on the 24th, which was followed by a Chinese counter-attack on the 26th. On the east coast, the UN was forced to evacuate Hungnam and Wonsan by sea and air, and on Christmas Day the Chinese crossed the 38th Parallel.

A fresh Communist offensive began on New Year's Day, and within three days Seoul was once more in Communist hands. By the middle of the month the Chinese were halted at a line from Suwon to Wonju. The UN Eighth Army in turn counter-attacked, retaking Seoul on 13 March and recrossing the parallel on the 22nd. On 11 April MacArthur was relieved of his command after public criticism of President Truman's concept of limited war, and General Ridgway was appointed to succeed him.

The Chinese then began their spring offensive, and after the Battle of Imjin River the Eighth Army was pushed back to a position north of Seoul. The front line now stabilised as UN Air Forces began Operation *Strangle* in an endeavour to cut the Chinese supply routes, but without a committed ground offensive the CPVA was able to conserve its stocks and the operation failed to meet its objectives through no fault of the Air Forces.

Moves were now made to arrange a ceasefire, and armistice negotiations began at Kaesong on 10 July, discussions which were to drag on for two years. Henceforward, much of the air effort would be directed to forcing the Chinese to maintain the negotiations. The first sticking point came over the repatriation of prisoners of war. Nearly half of those taken by UN forces did not wish to return, but the Chinese rejected the idea of voluntary repatriation.

By May 1952 the talks were at a stalemate, so to concentrate the Communist mind major air strikes on the North Korean power system began on 23 June. Then, on 11 July, and again on 29 August, Pyongyang was subjected to the heaviest air raids of the war. In October an indefinite recess in the talks was announced, but at the end of March 1953 the Chinese agreed to the voluntary exchange of sick and wounded prisoners. On 26 April armistice talks resumed at Panmunjom, but UN forces maintained pressure. On 13 May the North Korean irrigation dams were breached, and the following week the American National Security Council determined that, if conditions dictated, the war would be pursued into China.

The prisoner-of-war problem was finally resolved on 8 June, but two days later the Chinese launched yet another offensive at Kumsong, primarily for reasons of 'face' and to establish the most favourable ceasefire line. The armistice was signed on 27 July and became effective at 22.00 hrs.

This brief summary of events and the details of British involvement in the air war which follow necessarily make little reference to the war on the ground, which was as vicious as any in modern times. South Korean military casualties were put at 415,000 dead and 249,000 wounded, while the Americans, who bore the brunt of the fighting, lost 33,629 men with 105,785 wounded. The other UN participants lost over 3,000 dead and nearly 12,000 wounded; estimates of Chinese and North Korean dead range from 1 to 1.5 million.

UN Air Forces flew 1,040,708 sorties for the loss of 2,670 aircraft on operations, while North Korean and Chinese losses certainly exceeded 2,200 aircraft. North and South Korea remain technically at war, and from time to time there have been border incidents.

BRITISH INVOLVEMENT – THE CARRIERS

As has already been mentioned, the RAF played a limited role in the Korean War, but the geography of the country was such that naval power, and especially air power, was in its element. Thus there was a continuing British carrier presence throughout the war, operating in concert with the US Navy. The Army operated two flights of Austers, maintained by the RAF, which also flew the Sunderland flying-boats on maritime patrol.

When North Korean forces invaded the South there were two Allied aircraft carriers in the region: USS *Valley Forge* was at Subic Bay in the Philippines, while HMS *Triumph* was *en route* to Hong Kong from Japanese waters. Both carriers were immediately stocked with emergency provisions, *Triumph* at Kure in Japan, and they sailed on 29 June for the Korean west coast.

Valley Forge, an Essex Class carrier, embarked Carrier Air Group (CAG) 5, comprising no fewer than five full squadrons and a photo-reconnaissance detachment. The mix of units, typical of the first two years of operations, comprised VF-51 and VF-52 with the F9F-2 Panther, VF-53 and VF-54 with the F4U-4 Corsair and VA-55 with the AD-2 Skyraider; the PR detachment of VC-61 flew the F4U-5P.

The Royal Navy was able to make a significant contribution to the Korean War. The light fleet carrier HMS *Theseus* (R64), 17,720 tons, is seen at Spithead about to depart for the Far East with Sea Furies of 807 NAS and Fireflies of 810 NAS embarked. Lurking in the background is the escort destroyer HMS *Ulster* (D83). *(Author's collection)*

Triumph was a Colossus Class carrier and embarked CAG-13 with just two units, 800 NAS with the Seafire FR.47 and 827 NAS with the Firefly FR.1, although the Royal Navy squadron inventory was greater than that of USN units. The US and British carriers were 890 ft and 690 ft in overall length and their displacements 33,250 and 13,350 tons respectively. The FAA Seafires were painted with black and white 'invasion' stripes to distinguish them from the broadly similar Yak-9.

On station the ships joined Task Force (TF) 77 as Task Group (TG) 77.4, and began operations on 3 July, initially against North Korean airfields and troop movements along coastal roads. The first strikes were against airfields at Pyongyang and Onjong-ni (CAG-5) and Haeju and Ongjin (CAG-13), and saw the first use of naval jet aircraft in combat. At least ten aircraft were destroyed on the ground and two Yak-9s were shot down by F9F-2 pilots flying cover for the strikes. The twelve Seafires and nine Fireflies from *Triumph* were less fortunate, and no aircraft were sighted on the ground although installations were bombed.

On 4 July the RN asked for Sunderlands to help in the anti-submarine role, and one was sent from 88 Sqn at Hong Kong to Iwakuni. For the next few weeks the Seafires flew fleet combat air patrols while the Fireflies maintained anti-submarine sorties. (The importance of Hong Kong to the war effort was high. It acted as a staging-post for transports from the west, as an important naval base and as a welcome rest and recuperation centre. It was thus of interest to the Chinese, and from summer 1949 two fighter squadrons remained based in the colony, initially with Spitfires, then with Vampires and Hornets. PR Spitfires of 81 Sqn were detached, and they routinely overflew China to check on possible preparations for assault.)

Throughout early July the pace was maintained, but as the North Koreans advanced, TG.77.4 demonstrated the flexibility of naval air power by covering, on the 15th, an amphibious landing at Pohang. The purpose of the landing was to secure the eastern end of the Pusan pocket, and as soon as the landing was completed the carrier units returned to attacking the eastern airfields, including Yonpo, Sandok and Hamhung. Altogether thirty-two

NKAF aircraft were destroyed and thirteen damaged in two days, after which the NKAF retreated to bases further north. Significantly, North Korean operations around the Pusan perimeter were made with very limited air cover after the first few days.

On 18 July CAG-5 units hit the Wonsan oil refinery with considerable success, and shortly after this TF.77 was given a free area around south-west Korea in which to operate independently, in order to maintain pressure on North Korean forces pending the Inchon landings.

The TF was joined by USS *Philippine Sea* at the end of July and USS *Boxer* from mid-September; the carriers joined the TF after having delivered 145 F-51Ds to Japan. The whole task force gathered off the west coast in September to support the Inchon landings on the 15th, where TG.90.51, comprising USMC units on the escort carriers USS *Badoeng Strait* and *Sicily*, was also stationed for close support; TF.77 units were in indirect support again, attacking airfields and hitting supply lines and bridges.

Aircraft from *Triumph* (TF.91) were also committed to bombardment spotting for the cruisers HMS *Jamaica* and HMS *Kenya* and flying combat air patrol (CAP) sorties. Patrol and reconnaissance was the function of TF.99 comprising VP-6 (P2V) and 88 and 209 Sqns RAF (Sunderland) as TG.99.1, and VP-42 and VP-47 (PBM-5) as TG.99.2. The ships were subjected to what is believed to be the only attack on vessels during the war when on the 17th a Yak-3 and an Il-10 bombed USS *Rochester*, one aircraft being shot down by AAA on HMS *Jamaica*, which was also attacked by cannon fire. By the end of September the scale of flying had been such that CAG-13 had only two Fireflies and one Seafire operational. Only one aircraft had been lost in action, however – a Seafire shot down by a B-29 in error on 28 July, the pilot being rescued from the sea.

On 25 September the British and Commonwealth TF.91 was renamed TG.95.1 and reverted to blockade tasks. (The Royal and Commonwealth navies provided many other warships, including frigates, destroyers and cruisers for the blockade and coastal bombardment task.) On 10 October *Triumph* was relieved by HMS *Theseus* with CAG-17 on board. Additional aircraft were transferred from HMS *Warrior* at Sasebo. CAG-17 comprised 807 NAS with the Sea Fury FB.11 and 810 NAS equipped with the Firefly FR.5. This combination was to be deployed for the remainder of the war by Commonwealth carriers. Together with the escort carrier USS *Bataan*, HMS *Theseus* began to effect a blockade of the Yalu estuary. The remit of the Group was set out as comprising:

1   Daily reconnaissance of the coast for enemy shipping.
2   Combat air patrol (CAP) and anti-submarine (AS) patrols over the Group.
3   Bombardment spotting.
4   Airfield surveillance.
5   Indirect close support to land forces.

In practice the carriers spent around eighteen days on station, then six days on passage to the Japanese bases at Kure and Sasebo. Here HMS *Unicorn* acted as a replenishment ship, ferrying aircraft to and from Sembawang. The carriers were in port typically for under a week to rearm, refuel and restock before transit to the operational area.

HMS *Theseus* was required to provide CAP and AS patrols, leaving around 50% capacity for offensive operations from her twenty-three Sea Furies and twelve Fireflies. First strikes were against airfields at Chinnampo and Haeju, and in thirteen days of the first operational period for the carrier 384 sorties were flown, two-thirds of them by Sea Furies. The Fireflies carried either two 500 lb or 1,000 lb bombs, while the Sea Furies tended to be armed with eight 60 lb rockets. Both types routinely carried drop-tanks to increase range.

On the third day of operations a Sea Fury was shot down, but the injured pilot was rescued from behind enemy lines by a USAF H-5A of 3 Air Rescue Squadron (ARS) courageously piloted by Lt Col J. Schumate, who was awarded the MC for his bravery. This gave the Royal Navy a foretaste of the versatility of the helicopter in this role; at that time the British carriers flew a single Sea Otter amphibian for air-sea rescue. From the *Theseus* deployment onwards, the RN carriers were supplied with a single USN HO3S-1 with pilot loaned from HU-1 to replace the Sea Otter for plane-guard tasking, but downed aircrew were picked up by helicopters from a variety of vessels and land bases.

MiG COMBAT

As UN forces moved into North Korea they were supported by naval aircraft, which by November had turned their attention to the Yalu river bridges as the Chinese invaded. During one such attack on 9 November the strike aircraft of CAG-11 from *Philippine Sea* were met by a number of MiG-15s. The covering F9F pilots were soon in combat, during which Lt Cdr W.T. Amen, the CO of VF-111, became the first pilot to bring down a victim in an all-jet dogfight. Although suspected from an early stage that at least some of the MiGs were operated by Soviet pilots, this was only confirmed after the end of the Cold War. The Korean War therefore comprised not just a United Nations police action but a direct confrontation between Russia and the United States.

Two more MiGs were shot down by naval pilots from *Valley Forge* on the 18th. From 9 to 21 November AD and F4U strike aircraft flew 593 sorties against the bridges, dropping 232 tons of bombs, and all but one was destroyed, but by now the river was freezing to the extent that rail lines could be laid over it. Naval aircraft then joined with those of the USMC to support the Marines' breakout from Chosen and generally harass the advancing Chinese.

At this stage it may be relevant to note briefly the contest between the UN fighters and the MiG-15. The latter was far superior to all Allied types except the F-86 Sabre with which it was roughly matched, although the later F-86E was generally superior. The MiG had heavier gun armament. The Americans claimed 792 MiG-15s brought down by the F-86 against seventy-eight F-86s lost in combat. In recent years, as Soviet files have been opened, it is known that Soviet claims were rather different, being 650 Sabres lost against 335 MiGs. Somewhere between lies reality.

As the land position stabilised, the task force was assigned the role of interdiction and attacking troop movements along the eastern coast. The carrier strength was maintained at four ships (three USN, one Commonwealth), but this demand initially stretched American resources. At the outbreak of the war there were only nine CAGs constituted, and on 20 July fourteen Naval Air Reserve squadrons were mobilised, with a further twenty-eight being called up from September. The first reserve CAG entered the war zone as CAG-101 embarked on USS *Boxer* on 27 March 1951, in time to take part in Operation *Strangle* designed to choke the Chinese supply system.

When HMS *Theseus* was relieved by HMS *Glory* in May, her aircraft had flown 3,489 sorties, averaging 2½ hours, off both coasts. Although not possessing the firepower of their American counterparts, the British aircraft were operated efficiently, and on one occasion a flight returning to HMS *Ocean* was landed on at 16 sec intervals. In general, the Commonwealth carriers operated off the west coast, where 30 ft tides and numerous islands, coupled with the risk of mining, made bombardment spotting largely unnecessary, especially when there were few coastal tactical targets. The American Seventh Fleet carriers sailed in the Sea of Japan with virtually no tide and a straighter coastline, with important coastal communications systems offering valuable targets.

From May to October the US attack-carrier strength was reduced to two, but from early 1952 there were never fewer than four US carriers in the theatre. In the year TG.96.7 based on the escort carrier *Bairoko* was formed, to counter a possible submarine threat. Between embarking USMC units, the escort carriers turned to anti-submarine work, and in August 1952 the AF-2W was introduced into the theatre by VS-931 on board *Badoeng Strait*.

Another change came in September 1951, when HMAS *Sydney* relieved *Glory* and began a tour of duty in the war zone. Slightly larger than the Colossus Class ships, she embarked two Sea Fury squadrons and one of Fireflies. From 15 January 1952 the naval fighters turned to night attacks on communications in Operations *Moonlight Sonata* and latterly *Insomnia*, but results were poor, and from March the roads and railways were again the main target. Then, in June, a switch was made to industrial targets.

HMS *Ocean* began her tour on 11 May, during which her aircraft set several notable records. On 17 May the ship put up 123 sorties in a day, to claim the record for the war. Then, on 9 August, when a flight of Sea Furies of 802 NAS was attacked by a number of MiG-15s north of Chinnampo, Lt P. Carmichael was able to put in several bursts on one machine to bring it down. By the end of the next day, several more MiGs were claimed as probables or damaged, and almost certainly at least one more was destroyed, although there was no third-party witness.

By 30 October, when *Ocean* withdrew, she had flown off more than 1,900 sorties, each averaging about 1 hour 40 minutes. No. 802 NAS, which included pilots from 1832 NAS Royal Naval Reserve, used 420 1,000 lb and 3,358 500 lb bombs, plus half a million rounds of cannon ammunition; 825 NAS used mainly rockets, firing nearly 16,000.

Night strikes against military installations on the east coast began again in October as the targets became too heavily defended for the slow B-29 bombers. Then, in November, matters became potentially complicated when there was an incident involving the Russians. USS *Oriskany* embarked CAG-102, which included VF-781 equipped with the more powerful -5 version of the Panther. During a bombardment south of Vladivostok on the 18th, four F9F-5s were attacked by seven MiG-15s of the Soviet Air Force, during which at least one of the latter was shot down. Fortunately there were no repercussions.

In the last two months of the war the fighting intensified, and the air groups were flying about one-third of their sorties in close-support as the Communists mounted their final offensives. When the war ended there were five carriers on station, and on the last full day of operations around 700 sorties were flown, over four times the average rate for May.

After three years of constant combat the overall naval record was impressive: TF.77 had flown 167,552 sorties and dropped 120,000 tons of bombs; fourteen enemy aircraft had been shot down, including seven MiG-15s, and around fifty destroyed on the ground. The roles were essentially attack, however, and 37,000 buildings and 4,500 trucks were among the final tally. The cost to the task force was 814 aircraft lost on operations and 354 men, of whom twenty-seven were FAA aircrew. The ten FAA squadrons involved flew a total approaching 23,000 sorties

RAF AND ARMY

The RAF did not send tactical combat units to Korea. However, the RAAF and SAAF both had fighter units operating in Korea and integrated into the USAF throughout the war. Both air forces began operations with the F-51D Mustang, the South Africans then upgrading to the F-86 while the RAAF opted for the slower and more vulnerable Meteor F8. After initial heavy combat losses the Meteor was used for close-support tasks.

The RAF did send advisers, aircrew on exchange postings to USAF and Commonwealth squadrons and specialised units, for example for photo intelligence. Eight RAF pilots served with the USAF, with a total of at least six MiG-15s claimed; one pilot was shot down. A number of RAF pilots and ground crew supported the introduction of the Meteor to RAAF service, and of the pilots three were killed in action. A number of RCAF pilots served with the USAF Sabre units and four Army pilots with the RAF's 1903 AOP Flight.

Brief mention has already been made of the Sunderland flying-boats, which during cover for the Inchon landings formed part of TG.99.1. This was the search and reconnaissance group, which also included USN P2V Neptunes of VP-6. The Sunderlands were under the control of Fleet Air Wing 6 and flew maritime patrol to enforce the blockade of North Korean ports, convoy protection, weather reconnaissance and mine-spotting sorties, as well as bringing supplies and mail in from Hong Kong. The aircraft were based at Iwakuni in Japan and completed 1,647 sorties. Because of the potential threat of attack by enemy aircraft, the air gunner role was reintroduced.

The RAF and Commonwealth air forces also provided transport support, although the only in-theatre transport was that of 30 Sqn RAAF, whose C-47s were attached to 21 TCS, 374 TCW. RAF Hastings of 53 Sqn repatriated wounded British and other European troops from Seoul to Iwakuni, from where they were flown back to Malaya or Europe by Dakotas and Hastings. Over 11,000 were evacuated to Japan. North Stars of 426 Sqn RCAF performed similar duties flying from Tokyo to McChord AFB in the US.

The air observation post squadrons equipped with the Auster AOP.6 were hybrid units maintained by the RAF but with Army (usually ex-artillery) pilots. No. 656 Sqn embraced several flights in the Far East, and of these 1903 Flt was sent from Hong Kong in July 1951 to provide artillery spotting for the Commonwealth Division. A second flight, 1913 Light Liaison Flight, was formed in the UK in June 1951 specifically for duties in Korea, where it became operational at Fort George from October. This unit, which acquired an L-19 from the US in addition to its Austers, broke the mould in that it was explicitly charged with liaison as opposed to AOP tasks. Hitherto, the RAF had claimed all flying as its own except for AOP and glider assault, and this loosening helped to lead the way to an independent Army Air Corps. By the end of the war the Army aircraft had flown 2,935 sorties with the loss of two aircraft brought down by light AAA and more lost to accidents.

SEQUEL

At the time of writing, South and North Korea remain technically at war. Significant US forces have remained in the south, and from time to time there are cross-border incidents. The border, though, remains heavily fortified on both sides. The United States also maintains a wide range of surveillance activities, and several aircraft have been brought down. (See Chapter 4, Section 5.)

SUPERMARINE SEAFIRE

In the early years of the Second World War naval fighters traded performance for ruggedness and were no match for their land-based equivalents. After successful use of the Hurricane at sea the decision was taken to convert the Spitfire for naval use. The first tests were carried out late in 1941 with a converted Spitfire Mk Vb, as a result of which the decision was taken to introduce the type to naval service. The early versions were only in second-line use by 1945.

Powered by the Merlin 55, the **Mark III** Type 358 had no RAF equivalent. It had four 20 mm cannon in a C-type wing, and the bomb-load was increased to two 250 lb or one 500 lb bombs. However, manual wing folding was employed for the first time in the Seafire, and over 1,000 were built.

Fighter units equipped – 887, 894, 1832

The Type 377 **Mk XV** was the next variant number applied, as Seafire variants were now given mark numbers interspersed with those applied to contemporary Spitfire variants. The Mk XV was the first Seafire to be fitted with the Griffon engine, but it appeared too late to see war service. It was essentially a navalized Spitfire XII with a folding, strengthened C wing with fuel tanks. A total of 392 was delivered, the Mk XV entering service with 892 NAS in May 1945.

Fighter units equipped – 800, 801, 802, 803, 804, 805, 806, 883, 1831, 1832, 1833

The Type 395 **Mark XVII** was a refined Mk XV with a clear-view canopy and an extra 33 gal of fuel in the rear fuselage. A total of 232 were produced, and the variant was the last Seafire type to remain in naval service. The Type 395 FR version comprised a limited number of Mk XVII variants fitted with two F.24 cameras (one vertical and one oblique) in place of the extra fuel tank. They were allocated to most of the units using the basic Mk XVII model.

Fighter units equipped – 800, 802, 803, 805, 807, 809, 879, 883, 887, 1831, 1832, 1833

The Type 388/474 **F Mark 47** was the final Seafire variant, being a navalised version of the Spitfire Mk 24 with wing folding, a six-blade airscrew and additional fuel. Powered by a Griffon 87/88, the Mk 47 served in Malaya and Korea. The FR model was fitted with a single F.24 camera, and most of the ninety Mk 47s were either built or converted to this standard.

Fighter units equipped – 800, 804, 1832, 1833

HAWKER SEA FURY

The P.1022 Sea Fury originated in the Fury land-based fighter intended to complement the Tempest in the long-range escort role, and based on it in many respects. The Fury, designed to meet Specification F.6/42, was a lightweight fighter utilising the Centaurus engine, which in the event was also used successfully in the Tempest Mk II. The main change was a reduced wing span and modified fin and rudder. In the event the Fury would offer little to the RAF, but the type was also designed to meet Specification N.7/43 calling for a naval fighter. The prototype flew on 21 February 1945, with a four-bladed propeller and non-folding wings.

Fine shot of Firefly FR.5 WB409/2920 of 825 NAS from HMS *Ocean* flying over Korea during her deployment in the summer of 1952. In the course of the tour of duty Fireflies of the unit fired nearly 16,000 rockets against ground targets in North Korea. *(Author's collection)*

The **F Mk 10** was the first Sea Fury variant, earlier mark numbers being reserved for RAF Fury variants. It was armed with four 20 mm cannon, and the first production aircraft flew on 30 September 1946. The first unit to receive the Sea Fury was 807 NAS at Eglinton in August 1947.

Fighter units equipped – 802, 803, 805, 807

The **FB Mk 11** differed from the first version in having provision for underwing weapons carriage, including twelve 60 lb RPs or two 1,000 lb bombs. The new variant complemented the Seafire 47, which had superior performance as an interceptor, and the Mk 11 came off the production line from TF956. The first unit to receive the type was 802 NAS, and it remained in front-line service until 1954, when it was replaced by the Sea Hawk or Sea Venom.

Fighter units equipped – 801, 802, 803, 804, 805, 806, 807, 808, 811, 898, 1831, 1832, 1833, 1834

FAIREY FIREFLY

The Firefly was designed to Specification N.5/40, which called for a fast, two-seat fighter aircraft, also capable of fulfilling the reconnaissance role, to replace the Fulmar. Broadly similar in design and dimensions, the prototype Firefly flew on 22 December 1941. It was fitted with the Griffon engine and armed with four 20 mm cannon. Although designed as a fighter-reconnaissance type, it was used in the fighter-strike role rather than as an air superiority fighter. There appear to have been two strands to mark numbers for the Firefly.

The Mk I saw service during the Second World War both off Norway and in the Far East. It was fitted with the Griffon IIB with a distinctive chin radiator, and had provision for eight 60 lb RPs or two 1,000 lb bombs. Several minor modifications were incorporated on the production line, including a revised cockpit canopy and faired guns.

By 1946 most had been converted to **FR Mk I** standard.

The FR variant was similar to the Mk I but with the addition of AN/APS4 ASH radar fitted on a rack under the nose. A total of 273 aircraft were built to this standard. The Mark IA designation was applied to a number of Mk I aircraft brought up to FR Mk I standard.

Fighter units equipped – 1830, 1841

The **Mk IV** was the first variant to be clean cowled, with a more powerful Griffon 74 engine and radiators in the wing roots. A four-bladed propeller replaced the three-bladed type of earlier versions. The wingtips were clipped, the ASH radar was housed in a pressurised container on the starboard wing with a counterbalancing fuel tank on the port wing, and a revised fin and rudder were fitted. Seventy-seven were built new and a further forty-three were converted from the Mk I.

Fighter units equipped – 810, 812, 814, 816, 825, 1830, 1840

The **FR Mk 5** was an improved version of the Mk IV with various minor equipment changes and, on later aircraft, powered wing folding. The variant was a true multi-role aircraft, and the designations AS Mark 5 and NF Mark 5 were also applied to reflect the speed with which the model could be adapted to roles with different equipment in both pilot and observer cockpits. Underwing stores included depth charges and sonobuoys. This mark of Firefly served extensively throughout the Korean War.

Fighter and ASW units equipped – 804, 810, 812, 814, 816, 817, 820, 821, 825, 880, 1830, 1841, 1844

The **AS Mk 6** was a development of the FR Mk 5 solely for anti-submarine warfare. The guns were deleted and the electrical equipment changed to accommodate a wide range of underwing stores. The type entered service with 814 NAS in 1951 and served until 1956, when it was replaced by the Gannet.

Anti-submarine warfare units equipped – 812, 814, 817, 820, 825, 826, 1830, 1840, 1841, 1842, 1843, 1844

The **AS Mk 7** was the last major variant, and as such it differed from all previous marks. The Gannet was found to be too heavy for the light carriers, and as an interim solution the Firefly was redesigned to accommodate two radar operators. The engine was switched to the Griffon 59 with the original chin radiator. The wings were also based on the elliptical form of the Mk I, and to improve directional stability a taller fin and rudder were incorporated. There was no provision for armament or stores, the type being intended for search only.

Anti-submarine warfare units equipped – 814, 824

Korea, 1950–53

Unit	Aircraft (code)	Base	From	To
RAF				
88 Sqn det	Sunderland GR.5	Iwakuni	7.50	
209 Sqn det	Sunderland GR.5 (WQ)	Iwakuni	10.50	
205 Sqn det	Sunderland GR.5	Iwakuni	00.51	
28 Sqn	Spitfire FR.18	Kai Tak	11.5.49	1.5.50
		Sek Kong	1.5.50	7.10.50
		Kai Tak	7.10.50	28.3.51
	Vampire FB.5	Kai Tak	1.51	28.3.51
		Sek Kong	28.3.51	2.52
	Vampire FB.9	Sek Kong	2.52	

Unit	Aircraft (code)	Base	From	To
80 Sqn	Spitfire F.24 (W2)	Kai Tak	20.8.49	12.51
	Hornet F.3 (W2)	(dets Sek Kong)	12.51	
81 Sqn det	Spitfire FR.18	Kai Tak	11.50	1.51
	Spitfire PR.19	Kai Tak	1.51	
53 Sqn	Hastings C.1	Iwakuni	9.50	
FAA				
CAG13 (P)		HMS *Triumph*	3.7.50	9.10.50
800 NAS	Seafire 47			
827 NAS	Firefly FR.1			
SF	Sea Otter ABR.1			
CAG 17 (T)		HMS *Theseus*	29.9.50	23.4.51
807 NAS	Sea Fury FB.11			
810 NAS	Firefly FR.5			
SF	Sea Otter ABR.1, HO3S-1			
SAG 14 (R)		HMS *Glory*	3.5.51	4.10.51
804 NAS	Sea Fury FB.11			
812 NAS	Firefly FR.5			
SF	HO3S-1			
CAG 21 (K)		HMAS *Sydney*	4.10.51	25.1.52
805 NAS	Sea Fury FB.11			
808 NAS	Sea Fury FB.11			
817 NAS	Firefly FR.5			
SF	HO3S-1			
CAG 14 (R)		HMS *Glory*	1.4.51	11.5.52
802 NAS	Sea Fury FB.11			
825 NAS	Firefly AS.5			
SF	Dragonfly HR3			
CAG 17 (O)		HMS *Ocean*	11.5.52	30.10.52
802 NAS	Sea Fury FB.11			
825 NAS	Firefly AS.5			
SF	Dragonfly HR3			
CAG 14 (R)		HMS *Glory*	1.11.52	15.7.53
801 NAS	Sea Fury FB.11			
821 NAS	Firefly FR.5			
SF	Dragonfly HR3			
CAG 17 (O)		HMS *Ocean*	15.7.53	31.7.53
807 NAS	Sea Fury FB.11			
810 NAS	Firefly FR.5			
SF	Dragonfly HR3			

During the infamous Yangtze incident HMS *Amethyst* was supported by a Sunderland flying boat from 88 Sqn. DP199/W of the squadron is here seen taxiing. *(Crown copyright)*

Army (Commonwealth Division)

1903 Flt	Auster AOP.6	Seoul	29.7.51	
		Fort George	7.11.51	
1913 Flt	Auster AOP.6, L-19A	Fort George	10.51	8.4.53
		Imjin River	8.4.53	
RAAF				
77 Sqn	F-51D	Pohang, Taegu	11.8.50	4.51
(35 FIG)	Meteor F.8	Kimpo	30.6.51	
30 Sqn	C-47	Ashiya	8.50	
SAAF				
2 Sqn	F-51D	Pyongyang,	22.11.50	52
(18 FBG)		Chinhae		
	F-86F	Osan	52	
RCAF				
426 Sqn	North Star	Tokyo	7.50	

2.5   HONG KONG, 1948–97

BACKGROUND

Hong Kong was part of the Chinese empire until 1842, when it was ceded to Britain as one outcome of the Opium wars, which Britain fought to ensure a local conduit for Indian opium. Kowloon was ceded in 1860 and the New Territories leased for ninety-nine years from 1898. In effect the whole of Hong Kong (410 sq m) would revert to Chinese rule in 1997, the colony being non-viable without the New Territories.

The Chinese civil war began in 1945 with the end of Japanese occupation, resulting by 1948 in the Communists occupying the mainland and the weaker Nationalists the island of Formosa (Taiwan). There was continuing British concern that the People's Republic of China would invade, coupled with a recognition that there could be no practical defence. From recovery of Hong Kong from the Japanese at the end of the war the British maintained a garrison of a division, which was soon reduced to a brigade of three to four infantry battalions with support.

Between 1948 and 1952 the population of Hong Kong quadrupled with refugees from Communism, and in due course the economy grew, based on cheap labour. During the Korean War (Chapter 2, Section 4) the RAF element was increased because of the added value of the colony.

RIOTS AND SIGINT

The first British military air presence in Hong Kong post war was a detachment of Corsairs from 1851 NAS, followed by 132 Sqn equipped with Spitfires which moved in from India shortly after the war's end. The unit was soon involved in anti-piracy patrols, and in some of these it co-operated with detached Corsairs from carriers anchored in Hong Kong. In support was the Fleet Air Arm's 1701 NAS, which acted in the air-sea rescue role,

In 1952 the Hong Kong Auxiliary Air Force took over the Spitfire F.24s of 80 Sqn, including VN318/E. The aircraft were useful for demonstration flights but would have stood little chance in the face of a Chinese invasion.

(Author's collection)

equipped with the Sea Otter, but its sojourn was brief and it disbanded in August 1946. RAF Sunderlands of 209 Sqn were also soon based at Kai Tak for maritime reconnaissance and transport duties, and recce Spitfires of 681 Sqn were based there for the last three months of 1945, although carrying out few operations. 132 Sqn disbanded in April 1946.

Hong Kong remained without any air defence cover until 1949, when the situation in China prompted first the transfer of Spitfires from Burma, followed shortly after by the arrival from the UK of the Mk 24s of 80 Sqn. With further tension during the Korean War both squadrons remained until 80 Sqn was disbanded in 1955, by which time it had converted to the Hornet. Throughout this period the fighter squadrons were joined by detachments of Spitfires and Mosquitos of 81 Sqn, whose aircraft no doubt kept a careful eye on developments on the mainland.

At some time in the late 1940s RAF signals took over signals intelligence collection for the newly formed GCHQ. Hong Kong was to become an important base for such activity, carried out jointly by the British and Americans against Chinese and Soviet communications, and this provided yet another reason for increased defence of the colony.

Kai Tak became very crowded – hence the construction of a second, purely military airfield at Sek Kong. The situation was exacerbated in late summer 1949 when no fewer than eighty C-46 and C-47 aircraft of CNAC and CATC, many carrying refugees from the civil war, arrived at Kai Tak. They were impounded, but eleven managed to leave for the mainland.

Legal battles over ownership continued until the aircraft were shipped out in late 1951. Kai Tak was also used occasionally by weather diversions, some of which, like the USN's eavesdropping PB4Y Privateers, were embarrassments to be swiftly escorted away in this sensitive and very public airport.

On 10 October 1956 there were serious riots by Nationalist supporters aimed at perceived Communist sympathizers. Much damage was caused, and the 7th Hussars' armoured cars were brought in to support the police; when the riots were over on the 12th there were fifty-nine dead and many wounded. No. 28 Sqn, which had progressed to Venoms via Vampires, was placed on alert.

Hong Kong was a critical listening post for British and American intelligence services. Here Wessex HC.2 XR527/C of 28 Sqn lowers a 4,000 lb sea container on to a hillside site where it will accommodate radio and TV transmitter equipment.
(Crown copyright)

Army deployments reflected the general situation in the region. There was no Army aviation presence until 1949, when the unfolding civil war caused concern about Communist ambitions. No. 1903 Flt with Austers was formed in the colony, later departing for Korea. There was then a gap of several years, after which the Army maintained a significant presence, for long periods at squadron level.

SEQUEL

There were further riots in 1966 and 1967, by which time the resident 28 Sqn had progressed to the Hunter FGA.9. It was clear that a few fighters would make little difference in the face of a Chinese attack, and they were of no use in managing local disturbances. In 1968 the unit was re-equipped with helicopters, which it retained until the peaceful handover of the colony in 1997.

In Army aviation, Scout helicopters replaced the Auster AOP.9 in 1967, to be supplemented by several Sioux platoons from 1967. Army pilots were heavily involved in internal security duties, and from the mid-1960s in the control of illegal immigrants. From 1970 the Army helicopters were integrated in terms of internal security tasking with those of 28 Sqn RAF, until they departed in 1994.

In support of the British Government's air arms was the Hong Kong Auxiliary Air Force, initially equipped with the Auster AOP.6 and then progressing through a range of support types, with the Spitfire thrown in for good measure between 1951 and 1955. The Auxiliary Air Force became Royal in 1970, and the Government Flying Service in 1993. The latter assumed the internal security work hitherto conducted by the Army in the run-up to transfer of the colony to the Chinese.

DE HAVILLAND VAMPIRE

While much energy was expended on the first British jet fighter, the Meteor, a second and smaller type was being built by de Havilland as the DH.100 to Specification E.6/41. Originally and unofficially named Spidercrab, the new fighter was eventually produced as the Vampire. The first prototype flew on 20 September 1943, some six months later than the Meteor. It was designed around a single H1 engine, later to become the Goblin; power was limited and a lightweight twin-boom configuration was employed. Armament was to be four 20 mm cannon.

The **F Mark I** first flew on 20 April 1945 with a square-cut tail fin after modifications to the prototype to establish the best fin and rudder configuration. The first aircraft went to 247 Sqn from March 1946, and as production progressed improvements were introduced on the line. From the fortieth aircraft the Goblin 2 of 3,100 lb thrust was introduced, together with auxiliary underwing fuel tanks, and from the fifty-first machine the type had a pressurized cockpit and bubble canopy.

Fighter units equipped – 3, 20, 54, 72, 130, 247, 501, 600, 605, 608, 613

The short range of the early aircraft was addressed in the **F Mark 3** which was built to Specification F.3/47 and carried more fuel in wing tanks, resulting in extended range (730 to 1,145 miles). The tanks caused stability problems which were cured by lowering the tailplane, extending its chord and changing the shape of the fin and rudder. The prototype flew on 4 November 1945 and the type joined 54 Sqn in April 1948.

Fighter units equipped – 5, 20, 32, 54, 72, 73, 247, 502, 601, 604, 605, 608, 614

The **FB Mark 5** resulted from capitalizing on the Vampire's sound handling qualities as a ground attack platform. The wings were clipped and strengthened to enable the carriage of two 1,000 lb bombs or eight rockets. To compensate for the additional wing loading a longer-stroke undercarriage was fitted. The prototype flew on 29 June 1948, and the first production aircraft followed a year later. The first aircraft were delivered to 54 Sqn.

Fighter units equipped – 3, 4, 5, 6, 11, 14, 16, 20, 26, 28, 32, 54, 60, 67, 71, 72, 73, 93, 94, 98, 112, 118, 130, 145, 185, 213, 234, 247, 249, 266, 501, 502, 602, 603, 605, 607, 608, 609, 612, 613, 614

The need for improved pilot comfort in the tropics resulted in the **FB Mark 9**. The basic FB Mk 5 was fitted with air conditioning, which resulted in an eight-inch increase in the starboard wing-root fillet.

Fighter units equipped – 4, 5, 6, 8, 11, 20, 26, 28, 32, 45, 60, 73, 93, 185, 213, 234, 249, 501, 502, 603, 607, 608, 613, 614

The DH.113 **NF Mark 10** was originally built as a private venture night-fighter equipped with the AI Mark 10 radar. The fuselage was widened and lengthened to accommodate pilot and navigator, and the tailplane was extended beyond the fins and rudders to compensate. The prototype flew on 28 August 1949, and pending the delivery of the Meteor night-fighters the type served with three UK-based units, starting with 25 Sqn in July 1951.

Night-fighter units equipped – 23, 25, 151

Hong Kong, 1948–97

Unit	Aircraft (code)	Base	From	To
RAF				
132 Sqn	Spitfire XIV	Kai Tak	15.9.45	15.4.46
681 Sqn	Spitfire XIX	Kai Tak	27.9.45	23.12.45
81 Sqn det	Spitfire PR.19			
	Mosquito PR.34	Kai Tak	1.10.47	54
	Spitfire FR.18	Kai Tak	7.48	54
28 Sqn	Spitfire F.14	Kai Tak	11.5.49	1.5.50
		Sek Kong	1.5.50	7.10.50
		Kai Tak	7.10.50	1.51
	Vampire FB.5	Kai Tak	1.51	28.3.51
		Sek Kong	28.3.51	2.52
	Vampire FB.9	Sek Kong	2.52	15.8.55
		Kai Tak	15.8.55	5.12.55
		Sek Kong	5.12.55	2.56
	Venom FB.1	Sek Kong	2.56	14.6.57
		Kai Tak	14.6.57	11.59
	Venom FB.4	Kai Tak	11.59	5.62
	Hunter FGA.9	Kai Tak	5.62	2.1.67
103 Sqn det[2]	Whirlwind HC.10	Kai Tak	10.67	1.3.68
28 Sqn	Whirlwind HC.10	Kai Tak	1.3.68	1.72
	Wessex HC.2	Kai Tak	1.72	17.5.78
		Sek Kong	17.5.78	6.97
80 Sqn	Spitfire F.24 (W2)	Kai Tak[1]	20.8.49	12.51
	Hornet F.3 (W2)	Kai Tak	12.51	1.5.55
209 Sqn[3]	Sunderland V (WQ)	Kai Tak	17.9.45	1.5.55
1430 Flt[4]	Sunderland V	Kai Tak	5.8.46	1.9.46
88 Sqn[5]	Sunderland V	Kai Tak	1.9.46	1.10.54
205 Sqn det	Sunderland GR.5	Kai Tak	15.9.49	1.3.58
96 Sqn[6]	Dakota	Kai Tak	16.4.46	1.6.46
110	Dakota	Kai Tak	1.6.46	18.9.47

FAA

1851 NAS[7]	Corsair IV	Kai Tak, HMS *Venerable*	3.9.45	18.10.45
1701 NAS	Sea Otter I, Tiger Moth II, Oxford	Kai Tak	13.10.45	27.8.46
846 NAS	Whirlwind HAS.7	Kai Tak, HMS *Albion*	22.12.63	12.1.64
847 NAS	Wessex HU.5	Kai Tak HMS *Triumph*	28.9.70	15.10.70

Army

1903 Flt	Auster AOP.6	Sha Tin	11.4.49	10.7.51
1900 Flt[8]	Auster AOP.6	Sha Tin	24.4.53	1.9.57
	Auster AOP.9	Sha Tin	56	1.9.57
20 Flt[9]	Auster AOP.9	Sha Tin	1.9.57	64
		Kai Tak	64	67
	Sioux AH.1	Kai Tak	7.66	1.4.70
	Scout AH.1	Kai Tak	67	1.10.69
49 Lt Rgt RA 656 Sqn	Sioux AH.1	Kai Tak	5.65	12.65
20 Flt[10]	Scout AH.1	Sek Kong	1.10.69	30.6.77
	Gazelle AH.1	Sek Kong	74	75
25 Lt Rgt RA	Sioux AH.1	Sek Kong	69	73
6 QOGR	Sioux AH.1	Kai Tak	6.67	73
10 PMOGR	Sioux AH.1	Sek Kong	7.67	70
7 DEGR	Sioux AH.1	Sek Kong	6.67	73
11 Flt[11]	Scout AH.1	Sek Kong	30.6.77	1.8.78
660 Sqn	Scout AH.1	Sek Kong	1.8.78	1994

HKAAF/RHKAAF/GFS

Auster AOP.9, Harvard II	1949	1967
Spitfire FR.18, Spitfire F.24, Spitfire PR.19	1951	1955
Widgeon	1958	1965
Alouette III	1965	1980
Musketeer	1971	1979
Islander	1971	1992
Bulldog	1977	1988
Dauphin 2	1980	1990
Super King Air	1987	
T67 Firefly	1987	
S-76, S-70	1991	

NOTES
1 Became 28 Sqn
2 With short spells at Sek Kong in Winter 1950
3 Moved to Seletar 28.4.46 but retained detachments at Kai Tak
4 Became 88 Sqn
5 Moved to Seletar 24.6.51 but retained detachments at Kai Tak
6 Became 110 Sqn

7   Numerous detachments from carriers were shore-based at Kai Tak, but this is believed to be the only unit which saw operational service
8   Became 20 (Independent Flt)
9   Became part of 656 Sqn
10 Became 11 Flt
11 Became 660 Sqn

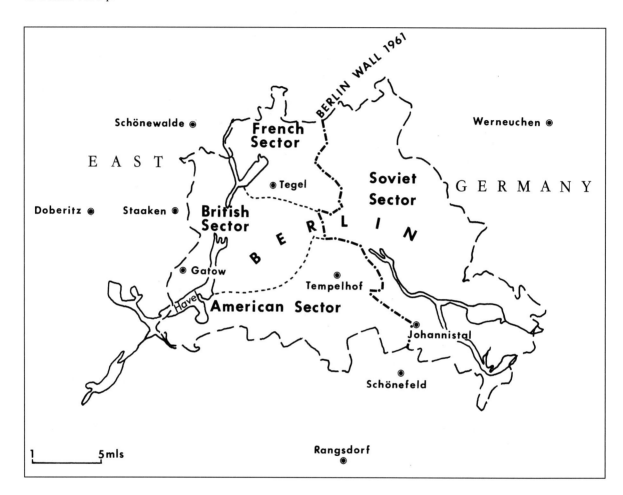

2.6   THE BERLIN WALL CRISIS, 1961–2

BACKGROUND

After the Berlin Airlift had demonstrated Western determination to maintain the integrity of West Berlin, the NATO allies pressed for the establishment of a tangible West German contribution to European defence; Britain, France and the US had many other commitments farther afield. On 5 May 1955 the German Federal Republic was declared, and just nine days later the formation of the Warsaw Pact was announced. The Soviet Union, mindful of the unthinkable prospect of a reunited Germany, kept a tight control on access to Berlin, and in 1958 suggested the handover of Berlin as a demilitarized city in exchange for concessions. The Western Powers rejected the proposal. Resenting the embedded example of Capitalism which Berlin represented, and which had encouraged no fewer than 2.25 million East Germans to cross to the West between 1949 and 1959, the Russians pressed for a resolution, and early in 1961 threatened a bilateral solution with East Germany.

During the Berlin Wall crisis RAF units in Germany were brought to a high state of readiness. The Canberra B(I)8 interdictor served with four squadrons on as many bases. Here WT340 of 16 Sqn tucks its undercarriage away as it departs Celle. *(Author's collection)*

These developments need to be seen in a wider context. For some time the USA had been keeping a watch on Soviet missile and bomber development, and on 1 May 1960 a U-2 reconnaissance aircraft was brought down over Sverdlovsk (see Chapter 4, Section 5). The result was the collapse of a planned summit meeting in Paris due to be held a few days later. New American President John F. Kennedy was sworn in on 20 January 1961 to find himself committed to an inherited plan for covert action in Cuba against the legitimate government of Fidel Castro. The attempted invasion of Cuba by US-backed rebels began in April 1961, and was doomed from the outset. Kennedy refused overt US involvement when the invasion foundered, and the action turned into a humiliating and public failure on the part of a green president.

ESCALATION

On 8 July 1961 the Soviet defence budget was increased by 25%, and on 25 July President Kennedy called for a build-up of conventional forces and the initial mobilization of Reserve and National Guard units. Then, on 13 August, sixty-three of the eighty entry points from East Berlin were sealed and the construction of a substantial physical barrier was begun, initially in the form of a fence. This act prompted moves to reinforce the US Army and Air Force in Europe.

The USA, having committed itself to a strong nuclear force, had no option but to rely on reserve units, because, as Kennedy said, '... we intend to have a wider choice than humiliation or all-out nuclear action'. At the end of August the Soviet Union resumed its nuclear test programme. On 1 October 1961 18,500 ANG officers and men reported for duty, while the six United States Air Force Europe (USAFE) tactical fighter wings, seven fighter squadrons and two reconnaissance wings were to be supplemented by a number of ANG units in Operation *Stair Step*. American reinforcements moved with the support of C-97 and C-124 transports of Military Air Transport Service (MATS).

In 1960 France had demanded the withdrawal of US nuclear-capable aircraft from French bases, but the reinforcements now flew into five French bases, as well as Ramstein in Germany and Moron AFB, Spain. Most of the tactical units flew the F-84F, still in service with a number of European air arms, and a wing of F-86H Sabres was also involved; in November a wing of F-104A Starfighters was flown over.

The RAF also made token gestures at the end of the year, with the temporary transfer to Germany of two squadrons of the new Lightning point-defence fighter and a Javelin operational-conversion unit. As diplomatic progress was made, the reserve units gradually withdrew to the UK and USA. The Western allies had again demonstrated support for the position of West Berlin and the importance to them of a strong foothold in West Germany, together with their ability to back that support with tactical, conventional forces.

SEQUEL

After the confrontation over the wall, Berlin remained stage centre for many years, but never again was there a stand-off. The ultimate confrontation was a year away over Cuba (see Chapter 2, Section 7), after which, while there was continued tension, the Cold War gently warmed. It may be significant that it was in Berlin that the wall literally came down in 1989, leading to a unified Germany and the end of the Cold War.

In the table that follows, only RAF units are listed as at October 1961, but the additional burden was primarily and extensively carried by the US. Based units are shown without dates. The USAF maintained three tactical-fighter, one recce and one medium-bomber wings in the UK, one recce wing in France, a fighter wing in Spain, two tactical-fighter wings and a squadron plus three air defence squadrons in Germany. For the period October 1961 to August 1962 there were in addition eight tactical-fighter, one recce and three air defence squadrons brought into Western Europe from the US.

The Berlin Wall Crisis, 1961–2

Unit	Aircraft (code)	Base	From	To
RAF				
118 Sqn	Hunter F.6	Jever		
2 Sqn	Hunter FR.10	Jever		
4 Sqn	Hunter FR.10	Gütersloh		
111 Sqn	Lightning F.1A	Gütersloh	12.61	12.61
5 Sqn	Javelin FAW.5	Laarbruch		
31 Sqn	Canberra PR.7	Laarbruch		
80 Sqn	Canberra PR.7	Laarbruch		
11 Sqn	Javelin FAW.4	Geilenkirchen		
3 Sqn	Canberra B(I).8	Geilenkirchen		
213 Sqn	Canberra B(I).6	Ahlhorn		
16 Sqn	Canberra B(I).8	Celle		
88 Sqn	Canberra B(I).8	Wildenrath		
17 Sqn	Canberra PR.7	Wildenrath		
56 Sqn	Lightning F.1A	Brüggen	10.61	10.61
228 OCU	Javelin FAW.5	Brüggen	10.61	10.61

2.7   THE CUBAN MISSILE CRISIS, 1962

BACKGROUND

Following the United States' humiliation over the Bay of Pigs incident and stalemate over Berlin, President Kennedy faced his toughest trial. Cuba had requested more arms from Russia to protect herself against the continuing threat of US interference, and by August 1962 the CIA was aware of significant arms shipments. On the 22nd of that month, the President was advised of the presence of large missiles on the island. Agency U-2 flights over Cuba were stepped up, and US Navy and US Air Force patrol and reconnaissance aircraft paid special attention to Soviet shipping.

MISSILES OF OCTOBER

On 29 August, a U-2 flight from McCoy Operating Location (OL), Florida, photographed two SA-2 sites on Cuba and six more under construction. Photo-interpreters became anxious when it was realized that the layout was similar to surface-to-air missile (SAM) sites associated with the protection of strategic missile bases in the Soviet Union. On 4 September Kennedy warned Khrushchev that the United States would not tolerate the siting of offensive weapons on Cuba, and Khrushchev replied by saying that the Soviet Union had no need to place such weapons in the Caribbean.

Just four days later, however, a P-2 Neptune of VP-44 photographed the freighter *Omsk* heading for Havana with large, oblong canisters on the decks. U-2 flights were again stepped up. On 19 September, the US Intelligence Board reported its view that Russia would not deploy nuclear weapons in Cuba, although four days earlier a second shipment of missiles had arrived in Havana. Further reconnaissance flights showed more construction work, and on 10 October the US Air Force's 4080th Strategic Reconnaissance Wing (SRW) formally assumed responsibility for overflights from the CIA.

The 4080th used CIA U-2E variants equipped with electronic countermeasures (ECM) equipment, and sorties were flown from McCoy, Barksdale and Laughlin AFBs. The primary reason for the transfer of responsibility to the USAF was the threat from SA-2 missiles. The first USAF flights were flown on 10 October, and highway construction was noted, but the flights were then halted for three days because of poor weather conditions associated with Hurricane *Ella*. Then, on 14 October, a second U-2E sortie out of Patrick AFB, Florida, secured 928 photographs of two sites at San Cristobal and Sagua la Grande. Processed the following day, they were rushed to President Kennedy on the 16th.

The photos clearly showed SS-4 *Sandal* medium-range ballistic missile (MRBM) sites in an advanced state of preparation and with missiles deployed, and what was to become known as the Cuban Missile Crisis had begun. A high-level Executive Committee was formed and low-level reconnaissance flights by RF-101Cs of the 29th Tactical Reconnaissance Squadron (TRS) from Shaw AFB in South Carolina were ordered.

The following day, what appeared to be intermediate-range ballistic missile (IRBM) sites were photographed at Guanajay and Remedios. On Thursday 18 October, Kennedy kept a prearranged meeting with the Soviet Foreign Secretary Gromyko, but, when warned of the perceived threat to US security, Gromyko told the President that defensive arms only were in Cuba. Meanwhile the Executive Committee was analysing Soviet intentions and debating responses. It seemed most likely that Russia was applying pressure to gain concessions over Berlin, and possibly the removal of forty-five Jupiter and sixty Thor IRBMs from Italy, Turkey and England.

The responses considered included invasion, air attack, ultimatum and blockade. On Monday the 22nd a quarantine (blockade) was announced, and 3,190 civilians were evacuated from the US Navy base at Guantanamo on Cuba. B-52 bombers of Strategic Air Command (SAC) were put on full alert and dispersed to civilian airports, while naval vessels raced to the Caribbean to enforce the blockade. Air Defense and Tactical Air Commands moved units south to Florida.

Guantanamo was reinforced with a garrison of 8,000 Marines and sailors, and Task Force 135 was established to defend the base. Ships in the force included the carriers *Enterprise* (CVN-65) and *Independence* (CVA-62), with a total of eight attack, four fighter and two photo-reconnaissance squadrons embarked. The quarantine was enforced by units of Task Force 136, which comprised 180 vessels, including the carriers *Essex* (CVS-9), *Lake Champlain* (CVS-39), *Randolph* (CVS-15), *Shangri-La* (CVS-38) and *Wasp* (CVS-18).

In the United Kingdom the RAF bomber force was placed on fifteen-minutes readiness, but significantly the aircraft were not dispersed as were their US counterparts. (There were two higher states of readiness – dispersal in small numbers to designated and widespread airfields with crews ready to take off within five minutes, and cockpit readiness.) Out of a total of 144 Valiant, Victor and Vulcan bombers, the expectation was that at any time 60% would be immediately serviceable, armed with the *Yellow Sun* thermonuclear weapon.

By 1962 the RAF also had a number of tactical medium-bomber squadrons equipped with the Canberra B.15

Among Bomber Command units placed on 15 minutes readiness by 28 October was 10 Sqn with the Victor B.1, part of the Cottesmore Wing. XA936 shows off well the early white overall anti-flash colour scheme, still with standard roundels and fin flash. *(Author's collection)*

and B.16 with the *Red Beard* bomb, which was also available to the FAA's Scimitar squadrons. The US Mk 7 nuclear bomb was accessible to the RAF Germany Canberra B(I).8 bombers.

From 1959 the USA based sixty Thor intermediate-range ballistic missiles in the UK, notionally under RAF command, but in reality under dual control. At 23 October all were on fifteen-minutes alert.

The quarantine was signed on the 23rd, creating a barrier 800 miles distant but reducing to 500 miles to give the Russians more time to signal their ships in transit. By Wednesday some vessels were stopping, only to resume the following day. During this time the US recce aircraft remained busy, and US Navy and Marine Corps aircraft flocked to the area.

On Friday, after the freighter *Marucla* had been stopped and searched, Khrushchev accepted the American terms for the removal of offensive weapons (which by now included forty-four Il-28s under construction at San Julian), but only in exchange for the Americans' removal of the Jupiter missiles, which had previously been ordered. Tension increased on the 27th as a USAF U-2 pilot was killed during an overflight of naval installations at Banes, his aircraft having been hit by an SA-2 missile.

Early the following day, Soviet intercontinental missiles (ICBMs) were readied as another U-2 inadvertently but embarrassingly overflew the Chukotka peninsula. At 10.00 hrs on the 28th the crisis ended as the Russians agreed to dismantle the missiles, under inspection. The freighter *Divinogorsk* sailed from Mariel with four SS-4s on 5 November, eight more missiles left on the 7th on the *Metallurg Anosov*, and six on the 9th on board the *Bratsk*. The Il-28s, however, were still under construction, and the quarantine was not lifted until 20 November, by which time the Russians had agreed to their removal. The first aircraft left Cuba in crates on 15 December aboard the *Kasimov*.

SEQUEL

Although the crisis centred around missiles, it was conventionally equipped aircraft that gave Kennedy a range of response options. Large numbers of machines were deployed by all services, and the whole Soviet withdrawal was monitored by aircraft. During the period 14 October to 6 December, the USAF flew 102 U-2 sorties over Cuba, but low-flying aircraft were able to supervise the operation with a versatility unmatched by more remote observation. The following year the Superpowers agreed to install the 'hot line' telephone link, and as further evidence of the thaw in relations a nuclear test ban agreement was signed in August 1963.

For the British, who played very much a supporting role, the concern was to ensure that her nuclear deterrent remained effective. Most importantly, perhaps, Prime Minister Harold Macmillan did not see Soviet intentions as sufficiently serious as to merit dispersal of the bomber force. British intelligence through this period was more concerned with intentions than capability or capacity, which drove US policy.

It is widely acknowledged that the world was closest to all-out nuclear war in 1962, after which, although the threat remained, there was a gradual thawing of relations, leading to the collapse of the Soviet Union and the Warsaw Pact. Soviet Premier Khruschev did agree to withdraw on the understanding that the US would not invade Cuba. In addition, the Americans agreed to withdraw Jupiter missiles from Turkey and Italy and Thor IRBMs from the United Kingdom, but in reality this withdrawal had been agreed a year previously.

As mentioned in the text, the confrontation was an essentially American operation, but with explicit British support. In the table that follows only British units placed on alert or potentially available for nuclear strike at 28 October are included.

Unit	Aircraft	Base
RAF Bomber Command		
1 Group Lincolnshire		
27, 83, 617 Sqns	Vulcan B.2	Scampton
9, 12 Sqns[1]	Vulcan B.2	Coningsby
44, 50, 101 Sqns	Vulcan B.1, B.1A	Waddington
230 OCU	Vulcan B.1	Finningley
98 Sqn[2]	Thor SSM	Driffield
102 Sqn	Thor SSM	Full Sutton
150 Sqn	Thor SSM	Carnaby
226 Sqn	Thor SSM	Catfoss
240 Sqn	Thor SSM	Breighton
97 Sqn[2]	Thor SSM	Hemswell
104 Sqn	Thor SSM	Ludford Magna
106 Sqn	Thor SSM	Bardney
142 Sqn	Thor SSM	Coleby Grange
269 Sqn	Thor SSM	Caistor
3 Group East Midlands, East Anglia		
100[1], 139 Sqns	Victor B.2	Wittering
10, 15 Sqns	Victor B.1, B.1A	Cottesmore
55, 57 Sqns	Victor B.1A	Honington
49, 148, 207 Sqns[3]	Valiant B.1, BK.1, BPRK.1	Marham
232 OCU	Victor B.1A	Cottesmore
77 Sqn[2]	Thor SSM	Feltwell
82 Sqn	Thor SSM	Shepherd's Grove
107 Sqn	Thor SSM	Tuddenham
113 Sqn	Thor SSM	Mepal
220 Sqn	Thor SSM	North Pickenham
144 Sqn[2]	Thor SSM	North Luffenham
130 Sqn	Thor SSM	Polebrook
218 Sqn	Thor SSM	Harrington

The Cuban Missile Crisis, 1962

Unit	Aircraft	Base
223 Sqn	Thor SSM	Folkingham
254 Sqn	Thor SSM	Melton Mowbray
RAF Germany		
16 Sqn	Canberra B(I).8	Laarbruch
59 Sqn	Canberra B(I).8	Geilenkirchen
88 Sqn	Canberra B(I).8	Wildenrath
213 Sqn	Canberra B(I).6	Brüggen
FAA		
800 NAS	Scimitar F.1	HMS *Ark Royal*
803 NAS	Scimitar F.1	Lossiemouth

NOTES
1   Still forming   2   HQ sqns   3   Assigned to SACEUR on a dual-key basis

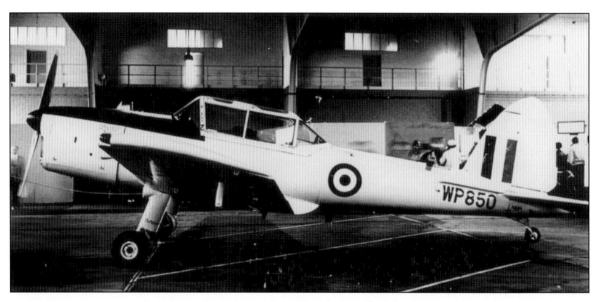

The British, American and French occupying powers in Berlin were entitled to use light aircraft across the capital, notionally for continuity training. WP850 based at Gatow was one of a number of Chipmunks used for photography over the eastern sector. *(via A S Thomas)*

2.8   BERLIN SPYING, 1953–89

BACKGROUND

With the isolation of Berlin within the Soviet Zone of Occupation of Germany and the division of the city itself, almost surreal arrangements were made for the examination of all the occupied zones. The British Mission involved, based in East Berlin, was known as BRIXMIS, and among its 200 members it included a strong RAF contingent. Although established for a plethora of immediate post-war tasks in Germany, the mission's staff were able to rove relatively freely in East Germany and were involved in much intelligence gathering. From 1958 BRIXMIS had the use of RAF Chipmunks from RAF Gatow's Station Flight, and Army helicopters.

Chipmunk WZ862 was one of a number of light 'spyplanes', based at Gatow in Berlin. It is seen overflying the Siegessäule Victory column in West Berlin. See Section 2.8. (*A S Thomas*)

Superb shot of four Vampire FB.9s of 213 Sqn in Egypt. Nearest the camera is WL562/C, then camouflaged WX207/F and behind that WL615. See Section 3.3. (*A S Thomas*)

After the nuclear deterrent responsibility was transferred to the Royal Navy the RAF retained a nuclear strike capability with the Tornado GR.1. An early recipient of this aircraft was 27 Sqn whose ZA585 coded 05 makes a low pass at RAF Marham. See Section 4.1. (*Author*)

Blue Streak was displayed at Farnborough in 1959. See Section 4.2. (*Author*)

The Douglas *Skybolt* air launched ballistic missile was ordered by Britain in 1960, but after cancelling her own *Blue Streak* and advanced *Blue Steel* programmes the American government pulled the plug and cancelled the missile. It would have been carried in pairs by Vulcans. This test vehicle is preserved at Cosford. See Section 4.2. (*Author*)

Yellow Sun was the thermo-nuclear deterrent device carried by Vulcan and Victor bombers in the 1960s. This example is preserved at the RAF Museum, Hendon. See Section 4.3. (*Author*)

Another nuclear weapon preserved at Hendon is the WE-177, which was in service from 1966 to 1998. Used in anger it would have been carried by Vulcans and latterly Tornadoes. See Section 4.3. (*Author*)

The Lightning was designed as a point defence interceptor with a phenomenal climb rate but very short range. The 'sports car' version was the light F.3 which typically wore bright markings as exemplified by XP740/J of 111 Sqn. See Section 4.4. (*Author*)

The F.6 version of the Lightning was heavier than earlier marks but had longer endurance. XR753/A of 23 Sqn based at Leuchars escorts a Soviet 'Bear' reconnaissance aircraft over the North Sea. See Section 4.4. (*Author*)

Fine shot of Phantom FGR.2 XT903/X of 23 Sqn. The Phantom succeeded the Lightning in the air defence role. See Section 4.4.
(Keith Maxwell)

The 1957 defence white paper determined the end of the manned fighter with air defence the preserve of guided missiles: by 1960 there were eleven *Bloodhound* missile squadrons defending the V-bomber bases. In the event, the manned fighter survived, but the *Bloodhound* remained in service for some years, both at home and abroad. See Section 4.4. *(Author)*

The Army also provided local and mobile air defence with the *Thunderbird* missile between1959 and 1977. This 36 Regt. Mk I was demonstrated at Farnborough in 1959. See Section 4.4. *(Author)*

51 Sqn operated specially modified Comets and then Nimrods for electronic intelligence gathering. Three Nimrod R.1s were operated including XW665 seen here in original form. See Section 4.5. (*Author*)

The Nimrod R.1s were later fitted with in-flight refuelling probes as seen on XW664 here landing at Wyton after a sortie. See Section 4.5. (*Author*)

In 1959 and again in 1963 Shackletons of 224 Sqn were detached to Khormaksar from the UK. See Section 5.1. (*via A S Thomas*)

The Comet was introduced into RAF service in 1956 in C.2 form with 216 Sqn which was the first jet transport unit in the world. The early version was used until 1967 across the world and in 1958 transported troops to Cyprus in support of the operations in Jordan. XK696 *Orion*. See Section 5.2. (*Author*)

Hunters of 229 OCU, operating from Brawdy, attacked the *Torrey Canyon* with *Avtur* aviation fuel to stimulate fires started by conventional bombs. F.6 XJ637/10 of 73 Sqn, 226 OCU. See Section 6.3. (*Author*)

XF516/49 displays the markings of 234 Sqn of the Tactical Weapons Unit at Brawdy. It was from this base that instructors flew sorties to the Scillies to hit the *Torrey Canyon* with *Avtur* and rockets. See Section 6.3. (*Author*)

The newly acquired Hercules were soon put to use in support of peacekeeping and humanitarian aid. First use was in the evacuation from Aden in 1967. Seen here in the original Dark Earth and Stone camouflage scheme is XV302/302. See Section 6.3. (*Author*)

Whirlwind HAR.10 XP329/V of 84 Sqn was one of a handful based at Akrotiri in Cyprus. When Turkey invaded the island in 1974 the based units were supplemented by a number of Naval and RAF helicopters to help with the evacuation of British and other foreign nationals. See Section 6.4. (*Rolls Royce*)

The VC-10 entered RAF service with 10 Sqn in 1967 in the transport role. C(K).1 XV109/109 was one of thirteen converted for air-air refuelling while retaining the passenger configuration. Second-hand Super VC-10s were later bought and equipped as tankers for 101 Sqn. See Section 6.4. (*Crown copyright*)

The RAF bought two versions of the Hercules in 1966 with service entry the following year. The C.1 was the C-130K (XV217/217 front) while the C.3 (XV223/223) had a 15 ft fuselage extension and was used on longer routes. See Section 6.4. (*Lockheed*)

The Hercules came into its own in relief operations in Ethiopia in 1984. XV178 of the Lyneham Wing was one of the aircraft detached: it is seen here dropping food aid at a remote site. See Section 6.5. (*Crown copyright*)

Tristars of 216 Sqn made two aid trips to Ethiopia in 1984 taking food and medical supplies. ZD952 is a passenger/tanker KC.1. See Section 6.5. (*Author*)

Nine ex-airlines Tristars were bought for the RAF to supplement the ageing Victor tanker fleet. This example, with refuelling probe, is transferring fuel to a Hercules during trials. See Section 6.5. (*Lockheed*)

Whirlwind HAR.10 XJ729 in 22 Sqn markings. See Section 6.6. (*Author*)

The Wessex complemented the Sea King with the UK based SAR units, being used for shorter-range tasks. HAR.2 XT604 of 22 Sqn. See Section 6.6. (*Author*)

The Royal Navy also used the Wessex in the UK SAR role, covering the South-West peninsula. HU.5 of 771 NAS Culdrose. See Section 6.6. (*Author*)

Both 22 and 202 Sqn eventually operated the Sea King HAR.3 across the UK for longer-range tasks. XZ589 demonstrates the large access door. See Section 6.6. (*Author*)

Sea King HAS.5 XV666/823 of 771 NAS at Culdrose in Cornwall. See Section 6.6. (*Author*)

Superb shot of a four aircraft flight of Javelin FAW.9s of 60 Sqn: XH956/W nearest. See Section 7.2. (*G Pitchfork*)

Fully armed Javelin FAW.9 XH777/R of 60 Sqn on patrol over the inhospitable terrain of Borneo. See Section 7.2. (*G Pitchfork*)

Showing the Javelin *Firestreak* fit is XH956/W. Of note is the lightning flash symbol on the outer pylon. See Section 7.2. (*G Pitchfork*)

Armed with a pair of *Firestreaks*, Javelin XH841/D waits at readiness at Kuching, while behind is a Belvedere 0f 66 Sqn. See Section 7.2. (*G Pitchfork*)

INTELLIGENCE GATHERING

On 5 September 1950 Meteor T.7 WA695 of 2 Ferry Pool crash-landed several miles inside the East German border near Redefin, reportedly having suffered radio failure. It appears that there was only the pilot in the aircraft, and he was held for several months by the Soviets. BRIXMIS staff were early on the scene, but were unable to recover the damaged aircraft.

On 12 March 1953 Lincoln B.2 RF531/C of the Central Gunnery School was shot down by MiG-15 fighters over Eastern Germany. It had flown from Leconfield in Yorkshire for fighter affiliation sorties, and its route over East Germany is disputed. It is reported to have circled over Rostok, and from evidence taken by BRIXMIS staff at the scene of the crash, it had been armed and its guns fired, although the RAF had claimed that it was unarmed. In this instance the crew perished, four through alleged parachute malfunctions.

Both of these instances involved aircraft from support rather than operational units, and conceivably either may have been involved in some form of intelligence gathering.

A Chipmunk trainer had been based at RAF Gatow since 1956, ostensibly for use as a continuity trainer for RAF aircrews on ground tours. However, the aircraft was permitted to fly over Berlin within a twenty-mile radius of the centre, three times a week. Initially a flight was made every ten days or so, with a cameraman in the back seat, and in East Berlin there were numerous barracks and equipment to keep the photographers busy. On more than one occasion the Chipmunks were fired at, but none was lost. The aircraft included WD289, WG466, WG486 and WZ862. Also involved in reconnaissance were the Sioux, then Gazelle helicopters of 7 Flt based at Gatow from 1970. The US Army operated L-20 Beavers for similar purposes from Tempelhof.

BRIXMIS was involved in many forays in East Germany to photograph Soviet and East German aircraft and airfields at close quarters. So important was the opportunity to gather material on air and related assets that the Deputy Mission Chief role was occupied by an RAF general-duties officer with the rank of group captain from 1956.

At very close proximity RAF intelligence officers and scientists from Farnborough were able to examine key features of a Yak-28P *Firebar* all-weather interceptor which had crashed in Lake Havel. The aircraft had suffered a flame-out, but the Soviet controllers denied the pilot the chance to land at Gatow; the crew were killed in the crash. BRIXMIS staff were immediately involved, keeping the Soviet military at bay, and once the type was identified, experts were brought in to direct recovery and examination of an engine and the radar at Gatow. After inspection, the removed items were replaced in the lake and the remains at last handed over.

SEQUEL

Berlin was a focal point for espionage and intrigue. Much important aeronautical intelligence was gathered before the collapse of the Berlin Wall and unification. BRIXMIS was de-activated on 2 October 1990.

Unit	Aircraft	Base
RAF		
SF	Chipmunk T.10	Gatow
Army		
7 Flt	Sioux AH.1	
	Gazelle AH.1	Gatow

CHAPTER THREE

Colonial Conflicts in the 1950s

Through the 1950s Britain was involved in containing uprising or insurgency, not only in colonies but in areas for which she held a mandate under the United Nations. Thus there were minor skirmishes with nomadic tribesmen in Eritrea and Sudan – subsequently and sadly both the focus of continued fighting ever since. Britain also had to contend with attempts to remove her forces from Egypt at a time when bases in the Middle East were critically important.

It was from these bases that troops were transported to Kenya during the emergency there from 1952, a campaign fought like others in the period by a mixture of regulars and national servicemen. The role of the RAF in Kenya has been the subject of much debate about the value of bombing unseen and elusive targets in the jungle. This was also the case in the long Malayan emergency, but in that theatre a greater diversity of aircraft was on hand to support forces on the ground, including helicopters for casualty evacuation.

Helicopters also came into their own in Cyprus, where Greek Cypriot Nationalists capitalized on Britain's problems with Egypt and the search for new bases to start their own insurgency.

During the period in question the importance of both strategic and tactical transport aircraft was manifest, in getting forces to problem areas fast and then moving and resupplying them in theatre. Throughout the 1950s the principle strategic transport was the Hastings, while the Valetta served as the primary tactical type. They were both based on 1930s/1940s technology, sharing features of the Halifax and Wellington bomber respectively. Although the Comet jet transport entered service in 1956, in its original Mark 2 form it only carried forty-four passengers, and with only ten aircraft in service it did not contribute significantly to the campaigns described.

Containment of the insurgency in Malaya was one of the great success stories of the British military after the war. The campaign lasted for twelve years, during which combined tactics were devised to counter the terrorists. After initial setbacks, military operations were conducted within clear policies of governance and an explicit strategy. Innovations included the creation of the first helicopter casualty evacuation unit in 1950, followed by widespread use of helicopters, including the insertion of special forces into the jungle. The campaign was the more remarkable in that a significant proportion of those involved were national servicemen. Of the total 1,873 British and Commonwealth troops who died on active service, 295 were RAF, 341 from the Brigade of Gurkhas and around 200 national servicemen, mainly from the infantry regiments.

3.1   ERITREA, 1950–52

BACKGROUND

Eritrea, on the Red Sea, was colonized by Italy from 1882 but occupied by Britain in 1941, after which it was subject to British administration. From time to time there was civil unrest, and small British forces were deployed, although the main responsibility for order rested with the Eritrean Police Field Force (EPFF).

ACTION

To assist with the task a detachment of Mosquito PR.34s of 13 Sqn was sent to Asmara in April 1947, primarily to provide the basis for mapping. Then in April 1948 a detachment of Tempest F.6s of 39 Sqn, recently re-formed at Nairobi, was sent to Asmara to support ground forces as rebel Shifta nomads made a number of guerrilla attacks.

The Tempests were in action late in the year rocketing rebel positions.

Matters became worse from 1950 as there was discussion about the future of the territory. No. 1910 Flt, equipped with Auster AOP.6s, was sent from Tripoli to operate in a variety of roles. The unit sent permanent detachments to Agordat and Barentu and flew reconnaissance sorties, also providing liaison, light resupply and occasionally casualty evacuation services. Primarily the flight kept mobile ground units in touch with base and acted to bring heavier air support to bear when required.

To provide firepower, Brigand light bombers of 8 Sqn and Spitfire FR.18s of 208 Sqn from Aden and Fayid respectively were detached to Asmara from August. Detachments remained in Eritrea to contain guerrilla activity until summer 1951. The Spitfires of 208 Sqn were retired in favour of the Meteor FR.9, and these aircraft maintained the fighter support role until late in the year. By early 1952 it had been decided by the UN that Eritrea should become federated to Ethiopia, and before withdrawal the RAF deployed

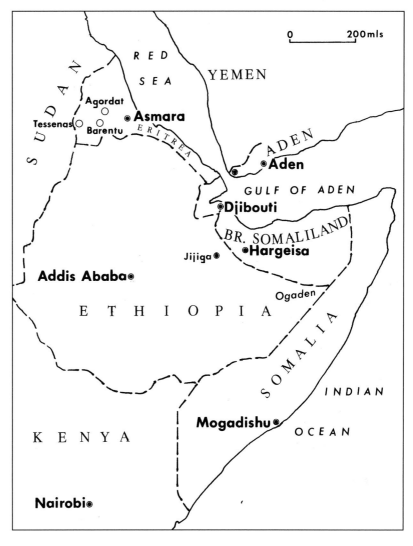

several Lancaster GR.1s of 683 Sqn to Hargeisa for survey work. British forces generally left Eritrea in June 1952, although 1910 Flt operated until September, when it departed to join the parent 651 Sqn at Ismailia.

SEQUEL

In 1952 the United Nations established Eritrea as an autonomous entity federated with Ethiopia. This tried to balance Ethiopian claims for sovereignty and Eritrean desire for independence. Ten years later Ethiopia annexed it, starting a long war between Ethiopian regular forces and Ethiopian rebels and the Eritrean People's Liberation Front (EPLF), which was won by the Eritreans. In a 1993 referendum Eritreans voted for independence, leaving Ethiopia landlocked.

There has been continuing conflict, settled in 2000, but only with UN security forces involved and huge amounts of food aid.

BRISTOL BRIGAND

The Type 164 Brigand was originally designed as a torpedo-bomber successor to the Beaufighter to Specification H.7/42. It was intended that it would be powered by two Hercules engines, but as the latter were not adequate for

A detachment of Mosquitoes of 13 Sqn was sent to Asmara for mapping in support of operations across Eritrea. VL619 is here at Kabrit as L of 13 Sqn. *(via A S Thomas)*

the task the aircraft eventually flew with the Centaurus. By the time the type was in production there had been changes in the torpedo-fighter role, which transferred to ship-based fighters.

The first Brigand **TF Mk 1** flew on 27 October 1944. It was intended for 36 and 42 Sqns at Thorney Island and notionally allocated to the units between 1 and 15 October, at which time they were disbanded. Armament comprised four 20 mm cannon and a .5 in. machine-gun in the rear cockpit and provision for a single torpedo.

The **B Mk 1** bomber variant was a successful attempt to salvage something from the programme, given the change in the torpedo-fighter role. The Brigand was now intended to replace the Mosquito in the Far East, and it differed from the TF Mk 1 in the deletion of the rear machine-gun and a weapons load which comprised four 500 lb bombs or rocket projectiles. It joined 84 Sq in Iraq in June 1949.

Bomber units equipped – 8, 45, 84

Eritrea, 1950–52

Unit	Aircraft (code)	Base	From	To
RAF				
13 Sqn det	Mosquito PR.34	Asmara	21.4.47	28.4.47
39 Sqn det	Tempest F.6	Asmara	4.48	11.48
208 Sqn	Spitfire FR.18 (RG)	Asmara	8.50	1.51
	Meteor FR.9	Asmara	1.51	4.51
8 Sqn det	Brigand B.1	Asmara	8.50	9.52
Army				
1910 Flt	Auster AOP.6	Asmara, Massawa, Agordat, Barentu, Tessenas	20.7.50	16.9.52

3.2   CYPRUS, 1955–9

BACKGROUND

Subject to Turkish sovereignty until the First World War, Cyprus was annexed by Britain in 1914 and it became a colony in 1925. With four-fifths of the population of Greek origin, pressure grew for *Enosis*, or amalgamation with Greece. Recognizing the difficulty of getting the British to concede such an important base, the National Organization of Cypriot Fighters (EOKA), under the leadership of the ex-Greek Colonel George Grivas, resorted to arms. On 1 April 1955 a bombing campaign started with attacks on government buildings at Larnaca, Limassol and Nicosia.

There was already a large British Army presence following the departure in 1954 from Egypt, and in May a Sycamore helicopter flight was formed, initially for search and rescue duties, and based at Nicosia. After further attacks in the autumn, in which policemen and servicemen were killed, Field Marshal Sir John Harding arrived as Governor, declaring a state of emergency on 27 November 1955.

THE EMERGENCY

With the emergency declared, the number of troops was increased, with a number flown out from the UK in Shackleton aircraft of 42 Sqn, and the Sycamore flight split to provide an internal security unit. From late 1955 Operations *Foxhunter*, *Pepperpot* and *Lucky Alphonse* were mounted in vain attempts to locate Grivas and his supporters. From 21 July 1955 Shackletons from 38 Sqn based in Malta were detached in Maritime Search Operations (MARSO) tasking looking for arms smugglers from Greece. The operation ended on 14 December 1959 after some 824 sorties. To complement the Shackletons on 12 April 1956 the Fleet Air Arm (FAA) started operations from Nicosia with three Gannet AS.1 aircraft from 847 Naval Air Squadron (NAS), also to prevent the smuggling of arms by sea. Perhaps by way of protest, EOKA blew up a Dakota aircraft on the airfield on the 27th, a Hermes on charter having already been destroyed on 3 March.

September saw a further influx of troops prior to the Suez expedition, and during the month the first placement of soldiers by helicopter took place at Prodhomos. In October the Sycamore flights became consolidated as 284 Sqn with fourteen aircraft. On 10 November, EOKA took the opportunity caused by preoccupation with intense flying to plant a bomb on Hunter F.5 WP180 of 1 Sqn, causing it to be written off.

All three services operated aircraft throughout the Cyprus emergency. In September 1955, 1910 AOP Flt with Auster AOP.6s had transferred to Nicosia for general reconnaissance and liaison work; such was the demand that it

The Sycamore proved extremely useful in Cyprus serving with the Internal Security Flight then 284/103 Sqns for eight years. XG547/5 is seen here in the Troodos mountains disembarking irregular troops in an olive grove while another machine is nearly hidden from view in the background. *(Crown copyright)*

was joined by 1915 Light Liaison Flt in April 1956. Eventually some fifteen airstrips were prepared for Army use, and the robust Austers complemented the Sycamores admirably. From November 1956, when terrorist attacks increased to 416 in the month, several Whirlwind HAR.2s were added to 284 Sqn's inventory, and further attempts were made, with some success, to round up the EOKA cells. The helicopters were also invaluable in spotting ambushes.

On 27 November 1957 four Canberras (B.2 WF886 of 6 Sqn, T.4 WJ858 of 13 Sqn, B.2 WP514 of 9 Sqn and PR.7 WT508 of 13 Sqn) were destroyed in a hangar fire at Akrotiri, the result of an EOKA bomb. Although fighter aircraft were of little value in the cordon and search operations conducted by the Army, the RAF retained a flight of Meteor NF.13s of 39 Sqn at Nicosia when the squadron transferred to Malta in March 1957. The only use of fighters is believed to have been in October 1958, when Sea Venom FAW.21s of 809 NAS, flying off HMS *Albion*, attacked hideouts in the Troodos Mountains.

The light-aircraft resource was increased from November 1958, with 230 Sqn's Pioneer CC.1s based on Nicosia supplementing the Austers which had re-formed as 653 Sqn AAC in September 1957. With a greater payload, the short take-off and landing (STOL) Pioneers were able to use the Auster strips. During 1958, as the British military strength increased, there were diplomatic moves to end the conflict. The spiritual leader of the Greek community, Archbishop Makarios, suspected of supporting EOKA, had been deported in 1956, but he was released to Athens in April 1957. He announced his abandonment of support for Enosis in September 1958, and after a London conference in February 1959 he returned to the island.

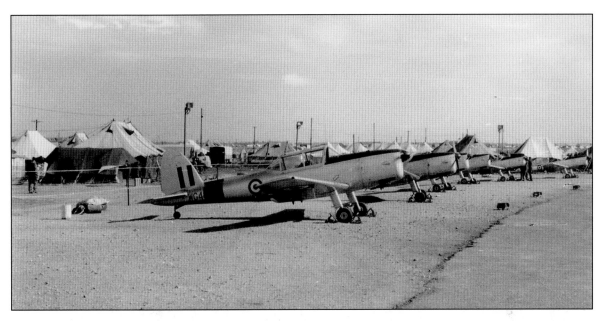

In the winter of 1959 Chipmunks served briefly with 114 Sqn in an unsuccessful attempt to provide anti-terrorist patrols. At Nicosia are six of the unit's aircraft with WG486/G in the foreground. *(A S Thomas)*

From the previous autumn there had been outbreaks of violence between the Greek and Turkish communities, and in December five Chipmunk T.10s, making up 114 Sqn, operated unsuccessfully, flying anti-terrorist patrols for which they were not suited. The unit disbanded on 14 March 1959. Cyprus was a conflict in which the helicopter came into its own. Despite the fact that the Sycamores had a limited payload, they were able to place troops quickly in inaccessible parts of the mountainous countryside, thus keeping EOKA units constantly on the move. By the time the emergency ended in December 1959, 284 Sqn had been renumbered 103 Sqn, having been operating continuously in support of the Army since 1955. In all, the squadron flew 9,792 hours in 19,375 sorties, dropping 4,000 troops and 120 tons of supplies and lifting 268 casualties. In the four years 1955 to 1958 284 Sqn lost seven Sycamores, mainly in landing accidents. Four Austers of 1910 Flt were also lost.

SEQUEL

Cyprus was granted independence in 1960, but with two British sovereign bases at Akrotiri and Dhekelia. Early in 1963 armed violence broke out between Turks and Greeks, leading eventually into war and partition, described in Chapter 6, Section 3.

FAIREY GANNET

The Gannet was one of three types constructed to Specification GR.17/45 (the others were the Blackburn YB1 and Short SB3), and it had its origins in a unique project pioneered by Fairey early in the war. A 24-cylinder P.24 Prince engine had been fitted to a Battle test-bed, each half of the engine driving one of two contra-rotating propellers. In this way twin-engined power was offered with single-engined bulk and no assymetric flight problems. Further, the aircraft could be flown economically on half an engine with full power being engaged when necessary. The Fairey Q, later known as the Fairey 17 and then the Gannet, was designed originally to take a Rolls-Royce Tweed turbine, and, when that was cancelled, the Double Mamba.

The Fairey Q AS Mk 1 was a two-seat anti-submarine aircraft, and the first of three prototypes flew on 19 September 1949. In the third prototype a third seat was installed, finlets fitted, the ASV radar 'dustbin' moved further back and the bomb-bay lengthened. No armament was fitted, but the bomb-bay accommodated two torpe-does or mines, and depth charges and eight 60 lb RPs could be fitted under the inner wing sections. The first production aircraft flew on 9 June 1953 and the type entered service with 826 NAS in January 1955.

Anti-shipping units equipped – 812, 815, 820, 824, 825, 826, 847, 1840, 1842

Early in the development of the Gannet it had been intended to design an early-warning variant, but it was not flown until some time after the AS Mk 4. The **AEW Mk 3** variant was significantly different from other models. The more powerful Double Mamba 112 was fitted further forward and the exhausts shortened to exit under the wing leading edge. A large radome housed the AN/APS radar retrieved from the Skyraider and a single cockpit housed the pilot, the observers being completely enclosed. To counter the bulk of the radome the fin and rudder were completely redesigned, and the undercarriage was lengthened to provide adequate clearance. The AEW Mk 3 joined 849 NAS in 1960 and served until 1978.

Warning unit equipped – 849

During development of the Gannet the weight had inevitably increased, and the initial variant was under-powered. This was resolved by fitting the more powerful Double Mamba 101 in the new **AS Mk 4**. The prototype flew on 12 March 1956, and service entry was with 824 NAS just five months later. The Gannet was to be the last fixed-wing anti-submarine aircraft, being succeeded by the Whirlwind helicopter.

Anti-shipping units equipped – 810, 814, 815, 824, 825

Cyprus, 1955–9

Unit	Aircraft	Base	From	To
RAF				
SAR Flt	Sycamore HR.14	Nicosia	5.55	15.10.56
Internal Security Flt	Sycamore HR.14	Nicosia	7.55	15.10.56
284 Sqn	Sycamore HR.14	Nicosia	15.10.56	31.7.59
103 Sqn	Sycamore HR.14	Nicosia	1.8.59	31.7.63
38 Sqn det	Shackleton MR.2	Akrotiri	21.7.55	14.12.59
230 Sqn	Pioneer CC.1	Nicosia	27.11.58	7.4.59
13 Sqn	Meteor PR.10	Akrotiri	10.2.56	8.56
	Canberra PR.7	Akrotiri	10.2.56	12.61
39 Sqn det	Meteor NF.13	Nicosia	9.8.56	17.6.58
114 Sqn	Chipmunk T.10	Nicosia	15.12.58	14.3.59
FAA				
847 NAS	Gannet AS.1	Nicosia	8.4.56	6.58
	Gannet AS.4	Nicosia	6.58	30.11.59
809 NAS	Sea Venom FAW.21	HMS *Albion*	23.10.58	22.11.58
Army				
1910 Flt	Auster AOP.6	Nicosia	15.11.55	17.4.56
	Auster AOP.6	Lakatamia, Kermia	18.4.56	31.8.57
10 Flt	Auster AOP.6	Kermia	1.9.57	11.5.58
1915 Flt	Auster AOP.6	Nicosia, Lakatamia	4.4.56	18.9.56
	Auster AOP.6	Kermia	18.9.56	31.8.57
15 Flt	Auster AOP.6	Kermia	1.9.57	11.5.58
653 Sqn	Auster AOP.6	Kermia	11.5.58	1.60

3.3 EGYPT, 1951–6

BACKGROUND

Britain had had a significant interest in Egypt through the nineteenth century, in terms of both trade and the strategically important Suez Canal, which was jointly owned with France. At the outset of the First World War Britain had declared Egypt a protectorate when Turkey sided with the Central Powers. In 1922 Egypt was granted nominal independence, but with a strong British military presence, especially in the Canal Zone, including No. 4 FTS formed in 1921 at Abu Sueir.

In 1936 a formal treaty was concluded allowing Britain to retain forces in Egypt, which through the Second World War became critical as an Allied stronghold from which to defeat the Axis Powers in North Africa. For several years after the war the RAF presence in Egypt was largely confined to transport units, given the location of the country, while combat squadrons were busily engaged close to where there was action – Palestine, Eritrea, Somaliland, Greece and Iraq. The base at Shallufa was host to Lincoln bombers on *Sunray* detachments, designed to provide training in rapid deployment of strategic bombers.

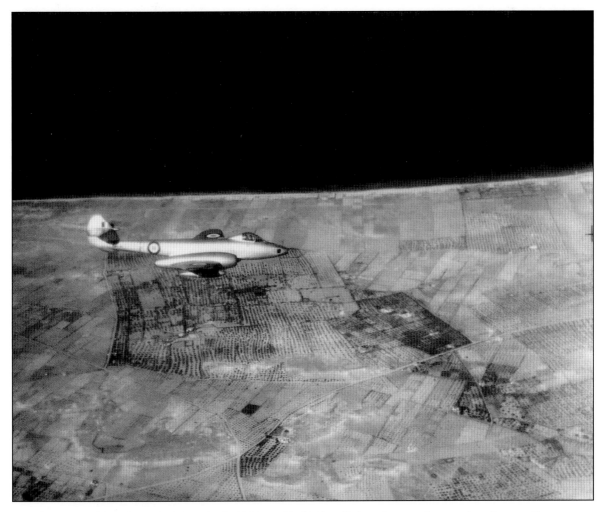

The Meteor PR.10 replaced the Mosquito in 13 Sqn at Fayid. Locally based reconnaissance aircraft were of importance in the Middle East; WB172/F overflying the Nile delta is in bare metal finish. *(via A S Thomas)*

RAF PRESENCE, JULY 1947

Unit	Aircraft	Base	Function
RAF			
70 Sqn	Dakota	Kabrit	Transport
78 Sqn	Dakota	Kabrit	Transport
114 Sqn	Dakota	Kabrit	Transport
204 Sqn	Dakota	Kabrit	Transport
216 Sqn	Dakota	Kabrit	Transport
MedME CS	Anson C.19, Proctor C.4	Kabrit	Communications

RIOTING AND RESPONSE

Immediately after the war, Egypt began a process of demanding British withdrawal. When the Egyptian Prime Minister abrogated the treaty in 1951 he was dismissed by King Farouk, which started a series of anti-British riots. The British bases were highly dependent on local labour, most of which ceased working. Egypt was not only an important base in respect of local British interest, it was also pivotal in terms of containing Soviet expansion in the Middle East, with the Suez Canal vital for access to oil and the Far East. The congested area along the Canal had thus become a key British base.

As the Canal Zone was consolidated, several RAF Regiment LAA squadrons were brought in to defend the airfields. In June 1951 16 Independent Parachute Brigade was shipped from the UK to Cyprus in HMS *Ocean* and HMS *Warrior*, initially for possible deployment to Iran. In the event the troops were flown from Nicosia to Kabrit by aircraft of the five Valetta squadrons in October as the situation seemed to be deteriorating. They were not to leave until August 1954.

219 Sqn began replacing its night-fighter Mosquitos with the tropicalized Meteor NF.13 from late 1951. WM312 is in gloss dark green/ medium sea grey finish. *(Author's collection)*

Complementing the PR Meteors of 13 Sqn in Egypt were the fighter-reconnaissance FR.9 variants of 208 Sqn based at Abu Sueir. VZ593/Q is nearest the camera is this photo dated 21 January 1952. *(via A S Thomas)*

In November 1951 there were serious riots in Ismailia, which were put down by the military while the Egyptian police stood by. On 25 January 1952 the situation escalated, resulting in a British attack on the police barracks in the town. An Auster of 1908 Flt maintained a constant watch on the situation, directing mortar fire onto the barracks roof from where police were firing on British troops. *Sunray* exercises were halted and dependants were evacuated to the UK. The threat was considered so serious that plans were made for an assault on Cairo and air raids on Egyptian Air Force bases.

The RAF received reinforcements in the shape of eight Lincolns of 148 Sqn plus two squadrons of Vampire fighters. The Canal Zone was sealed off, resulting in increased violence and sabotage. By now some forty British servicemen had been killed. Throughout the period Austers had been keeping a careful watch on proceedings, while the faster PR Meteors were also active. Fighters were held at readiness for immediate action.

In July 1952 there was a *coup d'état* by the military in Egypt, which paradoxically resulted in an improvement in relations. Notwithstanding this, while negotiations for a British withdrawal continued, there was a contingency plan to deploy three squadrons of Lincolns to Shallufa.

SEQUEL

In due course agreement was reached in July 1954 for British departure within twenty months, albeit with retention of two bases, to be maintained by civilians, for use in the event that the area was threatened by hostile forces. A new base at Akrotiri, Cyprus, was prepared, and the last British troops left Egypt on 26 March 1956.

Another NF.13 of 219 Sqn, this time WM321 displaying the unit's markings of two red chevrons on a black background. *(Author's collection)*

RAF AND ARMY PRESENCE, 1952

Unit	Aircraft	Base	From	To
RAF				
32 Sqn	Vampire FB.5	Deversoir	Based	
213 Sqn	Vampire FB.5	Deversoir	Based	
249 Sqn	Vampire FB.5	Deversoir	Based	
39 Sqn	Mosquito NF.36	Fayid	Based	
219 Sqn	Mosquito NF.36	Kabrit	Based	
13 Sqn	Meteor PR.10	Fayid	Based	
208 Sqn	Meteor FR.9	Abu Sueir	Based	
70 Sqn	Valetta C.1	Kabrit	Based	
114 Sqn	Valetta C.1	Kabrit	Based	
78 Sqn	Valetta C.1	Fayid	Based	
204 Sqn	Valetta C.1	Fayid	Based	
216 Sqn	Valetta C.1	Fayid	Based	
MEAFCF	Dakota C.4, Proctor C.4	Fayid	Based	
205 GCF	Anson C.12, C.19, Meteor T.7	Fayid	Based	
148 Sqn	Lincoln B.2	Shallufa	30.1.52	
6 Sqn	Vampire FB.5, FB.9	Abu Sueir	28.1.52	31.5.52
73 Sqn	Vampire FB.5, FB.9	Kabrit	1.2.52	30.9.52
Army				
1908 Flt	Auster AOP.6, T.7	Ismailia	Based	

3.4   KENYA, 1952–6

BACKGROUND

For many years before the Second World War there was dissension in Kenya on the part of the Kikuyu tribe in the central province to the north of Nairobi. Essentially it was felt, perhaps not without some justification, that Europeans had deprived them of their lands. After the war the Kenya African Union (KAU) was formed, and from it sprang an extremist group, Mau Mau, otherwise calling itself the Kenya Land Freedom Party. As the population grew, pressure on the land was such that the indigenous peoples found themselves working on increasingly less advantageous terms for European farmers. In 1948 and 1949 there was discontent among the labour force, and the East Africa Communications Flight (EACF) was involved in leaflet dropping.

THE EMERGENCY

Throughout 1952 there were isolated attacks on white farmers. However, by no means all Kikuyu supported Mau Mau, and it was the murder of Chief Waruhiu, a close British ally, on 9 October 1952 that led to a state of emergency being declared on 21 October. The previous day the 1st Bn Lancashire Fusiliers departed Fayid via Khartoum on Valettas of 204 Sqn. On the 21st the 1st Bn Royal East Kent Regt was flown into Nairobi on Hastings transports of 511 Sqn. The two infantry battalions, forming 39 Infantry Brigade, joined 3 and 5 Bns King's African Rifles (KAR), which were already in Kenya. The 4th Bn and 6th Bn were flown in in DC-3s from Uganda and Tanganyika respectively.

The first operation, *Jock Scott*, was the rounding up and internment of eighty-three known Mau Mau leaders. A large region north of Nairobi was declared the operational area, and within that were two prohibited tracts within which the security forces could work freely on the assumption that anyone found within them could be deemed to be a terrorist. One area, of 820 square miles, was in the Aberdare Mountains, while the second, of 780 square miles, was around Mount Kenya.

Without their leaders the Mau Mau were inactive for a few weeks, but on 1 January 1953 the first white farmers were killed. At the time the strength of the RAF in Kenya amounted to six aircraft in the EACF based at Eastleigh, and these included two Dakotas left by 82 Sqn when it had returned to the UK in October, following a survey. Plans were put in hand to improve the position, and as the Rhodesian Air Training Group (RATG) was being disbanded, a number of its Harvard IIBs were

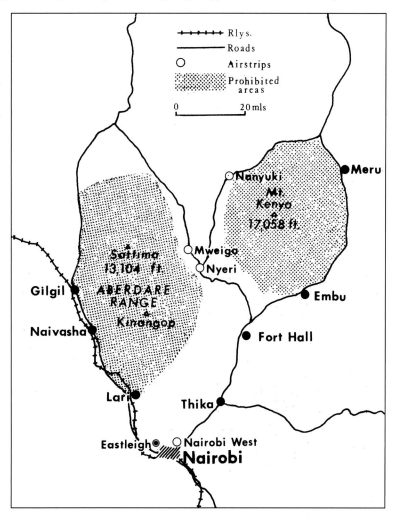

Lancaster PR.1s of 82 Sqn were detached from Benson to Eastleigh for survey tasks in 1952. TW658/J is seen in white over/black under finish. *(Author's collection)*

formed into 1340 Flt at Thornhill. The flight moved to Eastleigh on 23 March 1953, and it immediately began bombing operations, using 19 lb fragmentation bombs. The aircraft were equipped with carriers for eight bombs and a single .303 in. machine-gun in the starboard wing.

There was one other air unit that was to prove of immense value to the security forces – the Kenya Police Reserve Air Wing (KPRAW), which had been formed in 1949. By 1953 it comprised several Austers and some Piper Pacers and Tri-Pacers, and these were soon put to work supporting police and army outposts and searching for signs of the elusive enemy. The Tri-Pacers were soon fitted with under-fuselage bomb-racks accommodating four 19 lb anti-personnel bombs.

There was an outrage on 26 March when eighty-four loyal Kikuyu were massacred at Lari, only twenty miles out of Nairobi, and the same day guns were stolen from a police station at Naivasha. The military commander called for more units from Britain, and on 7 June HQ 39 Brigade, with battalions from the Royal East Kent Regiment and the Devon Regiment, was flown in and a separate East Africa Command established.

The security forces now began a series of intense operations in and around the prohibited areas. The KPRAW and 1340 Flt moved up to Nyeri, then Mweiga, where a Joint Operations Centre (JOC) was established to co-ordinate bombing in support of ground forces. The KPRAW was invaluable in that its pilots were familiar with the local geography and were able to reconnoitre for the Harvards. So important was the unit that its CO, an RAF reserve officer, was given tactical command under the RAF Commander of Air Forces. The Harvards were not ideal for counter-insurgency, being light on power for hot and high operations. At least six were lost in tight valleys, being unable to climb their way out of difficulty; three (KF348, 382 and 985) were lost in a single operation on 19 April 1954. The crews survived to be recovered, but the crashed aircraft were a source of rich picking for the insurgents.

The situation became worse through the summer of 1953, with the Mau Mau building up a town-based infrastructure of support for operational groups in the mountains. Savage atrocities were committed against any loyal Kikuyu in order to ensure support and neutralize local opposition. A second brigade HQ and two more infantry battalions were flown into Kenya from 29 September 1953 on forty-one RAF Hastings and civilian charter flights. In September the Harvards flew 332 sorties, dropping 2,555 bombs, but their limitations soon became apparent in attacking small, elusive Mau Mau groups working from mountain hideouts. From November 1953 Lincoln bombers were rotated into Eastleigh to provide for pattern bombing of known terrorist camps, the first detachment being provided by 49 Sqn.

In January 1954 100 Sqn took over from 49 Sqn, and in March it was replaced in turn by 61 Sqn, which lost RE297 when it crashed on a night operation on 22 March with the loss of five crew. The Lincolns normally worked early in the morning before clouds and turbulence had built up, or at night, and the sortie rate was about twenty to twenty-five a month. Their loads generally comprised five 1,000 lb and nine 500 lb bombs, although on occasions 350 lb cluster bombs were carried. The supply of bombs was a problem throughout the campaign and many were unreliable. In the early stages of the operations Lincolns had to fly up to Khormaksar to pick up bombs before each sortie.

Bomb fuses were normally set at 25 seconds because of the low altitudes often required. On one urgent raid on 14 August 1954 three Lincolns of 214 Sqn were required to bomb a concentration of Mau Mau near Nyer. The aircraft were already bombed up, but the cloud ceiling meant that the weapons had to be released at only 900 ft. The first bomb detonated on impact, and the shock waves set up sympathetic explosions among the succeeding bombs until one exploded just below the bomb-bay of the third aircraft, SX976, causing considerable damage and killing the flight engineer.

The bombing was not without constraint and problems on the ground. Distressed animals attacked troops, who also found the craters impossible to search and difficult to bypass. There was also considerable loss of valuable trees.

The KPRAW generally undertook spotting and target marking as for the Harvards. Early in the year Eastleigh acquired two Auster AOP.6s and a Pembroke fitted with loudspeakers for use in post-bombing sorties, to encourage surrender while the terrorists were still confused. In addition, Lincolns and Valettas dropped leaflets promising safe conduct for those surrendering. Sycamore XG309 was added to the Station Flight to enable the speedy recovery of casualties in terrain where surface transport could take many days to cover a few miles. Individual infantry platoons or companies were given responsibility for defined areas, staying in the bush for long periods and

Lincoln squadrons were rotated into Eastleigh from November 1953 to June 1955 for bombing dissident camps. SX976 of 214 is at Nairobi in 1954; in the background is a Dakota of the resident Communications Flight.
(Author's collection)

being supplied by air by light aircraft of the KPRAW, which typically carried up to eight 30 lb packs. The light aircraft, which were often flying upwards of ten sorties a day, were also invaluable in being able to maintain radio contact with ground forces and helping to give their locations with a high degree of accuracy.

By 1954 it had been appreciated that the light aircraft had limited capacity for resupply, although they could manoeuvre in very tight spaces. Thus the sole Valetta of EACF (VW814) was used for delivering up to 6,000 lb of supplies per sortie to isolated ground units. A team of RASC dispatchers was provided, and the aircraft operated from Eastleigh from 06.00 hrs to complete tasking before clouds obscured the mountains from 09.00 hrs. The Valetta used the forward strip up-country at Nanyuki to ensure that two sorties a morning were flown. These missions were dangerous, being flown at altitudes of up to 13,000 ft in turbulence, but they were undertaken without loss.

As intelligence improved, the Mau Mau dependence on town-based supporters for supplies became clearer, and Operation *Anvil* between 24 April and 7 May led to 16,538 suspects being detained in sweeps around Nairobi. Coincident with this operation, a detachment of Vampire FB.9s of 8 Sqn was sent to Eastleigh from Aden to support the operation. During the detachment the Vampires fired 111 60 lb rockets and used 12,700 rounds of 20 mm shells.

One problem identified in early 1953 had been the lack of photo-reconnaissance aircraft to provide post-attack information on the success of strikes. This was remedied from August when two Meteor PR.10s were detached from 13 Sqn, then based at Fayid in Egypt. September 1954 was the month of heaviest bombing; even then by the beginning of the month some 1m lb of bombs had been dropped. From the end of 1954, by which time 49 Sqn had begun its second Kenyan tour, the Mau Mau were demonstrably weaker.

Operation *Hammer* in January 1955 in the Aberdares and Operation *First Flute* from February around Mount Kenya resulted in 161 and 277 Mau Mau dead respectively; during these sweeps 49 Sqn lost SX984 after it hit a police post during a demonstration. The terrorists were now effectively defeated, but the Lincolns did not depart until July 1955, and at the end of September 1340 Flt was disbanded. During the emergency its aircraft had dropped 21,936 19 lb bombs and lost eight aircraft out of nineteen in accidents. On 17 November 1956 the Army withdrew, and in December the operational phase ended. By then the war had cost the Mau Mau 10,527 dead and 2,633 captured; the security forces had lost 602 dead, of whom 534 were Africans. The British Government calculated the cost at precisely £55,585,424!

SEQUEL

One of the key figures in Kenyan politics was Jomo Kenyatta, arrested in the *Jock Scott* operation and sentenced to seven years' hard labour for alleged Mau Mau membership. From elections held in 1957 he led his country to independence on 12 December 1963, but almost immediately he had to ask for British support in quelling an army mutiny (described in Chapter 7, Section 4).

There has been controversy about the value of expending large quantities of bombs and other weapons against elusive targets in the jungle. In terms of eliminating Mau Mau members the bombing had little merit. Where it did make a contribution was in disrupting Mau Mau activities and diverting attention away from creating mayhem to survival. In March 1955, towards the end of the campaign, four Canberras of 21 Sqn were sent to Kenya simply as a show of force and not to apply weapons. It is conceivable that more displays and intermittent bombing would have had the same gang dispersal effect as the level of heavy bombing undertaken by the Lincolns.

Kenya, 1952–6

Unit	Aircraft	Base	From	To
RAF				
EACF	Anson C.21, Proctor C.4, Valetta C.1, Dakota C.3, Auster AOP.6, Pembroke C.1, Sycamore HR.14	Eastleigh	Based	
82 Sqn	Lancaster PR.1, Dakota C.3	Eastleigh	1.7.52	31.10.52

Unit	Aircraft	Base	From	To
1340 Flt	Harvard 2B	Eastleigh	31.3.53	6.53
	Harvard 2B, Auster AOP.6	Marrian's Farm	6.53	2.54
		Nanyuki	2.54	4.54
		Eastleigh	4.54	30.9.55
49 Sqn	Lincoln B.2	Eastleigh	11.11.53	6.1.54
100 Sqn	Lincoln B.2	Eastleigh	1.54	3.54
61 Sqn	Lincoln B.2	Eastleigh	3.54	19.6.54
214 Sqn	Lincoln B.2	Eastleigh	6.6.54	10.12.54
49 Sqn	Lincoln B.2	Eastleigh	30.11.54	7.2.55
21 Sqn	Lincoln B.2	Eastleigh	6.3.55	13.6.55
8 Sqn det	Vampire FB.9	Eastleigh	4.54	5.54
13 Sqn det	Meteor PR.10	Eastleigh	18.8.54	25.7.54
KPRAW				
Pacer, Tri-Pacer, Cessna 180		Nairobi West, Marrian's Farm, Nanyuki		Based

NOTE

Kenya Police Reserve Air Wing aircraft included Tri-Pacer VP-KKY, KMH, KPF, KPS, KXP, KXX

3.5   SUDAN, 1955

BACKGROUND

The Sudan is the largest country in Africa, embracing many tribes and with a critical division between north and south: the north is essentially Arab, while the poorer south is peopled by black Christians or Animists. The country was ruled as an Anglo-Egyptian condominium from 1896 until 14 December 1955, when it achieved independence.

REVOLT

In the period 1947–9 the RAF based three Tempest squadrons at Khartoum – 6 and 213, as 324 Wing, from October 1947 to October 1948, and then 39 Sqn for a period in 1949. These units were on hand either to support Egyptian units or to assist ground forces dealing with dissidents in Somaliland or Eritrea.

In the spring of 1955 there was unrest in the south, and the decision was taken to fly northern troops to quell the revolt rather than trust the local Equatoria Corps, which

Tropicalised Tempest F.6ss of 6, 39 and 213 Sqns were on hand to support Egyptian ground forces dealing with dissidents in the late 1940s. NX229/AK-R wears the wartime codes of 213 Sqn, which was the only RAF unit to retain its pre-war code through the Second World War and beyond. *(via A S Thomas)*

was ordered to prepare for northern posting. On 18 August the southern troops revolted and 8,000 government troops were flown in from Khartoum in RAF Valettas drawn from 70 and 84 Sqns based at Fayid and 114 and 216 Sqns based at Kabrit. Although the revolt was put down, many Equatoria troops deserted into the bush with their weapons.

Over the next few years the new government ignored the calls for a degree of southern autonomy, while the rebels grew in strength. With British help the embryo Sudanese Air Force (SAF) was established from 1957 with four Provost T.53s, later supplemented by five ex-RAF aircraft, and four Gomhourias from Egypt. In 1962 the SAF acquired four Jet Provost T.51s and eight T.52 trainers. The southern rebels unified in 1963 as the Land Freedom Army, more popularly known as Anya-nya. From January 1964 Anya-nya, with support from Ethiopia, Uganda and Zaire, began a series of attacks on government posts.

SEQUEL

As the position deteriorated there was civil unrest, leading to political chaos in the north and famine and the collapse of government in the south. After several changes in central government there was a coup in May 1969 which brought Colonel Jaafar Numeiri to power. The British withdrew training teams and the Russians moved in. However, Numeiri secured covert British support to contain a counter-coup in 1971, and relations improved to the extent that in Exercise *Jowar* in 1975 a detachment of Alouettes from 7 Regt AAC was involved. It is also understood that some ex-RAF Jet Provosts were supplied with British mercenary personnel in support.

Sudan, 1955

Unit	Aircraft (code)	Base	From	To
RAF				
213 Sqn	Tempest F.6 (AK)	Khartoum	22.10.47	17.8.48
		Mogadishu	17.8.48	21.10.48
6 Sqn	Tempest F.6 (JV)	Khartoum, det Mogadishu	26.11.47	5.5.48
39 Sqn	Tempest F.6	Khartoum, det Asmara	1.4.48	28.2.49

Hastings of 48 Sqn brought troops of the Cheshire Regiment to quell a rebellion on the Maldives. Pictured is WJ332 with spinners removed, presumably to aid cooling. *(Author's collection)*

3.6   THE MALDIVES, 1959–75

The British occupied Ceylon from 1815, and thus in due course assumed responsibility for the Maldives in 1887. The Maldives are a range of 1,196 atolls in the Indian ocean, of which 203 are inhabited by a total population of around 300,000. When Ceylon gained independence in 1948, there was a new agreement confirming British protection, and in 1956 negotiations were concluded for a 100-year lease of the airfield on Gan in the south. The islands are some 500 miles from north to south and the airbase was about 300 miles from the relatively isolated capital, Male. There was dissension in the south when locals were precluded from dealing with the British, leading to a local rebellion.

The more southerly atolls declared an independent republic early in 1959, and the British largely ignored the situation at the time. In June there was an attempt by the Maldivian government to regain full control, and as there was only a staging-post at Gan, with no garrison, in August a company of 1st Bn Cheshire Regt was flown to Gan from Singapore in Hastings aircraft of the resident 48 Sqn. Two Shackleton MR.2 aircraft of 210 Sqn based at Ballykelly flew out to Gan on 5 August via Orange, Kano and Nairobi, arriving eleven days later. They returned after a short sojourn.

In due course there was a peaceful conclusion to the problem, and the short-lived republic of United Suvadiva was dissolved in 1964. The British Government vacated Gan in 1975 in favour of Diego Garcia.

3.7   MALAYA, 1948–60

BACKGROUND

Although the Malayan Communist Party (MCP) was formed in 1929, mainly from among the 38% of the Malayan population who were ethnic Chinese, during the Second World War its members supported the Allies against Japan. In 1942 the Malayan People's Anti-Japanese Army (MPAJA) was formed from among MCP members, who were armed by the British in order to harass the enemy and provide intelligence, and from 1943 the MPAJA worked with the British covert Force 136.

When the war ended, the MPAJA was disbanded and expected to surrender its weapons, and although the majority were recovered, several hundred committed and armed members of the MCP took to the jungle to prepare for a guerrilla war against the British. A Malayan Union was introduced in April 1946, but this was unpopular because the Malays resented representation of Chinese and Indians, while the Communists opposed any central government.

There were demonstrations through 1946, and in 1947 over 300 strikes were called. By early 1948 serious riots had begun, and these increased after strikes were made unlawful in the spring. In June the Malayan People's Anti-British Army (MPABA) was formed out of elements of the defunct MPAJA and the MCP. As the position deteriorated, a state of emergency was declared on 17 June, and on 23 July the MCP was banned. Operation *Firedog*, which was to last for twelve years, had begun.

THE DEFENSIVE PHASE

At the start of the emergency there were two British, five Gurkha and three Malay battalions in Malaya, and some 9,000 police. Intelligence was poor, despite the fact that the Communists operated widely in the populated coastal plain. On 1 February 1949, the Malayan Races Liberation Army (MRLA) was formed from MCP and MPABA elements. In June 1948 the RAF presence in Malaya was limited. Elements of two air defence squadrons, 28 and 60, both equipped with the Spitfire FR.18, moved up to Kuala Lumpur from Tengah.

84 Sqn at Changi, with the Beaufighter X, was the only available strike unit, although the Sunderlands of 209 Sqn could be called on for heavy support. In the reconnaissance role, 81 Sqn with Spitfire FR.18s and PR.19s and Mosquito PR.34s was also at Changi. The transport units were based at Changi and comprised 48, 52 and 110 Sqns, all equipped with the Dakota. They were supplemented by a variety of aircraft of the Far East Communications Squadron (FECS). Last, there were the Austers of 1914 Flt, which was soon expanded to form 656 Sqn.

The war in Malaya went through three phases, the first of which, the defensive phase, lasted from 1948 to 1951. During this period the population was subjected to attack by guerrillas, who then simply disappeared into the jungle. The ground forces were inexperienced at handling this type of fighting and, as already indicated, were poorly served with intelligence. The first RAF strike against Communist terrorists (CT) was on 6 July, when a CT camp near Ayer Karah in Perak was attacked by Spitfires of 60 Sqn.

A second strike was mounted on the 15th, and a third the following day against a camp situated in swamps at Telok Anson, where ten CT were killed. The strikes continued into August, but the accidental firing of a rocket on the ground which killed a civilian brought a temporary ban on the use of underwing stores on the ageing Spitfires.

At the outset of the war in Malaya the Spitfire was the only available fighter. While 28 Sqn soon departed for Hong Kong, 60 Sqn remained at Kuala Lumpur, flying its last Spitfire sortie on 1 January 1951. In this line-up FR.18 TP197 is in the foreground showing the unit's distinctive nose stripes. On the far right are two Tempest F.2s of 33 Sqn. *(Crown copyright)*

Final checks on the rocket fit on Brigand B.1 RH82?/A of 84 Sqn at Tengah; in addition to eight rockets the aircraft is carrying at least one 500 lb bomb under the fuselage. Prominent on the fin is the playing card 'hearts' emblem first worn by DH9As in Iraq. *(Crown copyright)*

Another Brigand of 84 Sqn, RH776/K firing rockets at a suspected terrorist hideout. With a high stalling speed the Brigand was not universally popular and several broke up in the air during rocket attacks. *(Crown copyright)*

Two Beaufighters of 84 Sqn were brought up to Kuala Lumpur from Tengah, from where they continued to mount offensive sorties, being supplemented by a trio detached from 45 Sqn based in Ceylon.

Throughout the war the RAF mounted two types of air strike. When intelligence indicated the precise location of a camp or other known target, pinpoint attacks were made, but with the prevailing weather conditions, which meant that the early mist did not clear until mid-morning, these operations were limited. Most of the successful strikes were made early in the war before the CT realized the potential of air power; by the end of 1948 they reduced the size of their camps, camouflaged them and became more mobile.

The second type of air strike was the use of area bombing in regions believed to be occupied by the CT. Throughout the war an enormous tonnage of bombs was used to relatively little effect against the jungle. The guerrillas employed only hit-and-run tactics, never gaining sufficient strength to stand and fight set-piece battles. For this reason, close-support strikes were rarely flown, since by the time aircraft were alerted the enemy would have vanished. Escort patrols were flown, however, as in the early stages of the emergency the CT set many ambushes on road and rail convoys.

In October 84 Sqn departed for Iraq, where it re-equipped with the Brigand; it was replaced by 45 Sqn, which was fully operational by May 1949. After August there was a lull in operations as the guerrillas re-formed after initial setbacks, but as the civilian authorities began a resettlement programme, intelligence improved, and on 28 February 1949 one of the most successful strikes of the campaign was mounted. To date, operations had been hampered by the CT having advance warning of strikes by reconnaissance flights, and especially by the noise of troops setting up ambushes. The strike against a target in Mengkuang by eight Spitfires using fragmentation bombs and four Beaufighters killed nine out of a total of fifteen in the combined operation.

BOMBING THE JUNGLE

The Sunderlands also occasionally took to bombing the jungle, but they spent most of their time on maritime reconnaissance, searching for vessels bringing arms up the coast. The apparently indiscriminate area bombing based on dated intelligence did have the effect of keeping the guerrillas on the move, however. The pattern bombing required larger aircraft than those permanently based in the theatre, and in January 1947 Lancasters of 7 Sqn had detached to Changi from the UK in Operation *Red Lion*; in *Red Lion II*, Lincolns of 97 Sqn also gained experience of detaching.

On 28 November 1949, in Operation *Centipede*, Lancasters of 210 Sqn spent two weeks at Tengah, where it is understood they dropped bombs on areas believed to be occupied by CT. These early detachments paved the way for a series of operations from March 1950 involving detached Lincolns (Operations *Musgrave* and *Bold*) and then Canberras (Operation *Mileage*). From 1957, in the *Profiteer* series of exercises, Valiant and Vulcan bombers from the V-force also flew sorties from Changi, then Butterworth. On a more permanent basis, the Lincolns of 1 Sqn RAAF arrived at Tengah in July 1950, from which base they were to operate until 1958.

The fighters had been depleted when 28 Sqn departed for Hong Kong, along with 656 Sqn's 1903 Flight, as the position in China worsened. Reinforcement came in August 1949 in the shape of Tempests of 33 Sqn, shipped from Germany aboard HMS *Ocean*. Over the next twenty-one months these aircraft flew nearly 2,000 sorties. There was further (albeit temporary) support when the Seafires of 800 NAS and Fireflies of 827 NAS disembarked from HMS *Triumph* in October. Throughout the emergency, Royal Navy carriers stopped off at Singapore, enabling their aircraft to add to the RAF and Commonwealth Air Forces in the theatre.

The elegant Hornet fighter was just too late to see war service as an air defence fighter, but the type came into its own in Malaya in F.3 guise. While the Brigand had a short service life, the Hornet served for five years – surprising for a wooden airframe in tropical climes. Aircraft O of 33 Sqn armed with four rockets and two 250 lb bombs is readied for take-off at Butterworth. *(Crown copyright)*

The Casualty Evacuation Flight was formed at Changi in May 1950 with three S-51s and in its first two years of operations lifted 265 casualties. Initially the injured were transported in oversize Moses baskets which were difficult to load in confined clearings, as seen here. *(Crown copyright)*

STRUCTURAL CHANGE

The mistakes made by the Government in the early stages were soon recognized and gradually rectified. In April 1950, Sir Harold Briggs was appointed Director of Operations in Malaya, a distinct appointment from that of High Commissioner held by Sir Henry Gurney. The Director of Operations was responsible for all security forces, including the police, the Army and the air forces, and he had authority to co-ordinate the work of those civil agencies whose actions affected the outcome of the war. Briggs recognized two problems. The first was the need for co-ordination between agencies, especially in the area of intelligence, and the second was the vulnerability of displaced Chinese villagers as Communist tools. Thus a three-tier committee system was set up.

At the top a War Council was established, with the Director of Operations in the chair and consisting of the Secretary of the Malayan Federation and Police, Army and Air Force commanders. Next were the State War Executive Committees, comprising the State Prime Minister and Police and Army representatives. At local level, District War Executive Committees were established, comprising the District Officer and local police and Army representatives. While at each level civilians took the chair, the most important contribution came from the police, who were responsible for intelligence.

There was a further development from February 1951. Sir Henry Gurney was killed in a road ambush in October 1950, and shortly afterwards Sir Harold Briggs died. It was decided to combine the posts of High Commissioner and Director of Operations, and Sir Gerald Templar was the first appointee. From this date the situation improved rapidly: by the end of 1952, civilian deaths from CT raids were down from ninety a month to

The certainty of early evacuation in the event of injury was a great morale booster and in 1952 the CEF was disbanded into the larger 194 Sqn. The wicker baskets were replaced by externally carried metal panniers, but the unit took on a wider range of tasks including troop movement and supply. *(Crown copyright)*

fifteen, and the CT strength was reduced from 8,000 to 2,800. The Communists withdrew to the hills, where they pressed aboriginals to supply them with food.

RE-EQUIPMENT

The RAF, meanwhile, had received new equipment. 45 Sqn had re-equipped with the Brigand from 6 December 1949, and in April 1950 84 Sqn, similarly equipped, had returned from Iraq in Operation *Tireless*. Early in 1951, 60 Sqn lost its Spitfires for the first jet in the theatre, the Vampire FB.5, although the squadron's primary function was air defence and the commitment of the unit to *Firedog* was limited. The last Spitfire fighter sortie of more than 1,800 in the campaign was flown against a target in Johore on 1 January.

Through 1951 the Brigand was plagued with troubles and grounded on several occasions. 33 Sqn exchanged its Tempests for the long-range Hornet in mid-1951, the type having gone out of service in Fighter Command. At the end of January 1952, 45 Sqn also received Hornets, transferring its remaining Brigands to 84 Sqn. The number of equipment changes, coupled with weapons problems on the Brigands, Vampires and Hornets, had a serious effect on availability through 1950 and 1951, and Harvard communications aircraft of the station flights and fighter squadrons were fitted with bomb-racks and pressed into service as dive-bombers.

The onset of the Korean War also reduced the availability of Sunderlands, which had played their part in the pattern bombing. Then, in March 1951, the Air Ministry blocked further detachments of Lincolns under Operation *Musgrave* after 61 Sqn departed. It was the view of Bomber Command that the detachments provided little in the way of proper training for the crews, and the number of squadrons available to NATO was to be reduced temporarily as the command converted to the Washington. In any event, the cost of the bombing campaign was extremely high with little tangible result, and there was a shortage of 1,000 lb bombs. To a limited extent, the, loss was made good by an increase in the establishment of 1 Sqn RAAF.

The Lincolns generally operated from Tengah, which was acceptable given that they usually took part in planned operations. The lighter units were based at Tengah but operated from Kuala Lumpur and Butterworth, with aircraft held on two-hour standby, primarily to provide relief to police posts under attack, and with the Brigands covering the south and the longer-range Hornets the north. The Hornets were particularly valuable in convoy support. The main weapons employed, apart from guns, were 1,000 lb and 500 lb high-explosive (HE) and 20 lb fragmentation bombs. Rockets were generally ineffective, except when used against a specific hard target. Features of the main weapons used are set out below.

Weapon	MAE[1]	Usage (1951)	Unit Cost[2]
1,000 lb bomb (nose-fused)	75,000	5,080	£125
1,000 lb bomb (tail-fused)	6,000		£125
500 lb bomb (nose-fused)	15,000	14,309	£56
500 lb bomb (tail-fused)	3,000		£56
20 lb fragmentation bomb (fb)	1,000	34,618	£4.50
350 lb clusters of 19 lb fb	27,500	384	£90
60 lb rocket	1,500	19,961	£18.50
20 mm cannon shell	400	60,000	
0.5 in. ammunition	4	550,000	
0.303 in. ammunition	4	700,000	

NOTES
1 Mean area of effectiveness in square feet
2 Costs at 1951 prices

The most effective way of achieving a mean area of effectiveness was to use one Lincoln bomber loaded with fourteen nose-fused (and therefore air-bursting in the jungle) 1,000 lb bombs. The total cost was £2,500, comprising £750 per sortie operating costs plus ammunition. In contrast, using tail-fused 500 lb bombs, 80 Brigand sorties would be needed to cover the same area, at a cost in excess of £32,000.

Other types of weapon were tried and rejected. Napalm was tested in 200 lb canisters in 1950, but it was ineffective in the jungle, and depth charges also proved of little value. From 1953, 4,000 lb HE bombs were used very occasionally, and smoke markers were dropped to move aborigines without causing lasting damage. From around 1954, 'screamers' in the form of empty beer bottles were dropped with conventional weapons, to economize on cost while still creating fear.

Initially, targets were passed through the RAF command chain from local ground forces, but this time-wasting procedure soon changed so that targets were allocated through a Joint Operations Centre. This procedure facilitated the speedy preparation of the best aircraft and weapons combination for the task and took full account of the need for care in minimizing the risk to civilians or ground forces. Occasionally local ground commanders were authorized to call for direct air support in conjunction with planned full-scale operations. As a result, accidents were few. It is a fact, however, that piston-engined aircraft were more suitable for attacking targets in the conditions of Malaya, where there was no effective anti-aircraft opposition, than the faster and less accurate jets.

In the early days of the campaign, Army cars equipped with radios directed strike aircraft to the target, with Dakotas acting as relays, but by 1950 this method was rarely used as the cars had difficulty reaching the sites of attacks. Working from aerial reconnaissance photos, from early on in the campaign the strike aircraft were guided by Austers of 656 Sqn flown by pilots with local knowledge. Targets were then marked by the Austers using phosphorus grenades or flares. Over the years numerous other methods and devices were tried, but although some increased accuracy, they often meant moving heavy equipment in the jungle near to the scene of action.

In a sizeable operation, the area to be attacked was first bombed by medium bombers using 500 lb or 1,000 lb bombs. This strike, of perhaps six to ten aircraft, would be followed immediately by fighters using lighter bombs, rockets and guns. Precise timing was important, to preserve the element of surprise. Raids would then be followed up by Sunderlands dropping fragmentation bombs over the next twenty-four to forty-eight hours to keep the CT in a state of shock and to inhibit the removal of the wounded.

The first major operation involving the Lincolns was *Jackpot*, mounted between 15 March and May 1950 in south-east Selangor. On 14-16 April ninety-eight sorties were made, and after a further series of raids later in the month involving 108 sorties, forty-four CT were eliminated. In 1950, 687 strikes were made, involving 4,938 sorties. The largest operation of 1951 was *Warbler*, mounted in Johore.

The air forces were employed in harassing the CT and denying escape routes and assembly points and by attacking clearings and camps away from the area of operations of the ground forces. During two months 145 strikes involving 610 sorties were flown, despite the RAF Lincolns having returned to the UK. Major strikes continued through the year, but the results were out of proportion to the effort involved. Particularly disappointing were the attempts to cut off and round up the CT responsible for the murder of the High Commissioner.

The year 1952 saw a change in the nature of targets as intelligence and reconnaissance photos indicated CT camps and cultivation clearings. Thus the air forces turned to a higher level of pinpoint attack. In February, in Operation *Puma*, the first air-only attack, was carried out against up to 400 CT in western Pahang, who could not be approached by ground forces. Eighteen Lincoln and thirty-five Brigand sorties were flown, with 132 1,000 lb and 216 500 lb bombs dropped and 6,800 rounds of 20 mm ammunition expended in six days from 13 February, but because of the absence of ground forces in the area no evaluation of the strikes was possible. By the end of 1952, 676 targets had been attacked in 3,699 sorties.

The same year also saw the start of USAF bomber detachments, beginning in December with three aircraft from Clark AB deploying to Changi. It is not clear whether or not they took part in bombing terrorists, but they certainly used the bombing range at Song Song Island. The detachments continued through the 1950s under the serial *Josstick* with one a year to 1959, when B-57s of the 13th Bomb Squadron based in Japan were deployed, starting with a detachment in July 1959.

RESUPPLY

When the campaign began, the transport force comprised three Dakota squadrons – 48, 52 and 110. They were all based at Changi, but one squadron was detached to Kuala Lumpur to provide direct support for ground operations on a rotational basis. As necessary, the detached aircraft were supplemented by Dakotas from Changi which were otherwise involved in flying the trunk routes. The RAF units were supported by aircraft from 41 Sqn RNZAF and 38 Sqn RAAF from December 1949 and June 1950 respectively.

The plan devised by Briggs for defeating the CT was to clear areas from the south northwards while dealing with any local problems anywhere in the Federation. As areas were deemed to be clear, they were described as 'white'; thus many early operations were conducted within reach of the airfields on Singapore. As the campaign developed and the CT took to the mountainous jungle, they applied pressure on aboriginals to give them support,

The first transport helicopters in Malaya were ten S-55s of 848 NAS based at Sembawang and designated Whirlwind HAR Mk 21. Finished in midnight blue is WV224 which is a HAS Mk 22 which supplemented the earlier variant.

(Author's collection)

so from 1953 a series of hill forts, usually with their own airstrips, was constructed, and the transport force not only supplied patrols in the jungle but also kept the hill forts supplied.

The importance of air supply in Malaya cannot be overstated. Without fresh stocks of food and ammunition the patrols would have been limited to four days' duration, while air drops allowed patrols lasting up to three months. The conditions for drops were far from ideal. Many were made into small clearings among 200 ft trees or swamps, where a margin of error of more than 50 ft could mean the loss of the supplies. Weather added to the problems, and it is remarkable that only 1.5% of all supplies were not retrieved. The work of packing and dispatching fell to 55 Coy Royal Army Service Corps (RASC).

The average weight of the packs was 270 lb, and it was usual for crews to lose over 3 lb in body weight through perspiration on a single sortie. Parachutes used were the 18 ft 'Irvin' costing £15 (weight limit 180 lb) and the 24 ft 'R' type costing £32 (weight limit 450 lb); each could be used up to three times and were to some extent replaced by a 28 ft 'Utility' disposable parachute costing £25. As 18,000 parachutes a year were used, the introduction of the later type resulted in considerable savings.

The first drops were made in support of Operation *Haystack* in northern Perak between 25 April and 27 May 1948, during which time a Dakota of 110 Sqn detached to Taiping dropped 222 containers in fifteen sorties. The work was dangerous, and several Dakotas were lost early on in the war. KJ962 of 110 Sqn crashed near Batu Melintang on 19 August 1948, followed on 12 November by KM633 of the same unit, in which the CO was killed; 52 Sqn lost KN536 on 7 September 1949, and KN630, in which twelve were killed, on 25 August 1950. Activity increased steadily to August 1951, when the number of patrols dropped and certain posts were supplied by road, but in January 1952 flooding resulted in a temporary increase. In February the Valetta, with a 50% increase in payload over the Dakota, was used for the first time on supply drops.

The construction of hill forts from 1953 placed an extra burden on the transport units, since all equipment, including tractors for clearing airstrips, was dropped by air. Moreover, from July 1953 to March 1954, two battalions of infantry operated continuously in southern Kedah in Operation *Sword*, while from October to December 1953, in Operation *Valiant*, a further four battalions were deployed in north-west Pahang. Both operations were completely supplied by air. To the end of 1954 the annual air supply activity is set out below.

Year	Sorties	Weight dropped (lb x 1,000)	Amount per sortie (lb)
1948	46	c.62	1,348
1949	875	2,045	2,337
1950	1,421	3,724	2,637
1951	1,289	3,465	2,688
1952	988	3,013	3,050
1953	1,346	4,462	3,315
1954	2,080	6,793	3,266

The medium-range transport units were also employed on communications work, especially in moving troops and police around the country, but also in evacuating wounded personnel and providing a courier service. They also played an important part in several operations where paratroops were deployed. Members of 22 Regt Special Air Service (SAS) were dropped on several occasions, the first being during Operation *Helsby* in February 1952, when fifty-four men of B Squadron were dropped near the Thai border. Because of local conditions, the four Dakotas employed dropped forty-four paratroopers beyond the drop zone into 150 ft trees, but all recovered.

Thought was now given to the provision of improved equipment for paratroops dropping into and recovering from trees. Eventually several forms of abseiling gear were developed and used with success, although there were several fatalities during Operation *Sword*. Operations were halted for a time while improvements were made, and then, in the largest operation of the campaign, *Termite*, 180 men of 22 SAS Regt were dropped into the Kinta and Raia valleys east of Ipoh. The paratroops took in equipment for cutting trees to make clearings for helicopter landings, by which means many additional troops were brought in.

THE HELICOPTER COMES INTO ITS OWN

After *Termite* there were relatively few paradrops as the helicopter became available in greater numbers, although there were occasions when they were made from helicopters hovering at 750 ft over particularly small and difficult drop zones. The first helicopters in the theatre were three S-51 Dragonflies of the newly formed Far East Casualty Air Evacuation Flight (FECAEF). They became operational on 1 April 1950 at Seletar, soon moving to Changi, and the first casualty to be evacuated by helicopter was a policeman flown to Johore hospital on 6 June.

By the end of 1950, twenty-six casualties had been evacuated; although the initial numbers were small, the improvement in morale resulting from the knowledge that medical treatment was never far away was important. Fifty-five evacuations were made in 1951, but with more helicopters available from 1952 the number increased to 144, although one Dragonfly was lost in a crash. Late in 1952 it was decided to disband the Evacuation Flight and replace it with 194 Sqn, which, equipped with twelve aircraft, was to operate in a range of roles, including troop movement. The unit shared this task with 848 NAS, which brought its S-55 helicopters to Sembawang from the UK aboard HMS *Perseus* in January 1953. Both units operated within 303 (Helicopter) Wing, with detachments at Kuala Lumpur but with helicopters positioned at other bases as necessary.

Serviceability problems with the S-51 resulted in the type being progressively replaced by the Sycamore with 194 Sqn. Gradually the restrictions on the use of helicopters for work other than casevac were relaxed, and the units available undertook an increasing share of troop movements. The Fleet Air Arm's 848 NAS carried out its first troop lift on 16 February 1953 when three machines transferred twelve men of the Worcestershire Regiment to a hideout near Port Swettenham in search of a local CT commander.

Nearly 12,000 troops were moved into operational areas by helicopter during 1953, but the small numbers of machines available placed heavy demands on aircraft and crews, and at one stage in August 1954 only one S-55 and one S-51 were serviceable. To some extent the position was rectified by the establishment of 155 Sqn with the Whirlwind, an inadequate licence-built version of the S-55 which was plagued with problems during its career in Malaya.

Although 848 NAS had been due to return to the UK in August 1954, it was retained in the theatre until the RAF was able to meet all the demands; the unit was disestablished on 10 December 1956. As the range of work

The RAF caught up with the Fleet Air Arm in September 1954 when 155 Sqn formed with the Whirlwind HAR.4 at Kuala Lumpur. XD163 sits on the apron waiting for another sortie. *(Author's collection)*

undertaken by the helicopters increased, the rules for their use were again tightened, and from 1953 the first Pioneer short take-off and landing (STOL) light transports appeared in the theatre. Able to carry four passengers and with a take-off run of only 75 yd, they were able to assume some of the roles hitherto reserved for the helicopters, especially in reinforcing and supplying the chain of hill forts. From 1955, as areas were declared clear, the helicopters were mainly confined to work in the north and south of Malaya. It was planned to replace the early Whirlwinds with Sycamores, but problems with the rotors of the latter led to both types remaining in service, 155 and 194 Sqns being merged into 110 Sqn in June 1959. The peak month for troop lifting was October 1958, when, in support of Operation *Tiger* in South Johore, 4,133 fully equipped troops were airlifted in and out of jungle clearings, 60% of them by Sycamore.

Another important role carried out by the helicopter was crop spraying. As the CT were denied access to the coastal towns and villages under the Briggs Plan, they lost much of the support from their Min Yuen (People's Movement) civilian branch and therefore of their supplies of food. As they took to the hills they were obliged to cultivate crops in jungle clearings only identifiable from the air, and it was these clearings that were the target of the crop-spraying effort. Development work was undertaken in the UK using Auster Autocar J/5G G-ANVN, registered with the Secretary of State for the Colonies.

The aircraft was subsequently brought into service with the RAF as XJ941 and sent to Malaya in 1956. Austers of 656 Sqn were also used to spray verges of roads to reduce cover to CT preparing to ambush vehicles. Initially sodium arsenite was used, but since this was poisonous and might affect the indigenous population, a change was made to a mixture of trioxene and diesolene, which killed all vegetation and was non-poisonous but effective over a long period. The first operation was *Cyclone 1*, mounted on 31 August 1953 in the Kluang and Labis areas.

Ten noted cultivation sites were sprayed after being marked by Austers of 656 Sqn, and over several days two S-55s and one S-51 had destroyed thirty cultivations. Operation *Cyclone II* followed shortly after this, and by the end of 1953, eighty-eight cultivations had been sprayed. Work carried on into 1954, but the shortage of helicopters led to the work being taken over by aircraft of 267 Sqn. Helicopter operations through the period of the Emergency are summarized below.

Year	Casevacs	Troops	Passengers	Freight (lb x 1,000)
1950	26			
1951	55			
1952	144			
1953	518	10,098		164
1954	743	8,829	3,033	238
1955	793	27,887	4,387	593
1956	701	25,890	3,769	439
1957	632	19,752	2,875	415
1958	752	26,767	2,709	629
1959	136	2,397	324	76
1960	173	4,033	369	92

LIAISON, AUSTERS AND THE PSYWAR

In the early years of the campaign the brunt of liaison work was borne by the Austers of 656 Sqn. Originally based at Sembawang, the squadron comprised four Flights, 1902 at Taiping, 1903 at Seramban, 1914 at Kluang and the RAF Communications Flight at Kuala Lumpur. The last was disbanded in July 1948 and replaced by 1907 Flt at the end of August. Then, in July 1949, 1903 Flt was sent to Hong Kong, to be replaced in July 1950 by 1911 Flt at Changi. The squadron now comprised about thirty Austers, mostly in the observation role, but in May 1952 1902 and 1914 Flts remained designated AOP while 1907 and 1911 became Light Liaison Flights to reflect the balance of work undertaken.

Supply drop by Dakota KN310 of 52 Sqn alongside a main road. The Dakotas were replaced by the Valetta from 1951 which were more powerful and carried a greater payload. *(Crown copyright)*

The Austers were used extensively for a range of work, often in direct support of Army units, and their value was limited only by their payload. No. 656 Sqn was one of the few flying units to be continuously employed throughout the Emergency, being equipped for most of the time with the Auster AOP.5 and 6. Its roles included communications, reconnaissance, target-marking, supply dropping, leaflet dropping, AOP and liaison, and at the peak of the campaign it was flying nearly 23,000 sorties a year.

The first Pioneers reached Malaya in early 1953, and by October they formed 1311 Transport Flight of 303 (Helicopter) Wing; they then formed part of the original equipment of 267 Sqn. As already mentioned, the Pioneers fulfilled some of the tasks previously undertaken by helicopters, especially in resupplying the forts. In 1954 the costs of flying the S-55 and S-51 were £73 and £53 per hour respectively, whereas the cost of operating the Pioneer and Auster were £35 and £15 per hour. As the short-range transport unit in Malaya and because it was based at Kuala Lumpur, 267 Sqn was required to handle as wide a range of tasks as 656 Sqn. One of the new roles it assumed was leaflet dropping and broadcasting.

Throughout the conflict an extensive campaign of psychological warfare was mounted. The objective was to encourage the surrender of CT through disaffection, especially in junior ranks, and to win the hearts and minds of the uncommitted population. In the first instance the leaflet-drops were of a strategic nature, advising the population of the emergency, but the emphasis quickly turned to tactical drops, often in association with operations, and the majority called for the surrender of CT, often naming individuals. Surrendered CT were used to draft the leaflets. As an indication of the effort involved, during the peak month for leaflet dropping, October 1953, 19,536,000 leaflets were dispersed in fifty-one sorties, many in association with Operation *Bison I*. Loud-hailer aircraft were also used in this operation.

The use of broadcasts from aircraft was first tested in October 1952 using a borrowed US Army C-47. From these trials and similar experiments with two 100-watt speakers tested on Auster J/1 Autocrat G-AJIZ, the RAF fitted equipment in two Valettas, which were used from early 1953. The Valetta suffered from excessive engine

The Dakota remained in service beyond 1951 with 267 then 209 Sqns which used the aircraft for specialised purposes. KP277 is fitted with eight loudspeakers in the psychological warfare role. *(Crown copyright)*

noise, however, limiting the range of broadcasts, so the RAF turned to the Dakota, three of which were fitted with a battery of speakers.

Whereas the Valetta had to fly at 1,500 ft to be heard over a 1,500 yd range, the Dakota could fly at 2,500 ft and be heard over 2,500 yd. Flying on a creeping, left-handed, square circuit at little over stalling speed, the Dakota could remain within earshot for the thirty seconds necessary to get its message across. The Austers, with their shorter broadcast range, were used for known pinpoint targets. Initially they covered nearly half of the all sorties flown, but gradually, as the war drew to a close, they were used less and less and in 1958 were removed from the role.

The psychological warfare tasks were shared between the theatre transport units and first the FECS and then 267 Sqn until, in 1958, it was renumbered 209 Sqn. The Voice Flight of 267 Sqn only comprised at its peak three Dakotas and two Austers, which were normally based at Kuala Lumpur, but when 267 Sqn was renumbered the Dakotas operated from Bayan Lepas, Penang, to be within reach of the remaining CT enclaves. A summary of psychological warfare sorties throughout the campaign to 1958 is set out below, bearing in mind that only dedicated leaflet-dropping sorties are listed; many leaflet drops were made in conjunction with other tasks.

Year	Leaflet sorties	Broadcast sorties
1948	10	
1949	69	
1950	168	
1951	261	
1952	53	
1953	184	327
1954	240	666
1955	365	922
1956	331	777
1957	348	821
1958	314	686

The psychological warfare campaign was most successful in complementing the war on the ground. Intensive leaflet operations offering rewards for information resulted in significant increases in valuable intelligence, and there is no doubt that the effort played a major part in isolating and demoralizing the CT.

RECONNAISSANCE

Another important contribution to the intelligence war was the work of 81 Sqn in its reconnaissance task. Initially the unit comprised two Spitfire PR.19s and nine Mosquitoes. One Spitfire was detached to Taiping in support of police operations in northern Perak in May 1948, but the Mosquitoes remained in Singapore throughout the campaign until their replacement in 1955. For a time, from March 1950, the Spitfires were transferred to 60 Sqn at Tengah, but they returned to 81 Sqn in November.

The role of the PR squadron was both strategic and tactical. In the former role, maps had to be produced and revised, while, tactically, photographs were required for intelligence and briefing purposes. 81 Sqn worked in close concert with the Army, both in the production of maps and in briefing; detailed photographs could highlight paths otherwise unseen, and save ground forces much time in reaching targets. Regular PR flights were flown from July 1948 by the Spitfires, while the Mosquitoes maintained the task of completing the survey of Malaya. In the target and briefing work the aircraft took obliques at low level, while the mapping was carried out at around 16,000 ft. Both aircraft types suffered from maintenance problems, but by the end of December 1950 the monthly output of photographs was 83,000.

The Spitfires flew on until 1954, the last sortie being flown in PS888 on 1 April of that year. The type was

As in Kenya and Aden Lincolns were detached from the UK for bombing dissident camps. From the cheerful looks on the faces of these air and ground crew of 57 Sqn aircraft DX-L their long detachment through 1950 and 1951 may be coming to an end. Behind is RF301/DX-J. *(Crown copyright)*

replaced by the Meteor PR.10 from late 1953, and when the Mosquitoes retired in 1955 they were replaced by four Pembroke C(PR).1s. Because of the limited availability of aircraft and the conflicting demands of the survey and tactical reconnaissance, from 1955 PR Canberras from 3 Group Bomber Command were detached from the UK in Operation *Planter's Punch*. The detachments were maintained to October 1956; from then, two UK-based Canberras were detached for two-month periods twice a year. The total of PR sorties flown by 81 Sqn to 1958 is set out below.

Year	Sorties	Year	Sorties
1948	271	1954	945
1949	612	1955	833
1950	642	1956	974
1951	1,135	1957	709
1952	1,172	1958	725
1953	1,335		

As important as photo-reconnaissance in Malaya was visual reconnaissance, normally conducted by the Austers of 656 Sqn. The work was demanding and expert, for the pilots had to identify and interpret while trying not to arouse suspicion by circling. The squadron also provided contact reconnaissance support for the ground forces by confirming locations and bearings accurately in the featureless jungle. There were occasions when the Austers acted in their primary role of artillery spotting, both for field artillery and naval guns.

As an indication of the value of visual reconnaissance, between March and August 1955 the Austers of 656 Sqn located 155 CT camps, seventy-seven possible camps, 313 cultivations, thirty-one recultivations, 194 man-made clearings and twenty-one aboriginal farms under CT control. At the other end of the scale, to about 1952 the

Early deliveries of the Lincoln were finished in the white upper surface scheme for Far East use, as illustrated by RF385/DX-G also of 57 Sqn. *(Author's collection)*

Sunderland squadrons, in conjunction with naval vessels, conducted maritime reconnaissance patrols along the eastern coast of Malaya to prevent illegal immigration or arms-smuggling.

THE OFFENSIVE PERIOD

The defensive period for the security services ended in July 1951, which year saw a peak of violence. The next three years were the offensive period. By July 1954 the crisis was over and the CT confined to jungle along the central spine of Malaya, but the Emergency was far from finished, and for the next six years the security services methodically eliminated the threat during the consolidation period. A table showing the CT strength, incidents and casualties is set out below.

Year	MRLA Strength	Incidents	Losses MRLA	SF	Civilian
1948	2,300	1,274	693	360	554
1949	2,550	1,442	1,207	476	694
1950	3,923	4,739	942	889	1,161
1951	7,292	6,082	1,399	1,195	1,024
1952	5,765	3,727	1,527	664	632
1953	4,373	1,170	1,392	209	143
1954	3,402	1,077	971	241	185
1955	2,798	781	709	182	143
1956	2,566	435	473	126	92
1957	2,066				
1958	1,681				
1959	868				
1960	623				

NOTE
Figures for losses from 1957 to 1960 are not available

During the offensive period there was some reduction in the number of air strikes but an increase in their effectiveness. The period also saw further re-equipping and changes in units committed to the Emergency. 84 Sqn disbanded on 20 February 1953, having completed 2,038 sorties and dropped 1,883 tons of bombs. The RAF said goodbye to the Brigand with few regrets, and the unit was not replaced.

On 31 March 1955, 33 and 45 Sqns amalgamated, losing their Hornets at the same time to the Venom FB.l; when the dual-numbered squadron was again operational by October, it was renumbered 45 Sqn. To make good the loss of 33 Sqn, the Venoms of 14 Sqn RNZAF entered the campaign, flying from Tengah. Finally 60 Sqn, having progressed to the Vampire FB.9, also changed to the Venom in May 1955, and with the exception of the Lincoln, the air strike capability was now all-jet.

There were also changes with the Sunderland squadrons: 88 Sqn disbanded in October 1954, and in December 205 and 209 were merged, the unit remaining dual-numbered until 1958. Although the Lincolns of 1 Sqn RAAF remained in the theatre until 1958, the RAF began to deploy Canberras from 1955 in Operation *Mileage*. The first unit detached was 101 Sqn, which arrived at Butterworth in March.

The Canberras were never as successful as the Lincolns in Malaya. Their range at operating height was limited, navigation was more difficult and the weapons load was less. In addition, they were unable to operate at night. During 1955, because of the introduction of new equipment, training demands and the need for economy, the number of strike sorties dropped significantly. Intelligence remained a problem on occasions; in Operation *Beehive* for example, against an alleged concentration of 200 CT in the Bukit-Resam Ambat area on 4 April, eleven Lincolns, four Canberras and twelve Hornets bombed and strafed the target, but the follow-up paratroopers found no evidence of the enemy.

From 1956 81 Sqn employed the Pembroke C(PR).1 for photo reconnaissance tasks in addition to the Meteor PR.10.
The Pembroke, typified by XF796, was a stable platform when there was minimal threat from the ground.
(Author's collection)

From 1956 the air offensive was confined to promising targets where hard-core CT were likely to be located. On 21 February Operation *Kingly Pile* was mounted by 1 Sqn RAAF and 12 Sqn Canberras. The target was a camp near Kluang, Johore, which was known to be occupied. In the attack twenty CT were killed by accurate bombing, including a notorious local commander. For the remainder of the year sorties were flown in support of ground operations, and the pattern continued through 1957. 1 Sqn achieved another success on 15 May when four CT, again including an important local leader, were killed in the Jelebu district. During the year 45 Sqn re-equipped with the Canberra. As the CT units were gradually eliminated and those remaining became more elusive, the number of pinpoint targets became fewer.

1 Sqn RAAF finally left Malaya on 30 June 1958 after eight years of continuous flying, having made a superb contribution to the war. In that time the unit had flown over 3,000 strikes, dropping 33,000,000 lb of bombs. 1 Sqn RAAF was replaced by 2 Sqn, flying the Canberra B.20 from Butterworth, and the strike force became all-Canberra when 75 Sqn RNZAF replaced 14 Sqn in July. Later in 1958, 3 Sqn RAAF deployed to Butterworth with its Sabres; it was joined early in 1959 by the similarly equipped 77 Sqn. Only forty-seven strikes were ordered in 1958, by the end of which it was clear that mopping-up operations could be achieved without air support. The only two strikes of 1959 were on 13 and 17 August, when camps at Bentong (Pahang) and Bukit Tapah (Perak) respectively were attacked, giving the Sabres their only taste of action.

Throughout the campaign 23,004 sorties were flown in 4,063 strikes, during which 34,500 tons of bombs were dropped and 74,000 rockets and 9.8 million rounds of ammunition fired.

The transport units maintained a high rate of activity throughout the Emergency. From 1955 there was an increasing amount of work associated with the dropping of SAS units and their resupply, and each year the number of hill forts increased.

The transport squadrons remained based at Changi, and through 1956 and 1957 only three Valettas and one or two Bristol Freighters of 41 Sqn RNZAF were available for supply dropping at Kuala Lumpur. In 1958 the transport force was stretched when the Pioneers had to be withdrawn from their resupply work through serviceability problems, but from 1959 there was relief as the fledgling Royal Malayan Air Force (RMAF) took over this work.

The reliability of the Valetta was never as good as that of the Dakota, although its climb rate was better, allowing its use in valleys where the American aircraft would have been in difficulty. After 110 Sqn disbanded in December 1957, although its aircraft went to 52 Sqn, the latter unit took two Dakotas on strength in 1960. Other changes in equipment towards the end of the campaign were the introduction of the Hastings by 48 Sqn from May 1957 and the Beverley by the same unit from June 1959. Both types offered considerable increases in payload and were used in support of operations in the north after the Emergency had ended.

The transport units made perhaps the most significant contribution to the prosecution of the anti-terrorist campaign, enabling ground forces to operate in inhospitable regions independent of normal supply lines. When the need for air support diminished the demand for air supply did not.

No account of Operation *Firedog* would be complete without reference to the locally raised air forces. The Malayan Auxiliary Air Force (MAAF) was formed in 1950 with a view to augmenting the RAF air defence units. Four squadrons were formed, but they were unable to progress to fighters in a reasonable time. Using Tiger Moths and Harvards, the squadrons did, however, participate in a limited amount of leaflet dropping and visual reconnaissance. Malaya achieved independence on 31 August 1957, and the MAAF paved the way for the establishment of the Royal Malayan Air Force (RMAF) from 1958. Initially equipped with four Twin Pioneers, four Pioneers and four Chipmunks, the RMAF assumed the responsibility for resupplying the hill forts from March 1959, relieving the RAF short-range transport force. Although it made a valuable contribution to the war effort, the RMAF found difficulty in meeting all the demands placed upon it.

SEQUEL

The end of the Emergency was declared from 31 July 1960, by which time about 500 CT were still operating from a salient within Thailand. Policing continued, as did mopping-up operations, but the armed services were gradu-

With a take-off run of just 75 yds the five-seat Pioneer was ideal for flying patrols and supplies into extreme jungle strips. XE512 operated with 267 Sqn and the successor 209 Sqn from 1953. *(Author's collection)*

The Navy also contributed to the occasional attack mission when aircraft were disembarked from their carriers. 811 NAS Sea Furies from HMS *Warrior* lined up at Tengah in the summer of 1954. *(Crown copyright)*

Each winter B-29 units were detached to Malaya from the Philippines. Even if they did not actively participate in offensive operations their presence would have been intimidating to terrorists. *(Author's collection)*

ally withdrawn. Throughout the twelve-year war, the security forces lost 1,865 killed and 2,560 wounded, while 2,473 civilians were killed, 1,385 wounded and 810 missing. Of the estimated 12,000 members of the MRLA, 6,698 were killed, 2,819 wounded, 1,286 captured and 2,696 surrendered.

From a British point of view, the campaign was a total success, but many hard lessons were learnt. The war was, probably, unnecessarily extended because of the slow initial response and the lack of sound intelligence. Many comparisons have been made with Vietnam, but although in the early stages of the latter war British advisers were employed, the situation was fundamentally different.

The region had gone through a succession of constitutional changes from 1946 when the Malayan Union was formed. This was opposed by Nationalists, so a Federation was declared on 31 January 1948. The Federation of Malaya secured independence on 31 August 1957, expanding as a fourteen-state Federation of Malaysia, now including Borneo and Sarawak, on 11 August 1963. In the run-up to this wider state, Indonesia began military confrontation (Chapter 7, Section 2). In 1964 there were race riots in Singapore, which had left the Federation on 9 August 1965. On 13 May 1969 there were serious race riots in Kuala Lumpur and a state of emergency declared to 1971. It can justifiably be said that the British legacy enabled continued stability in the region.

DE HAVILLAND HORNET

The DH.103 Hornet was designed as a private-venture, lightweight, twin-engined fighter, optimized for use in the war against Japan. Specification F.12/43 was written around the type, which first flew on 28 July 1944. In design it resembled a scaled-down Mosquito, and like its forebear it was remarkably fast, the prototype exceeding 485 mph. The Hornet equipped Fighter Command day-fighter units in the UK and later was used with success as a strike fighter in Malaya. It was the fastest piston-engined fighter in Royal Air Force service.

The F Mark 1 was armed with four 20 mm cannon, and it entered service with 64 Sqn in May 1946. Like all variants it was powered by the Merlin 130/131 driving handed propeller units. The first production machine flew on 1 March 1945, and the Mark 1 served only in the UK, lacking the range of later variants.

Fighter units equipped – 19, 41, 64, 65

The F Mark 3 variant was provided with increased internal tankage (from 360 to 540 gal) plus a further 400 gal in underwing tanks. To improve lateral stability a dorsal fillet was introduced, and provision was made for two 1,000 lb bombs or eight 60 lb RPs under the wings. It entered service with 19 Sqn in March 1948, and when replaced by jet types in the UK this variant, together with the FR.4, served in Malaya and Hong Kong.

The FR Mark 4 was the last of the Hornets, and it was used exclusively in the Far East. It was basically an F Mk 3 equipped for photo-reconnaissance with an F.52 camera displacing 21 gal of fuel. Some were built on the production line, while others were F Mk 3 conversions. It served with 33, 45 and 80 Sqns.

Fighter units equipped – 19, 33, 41, 45, 64, 65, 80

SCOTTISH AVIATION PIONEER

The Pioneer short take-off and landing utility first flew in May 1950, initially powered by a single 240 hp Gipsy Queen. Built to Specification A.4/45, the influence of the Fieseler Storch was evident, but the newer type was underpowered. A civil version followed, and when its potential was appreciated the type was ordered for RAF duties.

The Pioneer CC.1 was a five-seat utility aircraft powered by the Alvis Leonides 502 of 520 hp. It had quite remarkable short-field performance; take-off was in seventy-five yards and landing in only sixty-five. Stalling speed was just 43 mph. The Pioneer joined 1311 Flt in Malaya in September 1953, and it remained in service until 1969, serving latterly in Borneo in the Forward Air Control (FAC) role with 20 Sqn, supporting its Hunters.

Units equipped – 20, 78, 209, 215, 230, 267; 1311 Flt

MALAYA TABLE OF UNITS, 1948–60

Unit	Aircraft (code)	Base	From	To
Royal Air Force				
28 Sqn	Spitfire F.14, FR.18	Tengah	26.1.48	
		Sembawang	26.1.48	11.5.49
60 Sqn	Spitfire FR.18	Tengah	24.1.48	
		Sembawang	24.1.48	31.8.49
		Tengah	31.8.48	15.10.49
		Butterworth, Kuala Lumpur	15.10.49	31.5.50
		Tengah	31.5.50	12.50
	Vampire FB.5		12.50	3.52
	Vampire FB.9		3.52	8.55
	Venom FB.1		4.55	4.57
	Venom FB.4		4.57	12.59
	Meteor NF.14		1.10.59	
45 Sqn	Beaufighter X (OB)	Kuala Lumpur	28.5.49	5.12.49
	Brigand B.1 (OB)	Tengah	5.12.49	2.52
	Hornet F.3 (OB)		1.52	5.55
	Vampire FB.9			
	Meteor F.8	Butterworth	21.3.55	1.56
	Venom FB.1		9.55	11.57
	Canberra B.2	Tengah	11.57	
33 Sqn	Tempest F.2 (5R)	Butterworth	10.9.49	13.10.49
		Changi	13.10.49	18.3.50
	Hornet F.3 (5R)	Tengah	18.3.50	31.3.55
		Butterworth		
84 Sqn	Beaufighter X	Changi	1.2.48	
		Tengah	1.2.48	11.10.48
	Brigand B.1	Tengah	8.4.50	20.2.53
81 Sqn	Spitfire PR.19	Changi		1.2.48
	Mosquito PR.34			
	+ Spitfire FR.18	Tengah	1.2.48	16.3.50
	As above	Seletar	16.3.50	1.54
	Meteor PR.10		1.54	
	Pembroke C(PR).1		1.56	7.60
	As above	Tengah	1.4.58	
	Canberra PR.7		2.60	
209 Sqn	Sunderland GR.5 (WQ)	Seletar	1.1.55[1]	
205 Sqn	Sunderland GR.5	Seletar	15.9.49	1.5.58
	Shackleton MR.1	Changi	1.5.58	
88 Sqn	Sunderland GR.5	Seletar	24.6.51	1.10.54
48 Sqn	Dakota	Changi, Kuala Lumpur	9.50	
	Valetta C.1		9.50	12.57
	Hastings C.1, C.2		5.57	
	Beverley C.1		6.59	

Unit	Aircraft (code)	Base	From	To
52 Sqn	Dakota	Changi,		
		Kuala Lumpur	21.11.48	31.5.49
		Seletar	31.5.49	27.8.49
		Changi, Kuala Lumpur	27.8.49	9.51
	Valetta C.1		6.51	
	Dakota mod	Kuala Lumpur	11.59	
110 Sqn	Dakota	Changi, Kuala Lumpur		27.5.49
		Seletar	27.5.49	27.8.49
		Changi, Kuala Lumpur	27.8.49	5.52
	Valetta C.1	As above	10.51	31.12.57
HQFETW	Valetta C.1, C.2	Changi, Kuala Lumpur	1.7.53	15.2.56[2]
FECS, FETW	Anson C.19, Harvard, Dakota, York C.1, Valetta C.1, C.2, Spitfire FR.14, Auster AOP.5, AOP.6, Pembroke C.1, Hastings, C.1, Vampire FB.9, Meteor T.7, F.8, Devon C.1	Changi		
1311 Flt	Pioneer CC.1, Auster AOP.6	Kuala Lumpur	1.9.53	15.2.54[3]
267 Sqn	Dakota, Auster AOP.6, Pioneer CC.1, Pembroke C.1, Harvard T.2B	Kuala Lumpur	15.2.54	1.11.58[4]
209 Sqn	Auster AOP.6 Dakota, Pembroke C.1, Pioneer CC.1,	Kuala Lumpur	1.11.58	1.10.59
	+ Twin Pioneer CC.1		3.59	1.10.59
	As above	Seletar	1.10.59	
CAEF	Dragonfly HC.2, Tiger Moth T.2	Kuala Lumpur, Seletar	1.5.50	22.5.50
FECEF	Dragonfly HC.2, HR.4	Changi	22.5.50[5]	2.2.53[6]
194 Sqn	Dragonfly HC.2	Sembawang	2.2.53	1.5.53
		Kuala Lumpur	1.5.53	6.56
	Sycamore HR.14		4.54	3.6.59[7]
155 Sqn	Whirlwind HAR.4	Kuala Lumpur	1.9.54	3.6.59[7]
110 Sqn	Whirlwind HAR.4	Kuala Lumpur	3.6.59	1.9.59
		Butterworth	1.9.59	
	Sycamore HR.14		4.60	

RAF detachments ex-United Kingdom

Red Lion, Red Lion 2

7 Sqn	Lancaster B.1 (MG)	Changi (Upwood)	1.47	2.47
97 Sqn	Lincoln B.2 (OF)	Tengah (Hemswell)	30.4.48	15.6.48

Unit	Aircraft (code)	Base	From	To
Exercise *Centipede* (ex-St Eval)				
210 Sqn	Lancaster GR.3 (OZ)	Tengah	28.11.49	12.12.49
Musgrave (all ex-Waddington)				
57 Sqn	Lincoln B.2 (DX)	Tengah	20.3.50	7.51
100 Sqn	Lincoln B.2 (HW)	Tengah	30.6.50	12.50
61 Sqn	Lincoln B.2 (QR)	Tengah	12.50	29.3.51
Bold				
83 Sqn	Lincoln B.2	Tengah (Hemswell)	28.8.53	7.1.54
7 Sqn	Lincoln B.2	Tengah (Upwood)	1.54	4.54
148 Sqn	Lincoln B.2	Tengah (Upwood)	4.54	7.54
7 Sqn	Lincoln B.2	Tengah (Upwood)	15.7.54	10.54
148 Sqn	Lincoln B.2	Tengah (Upwood)	15.10.54	28.2.55
Mileage (all ex-Binbrook)				
101 Sqn	Canberra B.6	Butterworth	1.3.55	7.55
617 Sqn	Canberra B.6	Butterworth	7.55	11.55
12 Sqn	Canberra B.6	Butterworth	10.55	3.56
9 Sqn	Canberra B.6	Butterworth	3.56	7.56
101 Sqn	Canberra B.6	Butterworth	31.8	9.56

Profiteer detachments were primarily to give the crews overseas operating experience and the aircraft did not participate in the anti-terrorist campaign, although they did give a clear indication of the ability of the RAF to deploy widely and speedily

Unit	Aircraft (code)	Base	From	To
214 Sqn	Valiant B.1	Changi	29.10.57	14.11.57
90 Sqn	Valiant B.1	Changi	2.3.58	16.3.58
148 Sqn	Valiant B.1	Butterworth	3.2.59	24.2.59
138 Sqn	Valiant B.1	Butterworth	1.7.59	14.7.59
617 Sqn	Vulcan B.1	Butterworth	14.10.59	4.11.59
101 Sqn	Vulcan B.1	Butterworth	15.1.60	7.2.60
83 Sqn	Valiant B.1	Butterworth	4.60	4.60
Planter's Punch (all ex-Wyton)				
542 Sqn	Canberra PR.7	Changi	13.5.55	10.55
540 Sqn	Canberra PR.7	Changi	11.55	3.56
82 Sqn	Canberra PR.7	Changi	3.56	7.56
58 Sqn	Canberra PR.7	Changi	8.56	10.56
Fleet Air Arm				
848 NAS	Whirlwind HAR.21	Sembawang	8.1.53	20.5.53
	+ Whirlwind HAR.1	Dets Kluang,	20.5.53	18.12.56
		Kuala Lumpur		

The following units were shore-based from their carriers and are believed to have participated in strikes on Malayan targets

Unit	Aircraft (code)	Base	From	To
800 NAS	Seafire FR.47	HMS *Triumph*		
827 NAS	Firefly FR.1	To Sembawang	3.10.49	1.11.49
807 NAS	Sea Fury FB.11	HMS *Theseus*		
810 NAS	Firefly FR.5	To Sembawang	12.9.50	20.9.50
804 NAS	Sea Fury FB.11	HMS *Glory*		
812 NAS	Firefly FR.5	To Sembawang	9.51	11.10.51

Unit	Aircraft (code)	Base	From	To
802 NAS	Sea Fury FB.11	HMS *Ocean*		
825 NAS	Firefly FR.5	To Sembawang	10.52	10.52
811 NAS	Sea Fury FB.11	HMS *Warrior*		
825 NAS	Firefly FR.5	To Tengah	16.8.54	23.9.54
801 NAS	Sea Hawk FGA.4	HMS *Centaur*		
811 NAS	Sea Hawk FB.3	To Tengah	4.4.56	19.4.56
804 NAS	Sea Hawk FGA.6	HMS *Albion*		
809 NAS	Sea Venom FAW.21	To Seletar	25.3.59	14.4.59
891 NAS	Sea Venom FAW.22	HMS *Centaur*		
810 NAS	Gannet AS.4	To Seletar	4.9.59	30.9.59

Army

At the beginning of the campaign 1914 Flt was extant at Changi. 656 Sqn was formed on 29 June 1948, with three further flights added the following month. Throughout the campaign there were usually four flights rotating between eight airfields or airstrips, but using many more in the course of their tasking. These main bases were Benta, Changi, Kluang, Kuala Lumpur, Sembawang, Seremban, Taiping and Temerloh, with occasional basing at Ipoh, Johore Baru and Port Dickson.

Unit	Aircraft (code)	Base	From	To
1914 Flt	Auster AOP.5, 6	Changi		1.2.48
		Sembawang	1.2.48	13.7.48

656 Sqn formed Changi 15.7.48 embracing 1902, 1903, 1907 and 1914 Flts

Unit	Aircraft (code)	Base	From	To
1902 Flt	Auster AOP 5, 6	Taiping etc	15.7.48	1.56
	Auster AOP.9	Ipoh	1.56	1.9.57
1903 Flt	Auster AOP.5	Seremban	15.7.48	11.4.49
1907 Flt	Auster AOP.5	Sembawang	15.7.48	56
	Auster AOP.9	Taiping	56	1.9.57
1914 Flt	Auster AOP.5, AOP.6	Kluang	13.7.48	1.9.57
1911 Flt	Auster AOP.5, AOP.6	Changi	6.50[8]	56
	Auster AOP.9	Sembawang	56	1.9.57

The Army Air Corps was formed on 1 September 1957, after which the flights were renumbered, still within 656 Sqn, now based at Noble Field, Kuala Lumpur.

Unit	Aircraft (code)	Base	From	To
2 Flt	Auster AOP.9	Ipoh	1.9.57	
7 Flt	Auster AOP.9	Taiping	1.9.57	
11 Flt	Auster AOP.9	Sembawang	1.9.57	
14 Flt	Auster AOP.9	Kuala Lumpur	1.9.57	

Royal Australian Air Force

Unit	Aircraft (code)	Base	From	To
1 Sqn	Lincoln Mk 30	Tengah	16.7.50	30.6.58
2 Sqn	Canberra Mk 20	Butterworth	1.7.58	
3 Sqn	Sabre Mk 32	Butterworth	11.11.58	
77 Sqn	Sabre Mk 32	Butterworth	11.2.59	
38 Sqn	Dakota	Changi, KL	1.6.50	30.11.52

Royal New Zealand Air Force

Unit	Aircraft (code)	Base	From	To
14 Sqn	Venom FB.1	Tengah	10.4.55	1.9.58
75 Sqn	Canberra B.2	Tengah	1.7.58	

Unit	Aircraft (code)	Base	From	To
41 Sqn	Dakota, Bristol Freighter	Changi, KL	1.9.49	

Malayan Auxiliary Air Force

The Singapore Auxiliary Fighter Squadron was formed on 1 March 1950, followed by the Penang Squadron in June and the Kuala Lumpur Squadron in December 1951. The Malayan Auxiliary Air Force was formed on 1 October 1951, absorbing the units plus two fighter control units. The MAAF was disbanded on 30 September 1960.

Unit	Aircraft (code)	Base	From	To
Sing Sqn	Tiger Moth	Tengah	1.3.50	5.57
	Harvard 2B		7.51	5.57
	Spitfire FR.18, F.24		10.5.51	7.52
	Chipmunk T.10	Seletar	1.4.58	
Pen Sqn	Tiger Moth	Butterworth	1.3.50	5.57
	Harvard 2B		7.51	5.57
	Spitfire FR.18		7.51	7.52
	Chipmunk T.10		3.57	
KL Sqn	Tiger Moth	Kuala Lumpur	1.12.51	5.57
	Harvard 2B		7.51	5.57
	Chipmunk T.10		3.57	

Royal Malayan Air Force

Unit	Aircraft (code)	Base	From	To
1 Sqn	Pioneer, Twin Pioneer, Chipmunk	Kuala Lumpur	1.6.58	

United States Air Force

Like the RAF *Profiteer* detachments, the USAF *Josstick* deployments were to give crews the opportunity of operating in a different environment in collaboration with unfamiliar operating procedures. The detachments terminated before B-57 involvement in Vietnam, and it is unlikely that the American bombers flew operational sorties in Malaya. All B-29 deployments were ex-Clark AB, Philippines.

Unit	Aircraft (code)	Base	From	To
	B-29	Changi	12.52	12.52
	B-29	Changi	10.53	10.53
	B-29	Tengah	1.54	1.54
	B-29	Tengah	12.54	12.54
	B-29	Tengah	1.56	1.56
	B-29	Tengah	3.56	3.56
13 BS	B-57	Tengah	7.59	7.59
13 BS	B-57	Tengah	60	60

NOTES
1 Merged with 205 Sqn and dual-numbered to October 1958
2 Psywar role assumed by 267 Sqn
3 To 267 Sqn
4 To 209 Sqn
5 Casualty Air Evacuation Flight to FECEF
6 Far East Casualty Evacuation Flight to 194 Sqn
7 Merged to form 110 Sqn
8 Replaced 1903 Flt

CHAPTER FOUR

The Airborne Nuclear Deterrent

At the outset it needs to be said that much of what is set out in this chapter was extremely sensitive at one time, and much remains classified. The author has tried to steer a fine course between describing as accurately as possible what was deployed, and why, on the one hand, and not disclosing any information which might be of value to any present or potential enemy on the other hand.

There is nothing in the chapter which is not already in the public domain somewhere, and every attempt has been made to verify facts. Some topics, like nuclear weapons, missile technology and signals intelligence, are the subjects of much speculation and disinformation. On matters of deep history where facts may still be inaccessible, it appears reasonable to speculate; however, it would seem unwise to speculate about capabilities where they have current application.

There are several important areas of military activity and competence, developed over the period covered by this book and still being refined, which quite properly should be shielded from public view, and these are not mentioned. The author will run the risk of appearing naïve through some, albeit few, deliberate omissions. The story is not complete, especially in respect of intelligence gathering, and it is better that it remains so.

RAF Bomber Command through the strategic bombing campaign had made a major contribution to bringing victory to the Allies in the Second World War. It was thus inevitable that the post-war Government would see the retention of a strategic bombing capability as being an essential counter to Soviet ambition. Over time there were five inter-related dimensions to ensuring that the United Kingdom retained a credible strategic force. These dimensions were the bomber force, guided missiles, the weapons they would carry, their defence, and finally in--telligence to maintain the first four at the right level and at the right capability.

The deterrent against Soviet expansion in the West was based until 1969 upon airborne weapons of incredible power. The RAF brought the first nuclear bombs into service in November 1953, but nuclear weapons had been maintained at British bases since 1950. The USAF stored eighty-nine sets of casings in the UK from July 1950, with the warheads in the USA for speedy dispatch and mating should the need arise. From December 1954, with no formal authority, the USAF stored complete weapons at British bases, in greater numbers than the host nation could deploy. B61 bombs were still in the UK in 1995, by which time the RAF was planning to phase out its own bombs.

In the sections which follow, reference is made to tactical aircraft and weapons in a strategic context. Broadly, strategy is the approach, or approaches, to winning war or converting policy into action at the highest level. Tactics are the mechanisms for securing short-term advantage or winning battles. In reality there is no such thing as a tactical nuclear weapon, at least in respect of a conflict involving nuclear powers. Subject to the proximity to target, relatively short-range aircraft with low-yield weapons can make strategic impact with the likelihood of immediate escalation.

Academics will argue for ever about the effectiveness of the British independent nuclear deterrent. It is a fact that through nearly forty years of Cold War, although there were provocations and confrontation, the major Powers did not use weapons of mass destruction nor engage in head-on conflict. The records can never show what might have been, only what was, and then sometimes in a sanitized version. That Britain developed her own weapons was critical in maintaining a balance between the Superpowers and retaining some influence – quite probably a constraining one – on the world stage.

4.1   THE BRITISH STRATEGIC NUCLEAR BOMBER FORCE

INTRODUCTION

At the end of the Second World War the RAF possessed a large strategic bomber fleet, but one which was increasingly vulnerable to modern fighters. As the Lancaster/Halifax fleet was disbanded it was replaced by a smaller number of Lincoln squadrons. At the same time the unit establishment of aircraft was reduced considerably, from typically twenty to eight or fewer. Now with the British decision to proceed alone with nuclear bomb construction, there was a need for indigenous vehicles capable of delivery. Two parallel options were pursued – guided missile and strategic bomber.

The former option resulted in the Blue Streak and Blue Steel (described in Chapter 4, Section 2), while the latter produced the Valiant, Vulcan and Victor – the V-bombers. While the RAF was waiting for the first of these the Lincoln was complemented by the Washington (B-29) loaned by the USAF, while simultaneously the Canberra light bomber was coming on stream. Another US acquisition was the Thor intermediate-range ballistic missile (IRBM) which was in service between 1959 and 1963.

The Valiant entered service in 1955, the Vulcan in 1957 and the Victor in 1958. The V-bomber force was at its numerical peak in spring 1963, just as the Thor units were being dismantled, having served their purpose. The order of battle at the end of March 1963 was thus:

Sqns	Type	Base
1	Valiant B.1	Honington
1	Valiant B.1	Finningley
4	Valiant B.1	Marham
3	Vulcan B.1	Waddington
3	Vulcan B.2	Coningsby
3	Vulcan B.2	Scampton
2	Victor B.1	Cottesmore
2	Victor B.1	Honington
2	Victor B.2	Wittering
21	**Total**	

NOTES

Three of the Marham squadrons were assigned to Supreme Allied Commander Europe (SACEUR) and armed with US weapons

Of this total of twenty-one squadrons, two units operated in the tanker role, while one was a dedicated ECM squadron. This there was a nominal force of 144 aircraft, for which there were 158-megaton-range and 120-kiloton-range British bombs available. To these strategic bombers should be added the tactical aircraft, both RAF and FAA, which were equipped with nuclear weapons and which had potentially strategic reach.

Sqns	Type	Base
4[1]	Canberra B.6, B(I).8	German clutch airfields[2]
4	Canberra 15, B.16	Akrotiri
1	Canberra B.15	Tengah
1	Scimitar F.1	HMS *Ark Royal*, UK
1	Scimitar F.1	HMS *Hermes*, FE
2[3]	Buccaneer S.1	HMS *Ark Royal*, HMS *Victorious*, both UK
13	**Total**	

NOTES

1 Assigned to SACEUR   2 Brüggen, Geilenkirchen, Laarbruch, Wildenrath

3 Newly equipped and working up

AVRO LANCASTER

By January 1946, after the initial immediate post-war consolidation of the RAF, there were twenty-six Lancaster squadrons in Bomber Command, supported by three Mosquito pathfinder units. The Avro 683 Lancaster had a typical range of 1,750 miles and a bomb-load of 7,000 lb, but specials, with significantly reduced range and removed bomb-bay doors, could carry the vast 22,000 lb Grand Slam bomb. Although it equipped bomber squadrons after the war's end, the Lancaster only flew operationally post war in the maritime and photo-reconnaissance roles. In the bomber role it remained in front-line service until 1949.

Bomber units equipped – 7, 9, 12, 15, 35, 40, 49, 50, 61, 70, 83, 90, 97, 100, 101, 104, 106, 115, 138, 149, 207, 214, 300, 427, 429, 617

AVRO LINCOLN

The successor to the Lancaster, the Avro Type 694 Lincoln, started life as the Lancaster Mk IV built to Specification B.14/43 and designed to complement the USAAF heavy bombers in the Far East and to replace the Liberator in RAF service there. The Lincoln had high-aspect-ratio wings and much longer range than the Lancaster, but production versions flew too late for wartime service. It had been intended that the Lincoln would be faster, with either Griffon or Centaurus engines, but neither was available for bomber application. Pairs of .50-calibre guns were fitted in nose, dorsal and tail turrets, and with a full bomb-load of 14,000 lb the aircraft could fly 2,640 miles at 20,000 ft. The Lincoln entered service with 57 Sqn in August 1945.

The advance on the Lancaster, then, was in range and defensive armament, but it was soon realized that the Lincoln would be no match against new fighters being developed at home and abroad. It was therefore recognized that the Lincoln would not be used to carry the atomic bomb, being too vulnerable, and in any event the new jet bombers were expected to come on line at the same time as an operational bomb. Further, the Lincoln's range would only have permitted a one-way flight to the inner reaches of the Soviet Union.

In July 1948 there were still twenty-four heavy-bomber squadrons, but of these sixteen were equipped with the Lincoln, with the Lancaster units concentrated in 3 Group. By now, the squadrons were typically based three or four to an airfield to ease maintenance and reduce expenditure on infrastructure. The Lincoln remained in service with RAF bomber squadrons until 1955. It was not called upon to fly strategic bombing sorties, but did undertake tactical bombing in support of ground forces in Aden, Malaya and Kenya. The type also served with several electronic intelligence gathering (ELINT) units and the Radar Reconnaissance Flight. The last unit to fly the Lincoln was 151 Sqn on radar development work.

Bomber units equipped – 7, 9, 12, 15, 35, 44, 49, 50, 57, 61, 75, 83, 90, 97, 100, 101, 115, 138, 148, 149, 207, 214, 617 Sqns; 1426 Flt
Signals units equipped – 116, 192, 199, 527; 1321 Flt

BOEING WASHINGTON

The immediate post-war Government decided in 1947 to apply the 'ten-year rule' to the defence of the realm, while recognizing that the main threat to peace would be the Soviet Union. In essence, this crude approach, based on guesswork, dictated that the United Kingdom would not be subject to attack for at least ten years. That period then gave the armed forces the opportunity to re-equip while being hopelessly under-resourced in the event of a major conflict within that timescale.

Towards the end of the war the Soviets had reverse-engineered the B-29, several examples of which they had acquired intact through diversions, and which were built as the Tu-4. Further, in September 1949, Russia surprised the West by exploding a nuclear device well in advance of any date predicted by Western intelligence. This had prompted the urgent need for additional strategic bombers capable of striking at the heart of the Soviet Union, which as already explained the Lincoln could not. There was also concern to supplement the Lincolns pending the introduction of the Canberra light bomber into service in the early 1950s.

The Korean War, which started in 1950, was a real shock, both in timing and in the introduction of the MiG-15 fighter. (This latter used the VK-1 engine, which was an unlicensed copy of the Rolls-Royce Nene, twenty-five examples of which had been sold to the Soviet Union by the British Government. However, the Government was at least even-handed in that the Nenre and Goblin engines were developed under licence in the USA as the Pratt and Whitney J42 and Allison J33 respectively, powering the first-generation of US fighters. The war vindicated arrangements made earlier in 1950 for the loan of eighty-seven American B-29 Superfortress bombers. The aircraft, provided free of charge under the Mutual Defense Assistance Program, were ex-stock B–29As, and they were delivered by USAF crews from the 307th Bomb Wing, which also set up the initial training programme. The Washington entered service with 115 Sqn in May 1950, in which unit it replaced the Lincoln.

Although popular with crews in respect of comfort, the type suffered from low serviceability in RAF service, mainly through spares shortages, and it was very expensive to maintain and fly. While involved in exercises, it was not used operationally, and the last Washington in bomber service was retired in March 1954. Four aircraft were lost in service, nine were sent to Shoeburyness as targets on the trial gunnery ranges, and the remainder were returned to the USA.

Given their sourcing under the MDAP, it was confined to the strategic bombing role in line with US policy, which denied their use in support of colonial policing. It was rumoured that the Washington stations held nuclear bombs, and certainly the air planners had considered the possibility of securing some from the US. However, the United Kingdom had no nuclear weapons of her own, and the American McMahon Act of 1946 forbade the sharing of nuclear technology with any foreign power.

Bomber units equipped – 15, 35, 44, 57, 90, 115, 149, 207
Signals unit equipped – 192

The Vickers Valiant was the first of the V-bombers into service with 138 Sqn in February 1955. It was designed around the need to carry a 10,000 lb nuclear bomb. XD820 of 148 Sqn is caught in landing configuration in 1960 just before high level bombing was abandoned. The unusual tandem main landing gear and large flaps are noteworthy.
(Author's collection)

OPERATIONAL REQUIREMENTS, SPECIFICATIONS AND THE SPERRIN

Soon after the war, the decision was taken to pursue the development of an independent British nuclear bomb. It was quickly appreciated that missile delivery was beyond any prospect of early achievement, so that aircraft delivery was inevitable. It was anticipated that the nuclear device would measure 10 ft by 30 ft and weigh 10,000 lb, and accordingly Operational Requirement OR.229 was drafted for a four-jet aircraft which could carry such a weapon. OR.229 also specified a speed of 500 knots at 45,000 ft ceiling over a range of 3,500 miles, which in OR.230 for a long-range bomber was adjusted to 50,000 ft over 4,000 miles. H2S radar was specified and the aircraft would have a crew of five – two pilots, two navigator/bomb aimers and a radio operator.

The long-range OR.230 was dropped as being too ambitious in relation to the ability of industry to produce a response. However, OR.229 was retained and six companies were invited to submit tenders. Of these, four were further invited to submit detailed proposals against Specification B.35/46. The Shorts response, the SA.4, was seen as conventional and unlikely to meet the requirement, but it had the advantage of being easy to produce in a very short time. Thus Specification B.14/46 was produced based on a new OR.239 for the Shorts design as an 'insurance' bomber, in the event that the more advanced designs proved too problematical or were too far delayed into service: as has been said, the expectation was a nuclear attack by the Soviet Union in 1957. The S.A.4 would be required to cruise at 390 knots to 45,000 ft, and a contract was let for two prototypes.

The first Sperrin, as the SA.4 had been named, flew on 10 August 1951, but it had by then been cancelled since the more advanced Valiant had flown some three months earlier. The two prototypes produced were used for trials, including ballistic tests of dummy nuclear weapons, and both were scrapped by 1958.

VICKERS VALIANT

Although not originally invited to respond to OR.230, Vickers produced a proposal which attracted serious consideration. It was seen as being more advanced than the 'insurance' Sperrin but less risky than the Avro and Handley Page submissions. Accordingly a revised specification, B.9/48, was issued demanding a speed of 435 knots to 45,000 ft over a range of 3,350 nm, and the Vickers Type 660, later named Valiant, was ordered from the drawing-board as an interim design. It was a shoulder-wing design with compound wing sweepback averaging 20° and embedded engines. Originally intended to use the Sapphire engine, the first prototype, powered by four Avon R.A.3 engines of 6,500 lb thrust, flew on 18 May 1951, just over two years from the initial order being placed.

Development of the Valiant proved relatively trouble-free, and production aircraft (by now Type 706) joined 138 Sqn at RAF Gaydon in July 1955. The production aircraft were powered by the Avon R.A.7s offering 7,500 lb thrust. Initially 138 Sqn acted as the training unit, and squadrons formed at Gaydon prior to moving to their permanent bases. At the outset a dedicated PR variant, the B(PR) Mk 1 (Type 710), was produced with the R.A.14 engine of 9,500 lb thrust. Three of the initial production batch of twenty-five were delivered in this model to 543 Sqn. The Valiant had a service ceiling of 54,000 ft and a range, with underwing tanks, of 4,500 miles.

Eventually 104 Valiants equipped eight bomber squadrons in four variants, but unlike the later Vulcan and Victor, it was not developed to a more powerful Mark 2 version. Valiants of four squadrons based on Malta dropped conventional 1,000 lb bombs on Egyptian targets during the Suez campaign, while at the same time a fifth unit was engaged on atomic bomb tests in Australia and the Pacific. While the Suez campaign was a flawed operation, it did give RAF Bomber Command the opportunity to review its procedures in the light of experience. Especially important was the ability to deploy overseas effectively and to undertake conventional bombing by night and in all weather conditions.

In 1955 it was decided to confer in-flight refuelling capability on the V-bomber force and to create dual bomber/tanker role Valiants from the second production batch onwards. These aircraft had yet more powerful engines in the form of the R.A.28 at 10,500 lb, and they entered operational service with 214 Sqn in January 1959. Two tanker variants were produced – the Type 733 B.PR(K) Mk 1 and the Type 758 B(K) Mk 1.

The Valiant had been designed to carry one 10,000 lb nuclear bomb or twenty-one 1,000 lb conventional bombs. The first atom bombs were delivered to RAF Wittering as early as November 1953 for the Bomber Command Armament School, and Valiants of 1321 Flt undertook trials on weapon delivery from August 1954. The Valiant

XD823 of 49 Sqn RAF Wittering is seen in clean configuration. At its peak there were eight Valiant squadrons, mainly in 3 Group RAF Bomber Command and based in East Anglia; four of these deployed aircraft to Malta during the Suez campaign of 1956. By 1962 there remained four squadrons at RAF Marham in the air refuelling and tactical nuclear roles. *(Author's collection)*

18 Sqn was the sole 1 Group unit operating the Valiant at Finningley which it shared with several Vulcan units. Aircrew are hurrying to WZ365 ready for a speedy departure from what looks to be a deployment airfield. The Valiant was suddenly withdrawn from service in 1965 after the stresses of low-level flying resulted in fatigue cracks in the wing spars. *(Author's collection)*

would have carried the Blue Danube nuclear bomb of 40-kiloton yield, and in tests it dropped the Yellow Sun thermonuclear bomb to be carried by the Vulcan and Victor.

In its intended deterrent role the Valiant was withdrawn from use from April 1962, but the Marham Wing comprising 49, 148 and 207 Sqns was assigned to SACEUR in a tactical role, to carry, intially, the US, and later the Mks 28 and 43 tactical nuclear weapons. From 1960, when a high-flying American U-2 reconnaissance aircraft had been brought down by a surface-to-air missile over Russia, the decision had been taken to operate the V-force from low level. The Marham Valiants thus had their white anti-flash paintwork replaced by gloss grey/green camouflage, as did the two surviving tanker units, 90 and 214 Sqns.

Sustained low-level flying was to bring about the premature retirement of the Valiant fleet, when in the summer of 1964 serious fatigue cracks were identified in the wing spar. The type was withdrawn from service in February 1965. There is a fine irony to the situation, for Vickers had produced the Type 673 B Mk 2 version designed as a fast, low-level, pathfinder. The undercarriage was revised to fold backwards into a fairing behind the wing, enabling much stronger wing construction to cope with buffeting at low levels. The Air Ministry was not interested, and the sole prototype, WJ954, was scrapped in 1958.

The Valiant was a first-class aircraft with which the RAF embraced the nuclear deterrent role at a very low price, even by contemporary standards. It was delivered on time at a total cost including development of just £67 million, enjoyed high serviceability, saw action in the conventional bomber role and conducted the tests of British atom and hydrogen bombs. The type also pioneered operational in-flight refuelling between jet-powered aircraft and acted as a test-bed for the Pegasus engine and Blue Steel missile. Squadron aircraft ventured far and wide across the globe; indeed two aircraft of 543 Sqn were reported to have operated briefly in Laos in 1958 in the recce role. One Valiant, XD816, continued to fly from Wisley on tests until 1968.

Bomber units equipped – 7, 18, 49, 90, 138, 148, 207, 214
Signal units equipped – 18, 199

AVRO VULCAN

The Avro 698 Vulcan was the second of the new V-bombers built to the original Specification B.35/46 to fly. Because of the revolutionary design several scale 'models' were produced in the form of the Avro 707, a total of

Although devoid of unit markings – apart from a USAF SAC zap on the fin – Vulcan B.2 XH539 gives a very good impression of the toned down national markings on a white overall finish. This finish was reflective and designed to protect the aircraft against nuclear flash. *(Author's collection)*

The Vulcan was the second V-bomber to enter service, with 83 Sqn in 1957. In the more powerful B.2 form it was operational from 1960. The *Blue Steel* stand-off missile was operated by three squadrons including No 27 whose XL446 shows the clean fitting of the missile. *(Author's collection)*

four of which were eventually flown. The prototype Avro 698 flew on 30 August 1952 powered by four Avon RA.3 engines, each of 6,500 lb thrust. The wing was a simple delta of 99 ft span, changed early in production to a compound shape to overcome an aerodynamic problem causing buffet at high Mach numbers. The prototypes were later fitted with the Sapphire of 8,000 lb thrust.

The first production aircraft flew on 4 February 1955, and the type entered service with 230 OCU in May 1956. The first operational unit was 83 Sqn, formed on the Vulcan at Waddington in July 1957. The Vulcan had a crew of five, and was unarmed with an H2S Mk 9 radar and a weapons load of twenty-one 1,000 lb bombs carried internally. The definitive engine was the Olympus 102 of 12,000 lb thrust, which almost doubled the power of the aircraft from the original prototype. The Vulcan was equipped to carry the Yellow Sun, Blue Danube, Violet Club, Red Beard and the much smaller WE 177 nuclear weapons.

Thirty **B Mk 1** aircraft were rebuilt as the Mark 1A with ECM equipment in an extended tailcone and an aerial plate between the starboard jetpipes. Four of the five original B.1 units were equipped with the new variant, though it was soon superseded by the Mk 2.

The **B Mk 2** employed a significantly larger wing than the B Mk 1, together with the much more powerful Olympus 201 engine of 17,000 lb thrust. No. 230 OCU re-equipped in 1960, followed by 83 Sqn in October of that year. Nine were converted for maritime and strategic reconnaissance. In **B Mk 2A** form the Vulcan was adapted to carry a single Blue Steel stand-off missile semi-recessed into the bomb-bay. Some were fitted with the Olympus 301 of 20,000 lb thrust (Coningsby Wing (9, 12, 35 Sqns)), but only the Scampton Wing (27, 83, 617 Sqns) with the slightly lower rated engines was supplied with the weapon. Some Vulcans were wired for the AGM-87A Skybolt stand-off missile ordered from the United States but cancelled.

In bomber form the Vulcan finally left RAF service in December 1982 (44 Sqn). Six of these aircraft had been hastily adapted to carry up to four Shrike ARM missiles and the AN/ALQ-101 jamming pod under the wings for use in the Falklands campaign. They were involved in the *Black Buck* missions bombing Stanley airport from Ascension Island, the only time the Vulcan dropped bombs in action.

Following the campaign and as a temporary expedient to make good a shortage of tankers, six aircraft were converted from B Mk 2 with tankage in the bomb-bay, and a single Mk 17B HDU was carried in the redundant ECM tailcone. The first conversion flew on 18 June 1982 and the version was the last in RAF service, finally departing on 31 March 1984.

Bomber units equipped – 9, 12, 27, 35, 44, 50, 83, 101, 617

HANDLEY PAGE VICTOR

The Victor was Handley Page's response to Specification B.35/46, and with the Vulcan it maintained the Avro/Handley Page (Lancaster/Halifax) partnership. It incorporated a wing of unusual crescent compound sweep design. The wing was first tested in the wind tunnel from 1947 and then on a 40%-scale model, the HP.88, which was based on the Attacker fuselage and built by Blackburn to Specification E.6/48. This flew on 21 June 1951 and broke up shortly after, but the prototype Victor was almost complete, flying for the first time on Christmas Eve 1952.

The HP.80 Victor was the last of the V-bombers to enter service, and its operational life – albeit latterly in the tanking role – was longer than that of the Valiant and Vulcan. However, although the most potent, it did not drop bombs in anger, but served with distinction as a tanker in the Falklands and Second Gulf wars. The nearest the Victor got to action as a bomber was during the confrontation with Indonesia in the 1960s.

The first production Victor flew on 1 February 1956, and was 40 in. longer than the prototypes. It was powered by four Sapphire engines of 11,050 lb thrust, and compared to the Vulcan had much greater load-carrying capability, being able to carry thirty-five 1,000 lb bombs. In fact the bomb-bay was designed to accommodate four nuclear weapons, but the early Blue Danube bomb was so large that only one could be carried. The aircraft was unarmed and had H2S radar. It entered squadron service with 10 Sqn in April 1958, although the Radar Reconnaissance Flight was the first unit to receive Victors. Four aircraft were fitted at an early stage with H2S Mk 9 Yellow Aster radar to support reconnaissance tasks, details of which have not been released.

Twenty-four **B Mk 1** aircraft were fitted with a blunter tail cone incorporating ECM equipment as the Mark 1A. Some of these aircraft were converted to two-point tankers when the Valiant tankers were withdrawn from service at short notice in 1965, while yet others were converted to three-point tankers.

The **Mark 2** was a completely new model, employing the more powerful Conway engine and with increased

Victor B.1 XH648 of 15 Sqn apparently releases all 35 1,000 lb bombs simultaneously, but the photograph is probably retouched. The aircraft is in the original white anti-radiation colour scheme. In its later tanker form it is preserved at the Imperial War Museum, Duxford. *(Handley Page)*

The Victor was the third of the RAF's V-bombers and the second to be converted to accommodate the *Blue Steel* stand-off missile. B.2 XL190 of 139 Sqn – one of only two units which operated the missile – is seen making a slow fly-by.
(Author's collection)

wingspan. Further changes to the wing included revised intakes, Küchemann wing fairings and large, fixed, under-wing fuel tanks. This variant was adapted to carry the Blue Steel stand-off bomb, and entered service with 139 Sqn in February 1962, but production was limited, despite superior performance to the Vulcan.

The **B Mk 2R** was a retrofit of some twenty-one B.2 airframes with the Conway 201 of 20,600 lb thrust, with an increase in take-off weight to 223,000 lb. In addition, two Spectre rocket motors could be fitted and Red Steer ECM equipment installed. When high-flying bombers became vulnerable to SAM defences and the role shifted to low level, the Victor was soon retired in favour of the Vulcan, which had better fatigue resistance; the Victor remained in service only until 1968 as a bomber, but with its capacious fuselage it continued as a tanker for many years.

Bomber units equipped – 10, 15, 55, 57, 100, 139
Reconnaissance units equipped – 543; RRF

ENGLISH ELECTRIC CANBERRA

Specification B.3/45 was issued in the summer of 1945, calling for a light jet bomber capable of carrying a 4,000 lb bomb-load to at least 50,000 ft over a 1,400 nm range. The aircraft, which would be unarmed and equipped with a radar bombing system, was to be a Mosquito replacement. The English Electric design was accepted and an order placed for four prototypes in January 1946.

Originally designated E.A1, the designation was amended to E.A3 to meet Specification B.5/47 when delays in the bombing radar necessitated a glazed nose and a third crew member. The bomber was designed to carry six 1,000 lb conventional bombs, and the original specification did not require nuclear weapon capability. In due course further specifications were issued for a photo-reconnaissance variant (PR.31/46) and a trainer (T.2/49), which in the short term became the E.A2 and E.A4 respectively. It is of note that the PR variant was ordered before the production bomber type.

The prototype (VN799), later formally named Canberra B Mk 1, first flew on 13 May 1949, while VX181, the **PR.3** prototype, flew on 19 May 1951. Service entry of the B.2 was with 101 Sqn in January 1951, less than two years from the type's first flight. By the end of 1953 there were eighteen Canberra bomber squadrons based in the UK and Germany to complement the long-range but more vulnerable Lincolns and Washingtons, pending the introduction of the V-bombers.

The **B Mk 5** was designed to Specification B.22/48 for a target marker and a range increase to 2,500 miles. One prototype was built and flown in July 1951, but the type was cancelled. The **B Mk 6** had most of the features of the B.5 fitted with the RA.7 Avon of 7,500 lb thrust, and was the definitive Bomber Command version. Some twenty-five were fitted with Blue Shadow radar, and the light bombers remained in service until 1961, when they were supplanted by V-bombers. Throughout its life the Canberra was used as a trials aircraft, and from 1955 to 1963 there were various attempts to apply radar-absorbent materials to B.6 WK161, but these came to nothing.

There were several further bomber variants, including the interdictor **B(I).6** variant and the **B(I).8** with a fighter-type canopy, both used solely in RAF Germany between 1958 and 1972. These short-range types were initially equipped to carry the US Mk 7 tactical nuclear bomb, and were spread around the four 'clutch' airfields; in operation they would have used a low-altitude bombing system (LABS) or toss-bombing technique, pulling up from low level to release the weapon on the climb before turning rapidly for home. From 1966 the Mk 7s were supplanted by US Mk 43 'laydown' weapons. The **B Mk 15** and **Mk 16** were B.6 conversions fitted for the tactical nuclear role and equipping four squadrons in the Middle East and one in the Far East in the period 1961 to 1970. In this period these bombers were armed with the British Red Beard atomic bomb. Given their basing and range, the Canberras equipped with independent nuclear weapons could easily have operated in the strategic role.

Numerous other versions of the Canberra were produced, mainly for training, photo-recce or trials tasks, and the type was extensively used as a test-bed; the activities of the PR types are described elsewhere in this chapter. A total of 512 bomber Canberras was built for the RAF, and they played an active part in the Suez operation, in Malaya and the Borneo confrontation. The Canberra was also exported widely and used operationally by numerous air forces, including the USAF and RAAF in Vietnam. Perhaps the ultimate accolade is that the type remained in service with the RAF for fifty-five years in a variety of roles.

Bomber units equipped – 3, 6, 9, 10, 12, 14, 15, 16, 18, 21, 27, 32, 35, 40, 45, 50, 57, 59, 61, 73, 76, 88, 90, 100, 101, 102, 103, 104, 109, 139, 149, 199, 202, 207, 213, 249, 617

SUPERMARINE SCIMITAR

The Supermarine Scimitar was produced to Specification N.113D as a naval fighter. In the event the Sea Vixen was developed into a fleet fighter, primarily as an interceptor but fitted for a wide range of underwing stores. The Sea Vixen was in service, in two marks, from 1959 to 1971. Since it was equipped with a low-altitude bombing system (LABS), it would have been capable of carrying the Red Beard bomb, but training for, and carriage of, that weapon was confined to the Scimitar.

As the Sea Vixen was developed, so the Scimitar specification evolved to provide for a single-seat, fast, low-level strike fighter, powered by two Avon RA.24 engines of 11,250 lb thrust. Range was around 1,400 miles and the armament included four 30 mm Aden cannon, plus up to 4,000 lb of underwing stores, including the Red Beard nuclear weapon. The latter in its Mk I form had a 15 kt yield, and although a tactical weapon its destructive power was in the same range as the Hiroshima and Nagasaki bombs.

The Scimitar entered service in 1958 as an interim strike aircraft pending delivery of the Buccaneer, which had replaced it by 1966. In the event of global conflict, the Fleet Air Arm's Scimitars aboard HMS *Ark Royal* and HMS *Victorious* would have been capable of mounting sorties against targets within the Soviet Union or China. Scimitars were active during the blockade of Rhodesia in 1965–6.

Strike units equipped – 800, 803, 804, 807

The BAC TSR.2 was intended as a long-range tactical strike aircraft with a 10,000 lb munitions load. The prototype, XR219 seen here, first flew in September 1964, but the type was cancelled in 1965 in favour of the American F-111K, which was in turn cancelled. *(BAC)*

BAC TSR.2

The operational requirement for the Canberra replacement, OR.339, was issued in 1956, and resulted in the Tactical Strike and Reconnaissance (TSR).2. It called for an aircraft capable of operating from small airfields at supersonic speeds and at all levels, especially close down; already the threat to high-flying aircraft was appreciated. The complexity of the requirement was such that no single aerospace company, except possibly Hawker Siddeley, was capable of designing and producing a solution. Therefore Bristol, English Electric and Vickers merged to form the British Aircraft Corporation in 1960.

The accepted Vickers design, built to the revised GOR.343, was nearly 90 ft long, with a shoulder wing and two Olympus engines, each delivering 30,610 lb thrust. Intended performance was Mach 2.25 at above 36,000 ft and Mach 1.1 at sea level, with a tactical operating radius of around 800 miles. Maximum weapons load would have been 6,000 lb internally and 4,000 lb on underwing pylons; munitions would have included the Red Beard nuclear weapon.

The aircraft was constructed at Weybridge and transported to Boscombe Down for the first flight on 27 September 1964. For a variety of reasons, political and military, the TSR.2 was cancelled in April 1965, by which time over thirteen hours of flight had been achieved in twenty-four sorties. Five airframes were complete, four were nearly completed and eleven pre-production aircraft and thirty production aircraft were on the production line. Although essentially a relatively short-range tactical strike aircraft, the TSR.2 would have contributed to the United Kingdom's independent nuclear deterrent.

GENERAL DYNAMICS F-111

Replacement of the TSR.2 programme was determined in the form of the Anglo-French variable-geometry (AFVG) aircraft, which circuitously became the Tornado, and as an interim measure fifty F-111Ks were ordered from the United States. The intended British F-111 was based on the F-111A with a strengthened undercarriage, changed avionics, a high-level range of 3,800 miles and a theoretical 30,000 lb weapon load, nearly all of which would have been carried on wing pylons. It would have been based in Germany as a tactical aircraft, but probably only fitted to carry US nuclear weapons. The AFVG as such was abandoned in 1966, and the F-111 order was cancelled in 1968.

McDonnell Douglas Phantom

The next step in the tactical nuclear progression was the F-4 Phantom, ordered in 1965 to replace the cancelled Hawker P.1154 vertical take-off and landing (VTOL) fighter. This latter was intended to be a Hunter ground attack and Royal Navy Scimitar replacement, but the compromise specification resulted in uncertainty, with the inevitability of cancellation. The F-4K and M, originally for the Fleet Air Arm and RAF respectively as the **FG.1** and **FGR.2**, entered operational service, first with the FAA's 892 NAS in 1969 and then with 6 Sqn RAF, also in 1969.

While the Navy's priority was for a fleet defence fighter, the RAF needed a tactical attack aircraft to replace the Canberra. Three squadrons, 14, 17 and 31, were based in Germany at RAF Brüggen, and these were fitted to carry a single US B57 nuclear bomb on the centre-line; the bombs were held under dual-key arrangements. The Phantom was very much an interim aircraft in this role, pending the arrival of the Anglo-French Jaguar, which replaced it in Germany between 1975 and 1976. Although fast and with a maximum weapon load of around 11,000 lb, with a full load the radius of action was only 150 miles, but with a light Mk 57 bomb its range would have been rather greater. The FGR.2 began its operational RAF career in January 1969, and it was used primarily in the tactical role until replaced by Jaguars. The last tactical operator was 41 Sqn, which replaced its aircraft in September 1977. Two units, 2 and 41 Sqns, had a primary reconnaissance role. The Phantom did not see action in British service: it is described more fully in Chapter 4, Section 4.

Attack units equipped – 2, 6, 14, 17, 31, 41, 54

In the hiatus following the search for Hunter ground attack and Canberra light-bomber replacements, the RAF secured the interim Phantom as described, and then operated several types simultaneously that had a nuclear capability. These were the Jaguar, Buccaneer and Tornado. Although capable of carrying the WE 177 nuclear bomb, the Jaguar was only ever a tactical aircraft with a comparatively short range, but it did re-equip some of the Canberra/Phantom units in Germany pending the longer-range Tornado coming into service.

Hawker Siddeley Buccaneer

The Buccaneer was built to naval Specification NR/A.39 for a fast carrier-borne low-level strike aircraft. First flight was in April 1958, with service entry in July 1962 with 801 NAS. The **S Mk 1** was underpowered and was only capable of carrier launch at significantly less than the designed operational weight, which at least resulted in the 'buddy' refuelling system, whereby post launch the aircraft was refuelled by another Buccaneer. The long-term solution was the **S Mk 2**, wherein the original 7,500 lb thrust Gyron Junior engines were replaced by two Spey Mk 101s of 11,100 lb. The S.2 replaced the S.1 in FAA service from 1965 until retirement in 1978.

In naval service the Buccaneer could carry up to 16,000 lb of ordnance within its rotating bomb-bay and on wing pylons; weapons included the Red Beard tactical bomb. As with the Scimitar, which it succeeded, the aircraft could strike at many strategic targets from its mobile carrier base. With an unrefuelled range of 2,300 miles, it added to the United Kingdom's options and thus the strength of its nuclear deterrent. FAA Buccaneers were active in the blockade of Rhodesia in 1965–6.

Naval strike units equipped – 800, 801, 803, 809

After cancellation of the TSR.2 and then the F-111K, the RAF was lacking a medium-range strike aircraft, pending development and production of the multi-role combat aircraft (MRCA) – eventually the Tornado. As an interim measure forty-nine Buccaneer S.2 aircraft were ordered, in addition to which the RAF acquired many ex-FAA machines as the Navy lost its carriers. The type entered RAF service in 1969, and it equipped three UK-based squadrons in the maritime strike role, plus two in Germany in the tactical nuclear role. In the main the RAF operated the **S Mk 2B**, which had a bulged 425 gal fuel tank under the bomb-bay.

In FAA service the Buccaneer was the first type to carry the British WE 177 nuclear bomb. In the maritime role the -A version was used, while the RAF's tactical strike units used the much more powerful WE 177C of 200 kt yield. Again, these forward-based units gave some additional flexibility in the event of major conflict, and with their ECM fit could have penetrated well into Russia. For protection AIM-9L Sidewinders were carried.

RAF Buccaneers were operational in Lebanon in 1983–4 and in the Second Gulf War in 1991, where they designated targets for Tornado attack.

Strike units equipped – 12, 15, 16, 208, 216

PANAVIA TORNADO

With the collapse of the TSR.2 project, the British Aircraft Corporation initially looked to France to develop the Anglo-French variable-geometry (AFVG) aircraft, but with the French insistence on industry domination this came to nothing. In due course the British outline plan for a variable-geometry aircraft resulted in a tri-nation strike aircraft produced by Britain, Germany and Italy, known initially as the multi-role combat aircraft (MRCA), and eventually as the Tornado.

First flight of the twin 16,800 lb thrust Turbo-Union RB199-engined aircraft was in August 1974, with RAF service entry with 9 Sqn in 1982. In due course it equipped twelve strike squadrons – two of which, 2 and 13 Sqns, were primarily dedicated to the tactical reconnaissance role – plus the weapons conversion unit and OCU. In the strike role the Tornado replaced the Vulcan (two squadrons), Jaguar (five squadrons, all in Germany) and Buccaneer (three squadrons, two in Germany); two further squadrons were re-formed after long disbandment. The Tornado was also developed as a long-range fighter for the RAF, in which role it has served with eight operational squadrons.

In terms of performance the Tornado could fly at 1,450 mph at height and Mach 0.92 on the deck. Radius of action is 810 miles unrefuelled, but that range has to be traded for a reduction in armament. All weapons are carried externally, apart from a pair of 27 mm Mauser cannon, with up to eight 1,000 lb bombs or two JP-233 runway-denial-munitions dispensers on under-fuselage racks and up to 11,840 lb on the four underwing pylons.

In practice the Tornado typically flew with bombs on the fuselage racks, two 330 gal tanks on the inner pylons and a BOZ-107 chaff/flare dispenser and Sky Shadow jamming pod on the outer pylons. This would have been the configuration when carrying the 450 kt WE 177B nuclear bomb. The **GR Mk 1A** was a dedicated reconnaissance version, while the **GR.1B** was optimized for maritime strike.

Within the timescale covered by this book, RAF Tornado strike aircraft flew operationally with great effect in the Second Gulf War.

Strike units equipped – 2, 9, 12, 13, 14, 15, 16, 17, 20, 27, 31, 617

4.2 STRATEGIC GUIDED MISSILES

INTRODUCTION

Apart from the use of small solid-propellant rockets used for short-range attack, British experience with missiles prior to the end of the Second World War was on the receiving end.

The subsonic V-1 was a cruise missile fired from fixed sites and with a range of up to 150 miles. It was unguided, and flying at 350 mph at 4,000 ft it was vulnerable to conventional defences. In all, 9,251 were plotted over England between June 1944 and March 1945, of which 4,261 were destroyed, mainly by AAA fire and aircraft.

Defences were powerless against the V-2 ballistic missile which travelled at 3,600 mph and reaching sixty miles at its apogee; the rocket, referred to in Britain by the code *Big Ben*, defied interception. Attempts were made to attack launch sites, initially using a Liberator/Tempest combination. It had been assumed that the V-2 used radio command guidance, and 100 Group radio-countermeasures-equipped Liberators of 223 Sqn, based at Oulton in Norfolk, flew along the Dutch coast searching for transmissions. Tempests of 150 Wing (3, 56 and 486 Sqns) detached from Newchurch to Matlaske, were on hand to attack any identified launch sites.

When it was clear that radio command would not lead to V-2 launch sites, the Tempests were cleared for transfer to the Continent, their place being taken by Spitfires. Additional radar, sound-ranging and flash-spotting units were deployed under 105 Mobile Air Reporting Unit with headquarters near Brussels. Fighter Command in the UK was tasked with attacking *Gruppe Nord* mobile launch sites on the Dutch coast, while 2 Tactical Air Force attacked V-2 related targets of *Gruppe Sud* on the Dutch–German border.

Results of the Allied counter-offensive were poor. The cost was high, with typically 933 sorties flown by Fighter Command fighter-bombers in February dropping 192 tons of bombs and expending thousands of rounds of cannon shells. The last of 1,115 V-2s fell on the UK at the end of March 1945, by which time 2,754 civilians had been killed in England alone, with a further 6,523 injured. Several hundred remain missing to this day. By 7 March 1945 the Germans reported fifty-one rocket troops killed and 117 wounded, and fifty-eight lorries, eleven oxygen trucks and forty-eight missiles damaged in the Netherlands.

The victorious Allies were generally not slow to take full advantage of the weapons, research and scientific personnel which fell into their hands. However, Britain missed the boat. After the Americans had removed a hundred complete missiles from the Nordhausen factory for shipping to the USA, the British recovered a considerable number of unassembled rockets. These were taken to Altenwalde, near Cuxhaven, for testing as part of Operation *Backfire*, the first successful firing taking place on 2 October 1945. However, the post-war British Government was not prepared to engage in rocket research with a former enemy, so all post-war developments were based on captured material and original work.

What follows is a brief history of UK engagement with missiles, including for the sake of completeness the submarine-launched Polaris and Trident. The history highlights especially the peculiarities of the UK–US relationship, which, while allegedly special, certainly is not always friendly. Indeed, the avowed British intent in retaining an independent deterrent has been to be able to apply pressure on the United States when necessary.

FIRST SHORT-RANGE MISSILES

With the experience of the V-1 pilotless bomb, the Air Ministry expressed interest in a similar weapon, but one potentially carrying a nuclear warhead. In the early years of the Cold War a need was perceived for an inexpensive guided cruise missile to saturate enemy forces advancing westwards through Europe. Range was set at around 450 miles with a 600 miles range in Specification UB (unmanned bomb) 109T, which became OR.1097 in December 1950.

Bristol proposed the Type 182, which incorporated a Gnat fighter wing and was powered by a single BE.17 engine of 3,000 lb thrust. As the Blue Rapier, this latter incorporated a fuselage of plastic and would be produced at a very low unit cost. This first flying-bomb was cancelled in June 1953.

Vickers proposed the Type 825 powered by three Rolls-Royce Soar engines of 1,750 lb thrust, and this missile was built and tested at Woomera in Australia as the Red Rapier. Although it showed promise, it was considered to be too slow, too short-ranged and too inaccurate for the delivery of small nuclear warheads. It was cancelled in March 1956.

There were other developments which had the potential for extending the strategic reach of the bomber force. From 1950 this had been a major concern, given the introduction of the Soviet MiG-15 and the vulnerability of the bombers then in service.

Blue Boar was a TV-guided air-to-surface missile designed by Vickers to OR.1059. The warhead would have been a modified Blue Danube package, and the missile was fitted with Smiths autopilot and an EMI TV scanner. It was dropped from Valiant trials aircraft at Woomera, but cancelled in June 1954; the main concerns were that it was too heavy for use by naval aircraft and also that cloud negated the TV guidance system.

Originally known as Fairey Project 7, Green Cheese was developed in the 1950s to OR.1123, and was also intended for use on naval attack aircraft. It comprised a modified Blue Boar casing fitted with the X-band seeker from a Red Dean air-to-air missile. The Red Beard nuclear warhead was also intended to be fitted to the missile, but at nearly 4,000 lb Green Cheese was too heavy to be carried by the Gannet. Although it showed promise, and was developed into several successive intended variants, it was eventually cancelled in favour of the Red Beard in toss-bomb format.

BLUE STREAK

After the war the British fired several captured V-2 rockets in Germany in Operation *Backfire*. No explicit requirement for a ballistic missile was issued, but Government interest was kept alive under the codename *Hammer*. More specifically, as various research establishments began to identify possible solutions to problems of construction, propellant, guidance and warheads, so the interest was embraced within a broad new project, *Menace*. Some of the most important work was undertaken at the Rocket Propulsion Establishment, where rockets were designed and tested for aircraft and missile application.

The Royal Aircraft Establishment (RAE) at Farnborough was given the task of examining ballistic missile possibilities in December 1953, by which time British interest in a strategic missile system had been publicly announced in Australia. Furthermore, in March the following year a US/UK agreement was reached on missile technology exchange. In the summer of 1954 de Havilland Propellers was given the key contract to begin studies of a missile system with a range of 1,000 nautical miles (eventually stretched to 2,500 nm). Rolls-Royce was to handle motor development and Sperry the inertial guidance system.

de Havilland was in contact with Convair, from whom it secured information about the intended Atlas missile, which was very similar in size and construction to what was now to become Blue Streak. Rolls-Royce had already arranged a licence with North American for development of the Rocketdyne engine, which it improved as the RZ.12 sustainer motor and the RZ.2 booster. Blue Streak was to have one of the former and two of the latter.

The intention was to base the missile in underground silos from which they would be hot-launched. Sixty missiles would be deployed in ten widespread clusters of six. Apart from the design of the missile itself – which was basically a flexible stainless-steel cylinder – challenges faced included silo design and protection, warhead integration,

de Havilland Propellers was contracted in 1954 to begin work on a strategic missile. The outcome was *Blue Streak* which was test-fired at Spadeadam and scheduled for launch at Woomera. However, the silo-based missile would have been vulnerable to any pre-emptive strike and as a military vehicle was cancelled in 1960 just prior to the first launch. *(Author's collection)*

payload re-entry and guidance. Blue Streak was designed and constructed at Hatfield, where an assembly rig was built, with a further rig at Luton and a vast engine test-site at Spadeadam Waste. Live firings were to be conducted at Woomera in Australia.

Needless to say, there were problems with such a vast undertaking, but the first missile was erected at Hatfield in 1958 with test firings at Spadeadam in 1959. At 62 ft, the size of the weapon was determined by the likely weight of the warhead; the decision to build had been taken some four years before Britain's first thermonuclear weapon had been tested. In due course the Red Snow warhead was selected, but by 1959 it was becoming clear that Blue Streak would never be a credible deterrent in a United Kingdom setting. It was cancelled in April 1960, just before the first flight was due.

Britain's ICBM was cancelled, not through any failing of design or development, but rather because it was outdated. The weapon in its fixed silo, concentrated in such a relatively small area as England, would have been vulnerable, especially to any Soviet nuclear pre-emptive strike. Further, after any such first strike there would have been insurmountable control and command problems. All was not lost, since Blue Streak, mated to the smaller Black Knight rocket, served for some years as a satellite launcher, while the silo design was applied to the US Titan II ICBM.

THOR

Anglo-American relations reached an all-time low in the autumn of 1956 during the Suez adventure. In the post-Suez period after the British climb-down, President Eisenhower went some way to attempt to appease Prime

Minister Harold Macmillan by offering new Douglas SM-75 Thor missiles for basing in the United Kingdom. British projects, primarily Blue Steel and Blue Streak, were some way from fruition, and the offer was accepted with alacrity. The first missiles arrived as quickly as September 1958.

The Douglas Thor nuclear-tipped IRBM was one of two intermediate US ballistic missile types (the other was Jupiter) developed and brought into service quickly and to be delivered by 1959. It was 65 ft long with a one-megaton warhead, and with a single Rocketdyne MB-3 engine fuelled by liquid oxygen and kerosene it had a range of around 1,500 miles. Work started late in 1955, and the weapon was in USAF hands within a year. Notwithstanding commonality of parts with other weapons, this was a remarkable

In 1958, when deployment of *Blue Streak* was still well in the future, the US Government forward-based some 60 intermediate-range *Thor* missiles in the UK under a dual-key agreement. The first unit equipped was 77 at Feltwell, one of whose missiles is seen being erected. The *Thor*s were withdrawn by 1963 by which time the USAF was deploying ICBMs on US soil. *(C G Jefford)*

achievement. However, with its restricted range and vulnerable fixed surface sites, the missile had limited value – unless it could be based abroad. Subject to the general state of alert, Thor could be brought to readiness in as little as fifteen minutes: too long to prevent its destruction on the ground by incoming ICBMs.

The US offer, then, was rather less generous even than the basing of US-operated Jupiter IRBMs in Italy and Turkey. In the case of the Thors, sixty missiles were funded by the United States, while the RAF provided the base infrastructure and manpower. The missiles could only be fired by joint agreement through a 'dual-key' system, with USAF officers based at every RAF unit. The deployment of Thor under notional RAF control may have created the impression that the United Kingdom was getting early hands-on experience of new advanced technology. The reality is that the UK just became a US forward base, with no perceptible benefit and leaving eastern England extremely vulnerable to pre-emptive strike.

The sixty weapons were allocated to a total of twenty squadrons in four complexes or clusters based on wartime airfields in East Anglia and Yorkshire. Together with support equipment they were delivered in some 300 sorties to airheads at Lakenheath, Scampton, Leconfield and Cottesmore by C-124 and C-133 transports of the 1607th Air Transport Wing. To provide UK support and the USAF launch controllers, to monitor progress and control the warheads, the 705th Strategic Missile Wing (SMS), USAF, was established at Lakenheath, while in the USA the 704th SMS was formed to train RAF crews. No. 77 Sqn at Feltwell was the first unit activated, in September 1958, and within a year all twenty squadrons were equipped. However, the warheads were not mated with the rockets until 1960, when the system became operational.

In August 1962 the UK announced that the Thors would be deactivated by the end of 1963. Although the RAF Thors were brought to readiness during the Cuban Missile Crisis of October 1962, the USAF deployed its first ICBMs the same month. The USA no longer needed to rely on short-range missiles established at overseas bases, and the RAF could not afford to maintain a weapon which detracted from the manned bomber. The RAF squadrons were disbanded by August 1963 and the hardware was returned to the US.

Squadron	Station	Activated	Operational	Disbanded
Feltwell Wing (airhead Lakenheath)				
77	Feltwell	9.58	6.59	7.63
82	Shepherd's Grove	7.59	7.59	7.63
107	Tuddenham	7.59	7.59	7.63
113	Mepal	7.59	7.59	7.63
220	North Pickenham	7.59	7.59	7.63
Hemswell Wing (airhead Scampton)				
97	Hemswell	12.58	9.59	5.63
104	Ludford Magna	7.59	9.59	5.63
106	Bardney	7.59	9.59	5.63
142	Coleby Grange	7.59	9.59	5.63
269	Caistor	7.59	9.59	5.63
Driffield Wing (airhead Leconfield)				
98 Sqn	Driffield	8.59	12.59	4.63
102 Sqn	Full Sutton	8.59	12.59	4.63
150 Sqn	Carnaby	8.59	12.59	4.63
226 Sqn	Catfoss	8.59	12.59	4.63
240 Sqn	Breighton	8.59	12.59	4.63
North Luffenham Wing (airhead Cottesmore)				
144 Sqn	North Luffenham	12.59	4.60	9.63
130 Sqn	Polebrook	12.59	4.60	9.63
218 Sqn	Harrington	12.59	4.60	9.63
223 Sqn	Folkingham	12.59	4.60	9.63
254 Sqn	Melton Mowbray	12.59	4.60	9.63

BLUE STEEL

By the time Thor was coming out of service, the Blue Steel stand-off missile was already equipping RAF bomber squadrons. Work on a stand-off bomb had started in 1947 with the *Blue Boar* project, which was cancelled in June 1954, but which resurfaced as OR.1132 in September 1954 for an inertia-controlled weapon for use by the V-bombers. The main contract was let to Avro for a missile capable of flying a hundred miles with a 1 Mt warhead. Power was through a Bristol Stentor engine of 16,000 lb thrust, but initially scale models were test-flown in 1956, leading up to live firings of full-scale rockets by 1957 powered by the de Havilland Double Spectre motor.

Blue Steel was developed in a relatively short period of time, given its complexity and novelty. It weighed 16,000 lb and had a 35 ft long steel body, rear main control surfaces with a 13 ft span and delta foreplanes. From launch it accelerated to M2.3 in the climb to 70,000 ft, then dived steeply over the target. With its carrier aircraft – either Vulcan or Victor – the missile comprised a weapons system with internal autopilot interlinked to the aircraft's Green Satin Doppler radar. The warhead was originally to have been Green Bamboo, which was upgraded to Red Snow.

A small number of Vulcan and Victor bombers were modified as the B Mk 2A and B Mk 2R respectively. Both types were fitted with engines of 20,000+ lb thrust and had their bomb-bays adapted to accommodate the missile with minimum drag.

Service entry was with the Vulcan-equipped 617 Sqn at Scampton in June 1962, followed by 27, then 83 Sqn. The Victors of 139 Sqn at Wittering achieved operational status with the weapon in February 1964, followed by 100 Sqn. Blue Steel was both temperamental, with its liquid propellant fuel, and not always easy to fit to the parent aircraft, which had been modified individually post-production. Fitting was therefore time-consuming, and although there were proposals for improved versions these came to nothing and the weapon was withdrawn from

Blue Steel armed Vulcan B.2 XM594 of 27 Sqn climbs out from a practice scramble. *Blue Steel* carried a 1 MT warhead and from launch had a range of 100 miles. Climbing to 70,000 ft at M2.3 it was virtually invulnerable to interception by contemporaneous weapons systems. *(Author's collection)*

Preserved *Blue Steel* missile at Duxford. By the time the *Thors* were being removed *Blue Steel* was in service, ultimately with three Vulcan and two Victor squadrons. The missile was 35 ft long and weighed 16,000 lbs. *(Author)*

use in 1970. With its range limitations in mind, OR.1159 had been issued in 1957 for a weapon with a range of 300 miles, but this was cancelled in December 1959 when it was clear that Avro was struggling to perfect the basic Blue Steel.

SKYBOLT

As the relationship between the US and UK seemed to be improving in the late 1950s, discussions turned to improving the UK nuclear deterrent. In March 1960 President Eisenhower offered the UK the intended Douglas GAM-87 Skybolt air-launched ballistic missile (ALBM) being developed for the B-52. The GAM-87 was a 38 ft long solid-fuel, two-stage missile intended to carry a 1.2 Mt warhead 1,000 miles at 9,500 mph. It was intended to be in service by 1965.

As Soviet defences were improving, coupled with a serious pre-emptive strike capability, there was a need for a flexible, fast-response and credible weapon. A long-range missile, air launched with minimum preparation and travelling very fast, was one obvious answer. The Skybolt deal was not without strings, of course: in exchange the Americans required the use of safe anchorages in Scotland for the USN's Polaris missile submarines.

At the time of the offer the USA had only just decided to order the missile, but by June 1960 the British Government had ordered one hundred for carriage in pairs by the Avro Vulcan. By this time Blue Streak and Blue Steel Mk 2 had both been cancelled, so apart from the limited-range Blue Steel Mk 1 and free-fall nuclear weapons the future of a credible deterrent rested on Skybolt.

Vulcan B Mk 2 XH537 was modified to carry one missile under each wing, and the first test body was dropped in January 1961. Initial compatibility tests showed that the Vulcan would have been better suited to the missile than the B-52H, especially in respect of electronics. Avro even worked up plans for a Phase-6 Vulcan with increased wing area and capable of carrying six missiles. The first live firing of a Skybolt, from a B-52, was in April 1962, but the test, in common with the next four, was a failure. The weapon was cancelled by the US administration on 8 November 1962, although just a few weeks later, on 19 December 1962, the sixth test was satisfactory.

President John F. Kennedy had kept Britain poorly informed through the Cuban Missile Crisis two months earlier, and his advisers were totally opposed to any other country possessing a nuclear capability. Indeed, on 16 June 1962, Defense Secretary Robert McNamara had made a speech in which he said, *inter alia*, 'Limited nuclear capabilities, operating independently, are dangerous, expensive ... and lacking in credibility.' Although subsequently alleged to have been directed at France (another supposed ally), it is known to have represented the official line on the UK.

The US Government had not given any formal indication that cancellation was imminent, and Kennedy seemed surprised at the UK reaction, which was one of extreme hostility. Having ensured that the United Kingdom's own efforts at deterrence had been abandoned, the United States appeared to have achieved the objective of reducing at least the British nuclear capability. However, in subsequent discussions Kennedy agreed to sell Britain the Polaris missile, which certainly offered a truly credible and virtually undetectable deterrent. Therefore, from 30 June 1969, when Polaris entered service with the Royal Navy in the submarine HMS *Resolution*, responsibility for the strategic deterrent transferred to the senior service.

POLARIS AND TRIDENT

In the period 1960–62 there were concerns over the agreement reached between Kennedy and Macmillan at Camp David in March 1962. The essence of the agreement was that the UK would buy Skybolt in return for a USN submarine base on the Clyde at Gareloch, but the timings were unclear, and the US wanted the base before agreeing a signed contract for Skybolt. In the event the US pulled out of Skybolt, and so were obliged to offer a replacement in the form of the Polaris submarine-launched ballistic missile (SLBM).

Originally Kennedy wished the missiles to be under NATO control as part of a European component to nuclear deterrence. However, during the talks at Nassau in December 1962, it was agreed that, although part of a NATO multilateral force, the weapons could be used independently by Britain where her '... supreme national interests are at stake'. The formal agreement was signed in April 1963, resulting in France twice blocking UK entry to the European Economic Community, in 1963 and 1967.

At 32 ft long, the solid-fuel UGM-27C Polaris was launched from below the surface, and in A3 form as bought by Britain each carried three 200 kt warheads 2,500 miles. Sixteen were carried in each submarine and a total of around a hundred was acquired. Originally it was intended to build twelve Polaris submarines for the Royal Navy, but this was soon reduced to four, allowing at least one, and usually two, to be on station at any time. The *Resolution*-class vessels, which displaced 8,400 tons dived, and were 425 ft long, were on duty from June 1969 to 1996, by which time they were replaced by the much larger Vanguard class. In total the four submarines maintained 229 overlapping patrols.

Polaris employed a warhead based on the US W-58 of 200 kt. A mid-life extension was planned from early in the programme, based on the US Antelope scheme, as Chevaline. While the missile itself was not changed, seventy-two new re-entry vehicles were built with two warheads and four decoys each, and these were in service from 1982.

That year the Polaris Sales Agreement was modified to allow the UK to lease the more capable Trident system. Seventy of the D5 version were ordered, and in an unusual arrangement the missiles are collected by the user submarines from US stock in Georgia. The warheads remain British, although based on the American W-76, and 192 have been built. Each is of variable yield, selected as required.

The new missiles were deployed sixteen at a time on the Vanguard class of submarines which entered service in December 1994. Again just four were built, and although twice the displacement of the Resolution class, they had a very slightly smaller crew. Their warheads and tasking reflect the quite different challenges of a post-Cold-War world.

In service	From	To
HMS *Resolution* S22	6.68	10.94
HMS *Repulse* S23	69	8.96
HMS *Renown* S26	70	2.96
HMS *Revenge* S27	9.70	7.94
HMS *Vanguard* S28	12.94	date
HMS *Victorious* S29	12.95	date
HMS *Vigilant* S30	6.98	date
HMS *Vengeance* S31	2.01	date

4.3   NUCLEAR BOMBS AND WARHEADS, AND INDEPENDENCE

Throughout this section there is reference to yields of weapons, and these used need to be treated with caution. Where quoted, yields should be seen as indicative and not definitive: the intended or design yields of most of the weapons described have not been officially confirmed.

WARTIME ORIGINS

From the late nineteenth century a number of scientists across the world had explored aspects of physics which would eventually lead to the atom bomb. In March 1940 two émigrés, Otto Frisch and Rudolf Peierls, working at Birmingham University, produced a paper describing in outline the principles of an atom bomb based on uranium 235. A complementary paper, written for a lay audience, set out the case for possession of such a weapon as a deterrent to its use by an enemy. On 10 April 1940 the Government set up a committee to oversee work on related challenges, which in due course became the Maud Committee (named almost randomly, Maud being neither an acronym not the name of the chairman, who was G.P. Thompson). The committee comprised eminent scientists and was accountable to the Ministry of Aircraft Production.

In July 1941, the Maud Committee produced two reports, one of which was *The Use of Uranium for a Bomb*. It was recommended that the atom bomb project should be given the highest priority, and in the summary said, '... the scheme for a uranium bomb is practicable and likely to lead to decisive results in the war.' This led to the establishment of a new secret organization known as the Directorate of Tube Alloys, set up within the Department of Scientific and Industrial Research (DSIR). At this stage British-based scientists were significantly ahead of the field in military nuclear research.

In his analysis of the Maud report, the Government's chief scientific adviser, Lord Cherwell, had urged the Government to undertake production of the necessary materials for an atomic bomb in the UK or Canada: 'Whoever possesses such a plant should be able to dictate terms to the rest of the world. However much I may trust my neighbour and depend on him, I am very much averse to putting myself completely at his mercy.' The Maud report had been copied to the US Government, which in October set up a policy committee chaired by the President.

After the Japanese attack on Pearl Harbor, the USA applied itself to research on bomb development and production, eventually drawing in British-based scientists who had been conducting research for the DSIR and copies of whose work had been sent to the USA. Through 1942 and 1943 it had become evident that although she had the scientists Britain had not the financial and possibly adequate skilled manpower resources to undertake development of the atomic bomb. In effect Tube Alloys moved across the Atlantic to play an important part in the *Manhattan* Project that produced the first such weapons.

THE BOMBS DESCRIBED

Nuclear bombs come in two forms. Atom bombs (A-bombs, fission bombs) are the easier to construct and are of the type used against Japan. Their power, or yield, is given in terms of thousands of tons of TNT, or Kilotons (kt). Hydrogen bombs (H-bombs, Super, thermonuclear bomb, fusion bomb) were developed after the war, are more difficult to construct and are much more powerful. Their yield is measured in terms of millions of tons of TNT, or Megatons (Mt).

The energy source for an atomic bomb is a mass of heavy, unstable, material like uranium or plutonium, which by its nature emits escaping neutrons as harmful radiation: the elements are radioactive. Routinely, this decay of the nuclei is casual, resulting in warmth. However, if the decay can be concentrated, a large explosion will result as a mass of atoms split (fission). The key to creating the explosion is to compress the core rapidly into a critical mass, where the escaping neutrons can only hit other nuclei and cause an instantaneous chain reaction.

The principles of the process were clearly understood before the war, but the most significant problem was an engineering one – how to compress the core. The first bombs used two systems. One, the Hiroshima bomb (Mk I, or *Little Boy*) used a 'gun' approach to drive two sub-critical masses of uranium 235 together. This system is wasteful of fissile fuel: 60 kg of uranium produced a yield of about 15 kt. The second approach, more complicated but more cost-effective, was used in the Nagasaki bomb (Mk III, or *Fat Man*). In this weapon the core was

Valiant XD823 was one of four 49 Sqn aircraft deployed to Christmas Island for the *Grapple* series of H-bomb tests in 1957. This aircraft dropped the third test weapon on 19 June. *(Author's collection)*

surrounded by a series of inward-facing explosive charges acting as a spherical set of lenses, which when simultaneously fired imploded on the core, compressing it; 6.2 kg of plutonium produced a yield of 23 kt. Subsequent atom bombs have used the latter plutonium/implosion principle.

Hydrogen bombs work on the principle of fusion of light atoms of hydrogen isotopes – deuterium and tritium – through intense compression. The compression is created by the placement of small atomic bombs around the core, and when these are triggered the resulting fusion of nuclei forms helium nuclei. The escaping energy is huge and is exaggerated in some designs by making the bomb casing of uranium, which in turn creates fission and very heavy radioactive fallout. Cleaner, or neutron, bombs, without this third stage, release vast amounts of energy, but with relatively little fallout.

US DUPLICITY

There had been an agreement on the exchange of scientific information between the UK and the USA since 1941, and numerous exchange visits to monitor developments at first hand. In retrospect, though, it seems that transactions were a little one sided. Britain had shared all information on the development of radar, the jet engine and the programmable computer (Colossus), in addition to work on the use of uranium in an atomic bomb. In return, the US could have made available, for example, the advanced Norden bombsight, but it did not.

An Anglo-American Combined Policy Committee had been formed to agree on key aspects of the atomic bomb development and application (the *Manhattan* Project), and it met on 4 July 1945 to agree on the use of the weapon against Japan. British scientists were involved in the *Trinity* test of the first bomb at Alamogordo, New Mexico, on 16 July 1945, but once the weapon was proved the British were marginalized and effectively isolated from the manufacturing process. Many of the discussions in 1945 seem to have revolved around sources of raw materials, including uranium and thorium, which would have been of special concern to the Americans.

In November 1944 the British Chiefs of Staff asked the Joint Technical Warfare Committee to advise on the future of warfare, given impending new weapons. Under the chairmanship of Sir Henry Tizard, the committee reported in July 1945. Perhaps anticipating a formal change in the US position, and although it was denied access to any information on atomic weapons or policy, the committee recommended research into atomic energy. It also anticipated jet bombers cruising at 500 knots at 40,000 ft, and refined thinking about the importance of a nuclear deterrent.

In August 1946 the United States Congress approved the Atomic Energy Act, commonly known as the McMahon Act. While primarily concerned with the control of atomic energy and research in the United States, it also explicitly prohibited the transfer of any nuclear technology to other nations. The whole assets of the *Manhattan* Project transferred to the Atomic Energy Commission (AEC) in December 1946.

Britain was shut out, and it is a fine irony that the Communist spy Klaus Fuchs, who was uncovered in Britain in February 1950, was able to use his extensive notes from the *Manhattan* Project to accelerate British research. (Security around the *Manhattan* Project had been high, and work was compartmentalized, so that scientists and engineers worked on a strict 'need to know' basis. Few Britons were involved in the engineering and manufacturing aspects of the bomb.)

THE BRITISH BOMB

One result of the Tizard Committee report was the specification for what became the V-bombers. Another was the formation of a Cabinet Committee, GEN.75, in August 1945 to consider the way forward. Yet another outcome was the foundation of the Atomic Energy Research Establishment (AERE) at Harwell under the aegis of the Ministry of Supply in 1946. This was an important step to the building of a reactor at Windscale to produce plutonium from uranium.

The Air Staff had issued OR.1001 for a nuclear fission bomb on 9 August 1946, and formal Government

As part of the support to the *Grapple* tests the Station Flight had in charge a couple of Auster AOP.9s for mosquito control. WZ698 is seen in action: colour scheme is believed to be black overall with a white nose. *(Crown copyright)*

approval to develop and produce Britain's own atomic bomb was given on 8 January 1947 through a one-off Cabinet committee, GEN.163. The reason for an independent line was twofold. First, there could be no telling when the United States might adopt an isolationist stance in the future, leaving the western European nations exposed. Second, the United Kingdom, with its secure geographical possition off mainland Europe, was singularly vulnerable to attack from the Soviet Union. Britain needed to hold key cards with which to protect herself and influence US policy and strategy.

With work on the reactors for plutonium production in hand, consideration turned to the design and manufacture of the bomb itself. This was undertaken by the Armament Research Department (ARD) at Woolwich Arsenal under the direction of William Penney, who had been more intimately involved in the *Manhattan* Project that any other Briton. He had been appointed Chief Superintendent from 1 January 1946, and despite the US stance on secrecy, so important was his work that he was invited to the first post-war US atom bomb tests at Bikini Atoll in July 1946.

At ARD a new division was set up – Basic High Explosive Research (BHER). While the principle of creating an imploding explosive sphere was understood, work had to start in the UK from scratch. Various aspects of design and testing were conducted at a number of locations, before all work transferred to the Atomic Warfare Research Establishment (AWRE) at Aldermaston in April 1950. By then the Soviet Union had exploded her first atom bomb at Semipalatinsk on 29 August 1949 to universal surprise and Western dismay. The event was only detected by air-sampling aircraft. In 1950 the first British reactor went critical, and by 1952 the materials and design were ready for full-scale testing.

The first British bomb, codenamed *Hurricane*, was similar to the US Fat Man bomb, and was exploded at Monte Bello Islands off the north coast of Australia on 3 October 1953. The bomb was detonated successfully in HMS *Plym*, a redundant frigate. Equipment had been taken out in several vessels, and the command ship was the escort carrier HMS *Campania*, which embarked two Dragonfly helicopters. The core was flown in a Hastings from Lyneham in England to Singapore, where it was transferred to a Sunderland flying-boat of 88 Sqn for the trip to Monte Bello, which had no airfield. Scientists were flown into the mainland airstrip at Onslow.

Britain was now a nuclear power, and the new bomb was rushed into service as the Blue Danube, test-carried by Valiant aircraft from November 1953. Within a month the Americans had tested a thermonuclear bomb, so the pressure was now considerable for a British H-bomb. There were further tests of atom bomb and thermonuclear components in Australia (*Totem* – two tests in South Australia; *Mosaic* two tests at Monte Bello; *Buffalo* – four tests at Maralinga; *Antler* – three tests at Maralinga). During one of these tests the bomb was air-dropped by Valiant WZ366 of 49 Sqn. From 1954 there was an amendment to the US Atomic Energy Act, and the US began to relax its stance on sharing; Britain derived some data from air sampling during the American *Castle* test series at Bikini in 1954, presumably conducted by Canberras of 1323 Flt.

To support the Australian tests several RAF units were formed: 1310 Flt with York transports operated from Mallala in 1953, followed by 1362 Flt with Whirlwinds from 1955 to 1958, and 1439 Flt with Valettas and Whirlwinds in 1957. No. 1323 Flt formed with the Canberra B.2 for sampling and photography tasks, becoming 542 Sqn at Laverton, returning to the UK in early 1957. Weather reconnaissance was handled by the Shackletons of 269 Sqn. Remaining in the UK for ballistic tests was 1321 Flt with two Valiants which were used for Blue Danube trials between August 1954 and March 1956, when these tasks were absorbed by 18 Sqn.

The British thermonuclear test programme was codenamed 'Grapple', and the tests were moved to remote sites in the Pacific. The first three tests in May and June 1957 at Malden Island were a qualified success, with very high yields from boosted fission warheads. The first successful H-bomb was dropped off Christmas Island on 8 November 1957 in *Grapple X*, producing a yield of 1.8 Mt; five more *Grapple* tests followed in 1958.

The first thermonuclear weapon in British service was Violet Club, followed by Yellow Sun Mk I built to Specification OR.1136. These weapons succeeded Blue Danube as strategic deterrent weapons, while the smaller Red Beard fission bomb to OR.1127 replaced it as a tactical weapon. The sum of British effort provided around 300 bombs by the mid-1960s.

Some idea of the complexity of developing and testing nuclear bombs may be judged from the RAF involvement alone during the *Grapple* tests on Christmas and Malden Islands. Aircraft were detached from the following units.

160 WING CHRISTMAS ISLAND

Unit	Type	Function
49 Sqn	Valiant B.1	Bomb drop
76 Sqn	Canberra B.6	Air sampling
100 Sqn	Canberra PR.7	Photo-reconnaissance
206 Sqn	Shackleton MR.2	Weather recce, patrol, ASR
240 Sqn	Shackleton MR.2	Weather recce, patrol, ASR
22 Sqn	Whirlwind HAR.2	SAR
99 Sqn	Hastings C.2	Transport link Hickam AFB, Hawaii
1325 Flt	Dakota C.4	Inter-island transport
SF	Auster AOP.9	Mosquito control spraying
Ship's Flt	Whirlwind HAR.3	SAR
HMS *Warrior*	Avenger AS.5	Patrol

CHARACTERISTICS OF BRITAIN'S NUCLEAR WEAPONS

Name	In service	Weight (lb)	Yield	Nos
Blue Danube	1953–62	10,250	15–40 kt	20
Violet Club[1]	1958–60	9,000	500 kt	12
Yellow Sun Mk 1	1958–60	7,000	400 kt	5
Yellow Sun Mk 2	1961–72	6,500	1 Mt	150
Red Beard	1961–71	2,000	5–20 kt	80 RAF
				30 FAA
WE 177A	1969–98	600	0.5–10 kt	Note[2]
WE 177B	1966–95	950	450 kt	
WE 177C	1973–98	950	200 kt	

NOTES
1   Used Blue Danube casing; converted to Yellow Sun Mk I
2   Total RAF stock of WE 177 around 250; FAA perhaps 20

British success with H-bomb development undoubtedly impressed the US, and there was now little reason for continued secrecy, especially given that the two nations would need to act in concert in any war involving the Soviet Union, and therefore nuclear weapons. Further revision of the Atomic Energy Act in 1958 led to meetings to exchange information as a result of which Britain ceased further national designs, instead adapting US weapons.

The first weapon to be designed in this way was Yellow Sun Mk.II, which incorporated the 1 MT US Mk 28 warhead as Red Snow. The Yellow Sun Mk II was used by the Vulcan and Victor B.2 force until supplemented by the Blue Steel stand-off bomb, which is believed to have used a similar warhead.

The final air-launched nuclear bomb type was the WE 177 series built to Naval and Air Staff Requirement (NASR) 1177, and initially intended for the TSR.2. Although a British weapon, it is believed to have been based on US warheads, constructed at Aldermaston. The thermonuclear WE 177B was the key strategic variant for the Vulcan force with a 450 kt yield. The warhead was tested underground in the USA in 1962, and it entered service in 1966. The single-stage lower yield and physically smaller WE 177A of 0.5–10 kt replaced Red Beard as a tactical weapon carried by Buccaneers. The later WE 177C was similar in size to the B version, but much less powerful; it equipped the RAF Germany Phantom, then Jaguar, squadrons.

For a time, until 1991, FAA Sea Harriers were nuclear capable, presumably with the WE 177C. The main customer for the WE 177 in RAF service was the Tornado. Not only did their bases incorporate a supplementary storage area, but weapons were also stored in pits below hardened aircraft shelters ready for speedy fitting and arming. The RAF eventually gave up a nuclear role in 1998, and the last WE 177s were decommissioned.

THE AMERICAN BOMBS

When Britain embarked on her programme of nuclear weapon development it was after having been shut out by the United States and before the advent of the North Atlantic Treaty Organization. In 1954 the US Department of Defense advised the UK that in the event of war certain US bombs might be made available to the RAF, and basic information on weights and dimensions was given. From 1958 there was a relaxation of technology transfer, coupled with a secure Western alliance, and a number of US bombs were made available for RAF use, but only on behalf of NATO, under Project E.

The first aircraft to benefit were the V-bombers, which gained access to US Mk 5 weapons, followed by the Canberras of RAF Germany and some of those of Bomber Command assigned to SACEUR, with the Mk 7 bomb. There were problems with the custody of these weapons since they were only to be released at short notice, which denied the RAF the ability to disperse its bombers in anticipation of attack.

Further special weapons were provided for anti-submarine warfare. Nuclear depth bombs were made available to UK-based Shackletons and Nimrods. These bombs were stored at UK bases (St Mawgan and Macrihanish) but were under US control.

CHARACTERISTICS OF US-SUPPLIED BOMBS

Name	In service	Weight (lb)	Yield	Carrier
Mk 7	1958–65	1,650	20 kt	Canberra
Mk 5	1958–60	6,000	40–50 kt	Valiant, Vulcan, Victor
Mk 28	1960–64	1,900	0.5–1 Mt	Valiant
Mk 43	1964–76	2,100	1–2 Mt	Canberra, Valiant, Phantom
W-34	1965–71	1,500	10 kt	Shackleton
Mk 57	1970–91	510	5–10 kt	Nimrod, Phantom

4.4   DEFENCE OF THE NUCLEAR DETERRENT

INTRODUCTION

Although the RAF has provided air defence of the UK throughout the period covered by this book, this section is concerned primarily with protection of the RAF nuclear deterrent force from 1957 to 1969.

From the end of the war the regular and auxiliary air forces continued to maintain an air defence capability within Fighter Command. (The auxiliary squadrons, which had had such a distinguished war, disbanded in May 1945 but re-formed in 1946.) The fighter force was composed of Spitfire and Meteor day-fighters and Mosquito night-fighters spread across the country within three groups. Through the late 1940s and early 1950s the fighter force was deployed primarily to protect the South-East and Midlands from attack from the East.

By 1950, when the threat was perceived as being from Soviet Tu-4 piston-engined bombers (B-29 copies) using conventional weapons, Fighter Command still operated Spitfires in most of the RAuxAF squadrons, plus four squadrons of Hornets in addition to Mosquito night-fighters. There simply was no urgency in bringing more modern aircraft into service.

The Korean War provided a jolt, and by 1952 the air defences, now operated within two groups, were all jet, comprising Vampires and Meteors in various marks. By 1955 swept-wing fighters had been introduced in the form of the Swift (56 Sqn), Hunter (43 and 222 Sqns) and Sabre (92 Sqn); the latter was also in widespread RAF use in Germany.

While radar played a crucial part in the defence of Britain through 1940 and 1941, developments in radar were across a wide spectrum, and the static air defence system in 1945 was little improved from that in 1940. There were then developments through the late 1940s in air defence radar capability. The Telecommunications Research Establishment (TRE) and Royal Radar Development Establishment (RRDE) were merged as the Radar Research Establishment (RRE) in 1953.

The organizations had supported improvements in radar technology and reporting systems, for which some limited stimulus had been given in the 1950 ROTOR plan for upgrading air defence radars and reporting. This plan envisaged a reduction in the number of radar sites from 170 to sixty-six, with improved radars and simpler reporting systems to a number of sector-based master ground-controlled intercept (GCI) centres. These were located in underground bunkers. The system was based on an assumption of 932 fighter aircraft in fifty-seven squadrons based on seventeen airfields, with a further forty-nine airfields available on a reserve or standby basis.

From 1953 it was clear that point defence was irrelevant against a nuclear threat, and the number of planned fighters was reduced to 736 in forty-six squadrons. The UK Defence Policy of 1954 stated that the primary role of Fighter Command was the protection of Bomber Command, and in the 1956 Defence White Paper (Cmd 969) the policy of close defence was abandoned in favour of defence of the V-bomber bases by surface-to-air guided weapons (SAGW), then fighters. The 1957 White Paper (Cmd 124) filled in the details. By now ROTOR Stage 1 was complete, with thirty-nine new radar stations covering the south and east of England; however, they did not routinely operate at night and weekends!

DETECTION, WARNING AND CONTROL

There are two essential components of an effective system, each of which requires critical sub-elements if they are to function properly. The first component is a detection system to identify incoming threats; the faster and higher-flying the threat, the greater the distance over which it must be detected. The second component is a control system for the air defences in order to bring them most effectively to bear on hostile targets.

During the Second World War the detection system comprised radar and then overland human observation (the latter subject, of course, to weather). The defences comprised fighters, barrage balloons, anti-aircraft artillery and searchlights. The control system was sufficient to get numbers of fighters in the right place for interception during daylight, but was not really adequate for placing any numbers of aircraft accurately in poor weather or at night. One critical element supporting control is the process for separating radar plots of hostile aircraft from friendly ones. The system in use is identification friend or foe (IFF), which has remained problematical in relation to emulation, jamming and its use by hostile aircraft as a homing device.

The ROTOR plan in effect in 1957 was Plan 1½, with mainly improved wartime radars plus the new Air Ministry Experimental Station (AMES) Green Garlic Type 80 with much improved performance. The UK was divided into six sectors, each with an underground sector operations centre (SOC), and between them a total of twelve GCI stations. These latter had a Type 7 radar for control, two Type 14 sets for high and low surveillance and four Type 13 height-finding radars. The stations feeding into the SOCs were either chain home (CH) or chain home extra low (CHEL), of which there were twenty-one, and centimetric early warning (CEW), of which there were eight, equipped with the Type 80 radar. The RAF bought some AN/FPS-6 height-finding radars to match the range of the Type 80.

At this stage of the ROTOR plan, the total number of radar stations had decreased considerably with improved performance and communications, but although coverage was extended from the earlier defended area, the system still only ran from South Devon up to Peterhead. While there were stations covering the western side of the UK they were not operational.

As radars improved in range, discrimination and reliability, so the options for the early warning and control system developed, and the next proposal was *PLAN AHEAD*, which envisaged far fewer radars and control centres. It was also planned around the use of mainframe computers. In due course, after modification of the plan to accommodate integration with civilian air traffic control, the scheme became *Linesman*. It was at this stage that computerization played a part in tracking and in communications, making a real improvement in reliability and efficiency.

Three radar sites were improved to take the Type 84 surveillance radar at Boulmer, Northumberland, Staxton

Wold, North Yorkshire and Neatishead, Norfolk. As radar tracking stations (RTS) they were operational from 1964, and were supplemented by similar equipment at Bishops Court, Northern Ireland, Buchan, Aberdeenshire and Saxa Vord, Shetland. All data fed to a master control centre (MCC) at West Drayton near Heathrow. At each RTS there were several HF200 height-finding radars and one Type 85 Blue Yeoman radar which was particularly resistant to jamming. In addition, eight civil radar sites around the country fed into the system.

RADAR PERFORMANCE

AMES type	Function	Wavelength	Range (miles)	at height (ft)
Type 7	GCI	1.5 m	90	20,000
Type 13 Mk V	Height finding	10 cm	50	1,000
Type 14 Mk VI	CHEL	10 cm	50	1,000
Type 80	EW	10 cm	240	40,000
AN/FPS-6	Height finding		200	75,000
Type 84	EW	50 cm	240	40,000
Type 85	Tracking	10 cm	400	60,000
HF200	Height finding		180	40,000

BMEWS

From November 1958 the UK was briefed about an intended American ballistic missile early warning system (BMEWS), which with appropriately sited long-range radars would give the USA up to fifteen minutes' warning of incoming long-range missiles. This would give time for retaliatory strikes to be launched, even if there would be little time to protect the civilian population.

The problem for the Americans was that they required a European base to complete the network of three stations, and in due course a site on Fylingdales Moor, North Yorkshire, was identified and formal agreement made in 1960. The new high-powered radars there became operational as project *LEGATE* in September 1963, giving the UK a rather meagre three to four minutes' warning. The other stations were at Clear, Alaska, and Thule, Greenland. About 70% of the cost of Fylingdales (the equipment) is met by the US Government, while the balance for infrastructure is provided by the UK. A US liaison officer from the 21st Operations Group is present on site.

In 1992 the system at Fylingdales was upgraded from three steerable AN/FPS-49 radars housed in large 'golf-balls' to a single three-faced AN/FPS-126 large phased-array radar based on a truncated pyramid. The range remains 3,000 miles, and the system identifies not only any missile threat, but also a wide variety of space objects, and gives warning of overflying reconnaissance satellites.

The Fylingdales system warning time dictated RAF response policy for some years. While the system connected directly to the USA by the North Atlantic Radio System (NARS) it interestingly also gave USAF bases in southern England simultaneous warning.

UKADGE

By the time that the *Linesman* system was operational there were serious discussions about an integrated NATO system of warning, to become described as NATO Air Defence Ground Environment (NADGE). In due course the UK system (UKADGE) became a part of a wider network from which the UK benefited by being the westernmost outpost and thus receiving longest warning of impending conventional attack.

At the same time there were significant changes in the designation and control of airspace in the UK as commercial traffic increased, with military and civil integration. By 1971 there were military radar stations at Faroes (Danish), Saxa Vord (NATO), Buchan, Boulmer, Patrington, Staxton Wold, Neatishead and Bawdsey serving the

UK air defence region (UKADR). These linked through West Drayton, which also incorporated civil radars generally covering the west, although a new RAF station at Benbecula was added in 1973. In the control and reporting system, all radars fed into West Drayton for reporting, but fighters were controlled from Boulmer (Leuchars), Staxton Wold (Binbrook), Neatishead (Coltishall and Wattisham) and West Drayton (Coningsby).

The eventual configuration of UKADGE was two sectors, north and south of Newcastle, with sector operations centres (SOC) at Buchan and Neatishead respectively. Each was served by a further fixed control and reporting posts/centre, which with mobile radars gave complete coverage of the UK. Both fixed and mobile units were by the 1980s equipped with powerful but mobile radars, including the Types 91 (Marconi Martello), 92 (GE 592), 93 (Plessey AR320), 95 (Marconi S259) and 96 (GEC-Marconi S648). These were all jam resistant and worked with high definition to between 200 and 300 miles' range.

AIRBORNE EARLY WARNING

In 1972, after responsibility for the nuclear deterrent had transferred to the Royal Navy, one further dimension was added when 8 Sqn was re-formed at RAF Kinloss with the Shackleton AEW Mk 2. Hitherto the Royal Navy had provided radar warning of threats to surface vessels through 849 NAS, equipped with the Gannet AEW Mk 3 with the dated but reworked AN/APS-20 airborne radar. However, with the demise of the fixed-wing aircraft carrier there was a need for a successor. The RAF had tried unsuccessfully to operate four Neptunes of 1453 Flight in the AEW role between 1953 and 1956.

The Shackletons were on two-hour 'quick' reaction alert, and were scrambled through RAF High Wycombe when Norwegian NADGE radars detected a likely incoming target, usually Soviet reconnaissance aircraft. The 8 Sqn aircraft would then take over control of air defence fighters, initially controlled from Buchan. The AN/APS-20 had a range of around a hundred miles. Efforts were made to produce a Nimrod AEW variant, but in due course this was cancelled due to what appeared to be insurmountable problems with the radar. In the event the American E-3D was bought and operated as the Sentry, replacing the Shackleton in 1991.

FIGHTERS

As mentioned above it was envisaged in 1950 that there would be fifty-seven fighter squadrons defending the UK, and this number was reduced to forty-six in 1953. In fact, in 1950 there were fourteen Meteor squadrons (Marks 3 and 4), seven Vampire squadrons (Marks 1, 3 and 5), thirteen Spitfire squadrons (mainly Marks 21 and 22 in auxiliary units), six Mosquito night-fighter squadrons and, solely in 12 Group, four Hornet Mk 3 squadrons, making a total of twenty-five regular and nineteen volunteer squadrons. The regular units were located as shown, while the auxiliary squadrons were widely distributed, especially in the west and north, reflecting their personnel catchment areas.

Air Defence – regular units 1950

Sqns	Type	Base
11 Group		
2	Meteor F.4	Tangmere
3	Meteor F.4	Thorney Island
3	Vampire F.3, FB.5	Odiham
3	Mosquito NF.36	West Malling
12 Group		
2	Meteor F.4	Linton-on-Ouse
2	Hornet F.3	Linton-on-Ouse
4	Meteor F.4	Horsham St Faith
2	Hornet F.3	Church Fenton
3	Mosquito NF.36	Coltishall
25	**Total**	

By 1957, by which time the V-bomber force was operational with nuclear weapons, RAF Fighter Command was equipped with the Hunter (seventeen squadrons), Javelin (three squadrons), Meteor night-fighter (eight squadrons) and Venom night-fighter (five squadrons). These thirty-three squadrons in two groups, by now all regular, were mainly spread across bases in eastern England, with just seven south of the Thames. Whereas in 1950 stations generally hosted similarly equipped units, by 1957 day- and night-fighters were co-located.

Sqns	Type	Base
11 Group		
2	Hunter F.1, F.6	Odiham
1	Javelin FAW.1	Odiham
2	Hunter F.5	Tangmere
1	Hunter F.5	Biggin Hill
3	Meteor NF.12, NF.14	West Malling
1	Hunter F.6	North Weald
1	Hunter F.6	Wattisham
1	Meteor NF.12, NF.14	Wattisham
1	Hunter F.6	Duxford
1	Meteor NF.14	Duxford
2	Hunter F.5, F.6	Waterbeach
1	Venom NF.2A	Waterbeach
12 Group		
1	Hunter F.4	Stradishall
1	Venom NF.3	Stradishall
1	Hunter F.4	Horsham St Faith
1	Javelin FAW.4	Horsham St Faith
1	Javelin FAW.4	Coltishall
1	Hunter F.6	Church Fenton
1	Meteor NF.12, NF.14	Church Fenton
1	Hunter F.6	Linton-on-Ouse
1	Hunter F.6	Middleton St George
1	Meteor NF.14	Middleton St George
1	Meteor NF.11	Acklington
2	Venom NF.2, NF.2A	Driffield
2	Hunter F.4	Leuchars
1	Venom NF.3	Leuchars
33	**Total**	

The 1957 Defence White Paper produced a bombshell for the RAF. There was a need to reduce dramatically defence expenditure, and the White Paper signalled the end of the manned fighter in favour of guided missiles. In reality the Government was to some extent bowing to reality by recognizing that any attack by the Soviet Union was likely to be a nuclear strike with little, if any, warning. In those circumstances, the only response was a credible nuclear deterrent, so the investment was in the V-force and a mixture of guided missiles and manned fighters (in the short term) to protect the bomber bases.

A number of very promising fighter aircraft like the SR.177 rocket-propelled fighter fell victim to the needs of economy, although no doubt some would have been extremely effective. However, one potent point-defence fighter, the Lightning, was spared. Together with the Javelin all-weather fighter and the Bloodhound surface-to-air guided weapon (SAGW), it provided the air defence of the UK through most of the airborne nuclear deterrent period.

GLOSTER METEOR

The Gloster Aircraft Company was responsible for building Britain's first jet aircraft, the G.40 built to Specification E.28/39. First flight of the prototype was from Cranwell on 15 May 1941. Before this date Specification F.9/40 was issued, calling for a twin-engined jet fighter. The specification was written around Gloster experience with the low-powered G.40 (one WI engine of 860 lb thrust), and the company proceeded with development. An order for twelve aircraft was received in February 1941. First flight was by the fifth prototype, with a Halford H.1 engine, at Cranwell on 5 March 1943.

Gradually more prototypes were brought into the flight test programme, and as problems were identified, so great effort was made to address them. The first aircraft built to the **Mark I** (Type G.41) standard flew on 12 January 1944. Twenty production machines were produced, twelve being issued to 616 Squadron at Culmhead in July. Armament was four 20 mm Hispano Mk 5 cannon in the nose, and the engine was the Welland Series 1 of 1,700 lb thrust. The type was used to counter the V-1 flying-bombs, 616 Sqn moving to Manston for Diver patrols. The first V-1 was brought down on 4 August 1944. One flight was moved into Nijmegen in January 1945, although the Meteor was not to be flown over enemy territory. The Mark I was withdrawn at the end of January.

The **F Mark III** was generally similar to the Mark I but it incorporated numerous refinements, including a sliding canopy, increased fuel capacity and airframe strengthening. The first fifteen were fitted with the Welland, while the remainder of the total of 210 had the improved Derwent I of 2,000 lb thrust. A ventral fuel tank was fitted. The Mark III began coming off the production lines in early 1945, and the first were issued to 616 Sqn, and then 504 Sqn. Both units were disbanded in August 1945 in common with all Auxiliary Air Force squadrons, although 616 was to be re-equipped with the F.3 in 1949, after re-formation. On 7 September 1946 Gp Capt E.M. Donaldson raised the world air speed record to 615.78 mph in a specially modified aircraft.

Fighter units equipped – 1, 56, 63, 66, 74, 91, 92, 124, 222, 234, 245, 257, 263, 266, 500, 616

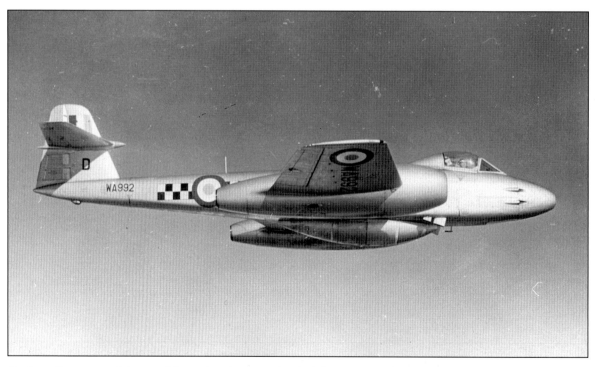

In the earliest stages of the era of the nuclear deterrent the air defence was provided by 1940s technology. Standard day fighter was the Meteor, typified by F.8 WA992/D of 43 Sqn. From the late 1940s the RAF fighter squadrons reverted to the pre-war silver finish with bright squadron markings – in this case black and white checks. *(Author's collection)*

The **F.4** evolved through the special Mark III designed to secure the world air speed record. The Mark 4 employed the Derwent 5 of 3,500 lb thrust with extended engine nacelles, and in later models wings clipped from 43 ft to 37 ft 2 in. Top speed at sea level increased from 420 to 585 mph. The first squadron to equip with the Mark 4 was No. 92, and some aircraft of 245 Sqn were modified with probes for in-flight refuelling trials.

Fighter units equipped – 1, 19, 41, 43, 56, 63, 64, 65, 66, 74, 92, 111, 222, 245, 257, 263, 266, 500, 504, 600, 609, 610, 611, 615, 616

The **F Mark 8** was the result of increasing the nose of the Mark 4 by 30 in. to improve directional stability and add fuel capacity. Unfortunately, expenditure of the ammunition, which was also moved forward, resulted in some loss of stability, so a new tail unit was fitted. Further improvements included a retractable gunsight and Martin Baker ejection seat. A total of 1,079 was built, making this the most popular version of Gloster's now ageing fighter. The last F.8s in front-line service were withdrawn from 245 Sqn in April 1957; the unit had been equipped with Meteor fighters continuously since August 1945.

Fighter units equipped – 1, 19, 34, 41, 43, 54, 56, 63, 64, 65, 66, 72, 74, 92, 111, 222, 245, 247, 257, 263, 500, 504, 600, 601, 604, 609, 610, 611, 615, 616

To provide a tactical reconnaissance platform the **FR Mark 9** was based on the F.8, but with a new nose retaining the four cannon of the fighter but incorporating glazed panels either side of the nose, and with a remotely controlled F.24 camera. Heating was provided by hot air bled from the starboard engine. The prototype flew on 22 March 1950, and 126 were produced, serving with the RAF from 1951 to 1957.

The night fighter units of the early 1950s were equipped with a mix of Meteor and Vampire fighters. NF.14 WS776/K of 25 Sqn at West Malling illustrates well the night fighter camouflage scheme. *(Author's collection)*

Fighter reconnaissance units equipped – 2, 79, 208, 541; FR Flt Aden

The **NF Mark 11** was based around the T.7, but with longer-span wings to house four 20 mm Hispano cannon and a 5 ft fuselage extension to accommodate the Mk X nose radar. It was powered by two Rolls-Royce Derwent 8 engines delivering 3,700 lb of thrust each, and top speed was 554 mph, with a service ceiling of 43,000 ft and endurance of around 1.5 hours. The Mk 11 remained in service until June 1960

Night-fighter units equipped – 5, 11, 29, 46, 68, 85, 87, 96, 125, 141, 151, 219, 256, 264

The **NF Mark 12** was similar to the NF.11 but with the US APS-21 radar fitted; fin area was extended to counteract the 17 in. longer fuselage. It was powered by the slightly more powerful Derwent Mk 9 engine, and was only used in the UK.

Night-fighter units equipped – 25, 29, 46, 64, 72, 85, 152, 153

The **NF Mark 13** was a tropicalized version of the NF.11 for use in the Middle East. It had larger engine nacelles, a cold air unit and modified radio.

Night-fighter units equipped – 39, 219

The final night-fighter variant was the **NF Mark 14**, which also employed the Derwent 9, giving a top speed of 580 mph. It had a completely new clear blown canopy, and was the first night-fighter variant with ejection seats. All were used in the UK apart from one unit in the Far East, which retained the type until August 1961.

Night-fighter units equipped – 25, 33, 46, 60, 64, 72, 85, 152, 153, 264

DE HAVILLAND VENOM

The DH112 Venom was a development of the Vampire with more power and a new, thinner, wing. In ground attack form it flew on 2 September 1949 and entered service in 1952 as the FB Mark 1. The night-fighter variant was a natural successor to the Vampire, but was produced as a private venture with side-by-side seating and wartime AI Mk X radar in the nose.

The prototype **FB Mark 1** first flew on 2 September 1949. Performance was much improved over the Vampire due to the engine/wing combination. Armament was four 20 mm guns (150 rounds each), with provision for 2,000 lb of bombs or eight RPs; as in the Vampire, no ejection seat was fitted. Service entry was with 11 Sqn in Germany in August 1952.

Fighter units equipped – 5, 6, 8, 11,14, 16, 28, 32, 45, 60, 73, 94, 98, 118, 145, 249, 266

The *NF Mark 2* night-fighter variant was built with side-by-side seating for pilot and navigator, and was equipped with AI Mark X radar. The prototype flew on 22 August 1950, only a year after the Vampire NF Mark 10 which it superseded. Many NF.2 aircraft were converted to Mark 2A standard to counter stability problems. The fin and rudder shape was changed, and the dorsal fillet of the Vampire T.11 was added; in addition a clear-view canopy was incorporated.

Night-fighter units equipped – 23, 33, 219, 253

The **NF Mark 3** was an upgraded night-fighter equipped with powered ailerons, ejection seats and a more bulbous nose to accommodate the American AI Mk 21 (APS-57) radar. Power was provided by the slightly more powerful Ghost 104, and the tailplane extension beyond the fin and rudders was deleted.

Night-fighter units equipped – 23, 89, 125, 141, 151

The **FB Mark 4** was an improved single-seat fighter similar to the FB.1 but with the Ghost 104, powered ailerons, ejection seat and revised fin and rudder. The FB Mk 4 entered service with 123 Wing, Wunstorf, in July 1955.

Fighter units equipped – 5, 6, 8, 11, 28, 60, 73, 94, 142, 208, 249, 266

HAWKER HUNTER

This most handsome of aircraft started life as the Hawker response to Specification F.3/48, which was to be a replacement for the Meteor. The appearance of the MiG-15 in 1949 had shaken Western governments, and there was some urgency to produce a fighter that could match the Soviet type and intercept potential jet bombers. The new fighter was to be capable of flying at Mach 0.90 and was armed with four 30 mm cannon.

The prototype Hawker P1067 (Avon 107, 7,550 lb thrust) flew on 20 July 1950, and the first Avon-powered **F Mark 1** production aircraft joined 43 Sqn four years later. In the meantime the sole F Mark 3, powered by an Avon RA7R with reheat, set a world air speed record of 727.6 mph in September 1953. The Wattisham wing acquired the **F Mark 2**, powered by the slightly more powerful Sapphire engine (8,000 lb thrust), from September 1954. Top speed was in the region of 675 mph, endurance less than an hour, in practice, and service ceiling 51,500 ft. The initial Hunter units were soon re-equipped with later variants, partly due to the Avon engines surging when the guns were fired at altitude.

Fighter units equipped – 43, 54, 222, 257, 263

The **F Mark 4** employed the Avon 115, which cured the surging problem, and equally importantly fuel capacity was increased both internally and through the use of wing tanks. Similar improvements were applied to the Sapphire-engined aircraft as the **F Mark 5**. These two variants joined operational squadrons in the spring of 1955, and with their much better endurance they soon became the day-fighter backbone of the RAF, replacing the Meteor, Venom, Sabre and short-lived Swift by 1957.

Fighter units equipped – 1, 3, 4, 14, 20, 26, 34, 41, 43, 54, 56, 66, 67, 71, 74, 92, 93, 98, 111, 112, 118, 130, 208, 222, 234, 245, 247, 257, 263

The final Hunter air defence day-fighter was the **F Mark 6** powered by the Avon 203 with 10,150 lb of thrust. Apart from the more powerful engine, it differed from earlier versions in having underwing hardpoints, faired link collectors for the guns (to avoid damage to underwing stores by ejected debris) and a wing leading-edge extension. The F.6 entered service with 19 Sqn in October 1956, but with the introduction of the Lightning from 1960 it was phased out by the end of 1962.

Fighter units equipped – 1, 4, 14, 19, 20, 26, 34, 43, 54, 56, 63, 65, 66, 74, 92, 93, 111, 208, 247, 263

The **FGA Mark 9** was an F.6 conversion originally built to replace Venoms in the Middle East after competition with the Gnat. Braking parachutes were fitted, and the aircraft was equipped with large 230 gal drop-tanks and cockpit ventilation and refrigeration. The Avon 207 engine was selected, but pending deliveries the 203 was fitted in an interim version; all aircraft were retrospectively fitted with the later engine. The Hunter FGA.9 entered service with 1 and 8 Sqns in January 1960, and the type remained in front-line service until 1968. A total of 126 conversions was built.

Ground attack units equipped – 1, 8, 20, 28, 43, 45, 54, 58, 208

The **FR Mark 10** was yet another F.6 conversion originally designed to Specification FR.164D. The first of thirty-three conversions flew on 7 November 1958. Two ex-Swift units were equipped with the type, and several were flown by 8 Sqn in Aden.

Fighter reconnaissance units equipped – 2, 4, 8; 1417 Flt

The elegant Hunter followed the Meteor into service, initially with 43 Sqn in 1954. At readiness at Horsham St Faith is F.4 WV272/L of 74 Sqn seen clean, although this variant was fitted with pylons for wing tanks to offer extended range.
(Author's collection)

GLOSTER JAVELIN

The Gloster GA.5 was designed to meet Specification F.4/48 for an all-weather fighter capable of 600 mph with a ceiling of 40,000 ft. Intended to replace the Meteor and Venom night-fighters, the prototype flew on 26 November 1951, and after evaluation it was selected over the DH110, which in naval service was to become the Sea Vixen. Two Sapphire Sa6 engines of 8,000 lb thrust were selected, and armament was four 30 mm Aden cannon in the wing.

The first two marks differed only in the radar fit. The **F(AW) Mark 1**, which joined 46 Sqn at Odiham in February 1956, had the AI17 radar, whereas the **FAW Mark 2** used the US AN/APQ-43 (AI22) radar.

Night-fighter units equipped – 46, 85, 87, 89

The Mark 3 was a trainer variant, while the Marks 4 and 5 were as the F(AW).1 but fitted with an all-moving tailplane, and then a new wing, with an additional 250 gallons of fuel respectively. The **F(AW) Mark 6** was as the F(AW).5 but with the AI22 radar of the Mark 2.

Night-fighter units equipped – 3, 5, 11, 23, 29, 41, 46, 72, 85, 87, 89, 96, 141, 151

The Javelin **F(AW) Mark 7** introduced the Sapphire Sa7 with 11,000 lb thrust, giving a top speed of 700 mph at sea level and a service ceiling of 52,000 ft. Armament extended to four Firestreak AAMs plus two cannon, and the fuel load was increased through ventral and underwing tanks. Service entry was with 33 Sqn in July 1958.

The **F(AW) Mark 8** employed limited-reheat Sa7R engines offering a maximum 12,300 lb thrust each, and the AI22 radar. It also had a revised wing with drooped leading edge and vortex generators. Some Mark 7 aircraft were brought up to Mark 8 standard while retaining their British radars, and as such became the **F(AW) Mk 9**. Finally, some Mark 9 aircraft were fitted with refuelling probes for overseas deployment, presaging the lengthy sortie times required for intercepting Soviet intruders up to the Arctic. The last Javelin unit based in the UK was 64, which departed for Cyprus in April 1965.

UK night-fighter units equipped – 5, 11, 23, 25, 29, 33, 41, 60, 64, 85

THE 1960s

In 1960 the plan was for twelve fighter squadrons and twelve SAGW fire units (sixteen missiles each) for Air Defence United Kingdom (ADUK). Therefore, by October 1962, at the time of the Cuban Missile Crisis, RAF Fighter Command was on the verge of reform. In 1961 the command became one of four NATO air defence regions, and on 1 May 1962 it became subordinate to Supreme Allied Commander Europe (SACEUR). Standing at the determined twelve squadrons, its groups were shortly to stand down, the squadrons reporting at command level in the short term.

The potent Lightning was introduced from 1960 to replace the Hunter, with the Javelin complementing it in the night-fighter and all-weather fighter role. These aircraft were deployed to protect the V-bomber bases and main industrial centres, while four new Bloodhound SAM wings had been formed in clusters around the Thor strategic missile complexes from 1959.

The specialized needs of all-weather and night-fighting resulted in aircraft designed for the role, rather than adaptions of day fighters like the Vampire, Venom and Meteor. The delta wing Javelin was built from the outset to such a specification, being the first aircraft in RAF service to feature missile armament. It entered service with 46 Sqn in 1956 and in this photo FAW.2s XA773/S and XA812/B of the squadron depart Odiham in 1958. *(Jack Murray)*

FIGHTER COMMAND, OCTOBER 1962

Sqns	Type	Base
2	Lightning F.1A	Wattisham
1	Javelin F(AW).8	Wattisham
1	Lightning F.1	Coltishall
1	Javelin F(AW).7	Coltishall
1	Javelin F(AW).8	West Raynham
1	Javelin F(AW).9	Binbrook
2	Hunter F.6	Leconfield
1	Javelin F(AW).9	Middleton St George
2	Javelin F(AW).9	Leuchars
12	**Total**	

THE ENGLISH ELECTRIC LIGHTNING

The P1 was built originally to a research Specification ER.103, subsequently modified to F.23/49, which called for an operational fighter. A manned model was built in the form of the Shorts SB.5 to test tailplane location and wing sweep, and the first P.1A flew on 4 August 1954. The first P.1B, which more approximated the eventual design, flew in 1957, and, unusually, twenty pre-production aircraft were ordered for various aspects of systems development and evaluation.

Power was provided by two reheated Avon engines, and initially armament was two 30 mm Aden cannon and two Firestreak AAMs. Time to 60,000 ft was just over a minute, but endurance was very limited – the Lightning was built as a point-defence fighter. The **F Mark 1** entered service with 74 Sqn in July 1960, and with the F Mark 1A with in-flight refuelling provision it served with three squadrons until replaced by later variants.

Fighter units equipped – 56, 74, 111

The **F Mark 2** was externally virtually similar to the F.1A, but it incorporated several internal changes. These included improved navigation equipment, a steerable nosewheel, offset TACAN, liquid oxygen breathing and variable-nozzle reheat. The only external difference was a small intake scoop on the fuselage spine for a DC standby generator. The first F.2 flew on 11 July 1961, and the version entered service with 19 Sqn at Leconfield in December 1962.

Fighter units equipped – 19, 92

The **F Mark 2A** was rebuilt to incorporate some F.6 features. Thirty-one of the original forty-four F.2s were converted from 1968. The engines fitted were the Avon RA211R, but the F.2 armament fit was retained. External features of the F.2A were the most noticeable, comprising the cambered wing, square-cut fin and much enlarged ventral tank of the F.6.

Fighter units equipped – 19, 92

F Mark 3 had two Avon 301R engines of 12,690 lb thrust, giving a 1:1 thrust-to-weight ratio, making it the fastest of all variants. The cannon were deleted, with the armament confined to two Red Top AAMs, and the fin was enlarged by 15%. It began to replace the Mk 1 in 1964.

Fighter units equipped – 23, 29, 56, 74, 111

The **F Mark 6** was the ultimate Lightning, with even more powerful Avons, a cambered wing and much larger ventral fuel tank, with two Aden cannon in the forward section. It joined 5 Sqn in December 1965, finally being withdrawn from service in December 1987.

Fighter units equipped – 5, 11, 23, 56, 74, 111

By 30 June 1969, when the RAF handed over responsibility for the nuclear deterrent to the Royal Navy, the RAF air defence units were at a disgraceful all-time low. There were just five Lightning squadrons (two each at Wattisham and Binbrook, and one at Leuchars) and one Bloodhound II base at West Raynham, with sixteen missiles.

Later in 1969 the first Phantoms joined 43 Sqn in the air defence role, slowly increasing the number of squadrons to seven by 1980 and, with the introduction of the Tornado, nine by 1990.

McDonnell Douglas Phantom

First flight of the F4H-1 was on 27 May 1958. The first F4H-1 Phantoms entered USN service with VF74 in July 1961. The new comprehensive designation system introduced in 1962 resulted in the F4H becoming the F-4. Before that time the F4H had been selected by the USAF as a tactical fighter designated F-110. Subsequently the Phantom served with distinction in a range of roles with US air arms and further afield.

From 1962 McDonnell had been studying F-4 and Rolls-Royce Spey compatibility, and orders for the type for both British air arms specified the Spey engine. In addition, British avionics were specified, although the Westinghouse AWG-10 radar was retained, albeit built in the UK under licence. The Royal Navy's requirement was subsequently reduced in size when the Government in 1968 decided to scrap the carrier force. Phantoms in British service (except the F-4J) were easily distinguished from other variants. The Spey installation resulted in a 20% larger air intake and quite different, drooping jetpipes. From 1976 the distinctive Marconi ARI18228 RWR was added to the fin-tip.

The **FG Mark 1** was the Royal Navy version of the Phantom, the original order for which was 140. The type was based on the F-4J, and was designated F-4K. The nose cone was hinged to allow the use of British carrier lifts, and the nosewheel leg was increased in height to 40 in. to increase the angle of attack at launch. Other devices to ease operation from small carriers included a strengthened undercarriage and arrester hook, drooped ailerons and enlarged leading-edge flaps.

The Phantom was not built with internal armament, and the naval aircraft were not fitted for the SUU-23A under-fuselage gunpack. In the air defence role armament options were four AIM-9 Sidewinders and four AIM-7 Sparrow air-to-air missiles. In the ground attack or strike roles there was provision for the carriage of up to 16,000 lb of stores on eight underwing and one fuselage hardpoints. A wide range of stores could be carried, and on British aircraft the wing points were capable of taking 1,000 lb bombs. In the air defence role the eight-missile fit would typically be complemented by two 370 gal wing tanks and one 600 gal centre-line tank. In the attack roles stores would normally be confined to around 6,000 lb plus fuel tanks. The FG.1 entered naval service in April 1968 and equipped just one unit – 892 NAS. With the decision to reduce the naval requirement, some went direct to the RAF (43 Sqn) from September 1969.

Fighter units equipped – 43, 111

The **FGR Mark 2** was the RAF version of the Phantom, the F-4M. It was similar to the FG.1, but lacked the extendable nose leg and had a standard stabilator. The version was also fitted for the SUU-23A gun-pod, and some were wired for the EMI reconnaissance pod carried on the centre-line. The RWR was also fitted from 1976, and some aircraft were equipped with dual controls. The FGR.2 began its operational RAF career in the tactical role until replaced by Jaguars. From 1974 the FGR Mk 2 was switched to the air defence role; the last was withdrawn from UK service with 56 Sqn in June 1992, while 1435 Flt in the Falklands converted to the Tornado two months later.

Air defence was not the preserve of the RAF alone. When carriers were in home waters their fighters also occasionally intercepted Soviet aircraft. In this instance Phantom FG.1 XT864/007 of 892 NAS from HMS *Ark Royal* accompanies a prowling Bear D during the *Northern Wedding* exercise of September 1978. *(Crown copyright)*

Fighter units equipped – 19, 23, 29, 43, 56, 74, 92, 111; 1435 Flt

The F Mark 3 was the initial designation applied to fifteen F-4J aircraft (F-4JUK) purchased to address the reduction in air defence capability when one unit had to be based in the Falklands. The aircraft retained their American engines and equipment and were operated by one unit, 74 Sqn at Wattisham, from July 1984 to early 1991.

Fighter units equipped – 74

MISSILES

In 1953 the decision was taken to disband Anti-Aircraft Command and to scrap medium- and high-level AAA. Work had started in 1949 by Bristol and Ferranti on a surface-to-air guided weapon (SAGW) system, and the first *Red Duster* missile was tested in Australia in 1953. A parallel development by English Electric was *Red Shoes*, which became the mobile Thunderbird used by the Army in Germany. In due course 800 *Red Dusters*, now named Bloodhound, were ordered for deployment in eighteen fire units defending London and the V-bomber bases. The order was cut to 330 in 1958, and the fire units were to be grouped around the Thor missile complexes, leaving the cities unprotected.

The fire units comprised a launch control centre, sixteen missiles on fixed sites and two Type 83 *Yellow River* tracking and illuminating radars. The Bloodhound was a semi-active radar homing (SARH) weapon, which relied on mid-flight guidance until its radar picked up the returns from the illuminating ground-based trackers. North Coates was the first base, and it was also used as a trials centre for systems, but not for live firings.

The Bloodhound was fired at a 45° angle from the launcher with the power of four Gosling boosters, which fell away shortly after firing. Power was provided by two Thor ramjets which would carry the Mk 1 missile to a range of fifty miles at Mach 2.2. The pulse radar was prone to jamming, so the improved Mk 2 used the Type 86 *Blue Anchor* continuous-wave radar. Combined with improved Thor engines, it had much better low- and high-level performance, and range was increased to 110 miles at Mach 2.7. The first missiles were deployed with 264 Sqn at North Coates on 1 December 1958, but all units were disbanded by September 1964.

BLOODHOUND MK 1 SAGW UNITS

21 Wing Lindholme		148 Wing North Coates	
(Yorkshire Thor complex)		**(Lincolnshire Thor complex)**	
94 Sqn	Misson	264 Sqn	North Coates
112 Sqn	Breighton	141 Sqn	Dunholme Lodge
247 Sqn	Carnaby	222 Sqn	Woodhall Spa
151 Wing North Luffenham		**24 Wing Watton**	
(East Midlands Thor complex)		**(East Anglia Thor complex)**	
62 Sqn	Woolfox Lodge	263 Sqn	Watton
257 Sqn	Warboys	242 Sqn	Marham
		266 Sqn	Rattlesden

The Mk 2 was brought into service with 41 Sqn at West Raynham in July 1965 in two fire units. The squadron was disbanded in 1970, but after three years the missiles were brought out of storage for use by 25 Sqn in RAF

These Mk 2 missiles of 85 Sqn were deployed at West Raynham in 1976. *(Crown copyright)*

Germany. 85 Sqn with fire units at West Raynham, North Coates and Bawdsey formed in December 1975. 25 Sqn returned to the UK in 1983 to be absorbed into 85 Sqn in 1989. The Bloodhounds were by then also deployed at Barkston Heath and Wattisham until disbandment in 1991.

Quite what the strategy was for the deployment of the Mk 2 missiles – if indeed there was one – is not clear, given the gaps in coverage over time. From the bases used it must be assumed that they were protecting the metropolis and/or airfields from high-level attack, since by now the Rapier SAM missile was in service to defend against low-flying intruders.

4.5   PHOTO-RECONNAISSANCE AND THE BLACK ARTS

THE 'INTS'

In order to target deterrent weapons and to enable their carriage to the target with minimum risk, various forms of intelligence gathering were essential. They were also critical in respect of enabling the defence system to function effectively.

Intelligence, in respect of the deterrent, may be considered in the terms of what, where, how and when:
- What the enemy's offensive and defensive weapons and support systems are, and of what they are capable
- Where they are located
- How they function
- When or in what circumstances they might be used

In order to determine the answers, a range of intelligence processes is used, including the following:
- Agents in place, observers or enemy personnel under questioning – human intelligence, or HUMINT
- Photographic or other imaging (for example IR or radar) reconnaissance, or PHOTINT
- Signals intelligence, or SIGINT, which may be sub-divided into communications intelligence (COMINT) and electronic intelligence (ELINT), within which is intelligence gathered from telemetry (TELINT) and radar transmissions (RADINT)
- Atmospheric sampling

During the period covered by this book the means for gathering intelligence remotely improved dramatically, since human intelligence from behind the Iron Curtain was singularly lacking. Further, whereas at the political level there were serious tensions between the UK and the USA over nuclear weapons and missile technology, in respect of intelligence there seems to have been remarkable cohesion, but at the senior operational level.

It would appear that the United States relied on Great Britain to undertake some photo-reconnaissance sorties over the Soviet Union, and it must be assumed that there was a quid pro quo whereby the product of later US sorties was also shared. In respect of ELINT sorties, it is an open secret that there has been a succession of formal agreements engaging the US, the UK and most of the former dominions. These agreements involve extensive if not total sharing of SIGINT products. The first such was the BRUSA agreement of 1943, followed more formally by the UKUSA agreement of 1947. The existence of the agreements has never been publicly admitted in the UK, but it is known that the parties and their fields of responsibility are:
- US   Soviet Union, the Americas, China
- UK   Soviet Union west of the Urals, Africa, China
- Canada   northern Soviet Union
- Australia   south-east Asia
- New Zealand   west Pacific

In addition, China, Germany, Japan, Norway, South Korea and Turkey are also involved. Many other countries must also be more or less actively engaged, given that the United States National Security Agency (NSA) is alleged to have had around 2,000 listening posts in 1999 intercepting some two million signals an hour.

In respect of this book, human intelligence and much signals intelligence (managed as it is through ground stations) are beyond its scope. What is covered are those intelligence activities which rely at least in part on aircraft for collection.

PHOTO-RECONNAISSANCE

The primary needs for photographic reconnaissance in terms of the deterrent were to establish the size and nature of the threat that needed be countered, to identify targets for annihilation, to identify defences and to undertake post-strike assessment.

The Western Allies were fortunate at the end of the war in that they captured a huge amount of German reconnaissance photographs covering the Soviet Union west of the Urals. This was shared with the United States, sorted in Operation *Dick Tracey* and used for target information until the advent of reconnaissance satellites. However, by 1947 RAF Mosquitoes of 13 Sqn were undertaking flights around the Caspian Sea from bases on Crete, and between October and December 1948 from Tabriz in Iran. In the meantime RB-29 aircraft of 46 SRS of the newly formed Strategic Air Command of the USAF were also flying reconnaissance sorties over northern Russia.

Two events prompted the need for more up-to-date information about Soviet capability. At the Tushino air display in August 1947 three examples of the Tu-4 (reverse-engineered B-29) strategic bomber were flown, and on 29 August 1949 the Soviet Union exploded its first nuclear weapon. For a time the Western Allies were preoccupied with the war in Korea, and then as Soviet involvement became evident the US Joint Chiefs of Staff prohibited any further overflights on 5 May 1950.

In December of that year President Harry Truman met Prime Minister Clement Attlee to discuss a range of strategic military issues. At that meeting it was agreed to share photo-reconnaissance tasks and product. At around this time there was agreement between the RAF and USAF that in the event of nuclear war strategic targets would be shared between the two services, with the USAF taking the lead in identification and allocation.

Thus in spring 1951 a small RAF special-duties flight (SDF) was formed at RAF Sculthorpe to train to fly the American RB-45C reconnaissance aircraft. At this stage just in service, the type was being used by 91 SRW temporary-duty units at Sculthorpe to photograph areas of interest in western Europe. This was so that target maps would be available in the event of Soviet invasion and occupation.

The SDF comprised just three crews, and in August they went to Barksdale in the USA for training, returning in December. By now Churchill was again Prime Minister, and he agreed to an early set of overflights. These were to take place at night over several routes in order that the radarscopes could be photographed over a large number of critical targets to provide radar maps for Strategic Air Command and presumably Bomber Command, RAF.

On 12 March 1952 a dry run was conducted at speed and altitude along the Berlin Corridor and back. This was closely monitored for signals intelligence in order to understand the nature of Soviet reaction. The true overflights were then planned for April. Three aircraft in RAF markings, but without either British or American serials, were to fly simultaneously on three separate tracks, all refuelling on the outbound leg over the North Sea or Baltic.

The northern flight was to route from Denmark up to Tallinn in Estonia, across towards Leningrad, down through Latvia and Lithuania and home across northern Poland. The centre sortie was to route across central Poland towards Moscow then south-east to Orel, returning across Belorussia and Poland. The third, and longest, sortie was to the south over Germany, Czechoslovakia and the Ukraine to Rostov on the Black Sea and then a return route just to the south.

The three aircraft departed Sculthorpe in the afternoon of 17 April 1952 and flew the sorties at 36,000 ft in radio silence; all returned safely after flights lasting all night. Although they were detected, it appears that no real effort was made to intercept the aircraft. The RAF crews returned to their units, but another mission was planned for December 1952. In the event it was cancelled, and the aircraft returned to the USA, still in RAF markings.

KAPUSTIN YAR

Through the late 1940s and early 1950s hundreds of thousands of POWs and refugees returned to Germany, having been used as slave labour in the Soviet Union on a wide range of projects. In Operation *Wringer*, a joint Anglo-American project, they were interrogated to provide information about areas of potential interest. One outcome, confirmed by telemetry intercepts in the Middle East, was the identification of a missile test site at Kapustin Yar, some sixty miles south-east of what had been Stalingrad.

It was deemed essential to find out more, and it appears that an RAF Canberra of 540 Sqn, then based at RAF Benson, undertook a long overflight in August 1953. Although this has never been confirmed, and there is uncertainty as to whether the aircraft was a PR.3 or a modified B.2, the flight has been formally referred to in the USA. The route, flown at between 46,000 and 48,000 ft, took the aircraft from Giebelstadt in West Germany across Prague, Krakow and Kiev, and then, after overflying the target, on to Tabriz in Iran. It has been reported that the aircraft was intercepted by MiG-15s, which caused some damage, but not sufficient to abort the sortie, although the quality of the resulting prints was poorer than had been hoped due to resulting vibration.

From 1953 to 1956, 540 Sqn Canberras undertook a number of sorties along the Iron Curtain in Project *Robin*. The aircraft, probably converted B.2s of which the squadron had three on charge, used a K-30 camera with a lens of 100 in. focal length provided by the US. It was fitted in the bomb-bay for oblique photography, and from 40,000 ft had a slant range of about sixty miles in good weather. One 540 Sqn B.2, WH726, was fitted with a 240 in. LOROP camera in the USA. Over several years a careful watch was maintained on airfields and other potential targets close to the border.

At the war's end there were PR squadrons in every theatre. In the UK, strategic reconnaissance operated within 106 Group of RAF Coastal Command with the Central Interpretation Unit (CIU) at RAF Medmenham and Nuneham Park. Flying units were based at RAF Benson, which had been the home of PR through much of the war. No. 106 Group disbanded on 15 August 1946 and became the Central Photographic Establishment (CPE). Through several changes the CIU became the Joint Air Photographic Intelligence Centre (JAPIC), which embraced both Army and Air Force elements.

Equipment at this time was installed in the Spitfire XIX, Mosquito XXXIV and Lancaster, the last generally for survey work. In due course some units re-equipped with the Meteor PR.10, while the Canberra was to become the mainstay of photo-reconnaissance for over fifty years! The focus for photo-reconnaissance shifted in 1953 when the flying units moved to RAF Wyton and JAPIC became the Joint Air Reconnaissance Intelligence Centre (JARIC) at nearby RAF Brampton. The USAAF had been closely involved in the CIU and probably remained so with its successors; Brampton was conveniently close to the USAF base at RAF Alconbury, which for some time hosted USAFE and then USAF reconnaissance units.

The SDF was reformed early in 1954 in Project *Ju Jitsu* for one more overflight. Four RB-45Cs were flown from Shaw AFB to Wright-Patterson AFB, where the radars were modified by British experts to provide a crisper image. They were then flown to the UK in April and again repainted in RAF markings. The routes were to be similar to the original routes some two years previously, and designed to cover as many airfield targets as possible, and the sorties were flown from RAF Sculthorpe on 28 April.

The southerly sortie was extended and ran into serious flak around Kiev, at which point the aircraft commander followed instructions and completed a 180° turn. The mission was apparently completely successful, and the flight was finally disbanded in May. It was becoming clear that overflights were increasingly risky, but in any event new tools were on the way.

In the United States the CIA had commissioned from Lockheed an aircraft capable of flying at unprecedented heights. The U-2 first flew in 1955, and the first two aircraft were airlifted to RAF Lakenheath to begin operations in April 1956. However, the project was compromised by British aircraft spotters, and the parent unit with aircraft moved to Giebelstadt in Germany, from where the first overflights were made in June or July. (As an indication of the close relationship between the UK and the US at the operational level, the RAF was handed post-attack U-2 photographs of the RAF attacks on Egyptian airfields during the Suez action in November 1956. This was at a time when governmental relations had fallen to an all-time low.)

This was not the end of British involvement in the programme. In 1958 four RAF pilots were selected for training in the USA, subsequently to be based with the CIA unit at Incirlik in Turkey. Responsibility for over-flights, which were closely controlled and required presidential sanction, could thus be shared, and the RAF pilots made at least two deep-penetration sorties. A further two pilots were attached at three-yearly intervals in 1961, 1964 and 1967, the later crews flying out of RAF Akrotiri. On 1 May 1960 an aircraft based at Incirlik was brought down by Soviet surface-to-air missiles (SAMs) over Sverdlovsk, and this signified the end of such sorties.

The Russian *Sputnik* satellite was launched in 1957, and this pointed the way for the future. While there are limitations to photo-reconnaissance from space, especially in overcast weather, during peacetime sufficient intelligence is gathered to satisfy demand. High-flying reconnaissance aircraft remain essential, though, for use in times of war or when the threat of interception is limited. Their flexibility is unparalleled. While the RAF does not have its own reconnaissance satellites, it is believed that at least through the Cold War the US shared target information.

It was not only in the West that the RAF was active in penetration missions. Another result of the Truman–Attlee agreement was a series of overflights of mainland China by Spitfire PR.19s of the 81 Sqn detachment at Kai Tak, Hong Kong. The flights were flown at the request of the US Navy and were conducted between January 1951 and June 1952. One pilot alone is reported to have flown sixty-three sorties by the end of 1951.

In the Middle East there is every reason to believe that the RAF used its Canberras for border surveillance, perhaps with some limited overflights. Certainly aircraft of 13 and 39 Sqns were tasked with photographing Soviet merchantmen bound for, or returning from, Cuba in the Mediterranean during the Cuban Missile Crisis in October 1962.

In 1955 543 Sqn re-formed at RAF Gaydon with the Valiant B(PR).1 and later the Victor B(SR).2. The squadron soon moved to RAF Wyton, where it joined 58 and 540 Sqns, the latter of which it had replaced by 1956. The Valiants carried eight cameras in addition to *Yellow Aster* H2S Mk 9 radar which enabled all-weather reconnaissance. The aircraft also carried sideways-looking radar, and apart from flying sorties close to the Black Sea, they photographed much of Europe in connection with the Blue Steel missile navigation system.

When wing spar failure resulted in the Valiant fleet being grounded late in 1964, the Victor B(SR) Mk 2 was brought into service. There was increasing demand for maritime reconnaissance, and this became a more important demand on tasking. When 543 Sqn disbanded in 1974, the Vulcans of 27 Sqn had already taken responsibility for the maritime radar reconnaissance role, which they only relinquished in 1982.

Although dangerous, the strategic photographic sorties resulted in remarkably few casualties. The USAF/CIA lost aircraft over China and the U-2 over Russia in 1960. Apart from one Canberra during the Suez campaign, the RAF appears not to have lost aircraft on operational missions.

RAF STRATEGIC RECONNAISSANCE UNITS, 1945–90

Unit	Type (code)	Base	From	To
United Kingdom				
541 Sqn	Spitfire XIX (WY)	Benson	at 6.45	1.10.46
	Lancaster PR.1		2.46	1.10.46
	Spitfire PR.19 (WY)	Benson	1.11.47	7.6.51
540 Sqn	Mosquito XVI, PR.34	Benson	6.11.45	30.9.46
	Mosquito PR.34 (DH)	Benson	1.12.47	26.3.53
	Canberra PR.3, PR.7	Wyton	26.3.53	31.3.56
58 Sqn	Mosquito PR.34 (OT)	Benson	1.10.46	12.53
	Lincoln B.2 (OT)		11.50	10.51
	Mosquito PR.35		11.51	31.3.53
	Mosquito PR.35	Wyton	31.3.53	30.9.70
	Canberra PR.3		12.53	10.55
	Canberra PR.7		1.55	30.9.70
	Canberra PR.9		1.60	30.9.70
82 Sqn	Spitfire PR.19 (ES), Lancaster PR.1	Benson dets W Africa	1.10.46	31.10.47
	Lancaster PR.1	Benson	30.10.52	31.3.53
	Canberra PR.3	Wyton	31.3.53	2.55
	Canberra PR.7		10.54	1.9.56
542 Sqn	Canberra PR.7	Wyton	15.5.54	1.10.55

Unit	Type (code)	Base	From	To
RRF	Lincoln B.2	Benson	1.10.51	27.3.52
	Canberra B.2	Upwood	27.3.52	17.10.55
	Canberra B.2	Wyton	17.10.55	1.9.61
	Victor B.1	Gaydon	1.9.61	1.11.63
543 Sqn	Valiant B(PR).1,	Gaydon	1.4.55	18.11.55
	+ Valiant B(PR)K.1	Wyton	18.11.55	12.64
	Victor B.1, B.2(SR)		12.64	24.5.74
39 Sqn	Canberra PR.7, PR.9	Wyton	1.10.70	1.6.82[1]
27 Sqn	Vulcan B.2(MRR)	Scampton	1.11.73	31.3.82
13 Sqn	Canberra PR.7, PR.9	Wyton	3.10.78	1.1.82
1 PRU	Canberra PR.7, PR.9	Wyton	1.6.82[2]	1.7.92[3]
39 Sqn	Canberra PR.7, PR.9	Wyton	1.7.92	3.12.93
Germany				
541 Sqn	Meteor PR.10 (WY)	Bückeburg, Gütersloh, Laarbruch, Wunstorf	7.6.51	7.9.57
69 Sqn	Canberra PR.3	Gütersloh, Laarbruch	1.10.54	1.4.58
31 Sqn	Canberra PR.7	Laarbruch	1.3.55	31.3.71
214 Sqn	Canberra PR.7	Laarbruch	15.6.55	1.8.55[4]
80 Sqn	Canberra PR.7	Laarbruch, Brüggen	1.8.55	30.9.69
17 Sqn	Canberra PR.7	Wahn, Wildenrath	1.6.56	31.12.69
Middle East and Africa				
680 Sqn	Mosquito IX, XVI	Deversoir	at 6.45	9.7.46
	+ Mosquito PR.34	Ein Shemer	9.7.46	1.9.46[5]
13 Sqn	Mosquito PR.34	Hassani	13.9.45	19.4.46
		Ein Shemer	1.9.46[6]	14.12.46
		Kabrit	14.12.46	5.2.47
		Fayid	5.2.47	21.2.51
	Meteor PR.10	Kabrit	21.2.51	30.12.54
		Abu Sueir	30.12.54	1.2.56
	Canberra PR.7	Akrotiri	1.2.56	1.9.65
	Canberra PR.9	Luqa	1.9.65	6.1.72
		Akrotiri	6.1.72	3.10.78
82 Sqn	Lancaster PR.1	Eastleigh, Takoradi	31.10.47	30.10.52
683 Sqn	Lancaster PR.1	Fayid, Kabrit, Eastleigh, Khormaksar, Habbaniya	1.8.50	30.11.53
69 Sqn	Canberra PR.3	Luqa	1.4.58	1.7.58[7]
39 Sqn	Canberra PR.3	Luqa	1.7.58	4.63
	Canberra PR.9		11.62	5.82
	Canberra PR.7		10.70	2.72

Unit	Type (code)	Base	From	To
Far East				
681 Sqn	Spitfire XIX	Mingaladon, Kai Tak, Seletar, Palam	at 6.45	1.8.46[8]
34 Sqn	Spitfire PR.19	Palam	1.8.46	1.8.47
684 Sqn	Spitfire XIX	Tan Son Nhut	11.10.45	27.1.46
	+Mosquito PR.34	Don Muang	27.1.46	1.9.46[9]
81 Sqn	Spitfire PR.19, Mosquito PR.34	Seletar	1.9.46	1.10.47
		Changi	1.10.47	1.2.48
	+ Spitfire FR.18	Tengah	1.2.48	16.3.50
		Seletar	16.3.50	1.54
	Meteor PR.10		1.54	1.4.58
		Tengah	1.4.58	7.61
	Canberra PR.7		2.60	16.1.70

NOTES
1 retitled 1 PRU
2 ex-39 Sqn
3 retitled 39 Sqn (1PRU)
4 renumbered 80 Sqn
5 renumbered 13 Sqn
6 ex–680 Sqn
7 renumbered 39 Sqn
8 renumbered 34 Sqn
9 renumbered 81 Sqn

SNIFFING THE ATMOSPHERE

One key method of intelligence gathering in relation to nuclear weapon tests is upper-atmosphere air sampling. This was critical after the war in order to maintain a watch on Soviet developments, because there were few if any agents in place, overflights were difficult when the location of any test site was not known, and local communications were by secure land-line.

Two days before it was formally established on 18 September 1947, the nascent USAF was tasked with monitoring the atmosphere for signs of Soviet atom bomb tests in the *Constant Phoenix* programme. On 3 September 1949 the search paid off when a WB-29 of the 59th Weather Reconnaissance Squadron (WRS) flying from Yokota in Japan to Eielson AFB, Alaska, picked up debris from the first Soviet nuclear weapon test. It is believed that their efforts were backed by RAF operations conducted by Halifax meteorological flights flying from Aldergrove, Northern Ireland (202 Sqn), and North Front, Gibraltar (224 Sqn).

The first dedicated RAF upper-air sampling unit was 1323 Flight, established in 1953 to undertake radiological monitoring around the world. It also supported the British nuclear tests in Australia, to where its Canberra B.2 aircraft were detached between March and June 1954. It was at this time that the first Soviet thermonuclear bomb test was confirmed by USAF 'sniffers', but it appears that RAF activity was mainly confined to work relating to UK tests, including flying through the nuclear cloud.

76 Sqn was formed in December 1953, primarily to support the nuclear tests in Australia and at Christmas Island in the Pacific, where it supplanted 1323 Flt. The latter achieved squadron status in November 1955, when it was renumbered 542 Sqn, and also supported the *Grapple* series of tests in 1957. In turn the unit was renumbered 21 Sqn for just a few months. 542 Sqn had worldwide commitments monitoring Soviet, and probably French, tests.

It appears that the RAF then lacked any upper-air sampling capability until 1973, when maritime radar reconnaissance Vulcans of 27 Sqn were fitted with underwing sampling pods. These were adapted from Sea Vixen underwing fuel tanks.

RAF AIR SAMPLING, 1948–90

Unit	Type	Base	From	To
202 Sqn	Halifax GR.6, A.9	Aldergrove dets Gibraltar	1.10.46	5.51
	Hastings Met.1	Aldergove	10.50	28.8.64
224 Sqn	Halifax Met.6	Aldergrove, det Gibraltar	1.3.48	3.52
76 Sqn	Canberra B.2	Wittering	9.12.53	15.11.55
	Canberra B.6	Weston Zoyland dets Pearce, Christmas Is	12.55	1.4.57
		Hemswell, Upwood	1.4.57	30.12.60
1323 Flt	Canberra B.2	Wyton	20.10.53	3.54
		Laverton	3.54	6.54
		Wyton	6.54	1.11.55[1]
542 Sqn	Canberra B.2, B.6	Wyton	1.11.55	15.12.55
		Weston Zoyland dets Darwin		
		Laverton	15.12.55	31.3.57
		Hemswell	31.3.57	17.7.58
		Upwood	17.7.58	1.10.58[2]
21 Sqn	Canberra B.2, B.6	Upwood det Laverton	1.10.58	15.1.59
27 Sqn	Vulcan B.2(MRR)	Scampton	1.11.73	31.3.82

NOTES
1   retitled 542 Sqn
2   renumbered 21 Sqn

SIGNALS INTELLIGENCE

At the end of the Second World War the RAF's radio countermeasures (RCM) units of 100 Group were disbanded into the Radio Warfare Establishment (RWE) at RAF Watton within 60 Group RAF Fighter Command. However, early the following year 26 and 60 Groups merged into 90 Group, with headquarters at RAF Medmenham, and this now became a directly reporting group. In September 1946 the RWE became the Central Signals Establishment (CSE) based at Watton and with a number of functions.

There was a development squadron and three operational arms. Y Wing undertook signals intelligence gathering, the Signals Flying Unit undertook training of ground control approach (GCA) operators and calibrated radars, and the RCM squadron provided jamming aircraft, which during this period were heavily involved in exercises. By 1948 there were three un-numbered squadrons operating within CSE – Signals Research Squadron, Monitoring Squadron and RCM Squadron.

The tasks of the Watton units were first to help identify Soviet communications and air defence systems. (It must be assumed that there were also other agencies involved in this work.) The product of this work would have been passed on to other agencies, but also used internally to test opportunities and systems for signals jamming. CSE thus provided an airborne jamming service for RAF Bomber Command. The establishment worked closely with the Telecommunications Research Establishment (TRE) at Malvern (later the Radar Research Establishment (RRE)) and with GCHQ. Probably little in the way of communications intelligence by aircraft took place in the early post-war years.

The method of gathering electronic intelligence was to fly along, or sometimes over, the borders of unfriendly territory, identifying signals and radars in terms of both type and source location. Thus a map of where the systems were located, an understanding of how the components interacted and knowledge of how they worked could all be generated. Aircraft carrying the requisite equipment and operators would generally be heavy and relatively slow, so other aircraft could be involved in probing flights to stimulate a response by the air defence systems. As time went by, the importance of monitoring communications – the content of signals – increased, with GCHQ the major client. As an example of signals intelligence conducted by Y Wing, a Halifax flew at least one ELINT sortie over East Germany in May 1948 in connection with the Berlin crisis in order to determine how the Soviet air defence system responded to flights from the West to Berlin.

The work of CSE eventually settled to numbered squadrons. The Radio Warfare Squadron was split into 192 and 199 Sqns, the former involved in SIGINT and the latter in operational countermeasures. SIGINT had been the function of Y Wing with Halifaxes and Fortresses, whose role was gradually assumed by Lancasters. In 1948 Y Wing became the Monitoring Squadron, which in 1950 acquired four Lincoln B.2 bombers. As 192 Sqn it received Washingtons in 1952 and Canberras a year later; as a matter of note it is interesting that several of the very early Canberras were issued to TRE for trials duties in advance of delivery to bomber units.

The most significant development for 192 Sqn was the receipt in April 1957 of three special Comet Series 2 aircraft, which had the size and electrical power to manage a wide range of eavesdropping equipment, together with operators. 192 Sqn flew numerous sorties referred to in the operations book only as 'Air Ministry' sorties, usually along the East European border, and most of these were probably flown on behalf of GCHQ. Sorties were also flown routinely from Cyprus to the Black Sea, and one of these missions in May 1965 resulted in Category 3 damage to a Comet when it was hounded by five Tu-28 fighters and had to escape at high speed, eventually recovering to el Adem in Libya.

In August 1958 192 Sqn was renumbered 51 Sqn, and later in the year 90 Group attained command status as Signals Command. At around this time there was a CIA detachment of SIGINT-configured U-2s, indicating how closely British and American monitors were working.

Several Canberra B.6 aircraft were acquired and soon modified for signals collection, and in 1963 51 Sqn moved to RAF Wyton, where it exchanged the ageing Comets for three specially modified Nimrods. Ten years later 90 Group was absorbed into Strike Command. Since then not only has 51 Sqn borne the brunt of British airborne long-range SIGINT work, it has also been involved in a number of specific conflicts.

These activities were necessarily most sensitive and also of extreme importance. They were also very risky, but the RAF only lost several aircraft which *might* have been involved in probing. For example, there are some peculiarities relating to the loss of the CGS Lincoln in 1953, and on 27 July 1954 Meteor NF.11 WM1884 of 527 Sqn ran out of fuel and force-landed at Gardelegen in East Germany. One might have thought that a Watton-based unit would have been more circumspect! The USAF and USN, plus client operators like Nationalist China and Pakistan, lost numerous aircraft involved in intelligence gathering, either PR or ELINT, and for the sake of illustration these are noted in the table that follows.

While much COMINT work is conducted through satellites and ground station intercept, this sensitive work has also been undertaken by aircraft. With phenomenal growth in the use of mobile telephones since 1986, both the Army and RAF have developed the capability of a wide range of message monitoring.

JAMMING

After the war, radio (later electronic) countermeasures, or jamming, became absorbed into the Development Wing and part of the Signals Flying Unit (SFU), which for a time was based at Shepherd's Grove. In March 1947 the Naval Air Radio Warfare Unit moved into Watton in the guise of 751 NAS, although it was only to remain until September. In February 1948 the RCM Squadron was formed, and its aircraft included Mosquitoes, Lancasters and Lincolns.

The RCM squadron was increasingly involved in exercises, and there was constant pressure for a mainstream specialist unit to support the bomber force. This prospect seemed further than ever when the monitoring and RCM squadrons merged as RW Squadron in June 1950, only to separate into 192 and 199 Sqns in November 1951. The latter provided jamming for exercises, and also specialist operator training, and the demand for exercise support was such that the Development Squadron also participated. In April 1952 199 Sqn moved to Hemswell.

In 1956 Watton received its first Valiant for trial installation of ECM kit. This type then equipped 199 Sqn from May 1957, and in 1958 it became 18 Sqn, embedded in Bomber Command as a specialist jamming unit until 1963. In 1957 the Lincoln element of 199 Sqn had become 1321 Flt for a few months before its tasks were absorbed by C Flight of 138 Sqn. However, with the development of effective ECM equipment for a range of V-bombers and indeed Canberras, the need for specialized units ended.

In 1957 751 NAS had moved to Culdrose with the Sea Venom ECM.21, where in May 1958 it was renumbered 831 NAS. In July 1963 it returned to Watton with a wider range of types, and was disbanded there in August 1966, many of its personnel transferring to the newly forming and bi-service 360 Sqn, which was created from B Flight of 97 Sqn. The various marks of Canberra used by the squadron were involved in training and exercises until disbandment in October 1994. To complete the picture a second bi-service unit, 361 Sqn, was formed for service in the Far East, but it was disbanded before becoming operational.

CALIBRATION AND DEVELOPMENT

The calibration and development units are also listed in the attached table. While their roles were not overtly warlike, their wide-ranging duties on signals-related tasks gave opportunity to probe and spy. Their main task, though, was calibration of ground radars for the armed services throughout the world, a task put to civilian contract in 1993.

ELECTRONIC INTELLIGENCE, 1945–90

Unit	Type	Base	From	To
SIGINT, including ELINT and COMINT				
Y Wing RWE/CSE	Halifax III, Fortress III	Watton	22.10.45	11.48
	Mosquito B.16, PR.34		22.10.45	15.7.51
	Lancaster, Anson 19		46	1.51
	Lincoln B.2		50	15.7.51
192 Sqn	Mosquito PR.34, Lincoln B.2	Watton	15.7.51	9.52 3.53
	Washington B.1		4.52	2.58
	Canberra B.2		1.53	21.8.58
	Varsity T.1		4.54	21.8.58
	Canberra B.6(RC)		12.54	21.8.58
	Comet C.2(RC)		4.57	21.8.58
51 Sqn	Canberra B.2	Watton	21.8.58	7.59
	Comet C.2(RC)			1.75
	Canberra B.6(RC)			10.76
	Nimrod R.1	Wyton	31.3.63	28.4.95
Electronic warfare and training				
SFU	Halifax, Lancaster B.1	Shepherd's Grove	6.46	2.48
RCM Sqn	Mosquito B.35, Lincoln B.2, Lancaster B.1	Watton	2.48	1.11.51
199	Lincoln B.2, Mosquito NF.36	Watton	1.11.51	17.4.52
	Lincoln B.2, Canberra B.2	Hemswell	17.4.52	1.10.57
	Valiant B.1		5.57	1.10.57
	Canberra B.2, Valiant B.1	Honington	1.10.57	17.12.58

Unit	Type	Base	From	To
18 Sqn	Valiant B.1	Finningley	17.12.58	31.3.63
1321 Flt	Lincoln B.2, Canberra B.2	Hemswell	1.10.57	23.1.58
C Flt 138 Sqn	Valiant B.2	Wittering	23.1.58	1.4.62
751 NAS	Seafire XV, Anson I	Watton	1.3.47	30.9.47
	Mosquito FB.6, PR.34	Watton	3.12.51	11.54
	Sea Fury FB.11		8.52	3.56
	Firefly AS.6		9.52	3.56
	Anson I		2.53	8.55
	Avenger AS.4		12.52	7.57
	Sea Venom ECM.21		6.57	27.9.57
	Sea Venom ECM.21	Culdrose	27.9.57	1.5.58
831 NAS	Sea Venom ECM.21, ECM.22	Culdrose	1.5.58	26.7.63
	Sea Venom ECM.21, ECM.22, Sea Vampire T.22, Gannet ECM.4, ECM.6, Sea Prince T.1	Watton	26.7.63	26.8.66
360 Sqn	Canberra B.2, B.6, T.17	Watton	23.9.66	21.4.69
		Cottesmore	21.4.69	1.9.75
		Wyton	1.9.75	31.10.94
	+ Canberra PR.7, E.15	Wyton	9.91	31.10.94
361 Sqn	Canberra T.17	Watton	2.1.67	14.7.67
Calibration				
527 Sqn	Spitfire VB, Oxford, Wellington X, Dominie	Watton	12.11.45	15.4.46
Cal Sqn	Oxford, Anson, Lincoln B.2, Mosquito B.35		15.4.46	1.11.51
N Sqn	Anson, Lincoln B.2		1.11.51	1.8.52
116 Sqn	Anson C.19, Lincoln B.2	Watton	1.8.52	54
	Hastings C.1		9.53	4.56
	Varsity T.1		12.53	21.8.58
115 Sqn	Varsity T.1	Tangmere	21.8.58	1.10.63
	Varsity T.1, Valetta C.1	Watton	1.10.63	8.70
	Hastings C.2		1.67	1.69
	Argosy E.1		2.68	1.78
	Varsity T.1, Argosy E.1	Cottesmore	9.4.69	23.2.76
	Argosy E.1, Andover E.3	Brize Norton	23.2.76	4.1.83
	Andover E.3	Benson	4.1.83	1.10.93
R Sqn	Mosquito B.35, Anson, Lincoln B.2		1.11.51	1.8.52
527 Sqn	Mosquito B.35	Watton	1.8.52	1.54
	Anson C.19			3.54
	Lincoln B.2			9.54
	Meteor NF.11		6.53	11.57
	Varsity T.1		1.54	3.56
	Meteor NF.14		8.54	10.55

Unit	Type	Base	From	To
	Canberra B.2, PR.7		12.54	21.8.58
245 Sqn	Canberra B.2	Tangmere	21.8.58	19.4.63
98 Sqn	Canberra B.2	Tangmere	19.4.63	1.10.63
		Watton	1.10.63	17.4.69
	Canberra B.2, E.15	Cottesmore	17.4.69	27.2.76
Development				
Dev Sqn	Anson I, C.19, Lincoln B.2, Meteor F.8, NF.14, Canberra B.2	Watton	22.10.45	1.1.62
151 Sqn	Lincoln B.2, Hastings C.1, C.2, Varsity T.1, Canberra B.2	Watton	1.1.62	25.5.63
97 Sqn	Varsity T.1, Hastings C.2, Canberra B.2	Watton	25.5.63	2.1.67

POSSIBLE INTELLIGENCE-GATHERING-RELATED LOSSES OF AIRCRAFT OPERATED BY US AIR ARMS, ALLIES OR CLIENT AIR FORCES, 1945–95

Date	Aircraft	Unit	Location
8.4.50	PB4Y-2 (59645)	VP-26	Leyaya, Latvia
6.11.51	P2V-3W (124284)	VP-6	Vladivostok
13.6.52	RB-29	91 SRS	Sea of Japan
13.6.52	DC-3/Tp-79 (79001)	Swedish AF	Gotland, Baltic
3.7.52	RB-29	91 SRS	Far East
7.10.52	RB-29A (4461815)	91 SRS	Kuriles
29.11.52	B-29	?	Manchuria
12.1.53	RB-29A	581 ARCS	Manchuria
18.1.53	P2V-5 (127744)	VP-22	Swatow, Formosa
12.3.53	Lincoln B2 (RF531/C)	CGS RAF	East Germany
10.3.53	F-84E	USAFE 53 FBS	West Germany
28.7.53	RB-50	55 SRW	Vladivostok
4.1.54	P2V-5 (127752/CC-3)	VP-2	Yellow Sea
4.9.54	P2V-5	VP-19	Sea of Japan
17.4.55	YRB-47B (512054)	26 SRW	Kamchatka
22.8.56	P4M-1Q (124362)	VQ-1	Wenchow, China
10.9.56	RB-50	? 55 SRW	Sea of Japan
18.2.58	RB-57A (CNAF 5642)	CNAF	Yellow Sea
27.6.58	C-118A (513822)	USAF/CIA 7405 SS	Soviet Armenia
2.9.58	C-130A-II (560528)	7406 CSS	Yerevan
16.6.59	P4M-1Q (122209)	VQ-1	Sea of Japan
7.10.59	RB-57D (CNAF 5643)	CNAF	Nr Peking
1.5.60	U-2C (566693)	WRSP-2/CIA	Sverdlovsk
1.7.60	ERB-47H (534281)	55 SRW	Barents Sea
9.9.62	U-2C	CNAF	Eastern China
24.1.64	T-39 (624448)	701 ABW	East Germany

Date	Aircraft	Unit	Location
10.3.64	RB-66C (54451)	19 TRS, 10 TRW	Gardelegen, Germany
7.7.64	U-2G (3514)	CNAF	Southern China
8.9.64	P-2	VP-42	South China Sea
10.1.65	U-2C (3512/566691)	CNAF	South of Beijing
27.4.65	ERB-47H	55 SRW	North Korea
11.9.65	RB-57F	24 Sqn PAF	India
14.12.65	RB-57F (6313287)	7407 CSS	Black Sea
8.10.66	U-2A (566690)	4080 SRW	Bien Hoa
0.0.67	Boeing 707	PanAm	Kamchatka
9.9.67	U-2	CNAF	Eastern China
2.4.68	U-2	CNAF	China
5.6.68	A-12 (606932)	CIA (9 SRW)	South of Philippines
0.1.69	U-2	CNAF	China
0.3.69	U-2	CNAF	Inner Mongolia
15.4.69	EC-121M (135749)	VQ-1	SE Chongjin North Korea
0.0.70	U-2	CNAF	China
21.10.70	U-8	USAF	Soviet Armenia
13.10.74	WC-130H (650965)	54 WRS	South China Sea
15.8.75	U-2R (6810334)	99 SRS	Gulf of Siam
23.4.78	Boeing 707	Korean Air Lines	Murmansk
1.9.83	Boeing 747 (HL7442)	Korean Air Lines	Sakhalin
7.6.94	Lockheed L-100	? (US contract)	Adler (Black Sea)

THE AIRCRAFT

Avro Lancaster PR.1

The Lancaster **PR Mark 1** was powered by four Rolls-Royce Merlin engines and had a range of 2,500 miles at 234 mph. Ceiling was 23,000 ft. Fitted with F24 cameras in the bomb-bay and with the gun turrets faired over, the Lancaster was a sound survey platform, but of little value on 'hot' operational sorties by the time it came into service with 541 Sqn immediately after the war. The Lancaster remained in service in the survey role until 1953.

Survey units equipped – 82, 541, 683

de Havilland Mosquito PR.34/35

The **PR Mark 34** was a development, with a 3,500-mile range, of the PR Mk XVI with Merlin 113/114 engines. Additional fuel was contained in a bulged bomb-bay, and four vertically mounted F52 cameras and one oblique F24 were carried. The aircraft were unarmed and unarmoured, and the ceiling was 36,000 ft, with a maximum speed of 422 mph. A total of 181 were built, and they joined the RAF with 544 Sqn in April 1945; the last sortie was with 81 Sqn in December 1955. In **PR.35** form the bomber was converted for night photography and operated by B Flt of 58 Sqn.

Strategic reconnaissance units equipped – 13, 58, 81, 540, 680, 684
SIGINT units equipped – 192, 199, 527; 751 NAS

Vickers Armstrong Spitfire PR.19

The Type 389 Spitfire was a Griffon-engined hybrid for unarmed photo-reconnaissance, comprising the Mk XIV fuselage mated to Mk Vc wings. In all, 225 were built, and the variant entered service in June 1944, being withdrawn from use in the PR role in June 1951. Camera fit comprised one or two F52 or F8 vertical cameras and one F24 oblique, and the version was used by both tactical and strategic reconnaissance units. Service ceiling was 30,000 ft, endurance three hours and top speed 446 mph.

Strategic reconnaissance units equipped – 34, 81, 541, 681, 683

Gloster Meteor PR.10

The Type G.41M Meteor PR.10 was also a hybrid design, comprising the F.8 fuselage, long-span F.3 wing, F.4 tail unit and FR.9 nose, less the guns. It was intended as a replacement for the Spitfire. It carried one F24 camera in the nose which could take photographs obliquely on either side or forward, plus two F52 cameras in the rear fuselage. Powered by two Rolls-Royce Derwent 8 engines, the first of fifty-nine built entered service with 541 Sqn in December 1950. The service ceiling with internal fuel only was 47,000 ft, at which height it achieved 545 mph with a range of 700 miles. It was replaced by the Canberra.

Strategic reconnaissance units equipped – 13, 81, 541

English Electric Canberra

The **B Mark 2** (two Avon RA.3 engines of 6,500 lb thrust) and B Mark 6 were both used in modified form as ELINT platforms, the latter having more powerful Avon RA.7 engines of 7,500 lb thrust each. The first B.2 aircraft reached the Telecommunications Research Establishment (TRE) in advance of operational bomber squadrons.

Signals units equipped – 51, 97, 98, 151, 192, 199, 245, 360, 527; 1321 Flt

The prototype Canberra **PR Mark 3** was built to Specification PR.31/46. It differed from the B.2 on which it was based in a fuselage fourteen inches longer to accommodate extra fuel tanks, seven cameras (six F52 and one F49) and flares. It first flew in March 1950, and joined 540 Sqn in December 1952 after buffeting problems had been corrected. Range was 3,000 miles, maximum speed 570 mph and service ceiling 47,000 ft. Thirty-five were built, and it was finally retired in 1958, being replaced by the PR.7.

Units equipped – 39, 58, 69, 82, 540

The **PR Mark 7** was to the B.6 as the earlier version related to the B.2. It had more powerful Avon engines and extra fuel in internal wing tanks, and performance and camera fit were similar to those of the PR.3. It joined 540 Sqn from May 1954, and as the most widely used (seventy-four built) it eventually equipped eleven squadrons, including four in Germany.

PR units equipped – 13, 17, 31, 39, 58, 69, 80, 81, 82, 214, 360, 540
Signals units equipped – 360, 527

The **PR Mark 9** was perhaps the most developed Canberra. It had the fighter-type cockpit of the B(I).8 and a much larger wing of increased span (4 ft) and chord inboard of the engine nacelles. Power was provided by two Avon 206 engines of 10,050 lb thrust, which reportedly conferred a ceiling in excess of 70,000 ft. A crew of three was carried, and service entry was with 58 Sqn in 1960.

Units equipped – 13, 39, 58; 1 PRU

Initially specially equipped piston-engined aircraft like the Lincoln and Washington were used for electronic intelligence gathering. The Comet, as seen here in the form of R.1 XK695 of 51 Sqn, represented a dramatic improvement in terms of speed, ceiling and range. The aircraft were used to harvest *Warpac* frequencies and communications. *(51 Sqn records)*

The **T Mark 17** was a conversion of the B.2 fitted with various jamming equipment in an extended nose. It entered service with 360 Sqn in 1965 and was used primarily for training, although in a conflict the unit would no doubt have taken on operational bomber support tasks.

Units equipped – 360, 361

de Havilland Comet

The Comet jet airliner was first flown in 1949, and several examples of the Mark 1 and Mark 2 served as trials aircraft. Three Series 2 aircraft were converted for use by 51 Sqn as ELINT platforms, but one, XK633, was burnt out in a hangar fire at Watton in 1959. These first aircraft were fitted with US equipment to identify, locate and record Soviet radar and communications transmissions, but the replacement aircraft was to RAF C.2 standard and was fitted with British equipment. Three C.2 aircraft were also used sequentially as trainers.

Units equipped – 51, 192

Hawker-Siddeley Nimrod

The replacement for the Comets of 51 Sqn was in the form of the Nimrod R Mark 1, a much more comfortable aircraft, and one capable of greater endurance and capacity. A wide variety of classified detection and recording equipment is carried and regularly updated, and data are conveyed to the ground support station in real time. Three were acquired, and although significantly different in appearance from the MR.1, no new mark number was allocated, to avoid undue interest.

Unit equipped – 51

DETECTING AND JAMMING EQUIPMENT

The detailed operation of devices applied in electronic warfare is beyond the scope of this book. What follows is an outline of how the systems function, with examples of fit.

There are two aspects to airborne electronic warfare. First there is electronic support measures (ESM) equipment, which detects and/or locates signals, be they radars, radios or infra-red devices. Electronic countermeasures (ECM) then include confusion, deception – telling the source that the target is either somewhere or something different from reality – and jamming. Related is the process of using the source of transmissions to destroy the transmitters, usually by specialized units operating in the suppression of enemy air defence (SEAD) role. Electronic counter-countermeasures (ECCM) are approaches to overcome jamming or deception.

At the end of the war the RAF used strips of metal foil (*Window*, or *chaff*, to Americans) dropped from aircraft to confuse radars, and *Mandrel, Dina* and *Piperack* radar jammers. *Airborne Cigar* (*ABC*) and *Jostle* were the code-names for VHF communications jammers. Later radar jammers included *Potato* and *Indigo Bracket*.

A major problem for ECM vehicles was the power supply, and only when the Valiant entered service was there sufficient for a reasonable suite of jammers. A typical fit included AN/APR-4 and AN/APR-9 radar intercept receivers, six AN/APT-16 centimetric radar jammers, three AN/ALT-7 UHF communications jammers, six ABC VHF communications jammers, one APT-2 *Carpet* radar jammer and *Window*. What was now in the offing was new equipment for the V-force.

To give some idea of the ECM fit applied for self-defence on the V-bombers, the following equipment was fitted on later Vulcans. It comprised one ARI 18074 (*Green Palm*) VHF barrage jammer to disrupt air defence communications, later replaced by one ARI 18146, two ARI 18075 (*Blue Diver*) metric radar jammers to jam early-warning radars, three ARI 18076 (*Red Shrimp*) S-band radar jammers to block AAA and SAM radars. In addition was one ARI 18105 (*Blue Saga*) passive radar warning receiver, later replaced by the ARI 18228, one ARI 18051 *Window* dispenser, one ARI 18205 L-band jammer with infra-red decoys and one ARI 5952 (Red Steer) tail radar.

The Victor B.2 was adapted for strategic reconnaissance to replace the Valiant with 543 Sqn. Various cameras and the *Red Neck* radar were fitted. Illustrated is XL165. (*Author's collection*)

By the time the Tornado entered service in 1982, miniaturization had enabled much smaller packages, and very sophisticated equipment is now carried in two underwing pods. The Sky Shadow ECM pod identifies the type, source and location of emissions and then jams them accordingly. The Boz–107 dispenser automatically ejects chaff or flares to confuse airborne radars and infra-red seekers.

The Canberra was a remarkably versatile aircraft serving as a bomber but also, from the outset, as a reconnaissance platform. In its ultimate PR.9 format with extended wing area and powerful Avon 206 engines it could achieve a ceiling in excess of 70,000 ft for around 5,000 miles. The type joined 58 Sqn (whose XH136 is seen here) in 1960 and it remained in service until 2006. *(Author's collection)*

CHAPTER FIVE

The Middle East, 1950s and 1960s

The situation in the Middle East has in modern times been complex, to say the least. In the nineteenth and early twentieth centuries nations were created by the Turks, French and British, with artificial borders which respected neither tribal nor religious boundaries. The creation of the Suez Canal, followed by the exploitation of oil, resulted in the region being of paramount importance to the Major Powers. Their tasks were twofold – to prevent internal, inter-tribal, conflict, and to protect from physical invasion or influence.

The RAF had a long tradition of engagement in the Middle East through the policy of policing between the wars. After the war British involvement was both in respect of disengagement, as described in Chapters 1 and 3, and to maintain treaty obligations and protect oil interests.

Throughout the period covered in the present chapter, Anglo-American relations were often strained and never straightforward. The US idea of helping Middle East countries was to encourage and support Nationalists rather than what they saw as the old guard, non-reforming, puppet monarchs placed by the British. Their aim was to create allies in the fight against Communism, and in the process to diminish British and French influence in the region.

From 1950, having already vacated Palestine, Britain was now facing pressure to leave Egypt. The military coup in Egypt in 1952 was backed by the CIA, and in due course it led to the nationalization of the Suez Canal by Egypt, which in turn resulted in the ill-fated Anglo-French-Israeli Suez adventure. Not only was this unwise action a turning point in British fortunes worldwide, but it had a domino effect throughout the region for many years to come.

Within two years Iraq had witnessed a coup which led directly to collaborative action by the USA and Britain in Lebanon and Jordan respectively. A speedily placed and extensive military presence helped to stabilize the area.

Britain was already experiencing increasing insurgency in Southern Arabia, but post Suez, the Egyptians supported the government of Yemen in a continuing campaign of border incursions and in fomenting trouble among the Nationalist movements of Aden. There was clearly little point in remaining in Aden, and withdrawal was completed in 1967.

The United Kingdom provided protection for a number of Gulf states, including Oman and Kuwait. The former was threatened several times by interests in Saudi Arabia, and the Buraimi Oasis affair was a reminder of the difficulties of maintaining peace where there were either no formal boundaries or illogical ones. British forces supported the government for many years, both with British units and by manning Omani units as mercenaries, especially in the Dhofar region.

Kuwait further demonstrated the problems of artificial boundaries, and given the huge oil deposits there is little wonder that Iraq claimed the country when it declared independence of British protection in 1961. Kuwait had originally been a province, an area ill defined in terms of formal borders, and at the head of the Persian Gulf it had been settled by traders from across Arabia.

In coming to the assistance of Kuwait, Britain was fortunate in having a number of military assets in the region, some by design, as at Cyprus, Aden and Kenya, and some by accident aboard a commando carrier in the Indian Ocean. In this exercise the lessons of Suez had been learned and applied. The RAF's strategic transport fleet was now more fit for purpose, and the Navy was equipped with two commando carriers.

The events described in this chapter represent the swansong of empire in the Middle East. Apart from humanitarian actions, Britain was to remain largely uninvolved in further military action until the Second Gulf War of 1990–91.

5.1   SOUTHERN ARABIA (ADEN AND RADFAN), 1950–67

BACKGROUND

The early post-war years in Aden have been described in Chapter 1, Section 5.

TRIBAL TROUBLES POST WAR TO 1954

Within the Protectorate things were quiet for a year or two, but by August 1952 8 Sqn was involved in Operation *Firework*, an attack on Wadi Hatib. At the end of 1952 8 Sqn began converting to the Vampire FB.9, and in January 1953 a detachment of 32 Sqn from Deversoir was based at Khormaksar, undertaking several small operations. In May 8 Sqn used its Vampires to attack a fort at Mariba as part of Operation *West Bard*. These local forts were very strongly built, and armour-piercing rockets were often necessary to ensure their destruction. In November an airstrip was constructed at Am Ruseis in the Wadi Hatib to support the APL based in Nisab and Lodar engaged in keeping the trade routes open. Elements of the Shamsi tribe in the Wadi were bombed by Lincolns of 49 Sqn in January 1954.

YEMENI INVOLVEMENT

A more serious situation developed in May when troops had to be airlifted by Valettas of the Middle East Communications Squadron (MECS) to Am Ruseis to relieve the APL fort at Robat, which was under constant attack. The relief column was protected by overflying Vampires, and an air control post (ACP) was established to direct ground-attack strikes. The Vampires, in familiar territory, also marked targets for Lincolns of 49 Sqn. In

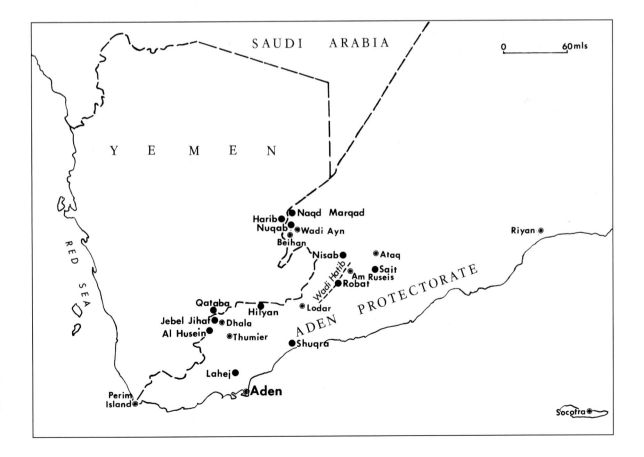

June action continued with raids against the Rabizi tribe around Nisab, who with Yemeni support were striking daily at Government targets. Vampires used 500 lb bombs, rockets and cannon fire in an attempt to force the dissidents into submission. In the month 8 Sqn flew for 483 hours, dropping 316 500 lb bombs and using 316 60 lb rockets and 9,000 rounds of ammunition.

Air strikes were highly accurate, but there was often confusion as to targets, and the siting of some meant hazardous approaches or exits. From May 1955 the first RAF intelligence officers (RAFIO) were based up-country to co-ordinate strikes, initially at Wadi Mirria, where 169 sorties were flown. The RAFIOs were highly successful, developing networks of intelligence sources and ensuring that only appropriate targets were selected for economic attack. In June 8 Sqn re-equipped yet again, this time with the Venom FB.1, which it changed a year later for the FB.4 fitted with ejection seats. These aircraft were in use in July in support of an operation from Ataq to relieve Robat yet again, and eighty sorties were flown against Wadi Hatib.

Sycamore helicopters of the MECS (re-formed as the Aden Search and Rescue Flight in 1958) were used for the first time for casualty evacuation. During 1955 Lincolns of 7 Sqn were detached to Khormaksar, and on 2 January 1956 the detachment became 1426 Flight. These aircraft were supplemented for a time by a detachment of Shackletons from 42 Sqn.

As 8 Sqn departed for Armament Practice Camp in July 1956, it was temporarily replaced by 73 Sqn, whose Venoms were soon in action supporting heavy strikes by Lincolns against targets at al Jaleleh, Boran and Khaura. Also in 1956, 78 Sqn was formed with six Twin Pioneer light transports to relieve the overworked Valettas and Pembrokes of the MECS. Target identification was always a problem in this desolate region, and maps were invariably inaccurate, so to assist in the reconnaissance role four Meteor FR.9s formed the Arabian Peninsula Reconnaissance Flight (APRF) in 1957.

From December 1956 throughout 1957 there was a succession of raids by tribesmen supported by the Yemeni government that required action in the form of reprisals. Targets for 8 Sqn, supplemented by 249 Sqn in July, included Saudaniya, Hadhaiya, Danaba, Lazarak and Huzarak. In March Venom FB.1 WR363 was damaged by small-arms fire, a not unusual event, but in this case sufficiently serious to cause the aircraft to be written off. March also saw Operation *Zipper*, which comprised concerted attacks on sangars around Dhala. During this operation WR357 was lost pressing home an attack near high ground at Lazarak.

Shackleton WL752/D of 37 Sqn on a support sortie over typical terrain. The Shackleton was a most versatile aircraft and it was used extensively for offensive strikes in Aden. (*via A S Thomas*)

At one stage there were three Hunter squadrons based at Khormaksar, all flying the FGA.9 variant. In addition 1417 Flt operated the FR.10 in the tactical reconnaissance role. These two Hunters of 43 Sqn are flying low down the Dhala road. *(Crown copyright)*

Further support was added in January 1957 with a detachment of Shackletons of 42 Sqn, followed by the establishment in August of 37 Sqn with four Shackleton MR.2 aircraft, which were to be used for bombing, reconnaissance, troop transporting, strafing, search and rescue, and, last, the role for which the aircraft were designed, maritime reconnaissance. Concurrently 1426 Flight disbanded. The Shackletons were used for the first time at Ghaniyah, strafing Yemeni attackers.

In December Operation *Muggah* comprised attacks against snipers in the Urqub Pass following ambushes of convoys. This was followed in January 1958 by Operation *Counter Battery* against Yemeni troops at Dhimra who had been using an old fort from which to bombard Protectorate forces and villages. A similar exercise was carried out the following month near Qataba. During April and May the Venoms struck rebel targets around Dhala and the Jebel Jihaf, while in July it was the turn of Qa'ashan and Ukaima to be on the receiving end. Venom WR375 was hit by ground fire on 1 July and damaged beyond repair. On the 8th a further Venom, WR503, was shot down with the loss of the pilot while attacking a Yemeni target at Harib.

With very poor surface communications, the need for heavy transports capable of using short strips became pressing as attacks from the Yemen increased. 84 Sqn, long associated with the Middle East, formed with Beverleys at Khormaksar in June 1958. In that month XH118 was lost making an emergency landing at Beihan. To support 8 Sqn, Vampires of 1 Sqn Royal Rhodesian Air Force (RRhAF) were detached from Salisbury in January, followed by 2 Sqn in August. To strengthen the political framework, a Federation of Emirates of the South was established in February 1959, and later in the year Air Forces Middle East (AFME) was formed as part of a unified Middle East Command covering East Africa, Aden, the Gulf and the Indian Ocean.

In October 1958 8 Sqn's Venoms were busy attacking targets in the Al Khabr region after a convoy had been ambushed. From 1958 use was also made of Royal Navy aircraft from carriers in Aden waters: in March 1960 Sea

This Hunter of 43 Sqn is seen landing at Thumier having expended its rockets during a strike. To enable longer range and loiter time the aircraft is fitted with 230 gal wing tanks. *(Crown copyright)*

For years the Beverley was the main in-theatre transport aircraft with 30 and 84 Sqns; the scorpion artwork on the nose of XM106/S indicates an aircraft with the latter unit. The Beverley was capable of using rolled stone airstrips and is here landing at Habilayn. *(Crown copyright)*

Venoms of 891 Naval Air Squadron from HMS *Centaur* participated in Operation *Damen* against targets in the Yemen, while Sea Vixen FAW.1 fighters of 892 NAS from HMS *Hermes* were to be used in 1963.

Hunters were introduced in January 1960 with 8 Sqn, and as activity increased, 208 Sqn, also with the Hunter, had a permanent detachment at Khormaksar from June, from Eastleigh in Kenya. The Hunters were busy from the outset, and in October they took part in Operation *Niggard*, designed to enable continued construction of the Rabizi road. The transport force was further enhanced by the creation of 233 Sqn with the Valetta C.1, taking over aircraft used by 84 Sqn.

The Army also introduced aircraft to the theatre in the form of the Auster AOP.9s of 16 Flight from April 1961. Army aircraft were based at Falaise airfield at Little Aden to lighten the now considerable load at Khormaksar, and another airstrip with a 1,400 yd tarmac runway was constructed up-country at Beihan in July. Eastern Aden Province was in part policed by the Hadrami Bedouin Legion (HBL), and on 19 July a post was attacked by dissidents, resulting in the death of sixteen HBL personnel. A force of Hunters, Meteors, Shackletons and Twin Pioneers was dispatched to Riyan to seek out and attack the culprits. Later in the year 208 Sqn moved permanently to Khormaksar.

In May 1962 an attempt was made to build an airstrip at Hilyan. A reconnaissance Shackleton in the area was hit by small-arms fire, and a Beaver which subsequently landed was fired upon. Hunters were called in to strike, but the site was not developed. A further change in the transport force was now made: although ideal for local use, the Beverleys were slow and short ranged, and they were supplemented in June by the less robust but faster Argosies of 105 Sqn for general theatre use.

ESCALATION

In October there was a revolution in the Yemen, which then claimed South Arabia. Attacks from Yemen increased, and on 22 October MiG aircraft of the Egyptian Air Force (EAF) struck at Nuqab near Beihan. The RAF set up patrols along the border, and some days later Hunters destroyed a fort in the Yemen in retaliation. A show of strength was made when a Valiant of 90 Sqn on a *Lone Ranger* exercise flew low along the frontier. Canberra PR.7 aircraft of 13 and 58 Sqns were detached to Khormaksar to track Egyptian arms supply vessels in the Red Sea.

The year 1963 saw Aden merged into the Federation, which then became known as the Federation of South Arabia. Tension increased between the tribes in the Protectorates and the townspeople of Aden, where, in addition, political groups set on independence were growing in strength, some supported by the Egyptian-backed Yemen Republic. The security forces thus had dissident tribes, incursions from the Yemen and terrorist action within Aden to contend with.

Further RAF re-equipment in the year included the establishment of 1417 Flt with the Hunter FR.10 and 26 Sqn with the Belvedere medium-lift helicopter and the transfer of 43 Sqn with the Hunter FGA.9 from Akrotiri, all in March. Khormaksar was now one of the busiest airfields in the world, sharing the single runway with civil movements. December saw a further temporary addition to the base in the form of Il-14 8411: on the 3rd a Yemen Air Force aircraft landed by mistake at Lodar, where its path was blocked to prevent it taking off. The aircraft was subsequently flown by an RAE crew to Khormaksar for evaluation, where it was eventually scrapped.

A state of emergency was declared after a hand grenade was thrown at the High Commissioner at Khormaksar. He and fifty-two others were injured and two died in the attack, which was apparently the work of the People's Socialist Party (PSP), which in 1963 merged with the South Arabian League (SAL) to form the Organization for the Liberation of the Occupied South (OLOS). The other major terrorist group was the National Liberation Front (NLF), which in 1966 was to merge with OLOS to become the Front for the Liberation of Occupied South Yemen (FLOSY).

RADFAN

Operations in 1964 were concentrated on the Radfan area to the east of Thumier. The Quteibi rebelled against the centralized collection of tariffs, and with arms and training from Egyptians in the Yemen they extended their action against traffic using the Dhala road. Some of this traffic was almost certainly arms and British Government-sponsored mercenaries *en route* for the Yemen in support of the Royalist cause in the civil war. Military action rather

On 21 June 1967 XM106 hit a landmine planted on the runway at Habilayn. The starboard undercarriage was blown off resulting in the wing striking the ground. The aircraft was bulldozed clear and stripped. Notable is the dark earth/light stone camouflage finish introduced from 1964. *(Crown copyright)*

than air control was decided upon, and Operation *Nutcracker* was launched on 4 January, its purpose to demonstrate the Government's ability to enter and control the Radfan at will.

Three battalions of the Federal Regular Army (FRA), as the APL had now been renamed, were assembled at Thumier with armoured cars, some British Army tanks and J Battery 3rd Regiment Royal Horse Artillery. One FRA battalion was airlifted by Belvederes and four Wessex HU.5s of 815 NAS from HMS *Centaur* to ridges overlooking Wadi Rabwa. As pickets were established and 105 mm howitzers lifted into position, a number came under attack, and the Hunters and Shackletons were called in for close support. The main force then worked along the Wadi, and engineers began the construction of a road to Wadi Taym. One battalion moved along the Bakn ridge to Jebel Haqla with helicopter support and Hunter cover.

The bulk of the forces then moved back on Thumier, and the Rabwa road was opened in February. By March it was clear that the area could be contained only at the expense of enabling more incursions from the Yemen, and the force withdrew, leaving Thumier garrisoned; shortly afterwards, the Rabwa road was closed by the Quteibi. A major raid across the border was launched on 13 March by armed Yemeni helicopters supported by MiG-17 fighters, the targets being the village of Bulaq near Beihan and a Frontier Guard (FG) post. On the 28th, eight Hunters retaliated by attacking and destroying Harib fort.

There were also reports of a group of 700 well-trained dissidents operating in the Radfan, and attacks on convoys on the Dhala road increased. The Government decided that further military action in strength was required, and the 'Radfan Force', abbreviated to 'Radforce', was established. The force comprised 45 Royal Marine Commando, a company of 3 Para, two FRA battalions, a Royal Tank Regiment squadron with armoured cars, J battery 3 RHA, a Royal Engineer (RE) troop, 3 Troop 22 Special Air Service (SAS) Regiment and, in due course, a battalion of the East Anglian Regiment. All RAF units were available for support, although by now 233 Sqn had disbanded.

The Argosy complemented the Beverley from 1962 with 105 Sqn. It was neither as robust as, nor did it have the short landing and take-off performance of, the older aircraft. XP439 is on the apron at Sharjah in 1966. *(Author's collection)*

Initially no Navy helicopters were in the theatre, but the Army now had the first Scout helicopters with 13 Flt; in addition, the SAR Flight had re-equipped with the more powerful Whirlwind HAR.10.

The objectives of the new initiative were to end the operations of dissidents in the area, to stop revolt spreading and to keep the Dhala road clear. The basic plan was for troops to dominate the Danaba basin and Wadi Taym, thought to be the centre of dissident occupation. Withdrawal to the Yemen would also be denied. The Commando force could not be lifted quickly enough to the heights with the available helicopters, so a landing of 120 Paras on a feature named 'Cap Badge' was planned, the target to be marked by the SAS lifted in by a Scout helicopter at last light on 29 April. Unfortunately the SAS group was discovered and subjected to intense opposition throughout the 30th. Hunters of 43 and 208 Sqns fired some 127 rockets and 7,131 rounds of ammunition in very close support, and the group withdrew at night, losing two members.

During the 30th the Marines had advanced along the Wadi Rabwa and branched north up the Wadi Boran to link up with the Paras, but the latter could not now be dropped, and the advance was halted. Some 105 mm howitzers were moved up, under Hunter cover, to positions from where they could fire on 'Cap Badge'. The 1st East Anglians were now released to the operation, and they moved from Thumier to the Marines' position, enabling the latter to take 'Cap Badge' on foot on the night of 4/5 May. 3 Para had also been brought up to Thumier and moved along through the Marines' positions to the Wadi Taym.

Out of effective artillery range, the Paras relied on Hunter support. Resupply was effected by the Belvederes, Scouts and, later, Beavers of 15 Flt flying into a newly created airstrip at Danaba, 'Monk's Field'. Thus all the initial objectives were achieved by 5 May. The difficulties experienced demonstrated the need for a stronger force, and on 11 May a regular Brigade HQ, 39 Bde from Northern Ireland, was established with additional infantry battalions – the balance of 3 Para, a second armoured-car squadron, 170 Battery 7 RHA with 5.5 in. guns and a Centurion tank troop of the 16/5th Queen's Royal Lancers.

From 24 May six Wessex helicopters of 815 NAS were available, and Thumier had been extended to take Beverleys. The Wessexes were a welcome addition, as the Belvederes, although essential for lifting large artillery pieces to otherwise inaccessible heights, were suffering from sand ingestion. In the relative lull a number of areas were identified for air attack, and the Hunter and Shackleton units carried out continuous air strikes. The Hunters worked by day, and the pressure was maintained at night by the Shackletons of 37 Sqn supplemented by two aircraft from 224 Sqn from Gibraltar.

The Belvedere twin-rotor helicopter served in Aden and Borneo, carrying up to 18 fully-equipped troops or 6,000 lbs of freight. It appears that XG467/C of 26 Sqn is being refuelled by hand during the Radfan campaign.
(J Manton via A S Thomas)

The new focus of enemy activity was deemed to be the Bakri ridge and Wadi Misrah to the south, and an exploratory drive was begun along the ridge from the 18th by men of 3 Para after reconnaissance by Scout helicopters. The Paras found little opposition until they reached Qudeishi. Resistance at this highest point on the ridge was heavy, and it fell only after repeated strikes by the Hunters. By 24 May the Paras were in control of the whole area. It was decided to push further south to occupy the dominant Jebel Huriyah, having first cleared the Wadis Misrah and Dhubsan.

All stores were manhandled, and again the Paras relied on Hunter close support to achieve their objectives. As they moved along the Wadi Dhubsan they were fired upon from a strong force of dissidents, and a Scout helicopter which had managed to support a reconnaissance was badly damaged by rifle and machine-gun fire. During this period the Scouts operated in threes, with one aircraft armed with three GPMGs and the other two carrying four soldiers, with a Wessex in support carrying up to fourteen men. Such groups could operate with a degree of independence, certainly until further support arrived.

By the end of May Radforce was in a position to attack Jebel Huriyah. The 1st East Anglians picketed the sides of Wadi Misrah while 4 RTR cleared the bed of the wadi. The advance continued to 4 June, by which time the foothills had been reached, and 2 FRA joined the assault force ready for the final attack. This began on 7 June, and the FRA was immediately pinned down by gunfire from a ridge. Despite concerted Hunter strikes and artillery assault, the insurgents held their position. The attack continued on the 8th, and it was found that the rebels had withdrawn, having suffered heavy losses. The final assault on the Jebel was made on the night of 10/11 June, the way being lighted by a succession of flares dropped by the Shackletons. The peak was reached before dawn.

XG461/G of 26 Sqn is seen preparing to lift what appears to be light field artillery at Khormaksar. The Belvedere was only built in small numbers and lasted in service only for eight years. *(J Manton via A S Thomas)*

All territorial objectives had now been met, but action continued until November. Air control was maintained, and gradually the tribes sued for peace. Hunters were directed by Beavers acting as forward-air-control (FAC) aircraft, and until retirement in September the Austers of 13 Flt operated in their designated role spotting for the artillery. The Army Air Corps was now operating from four strips in the region.

The Navy helicopters also performed magnificently in moving troops and supplies, often under fire. The Navy is also understood to have flown some strike sorties with the Buccaneers of 800 NAS from HMS *Eagle*. During May and June RAF Hunters flew 642 sorties, fired 2,508 rockets and used 183,900 cannon rounds. In the period the Belvederes flew 1,027 sorties, carrying 1,798 passengers and over 1 million lb of freight. During the year the Beavers of 15 Flt AAC made nearly 10,000 landings, with an average sortie time of just under twenty minutes. These figures convey some idea of the intensity of flying during the Radfan operations.

URBAN WARFARE AND INDEPENDENCE

In July 1964 the British Government announced its intention of granting independence by 1968, but with the retention of a military base. This resulted in fighting in and around Aden both between Nationalist groups and with the security forces. During 1965 equipment changes included the introduction of the Wessex with 78 Sqn, which transferred its Twin Pioneers to 21 Sqn which had moved up from Eastleigh, and the first AAC Sioux troop.

For a variety of reasons, not least the availability of small, relatively inexpensive, helicopters, the Army had decided to integrate its air assets primarily into field units. Thus from late 1964 infantry, armoured, engineer and artillery units operated their own airborne 'jeeps', while flights and squadrons were retained at theatre level. This organic scheme lasted only to 1972, but it affected Army flying through the later stages of the Aden campaign.

In urban guerrilla warfare, strike aircraft are of little use, but the Wessexs were able to place troops quickly where needed, while the Sioux were used for a range of reconnaissance and resupply tasks around the town. Twin Pioneers were used to drop leaflets.

During 1965 and 1966 operations continued up-country, and a mobile radar was set up at Mukeiras to warn of any air threat from the Yemen. On numerous occasions there were MiG attacks on villages in the Beihan area, although the RAF was now prevented from making retaliatory raids. As the situation in Aden deteriorated, the British Government announced in February 1966 that it would not retain a military presence after independence, and this only served to increase violence and lose all support for the British from hitherto friendly leaders. Those who remained loyal were attacked; several died when DC-3 VR-AAN of Aden Airways blew up on 22 November 130 miles east of Aden as a result of sabotage. As British forces prepared to leave in 1967, unrest spread from the mainland, and in March Beverleys of 30 Sqn flew to Riyan to lift an HBL force onto Socotra Island to quell a local revolt. In June there were mutinies both by the South Arabian Army (SAA), as the FRA had been renamed, and by the APL, which had become the South Arabian Police (SAP).

In July Wessex helicopters lifted a company of the Argyll and Sutherland Highlanders to the Crater district of Aden to regain control; earlier, on 20 June, Sioux XT173 had been brought down in the area by rifle fire on a resupply sortie. From now on RAF units disbanded or moved to airfields in the Gulf. By October 21, 37 and 30 Sqns had disbanded and 105 and 8 sqns had moved. The Beverleys of 84 Sqn were active in pulling back forces from the hinterland into Aden, and on 6 October XM106 was destroyed at Thumier when it ran over an anti-tank mine.

The RAF now prepared for its largest airlift since Berlin in 1948. Earlier in the year, more than 9,000 dependants had been flown out to Gatwick in RAF transports and VC-10 airliners of British United Airways (BUA). The military withdrawal was carefully planned, and from 1 November 5,800 men were flown out to Muharraq in stages on Hercules of 36 Sqn and Britannias of 99 and 511 Sqns, with Belfasts of 53 Sqn moving freight. The last Army units to move were the Argylls on the 26th, on which day 42 and 45 RMC moved into Khormaksar; 45 Commando was then airlifted to Muharraq. From Muharraq the men were flown directly to Lyneham by VC-10s of 10 Sqn, chartered VC-10s or Britannias. The final withdrawal was that of 42 Commando by Wessexes of 848 NAS to HMS *Albion*, covered by armed Wessexes of 78 Sqn, whose helicopters then embarked on assault ships and *Albion*. The final

The Wessex made a significant contribution to the campaign in southern Arabia, serving with 78 Sqn from 1965. XR508/B is placing a 105 mm lightweight pack howitzer on a mountain ridge. (*Crown copyright*)

To supplement the locally based Javelins of 60 Sqn reinforcements were sent from the UK. 64 Sqn flew out to Tengah from Binbrook in March 1965 where it was disbanded in 1967. FAW.9 XH874/H. See Section 7.2. (*Author*)

An Argosy of 215 Sqn based at Changi running up for take-off at Kuching. In the foreground is what – to the author's untrained eye – appears to be a light naval AA gun. See Section 7.2. (*G Pitchfork*)

Going.....What appear to be fuel drums about to be launched from the ramp of an Argosy over a small airstrip. See Section 7.2. (*G Pitchfork*)

Going.....The strip appears below. See Section 7.2.

(*G Pitchfork*)

Gone!.....Parachutes mushroom over the strip after another successful drop. See Section 7.2. (*G Pitchfork*)

Venerable Hastings TG525/525 of 48 Sqn with underwing tanks taxies in at Kuching. See Section 7.2. (*G Pitchfor*k)

The weather in Borneo made flying challenging as can be seen in the low cloud over the hills. A 52 Sqn Valetta lands at Kuching, demonstrating the high-visibility nose and fin panels. See Section 7.2. (*G Pitchfork*)

Busy scene at Kuching with Whirlwinds of 103 Sqn in the background and Hunter FGA.9 D of 20 Sqn nearest. See Section 7.2. (*G Pitchfork*)

Army Auster AOP.9 XN409 at Kuching. In the background is the wreck of 64 Sqn Javelin XH874, seen in happier times in an earlier photograph. See Section 7.2. (*G Pitchfork*)

Scout AH.1 XP906, probably of 14 Liaison Flight, receives attention on the apron at Kuching. See Section 7.2. (*G Pitchfork*)

From April 1967 the squadrons of the Ballykelly Wing took over responsibility for the Beira patrol. WL737?Z of 219 Sqn at Majunga 1970. See Section 7.5. (*A S Thomas*)

The Britannia was involved in the original oil-lift and then in re-supply of the RAF detachments in southern Africa. XM491 is at Majunga in 1970. See Section 7.5. (*A S Thomas*)

Several Hercules C.1 have been adapted for special forces use by 47 Sqn. XV213/213 is fitted with wingtip *Orange Blossom* ESM pod. See Section 8.2. (*Author*)

In the third Cod War the Nimrods of the Kinloss Wing were aided by ageing Hastings T.5s of 230 OCU, normally used to train V-bomber navigators. TG505 is wearing high visibility markings. See Section 8.3. (*Crown copyright*)

The Gazelle was a fine utility helicopter which saw extensive service in Northern Ireland. XZ309 was with 664 Sqn. See Section 8.4.
(*Westland Helicopters*)

Army Scout AH.1 XV126 of 666 Sqn. See Section 8.4. (*Author*)

The Gazelle was unique in that it served with the Army, the Royal Navy, the Royal Air Force and the Royal Marines. XX380/A is from 3 CBAS. See Section 8.4. (*Author*)

The Army is understandably coy about the full range of tasks undertaken by its Islanders and Defenders. ZG848 seen here at Middle Wallop employs a range of sensors. See Section 8.4. (*Author*)

From 1993 Chinooks of 7 Sqn were detached to Aldergrove in support of conventional and special forces. ZA711/ET shows to good effect the contemporaneous camouflage scheme. See Section 8.4. (*Author*)

In the event of a serious seaborne threat to British vessels or rigs, the Buccaneers of 12 and 208 Sqns at RAF Lossiemouth were designated in the maritime strike role. XX894/894 of 12 Sqn taxies out for a local sortie. See Section 8.5. (*Author*)

Nimrod MR.2 XV228/28 of 206 Sqn overflies and oil rig in the Moray Firth close to its Kinloss base at the height of Operation *Tapestry*. The aircraft is newly finished in the hemp camouflage scheme. See Section 8.5. (*Crown copyright*)

Responsibility for maritime strike passed from the Buccaneer to the Tornado. In banking over the Scottish coast this aircraft of 617 Sqn shows off its *Sea Eagle* anti-shipping missiles, long-range tanks and defensive suite. See Section 8.5. *(BAe Systems)*

Two Buccaneers of 208 Sqn swiftly depart Akrotiri for a demonstration flight over Beirut. The aircraft appear unarmed although fitted with the ALQ-101 ECM pod and *Pave Spike* laser designator. See Section 9.1. *(G Pitchfork)*

18 Sqn and 240 OCU provided Chinooks for support on Cyprus. Illustrated is HC.2 ZA670/BN of 18 Sqn. See Section 9.1. (*Crown copyright*)

With 42 mission symbols Tornado GR.1 ZA465/FK *Foxy Killer* of 16 Sqn topped the sortie ranking. Based at Tabuk the tally included 14 *Paveway* sorties and the nose marking also appear to include two *Scud* missile launchers. See Section 9.4. (*Author*)

Tornado GR.1 ZA447/EA *MiG Eater* of 15 Sqn also displays mission markings including three JP-233, 23 conventional bombing and fourteen *Paveway* attacks. See Section 9.4. (*Author*)

Minimally marked and un-named Tornado ZD810/AA of 9 Sqn completed 28 bombing missions and eight *ALARM* attacks. See Section 9.4. (*Author*)

ZA410/EX of 15 Sqn was a replacement aircraft which did not fly operationally during the Gulf War. It shows to good effect the pink camouflage scheme adopted and, unusually, carries a centre-line fuel tank. See Section 9.4. (*Author*)

Jaguar GR.1A XZ118/Y *Buster Gonad* displays an impressive mission tally including six 2 x 1,000 lb bomb, seven 4 x 1,000 lb bomb, eighteen 2 x CBU-87, two 4 x CVR-7 rocket sorties and one *Sidewinder* AAM fired. The underwing store seen here is the ALQ-101 ECM pod while *Sidewinders* are evident on the overwing rails. See Section 9.4. (*Crown copyright*)

Jaguar XZ367/P *Debbie* flew 40 missions. Underwing store on the right wing is the *Phimat* chaff pod. See Section 9.4. (*Author*)

Close-up of the stores carried by the Jaguar including overwing *Sidewinder* practice round, two 1,000 lb practice bombs on the centre-line and the Matra *Phimat* chaff pod and fuel tank below the wing. See Section 9.4. (*Author*)

Before the RAF Wessex helicopters arrived on the scene, the Royal Navy provided a detachment from 815 NAS to support ground forces in Operation *Nutcracker* in 1964. XM843/301B from HMS *Centaur* basks in the sun at Khormaksar. *(A S Thomas)*

phase was supported by Buccaneers and Sea Vixens of 800 and 899 NAS respectively, from HMS *Eagle*. Although there had been contingency plans in the event of fighting, the withdrawal took place without incident.

SEQUEL

Aden had been an important base until the British withdrawal of forces east of Suez, and an alternative staging post was retained on the island of Gan. The security forces had fought what turned out to be a number of pointless battles over the years in a hostile environment, with a loss of ninety dead and 510 wounded.

In the Yemen Arab Republic to the north, the civil war which had festered since 1962 continued until 1970, when the country – which has no formal north-eastern boundary with Saudi Arabia – was recognized by the latter. In the south, on the departure of the British, the People's Republic of South Yemen was declared on 30 November 1967, and this then became the first Arab Marxist government with the formation of the People's Democratic Republic of Yemen in 1970. There had been numerous border skirmishes between the two Yemens in 1972, 1978 and 1979, but in due course the countries were unified on 22 May 1990 as the Republic of Yemen.

There was no integration of government or armed forces, however, and in April 1994 serious fighting broke out between north and south. This war left the south defeated.

SCOTTISH AVIATION TWIN PIONEER

The Twin Pioneer was built on the success of the single-engine STOL utility Pioneer, and first flew as a sixteen-seat civil transport in 1955. The type, which used two of the same Leonides engine, was bought for the RAF to complement the Pioneer.

The Twin Pioneer **CC Mark 1** first flew in military form on 29 August 1957, and after A&AEE evaluation it joined 78 Sqn in Aden in October 1958. The Twin Pioneer could be armed with bombs on the undercarriage struts and a movable Bren gun in the rear door. Range was in the order of 400 miles loaded, and it could operate comfortably from 1,000 ft strips.

The **CC Mark 2** was similar in all respects to the CC.1, but with many machined and fabricated components replaced by forgings and castings. The final seven aircraft were built to this standard. The last three aircraft were fitted with the more powerful Leonides 531 engine, which was later retro-fitted to earlier machines.

Transport units equipped – 21, 78, 152, 209, 225, 230; 1310 Flt

DE HAVILLAND CANADA BEAVER

From 1952 a DHC.2 Beaver Srs 1 was evaluated by the RAF, and by 1954 it was joined by an Srs 2 aircraft. The Beaver had flown originally in 1947. As the time drew near for the Army to assume responsibility for its own flying in 1957, decisions about a utility aircraft were deferred, especially given the 4,000 lb weight limit initially determined for Army aircraft.

The AL Mark 1 Beaver was eventually ordered against Specification GSOR 342. Deliveries of forty-two aircraft (plus four for Oman with British serials) began in late 1961. The Beaver could accommodate four passengers in addition to a crew of two over a range of up to 700 miles. Underwing racks allowed supplies or markers to be dropped. First deliveries, after the AAC Centre, were to 15 Flight in the Middle East, and the Beaver was finally retired (in Northern Ireland) in 1989.

Liaison units equipped – 655, 667, 668; 6, 8, 11, 12, 13, 14, 15, 18, 19, 30, 31, 130, 131, 132 Flts; Beaver Flt NI (7 Regt); Laos Embassy

Southern Arabia (Aden and Radfan), 1950–67

Unit	Aircraft	Base	From	To
RAF				
8 Sqn	Brigand B.1	Khormaksar	6.49	1.53[1]
	Vampire FB.9		12.52	7.55[2]
	Venom FB.1, FB.4		3.55	1.60[3]
	Meteor FR.9		1.58	1.8.59[4]
	Hunter FGA.9		1.60	8.8.67[5]
	Hunter FR.10		4.61	1.3.63[6]
32 Sqn det	Vampire FB.9	Khormaksar	1.53	2.53
208 Sqn det	Meteor FR.9	Khormaksar	26.3.56	7.8.56
73 Sqn	Venom FB.1	Khormaksar	21.7.56	21.12.56
249 Sqn det	Venom FB.4	Khormaksar	13.7.57	15.10.57
208 Sqn	Hunter FGA.9	Khormaksar	15.11.61	8.6.64
43 Sqn	Hunter FGA.9	Khormaksar	1.3.63	14.10.67
SF	Meteor FR.9, PR.10	Khormaksar	1.9.58	31.7.59
APRF	Meteor FR.9	Khormaksar	1.8.59[7]	1.1.60
1417 Flt	Hunter FR.10	Khormaksar	1.3.63[8]	8.9.67
7 Sqn det	Lincoln B.2	Khormaksar	2.55	1.1.56[9]
1426 Flt	Lincoln B.2	Khormaksar	1.1.56	16.1.57
42 Sqn det	Shackleton MR.2	Khormaksar	7.1.57	9.57[10]
37 Sqn	Shackleton MR.2	Khormaksar	21.8.57	7.9.67
13 Sqn det	Canberra PR.9	Khormaksar	23.10.62	11.62
58 Sqn det	Canberra PR.9	Khormaksar	24.10.62	11.62
ACF	Ventura, Valetta C.1, Auster AOP.6	Khormaksar	00.1.46	1.12.51[11]

Unit	Aircraft	Base	From	To
ACS	Valetta C.1, Meteor T.7, Vampire FB.9	Khormaksar	1.12.51	31.8.55[12]
APSF	Anson C.19	Khormaksar	21.9.47	9.9.50[13]
	Anson C.19, Auster AOP.6, Pembroke C.1, Valetta C.1,C.2	Khormaksar	4.2.52[14]	31.8.55[12]
APC&SS[15]	Pembroke C.1, Sycamore HR.14	Khormaksar	1.9.55	31.12.56
30,47,53 Sqns det	Beverley C.1	Khormaksar		5.58
84 Sqn	Valetta C.1	Khormaksar	1.1.57	31.8.60[16]
	Sycamore HR.14		1.1.57	5.58
	Pembroke C.1		1.1.57	6.57
	Beverley C.1		5.58	8.67
30 Sqn det	Beverley C.1	Khormaksar	4.57	6.9.67
105 Sqn	Argosy C.1	Khormaksar	17.6.62	6.8.67
233 Sqn	Valetta C.1	Khormaksar	1.9.60	31.1.64
26 Sqn	Belvedere HC.1	Khormaksar	1.3.63	30.11.65
78 Sqn	Pioneer CC.1	Khormaksar	15.4.56	8.59
	Pembroke C.1		6.58	6.59
	Twin Pioneer CC.1		9.58	6.65
	Wessex HC.2		6.65	13.10.67
MEAF CF	Anson C.19, Dakota C.4, Canberra B.2, Andover CC.2, Hastings C.4	Khormaksar	4.63	1.6.65[17]
21 Sqn	Twin Pioneer CC.1	Khormaksar	1.6.65	9.9.67
	Dakota		8.65	9.9.67
	Andover CC.2		2.67	9.9.67
SAR Flt	Sycamore HR.14	Khormaksar	13.6.58	
	Whirlwind HAR.2			3.64
	Whirlwind HAR.4		2.64	6.67
MEC CS	Hastings C.4, Valetta C.2, Canberra B.2, Dakota C.4, Pembroke C.1	Khormaksar	1.10.61	1.9.67

RAF *Sunray* Lincoln detachments

49 Sqn	Lincoln B.2	Khormaksar	1.54	7.54

RAF Shackleton detachments in support of 37 Sqn; usually three aircraft

224 Sqn	Shackleton MR.2	Khormaksar	9.2.59	8.3.59
224 Sqn			6.63	31.7.63
42 Sqn			1.8.63	63
224 Sqn			20.5.64	8.64
42/206 Sqns[18]	Shackleton MR.3	Sharjah	8.67	29.11.67

NOTES

1 Detachments to Nicosia and Shaibah 1950, 1951 and 1952

2 To Nicosia and Egypt 7.7.53–23.11.53

3 To Iraq, then Akrotiri, 24.7.56–20.12.56 during the Suez war

4 To APRF
5 To Bahrain then Farwania 30.6.61–14.10.61 during the Kuwait crisis
6 To 1417 Flt
7 Ex-Station Flight and C Flt 8 Sqn
8 Ex-FR element of 8 Sqn
9 To 1426 Flt
10 To Oman – replaced by 37 Sqn
11 Aden Comms Flt became Aden Comms Sqn
12 ACS and APSF merged to form APC&SS
13 Absorbed into 8 Sqn
14 Ex-B Flt 8 Sqn
15 To 84 Sqn
16 To 233 Sqn
17 To 21 Sqn
18 To cover withdrawal after disbandment of 37 Sqn

Unit	Aircraft	Base	From	To
Fleet Air Arm				
801 NAS	Sea Hawk FGA.6	HMS *Bulwark*	7.58	9.58
891 NAS	Sea Venom FAW.22			
845 NAS	Whirlwind HAS.7			
801 NAS	Sea Hawk FGA.6	HMS *Centaur*	3.7.59	9.7.59
			3.60	3.60
891 NAS	Sea Venom FAW.22			
810 NAS	Gannet AS.4			
892 NAS	Sea Vixen FAW.1	HMS *Hermes*	7.63	7.63
803 NAS	Scimitar F.1			
892 NAS	Sea Vixen FAW.1	HMS *Centaur*	22.5.64	12.6.64
815 NAS	Wessex HAS.1			
899 NAS	Sea Vixen FAW.2	HMS *Eagle*	3.66	4.66
			9.67	9.67
800 NAS	Buccaneer S.1, S.2			
820 NAS	Wessex HAS.1			
848 NAS	Wessex HU.5	HMS *Albion*	10.67	10.67
Army 653 Sqn				
16 Flt	Auster AOP.9	Falaise	4.61	9.61
15 Flt	Beaver AL.1, Auster AOP.9	Falaise	9.62	14.10.67
13 Flt	Auster AOP.9	Falaise	9.62	9.64
	Scout AH.1		3.64	14.10.67
8 Flt	Beaver AL.1	Falaise	14.10.64	6.67
	Scout AH.1	Habilayn	6.67	
Army air platoons and troops				
Infantry regiments				
1 WG AP	Sioux AH.1	Falaise	4.66	10.66
1 IG AP	Sioux AH.1	Falaise	10.66	67
1 PoW AP	Sioux AH.1	Falaise	4.66	9.66
1 RNF AP	Sioux AH.1	Falaise	9.66	6.67
1 KOB AP	Sioux AH.1	Falaise	2.67	8.67
Armoured regiments				
QIRH	Auster AOP.9	Falaise	62	64

10 RH AT	Sioux AH. 1	Falaise	5.65	9.65
4/7 RDG AT	Sioux AH. 1	Falaise	8.65	9.66
5 IDG AT	Sioux AH. 1	Falaise	8.65	11.65
1 RTR AT	Sioux AH. 1	Falaise	12.65	10.66
QDG AT	Sioux AH. 1	Falaise	9.66	67
Artillery regiments				
19 LRRA AT	Sioux AH.1	Falaise	3.65	9.65
1 RHA	Sioux AH.1	Falaise	9.65	6.67
47 LRRA AT	Sioux AH.1	Falaise	6.67	8.67
Royal Marines				
45 RMC AT	Sioux AH.1	Falaise, Habilayn	6.66	21.11.67
Consolidated				
MELF AT	Sioux AH.1	Falaise	10.66	8.67
RAC/RA AT	Sioux AH.1	Falaise	8.67	10.67

Key

IDG – Inniskilling Dragoon Guards; IG – Irish Guards; KOB – King's Own Borderers; LRRA – Light Regiment Royal Artillery; MELF – Middle East Land Forces; PoW – Prince of Wales Own Regiment of Yorkshire; QDG – Queen's Dragoon Guards; QIRH – Queen's Irish Royal Hussars; RA – Royal Artillery; RAC – Royal Armoured Corps; RDG – Royal Dragoon Guards; RH – Royal Hussars; RHA – Royal Horse Artillery; RMC – Royal Marine Commando; RNF – Royal Northumberland Fusiliers; RTR – Royal Tank Regiment; WG – Welsh Guards

Royal Rhodesian Air Force

1 Sqn	Vampire FB.9	Khormaksar	1.58	20.3.58
2 Sqn	Vampire FB.9	Khormaksar	8.58	10.58

Airstrips – Am Ruseis, Ataq, Beihan, Dhala, Lodar, Mukeiras, Nisab, Perim, Thumier/Habilayn, Wadi Ayn

5.2   OMAN, 1952–9

INTRODUCTION

Britain has long maintained close links with Oman through a succession of treaties to protect her oil interests and sea routes. For many years Saudi Arabia had contested the border at the key crossroads of Buraimi Oasis, but when the area was thought to have potential oil reserves a Saudi Arabian party of about eighty settled in the village of Hamasa on 31 August 1952.

The British Government protested, and from 15 September a small force of Trucial Oman Levies (TOL) was dispatched to the village, and three Vampire FB.5s of 6 Sqn, supported by a Valetta, were flown to Sharjah from Habbaniyah. After demonstrations and leaflet drops, talks began, and the aircraft returned to Iraq in October.

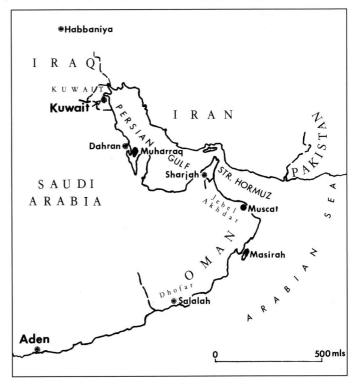

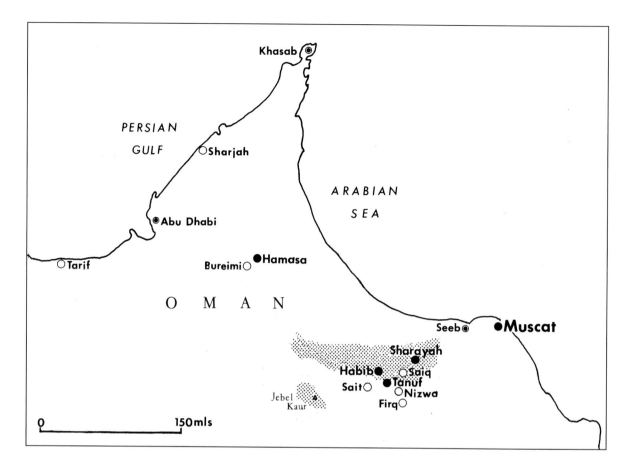

8 Sqn Venom FB.4s were operational at Sharjah through 1957 to 1959. *(via A S Thomas)*

Support in Oman was mainly from units based in Aden and detached. However, when Aden was relinquished, 152 Sqn moved down the coast to Sharjah. Twin Pioneer XM291 was one of its aircraft. *(Author's collection)*

INSURGENCY

The talks dragged on, and in March 1953 it was decided to mount a blockade of the Saudi investment. The Vampires returned, but because of runway corruption through jet efflux from the small aircraft they were replaced by four Meteor PR.9s of 208 Sqn. These aircraft treated the runway no more kindly, and from the end of April two Lancaster GR.3s each from 37 and 38 Sqns at Malta were detached to Habbaniyah to operate from Sharjah. The aircraft were used on reconnaissance duties but could barely be spared from NATO commitments in the Mediterranean. They were in turn replaced by Valettas from the Aden Communications Flight for a few weeks in July until two Lancaster PR.1s of 683 Sqn took over. With the imminent disbandment of 683 Sqn, 1417 Flt was formed on Ansons at Bahrein, and they supported the blockade until 15 August 1954, when the Saudi force withdrew.

Throughout the operation the use of offensive airpower was resisted as the Saudi party was almost certainly supported by US interests, critically the Arabian-American Oil Company (ARAMCO), which at the time operated not only C-46 transports but also B-26 light bombers. In addition, in June 1951 the US had concluded rights for the use of Dhahran airfield for five years, renewed in 1956.

In January 1955 there were reports of a Saudi Arabian group entering Oman in northern Dhofar. From 23 January Valettas from Aden, supported by two Lincoln B.2s of 7 Sqn, mounted reconnaissance sorties to no effect; they were called off in May. Then, in September, Saudi Arabian aircraft were sighted dropping 'civilians' at the airstrip at Buraimi. From 25 October a force of TOL, supported by Lincolns, Valettas, Ansons, Pembrokes and Venom FB.1s of 6 Sqn, surrounded the Saudi posts and removed the incumbents by Anson and Pembroke to Bahrein. To reinforce governmental authority, the Lincolns demonstrated over Hamasa. The operation ended on 27 October.

The Saudis next courted the Imam Ghalib bin Ah, based on Nizwa, who barely accepted the authority of Sultan Said bin Taimur. The Sultan decided to act, and on 15 December 1955 a force of Muscat and Oman Field Force (MOFF) and TOL occupied Nizwa, having been moved up by Valetta, 1417 Flt and 6 Sqn again supporting the operation. The Imam's brother Talib escaped to Saudi Arabia, where, possibly with ARAMCO help, he formed the Omani Liberation Army.

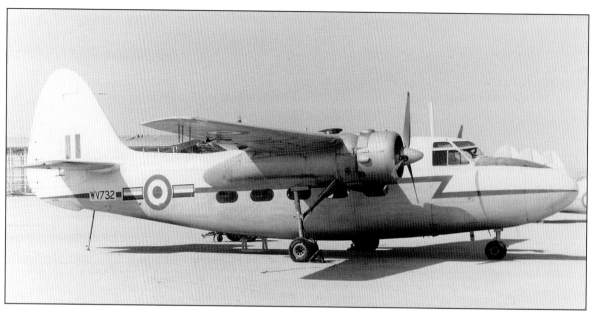

Another type serving with 152 Sqn was the eight-seat Pembroke. WV732 is seen sporting the unit markings abreast the fuselage roundel which was a relic of the days when as a fighter squadron 152 flew Meteors. *(Author's collection)*

Through 1956 the Oasis area was kept under scrutiny by Lincolns, Ansons and Pembrokes, but it was not until 14 June 1957 that Talib landed near Muscat, joining the Imam and moving up to the Jebel Kaur. Within a month the OLA had occupied many villages in the area, and with the potential loss of central Oman the Sultan sought British help. Venom FB.4s of 6 and 249 Sqns moved to Sharjah, and Beverleys and a Valetta of 84 Sqn and two Shackletons of 37 Sqn were detached to Sharjah and Bahrein. From 24 July the Venoms began attacking forts at six locations, including Nizwa, Tanuf and Firq. Forty-eight hours before the attacks, Shackletons dropped warning leaflets. A large area was proscribed, and all daylight movement resulted in strafing or bombing from patrolling aircraft.

The peak of air activity was on the 30th, when Meteor FR.9s of 208 Sqn and a Canberra PR.7, probably from 58 Sqn, also participated. After the period of softening up from the air, ground forces moved into the area on 7 August, and, with Venom support called in by air contact teams (ACT), first Firq then Nizwa were occupied. The OLA now withdrew to the impenetrable Jebel Akhdar, a fertile plateau above 7,000 ft with few, easily guarded approaches. From here the OLA presented less of a threat, and most British forces withdrew, leaving detachments of 8 Sqn and 1417 Flt. On 25 September the Trucial Oman Scouts (TOS), as the TOL had been renamed, made a probing reconnaissance of the lower slopes of Jebel Akhdar, supported by a Shackleton.

The rebels soon took the initiative, and in October nearly captured Tanuf. The Sultan's Armed Forces (SAF), with RAF help, attempted to force a route to Habib on the Jebel, but this failed, and so a blockade was attempted, to halt the flow of arms, although the British Government was keen not to get drawn into a major confrontation. In February 1958 two 5.5 in howitzers, with a range of 17,000 yd, were set up and began shelling the summit villages, while the RAF concentrated on attacking the water-supply system in the hope of so disrupting the pattern of life that the villagers would deny support to the OLA. Nevertheless, the supply of arms continued, and the rebels were able to mine approach tracks, making the prospect of assault virtually impossible.

Clearly, air control by itself would not contain, let alone eliminate, the OLA. From July the blockade was tightened, and, while plans for a paradrop or heliborne assault were considered (and rejected for a range of technical reasons), the RAF again increased their attacks. In one week in September Shackletons used 148 1,000 lb bombs, while Sea Hawk and Sea Venom fighters from HMS *Bulwark* joined the action for a few days, flying seventy-seven sorties. It was now decided to bring in D Squadron, 22 SAS Regiment, from Malaya.

As the unit settled down to probing the approaches and determining its tactics, it was joined by A Squadron and a number of Kenyan trackers. The final assault was made on the night of 26/7 January 1959, and the plateau was reached before dawn after a magnificent climb during which ropes were used. By the 30th the key villages of Saiq, Habib and Sharayah were occupied.

From 9 February the SAS and RAF units were withdrawn, but 152 Sqn, which had formed from 1417 Flt in September, remained at Muharraq to support the SAP. An airstrip was cleared near Saiq to help with the process of reconstruction. During the course of the campaign Shackletons of 37 Sqn flew 429 bombing sorties, while the Venoms of 8 Sqn flew 1,315 sorties.

SEQUEL

For several years insurgents continued to enter Oman from Saudi Arabia to lay landmines and harass the local population. To counter these actions was beyond the resources of the authorities, although the Oman Gendarmerie was formed in 1960 to complement the SAF. The incursions and landmine activity dwindled over time, although a Marxist group attempted to assassinate a senior government minister. Several bombs were also planted on civil aircraft around this time.

Oman, 1952–9

Unit	Aircraft	Base	From	To
RAF				
6 Sqn	Vampire FB.5	Sharjah	15.9.52	5.54
6 Sqn det	Venom FB.1	Sharjah	2.54	12.55
208 Sqn det	Meteor FR.9	Sharjah	4.53	4.53
		Sharjah	7.57	8.57
37 and 38 sqns det	Lancaster GR.3	Sharjah ex-Luqa	4.53	7.53
ACS det	Valetta C.1	Sharjah	7.53	7.53
683 Sqn det	Lancaster PR.1	Sharjah	7.53	30.11.53
1417 Flt	Anson C.19	Muharraq	9.53	10.55
	Pembroke C.1		10.55	29.9.58[1]
7 Sqn det	Lincoln B.2	Khormaksar	23.1.55	10.55
1426 Flt det	Lincoln B.2	Sharjah	2.56	12.56
249 Sqn det	Venom FB.4	Sharjah	7.57	8.57
8 Sqn det	Venom FB.4	Sharjah	7.57	9.2.59
37 Sqn det	Shackleton MR.2	Masirah	7.57	9.2.59
58 Sqn	Canberra PR.7	Bahrein	7.57	8.57
84 Sqn	Valetta C.1	Sharjah	7.57	2.59
	Beverley C.1	Bahrein	5.58	2.59
42 Sqn det	Shackleton MR.2	Masirah	58	58
228 Sqn det	Shackleton MR.2	Masirah	9.58	12.58
224 Sqn det	Shackleton MR.2	Masirah	1.59	2.59
SAR Flt det	Sycamore HR.14	Sharjah	7.57	2.59
152 Sqn	Pembroke C.1	Muharraq	1.10.58	
	Twin Pioneer CC.1		12.58	
Fleet Air Arm				
801 NAS	Sea Hawk FGA.6	HMS *Bulwark*	9.58	9.58
891 NAS	Sea venom FAW.22	HMS *Bulwark*	9.58	9.58
849 NAS (D)	Skyraider AEW.1	HMS *Bulwark*	9.58	9.58

NOTES

1 to 152 Sqn

5.3   SUEZ, 1956

INTRODUCTION

Having had a long-term interest in Egypt, the British withdrew forces in 1955, retaining stocks and an agreement for the use and defence of the critical Suez Canal. Under President Nasser Egypt looked to the West for arms. However, the West refused, so the Soviet Union, via Czechoslovakia, stepped in. The West withdrew financial support for the economically essential Aswan High Dam, and critically, on 26 July 1956, Nasser nationalized the Suez Canal.

The Canal provided an economic route from Europe to the Far East in terms of both time and money, as in the mid-1950s shipping was still the prime mover of men and *matériel*. On the day the Canal was nationalized the British Prime Minister, Anthony Eden, asked the Chiefs of Staff to plan for a military intervention, the first meeting at which the issue was considered being on 27 July. Not only had the UK to contemplate the loss of revenues, but Nasser might limit the Canal's use; in any event the Egyptians were considered technically incapable of operating and managing it.

The French Prime Minister, Guy Mollet, suggested to Eden a joint venture, and planning for an invasion of

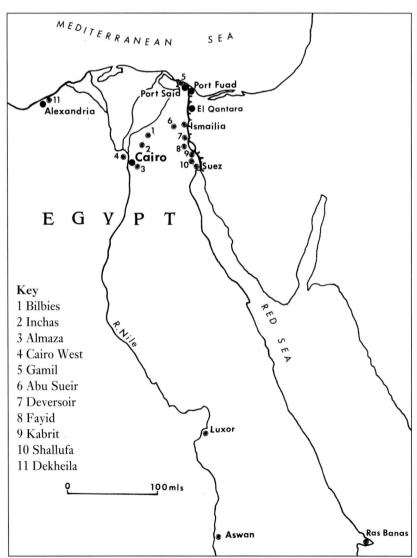

Key
1 Bilbies
2 Inchas
3 Almaza
4 Cairo West
5 Gamil
6 Abu Sueir
7 Deversoir
8 Fayid
9 Kabrit
10 Shallufa
11 Dekheila

Egypt followed, the operation to be headed by General Sir Charles Keightley. On 2 August it was announced that Canberra squadrons would be flown to Malta, UK reservists were called up, and at Toulon the French invasion force began forming. Three days later troops of the 16th Parachute Brigade left Portsmouth for Cyprus on board the carrier HMS *Theseus*, and a further four days later two infantry battalions were dispatched to Malta. No sooner had the Paras reached Cyprus than they were flown back to the UK for training, urgently needed both by the paratroopers and the transport pilots.

THE PLAN

The original plan, requiring some 80,000 troops, was for an assault on Alexandria, followed by a drive to Cairo. Known initially by the codename *Hamilcar*, and later *Musketeer*, a new, more realistic plan, *Musketeer Revise*, was offered in mid-August. This plan called for a seaborne and airborne assault on Port Said by the

Early to arrive on Malta were the Valiants of 207 and 214 Sqns. WP219 of 207 Sqn is at Luqa in the early bare metal finish. By way of contrast, in the background at right may be seen Beaufighters of the locally based target facilities flight. *(Crown copyright)*

combined French/British force, with a drive down the Canal to Ismailia. The assault would have to be preceded by the neutralization of the Egyptian Air Force (EAF) and interdiction missions to isolate the war zone. In August, 894 British civilians were evacuated from Egypt, many by Solent flying-boats of Aquila Airways.

The Israeli Chief of Staff, General Moshe Dayan, first heard of the joint invasion plan on 1 September, when French interests suggested that Israel join in. By 12 September the plans for *Musketeer* were ready, although their implementation depended on the very slow process of requisitioning, loading and sailing the large numbers of merchant vessels required. The Israelis flew to Paris for a further planning meeting on the 29th, and on 3 October Eden told close advisers that Israel had offered to collaborate.

The die was finally cast at a series of tripartite meetings at Sèvres between 22 and 24 October; concurrently, the French reached a private agreement with Israel for defensive support involving warships and fighter aircraft. The final plan was for the Israelis to invade Sinai on 29 October. When the Israelis reached the Canal the British and French Governments would issue an ultimatum requiring the Israelis and Egyptians to stop fighting and withdraw their forces ten miles east and west respectively. It was confidently predicted that the ultimatum would be rejected by Egypt, which would give the Allies a justifiable excuse for military intervention.

That the British did not trust the Israelis was evident by the preparation of Operation *Cordage*, designed to neutralize IDF/AF air bases in the event that Israel attacked Jordan. One senior RAF commander is on record as having said that he did not know whether his aircraft were to bomb Egyptian or Israeli airfields until twenty-four hours before the operation began. The military intervention in Egypt would initially take the form of bombing, and would be followed by a period of psychological warfare during which aircraft would be used to drop leaflets, and spurious radio broadcasts would deceive and confuse. The civilian population would also be warned of further impending bombing.

RAF bombers from Malta and Cyprus would attack airfields and military installations, initially by night and from high altitude. Further targets would be attacked by carrier-based strike aircraft, which would later be used to

Contrary to contemporaneous accounts, the Valiants did not carry the special black/yellow striped markings applied to all other aircraft involved. Flying at operational heights, recognition should only have been a problem for high-flying fighters. XD815 of 148 Sqn. *(Crown copyright)*

cover the invasion proper. Once the Egyptian Air Force had been neutralized and the population confused, the invasion would begin with paradrops to the west of Port Said (British) and on Port Fuad to the east (French); these drops would be followed up by seaborne troops who would push south down the Canal with armoured support.

PREPARATIONS

The French invasion convoy left its assembly port, Bone in Algeria, on 27 October. At 22.00 hrs on the 30th the British fleet, with a shorter sailing time, left Malta heading for Suez. The whole operation had nearly suffered a vital blow when the RAF Comet taking the Planning Group to Cyprus on 23 October lost all four engines at 45,000 ft. Fortunately they relit at lower altitude. With the Israelis spreading across Sinai towards the Canal, the Allies issued their ultimatum at 16.15 hrs on 30 October. The order to the RAF to commit itself to the bombing of Egyptian airfields was given at 15.00 hrs.

The ultimatum required the combatants to retreat to positions ten miles either side of the Canal; understandably, the Egyptians did not accept the ultimatum, which also required Allied occupation and maintenance of the Canal Zone. The first task in the 'police' intervention was to deal with the EAF. The Allies were most concerned about the strength of the EAF, the fighting capability of its aircrew and especially the preparedness of Czech and Soviet 'advisers' to fight. Allied intelligence was based on aerial reconnaissance, while Israeli assessments were probably the result of more direct espionage. The Israelis were thus aware that Egypt could at best use no more than fifty MiG-15s, about a dozen MiG-17s, thirty Vampire FB.52s, sixteen Meteors of several marks and forty Il-28s.

Allied estimates of Egyptian strength were roughly double those of the Israelis, while none of the parties could be confident of the role to be adopted by the 'advisers'. The British assessments almost certainly came directly from

The main bomber force was supplied by UK-based Canberras detached to Malta and Cyprus. WJ767 of 109 Sqn departing Luqa clearly displays the wing stripes applied to aircraft taking part in *Musketeer*. 91 Canberras were deployed in eleven squadrons, and a further three squadrons were involved in ferrying bombs to the island bases in the build-up. *(Crown copyright)*

In August the Meteors of 39 Sqn were re-deployed to Nicosia from Malta to provide a night fighter capability. Uncoded WM339 carried the identification markings in yellow and black. *(Crown copyright)*

the American CIA. A U-2A unit, WRS(P)-2, was formed in September 1956 at Incirlik Air Base, at Adana in Turkey, with three aircraft; for several months its aircraft overflew the eastern Mediterranean, and especially Egypt.

By the time of the invasion, relations between Britain and America were bad. The CIA, however, enjoyed a high degree of independence, and although informed had not advised President Eisenhower of the details of the Allied invasion plan. Throughout the Suez action the USAF's Strategic Air Command (SAC) was placed on alert, including the B-47-equipped 306 Bomb Wing (BW) at Ben Guerir in Morocco; on 26 October the RB-47s of 70 Strategic Reconnaissance Wing (SRW) arrived at Sidi Slimane, also in Morocco.

The destruction of the EAF became the responsibility of the Royal Air Force. Since August, Canberras from three units had been ferrying bombs to Malta, and from September Canberra and Valiant units began moving out to Mediterranean bases. By 30 October there were five squadrons of Canberra B.6s and four squadrons of Valiant B.ls on Malta, and seven squadrons of the shorter-range Canberra B.2 in Cyprus. Also in Cyprus were four reserve crews and aircraft of 35 Sqn.

By the beginning of the campaign there were no fewer than 112 aircraft at Akrotiri, 127 at Nicosia and forty-six at Tymbou. The Israelis were expecting the RAF attacks to begin at dawn on 31 October, but the first aircraft did not take off from Luqa until 19.30 hrs; two hours later the Cyprus-based aircraft began to take off. The targets were important air bases, including Abu Sueir, Almaza, Bilbeis, Cairo International, Cairo West, Dekheila, Deversoir, Fayid, Gamil, Inchas, Ismailia, Kabrit, Kasfareet, Luxor and Shallufa.

THE FIRST PHASE

The first bombs were dropped on Almaza by Canberra WH853 of 12 Sqn at about 22.30 hrs. The first wave of eight Valiants was recalled to Malta before reaching its target, Cairo West airfield. Late in the day the War Office had become aware that United States nationals were being evacuated through Cairo West, and radioed Keightley to

The Suez operation was very much a combined operation with five British and two French carriers involved. Tactical strike and later, air support, were provided by Fleet Air Arm fighters. Sea Hawk FGA.6 XE402/486J of 899 NAS carries drop tanks and eight rockets as she departs HMS *Eagle*. *(Crown copyright)*

This busy scene aboard HMS *Albion* shows, among other things, maintainers applying markings to XE391/109Z of 800 NAS. In the foreground ammunition boxes are being sorted. *(Crown copyright)*

prevent an escalation of the ill feeling between the Allies and the USA. The Valiants landed at Malta amid the second wave taking off for other targets. The delay was important: during the following day a number of Egyptian aircraft escaped south, with further aircraft destined for Syria. They were flown by Soviet instructors.

Despite the bombers having to operate from 45,000 ft, their job was made easy by the absence of blackout, clear skies and the lack of an Egyptian air defence system. Conventional 500 lb and 1,000 lb bombs were used, proximity fused. Target marking was undertaken by 18, 109 and 139 Sqns flying at low level and using two aircraft for illumination and two for marking. The first Valiant in action was XD814 of 148 Sqn in an attack on Almaza airfield. During the night the British cruiser HMS *Newfoundland*, part of an Allied task force in the Red Sea, engaged and sank the Egyptian frigate *Domiat*, but not without a short, sharp battle.

Reconnaissance was ordered at dawn on 1 November, and Canberra PR.7s of 13 Sqn, supplemented by aircraft from 58 Sqn plus RF-84Fs of EC 1/33 'Belfort', were dispatched from Akrotiri. The results were disappointing, with much cratering but no evidence of substantial aircraft losses. It has subsequently been concluded that the total tonnage of bombs dropped on all the airfields by the bomber force would have been required to guarantee neutralizing just one of them. The Canberra bombers were to return that night to attack concentrated targets, but much of the precision bombing work was subsequently handled by the lighter attack aircraft from Cyprus and the carriers.

Among subsequent targets was the group of 28 Il-28s that had fled south to Luxor. They were eventually destroyed on 4 November by F-84Fs of EC 1 based at Lydda, flying to the extremes of their range. Fitted with 450 gal tanks, twenty aircraft made the long flight in two waves. This was not before eight Ilyushins had departed for the greater safety of Riyadh, Saudi Arabia, to join a number that had earlier flown direct. Twenty MiG-15s destined for the SAF had flown to Hama, Syria, after the initial bombing.

During the daylight hours the Cyprus Canberras, and for good measure the Hunters of 1 and 34 Sqns and F-84Fs of EC 3, joined the fray. The Hunters quickly resorted to a defensive role. Without their 250 gal asbestos/phenolic drop-tanks, most of which had been destroyed by ejected shell casings in firing practice, their range limited time over target to no more than ten minutes. The F-84Fs flew protective top cover.

The British carrier force had sailed from Malta on 26 October and was on station, fifty miles off the Egyptian coast, almost due north of Cairo, by the 31st. Sea Hawks supported by Sea Venoms attacked airfields at Dekheila, Bilbeis, Abu Sueir, Inchas, Almaza and, for the first time, Cairo West. The last four airfields were all MiG-15 bases, and in due course twenty-seven aircraft destined for Syria were destroyed at Abu Sueir. Some 500 sorties were flown on this first day of the air offensive, without loss to the Allies. The naval pilots had not been briefed to avoid Cairo West, but fortunately spotted Pan Am airliners on the airfield before committing themselves.

Further photo-reconnaissance confirmed the effectiveness of the attacks, which were generally made with minimal civilian casualties. The British-run Sharq al Adna propaganda radio station had issued warnings to the Egyptian population well in advance of the raids. Control of this Cyprus-based organization was part of the remit of Brigadier Bernard Fergusson. His was also the task of organizing leaflet-dropping in Egyptian cities through the 'aeropsychological' phase of the operation. After several days of bombing it was clear that the British bomber force far exceeded the supply of suitable targets; this did not encourage volunteers for the task of leaflet dropping, traditionally seen as an unnecessary risking of resources.

It was also decided to bomb Cairo radio station, situated some fifteen miles outside the city, in order that Sharq al Adna could broadcast spurious messages on the same wavelength. The task fell to 27 Sqn, whose aircraft flew with F-84Fs as top cover on the morning of the 2nd; the station was off the air for two days following the attack. On this second full day of air attacks, attention turned to concentrations of ground forces, especially at Almaza, Cairo and Huckstep, the last being attacked continuously for three days.

As some indication of the intensity of flying, 6 Sqn's Venoms flew eighteen sorties on the 1st, mainly against

As HMS *Albion* turns into wind to prepare for a launch, her Whirlwind planeguard takes off. Sea Venom FAW.21s of 809 NAS (XG677/225Z nearest) and Sea Hawk FB.3s of 802 NAS (WN109/139Z at left) share the deck. These machines will all need to be moved forward or below deck before recovery of any launched aircraft. *(Crown copyright)*

On a strike on Almaza airfield on 2 November Sea Venom FAW.21 WW281/095 of 893 NAS was hit by flak which severely injured the observer and damaged the hydraulic system. Fearing an asymmetric wheeled landing the pilot skilfully belly-landed the aircraft on HMS *Eagle*, where it is being recovered. *(Author's collection)*

Dekheila airfield on the delta; 830 NAS's Wyverns flew a similar number of sorties on the same day against the same target. The day's activity was not without cost. A Canberra PR.7 of 13 Sqn was damaged by anti-aircraft fire, as was Sea Venom FAW.21 WW284/095-O of 893 NAS, which crash-landed on HMS *Eagle* with a damaged undercarriage and injured observer.

The French carriers had joined the action on 2 November, and by the following day, while the airfields and army concentrations remained important targets, a further change of approach was indicated. From this day specific tactical targets around Port Said were attacked, critically the Damietta road bridge to the west of the town and the only northern road link from the delta to the Canal. While attacking the bridge, 830 NAS Wyvern WN330, piloted by Lt McCarthy, was hit; the pilot ejected out at sea and was picked up by HMS *Eagle*'s plane-guard Whirlwind HAS.3. Less fortunate was the pilot of 8 Sqn Venom WR505, which struck the ground during a rocket attack, perhaps as a result of ground fire. Targets of opportunity were also attacked, but with great care to avoid civilian casualties.

During the day HMS *Albion* withdrew for refuelling. Mention should be made of the work of the carrier support aircraft, not only the plane-guard Whirlwinds but also the Avengers and Skyraiders. Each of the Royal Navy carriers had embarked a Whirlwind HAR.3 for rescue duties. The Skyraiders of 849 NAS flew airborne early warning (AEW) patrols over the task force; apart from Allied aircraft, they identified much traffic from the US Sixth Fleet, which was shadowing the carriers and flying numerous sorties, perceived by the French and British as disruptive. Both the USS *Coral Sea* and USS *Randolph* were operating close to the task force, while the anti-submarine carrier USS *Antietam* was further west, south of Italy. The Avengers of *Bulwark*'s ship's flight were used on anti-submarine patrols. French naval Avengers of *Flotille 9F* were of the ASW TBM-3E and AEW TBM-3W variants. Based on *La Fayette*, they also contributed to the patrol tasks.

The Malta- and Cyprus-based support units were also playing important roles. On Malta four Meteor FR.9s of 208 Sqn were maintained at readiness until 10 November, and during the critical period they made a number of intercepts. Also on Malta were four Hunter F.4s of 111 Sqn to supplement the Meteors. The other Malta support unit was 37 Sqn with Shackleton MR.2s, which provided cover for the convoys with, at one stage, a detachment based in northern Libya. Also involved, flying nine operational sorties, was 28F of the French Navy flying the PB4Y-2 from Karouba, Tunisia. The Cyprus air defence units were 39 Sqn, with the Meteor NF.13, and 1 and 34 Sqns detached from Tangmere flying the Hunter F.5, with flights at Amman, Jordan.

Also in Jordan throughout the crisis was 32 Sqn, equipped with the Venom FB.4. These Amman detachments were to protect Jordan in the event that Israel attacked her. At Akrotiri were the three RAF Venom units, 6, 8 and 249 Sqns, and the Canberra PR.7s of 13 Sqn. The French units at Akrotiri comprised EC 3 with F-84Fs and ER 1/33 with the RF-84F. It is understood that one other type was on Cyprus at the time. This was a Pembroke, believed to be WV700, released from the Kenyan emergency and used there for sky-shouting. It was required by Brigadier Fergusson for the aeropsychological phase, but the loudspeakers were removed *en route*, rendering the aircraft useless for its intended task.

Sunday 4 November saw no let-up in activity, and despite the fact that HMS *Eagle* was withdrawn for refuelling, the Royal Navy flew no fewer than 355 sorties. The Cyprus squadrons also remained busy, and much of the action was again in the vicinity of Port Said in preparation for the airborne assault due early the following morning.

AIRBORNE INVASION

The third and final phase of the operation, the occupation of Egyptian territory, began formally on the morning of 5 November with a parachute drop of 600 men of the 3rd Battalion the Parachute Regiment, part of 16 Para Brigade. Only a few days earlier they had been actively pursuing EOKA terrorists on Cyprus; it was from their base at Nicosia that they flew out before dawn in Valettas drawn from 30, 84 and 114 Sqns and Hastings of 70, 99 and 511 Sqns. In all, there were only thirty-four aircraft available: indeed, so short of transport aircraft was the RAF that Shackletons of 42 and 206 Sqns had been pressed into service to fly troops and RAF ground crews from the UK to Malta and Cyprus.

The target for 3 Para was Gamil airfield to the west of Port Said. The DZ had already been marked with flares by a Canberra B.2 from 115 Sqn. 'A' Company with sappers of 3 Troop, 9 Sqn, Royal Engineers, dropped first on the western edge of the airfield; the road link from Port Said to the delta had already been cut to the west of the airfield in attacks by FAA aircraft already described. 'C' Company then dropped near the control tower in the middle of the airfield, followed by 'B' Company, which had the unenviable task of holding the eastern edge of the airfield where it bordered a sewage farm. The opposition to Allied landings around Port Said had been assessed as one regular and two national guard battalions, with coastal and anti-aircraft artillery and with a few self-propelled guns in support.

In the event, the landing was totally successful, despite some resistance. This was both remarkable and fortunate. Such were the logistics problems suffered by the invasion force that the Paras could not benefit from a softening-up of Egyptian positions by naval bombardment, while the minesweepers necessary to clear channels were still one day's sailing from the area.

Further, for five hours the troops had to fight with a bare minimum of equipment and supplies. It was not until 13.45 hrs that a second drop of a hundred reinforcements was made, in addition to seven jeeps and six 106 mm recoilless anti-tank guns borrowed from NATO stocks. These items were dropped from under the wings of the Hastings; Valettas carried smaller, 300 lb loads under each wing. Despite their vulnerability, no transport aircraft were lost.

During the day the Paras made excellent progress, though not without casualties. FAA units flew continuous 'cab-rank' patrols and were called onto specific targets by a liaison team dropped with the first wave of troops. During one such attack on the coastguard barracks between Gamil and Port Said proper, Wyvern WN328/374-J was seriously damaged and was ditched in the sea, the pilot being rescued unharmed. Support throughout the day

The Wyvern was a powerful light strike aircraft powered by a 4,110 hp Python turboprop. Just one unit, 830 NAS, used the type operationally at Suez aboard HMS *Eagle*. Four aircraft are seen preparing to depart *Eagle*, each lightly armed with one 250 lb bomb under the fuselage. Parked aft are two Skyraiders of 849 NAS while the escorting planeguard destroyer closes up. *(Author's collection)*

was provided by the aircraft of *Albion* and *Eagle*, as HMS *Bulwark* finally took time off to refuel, and in excess of 400 sorties were flown.

While British troops were holding the airfield, their French counterparts had dropped at the same time to the east of the town to hold two key bridges and the waterworks. Five hundred men of the *2e Régiment de Parachutistes Coloniaux* (RFC), including a handful of British sappers and reconnaissance troops of the Guards Independent Parachute Company, were flown from Tymbou in Cyprus in a combined force of Noratlas and C-47 aircraft from ET 61 and ET 63.

The paratroopers landed from low altitude and achieved most of their objectives, although, again, not without resistance. One of the two bridges carrying the north–south Canal road over a feeder canal at Raswa was blown before it could be secured. With their basic objectives safe, the French used their second drop early in the afternoon to land a second battalion of 450 men of 2 RFC at Port Fuad. During the day they had had the benefit of their own air support from Corsairs of 14F and 15F from the carrier *Arromanches*, although one aircraft had been lost with its pilot, destroyed by gunfire.

Despite some heavy fighting, in terms of immediate military objectives the day must be judged a success. 3 Para suffered four killed and thirty-six wounded, while 2 RPC lost ten dead and thirty wounded. Possibly in excess of 200 Egyptians were killed. During the day a French C-47 landed at Gamil, and carrier-based helicopters were used for casualty evacuation. The Allied airborne troops effectively surrounded Port Said by nightfall; indeed, in the early evening, a tentative surrender had been organized, but it was not to be formalized.

SEABORNE INVASION

Standing off the Egyptian coast were the invasion fleets of Britain and France. They were to begin landing at dawn, but for political reasons were denied a preliminary naval bombardment. This directive did not prevent naval initiative from offering 'gunfire support', although with weapons of no more than 4.5 in. calibre. At 05.00 hrs on 6 November the first troops of 40 and 42 Commando, which had sailed from Malta, landed on the beach in front of Port Said; half an hour later, Centurion tanks of 'C' Squadron, 6th Royal Tank Regiment (RTR), were ashore. The Commandos and tanks made a concerted drive south through the town, often ignoring localized pockets of resistance.

No. 42 Commando was on the right flank, due to join up with 3 Para, while 40 Commando on the left flank was to press on down the Canal. No. 45 Commando had been held in reserve on HMS *Ocean* and HMS *Theseus*. It was becoming evident that it would take time to clear the city, and after an attempt to land helicopters at the sports stadium – obviously still held by Egyptian forces – a landing-ground in the square by de Lesseps' statue was selected. Whirlwinds and Sycamores of the Joint Helicopter Unit (JHU) on board *Ocean* ferried the soldiers in waves from 06.10 hrs.

This was the first time that helicopters had been used in this way, and on return journeys they were used most successfully to evacuate the wounded. The task facing the 417 men of the Commando, landed in just 1½ hours, was to contain the city centre and link up with 3 Para, who had had a busy morning, having been strafed by a solitary MiG-15. The helicopters, numbering just six Whirlwind HAR.2s of JHU, six Sycamore HC.14s of JHU and seven Whirlwind HAR.22s of 845 NAS at the start of the action, made no fewer than 200 deck landings during the day.

No. 40 Commando met stubborn resistance in its move south at Navy House, the previous headquarters of the Royal Navy in Egypt. A strong Egyptian force resisted assault, and aircraft from the cab-rank were called in to assist. The post eventually fell after a concerted rocket and bomb attack, but a Sea Hawk FGA.6 (XE377/195-J) from *Eagle* was shot down in the process. The pilot was recovered. Earlier, XE400/107-Z of 800 NAS had ditched after suffering engine failure. Late in the afternoon the British and French back-up force arrived by sea. The

The airborne early warning Skyraider AEW.1s of 849 NAS were deployed to HMSs *Albion* and *Eagle*. Much of their work involved keeping a watch on US 6th Fleet aircraft harassing the operation. WV178/424Z of C Flight launches conventionally from *Albion*. *(Author's collection)*

The Joint Experimental Helicopter Unit (JEHU) dropped the E just before the operation for obvious reasons. Whirlwinds (seen here at Gamil airfield) and Sycamores of JHU and Whirlwind HAR.22s of 845 NAS made the first heli-borne assault in history on 6 November. *(Crown copyright)*

remainder of 16 Para Brigade, 2 Para, was landed with the balance of Centurions from 6 RTR. On the Port Fuad side a battalion of the *1e Régiment Etranger Parachutiste* (REF), three naval commandos and a squadron of AMX light tanks of 7 Light Armoured Division were landed to consolidate positions on the eastern side of the Canal.

Time was running out, and the military leaders knew it: with increasing international pressure for a ceasefire, it was clear that further fighting was probably futile. Tanks of 6 RTR, carrying French paratroops from Raswa, pushed down the Canal road south to Quantara. In the course of the drive they moved through the forward position reached by the Guards the previous day. The whole Canal could easily have been taken, with French paratroops of *1e Régiment de Chasseurs Parachutistes* (RCP) standing by in Cyprus for a drop on Ismailia at the southern end. But it was not to be. A ceasefire was indeed ordered, with effect from 12 midnight GMT (02.00 hrs on 7 November local time), when the leading units were at El Cap, just a couple of miles north of Quantara.

Apart from the Sea Hawk lost from *Eagle*, two Whirlwinds are understood to have been damaged beyond repair. Canberra PR.7 WH799 of 58 Sqn was shot down off the coast of Syria, with the loss of the navigator, on 6 November by a MiG-17, having photographed a cut oil pipeline in Syria. Another casualty on the 6th was Canberra B.6 WT371 of 139 Sqn, which crashed on landing at Nicosia, killing the crew of three, after having been shot up over Port Said. Finally, at some stage in the previous few days, an F-84F of EC 1 in Lydda had been reported missing.

Pressure for the ceasefire had come from several directions. A run on sterling resulted in the need for a loan from the International Monetary Fund, in effect dominated by US interests. The Americans agreed to support a loan of $500 million – only against a ceasefire. On 5 November the Soviet leader, Nikolai Bulganin, had threatened to destroy London and Paris with nuclear missiles.

AFTERMATH

The plan was for a UN force to occupy Port Said and for French and British withdrawal, but components of the British 3rd Infantry Division continued to land. The Allied soldiers did their best to get things working again in

Port Said, but by 15 November UN forces were beginning to arrive in DC-4 and DC-6 aircraft of Swissair at Abu Sueir. From 7 November a miscellany of aircraft flew in the Port Said area, wearing the now irrelevant stripes, including a Hurel-Dubois HD.321, PV-2 Harpoons, and, reportedly, a Halifax and a Sea Vampire. Auster 6s of 1913 Light Liaison Flight (LLF) and Bell 47Gs of CH 2, French Army, were also in evidence.

On their island bases the bomber units were packing up to return home. The first to go, on the 7th, were the Valiants of 138 Sqn, followed by 10 Sqn's Canberras on the 9th. Most units were home by Christmas, but at least three – 15, 61 and 109 Sqns – did not return until the New Year. The last troops left Egypt on 22 December. The British suffered sixteen dead and ninety-six wounded, the French ten dead with thirty-three wounded. The total operational aircraft losses were one Canberra, one Venom, one Sea Venom, two Sea Hawks, two Wyverns, two Whirlwinds, one Corsair and one F-84F.

The Egyptians suffered considerably higher losses, with an estimated 650 dead in the Port Said area alone, as well as 900 wounded. Their air force reportedly lost 260 aircraft on the ground, including a number destined for the Syrian Air Force. Canberra sorties totalled seventy-two from Malta and 206 from Cyprus, while Valiants flew forty-nine. A total of 1,439 1,000 lb bombs were dropped, and forty-four photo-reconnaissance sorties were flown by the RAF. As a measure of the tactical air activity, the figures for HMS *Eagle* are valuable. The carrier made 621 launches of aircraft, which carried and used a total of seventy-two 1,000 lb bombs, 157 500 lb bombs, 1,448 3 in. rockets and 88,000 rounds of cannon ammunition.

SEQUEL

The Suez operation was little short of a catastrophe for Britain. More books have been written about the operation than about any other British post-war military/political campaign, and the subject remains both highly controversial and extremely complicated to analyse, and indeed summarize. However, it needs to be seen in context and not simply with the benefit of hindsight.

At the time, Britain was beginning to recover from post-war deprivations and there was a general mood of optimism. British forces were, or had recently been, active throughout Africa and Asia either in tough conventional fighting – as in Korea – or in the wearying tasks of countering insurgency, as in Malaya, Aden, Cyprus and Kenya. To the military, the challenge of preparing an invasion of a relatively small 'enemy' must have had the attraction of a major exercise.

American interests in the Middle East – always with an eye to oil – threatened British prestige. Here was the opportunity to put Britain back on the map, literally. Britain still had friends in the Middle East, not necessarily allies of Egypt, for whom a show of force might help further to cement relationships. Finally, there was genuine and understandable concern over future access to the Canal and the huge costs involved if its use was denied.

The total cost of the action to the British was estimated at £100 million. Middle East oil was cut off except by the long Cape route, Nasser having blocked the Canal with scuttled ships, and Syria had blown the land pipeline. Petrol was rationed for many months. Militarily, the operation was conducted indifferently at the strategic level, with command and control of British forces managed thousands of miles away in London. Logistics were difficult with much *matériel* unavailable when it should have been, through having been loaded on the wrong vessels many months earlier.

The operation highlighted the serious shortfalls in transport aircraft capability and availability and the need for relevant (in-theatre) training. Pilots used to flying in Europe experienced difficulty in adjusting to desert conditions without acclimatization. Military intelligence was poor in respect of the Egyptian forces, especially the air force, which, although notionally equipped with modern Soviet aircraft, was in a state of transition, with many pilots abroad in training. At the local level, soldiers, sailors and airmen performed with great competence and valour, let down by inadequate and insufficient equipment..

However, the political costs were probably infinitely greater, even though difficult to quantify. On the home front, British politicians and people were divided, with the issue of collusion being aired for the first time. (The exposure of collusion arose through reporters noting that British, French and Israeli aircraft carried the same special identification markings of three white or yellow bands and two black. Further, it was noted that French aircraft returning from the theatre showed evidence of Israeli markings hastily removed or over-painted.) National self-esteem and confidence plummeted.

French distrust of the British was confirmed, and the resultant split probably contributed significantly to long delays in Britain joining the Common Market. Shortly afterwards, the French began their withdrawal from NATO, citing the dominance of the USA and the UK in its organization. The humiliation accelerated French defeat in Algeria.

British relations with Arab countries in the Middle East suffered a serious setback, and in the longer term ensured the withdrawal from Aden, Iraq and Jordan. Relations with Israel have never been comfortable, but the Israelis were perhaps the only participant not to complain. They had been given Allied support in securing major territorial gains at little cost: however, under international pressure Sinai returned to Egypt only months later. The threat represented by the Egyptian Air Force was removed.

Although much has been made of the effect on UK–US relations, the fiasco probably made little impact on the 'special relationship'. The USA remained as duplicitous as ever, having been well aware from hard evidence that an invasion was to take place, but doing nothing in diplomatic terms to dissuade Britain. The affair also offers insight into US governance.

In contradiction of State Department policy, the CIA aided Britain by supplying U-2 reconnaissance photos (although the U-2 programme included British involvement from the outset). This was the same CIA that had backed Colonel Nasser in deposing King Farouk and was providing the Egyptians with details of Anglo-French planning. The US Sixth Fleet also appears to have had a mind of its own. Its carriers in the Eastern Mediterranean harried the Allied Task Force, while some of those serving on *Antietam* believed that it was placed south of Italy to guard against Soviet submarine intrusions through the back door!

Britain and France were probably ill advised to take military action against Egypt. The USA knew of the plans in July 1956 and did nothing to persuade the two countries of the folly of going to war. In the event, only once Britain and France were committed did the USA pull the plug, stepping neatly into British shoes in the Middle East in ensuing years. In pursuing the so-called 'police' action at Suez, in the mistaken belief that the USA would not intervene, but implicitly support, Britain sealed her own fate. From that time British influence in world affairs diminished to the extent that at the time of writing in 2008 Britain appears to be little more than a US puppet state.

DE HAVILLAND SEA VENOM

The DH112 Sea Venom was developed from the land-based NF.2 and was the Royal Navy's first jet all-weather fighter produced to Specification N.107P. The Navy used the NF.2 prototype for carrier trials, and the first Sea Venom prototype flew on 19 April 1951.

The **FAW Mark 20** was originally designated NF Mk 20, and was similar to the RAF's NF Mk 2A. It was fitted with AI Mk X radar and armed with four 20 mm cannon, with provision for eight 60 lb RPs or two 250 lb or 500 lb bombs. The Sea Venom entered service with 890 NAS in March 1954.

Fighter units equipped – 808, 809, 890, 891

The **FAW Mark 21** was fitted with the slightly more powerful Ghost 104 engine and powered ailerons, and had no extended tailplane outboard of the booms. It also had a clear view canopy, ejection seats and a longer-stroke undercarriage. It was the equivalent of the NF.3 and employed the AI Mk 21 (APS-57) radar.

Fighter units equipped – 809, 890, 891, 892, 893, 894

The **FAW Mark 22** was fitted with the Ghost 105, which gave a better climb rate, but in other respects it was similar to the FAW Mk 21. Thirty-nine were built as new, while an unspecified number were converted from the FAW.21. The Sea Venom was retired from front-line service in 1961, but it continued in second-line service to 1970.

Fighter units equipped – 891, 893, 894

HAWKER SEA HAWK

The Hawker P.1040 was Hawker's first jet aircraft, which became Specification N.7/46. The design began as a jet-engined Fury (P.1035), and then progressed to the P.1040 with a bifurcated jet pipe. The non-navalized prototype was powered by the Nene 1, and flew on 2 September 1947, and although in many respects the type was less advanced than the Attacker, its development was later and slower, and it eventually superseded the Attacker in service.

The **F Mark 1** had increased wingspan and tailplane area and a revised cockpit canopy. In the course of production an acorn fairing was fitted at the junction of the tailplane and fin to alleviate buffeting. The more powerful Nene 101 was fitted, and armament comprised four 20 mm Hispano Mk 5 cannon. The fully navalized prototype flew on 3 September 1948, and the Sea Hawk entered service with 806 NAS in 1953.

The **F Mark 2** variant was similar to the F.1 but with powered ailerons and provision for 90 gal wing fuel tanks

Fighter units equipped – 802, 804, 806, 807, 831, 1832

The **FB Mark 3** fighter-bomber reflected a production-line change, with the wing pylons adapted to carry two 500 lb bombs. The **FGA Mark 4** was similar to the FB.3 but with provision for four 500 lb bombs or up to sixteen rockets. The **FB Mark 5** comprised fifty upgraded FB Mk 3s fitted with the Nene 103 from 1955. The extra 200 lb of thrust conferred better low-speed performance and a slightly improved ceiling.

Fighter units equipped – 800, 801, 802, 803, 804, 806, 807, 810, 811, 895, 897, 898

The **FGA Mark 6** variant was the Nene 103 re-engined version of the FGA.4. About forty of the earlier version were converted, and in addition eighty-six new aircraft were built, the last coming into service early in 1956. Underwing stores included two 75 gal fuel tanks.

Fighter units equipped – 800, 801, 803, 804, 806, 810, 895, 897, 898, 899

Suez, 1956

Unit	Aircraft	Base	From	To
RAF				
Strike				
207 Sqn	Valiant B.1	Luqa ex-Marham	24.9.56	11.56
214 Sqn	Valiant B.1	As above	24.9.56	11.56
138 Sqn	Valiant B.1	Luqa ex-Wittering	26.10.56	7.11.56
148 Sqn	Valiant B.1	Luqa ex-Marham	26.10.56	11.56
Total 24 aircraft				
9 Sqn	Canberra B.6	Luqa ex-Binbrook	22.9.56	9.11.56
12 Sqn	Canberra B.6	As above	22.9.56	
101 Sqn	Canberra B.6	As above	22.9.56	
109 Sqn	Canberra B.6	As above	22.9.56	
Total 29 aircraft				
10 Sqn	Canberra B.2	Nicosia	10.56	
15 Sqn	Canberra B.2	Nicosia	10.56	1.57
18 Sqn	Canberra B.2	Nicosia	10.56	
27 Sqn	Canberra B.2	Nicosia	10.56	
44 Sqn	Canberra B.2	Nicosia	10.56	
61 Sqn	Canberra B.2	Nicosia	22.10.56	1.57

Unit	Aircraft	Base	From	To
139 Sqn	Canberra B.6	Nicosia	10.56	
35 Sqn[1]	Canberra B.2	Nicosia	10.56	
Total 62 aircraft				
6 Sqn	Venom FB.4	Akrotiri	based	
8 Sqn	Venom FB.4	Akrotiri ex-Habbaniyah	5.9.56	20.12.56
249 Sqn	Venom FB.4	Akrotiri ex-Amman	27.8.56	11.3.57
Total 47 aircraft				

Air defence

Unit	Aircraft	Base	From	To
208 Sqn	Meteor FR.9	Ta Kali	7.8.56	based
111 Sqn det	Hunter F.4	Ta Kali	9.56	11.56
39 Sqn	Meteor NF.13	Nicosia ex-Luqa	9.8.56	23.3.57
1 Sqn	Hunter F.5	Nicosia	8.8.56	20.12.56
34 Sqn	Hunter F.5	Nicosia	8.8.56	20.12.56
92 Sqn det	Hunter F.6	Nicosia	11.56	1.57
32 Sqn	Venom FB.1	Amman	28.8.56	28.10.56
		Mafraq	29.10.56	10.1.57
1 Sqn det	Hunter F.5	Amman ex-Nicosia	9.56	11.56

Reconnaissance

Unit	Aircraft	Base	From	To
13 Sqn	Canberra PR.7	Akrotiri	based	
58 Sqn det	Canberra PR.7	Nicosia	8.56	11.56
37 Sqn	Shackleton MR.2	Luqa	based	
37 Sqn det		El Adem ex-Luqa	10.56	11.56
38 Sqn	Shackleton MR.2	Luqa	based	
38 Sqn det		Idris ex-Luqa	10.56	11.56
192 Sqn	Washington B.1	Watton	based	

Strategic transport

Unit	Aircraft	Base	From	To
216 Sqn	Comet C.2	Lyneham		
24 Sqn	Hastings C.1, C.2	Colerne		

Plus 28 Shackleton MR.1s and MR.2s drawn from 42, 204, 206 and 228 Sqns, each transporting thirty-three troops to Cyprus via Malta from Blackbushe or latterly ground crew from Bomber Command bases to Malta and Cyprus. In addition, other Hastings units, as shown below, flew from the UK to the theatre.

Unit	Aircraft	Base	From	To
21 Sqn	Canberra B.2	Luqa ex-Waddington	8.56	9.56
15 Sqn	Canberra B.2	Nicosia ex-Honington	8.56	9.56
44 Sqn	Canberra B.2	As above	8.56	9.56

Aircraft used for bomb delivery from UK

Tactical transport and communications

Unit	Aircraft	Base	From	To
30 Sqn	Valetta C.1	Tymbou ex-Dishforth	10.56	12.56
84 Sqn	Valetta C.1	Tymbou ex-Nicosia	based	
114 Sqn	Valetta C.1	Tymbou ex-Nicosia	based	
Total 20 aircraft				

Unit	Aircraft	Base	From	To
70 Sqn	Hastings C.1, C.2	Tymbou ex-Nicosia	based	
99 Sqn	Hastings C.1, C.2	Tymbou ex-Lyneham	10.56	
511 Sqn	Hastings C.1, C.2	Tymbou ex-Lyneham	10.56	
Total 14 aircraft				
1913 Flt	Auster AOP.6	Akrotiri, Gamil		
SF	Pembroke C.1	Akrotiri	based	
SARF	Sycamore HC.14	Amman	based	

NOTES

1   Two aircraft and crew each for 18 and 61 Sqns

Unit	Aircraft	Code
Fleet Air Arm		
HMS *Eagle* In Mediterranean, to Malta 30 November. Carrier code J		
897 NAS	Sea Hawk FGA.6	19x-20x/B
899 NAS	Sea Hawk FGA.6	48x-49x
892 NAS	Sea Venom FAW.21	25x
893 NAS[1]	Sea Venom FAW.21	09x, 35x/O[1]
830 NAS	Wyvern S.4	37x
849 NAS A Flt	Skyraider AEW.1	41x-42x
SAR Flt	Whirlwind HAR.3	99x
HMS *Bulwark* Malta from 13 August, returned 1 December. Carrier code B		
804 NAS	Sea Hawk FGA.6	16x-17x/O[2]
810 NAS	Sea Hawk FGA.4	23x/ZB[3]
895 NAS	Sea Hawk FB.3	46x
Ship's Flt	Avenger AS.4	98x
SAR Flt	Dragonfly HR.3	98x
HMS *Albion* Malta from 17 September, returned 25 December. Carrier code Z		
800 NAS	Sea Hawk FGA.4	10x-11x
802 NAS	Sea Hawk FB.3	13x-14x
809 NAS	Sea Venom FAW.21	22x
849 NAS C Flt	Skyraider AEW.1	42x
SAR Flt	Whirlwind HAR.3	97x
HMS *Theseus* Malta 18 October 1956, returned 10 November 1956		
845 NAS	Whirlwind HAS.22	
HMS *Ocean* Malta from October 1956; returned November 1956		
JHU	Whirlwind HAR.2	
	Sycamore HC.14	

NOTES

1   Included aircraft and pilots from 890 NAS

2   Ex-HMS *Ark Royal*

3   Transferred from HMS *Albion*

Unit	Aircraft (Code)	Base	From	To
French air forces				
Armée de l'Air				
Musketeer (Cyprus)				
EC 1/3	F-84F (3-H)	Akrotiri	22.10.56	11.56
EC 2/3	F-84F (3-I)	Akrotiri	31.10.56	11.56
EC 3/3	F-84F (3-V)	Akrotiri	22.10.56	11.56
ER 4/33	RF-84F (33-C)	Akrotiri	22.10.56	11.56
ET 1/61	Noratlas (61-N)	Tymbou	10.56	11.56
ET 3/61	Noratlas (61-Q)	Tymbou	10.56	11.56
ET 1/62	Noratlas (62-W)	Tymbou	10.56	11.56
ET 2/63	Noratlas, C-47 (63-L)	Tymbou	10.56	11.56
CEAM	HD-32	Tymbou	11.56	11.56
ET 2/61	Breguet 761 (64-P)	Orléans	10.56	11.56
Kadesh (Israel)				
EC 1/2[1]	Mystère IVA (2-E)	Ramat David	23.10.56	13.11.56
EC 3/2[2]	Mystère IVA (2-S)	Ramat David	23.10.56	13.11.56
EC 1/1[3]	F-84F (1-N)	Lydda	23.10.56	13.11.56
EC 2/1[3]	F-84F (1-M)	Lydda	23.10.56	13.11.56
EC 3/1[3]	F-84F (1-P)	Lydda	23.10.56	13.11.56
ET 2/64[4]	Noratlas (64-L)	Haifa	23.10.56	13.11.56
Aéronavale				
14F	F4U-7	*Arromanches*	23.10.56	
15F	F4U-7	*Arromanches*	23.10.56	
23S	HUP-2	*Arromanches*	23.10.56	
9F	TBM-3	*La Fayette*	23.10.56	
23S	HUP-2	*La Fayette*	23.10.56	
21F	P2V-6	Karouba (Tunisia)	based	
28F	PB4Y-2	Karouba (Tunisia)	based	
Aviation Légère de l'Armée de Terre				
GH3	Bell 47G	Gamil	7.11.56	12.56

NOTES
1 Squadron 201 IDFAF while in Israel
2 Squadron 199 IDFAF while in Israel
3 Squadron 200 IDFAF while in Israel
4 Squadron 203 IDFAF while in Israel

Unit	Aircraft	Base	Comment
Israeli Defence Force Air Force			
Sqn 101	Mystère IVA	Hatzor	Some flown by French pilots. 16 aircraft
Sqn 199	Mystère IVA	Ramat David	French unit
Sqn 201	Mystère IVA	Ramat David	French unit
Sqn 200	F-84F	Lydda	French unit
Sqn 117	Meteor F.8, FR.9	Tel Nof	11 aircraft
Sqn 119	Meteor NF.13	Ramat David	Unit forming 2 aircraft
Sqn 113	Ouragan	Hatzor	22 aircraft
Sqn 69	B-17	Ramat David	3 aircraft

Unit	Aircraft	Base	Comment
Sqn 105	P-51D	Ramat David	13 aircraft
Sqn 116	P-51D	Tel Nof	16 aircraft
Sqn 110	Mosquito FB.6	Ramat David	Reserve unit 13 aircraft
Sqn 115	Meteor T.7, Mosquito PR.16	Tel Nof	5 aircraft
Sqn 103	Noratlas, C-47	Tel Nof	19 aircraft
Sqn 140	AT-6 Harvard	Sde Teyman	17 aircraft
Sqn 147	Kaydet	Ramleh	Primary training
Sqn 100	Cub	Sde Teyman	11 aircraft
Sqn 100 det	Cub	Eilat	4 aircraft
	S-55	Tel Nof	2 aircraft

Arab Air Forces

Egyptian Air Force

Unit	Aircraft	Base	Comment
1 Sqn[1]	MiG-15	Almaza	15 aircraft
20 Sqn	MiG-15	Kabrit	15 aircraft
30 Sqn	MiG-15	Abu Sueir	15 aircraft
5 Sqn	Meteor F.4, F.8	Fayid	12 aircraft
10 Sqn	Meteor NF.13	Almaza	5 aircraft
31 Sqn	Vampire FB.52	Kasfareet	15 aircraft
2 Sqn	Vampire FB.52	Cairo West	14 aircraft
40 Sqn	Vampire FB.52, Meteor F.4, F.8	Fayid	OCU: 20 aircraft
8 Sqn	Il-28	Inchas	12 aircraft
9 Sqn	Il-28	Inchas	17 aircraft
3 Sqn	C-47	Almaza	20 aircraft
7 Sqn	C-46	Almaza	20 aircraft
11 Sqn	Il-14	Almaza	20 aircraft
4 Sqn	Various	Dekheila	Comms unit
FTS	Spitfire F.22	Fayid	c 6 aircraft
	Sea Fury FB.11	El Arish	c 4 aircraft
	MiG-15UTI	Kabrit	OCU: 6 aircraft
	Il-28	Luxor	OCU: 20 aircraft

In addition there were numerous Gomhouria basic and Yak-11 advanced trainers

Syrian Arab Air Force

Unit	Aircraft	Base	Comment
1 Sqn	Meteor F.8, FR.9	Mezze, Nairab	8 aircraft
	Vampire FB.52	Mezze	c 20 aircraft
	Meteor NF.13	Mezze	6 aircraft
	AT-6		c. 10 aircraft armed
	C-47	Mezze	

Royal Jordanian Air Force

Unit	Aircraft	Base	Comment
1 Sqn	Vampire FB.9	Amman	
2 Sqn	Vampire FB.9, FB.52	Amman	
	Marathon, Viking	Amman	

NOTES

1   Reportedly beginning conversion to MiG-17 with 6-12 aircraft on charge

Unit	Aircraft	Code
United States Navy		
USS *Coral Sea* (CVA-43) with CVG-10 embarked. In Mediterranean September 1956 to January 1957		
VF-11	F2H-4	100 P
VF-103	F9F-8B	200 P
VA-106	F9F-8B	300 P
VA-104	AD-6	400 P
VAH-11 det 31	AJ-2	600 GN
VAW-12 det 31	AD-5W	NE
VA(AW)-33 det 31	AD-5N	SS
VFP-62 det 31	F2H-2P	PL
HU-2 det 31	HUP-2	UP
USS *Randolph* (CVA-15) with ATG-202 embarked. In Mediterranean August 1956 to January 1957.		
VF-102	F2H-3	100
VF-62	FJ-3	200
VA-46	F9F-8	300
VA-176	AD-6	400
VAW-12 det	AD-5W	NE
VA(AW)-33 det	AD-5N	SS
VFP-62 det	F2H-2P	PL
HU-2 det	HUP-2	UP
USS *Antietam* (CVS-36) In Mediterranean October 1956 to Mid 1957.		
VS-31	S2F-1	SP
HS-1	HSS-1	HU
VAW-12 det	AD-5W	GE
Land based Hal Far, Malta		
VP-24	P2V-5	LR

Unit	Type	Base
United States Air Force		
306 BW	B-47	Ben Guerir
70 SRW	RB-47	Sidi Slimane
WRS(P)2	U-2A	Incirlik

5.4   JORDAN, LEBANON AND IRAQ, 1958

BACKGROUND

From 1955 the Soviet Union gave military aid to both Egypt and Syria, including the supply of aircraft and, in the case of Syria, the building of new airfields during 1957 at Palmyre, El Rasafa and Hama. These airfields, some in the west of the country, threatened Lebanese and Jordanian integrity. After the Suez débâcle, the USA had offered financial assistance to Arab states in the Middle East to counter the prospective growth of Communist influence in the region, but only the Lebanese had shown any interest, the remainder wanting little to do with Western interests.

Britain had supported Jordan, bringing aircraft to protect her against potential aggression from Israel during the Suez action. Earlier in 1956, 114 Sqn Valettas moved troops from Habbaniya to Amman to counter rioting. However, Jordan and Britain had terminated the Anglo-Jordanian treaty on 13 March 1957, and in May six Valettas

Among aircraft engaged in supporting
British forces in Jordan were the
Beverleys of 84 Sqn based at
Khormaksar. XM109/U in the earlier
bare metal finish is dropping harness
packs. *(Crown copyright)*

of 114 Sqn moved to Habbaniya from
Cyprus ready to evacuate civilians in
the light of further unrest following an
Egyptian/Syrian-backed coup attempt.
On 1 February 1958 the United Arab
Republic (UAR) was formed between
Egypt and Syria; simultaneously, Iraq
and Jordan agreed to an anti-
Communist, anti-Nasser Federation,
the Arab Union which would have led,
inter alia, to a combined air force.

The situation at the eastern end of
the Mediterranean grew more tense
with the revolt in the Lebanon. The
country had been an independent
republic only since 1946, and comprised a range of Moslem and Christian

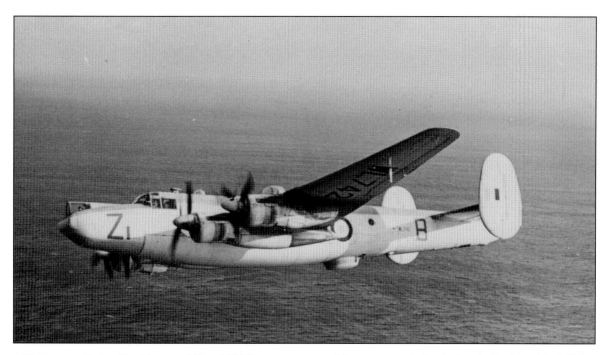

The long-suffering Shackletons of 42 and 204 Sqn were co-opted for transport duties during the Jordan crisis. MR.2 WL742 Z1/B of 42 Sqn. *(Author's collection)*

factions. Early in 1958 opposition to the Maronite Christian President Camille Chamoun hardened from all quarters in response to his pro-Western stance over the Suez affair. In May, Muslims in Tripoli revolted, and unrest soon spread to Sidon, Beirut and Baalbek; Syrian forces, in support of the Opposition, crossed the border.

King Hussein of Jordan, fearing growing hostility, sought help from the Iraqi government; King Faisal II was his cousin. The Iraqi response was a military coup in which Faisal, his uncle (the Crown Prince) and the Prime Minister were assassinated. Thus one revolt in Lebanon, plus a coup in Iraq, resulted in a Jordanian appeal to the UK for military assistance in maintaining stability.

The United States had foreseen the prospect of problems in the eastern Mediterranean, and had established a plan for operations in 1957, which excluded the British. However, by May 1958 there was a clear anticipation of the need for intervention in Lebanon and Jordan, at which time a broadly co-ordinated plan for an Anglo-American task force, *Blue Bat*, was conceived. In the event the USA and the UK were called upon simultaneously; but since the British were preoccupied with Jordan, the Americans acted alone in relation to Lebanon. In contrast to relationships two years previously, the British and Americans acted in collaboration, if not concert. Thus the two actions, so closely related, are described together.

THE US IN LEBANON

Through June there was heavy fighting in Tripoli and Beirut, and with the overthrow of the monarchy in Iraq, Chamoun appealed to the USA on 14 July for military intervention. The US Government response was immediate, ostensibly to protect the 2,500 US citizens in Lebanon, and 1,700 US Marines of 2 Bn 2nd Regt were landed at Beirut from units of the Sixth Fleet on 15 July.

The Sixth Fleet was composed of seventy-seven vessels, including the carriers USS *Essex* (CVA-9) and USS *Saratoga* (CVA-60), embarking Air Task Group (ATG) 201 and Carrier Air Group (CAG) 3 respectively. In addition, the anti-submarine carrier USS *Lake Champlain* (CVS-39) was on hand. On the 16th, 3 Bn 6th Marine Regt was landed as Military Air Transport Service (MATS) C-124s and C-130s of the 322nd Air Division (AD) flew in 2,000 paratroops from bases in southern Germany.

A minor diplomatic row broke out as the transports overflew neutral Austria without authority, in response to which the Austrian Air Force moved three Vampires to Innsbruck to intercept further transgressors. The final landings were on the 18th, when 1 Bn 8th Marine Regt beached at Beirut. By the 20th there were 10,000 US troops in Lebanon, and SAC was on full alert status; as a further precaution, the USAF's Composite Air Strike Force (CASF) 'Bravo' was activated, and detachments of tactical strike and reconnaissance aircraft were flown to Turkey from the USA.

Four squadrons of F-100Ds of the 354th TFW flew from their home base at Myrtle Beach, South Carolina, to Adana in Turkey, where troop reinforcements were held. A detachment of five RF-101Cs was sent from the 18th Tactical Reconnaissance Squadron (TRS) at Shaw AFB to Incirlik, where they were joined by a detachment of B-57Bs from the 345th Bomb Group (BG) from Langley AFB.

All landings were covered by USN fighters, which at that time were of a variety of types, as the Navy was in a transitional phase. The fighter units included VF-32 with F8U-1 Crusaders and VF-31 with F3H-2N Demons, both from USS *Saratoga*, and VF-13 with F4D-1 Skyrays and VF-62 with FJ-3M Furies from *Essex*. In addition, there were two squadrons of A4Ds of VA-34 and VA-83, a number of which were on standby armed with nuclear weapons. Later the A4Ds patrolled the Lebanese border, including that with Israel. The Sixth Fleet carriers withdrew on 23 August, leaving the Turkey-based CASF to cover the ground forces. As an indication of activity, VF-32 flew 533 hrs in July and 762 hrs by 23 August. During the course of a routine reconnaissance sortie one RF-101C was damaged by ground fire.

The US presence helped to stabilize the country, and on 31 July Gen Fuad Chehab was elected President. The new government was formed on 15 October, and the last US troops left on the 25th. The Lebanon crisis demonstrated the ability of the United States to bring enormous power to bear in the eastern Mediterranean at very short notice. Order was restored without bloodshed in one of the more successful Superpower interventions.

Jordan, Lebanon and Iraq, 1958

Unit	Aircraft (Buzz letters)	Base	From	To
United States Air Force				
Combined Air Strike Force Bravo				
354 TFW[1]	F-100D (FW)	Incirlik ex-Myrtle Beach AFB	18.7.58	10.58
355 TFS[2]	F-100D (FW)	Aviano	15.7.58	10.58
345 BG[3]	B-57B (BA)	Incirlik ex-Langley AFB	20.7.58	10.58
18 TRS[4]	RF-101C (FB)	Incirlik ex-Shaw AFB	17.7.58	10.58
Transport fleet				
322 AD	C-130A	Rhein-Main AB	based	
	C-119G	Evreux	based	
63 TCW	C-124B	Rhein-Main AB	based	

NOTES
1 20 aircraft drawn from 352, 353 and 356 TFSs
2 18 aircraft from 354 TFW
3 12 aircraft drawn from 498, 499, 500 and 501 BSs
4 5 aircraft (432 TRW)

Unit	Aircraft	Code
United States Navy		
USS *Saratoga* (CVA-60) with CAG-3 embarked.		
VF-31	F3H-2N	100 AC
VF-32	F8U-1	200 AC

Unit	Aircraft	Code
VA-34	A4D-1	300 AC
VA-35	AD-6	400 AC
VAH-9 det 43	A3D-2	700 GE
VA(AW)-33 det 43	AD-5N	800 GD
VFP-62 det 43	F9F-6P	900 PL
HU-2 det 43	HUP-2	UP
USS *Essex* (CVA-9) with ATG-201 embarked.		
VF-11	F2H-4	100 AP
VF-62	FJ-3M	200 AP
VA-83	A4D-1	300 AP
VA-105	AD-6	400 AP
VAH-7 det 45	AJ2	500 AP
VAW-12 det 45	AD-5W	GE
VA(AW(33 det 45	AD-5N	GD
VFP-62 det 45	F9F-8P	900
HU-2 det 45	HUP-2	UP
USS *Lake Champlain* (CVS-39)		
VS-27	S2F-1,2	MA
HS-3	HSS-1	HB
VAW-12 det 34	AD-5W	GE
HU-2 det 34	HUP-2	UP

BRITAIN IN JORDAN

The Jordanian appeal, which came on 16 July, was immediately supported, and at dawn on the 17th, in Operation *Fortitude*, 200 troops of the 2nd Bn the Parachute Regt were in Amman, having been flown in from Cyprus by Hastings of 70 Sqn. For a time they seemed to be isolated, since Israel temporarily refused permission for further overflights.

After pressure from the US Government, which was itself heavily involved in the Lebanon, the Israelis relented, and successive flights of RAF transport aircraft were escorted by American fighters from the Sixth Fleet; by the 18th, 2,200 troops of the 16th Independent Parachute Brigade were in Amman with light artillery support. Reinforcements had been flown into Cyprus from the UK by Comet C.2s of 216 Sqn and Shackletons, drawn from 42 and 204 Sqns; Beverleys of 84 Sqn flew in heavy equipment from Cyprus.

In all, 1,000 tons of freight was flown in, plus 120 vehicles and 6,000 gals of fuel. The troops were followed on the 20th by a detachment of Hunter F.6 fighters of 208 Sqn from Akrotiri. There was no British carrier in the area throughout the period of tension. The Royal Jordanian Air Force (RJAF) was no match in terms of equipment for those of Syria or Iraq. The combat element comprised a total of nine Vampire FB.9s and seven Vampire FB.52s, the latter ironically a gift from Egypt. The first of a batch of Hunter F Mk 6 fighters for 1 Sqn had been received but were not operational.

SEQUEL

King Hussein secured a pledge of loyalty from the powerful Bedouin tribes on 11 August, and British troops began withdrawing after the UN resolution calling for an end to Western intervention later in the month. The last British troops left on 2 November 1958. Although the Jordanian position was not as volatile as that in Lebanon, the British presence helped to stabilize the area and mended relationships with Jordan, which had deteriorated from 1956.

Jordan, Lebanon and Iraq, 1958

Unit	Aircraft	Base	From	To
RAF				
Air defence				
208 Sqn det	Hunter F.6	Amman	20.7.58	10.58
Transport				
70 Sqn	Hastings C1, C.2	Nicosia	17.7.58	2.11.58
84 Sqn	Beverley C.1	Khormaksar	17.7.58	10.58
47 Sqn	Beverley C.1	Abingdon	18.7.58	10.58
53 Sqn	Beverley C.1	Abingdon	18.7.58	10.58
99 Sqn	Hastings C1, C.2	Lyneham	17.7.58	10.58
216 Sqn	Comet C.2	Lyneham	18.7.58	8.58
42 Sqn	Shackleton MR.2	St Mawgan/Abingdon	18.7.58	8.58
204 Sqn	Shackleton MR.2	Ballykelly/Abingdon	18.7.58	8.58
Royal Jordanian Air Force				
1 Sqn	Vampire FB.9	Mafraq	based	
2 Sqn	Vampire FB.9, FB.52	Amman	based	
	Marathon, Viking	Amman	based	

5.5　KUWAIT, 1961

BACKGROUND

Britain reached an exclusive agreement for protection with the ruler of Kuwait in 1899, well before oil was discovered in the 1930s. By 1960 the agreement was dated, and an Exchange of Notes was signed in June 1961 agreeing, *inter alia*, that Her Majesty's Government would assist the ruler if requested. On 25 June the leader of

Transferred to Bahrein from Aden at the outset were the Shackletons of 37 Sqn including WR962/A. These aircraft were of great value in counter insurgency operations but would not have fared well against Iraqi Hunters.

(Author's collection)

Two Canberra squadrons from RAF Germany were deployed to Sharjah for interdiction tasks. WT342 was an 88 Sqn aircraft here seen prior to departure. *(Author's collection)*

To provide overall photo reconnaissance cover several Canberra PR.7s of 13 Sqn were detached from Akrotiri to Bahrein including WT530. Tactical reconnaissance was provided by Hunter FR.10s of 8 Sqn at Farwania.
(Author's collection)

Both of the local Beverley squadrons were heavily involved in Operation *Vantage*. Aircraft of 30 Sqn (XH120 here) were detached from Kenya to Bahrein. *(Author's collection)*

Another Middle East unit involved was 78 Sqn with the Twin Pioneer, extremely useful for short and rough strip operations. XL991 is readied for another sortie while '992 in the background is loaded with freight. *(78 Sqn)*

Much of the UK-based strategic transport fleet was committed to ferrying troops and equipment into Kuwait. The ageing Hastings of 24, 36 and 114 Sqns were all engaged. WJ330/330 of 24 Sqn was based at Colerne. *(Author's collection)*

The much newer and faster Britannia from 99 and 511 Sqns at Lyneham were also involved. XM519 is a C.1; aircraft were pooled rather than being allocated to a specific unit. *(Author's collection)*

Iraq, Abdul Qarim Qassem, declared Kuwait a part of Iraq, and troops began to move south from Baghdad.

The following day all UK forces in the Middle East were placed on four-day standby. There were three frigates in the theatre, and the commando carrier HMS *Bulwark*, with 42 RM Commando embarked, at Karachi. An amphibious warfare squadron was based on Bahrein, while Army units were located at Sharjah, Bahrein, Aden, Kenya and Cyprus. The RAF had two Hunter ground-attack squadrons at Aden and Nairobi, light transport and communications aircraft at Bahrein and Aden and heavier transports at Aden. Equipment reserves were stocked at Bahrein and in Kenya.

RESPONSE

A Reinforced Theatre Plan (RTF) for support to Kuwait had already been drafted as Plan *Vantage*. The plan envisaged supplementing the locally available forces with those on Cyprus, plus UK-based transport squadrons and Germany-based Canberra units. Problems anticipated were the lack of any surface routes into the area, the absence of air defence radar and restrictions on overflying many countries, including Saudi Arabia and Somalia.

On 29 June, in advance of a request for help, the first moves were made. Stockpiles at Bahrein were opened up and HMS *Bulwark* steamed from Karachi. The two Hunter squadrons, 8 and 208, were prepared and moved up to Bahrein on the 30th from Khormaksar and Eastleigh respectively; they were operational by the end of the day. Two Shackleton MR.2s of 37 Sqn moved up to Bahrein for reconnaissance duties, and 88 Sqn with Canberras at Wildenrath was ordered to Sharjah. Five Britannias in the area were cleared to join with Comet 4 and Argonaut aircraft of East African Airways in transporting HQ 24 Brigade from Kenya to the Gulf. Argonauts of 3 Sqn Royal Rhodesian Air Force (RRhAF) also supported the transfer.

The formal request for military support came late on the 30th, but early on the following day there was a setback when Turkey and Sudan refused permission for overflights. Both countries relaxed their positions later in the day.

The first unit to land in Kuwait on 1 July was 42 RM Commando, lifted from HMS *Bulwark* by Whirlwinds of 848 NAS. The Hunters landed at Kuwait New Airfield at Farwania later in the morning, and Britannias of 99 and 511 Sqns began lifting 45 RM Commando and the 11th Hussars from Aden. Four Canberras of 88 Sqn landed at Sharjah, where they were joined on the 2nd by eight B(I).6s of 213 Sqn from Brüggen, and Twin Pioneers of 78 Sqn from Aden joined those of B Flight of 152 Sqn at Bahrein, with elements operating from Farwania. Half a squadron of the 3rd Dragoon Guards was landed from HMS *Striker* with their Centurion tanks.

The build-up continued, with maximum RAF commitment by the 4th. By then Comets of 216 Sqn were involved, together with fourteen Britannias, in transporting elements of the 2nd Bn Parachute Regiment from the UK and Cyprus. Their equipment was moved by twenty-seven Hastings from three UK-based units and the Cyprus-based 70 Sqn, together with twelve Beverleys from 47 and 53 Sqns. The 1st Bn Royal Inniskillings was transported from Kenya in chartered aircraft and Beverleys of 30 Sqn, while two companies of the Coldstream Guards moved up to Kuwait from Bahrein with the help of six Valettas of 233 Sqn. Finally, several Canberra PR.7s of 13 Sqn flew into Bahrein from Akrotiri.

Once in Kuwait, the troops took up positions along the Mutla Ridge to the north-west of Kuwait Town. Conditions were appalling, with daytime temperatures of 120 °F and high winds creating sandstorms and a visibility often less than four hundred yards. During the emergency one Hunter of 208 Sqn was lost when it flew into the Mutla Ridge after the pilot was presumed to have become disorientated. Most RAF ground crew were already from the theatre, and they were to some extent acclimatized, but the men were rotated onto HMS *Bulwark* for rest. The carrier also provided the only air defence radar, with an effective range of about eighty miles, and complex communications to the Hunter squadrons.

Communications as a whole were a major problem. The headquarters was established at HMS *Jufair* at Bahrein, some 300 miles from Kuwait. Distances were too great for the use of landlines and radio-telegraphy, and most signals were delivered by air letter using the AOC's Canberra between Aden and Bahrein and Pembrokes of A Flt, 152 Sqn, between Bahrein, Sharjah and Kuwait. A further problem was that RAF aircraft were fitted with VHF radio, while those of the Fleet Air Arm (FAA) were UHF-equipped.

Air defences were improved from 9 July with the arrival of HMS *Victorious* with AEW Gannets and Sea Vixen all-weather fighters. The carrier's Type 984 radar extended cover to 150 miles. It was not until the 18th that the RAF had its own radar unit, a 'portable' Type SC 787, established, although that lacked a height-finding capability.

If an attack was to be made it might have been expected on Iraq's national day, the 14th, but no moves were made beyond Basra. From the 20th it was felt safe to withdraw forces, and 42 Commando and 2 Para moved to Bahrein, while 45 Commando returned to Aden.

SEQUEL

The Canberras returned to Germany, although a Cyprus-based unit was earmarked to reinforce if necessary, and 208 Sqn Hunters withdrew to Bahrein. The UK-based transport aircraft were released late in July, and on the 31st HMS *Centaur* relieved HMS *Victorious*. By the end of September all units had returned to their more usual policing tasks. It is not possible to say whether the reinforcement averted a war in the area. The speed of relocation in difficult circumstances was remarkable, and several important lessons about communications and stockpiling were learnt and subsequently applied. One result of the exercise was improvements to the airfields at Bahrein and Sharjah.

In August 1990 Iraq did invade Kuwait, which appealed to the West for help. A coalition was formed and a successful counter-invasion was launched on 17 January 1991 (Chapter 9, Section 4).

DE HAVILLAND SEA VIXEN

The twin-boom de Havilland DH110 was developed against RAF Specification F.44/46 for a night-fighter, and the prototype flew on 26 September 1951. In the event the specification was met by the Gloster Javelin, while a contemporary naval specification, N.40/46, was met by the de Havilland Sea Venom. Naval interest in the DH110 was kept alive, however, and after a swept-wing Venom development (the DH116) was rejected, work progressed on the DH110 prototypes. The prototype had crashed with appalling results at the Farnborough air show in 1952, but the second prototype was used for touch-and-go trials on HMS *Albion* in 1954. The third prototype flew in 1955 with a rounded nose and an arrester hook, allowing full carrier trials on HMS *Ark Royal*, but with no folding wing.

The **FAW Mark 1** was originally designated FAW Mark 20, and was produced against Specification N.139P. The first production aircraft flew on 20 March 1957, and the Sea Vixen entered operational service with 892 NAS in July 1959. It was the first British fighter aircraft to be designed without guns. Armament comprised four Firestreak AAMs or four Microcell rocket packs or two 1,000 lb bombs and two Bullpup ASMs. In addition twenty-eight 51 mm rockets were stored internally, and two underwing fuel tanks were also carried.

The **FAW Mark 2** version incorporated provision for 2,000 lb of extra fuel in slipper tanks within boom extensions projecting forward of the wing leading edge. In addition the armament was improved by the replacement of the Firestreak by the Red Top all-aspect AAM. Sixty-seven FAW.1 aircraft were converted, and these were supplemented by a number of new-build aircraft. The new arrangements were tested on two FAW Mk 1 aircraft, beginning in June 1962, and the first production FAW.2 flew on 8 March 1963.

Fighter units equipped – 890, 892, 893, 899

Kuwait, 1961

Unit	Aircraft	Base	From	To
RAF				
In theatre				
8 Sqn	Hunter FGA.9, FR.10	Farwania ex-Khormaksar	30.6.61	30.7.61
208 Sqn	Hunter FGA.9	Farwania ex-Eastleigh	30.6.61	22.7.61
88 Sqn	Canberra B(I).8	Sharjah ex-Wildenrath	1.7.61	20.7.61
213 Sqn	Canberra B(I).6	Sharjah ex-Brüggen	2.7.61	20.7.61
37 Sqn	Shackleton MR.2	Bahrein ex-Khormaksar	30.6.61	22.7.61
13 Sqn det	Canberra PR.7	Bahrein ex-Akrotiri	4.7.61	21.7.61

Unit	Aircraft	Base	From	To
Fleet Air Arm				
HMS *Bulwark* 1 July to 21 July 1961. Carrier code B				
848 NAS	Whirlwind HAS.7	/B		
HMS *Victorious* 9 July to 31 July 1961. Carrier code V				
803 NAS	Scimitar F.1	15x/V		
892 NAS	Sea Vixen FAW.1	20x-21x/V		
849 NAS B Flt	Gannet AEW.3	43x/V		
HMS *Centaur* 31 July to 24 August 1961. Carrier code C				
807 NAS	Scimitar F.1	19x/C		
893 NAS	Sea Vixen FAW.1	45x/C		
824 NAS	Whirlwind HAS.7	33x/C		
849 NAS D Flt	Gannet AEW.3	45x/C152 Sqn Twin Pioneer CC.1 Bahrein,		
Farwania	30.6.61	9.61		
	Pembroke C.1			
78 Sqn	Twin Pioneer CC.1	Farwania ex-Khormaksar	30.6.61	8.61
233 Sqn	Varsity C.1	Bahrein ex-Khormaksar	30.6.61	8.61
84 Sqn	Beverley C.1	Khormaksar	30.6.61	8.61
30 Sqn	Beverley C.1	Bahrein ex-Eastleigh	1.7.61	8.61
70 Sqn	Hastings C.1	Akrotiri	3.7.61	8.61
Strategic transport, UK based				
99 Sqn	Britannia C.1	Lyneham	1.7.61	26.7.61
511 Sqn	Britannia C.1	Lyneham	1.7.61	26.7.61
24 Sqn	Hastings C.1	Colerne	3.7.61	24.7.61
36 Sqn	Hastings C.1	Colerne	3.7.61	24.7.61
114 Sqn	Hastings C.1	Colerne	3.7.61	24.7.61
216 Sqn	Comet C.4	Lyneham	3.7.61	9.7.61
47 Sqn	Beverley C.1	Abingdon	3.7.61	26.7.61
53 Sqn	Beverley C.1	Abingdon	3.7.61	26.7.61
Royal Rhodesian Air Force				
3 Sqn	C-4 Argonaut	Salisbury	1.7.61	8.7.61

In addition, chartered Argonauts and Comet C.4s of East African Airways brought elements of 24 Brigade from Kenya

5.6   DHOFAR, 1965–75

INTRODUCTION

Oman was extremely conservatively ruled, and it was inevitable that frustration about relative taxation and deprivation would lead to rebellion. After the problems in the north in the 1950s the SAF had been strengthened and the Sultan of Oman's Air Force (SOAF) was formed in 1959, based at Muscat.

    But trouble was now to come in the Dhofar region in the south, where the Sultan Said bin Taimur lived. In 1962 the Dhofar Liberation Front (DLF) was formed, and with help from Egypt, Saudi Arabia and Iraq it formally began operations against the regime from 9 June 1965, with bases at Hauf and Al Ghayda in East Aden Protectorate. Soon the mountains behind the narrow coastal plain were under DLF control, and by 1966 Salalah,

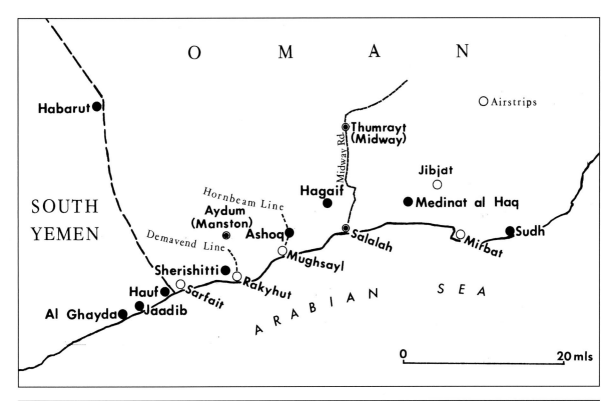

Beverley XM109/R of 84 Sqn kicks up dust taking off over SOAF Beaver AL.1 XR214 of 5 Sqn at Seeb. *(84 Sqn)*

the regional capital and RAF staging-post, was protected by a ring of defences, including wire; it was virtually isolated by road.

ACTION

Offensive air power was confined to five armed piston-engined Provost trainers flown by seconded RAF or direct-contract pilots. In the early days of the conflict there was no prospect of dealing with the situation through air control, especially when the population supported the DLF, whose base was better secured when Britain left Aden late in 1967. The following year it was absorbed into the People's Front for the Liberation of the Occupied Arabian Gulf (PFLOAG), sponsored not surprisingly by the People's Democratic Republic of the Yemen (PDRY). Britain was keen to retain influence and stability in the area, to guarantee the free flow of oil through the Straits of Hormuz.

With the withdrawal from Aden, several RAF units moved up into the Gulf area, including the two Hunter squadrons. It is not clear whether any of these units operated against targets in Dhofar before their disbandment in 1971. Certainly an increasing number of RAF pilots was seconded to the SOAF, but throughout the operations Britain went to some lengths not to appear publicly to be involved in the internal affairs of Oman.

The position deteriorated during 1968. On 7 August the rebels attacked the RAF camp at Salalah, and a Provost was hit by ground fire, Baghdad Radio claiming forty-nine British servicemen killed and a Hunter shot down. In this period 51 Sqn RAF Regiment was deployed to protect the airfield at Salalah. In August 1969 the rebels captured the coastal town of Rakhyut.

Also in 1969, the SAS Regiment saw action on the Musandam Peninsula overlooking the Straits of Hormuz. An Iraqi irregular group had infiltrated, and SAS soldiers were landed by sea and air to deal with the problem. To the

The Army Air Corps was active supporting ground forces in Dhofar. Poor but rare photo of Sioux AH.1 M of 668 Sqn hovers before another sortie. *(P R Grant)*

many British military and administrative advisers it now became clear that, if the integrity of Oman was to be preserved, radical changes in governance and military response were essential.

On 23 July 1970 the Sultan was deposed by his son, the Sultan Qaboos bin Said. Almost immediately plans for social change and military action were formulated, and SAS units were moved to Salalah to form British Army Training Teams (BATT) to work in the Jebel on a 'hearts and minds' campaign. Leaflet drops encouraged surrender, and many rebel supporters were eventually formed into tribal 'firqats' (paramilitary groups) to fight in support of the government.

In February 1971, with Strikemaster support, the SAS and a local firqat liberated the eastern town of Sudh. The overall plan was to secure areas to the east of Salalah and then to prevent supplies flowing from South Yemen, all in the context of denying the PFLOAC popular support. In Operation *Jaguar* from October to December 1971, key posts were established at Jibjat and Medinat al Haq, and sustained by helicopter supply. By now the SOAF could boast a squadron of Strikemaster light attack aircraft, one of which was brought down on 15 September 1971.

There was also a squadron of AB.205 and 206 helicopters and a large detachment of Skyvan light transports at Salalah. It was possibly the availability of these rugged and reliable short take-off and landing (STOL) aircraft that in the long term enabled the war to be won. They carted loads around the region using roughly and often hastily prepared strips only several hundred yards long. They were also used to destroy insurgent crops with makeshift 'bombs' made from drums of Avtur with dissolved polyurethane ignited by flares. The AB.205 version of the ubiquitous UH-1 also came into its own to ensure the deployment of troops, their resupply and, most importantly, speedy casualty evacuation.

The rebels, numbering about 2,500, were very well supplied with modern Soviet weaponry, including rifles, machine-guns, heavy mortars, 14.5 mm anti-aircraft MGs and Katyusha rockets. They were extremely mobile and could bring their weapons to bear on government forces from easily protected positions on the Jebel. But the key to supply was a single route from South Yemen through the Wadi Sayq, overlooked by Sarfait. In April 1972 the town was taken by the Desert Regiment of the SAF in a heliborne assault. Initially the SAF was supplied by Skyvan, but constant shelling from across the border made this method too dangerous, so for the next four years resupply was by helicopter. In April and May Strikemasters attacked targets in South Yemen, critically at Hauf, Jaadib and Habarut.

On 11 May the PDRY formally protested that British aircraft were violating Yemeni airspace and attacking towns and villages, including Socotra island. During the summer months Dhofar is subject to monsoons, during which air support is hazardous. In these conditions the PFLOAC prepared for a full-scale assault on the eastern coastal town of Mirbat, which was defended only by a small SAS unit, local gendarmerie and a firqat.

A force of 250 well-organized rebels attacked at dawn on 19 July 1972, having taken a small hill to the north of the town. The defenders held out through the initial attack, and within several hours Strikemasters flew in below the cloud to strafe enemy positions, while helicopters brought reinforcements and removed the injured. By mid-morning the battle was won, and the rebel forces not only lost face but were never able to mount a similar attack in the future.

During 1972 Oman received tangible external support from Jordan (a special-force battalion), Pakistan (a hundred Baluchi NCOs and officers) and, most notably, Iran (which eventually contributed 2,400 troops and several squadrons of fighters and helicopters). All of these forces were under SAF control and made a vitally important contribution to winning the war; indeed, through 1973 the Iranian AB.205s supported the supply of the Sarfait garrison. The SOAF lost its first aircraft on 9 July 1973, when Strikemaster '413' was shot down over western Oman and the British pilot was killed. When PDRY aircraft bombed Omani territory on 18 November, Iran guaranteed the integrity of Omani airspace.

In 1973, in an effort to restrict supply trains, construction began of the *Hornbeam* line. Completed in 1974, it ran inland from Mughsayl for some thirty-three miles, and was constructed of barbed wire and mines. Wessex helicopters of 72 Sqn were detached to Salalah from April 1974 to help with the project. The Imperial Iranian Battle Group (IIBG) was based around *Midway* (later renamed Thumrayt), and had responsibility for the Midway Road from Salalah. Although rebels were still operating widely in the area behind Salalah, the government's grip was tightening. In 1974 the PFLOAG assumed the less ambitious title of People's Front for the Liberation of Oman (PFLO).

There were many contacts with small groups of the PFLO through 1974, and plans were now drawn up to extend government control in the west. The IIBC evacuated Thumrayt in October, moving their main base of operations to *Manston* (Aydum), from where they reoccupied Rakyhut on 5 January 1975 with Strikemaster cover. Development of a second supply filter, the *Demavend* line, began. Operations were now focused on clearing rebel positions along the line. In each case the SAF would move on foot or by helicopter with Strikemaster support available at fifteen minutes' notice, and, subject to location, resupply would be by helicopter or Skyvan. Fighting was often intense, with PFLO fighters making optimum use of the difficult terrain.

In January fighting was concentrated around Sherishitti, followed in February by Operation *Himaar*, an attack on the 9 June Regiment's HQ north of Ashoq on the *Hornbeam* line. By now the helicopters were flying a total of 600 hours a month, and several were lost in accidents and to ground fire; on 8 March an AB.206 was shot down near Hagaif. Preparations were now made to clear the area west of the *Demavend* line.

On 10 May 1974 Strikemaster '410' had been shot down, but in August 1975 a new threat emerged when Strikemaster '406' was shot down by SA-7 on the 19th near Sherishitti. More rounds were fired at rescue helicopters and a circling Strikemaster, but no further hits were recorded and the pilot was picked up injured. In all, twenty-three SA-7 rounds would be fired for the loss of three aircraft, one being an IIAF gunship on 15 September.

From now on, aircraft operating patterns changed, with the slow helicopters keeping to altitudes above 10,000 ft. In October, what was to be the final major operation began as the plateau below Sarfait was invested. In order to counter the cross-border artillery fire, three 5.5 in. howitzers were flown in by IIAF CH-47C Chinooks and rapidly set up; in addition, newly delivered Hunters of 6 Sqn from Thumrayt attacked targets in South Yemen from 17 October to 21 November, concentrating on Hauf and Jaadib.

Despite losing two more AB.205 helicopters on 1 November and 25 December, the SAF was in a sufficiently commanding position that on 11 December the war was declared won, although the shelling of positions around Sarfait continued until a negotiated ceasefire in March 1976. There has been sporadic action since that time, and an IIAF F-4E was reported to have been shot down over eastern Yemen on 25 November 1976.

SEQUEL

The SAS Regiment, although formally withdrawn in March 1976, retained a strong presence for 'training' purposes, and for some time the SOAF continued to fly operational sorties against rebels. Oman has retained strong ties with Britain, and during the Second Gulf War (Chapter 9, Section 4) she hosted British and US forces. Thumrayt is a USAF storage base. In 2001, a large UK exercise, *Saif Sareea II*, was held jointly with Omani forces as a precursor to British involvement in Iraq and Afghanistan.

Dhofar, 1965–75

Unit	Aircraft	Base	From	To
RAF				
208 Sqn det	Hunter FGA.9	Muharraq	12.61	8.6.64
208 Sqn			8.6.64	10.9.71
8 Sqn det	Hunter FR.10	Masirah, Sharjah, Muharraq	14.10.61	5.63[1]
1417 Flt det	Hunter FR.10	As above	1.3.63	8.9.67
8 Sqn det	Hunter FR.10	Muharraq	9.67	21.12.71
8 Sqn det	Hunter FGA.9	Masirah, Sharjah, Muharraq	1.60	7.8.67
8 Sqn		Masirah	8.8.67	9.8.67
		Muharraq	8.9.67	21.12.71
210 Sqn	Shackleton MR.2	Sharjah	1.11.70	15.11.71
84 Sqn	Beverley C.1	Khormaksar	65	2.9.67
	+ Andover C.1	Sharjah	3.9.67	29.12.70
		Muharraq	30.12.70	1.10.71
78 Sqn	Wessex HC.2	Khormaksar	6.65	12.10.67
		Sharjah	13.10.67	21.12.71
72 Sqn	Wessex HC. 2	Salalah	6.4.74	11.74
British Army				
13 Flt	Beaver AL.1	Sharjah	11.67	30.9.68
13 Sqn	Beaver AL.1	Sharjah	1.10.68	30.11.69
688 Sqn	Beaver AL.1	Sharjah	1.12.69	11.71
MELF AT	Sioux AH.1	Sharjah	11.67	11.71
Infantry AP	Sioux AH.1	Sharjah	11.67	11.71
RAC/RA	Sioux AH.1	Sharjah	11.67	11.71
Sultanate of Muscat and Oman's Air Force (SOAF from August 1970)				
1 Sqn	Provost T.52	Muscat	59	73
	Pioneer CC.1	Muscat	59	62
	Strikemaster Mk 82	Salalah	1.69	
6 Sqn	Hunter F.6, FGA.9, Mk 73	Thumrayt	8.75	
5 Sqn	Beaver AL.1, Defender	Seeb, det Salalah	62	
2 Sqn	Skyvan 3M	Seeb	8.70	
4 Sqn	C-47, Caribou, Viscount, BAC.111, C-130H	Seeb	68	
3 Sqn	AB.205A, AB.206B	Salalah	10.70	
Imperial Iranian Air Force				
	F-5E	Thumrayt	74	74
	F-4E	Thumrayt	74	76
	C-130H	Thumrayt, Aydum	73	76
	AB.205	As above	9.73	76
	CH-47C	Aydum	9.75	12.75

NOTES
1 to 1417 Flt

CHAPTER SIX

Humanitarian Aid, Peacekeeping and Conflict Avoidance

The first significant airlift of civilians was conducted by the RAF in 1928, creating a precedent for support and aid across the world in ensuing years. In all, 586 people were evacuated from Kabul to Peshawar from 23 December by Victoria aircraft of 70 Sqn during tribal unrest and insurrection.

The services have a fine record of providing worldwide relief to civilians, either through evacuation or by the provision of supplies. At the end of the war the RAF played a major part in Operation *Manna*, in which thirty-three bomber squadrons dropped food to civilians starving in the Netherlands. Between 29 April and 8 May 1945, 6,685 tons were dropped in 3,205 sorties.

Subsequently, the RAF has been the service primarily involved in evacuation and supply simply because it is the only military arm which operates large transport aircraft. However, the Army and Royal Navy have frequently used their helicopters more locally and on a smaller scale to offer succour and relief.

Some of the support has been so immediate and local that it has barely been reported, while other operations, like the Berlin Airlift (Chapter 2, Section 2), merit books. What follows in this chapter is a year-by-year summary of airlift and aid operations, together with a section on the evolution of search and rescue around the United Kingdom.

Immediately after the war the emphasis was on the repatriation of servicemen from war zones and civilians and prisoners of war from occupied territories. The first post-war evacuation of civilians from conflict was in 1947, with the transfer of non-essential personnel from Palestine. This presaged a process continued through many years on any occasion that British nationals were under threat from insurgency or war. Thus, during the period covered by this book, the RAF was at hand in China (1949), Iran and Egypt (1951), Sudan (1955), Belgian Congo (1960), Indonesia (1963), Congo (1964), Aden (1967), East Pakistan (1971), Malta (1972), Bangladesh (1973), Cyprus (1974), Cambodia, South Vietnam and Angola (1975), Iran (1979), Lebanon (1984) and Yemen (1986).

The first post-war aid programme was in Burma, and it was to be the first of many famine-relief operations maintained to this day, mainly in Europe, Asia and Africa. These have included Berlin (1948), Hungary (1956), Kenya and Somalia (1961), Tanganyika (1962), Jordan (1970), East Pakistan (1970), Nepal, Mali, Senegal and Sudan (1973), Nicaragua and Cambodia (1979), Nepal (1980) and Ethiopia (1984).

Aid and evacuation was not confined to foreign climes. All services were heavily involved in the disastrous North Sea floods of 1953, and then from 1955 onwards the RAF dropped supplies, especially of animal foodstuffs, to isolated communities whenever severe weather cut them off. A more peculiar, but potentially just as humanitarian, operation was the destruction of the stricken and leaking tanker *Torrey Canyon* in 1967.

There is no geographical limit to the services' aid in the event of natural disaster, although in general the Pacific has been too distant for immediate response. The first post-war operation was to Turkey after an earthquake in 1953. This was followed by the Ionian Islands (1953), Algeria, Iraq and Haiti (1954), Mauritius, Morocco, Chile (1960), British Honduras and South Vietnam (1961), Bahamas (1963), South Vietnam (1965–6), Kenya (1967), Turkey and Peru (1970), East Pakistan (1971), Philippines and Nicaragua (1972), Australia (1974), Turkey (1976), Colombia (1985), Jamaica (1988) and Montserrat (1989).

The services have often been called upon either to provide troops in the colonies to avert insurrection or to transport foreign forces. These conflict-avoidance operations have included Trieste (1947), Uganda, Belgian Congo and Cameroons (1960), Rhodesia and Zanzibar (1961), Berlin, British Guiana and India (1962), Anguilla, Cyprus and Swaziland (1963), Berlin (1965), Basutoland (1966), Gibralter (1967), Anguilla (1969), British Honduras (1972), Egypt (1973), Falklands (1977), Zaire (1978), Rhodesia (1979), New Hebrides (1980), Gambia (1981) and Iran/Iraq (1987–90).

The air-sea rescue service started during the war with a combination of search and air-drop aircraft, light amphibians and launches. Its role was the discovery and rescue of downed Allied airmen. With the responsibilities associated with emerging commercial aviation and the advent of the helicopter, there was a dramatic shift in provision around the UK, but this had been preceded by the establishment of the FEAF Casualty Evacuation Flight formed in Malaya in 1950 to recover soldiers wounded in the insurgency.

The UK-based helicopter service started in 1952, but it was not until the mid-1970s that there was complete coverage of the mainland and coastal areas, supplemented by Shackleton and then Nimrod aircraft equipped for longer-range search support. By the 1990s, due to a consistent increase in leisure activities like sailing and climbing, coupled with a huge reduction in military flying around the UK, the service was primarily a broad humanitarian one, working closely with the RNLI and Mountain Rescue Services. While still having a primarily military remit, it now rescues far more civilians each year.

6.1   HUMANITARIAN AID AND PEACEKEEPING, 1940s

1945

Even before the war had ended, the Royal Air Force was engaged on its first major humanitarian relief project. For a variety of reasons, the population of the western **Netherlands** was starving, and between November 1944 and spring 1945 some 30,000, mainly the very young and very old, had died.

From 29 April to 8 May 1945, in Operation *Manna*, Lancasters of 1, 3 and 8 Groups RAF Bomber Command had dropped around 6,685 tons of food in some 3,181 low-level sorties. The operation was negotiated with the Germans, and six drop zones were marked by Mosquitoes, which flew 124 sorties. The USAAF joined the effort from 1 May in Operation *Chowhound*, flying 2,200 B-17 sorties and dropping a further 3,700 tons.

With the war in **Europe** ended a priority was the repatriation of a large number of Allied prisoners of war. On the night of 24/25 April 1945, leaflets had been dropped at eight POW camps advising of impending repatriation, and medical supplies had been dropped into one camp. Then in Operation *Exodus*, which started on 26 April, over 74,000 prisoners were returned to the UK in a month, mainly in Lancaster bombers adapted to carry twenty-five men. Some 2,900 sorties were conducted by aircraft of 1, 5, 6 and 8 Groups flying from B58 airfield (Melsbroek, near Brussels) to reception centres including that at Dunsfold.

The Lancasters were kept busy throughout 1945 and 1946 between the UK and bases at Bari and Pomigliano in **Italy**. In Operation *Dodge*, they transported 8th Army veterans, some of whom had been in theatre for five years, to and from the UK on leave. From early 1946 one-way trips were flown as troops were brought home for demobilization.

As soon as the war in the **Far East** was over, there was an urgent need to support an estimated 123,000 interned civilians and POWs who had endured so much at the hands of the Japanese. Initially, in Operation *Birdcage*, some 33 million leaflets were dropped advising that the war had ended. The most immediate need then was for medical teams and supplies, including food, clothing and medicines, which were dropped to prisoners of war in camps in Burma and Siam between 26 and 30 August 1945 in Operation *Mastiff*.

Then began the Recovery of Allied Prisoners of War and Internees (RAPWI) from Burma, Siam, Indo-China and Sumatra. Once the most immediate demands were met, supplies were flown out to internment and POW camps, and evacuees were flown back to Singapore. Priority was given to the sick and wounded. Key among the units involved was 31 Sqn, based at Kalang with Dakotas. In December Sunderlands of 230 Sqn began repatriating personnel from Batavia to Malaya. In addition some five Liberator (159, 203, 232, 321 and 355) and two Sunderland squadrons (205 and 240) were kept busy flying supplies out of Ceylon.

When 31 Sqn disbanded in September 1946, its aircraft had flown more than 11,200 sorties, carrying 127,800 passengers and 26,000 tons of freight in the year.

1946

Following widespread destruction of rice paddies in **Burma**, coupled with neglect and increased demand from the military, it became evident that many Burmese were in dire need of food. Relief sorties were flown by the RAF in Operation *Hunger* from January, with Dakotas of 62 Sqn and Liberators of 355 Sqn dropping more than 3,000 tons of rice by March. Demand continued, though, leading to Operation *Hunger II*, which involved Dakotas of 10 Sqn and Halifaxes of 298 Sqn: between them they dropped 2,650 tons. The task continued with Operations *Hunger III* and *IV*, the final sortie being undertaken in March 1947, by which time a further 740 tons had been dropped.

1947

In February, after two civilians had been kidnapped by Jewish extremists, non-essential civilians were evacuated from **Palestine** in Operation *Polly*. While some were flown to cities in Europe aboard chartered civilian aircraft, many more travelled by train to Egypt. Between the 5th and 6th 508 persons and 62,000 lb of baggage were taken from Aqir to Almaza aboard Halifax A.9 aircraft of 113 Sqn.

In July there was tension on the Yugoslavia-Italy border at Trieste over the former's post-war claim to the city. In Operation *Diagram* the RAF moved up 135 Wing, comprising 16 Sqn (code EG) and 26 Sqn (code XC) with the Tempest F.2, to Zeltweg in Austria from Fassberg. The detachment began on 13 July and ended on 12 August. During this period Mosquitoes of 21 Sqn (code YH) at Gütersloh were detached to Vienna-Schwechat.

1948

Berlin Airlift (see Chapter 2, Section 2)

1949

In April 1949 the frigate HMS *Amethyst* was sailing up the Yangtze River to relieve HMS *Consort*, the Nanking guard-ship. On the 20th she was fired on from Communist shore batteries and seriously damaged; her captain was killed. HMS *Consort* came to the rescue but was also shelled and damaged, being forced to retreat. The situation was obviously serious and the wounded needed urgent attention.

Sunderland ML772/D of 88 Sqn at Kai Tak flew to Shanghai on the 21st, and then on to *Amethyst*, where, despite gunfire, a doctor and supplies were dropped off. The aircraft returned the following day with more supplies and Navy personnel, but again had to beat a hasty retreat after dropping some supplies. The cruiser HMS *London* and frigate HMS *Black Swan* then tried to reach *Amethyst* upriver, but they were also shelled and damaged. In all, casualties on the four ships now totalled thirty-six dead and sixty-nine wounded. In due course, on 31 July, *Amethyst*, which had been grounded, slipped her moorings, and after a 104-mile dash reached safety.

From 15 May Sunderland flying boats of 88 Sqn based in Hong Kong evacuated 121 British nationals from Shanghai in the face of the Communist threat.

HANDLEY PAGE HALIFAX

Like the Stirling, the Halifax started life as a bomber, in which role it was highly successful. It was designed to a specification calling originally for a twin-engined bomber some 10,000 lb lighter than the Stirling. The bomber versions were out of front-line service by 1946.

The Mark III HP 61 was fitted with the Hercules XVI radial engine and was capable of carrying a heavier load. The **C Mark III** was a conversion of the B Mark III with the armament, mid-upper turret and H2S scanner removed; the conversion carried twenty-four troops up to 2,230 miles. The Met Mark III retained the armament but had minor changes in internal equipment.

The **Mark VI** (HP 61) employed the more powerful Hercules 100 and was the final bomber variant. Additional fuel in the wings conferred extended range: some were converted for meteorological use.

The **A Mark VII** HP 61 was similar to the Mark VI but with a Hercules XVI engine. There was no dorsal turret or radar scanner, and the type was fitted with a glider-towing hook. A total of 333 were built.

The **C Mark VIII** HP 70 was purpose-built as a transport, with no upper or rear turrets and dual control. The

Immediately after the war the Halifax served in several transport variants for several years until supplanted by the Hastings. Seen here is C Mk 8 PP245 of 298 Sqn, displaying the removable pannier capable of carrying 8,000 lbs of freight. *(Author's collection)*

variant was designed to carry a detachable freight pannier and up to eleven passengers. Many were later converted for civilian use as the Halton.

The **A Mk IX HP** 71 was built as an airborne forces variant, designed to carry sixteen fully equipped para-troopers. The prototype first flew in October 1945.

Transport units equipped – 47, 113, 202, 296, 297, 298, 301, 304, 620, 644

DOUGLAS DAKOTA

Surely the most famous of all transports, the Douglas Dakota was similar to the Douglas Commercial 3 (DC-3) of 1935. In all, 10,926 were built, of which more than 1,900 were supplied to the RAF; in USAAF service the DC-3 was designated C-47 and C-53. The type served in every theatre during the war and for many years after.

The **Mark III** was similar to the C-47A, powered by two Double Wasp engines of 1,200 hp and with a 24-volt electrical system rather than the 12-volt of the original model. The range was extended to 1,600 miles. It joined 31 Sqn in the Far East in early 1943 and served in all war theatres. The **Mark IV** was the equivalent of the C-47B, with high-altitude blowers and extra fuel to confer a higher operational ceiling. Many units were equipped with both Marks III and IV without distinction.

Transport units equipped – 10, 18, 21, 24,27, 30, 31, 46, 48, 52, 53, 62, 70, 76, 77, 78, 96, 110, 113, 114, 117, 147, 167, 187, 194, 204, 206, 209, 215, 216, 231, 233, 238, 243, 267, 271, 353, 435, 436, 437, 512, 525, 575, 620; 1315, 1325, 1359, 1359, 1680 Flts

SHORT SUNDERLAND/SEAFORD

The S.25 Sunderland was one of the longest-serving and most robust flying-boats; it was still in service some twenty years after first joining 230 Sqn in 1938. Originally designed to Specification R.22/36, the Sunderland was intended to replace the Singapore as a long-range maritime reconnaissance aircraft. The prototype Mark I, with four 1,010 hp Pegasus XXII engines, first flew on 16 October 1937, and the type was in service just eight months later. The Sunderland had a distinguished war, serving in fourteen squadrons in the United Kingdom, the Middle and Far East and Africa. The three early marks were out of service by the end of 1945.

The **Mark IV** was fitted with the much more powerful Hercules engine in order to improve speed. The hull was lengthened by 3 ft and the fin and rudder area was increased. The differences were sufficient to justify a new type number, and the S.45 Mark IV was renamed Seaford. The first prototype flew on 30 October 1944, and after protracted development only eight of the thirty ordered were completed. They entered service briefly with 210 Sqn in early 1946, but offered no improvement over the Sunderland V.

The **GR Mark 5** was the result of an Australian suggestion that the type would benefit from being re-engined with the Pratt and Whitney Double Wasp. The arrangement was first tried on a Mark III, and 150 production aircraft were built. A new radar, the ASV Mk VIC, was fitted in split scanners under the outer wings. Armament was four .303 in. guns in both nose and tail turrets, and two in the dorsal turret, plus two .5 in. manually operated guns in the beam position. Bomb load was 2,000 lb. The last GR.5 retired from RAF service with 205 Sqn in the Far East in 1959.

Operational units equipped – 88, 201, 205, 209, 230, 240

6.2   HUMANITARIAN AID AND PEACEKEEPING, 1950s

1950

From September, Hastings C.1s of 53 Sqn began routine casualty evacuation of wounded British military personnel from Seoul in **Korea** and Iwakuni in **Japan** to the United Kingdom. (See Chapter 2, Section 4).

1951

In June **Iran** nationalized the Anglo-Iranian Oil Company. The RAF deployed transport aircraft to the Canal Zone in Egypt, anticipating the need to fly in troops and to evacuate civilians. In the event some 900 civilians were flown out from Abadan by aircraft of British Overseas Airways Corporation (BOAC) and Trans-World Airlines (TWA) between 7 and 27 June.

Civilians were evacuated from **Egypt** (see Chapter 3, Section 3)

1953

On 31 January 1953 there was a storm surge sweeping down the North Sea associated with low pressure, strong winds and high tides. Sea defences crumbled and there was widespread flooding from Lincolnshire to Kent. In all, 307 lives were lost in the **United Kingdom**, including 133 when the Stranraer ferry sank in the Irish Sea. The situation was much worse in the **Netherlands**, where dykes broke and about 20% of the land was under water. Over several days some 1,800 died there.

Rescue in the UK was generally feasible by boat, and the only assets of immediate value were the Dragonfly HR.3s of 705 NAS based at Gosport. While a few Dragonflies remained in the UK, based at West Malling for reconnaissance and limited supply, most proceeded to Woensdrecht to support the Dutch authorities in their desperate situation. Between 2 and 19 February the ten pilots of 705 NAS rescued over 800 people in 402 flying hours, including sixty-four by winch, the vast majority in the first four days. One Dragonfly, WG748, was lost, but the crew escaped from the sinking machine to be rescued by a USAF S-55.

Aircraft from Transport Command were also involved in moving supplies to the Netherlands. In a reverse operation, *King Canute*, Hastings and Valettas flew eleven million US and NATO sandbags to the UK (Manston) between 13 and 15 February from as far afield as Zurich and Oslo to enable repair of sea defences. This was followed by the movement of heaters and pumps.

On 18 March there were serious earthquakes in **Turkey**. Valettas of 84 Sqn took relief supplies from Fayid to Istanbul.

The **Ionian Islands** were shaken by earthquakes on 13 August, with over 600 dead and many buildings destroyed. The cruiser HMS *Bermuda* (C52) was in Malta, and she sailed immediately with two Dragonfly heli-

The dreadful floods in the UK and the Netherlands in early 1953 saw the first significant use of helicopters in a major disaster. The Royal Navy deployed a number of Dragonflys to the Netherlands from 705 NAS at Gosport. WN493/534 is a machine from the unit. *(Author's collection)*

copters of 728 NAS at Hal Far aboard on the Y turret and quarterdeck. These were soon in operation, and additional crews and supplies were brought in by RAF Sunderland flying-boats.

As so often in these circumstances, the Americans came into their own, supplying fuel and tents for the British contingent, which had set up a convenient base on Zante. The helicopters were used for reconnaissance, rescue, leaflet dropping and supply. One aircraft was damaged and the remaining one embarked on HMS *Theseus* on 7 September for return to Malta after flying 114 sorties in seventy-five hours. In fact the carrier was diverted to Cyprus, where another earthquake had struck, and to 17 September a further twenty-two sorties were flown.

1954

In March the Euphrates and Tigris burst their banks, resulting in severe flooding in **Iraq**, especially around Baghdad. A total of about twenty-five Valettas of the Fayid Wing (70, 78, 84, 114 and 216 Sqns) flew numerous relief sorties, taking in tents, sandbags, food and medical supplies. The effort was not without cost: VW205 of 216 Sqn was lost when it flew into a mountain in Jordan on 2 April.

There were earthquakes in **Algeria** on 9 September, after which relief flights were flown by 224 Sqn Shackletons from Gibraltar to Orleansville.

The survey vessel HMS *Vidal* (A200), equipped with a Dragonfly HR1, was on hand to provide some support to **Haiti**, hit by Hurricane *Hazel* in October.

1955

In January, and again in February, maritime reconnaissance aircraft based at Kinloss were called upon to drop food and animal feedstuffs to farms in Caithness, **Scotland**, cut off by severe snowstorms. Involved in Operation *Snowdrop* were Shackletons of 236 OCU and Neptunes of 217 Sqn.

During an insurrection in **Sudan** (see Chapter 3, Section 5), the British Government was asked to provide support. From 28 August Valetta aircraft of 70 Sqn evacuated civilians caught up in the fighting from Juba to Khartoum.

1956

At the beginning of November, Beverleys of 47 Sqn transported eighteen tons of medical supplies to Vienna in two sorties. The supplies were for refugees escaping from **Hungary** in the uprising against Soviet occupation.

1958

With a worsening relationship between the United Kingdom and Guatemala over the status of **British Honduras**, a royal visit was conducted by Princess Margaret to show the United Kingdom's commitment to support the colony. In April the Viscount carrying the princess was escorted by two armed Canberra B(I).8 interdictors of 59 Sqn, with two Canberra PR.9s of 58 Sqn in support in Operation *Quick Flight*.

HANDLEY PAGE HASTINGS

Unlike the York, which it superseded, the HP 67 Hastings owed little to earlier designs apart from experience. The type was built to Specification C.3/44 which called for a four-engined transport, and the prototype, TE580, first flew on 7 May 1946. The Hastings entered service after the war, but was in time to see service through the Berlin airlift, Suez and in support of British troops in brushfire wars throughout the 1950s.

The **C Mark I** had a relatively high-set tailplane of short span. It carried fifty equipped troops, with power provided by four Bristol Hercules 101 engines, and it first equipped No 47 Squadron from September 1948. The **C Mark 1A** designation applied to some fifty C.1 models brought up to C.2 standard and fitted with the Hercules 216. Extra fuel was carried in underwing tanks, however, rather than in the wings as in the later variant. The Met variant was a conversion of the C.1 for meteorological work, with the seating replaced by crew positions and specialized equipment. The first conversion flew on 27 September 1950.

The **C Mark 2** was fitted with more powerful Hercules 106 engines and a wider, lower-set, tailplane to improve stability. Increased fuel capacity in internal wing tanks extended the range by some 40%. The prototype first flew

The Hastings entered service with the RAF in September 1948 and remained in front-line service for two decades. In that time they were to be seen across the world supporting troop movements and a variety of aid and peace-keeping campaigns. TG577/577 of 511 Sqn at Malta in 1958. *(Author's collection)*

on 23 October 1948, and the first production aircraft was built to Specification C.19/49.

The **C Mark 3** (HP 95) was as the C.2 but built for the Royal New Zealand Air Force: four were delivered. The **C Mark 4** (HP 94) was a VIP version seating up to twenty persons; four were built to Specification C.115/P, the original designation being C Mark 2A. The first flew on 22 September 1951.

The **T Mark 5** was a conversion of the C.1 with a ventral radome for bomber navigator/aimer training. Eight aircraft were converted and the variant was not retired until June 1977.

Transport units equipped – 24, 36, 47, 48, 51, 53, 70, 99, 114, 242, 297, 511; 1312 Flt; FECS

VICKERS VALETTA

The Valetta (Type 607) was the military version of the Viking transport, designed and built to Specification C.9/46. At first glance it was virtually indistinguishable from the civil type, apart from a blunt tail cone, but compared to the Viking it had a strengthened floor, large loading-doors on the port side and a revised undercarriage. The Valetta was equipped for troop transport, freight, air-dropping, paratrooping and air ambulance, and it entered service with 204 Sqn in Egypt in 1949. The aircraft operated in every RAF command, and supported operations in Malaya and at Suez.

The **C Mark 1** (Type 637, 651) carried thirty-four passengers or up to 8,000 lb of freight. The prototype flew on 30 June 1947, and within two years the type was in service. The powerplant was two Hercules 230, a more powerful version of the engine installed in the Viking. The C.1 was unique in that it equipped the sole Royal Auxiliary Air Force transport unit, 622 Sqn. The **C Mark 2** Type 659 was similar to the C.1 except that it was fitted as a VIP transport. It was distinguishable externally by having a pointed tailcone, and extra fuel provided a greater range than the C.1. Ten were built.

Transport units equipped – 24, 30, 48, 52, 70, 78, 84, 110, 114, 167, 204, 205, 216, 233, 622; 1312 Flt; APCS; EACF; FECS; MCS

The Vickers Valetta was very much a 're-fuselaged' Wellington generally replacing the Dakota in RAF service. The Valetta was widely used as a tactical transport seeing service in the Aden, Suez and Malaya campaigns as well as more low-key operations. VW831 was with the Malta Communications Squadron in 1958. *(Author's collection)*

BLACKBURN BEVERLEY

The B.101 Beverley was a developed version of the General Aircraft Company's Universal transport which had been designed in 1946 (Specification C.3/46), and flew in 1950, powered by four of the ubiquitous Hercules engines. The military variant, the Beverley, first flew on 17 June 1953, with the engines changed to the more powerful Centaurus.

The Beverley was the largest freighter aircraft to have been built in Britain, and it was to serve the RAF from 1956 to 1967 in most theatres. It came into its own in the Aden campaign with its excellent short-field capability. The **C Mark 1** was the basic and only version to enter service. The Beverley was designed for dropping heavy equipment through the rear detachable doors, and featured a fixed undercarriage. The total load was 45,000 lb, which could be flown over a range of 450 miles.

Transport units equipped – 30, 34, 37, 48, 53, 84

6.3   HUMANITARIAN AID AND PEACEKEEPING, 1960s

1960

Mauritius experienced a severe cyclone in February, following which relief supplies were flown in by Beverley transports of 30 Sqn based at Eastleigh in Kenya. The flights continued into April.

On 1 March there were severe earthquakes at Agadir in **Morocco**, which sadly resulted in the deaths of some 12,000 people. The following day Shackletons of 224 Sqn at Gibraltar joined aircraft from many nations in bringing food, tents, blankets and medical supplies into the surprisingly untouched local airport. Refugees were flown out to Istres, France.

An example of the more unusual aid delivered by British armed services was demonstrated in **Brunei** in March. The local cat population in inaccessible Bario had succumbed to an excess of DDT with a consequential increase of rats to plague proportions. At the request of the World Health Organization (WHO), a Beverley of 48 Sqn dropped a fresh load of healthy but hungry cats on the 13th.

There was a small-scale insurgency in **Uganda** in June. A number of airstrips was surveyed, and troops of the King's African Rifles were deployed by Beverleys of 30 Sqn. The squadron remained involved until early 1961, by which time the banditry was contained; three aircraft remained detached to Jinja.

On 30 June 1960 **Belgian Congo** became independent of Belgium. Shortly afterwards, the mineral-rich province of Katanga seceded, after which the Congolese Prime Minister sought United Nations help. In Operation *Half Cock* RAF Transport Command provided Comets of 216 Sqn, Britannias of 99 and 511 Sqns, Hastings of 24 and 36 Sqns and Beverleys of 30, 47 and 53 Sqns to fly Ghanaian troops and their equipment from Accra to Leopoldville in order to participate in the United Nations force in the Congo. On the return flights civilians were evacuated. The USAF also airlifted troops from across Africa and from Ireland. Subsequently two Handley Page Hastings of 114 Squadron supported the Ghanaian contingent. Further transfer of troops occurred in January and June 1961, but this time from Nigeria.

In July a Britannia of 99 Sqn, in Argentina for the 150th anniversary of independence celebrations, transported aid to Santiago, **Chile**, following an earthquake. Two sorties were conducted.

The **Cameroons** were a United Nations trust territory administered by the British in the north and the French in the much larger southern region. There was a revolt in the south in December 1956, and on the 20th French paratroopers were dropped at Eseka to help restore order. The French granted independence in 1960, and in the British-administered territory the constitutional position was due to be determined by plebiscite in 1961.

It was anticipated that there would be local disturbances, and accordingly 1 Bn The King's Own Royal Border Regt was flown to the Cameroons in September 1960, where it was supported by a detachment of three Twin Pioneer light transports from 230 Sqn based at nearby Mamfe in Nigeria. All equipment required was flown from the UK into the airstrip at Mamfe in Beverleys of 47 and 53 Sqns. Two 53 Sqn Beverleys and a Pioneer were detached to Kano in Operation *Private Eye* to help support the Nigerian authorities through forthcoming elections.

Order was maintained, but the Twin Pioneers were involved in combating smuggling as well as resupplying army outposts. The wishes of the people were respected, and in June and October 1961 respectively the northern region was ceded to Nigeria and the southern part joined the new republic. The 1st Bn Grenadier Guards took over internal security in May 1961, but in September British forces left, having enabled a peaceful transition to take place.

1961

There was disagreement between the UK Government and the **Rhodesian Federation,** which in January resulted in the RAF transporting troops into Nairobi, Kenya. The purpose was to enable Northern Rhodesia to secede if she wished. In the event, but not until after Rhodesian plans to counter any invasion, the issue was settled through diplomacy.

There was famine in **Kenya** early in the year, and during March and April food was dropped by aircraft of AFME and Transport Command. Seven Beverleys were detached from the UK to join aircraft of 30 Sqn in Operation *Oliver*, in which many tons of food were delivered to outlying areas.

There were disturbances in **Zanzibar** throughout 1961, but these came to a head in June. Seven Beverley aircraft of 30 Sqn transported troops of the King's African Rifles to contain the rioting. However, this escalated through the summer, and in September further troops were ferried to the island.

In October aircraft of RAF Transport Command and Air Forces Middle East began dropping food to communities isolated by floods in **Kenya** in Operation *Tana Flood*. Four Beverleys from Abingdon brought out Sycamore helicopters to Embakasi, where they joined aircraft of 30 Sqn. Some 7,273 tonnes of supplies were dropped by the Beverleys in very-low-level sorties.

In a related operation from 25 November, relief was extended to **Somalia**, which continued until January 1962. Most of Somalia's food crop was destroyed and more than 300,000 made homeless; in total approximately six million pounds of food were dropped. Beverleys transported the supplies from Nairobi to Mogadishu, where they

While their only operational engagement was during the Suez campaign, Valiants were used extensively for survey tasks, sometimes in the wake of natural disasters. Aircraft of 543 Sqn were deployed to Kingston for a survey of British Honduras following Hurricane *Hattie* in October 1961. WP223 was one of the squadron's aircraft.

(Author's collection)

were loaded onto Valettas for dropping in the Lower Juba province. At the outset the operation was hindered through a lack of aviation fuel. Royal Rhodesian Air Force C-54s and USAF transports were also involved.

On 31 October, **British Honduras** was devastated by Hurricane *Hattie*, which left 400 dead and 65,000 homeless. The 1st Battalion Royal Hampshire Regiment was already in the country and provided immediate support, while a second battalion arrived from Jamaica. In Operation *Sky Help* a battalion of the Worcester Regiment was flown from the UK in November in Britannias of 99 and 511 Sqns, together with 12 Field Squadron Royal Engineers. However, the Britannias could not use Stanley Field, so Shackletons and Hastings were used. Supplies from UK were flown to Kingston via the Azores and Bermuda by Shackletons of 42 Sqn and then shuttled to Belize by two aircraft of 204 and 210 Sqns. Two Hastings transports ferried spare crews and equipment while later two Valiant B(PR)K.1s of 543 Sqn were deployed for survey tasks.

The aid flights ended on 8 December, by which time 335,000 lb of freight and 1,050 persons had been moved.

There was severe flooding of the Mekong delta in **South Vietnam** late in the year. Relief supplies were flown into Saigon in three Beverleys of 34 Sqn and Bristol Freighters of 41 Sqn RNZAF.

1962

The floods affecting Kenya had resulted in a famine in **Tanganyika**. Between January and March 30 Sqn Beverleys dropped food in remoter areas.

The Soviet Union announced air exercises in February which would have the effect of closing the air corridors into **Berlin**. In Operation *Dark Bottle* Beverley transports were detached from Abingdon to Wildenrath, from where they made flights into the corridor throughout the exercise to maintain Allied rights of passage.

In 1953, elections in **British Guiana** brought a result that, it was feared by the Governor, might lead to a Communist government. The constitution was suspended, and two companies of the 1st Battalion Royal Welch Fusiliers were dispatched in Royal Navy frigates. There was continuing unrest, essentially between ethnic groups, since the majority People's Progressive Party (PPP) represented the Indian minority.

In February 1962 a general strike was called, and a company of the Royal Hampshire Regt was transferred from Jamaica. On the 15th two companies of the East Anglian Regt were flown out to Georgetown from the UK. A detachment of four Shackleton MR.2 aircraft of 204 Sqn (two lent by 210 Sqn) were sent from Jamaica in a show

In 1962 there was a general strike in British Guiana and Shackletons of 204 Sqn were sent from Jamaica in a show of force and to support British troops in the colony. Shackleton MR.2 WG555/K displays its ventral radar and capacious weapons bay. *(Author's collection)*

of force on the 19th, and they remained for five weeks. Rioting was contained but broke out again a year later in July 1963. Britannias flew out the 2nd Battalion the Green Jackets in Operation *Pedal*. In addition to ground forces, a small Royal Navy Wessex flight was based at Atkinson Field near Georgetown for support duties.

In July 1964 a state of emergency was declared after further lawlessness, and the garrison was reinforced by a battalion of the Devon and Dorset Regt flown from Northern Ireland.

In June several Alouette AH.2s were airlifted by Argosies to Atkinson Field where they formed 24 Flt. The detachment became 27 Flt in January 1965 then 25 Flt in June before disbanding in July 1966.

In September 1964 the Wessexes were replaced by three Whirlwind HC.10s of 1310 Flt RAF. In October they were joined by Auster AOP.9 aircraft of 24 Recce Flt for reconnaissance and liaison work under the overall control of 2 Wing AAC at Middle Wallop; at the same time, two Canberra PR.7s of 58 Sqn were detached from Piarco Airport, Trinidad, for survey work. The colony became independent of Britain as Guyana in May 1966 under a coalition government. Most British servicemen left, a few remaining in order to train local forces. Minimal military intervention over thirteen years prevented local insurrection and enabled the colony to progress to maturity.

China massed troops on the border with **India** north of Calcutta in November. A number of 34 Sqn Beverley transports were involved in ferrying Indian troops into the border area and evacuating refugees.

1963

The severe winter across the **United Kingdom** resulted in animal foodstuffs being dropped on farms in Devon by Beverleys of 47 and 53 Sqns.

A small Cuban task force landed on **Anguilla** to kidnap refugees on 15 August. Four Shackletons of 201 Sqn were detached from St Mawgan to Nassau to co-operate with the frigates HMS *Ursa* (F200) and HMS *Londonderry* (F108) in preventing further incursions. The aircraft stayed for eight weeks, during which they ferried aid to Mayaguana Island (**Bahamas**) in the wake of Hurricane *Flora*.

Cyprus was granted independence from Great Britain from 16 August 1960, but with little prospect of a lasting peace. 990 Greek and 650 Turkish troops were based on the island, and there were two British sovereign-base areas, at Dhekelia in the east and Akrotiri/Episkopi in the west. From 1962 Greek and Turkish Cypriot factions both began stockpiling weapons, and in early 1963 armed violence broke out, resulting in several hundred killed. On 27 March 1963 a UN peacekeeping force was established as United Nations Force In Cyprus (UNFICYP), comprising at its peak 7,000 troops, with air support provided by 19 Liaison Flight and 21 Recce Flight of 651 Sqn AAC operating Sioux helicopters and Auster AOP.9s.

In January 1964, in Operation *Hogmanay*, UK-based Beverleys of 47 Sqn and 242 OCU transported additional troops and associated equipment to Nicosia. In January two Shackletons of 210 Sqn were detached to Akrotiri for surveillance tasks, where they were replaced by aircraft from 42 Sqn in February. Also in February Whirlwind HAR.10s of 230 Sqn were detached from Gütersloh to Nicosia. The Shackleton detachment was followed by aircraft from 201, 206 and 38 Sqns through to June.

Premier George Grivas, not content with independence, still sought *Enosis*, or union with Greece, and in August 1964 he took command of the Greek Cypriot National Guard. On the 8th of the month, Greeks attacked three villages north of Nicosia, and the following day Turkish Air Force (THK) fighter-bombers struck targets in the immediate area. Fighting died down for some years, although THK F-100 fighters flew low over Nicosia on Christmas Day 1964.

On 20 May 1963 there was widespread unrest at the Havelock asbestos mine outside Mbabane, the capital of **Swaziland**, and this was followed by a call for a national strike by Nationalists seeking immediate independence from Britain. To maintain law and order in this most conservative of colonies, the 1st Bn Gordon Highlanders was lifted, with equipment, from Kenya on 13 June in Operation *Alfred*.

The aircraft involved, which operated out of Eastleigh, were Argosy C.1s of 105 Sqn, normally based in Aden, and Beverley C.1s of 30 and 84 Sqns. Bechuanaland Tribal Police were flown in and 128 Rhodesian SAS troops dropped by parachute. The position quickly stabilized without recourse to arms, and the troops withdrew on 20 June. Independence finally came in 1968.

The proclamation of the State of Malaysia on 16 September 1963 resulted in riots in Djakarta, **Indonesia**. The country was already in effect at war with Britain (Chapter 7, Section 2), although not acknowledged as such, and it was felt prudent to evacuate British personnel. Three Argosies of 215 Sqn, together with a Handley Page Hastings of 48 Sqn, airlifted 400 people over several days from the 19th.

1964

With the withdrawal of UN forces from the **Congo** in 1964, there was a further insurrection, and more than 1,500 white people were taken hostage. Mercenaries supported by US special forces fought the rebels, and on 24 November Belgian paratroopers dropped to recapture Stanleyville. While a number of hostages were murdered, more than 2,000 Europeans were evacuated, some 143 by a Beverley of 84 Sqn and an Argosy of 105 Sqn. Medical aid was provided by the RAMC.

1965

A 34 Sqn Beverley took flood relief supplies into Saigon, **South Vietnam**, in January.

A special session of the West German Bundestag was planned for **Berlin** on 7 April. The Soviet Union responded by announcing an army and air exercise to the west of Berlin between 5 and 10 April, clearly intended to intimidate both the West German government and NATO Powers. The exercise would potentially close the air corridors to the city from Western Germany.

The NATO response was to activate an element of contingency plans to keep Berlin accessible, and the *Jack Pine* HQ near Ramstein was opened in Operation *Gopherwood*. Two RAF Argosy transports from RAF Benson conducted ten flights along the corridors between 5 and 10 April, during which time fighters were brought forward. Five Mirage IIIs of the French Air Force moved up to Gütersloh, where they were joined by Javelin FAW.9s of 5 and 11 Sqns from Geilenkirchen. Six Javelins also detached to Celle; in the event fighter escorts to the transports were not required.

There were blizzards in the **United Kingdom** in December and January, cutting off many farms. RAF transports, including Argosies of 114 and 267 Sqns, dropped fodder on remote farms and communities.

1966

Yet again a Beverley of 34 Sqn was detached to Saigon, **South Vietnam**, to take flood-relief supplies to various bases in the region.

There was unrest in **Basutoland** in July, and a detachment of Royal Irish Fusiliers was supported by Beverley aircraft of 84 Sqn. The situation was soon in control.

1967

Further severe flooding in **Kenya** resulted in famine in the north, and relief sorties were flown by 84 Sqn Beverleys operating out of Nairobi.

Support to civilian powers does not always come passively. On 18 March 1967 the 974-foot, 118,000-ton super-tanker *Torrey Canyon*, chartered by BP, foundered on rocks at Seven Stones Reef between Land's End and the Scilly Isles, **England**, splitting her hull and spilling oil. Initially attempts were made to salvage the vessel, but she was stuck fast. During the early days Whirlwinds from 22 Sqn at Chivenor and St Mawgan and FAA Wessexes from 848 NAS Culdrose were active in monitoring and ferrying personnel.

By the 26th she was beginning to break up, and the decision was taken to fire her crude oil before there was further pollution of sea and coastline. In Operation *Mop-up* a task force was formed comprising eight FAA Buccaneer S.1s from 736 and 800 NASs at Lossiemouth and RAF Hunter F. 6s from 229 OCU, all operating from Brawdy. On 28 March the Buccaneers dropped forty-two 1,000 lb bombs on the stricken ship, at least thirty of which hit the target, although some failed to detonate. Hunters followed up with Avtur aviation fuel dropped from 100 gal wing tanks to fuel the fire now started.

High seas overnight quenched the fires, so eight Hunter FGA.9s from 1 and 54 Sqns West Raynham, plus no fewer than twenty-six F Mk 6s from 229 OCU, continued to attack with 3 in. rockets and Avtur. Later there were further Buccaneer strikes supported by Sea Vixen FAW.1s from 899 NAS at Yeovilton with napalm. *Torrey Canyon* still remained intact, and so on the 30th there were further Buccaneer and Sea Vixen attacks, and yet again the Hunters struck with thirty-six sorties, using rockets, incendiaries and kerosene. This had the desired effect.

In March 1967 the super-tanker *Torrey Canyon* ran aground off the Scillies splitting her hull. The stricken tanker is seen here spilling oil before she was attacked and eventually destroyed in a series of air strikes. *(Crown Copyright)*

Throughout the episode four Royal Navy frigates, some with Wasp helicopters aboard, plus a number of smaller ships, acted as range safety vessels. This was essential, given intense interest, not only by the media but by Soviet intelligence-gathering 'trawlers'. In the aftermath Argosy transports flew detergent and stores to RAF St Mawgan for use in cleaning beaches, while a 47 Sqn Beverley also brought detergent from Edinburgh to Culdrose. No. 72 Sqn Wessexes and Scouts of 3 Flt Army Air Corps at Perham Down were involved in spotting oil slicks and moving *matériel* around.

In all, the exercise cost 165 1,000 lb HE bombs, 30,000 gal of napalm, 20,000 gal of Avtur and numerous rockets. Although the press derided the bombing as a failure, it did achieve its objective, but perhaps not as quickly or as cheaply as had been expected. Sound lessons, militarily, politically and environmentally, were learned and applied.

After Spain had prohibited British flying over Algeciras in April two Hunter FGA.9s of 1 or 54 Sqn were detached to RAF North Front (Gibraltar) from West Raynham. The detachment extended to aircraft of the operational conversion units and tactical weapons units and they terminated in August 1978, after which Jaguars from RAF Germany were detached.

Relief supplies were delivered through **South Vietnam** by a 34 Sqn Beverley detached to Saigon during August.

British engagement in **Aden** is covered in Chapter 5, Section 1. The evacuation of British nationals in November, in Operation *Jacobin*, involved Hercules of the newly equipped 36 and 48 Sqns, and aircraft and crews from 242 OCU, plus Argosies of 70 Sqn. People and possessions were airlifted to Muharraq in forty-nine sorties, from where they were flown back to the UK in VC.10s of 10 Sqn, Belfasts of 53 Sqn or Britannias of 99 and 511 Sqns.

1968

Aid nearer to home was provided when a hurricane hit central **Scotland**, including Glasgow. With twenty dead and 1,700 homeless, a Hercules of 36 Sqn transported tarpaulins to the city to help protect buildings in the short term.

1969

With a population of 6,000, **Anguilla** has been linked with St Kitts and Nevis since 1822. From June 1967 there were negotiations with Britain after a local declaration of independence, but on 11 March 1969 the Parliamentary Under-Secretary responsible visited the island and was besieged by a crowd, some of whom discharged small-arms.

The British Government reacted by flying two companies of 2 Para to Anguilla – a total of 315 men – plus forty-seven policemen to restore order. Five Hercules of 24 and 36 Sqns left Lyneham at 02.35 hrs on 18 March, refuelling at Gander and landing at Antigua. They carried nine Land Rovers, six trailers, and signals equipment. The main force was flown in three VC-10s of 10 Sqn, a Comet C.4 of 216 Sqn and a Britannia of 99 Sqn, all of which made the non-stop flight from Brize Norton to Antigua later in the day. Also flown from the UK were two Andover C.1s of 46 Sqn, which flew from Abingdon for Antigua via Keflavik, Gander and Bermuda; they were joined by a third already in the Caribbean.

The men were landed on Anguilla at 03.15 hrs on the 19th from the frigates HMS *Rothesay* (F107) and HMS *Minerva* (F45). The ships' Wasps were busy from first light, dropping leaflets and later personnel. The heavy equipment was dropped on Wall Blake Airport by Hercules; an Andover later used the airport, which was too small for the larger aircraft.

In reality order had never been seriously threatened, and the troops left in September, although some Royal Engineers remained until 1971, undertaking civil projects on the neglected island.

AVRO SHACKLETON

The Type 696 Shackleton was the first British post-war type designed specifically as a land-based long-range maritime reconnaissance aircraft. The need for such a type was confirmed by the success of the Liberator and Lancaster in the role, and the Shackleton was to replace the latter type in service. It was originally to have been the Lincoln III, and it used the Lincoln's wing and undercarriage, but with a redesigned fuselage and with Griffon engines. The Shackleton was designed to Specification R.5/46, and the prototype flew on 9 March 1949; the type finally retired from RAF service, in AEW mode, in 1991.

The **MR Mark I** differed slightly from the prototypes in having twin 20 mm cannon in nose and dorsal turrets and twin .5 in. guns in the tail. Maximum weapons load was 15,000 lb. The first version, which entered service with 120 Sqn in 1951, carried its radar in a glazed chin mounting, which suffered somewhat from bird strikes. In the Mark 1 the outer and inner engines were not interchangeable, whereas in the Mark 1A they were. The change was introduced on the production line after twenty-seven of the total of seventy-seven had been built; most Mark 1s were subsequently brought up to the later standard.

The **MR Mark 2** incorporated a revised nose profile with the radar moved to a retractable 'dustbin' under the rear fuselage. The prototype flew on 17 June 1952, and the first production aircraft several months later. It was slightly heavier than the Mark 1 and was progressively upgraded over the years. Armament was twin .5 in. guns in the nose and dorsal turret, although the latter was removed on some later aircraft. The Phase I aircraft incorporated some changes from the subsequently introduced MR.3, including plotting table and ASV Mk 21 radar. The variant was also known as the MR.2C, and of the total of seventy MR.2 aircraft, fifty-two were updated. The Phase II represented yet another upgrade of the basic Mark 2 to incorporate Mark 3 features, in this case a new ECM and radio fit. Fifty-four aircraft were updated. The final MR.2 update was to MR.3 Phase III standard, enabling the aircraft to carry the Mark 10 nuclear depth charge. In addition Griffon 58 engines were fitted with a change in the oil feed system. Most of the Phase II aircraft were updated.

The airborne warning **AEW Mark 2** was a significant conversion of the Mark 2 Phase II version designed to Mod 1493. With the intended demise of the aircraft carrier, there was an urgent need for high-level radar surveillance to supplement ground-based radars in detecting low-flying intruders. Until 1971 the role was fulfilled by carrier-based Gannet aircraft. The older Mark 2 was chosen for conversion because of the availability of aircraft with low airframe hours, which had not been subjected to the stresses imposed on the later Mark 3 by heavier landing weights. The large AN/APS 20 radars from the Gannet were installed under the forward fuselage of the twelve aircraft converted.

The Type 716 **MR Mark 3** incorporated a number of improvements, and although retaining the same overall shape as the MR.2, a tricycle undercarriage was fitted to help cope with the higher all-up weight resulting from increased fuel capacity. The cockpit glazing was also improved and the dorsal turret of the Mark 2 deleted; weapons-load was 14,000 lb, carried in an internal bomb-bay, including mines, depth charges, sonobuoys, and 500 lb or 1,000 lb GP bombs. Thirty-four MR.3 aircraft were built for the Royal Air Force, and they were successively updated as anti-submarine warfare evolved to take account of new tactics and technology.

The Phase I was introduced on the production line, with six aircraft built as such and a further twenty-two converted. The changes included the ASV Mk 21 radar, ILS and VHF radio homer. Phase II aircraft incorporated ECM equipment (*Orange Harvest*), the Mk 1c sonics plotting table, UHF radio, TACAN and an improved radio compass. Twenty-nine aircraft were updated. The ultimate Shackleton, to which standard twenty-seven aircraft were upgraded, introduced the ability to carry and use the Mk 10 'Lulu' depth charge. The necessary equipment brought the all-up weight to a level where the safe take-off limit had to be traded for range, and it was decided to add two supplementary Viper turbojet engines of 2,500 lb thrust in the rear nacelles of the outer engines.

MR units equipped (supplementary transport role) – 37, 38. 42, 120, 201, 203, 204, 205, 206, 210, 220, 224, 228, 240, 269

Airborne Early Warning – 8

de Havilland Comet

The DH106 Comet was produced to Specification 22/46 as the first jet passenger aircraft in the world, and the Series 1 entered service with BOAC in 1952. The prototype, G-ALVG, flew on 27 July 1949 from Hatfield. It was powered by four Ghost 50 engines and accommodated thirty-six passengers. After two BOAC machines had crashed with considerable loss of life, the type was grounded; detailed examination of the wreckage and structural testing confirmed failure of the fuselage around a window. The Comet was withdrawn from service, and the Series 2 aircraft on the production line were strengthened.

The **C Mark 2** was delivered to the RAF in 1956, when the type went into service with 216 Sqn. This version seated forty-four, being powered by the Avon 117/118, and it remained in service until May 1967. The T Mark 2 trainer was a dual-control version, of which two were built. They were fully operational aircraft and formed part of the establishment of 216 Sqn.

R Mark 2 was the designation for three airframes converted for special ELINT work by Marshalls of Cambridge. The Comet remained in service with 51 Sqn until replaced by special Nimrods in 1971.

The Series 3 was an interim type with a stretched fuselage seating seventy-eight, and with Avon 502 engines. A single example was produced, but it led to the Series 4. The military **C Mark 4** was the 4C and was the natural successor to the C.2 on the RAF's trunk routes. It carried ninety-four passengers in rear-facing seats, and was powered by the Avon 350. Five were operated between 1962 and 1975.

Transport unit equipped – 216

Bristol Britannia

The Type 175 Britannia airliner was built to Specification 2/47 calling for a medium-range airliner for the Empire routes. The original design was for a thirty-six-seat aircraft powered by the Centaurus piston engine. The design was developed to accommodate the Proteus engine, and the prototype flew on 16 August 1952. Capacity of the early production aircraft was ninety passengers. In a significantly revised form the Britannia provided the basis for the Canadair Argus maritime reconnaissance aircraft. The Britannia entered RAF service in March 1959, and was withdrawn in early 1976 as an economy measure.

The Britannia Series 253 was ordered for the RAF as the **C Mark 1** mixed-traffic transport to support rapid deployment of the strategic reserve to the Far and Middle East, Africa and the West Indies. The Series 253 was powered by the Proteus 255, and featured a strengthened floor with tie-down points and a large cargo door; first production aircraft flew on 29 December 1958. The Britannia joined 99 Sqn in 1959.

C Mark 2 was the designation applied to three Series 252 Britannias originally ordered by the Ministry of Supply for leasing to charter companies charged for trooping contracts. In the event, policy changed and the aircraft were delivered to the RAF. They were similar in all important respects to the Series 253.

Transport units equipped – 99, 511

ARMSTRONG WHITWORTH (HAWKER SIDDELEY) ARGOSY

The Type 660 Argosy was a military development of the AW.650 civil transport which first flew in 1958. Built to OR 351, the military version differed from the original design in having split 'crocodile-jaw' rear doors for easy and fast loading and off-loading of bulky freight. It had excellent short and rough landing characteristics, and although flight refuelling trials were completed before introduction into service, the technique was not used operationally.

The **C Mark 1** was powered by four Dart 101 engines, and carried sixty-nine troops or 29,000 lb of freight 345 miles; the maximum useful range (20,000 lb load) was 1,070 miles. The first aircraft flew on 4 March 1961. The Argosy joined 114 Sqn in 1962, and was initially complemented by the Hercules from 1967 and finally supplanted by it in 1974.

The **E Mark 1** designation applied to C.1 conversions operated by 115 Sqn in the radar and navigational aids calibration role. They replaced Varsities from 1968 and were withdrawn from use in early 1978.

Transport units equipped – 70, 105, 114, 215, 267

6.4   HUMANITARIAN AID AND PEACEKEEPING, 1970S

1970

There was civil war in **Jordan** in 1970, prompted by an influx of Palestinian refugees from Israeli occupation of the West Bank. This resulted in an exodus of Western nationals through to Lebanon, where they were picked up from Beirut by a Britannia and flown to Cyprus. Despite Syrian intervention on the ground, the Jordanian government had US backing, and a ceasefire was forced in September. In the aftermath medical supplies were flown into Amman in specially marked Argosies of 70 Sqn flown by RAF crews in civilian clothing.

In November a cyclone devastated the coastal area of **East Pakistan**. In Operation *Burlap* VC.10 C.1s of 10 Sqn flew medical and other supplies to Dacca, from where they were distributed by Hercules C.1 transports of 48 Sqn based at Changi. These latter aircraft flew fifty-five sorties from Chittagong. Also involved were the Wessex HU.5s of 847 NAS based on HMS *Intrepid* (L11), which established several bases on the Ganges delta. The naval unit then deployed to **Malaya** for further flood-relief operations.

A Hercules flew relief supplies to **Turkey** following a local earthquake.

Hercules and Britannias flew relief supplies to **Peru** following an earthquake there.

1971

In March some one hundred British and other nationals were evacuated from **East Pakistan** during civil unrest. Britannias of 99 and 511 Sqns from Brize Norton conducted the flights.

Further heavy rains brought yet more flooding to **East Pakistan**. Some 400,000 lb of supplies were brought in by VC.10s of 10 Sqn, Belfasts of 53 Sqn and Hercules from 24, 30, 36, 47 and 48 Sqns. The latter brought in medical supplies to prevent a cholera epidemic.

Civil war between West and East **Pakistan** eventually involved India from November 1971. In what was to become Bangladesh in the east, Dacca was surrounded by Indian forces by 12 December. From now RAF Hercules of 70 Sqn from Akrotiri in Cyprus evacuated 409 Britons before Indian AF Hunters destroyed the runway. 925 evacuees were also airlifted from West Pakistan.

Britannias of 99 and 511 Sqns and VC.10s of 10 Sqn were also involved. Throughout the war the commando carrier HMS *Albion* (R07) was at hand in the Bay of Bengal with Wessex HU.5s of 848 NAS embarked.

1972

In **Malta** the government ordered the immediate removal of British troops from the island in January. Over two months 8,000 servicemen and women and dependants were airlifted to Cyprus, together with much equipment.

Flooding in East Pakistan in 1971 resulted in emergency supplies being flown in Belfasts of 53 Sqn based at Brize Norton. XR367/367 shares a ramp with Hastings of the Far East Air Force. *(Author's collection)*

VC.10s of 10 Sqn, Britannias of 99 and 511 Sqns, Belfasts of 53 Sqn and Hercules from 24, 30, 36, 47 and 48 Sqns were all involved.

In January Guatemalan troops massed on the borders of **British Honduras**, and invasion seemed imminent. The response was an airlift of troops and equipment involving Hercules aircraft from 24, 30, 36, 47 and 48 Sqns flying from Lyneham via the Azores and the Bahamas.

The carrier HMS *Ark Royal* was diverted from an American cruise with 809 NAS (Buccaneer S.1), 892 NAS (Phantom FGR.2), 824 NAS (Sea King HAS.1) and B Flt of 849 NAS (Gannet AEW.3). Buccaneer flights along the border helped to contain matters, and in February *Ark Royal* returned leading a task force including 2nd Battalion the Grenadier Guards.

RAF Hercules of 48 Sqn flew relief supplies to the **Philippines** in December, following devastation caused by Typhoon *Theresa*.

In December a Hercules flew relief supplies to **Nicaragua**, following an earthquake that resulted in around 6,000 deaths. Sadly, much of the aid did not reach those for whom it was intended.

1973

West **Nepal** was hit by famine early in the year, and in March four Hercules aircraft from the Lyneham Wing dropped 1,964 tons of food in Operation *Khana Cascade*. Also involved was a Puma helicopter of 230 Sqn.

There was also famine across west Africa following droughts for the previous five years. From March Hercules aircraft of the Lyneham Wing were involved in relief supply transport to **Mali** and **Senegal**. Supplies were also delivered to southern **Sudan**.

Following the establishment of **Bangladesh** after the Indo-Pakistan war, RAF Britannias from 99 and 511 Sqns transferred some refugees and prisoners of war between Karachi and Dacca. In Operation *Lucan*, Bengalis were

When Malta ordered the removal of British forces from the Island in 1972 all of the RAF's strategic transport fleet was involved. VC-10 XR810 of 10 Sqn. *(Author's collection)*

transferred to Bangladesh and Pakistanis repatriated on return flights. Between October and February 1974 some 30,000 persons had been conveyed in 148 round trips.

RAF Hercules transported 900 UN troops into Cairo, **Egypt**, as part of a peace-keeping force following the Yom Kippur war in October.

1974

With little warning, there was a coup in **Cyprus** on 15 July 1974, when President Makarios was deposed by the Greek National Guard. Two days later Nicos Sampson, a leading figure in EOKA-B, was declared president. The Turkish reaction was predictable, if leisurely.

On Saturday 20 July Turkish Army Bell UH-1 and AB.204 helicopters dropped troops behind Kyrenia, while parachute troops were dropped around Nicosia by Transall C-160s and Dakotas of 221 and 231 Sqns respectively; at the same time, a seaborne landing took place while THK F-100s of 111, 132 and 181 Filos and F-104Gs of 141 Filo attacked targets around Nicosia, including the National Guard barracks. During the air strikes the THK inadvertently sank the Turkish destroyer *Kocatepe* with one direct hit from a 1,000 lb bomb. Greek naval vessels were reported in the area; both navies used similar warships, hence the mistake.

The attacks caused great concern for the safety of foreign nationals caught up in the fighting. Phantom FGR.2s of 6 and 41 sqns were deployed from Coningsby to Akrotiri, while the RAF contingent at Nicosia Airport was evacuated to Dhekelia, as were the families of troops living in the east of the island. They were subsequently flown out from King's Field airstrip by RAF Hercules, although 500 US citizens were evacuated by Sixth Fleet CH-46 and CH-53 helicopters to the USS *Inchon* on the 24th. Cover was provided by fighters from USS *Forrestal*. Holidaymakers in the Kyrenia/Nicosia area were transferred to HMS *Hermes* (R12) from the beach at Kyrenia on the 23rd by Wessex HU.5s of 845 NAS and Sea King HAS.1s of 814 NAS, aided by HMS *Devonshire*'s (D02) Wessex HAS.3. By the end of the day, 1,630 people had been evacuated.

There was no Greek intervention, although on the 23rd seven F-4Es of 117 Wing, Greek Air Force (EA), took off from Iraklion to attack Turkish positions. After US intervention they were recalled. Fighting had apparently drawn to a halt. At Akrotiri the RAF was busy evacuating families of servicemen to the UK in Operation *Bold Guard*, while bringing in supplies and troop reinforcements. Also brought in were four Puma HC.1s of 33 Sqn to ease transport between bases. When the evacuation was complete on 8 August, 13,430 people had been returned in a well-organized operation, especially in respect of reception in England. The aircraft involved included Hercules (24, 30, 36, 47 and 48 Sqns), Belfasts (53 Sqn), Comets (216 Sqn), Britannias (99 and 511 Sqns) and VC.10s (10 Sqn).

August 14 saw a renewed Turkish offensive, with air strikes on Famagusta by F-100s. The following day a ceasefire was agreed, with the *Attila* ceasefire line cutting the island in two. Cyprus has remained partitioned, with large Greek and Turkish army contingents staying on the island.

Humanitarian Aid and Peacekeeping, 1970s

Unit	Aircraft	Base	From	To
RAF				
In theatre				
56 Sqn	Lightning F.6	Akrotiri	based	
9 Sqn	Vulcan B.2	Akrotiri	based	
35 Sqn	Vulcan B.2	Akrotiri	based	
70 Sqn	Hercules C.1	Akrotiri	based	
84 Sqn	Whirlwind HAR.10	Akrotiri	based	
112 Sqn	Bloodhound Mk 2	Episkopi	based	
Army Air Corps				
16 Flt	Sioux AH.1	Dhekelia	based	
UNFICYP Flt	Sioux AH.1	Nicosia	based	
RAF reinforcements				
6, 41 Sqns, 228OCU	Phantom FGR.2	Akrotiri ex-Coningsby	25.7.74	23.8.74
33 Sqn det	Puma HC.1	Akrotiri ex-Odiham	23.7.74	9.74
Strategic transport UK based all 20.7.74 to 8.8.74				
24, 30, 36, 47, 48 Sqns	Hercules C.1	Lyneham		
216 Sqn	Comet C.4	Lyneham		
99, 511 Sqns	Britannia C.2	Brize Norton		
10 Sqn	VC-10 C.1	Brize Norton		
53 Sqn	Belfast C.1	Brize Norton		
Fleet Air Arm all 20.7.74 to 23.7.74				
814 NAS	Sea King HAS.1	HMS *Hermes*		
845 NAS	Wessex HU.5	HMS *Hermes*		
SF	Wessex HAS.3	HMS *Devonshire*		
United States Marine Corps 20.7.74 to 23.7.74				
HMM-162	CH-46D (YS)	USS *Inchon*		
HMH-362	CH-53A (YS)	USS *Inchon*		
United States Navy cover 20.7.74 to 23.7.74 CVW-17 (AA)				
VF-11, -74	F-4J	USS *Forrestal*		
VA-81, -83	A-7E	USS *Forrestal*		
VA-85	A-6E, KA-6D	USS *Forrestal*		
RVAH-6	RA-5C	USS *Forrestal*		
VAW-126	E-2B	USS *Forrestal*		
HS-3	SH-3D	USS *Forrestal*		

At the end of December, Darwin, **Australia**, was struck by Cyclone *Tracy*, which made 20,000 homeless in addition to seventy-one killed. A Hercules of 48 Sqn was detached to support RAAF transports in bringing in relief supplies and evacuating the homeless.

1975

With the end of the war in Indo-China and with impending civil war, the RAF airlifted civilians from Phnom Penh, **Cambodia**, in April. A Hercules of 48 Sqn was diverted from Tengah for the task. An aircraft also evacuated Commonwealth personnel from Saigon, **South Vietnam**, while HMS *Lowestoft* stood by.

Independence from Portugal for **Angola** was set for 11 November. Immediately beforehand, some 300,000 Europeans departed in anticipation of the civil war, and during October VC-10s of 10 Sqn evacuated 5,700 people and 350,000 lb of freight from Luanda.

1976

A strong earthquake hit the Van area of **Turkey**, where it abuts north-west Iraq and Russia, in November, killing around 5,000 souls. Aid was flown out in Hercules of 24 Sqn.

1977

Fifty 'scientists' were landed from Argentina on **South Thule** in the South Sandwich group of islands and near the **Falklands** early in 1977. The British response was to send a small task force in November in Operation *Journeyman* to join HMS *Endurance*, already in the area. The task force was headed by the submarine HMS *Dreadnought* (S101), and included the frigates HMS *Alacrity* (F174) with a Wasp HAS.1 and HMS *Phoebe* (F42)

In 1977, in an operation not revealed for nearly 30 years, Argentine forces landed on South Thule. A small British task force, including warships embarking the Lynx HAS.2 of 815 NAS, was sufficient to ensure a discreet withdrawal. XZ676/336 is here seen in the UK. *(Author's collection)*

with a Lynx HAS.2. In attendance were the RFAs *Olwen* (A122) with Sea King HAS.1s of 819 NAS and *Resource* (S480) with Wessex HU.5s of 772 NAS.

When the presence of the force was made known to the Argentine government she withdrew the personnel, only to replace them shortly afterwards. The incident was only revealed in 2005, although the recovery of South Thule during the Falklands War was made public at the time.

1978

In March 1978 Katangese rebels struck into **Zaire** from bases in Angola, and soon occupied Kolwezi, where they held some 2,000 Europeans hostage. By May the situation was critical, and after a failed paradrop of Zairean troops, paratroops of the French Foreign Legion were dropped on 18 May. By the 20th they had occupied the city, but not before 130 hostages had been massacred.

The French were backed by Belgian paratroopers, and Italian Air Force and USAF transports brought in food supplies and equipment. The British contribution comprised a medical team and equipment brought into Lusaka by a VC-10 C.1 of 10 Sqn and three Hercules from the Lyneham Wing.

1979

In 1978 there was a revolution in **Iran**, resulting in the overthrow of the ruling monarch, Shah Pahlavi, after huge demonstrations in December. The USA had significant numbers of military advisers in Iran, and the government arranged the evacuation of dependants from Teheran in December. They were flown out in C-5A aircraft of the 436th MAW.

British nationals were evacuated in January 1979 by VC-10s of 10 Sqn and Hercules of the 24 Sqn.

In July a Hercules of 30 Sqn was detached to Panama to help with Red Cross famine relief in **Nicaragua** following the civil war there. The aircraft narrowly avoided being hijacked at Managua airport.

After an appalling civil war and wholesale genocide in **Cambodia**, Vietnamese forces invaded in December 1978, and had soon established control. There was severe famine caused by agricultural disruption, and by October 1979 significant food aid was reaching the country, mainly from Russia. However, a Hercules of 24 Sqn was also involved in transporting food.

In 1965 **Rhodesia** had made a unilateral declaration of independence, to which the British Government reacted with blockade and sanctions (Chapter 7, Section 5). By late 1979, with the Rhodesians attacking guerrilla bases in Mozambique and Zambia, the Rhodesian government was forced by international pressure to allow local elections, after which white minority rule collapsed.

A ceasefire between Rhodesia and Zambia came into effect on 28 December 1979, by which time a five-nation ceasefire-monitoring force was in place. The British contribution, deployed in Operation *Agila*, comprised seven Hercules operating from Salisbury, Pumas of 33 Sqn and Army helicopters, which remained in place until early 1980. Much equipment was brought from the UK in large transports of the USAF's Military Airlift Command, as well as VC-10s of RAF Transport Command.

The intention for the force was the overseeing, rather than enforcing, of the ceasefire. Sixteen assembly areas, generally close to the border, were identified as *Alpha* through *Romeo* less *India*. These camps, intended to receive and disarm guerrillas, were manned by British and New Zealand troops, and were supplied by air drop or air land from Hercules in 163 sorties.

Humanitarian Aid and Peacekeeping, 1970s

Unit	Aircraft	Base	From	To
RAF				
47, 70 Sqns	Hercules C.1	Lyneham–Salisbury	12.12.79	4.80
33 Sqn	Puma HC.1	Odiham–Salisbury	18.12.79	3.80
10 Sqn	VC-10 C.1	Brize Norton	12.12.79	3.80

Unit	Aircraft	Base	From	To
Army Air Corps				
656 Sqn	Gazelle AH.1, Scout AH.1	Various	18.12.79	4.80
USAF				
60 MAW	C-5A	Salisbury	16.12.79	4.80
437 MAW	C-141A	Salisbury	16.12.79	4.80
Royal Australian Air Force				
37 Sqn	C-130E	Richmond-Salisbury	25.12.79	2.80
Royal Canadian Armed Forces				
440 Sqn	CC-115 Buffalo	Salisbury	2.80	4.80
Royal New Zealand Air Force				
41 Sqn	C-130	Salisbury	2.80	4.80

SHORT BELFAST

The SC.5/10 Belfast was designed from the outset as a strategic transport, and was the first in the world to employ a fully automatic landing system. The design was broadly based on that of the Britannia, and similarity in the wings and tail unit are obvious.

The Belfast **C Mark 1** was built to Specification C.203, and the first aircraft – there were no prototypes – flew on 5 January 1964, five years after being ordered. All ten aircraft had been delivered to 53 Sqn by 1966. The Belfast was essentially a large freighter with a 10,000 cu ft hold, but it could be equipped to carry up to 150 troops. The type was withdrawn from service in 1976 in the light of defence cuts; the Ministry of Defence had to charter the aircraft from their subsequent owner, Heavylift, to support the Falkland operations in 1982.

Transport unit equipped – 53

The Short Belfast was the first transport aircraft in the world to employ a fully automatic landing system. The design was based on the Britannia's wing and tailplane and the type went straight into production. XR365/365 of 53 Sqn.

(Author's collection)

VICKERS VC-10

The Vickers VC-10 went into service with BOAC in April 1964, just six years after design work began, and only two years from the flight of the prototype on 29 June 1962. The type was ordered by the RAF to Specification C.239/60 for VIP duties and on the Far East routes. As a transport the VC-10 carried up to 150 passengers, while later versions were used for air-to-air refuelling.

The **C Mark 1** Type 1106 was similar to the Type 1103 for British United Airways with cargo door and floor. Fuel tanks were also fitted in the fin. The first RAF VC-10 flew on 26 November 1965, and the type entered service with 10 Sqn in 1967. In addition to the fourteen delivered for transport duties, one Type 1101 was used by RAF Brize Norton for ground training and one Type 1103 by the RAE. The **C(K) Mark 1** was the designation applied to the original aircraft converted from 1992 for supplementary air-to-air refuelling with FR Mk 32 refuelling pods under each wing. The passenger configuration was retained and no extra fuel was carried. By December 1995 all thirteen intended conversions had been made.

The **K Mark 2** Type 1112 were conversions of the civil Type 1101 bought from Gulf Air and fitted for air refuelling with two underwing pods and one under the rear fuselage. Total transferable fuel load was 70,000 gallons. The later **K Mark 3** Type 1154 was the first Super VC-10 variant used by the RAF, being a conversion of Type 1153 aircraft ex-East African Airways. Like the K.2, the stretched aircraft featured three refuelling points, but fuel load was extended to 80,000 gallons. The **K Mark 4** Type 1151 was the second Super VC-10 conversion. Some fourteen ex-BA aircraft had been bought and stored at RAF Abingdon for many years. Five were selected for conversion as mixed freighters/refuellers against ASR 415, and the first joined 101 Sqn in 1993. Fuel load was 66 tonnes.

Transport unit equipped – 10
Air–air refuelling – 101

LOCKHEED HERCULES

The Lockheed C-130 Hercules originated from a USAF design requirement issued in 1951 (during the Korean War) and intended to secure improvements over the contemporary C-46, C-47 and C-119. The prototype YC-130A first flew on 23 August 1954, just three years after the initial order. The Hercules must be the most successful transport type ever produced, having been in constant production for over fifty years and serving with more than fifty air forces. With the cancellation of the indigenous jet-propelled HS681, it was inevitable that the RAF would order the proven Hercules.

The **C Mark 1** (Type 382-19B) was essentially a C-130H, but with British instrumentation. It first flew on 19 October 1966, and the first of sixty-six ordered was delivered to 242 OCU in April 1967. The first squadron to receive the type was 36 Sqn, then based at Thorney Island. The Hercules served with distinction through numerous relief operations, and critically during and after the fight to retake the Falklands. The latter campaign prompted several important developments, all surviving C.1s being converted to C.1P, C.1K or C.3 standard.

The **C Mark 1P** comprised twenty-five C.1 aircraft fitted with probes above the cockpit for in-flight refuelling (Mod 5308) and the CMA 771 Omega navigation fit (Mod 5309). Several aircraft, including XV206, were fitted with the Racal *Orange Blossom* ESM pods under each wingtip to support special operations. Subsequently aircraft of this version have been fitted with AN/ALQ 157 IR jamming equipment and chaff and flare dispensers.

The **C Mark 1K** also originated in the Falklands War, with the need for additional tanker aircraft. Six aircraft with the extended internal fuel cells were fitted with a single Mk 17B HDU (Mod 5310), and they initially served in the Falklands with 1312 Flt. Three C.1Ks were equipped with the Racal *Orange Blossom* ESM for use in support of a supplementary maritime reconnaissance role in the Falklands.

The **C Mark 3** was a C.1 conversion with extended fuselage. The first conversion flew as such on 10 January 1980, and thirty aircraft were converted. The fuselage was extended by fifteen feet, with extensions fore and aft of the wings. The larger aircraft were mainly used on longer routes and for paratrooping, but they were not ideally suited for rough field performance. The -P variant is the C.3 retro-fitted with an in-flight refuelling probe above the cockpit. All thirty aircraft were converted.

The ubiquitous C-130 Hercules must be the most successful transport of all time. Although built in fewer numbers than the C-47, it has remained in continuous construction for over 50 years. Hercules C.1 XV218/218 of the Lyneham Wing drops a load during trials. *(Crown copyright)*

The later Marks 4 and 5 superseded the earlier versions from 2000, and their use is outside the scope of the present book.

Transport units equipped – 24, 30, 36, 47, 48, 70, LTW

6.5   HUMANITARIAN AID AND PEACEKEEPING, 1980s

1980

Western **Nepal** was again struck by drought and famine following monsoon failure in late 1979. The result was a 25% reduction in agricultural production. A Hercules of 70 Sqn dropped more than 1,005 tons of grain in seventy-seven sorties during May and June in Operation *Khana Cascade '80*. Initial drops were by parachute, but later drops were free drops of sacks on pallets, in up to three sorties a day, seven days a week.

In the **New Hebrides** there was an attempted coup on Vanuatu in June. Marines were transported by two Hercules drawn from the Lyneham Wing in Operation *Titan*, and order was quickly restored.

1981

There was an attempted coup by 400 rebels in **Gambia** in August. The safety of several hundred British nationals was threatened, and over several days from the 3rd a Hercules C.3 of 70 Sqn recovered more than 200 people from Banjul to Dakar in neighbouring Senegal.

1984

During the **Lebanon** war from 1978 (Chapter 9, Section 1) the situation became fraught for Westerners resident in Beirut. From February 1984 to the end of March Chinook helicopters of 7 and 18 Sqns evacuated Britons from the capital to Cyprus.

From 31 October two Hercules aircraft from the Lyneham Wing were involved in a major famine-relief operation in **Ethiopia**. In Operation *Bushell* the aircraft were based in Addis Ababa, situated at 8,000 ft AMSL. Tristars of 216 Sqn made two trips from Brize Norton, bringing in thirty tons of food and medical supplies. By the end of 1984 the Hercules had lifted some 3,500 tons of food to those most in need, and supplies were now being lifted at the rate of one million pounds a week.

The process was to collect grain at the Red Sea port of Assab and transport it to five airstrips around the country, from where it was distributed by road. Later, air drops were made to more remote areas, and 14,000 tons were dropped at very low level, the drop zones having been prepared by 47 Air Dispatch Squadron crews flown in by Polish Red Cross Mi-8 helicopters. In general the airlands were undertaken by 24 and 30 Sqn crews, while the drops were conducted by specially trained 47 and 70 Sqn personnel.

The operation continued until 18 December 1985, by which time 32,158 tons of food and medical supplies had been delivered in 2,152 sorties. Also involved in the relief effort were Transall C.160s of the German Air Force and Soviet An-12s.

1985

On 13 November Nevado del Ruiz volcano, **Colombia**, erupted with devastating results. The town of Armero was wiped out and 23,000 were killed, with many more made homeless. The RAF joined an international aid effort, supplying a Hercules, and two Pumas of 1563 Flt, from Belize between the 16th and 24th.

1986

There was a coup in southern **Yemen**, resulting in a short-term civil war. The destroyer HMS *Newcastle* (D87) and frigate HMS *Jupiter* (F60) were on hand by 16 January to evacuate British nationals to Djibouti across the Red Sea. Both were equipped with Lynx HAS.2 helicopters of 815 NAS.

1988

Hurricane *Gilbert* whipped across **Jamaica** in September, killing forty-five and leaving many homeless in the wake of floods. No. 30 Sqn Hercules brought in troops to assist from Belize and relief aid from the UK.

1989

In September Hurricane *Hugo* destroyed no less than 90% of the infrastructure in **Montserrat**, causing up to $300 million of damage. Relief aid was flown in by a Hercules of 30 Sqn to both Montserrat and Antigua. In twenty-four sorties 500,000 lb of aid was moved, together with 400 persons. HMS *Alacrity* (F174) was on station with her Lynx HAS.3s of 815 NAS.

LOCKHEED TRISTAR

Having reduced the tanker and long-range transport fleet, the RAF was in need of a complement to the Victor during the Falklands war. A decision was made to purchase second-hand L-1011-500 Tristars to meet the need. Six ex-British Airways and three ex-Pan American aircraft were bought and modified by Marshalls to three different configurations. All variants have twin hose-drum units mounted under the rear fuselage. Unlike other RAF strategic transports, the Tristar is unique in having forward-facing passenger seats.

The **K Mark 1** variant comprises two ex-BA machines which were tanker/passenger configured. In common with the KC.1, a total of 313,300 lb of fuel is carried. The Tristar entered RAF service in 1983. The **KC Mark 1** variant refers to the remaining four ex-BA machines, which are fitted with larger cargo doors and reinforced floors, and designed as tanker/cargo aircraft.

The **C Mark 2** passenger variant is a long-term interim version pending fitting of the HDUs to two of the ex-Pan American aircraft to bring them into the tanker role. It carries 10,000 lb less fuel, is not fitted with a refuelling probe and has different avionics. The **C Mark 2A** is similar to the C.2, but with full military avionics fit.

Transport unit equipped – 216

6.6   SEARCH AND RESCUE

INTRODUCTION – THE WARTIME LEGACY

The RAF's Air-Sea Rescue (ASR) service was formed in February 1941 as a series of flights attached to Fighter Command groups. These then formed the basis of the squadrons formed from November 1941. They comprised a miscellany of types able to locate, protect, drop aid to and recover downed airmen, especially in the waters around the United Kingdom. It operated both aircraft and high-speed launches (HSL) in the Marine Craft Section, and inevitably rescued a wide range of personnel. The short-range but fast HSLs were complemented by Royal Navy rescue motor launches (RML), which were slower but had a much greater range. During the course of the Second World War 13,626 persons were rescued, including 5,721 Allied aircrew.

The service was at its peak at the beginning of 1945, and the table shows the situation at that time. Since 1944 it has co-operated with UK-based American services, and these are shown for completeness.

For few months after the war's end the RAF maintained its wartime establishment of land-based search and rescue units. For short-range tasks the Walrus amphibian was invaluable – but only on calm seas! Walrus II HD908/BA-D of 277 Sqn at Hawkinge. *(Author's collection)*

Search and Rescue

Unit	Aircraft (code)	Base(s)
RAF		
275 Sqn	Walrus II, Spitfire Vb (PV)	Harrowbeer, Bolt Head, Portreath
276 Sqn	Walrus II, Spitfire Vb (AQ)	Andrews Field
277 Sqn	Lysander IIIa, Walrus II, Spitfire Vb, Warwick I (BA)	Hawkinge, Portreath
278 Sqn	Walrus II, Spitfire Vb, Warwick I (MY)	Bradwell Bay, Martlesham Heath, Hornchurch
279 Sqn	Warwick I, II (RL)	Thornaby
280 Sqn	Warwick I (MF)	Beccles
281 Sqn	Warwick I (FA)	Tiree
282 Sqn	Warwick I (B4)	St Eval
283 Sqn	Spitfire IX, Warwick I (LP)	Hal Far
284 Sqn	Warwick I, Hurricane II	Bone, El Aouina, Pomigliano, Elmas, Istres,
292 Sqn	Walrus II, Warwick I, Sea Otter II, Liberator VI	Jessore
293 Sqn	Walrus II, Warwick I (ZE)	Pomigliano
294 Sqn	Walrus II, Wellington XI, XIII, Warwick I (FD)	Idku, Palestine, Lakatamia, Nicosia
School of ASR	Anson	Calshot
USAAF		
5 ERS	P-47D, OA-10A (5F)	Boxted

The squadrons had all disbanded by the summer of 1946, some into flights which were themselves soon disbanded. The ASR services were confined to the HSLs, which became rescue/target-towing launches (RTTL) within the newly formed Marine Branch in 1948. The last of the RAF's marine units was disbanded in 1986.

For longer-range SAR tasks the Vickers Warwick was used, sometimes in conjunction with the Walrus. This was the case with 293 Sqn in Italy whose ASR.1 BV502/ZE-N is seen prior to a sortie. *(Author's collection)*

INTERNATIONAL OBLIGATIONS

In April 1947 the Chicago Convention came into effect, governing the way in which civil air transport was operated. Among other things it required signatories to provide a search-and-rescue service throughout their territories.

Through the late 1940s the RAF relied solely on its launches for air-sea rescue, while the Navy had Sea Otters based at shore stations and on aircraft carriers. On 13 January 1950, 705 NAS, which already operated the Hoverfly, acquired its first Dragonfly HR.1 helicopters, which were soon to replace the Sea Otters and complement the destroyers that conventionally accompanied active carriers on 'plane-guard' duties. On 12 January 1951 the first Dragonfly HR.3 provided the FAA's first SAR flight on HMS *Indomitable* (R92), with a second flight on HMS *Ocean* (R68) soon operational in Korean waters.

On 17 April 1951 the submarine HMS *Affray* (P421) was reported missing in the English Channel. Dragonflies of 705 NAS were involved in the search, which proved fruitless. The vessel was eventually located two months later, all on board having perished. No. 705 NAS, the FAA helicopter fleet requirements unit, provided some local SAR capability on the south coast until the role was assumed by 701 NAS in 1957.

Meanwhile the RAF, while operating Hoverfly helicopters with 1906 Flt of 657 Sqn and being generally interested in helicopters, saw little immediate need for them. This changed with the Malayan emergency (Chapter 3, Section 7), with an urgent call in 1949 for casualty-evacuation helicopters in the theatre. The result was the establishment of the Far East Air Force Casualty-Evacuation Flight formed at Changi on 1 May 1950 with three Dragonfly HC.2 machines. The first casualty was evacuated on 14 June. In the first two years of its existence it evacuated 265 casualties. However, the aircraft were far from ideal for the task, with minimal load capacity and wood and fabric blades that were a constant problem in the hot and humid climate of Malaya.

In the UK the RAF was slightly slower off the mark. In October 1952 a sole Sycamore was detached to Linton-on-Ouse to provide some rescue capability during Exercise *Ardent*. This resulted in the formation of 275 Sqn there in 1953 within 13 Group Fighter Command. Meanwhile on 3 December 1952 four Danish sailors were rescued by Flt Lt Daniel Kearns off Yarmouth in the first helicopter rescue in the UK. The first recovery by the unit was of a 14 Sqn Venom pilot at Boulmer on 15 August 1953.

The first practical helicopter used by British services in the rescue role was the Dragonfly which was the British-built version of the Sikorsky S-51 with a Leonides engine. HR Mk 1 VZ962/GJ703 of 705 NAS. (*Author's collection*)

The Sycamore was the first British-designed helicopter to enter RAF service. Although this HR.14, XE307, later served with 103 Sqn in Cyprus, it is here seen at Portland while with A&AEE. *(Author's collection)*

From 1953 the RAF re-launched search and rescue in the UK following the demise of the wartime structure in 1946. Initially equipped with the Sycamore the new units soon re-equipped with the larger Whirlwind, based on the Sikorsky S-55. XJ766/M is a HAR.2 of 22 Sqn. *(Author's collection)*

No. 275 Sqn soon had detachments across the country, initially in the north and then more widely. Because many aircraft crashes were occurring over land, from February 1954 the unit also took on charge an Auster AOP.5, two Anson T.21s, an Oxford, a Chipmunk T.10 and two Hiller HTE-2 helicopters to provide more varied coverage, but this was a short-lived process until more Sycamores came on line. Sycamores were also engaged in trials with the Air Sea Warfare Development Unit (ASWDU) at St Mawgan, and it was from here that the first aircraft were used to form 22 Sqn in February 1955 within 19 Group Coastal Command.

Responsibility for UK SAR transferred in full to Coastal Command in May 1958. As experience was gained, 275 Sqn was renumbered 228 Sqn in 1959, and then 202 Sqn within Coastal Command in 1964. In September 1959 the SAR in Northern Ireland was assumed by the short-lived 118 Sqn. The pattern was now set for the future, with 22 and 202 Sqns between them providing the RAF contribution to the UK SAR service.

To complement the relatively short-ranged helicopters, the Shackletons of Coastal Command provided the long-range search effort. They could remain airborne for twenty-two hours, covering wide areas, and were equipped with the Lindholme gear to aid survival. This comprised three canisters connected by floating lines, with the centre canister containing a dinghy and survival gear. They were dropped upwind of casualties, the intention being that the gear would drift across them for easy recovery.

EXPANSION ABROAD

In October 1952 the FAA formed its second helicopter unit, 848 NAS, with Sikorsky S-55 for use in Malaya. The unit was operational there from February 1953 under RAF control, primarily in the transport role but with casevac back-up to 194 Sqn Sycamores. In October 1954 Whirlwind HAR.1s were added for the search-and-rescue task. Sycamore SAR flights were also established at Sylt, where there were extensive ranges, and in Cyprus and Aden.

The Whirlwind, in HAR.3 form with a more powerful engine than the HAR.1, began to take over the FAA SAR role in ships and station flights from 1955, the first carrier to receive the new aircraft being HMS *Ark Royal* (R09). Gradually all FAA shore bases in the UK acquired their own SAR flights, which inevitably became engaged in local rescues.

Through the 1950s there was pressure on the relatively few helicopters in service, but small SAR detachments were established in the Middle East and in Kenya during the Mau Mau troubles (Chapter 3, Section 4). Gradually the Whirlwind replaced the Sycamore and itself went through change as more powerful variants were introduced. These critically allowed for greater range and/or payload.

Across the Middle East and Far East the Shackleton maritime reconnaissance units had an important – and much-called-upon – secondary role as search units, and there were permanent detachments at Ceylon to 1960, and then Gan. The conflicts in Malaya, Cyprus, Aden and Borneo all demanded numbers of helicopters, primarily in the troop movement and transport roles, but with casualty evacuation equally important. Some units held on charge one or two Whirlwind, or later Wessex, aircraft specifically equipped for the SAR role. Over time, as commitments abroad reduced, so did the demand for locally based SAR resources.

TRAINING

Training of RAF and FAA pilots was initially undertaken on Hoverflies of 43 OTU and 705 NAS respectively. The RAF continued with 'on-the-job' training within 1906 Flt (actually Army aircrew) and with 275 Sqn, but the Central Flying School (CFS) took on the task from 1955. In 1956 a separate squadron was formed within the CFS.

Initially crewmen to man the winches were recruited from volunteer ground crew, but the need for training was eventually recognized, and specialist courses were provided from 1961, still within the CFS, which formed an SAR training squadron on 23 April 1962. In due course the unit expanded, and on 31 March 1976 it became 2 Flying Training School (FTS) at Ternhill.

While 2 FTS concentrated on general helicopter-flying training, training for specialist SAR roles had been started in November 1958 with the formation of a training flight at St Mawgan, then maintained at RAF Valley. From December 1979 this became the Search and Rescue Training Unit (SARTU) operating the Wessex. When the Sea King entered service RAF crews were trained in the Sea King Training Unit (SKTU) from February 1978 at Culdrose, parented by, and using the expertise of, 706 NAS. In due course the SKTU transferred to St Mawgan.

TOTAL UK COVERAGE

By the mid-1970s the pattern of cover around the United Kingdom was complete, and involved primarily RAF, but also Royal Navy and some commercial assets contracted to the Board of Trade/Department for Trade and Industry. This ensured that the nation was able to meet its extensive ICAO and maritime commitments in conjunction with the Royal National Lifeboat Institution (RNLI) and HM Coastguard.

Very broadly the UK was split north and south. In terms of control there were two Rescue Co-ordination Centres (RCC) at Pitreavie Castle, Scotland, and Mount Wise, Plymouth. Nimrods had originally concentrated on the anti-submarine task upon their introduction to service in 1969, so Shackletons of 204 Sqn continued to provide a dedicated long-range over-sea search capability from RAF Honington between 1 April 1971 and 14 April 1972. After this date the Nimrods at Kinloss and St Mawgan assumed the responsibility.

No. 202 Sqn provided the northern helicopter cover, equipped with Whirlwinds, then Sea Kings from 1978, while 22 Sqn with generally shorter ranges employed the Whirlwind, then the Wessex from 1976. The Fleet Air Arm provided south coast cover; the rationale was simply that the helicopters were already there to support vessels operating out of Portsmouth and Plymouth. An operational anti-submarine Sea King unit which protected and supported the submarine base on the Clyde also provided long-range cover from Prestwick.

Finally, there were commercial contracts with Bristows to provide services in the Scottish islands and off-shore rigs, which made sense given the expertise of their mainly ex-service crews and their off-shore support contracts: they were there! In due course a commercial contract was also let to cover Lee-on-Solent, providing a service along the English Channel.

The description would be incomplete without mention of the RAF Mountain Rescue Service. Formed in 1943 there are now six teams based in Wales, the Midlands, Yorkshire and Scotland to provide a ground recovery service for aircrew crashing in remoter areas.

Some of the more significant rescues around the UK have involved more or less fixed 'vessels' associated with the North Sea oil and gas industry. In these the search element was relatively easy, albeit that the rescue element

The Royal Navy also used the Whirlwind, progressing from the piston-engined 'clockwork chicken' to the more powerful turbine-powered HAR.9. XM306/15BY served with the Brawdy SAR Flt in 1963. *(Author's collection)*

The RAF also upgraded its Whirlwinds, as exemplified by HAR.10 XP346 of 22 Sqn. *(Author's collection)*

84 Sqn in Cyprus operated the Whirlwind in several roles, that of rescue being paramount. Based at Akrotiri its aircraft included XJ437 and XR454; the former was a Mk 2 conversion. *(Crown copyright)*

was usually carried out at night or in appalling visibility. The first occasion was the recovery of injured from the sea after the collapse of legs on the oil rig *Sea Gem* off the north-east coast on 27 December 1965. Of the thirty-two crew, thirteen were killed, while the remainder were rescued by passing ships and helicopters, including a Whirlwind from 202 Sqn at Leconfield.

Major rescues included the evacuation of 150 personnel from two oil rigs in the North Sea in 1974 when they broke their moorings. *Trans World 62* and *Trans Ocean III* were involved, and the latter capsized after the rescue. On 15 December 1979, in appalling weather, the 100,000-ton derrick barge *Hermod* lost three of twelve anchors while next to the *Tartan* platform. The decision was taken to evacuate all 527 men aboard, a task completed by Bristows in twenty-five two-hour sorties over seven hours. In November 1981 forty-eight people were rescued from *Trans World 58* during a storm.

On 6 July 1988 there was an explosion of gases on the *Piper Alpha* oil rig some 120 miles out in the North Sea from Aberdeen. It was the largest and oldest rig operating in UK waters, and was manned by 229 workers. RAF helicopters were dispatched, and in due course sixty-two were rescued by helicopter and boat in what was to be the RAF's largest rescue operation, but sadly 167 perished. Most deaths were from carbon monoxide poisoning which took effect before rescuers could have reached the scene.

RAF, FAA and USAF UK-based SAR units, 1945–95

Unit	Aircraft	Base	From	To
RAF – UK				
ASWDU	Sycamore HC.12	St Mawgan	2.52	3.55
22 Sqn[1]	Sycamore HC.12			
	Whirlwind HAR.2	Thorney Island	15.2.55	3.6.56
	Whirlwind HAR.2, 10	St Mawgan[2]	4.6.56	31.3.74
	Whirlwind HAR.10	Thorney Island[3]	1.4.74	25.1.76
	Whirlwind HAR.10, Wessex HC.2	Finningley[4]	26.1.76	30.11.92
	Wessex HC.2	St Mawgan[5]	1.12.92	
275 Sqn	Sycamore HR.13, 14	Linton-on-Ouse Thornaby[6]	1.3.53	1.9.59
118 Sqn[7]	Sycamore HR.14	Aldergrove	1.9.59	31.8.62
228 Sqn[8]	Sycamore HR.14	Leconfield	1.9.59	6.60
	Whirlwind HAR.2, 4	Leconfield	1.9.59	12.62
	Whirlwind HAR.10	Leconfield	9.62	28.8.64
202 Sqn[9]	Whirlwind HAR.10	Leconfield	29.8.64	31.8.76
	Whirlwind HAR.10 Sea King HAR.3	Finningley	1.9.76	20.11.92
	Sea King HAR.3	Boulmer	1.12.92	
Bristows[10]	Whirlwind Sers 3	Manston	1.6.71	30.9.74
72 Sqn[11]	Wessex HC.2	Manston	10.74	6.76
72 Sqn[12]	Wessex HC.2	Aldergrove	12.11.81	
2 FTS (2 Sqn)	Whirlwind HAR.10	Shawbury	3.76	3.12.79
SARTF[13] Wessex HC.2	Whirlwind HAR.10,	Valley	3.12.79	31.3.97

NOTES

1   Formed with ex-ASWDU aircraft. A Flt Thorney Island, B Flt Martlesham Heath, C Flt Valley

2 A Flt St Mawgan (Chivenor from 11.58), B Flt Felixstowe (Tangmere from 6.61, Thorney Island from 5.64), C Flt Valley, D Flt Thorney Island (Manston from 6.61)

3 A Flt Chivenor, B Flt Coltishall, C Flt Valley, D Flt Brawdy

4 A Flt Chivenor, B Flt Leuchars, C Flt Valley, D Flt Brawdy (Leconfield from 10.79), E Flt Manston (Coltishall from 9.88), F Flt Coltishall (8.82-9.85)

5 A Flt Chivenor, B Flt Leuchars (Wattisham from 7.94), C Flt Valley, E Flt Coltishall

6 A Flt Linton-on-Ouse (Thornaby from 11.54, Acklington from 10.57), B Flt North Coates (Leconfield from 10.57), C Flt Leuchars, D Flt Horsham St Faith, E Flt Chivenor, F Flt Aldergrove

7 Ex-F Flt 275 Sqn

8 Ex-275 Sqn. A Flt Acklington, B Flt Leconfield, C Flt Leuchars, D Flt Horsham St Faith (Coltishall from 4.63)

9 Ex-228 Sqn. A Flt Acklington (Boulmer from 10.75), B Flt Leconfield (Brawdy from 10.79), C Flt Leuchars (Coltishall from 9.85, Manston from 9.88), D Flt Coltishall (Lossiemouth from 2.74), E Flt Leconfield (from 11.88)

10 On contract from HM Coastguard

11 Detachment from Odiham

12 SAR Flight within main unit

13 Ex-2 Sqn 2 FTS

Unit	Aircraft	Base	From	To
FAA – UK				
705 NAS	Dragonfly HR.1, 3, 5, Whirlwind HAR.1	Gosport	1.50	3.62
701 NAS	Dragonfly HR.5, Whirlwind HAR.1, 3	Lee-on-Solent	31.10.57	20.9.58
781 NAS	Whirlwind HAR.1, 3, Wessex HU.5	Lee-on-Solent	7.61	31.3.81
772 NAS C Flt	Wessex HU.5, Sea King HC.4	Lee-on-Solent	14.2.83	88
845 NAS	Whirlwind HAS.22	HMS *Theseus*	18.10.56	10.11.56
JHU	Whirlwind HAR.2 Sycamore HC.14	HMS *Ocean*	10.56	11.56
737 NAS	Whirlwind HAR.3	Portland	28.8.59	7.61
771 NAS	Dragonfly HR.5, Whirlwind HAR.3	Portland	11.7.61	1.12.64
	Whirlwind HAR.3, Wessex HAS.1, HU.5	Portland	23.6.67	3.9.74
772 NAS	Wessex HAS.1, HU.5, Sea King HC.4	Portland	6.9.74	
SF	Dragonfly HR.3, HR.5, Whirlwind HAR.3, HAS.7, HAR.9	Culdrose	55	74
771 NAS	Wessex HAS.1, HU.5, Sea King HAR.5	Culdrose	4.9.74	
706 NAS[1]	Sea King HAS.2, HAR.3	Culdrose	10.79	1.82
SARF	Whirlwind HAS.7, HAR.9	Brawdy	65	71
SARF	Whirlwind HAS.7, HAR.9	Lossiemouth	65	73
819 NAS[2]	Sea King HAS.1, 2, 5, 6	Prestwick	10.72	

NOTES

Dates shown above are those during which the unit provided an SAR service

1   Parented RAFSKTU and provided long-range SAR cover

2   Secondary role

Unit	Aircraft	Base	From	To
Commercial contracts – For H M Coastguard				
Bristows	WS55 Sers 3	Manston	1.6.71	30.9.74
BEA Helis	S-61N	Aberdeen	75	11.83
Bristows	S-61N	Sumburgh	12.83	
Bristows	S-61N	Stornoway	12.5.87	
Bristows	S-61N	Lee-on-Solent	15.5.88	
Commercial contracts – Bristows				
BP	S-61N	Aberdeen	2.78	83
Shell Expro	Bell 212	Off-shore	79	
USAFE – UK				
66th ARS	SA-16A, H-5H, H-19, C-82	Manston	11.52	54
67th ARS	H-19A	Sculthorpe	14.11.52	12.11.53
67th ARS	SB-29, SH-19B, SA-16B, SC-54,	Prestwick	12.11.53	6.60
	SC-54, HU-16, SH-19B	Prestwick	18.6.61	1.7.66
67th ARRS	HC-130H, N, P, HH-3E	Woodbridge	15.1.70	3.71
	HC-130H, N, P, HH-53C	Woodbridge	3.71	31.5.88
67th SOG		Woodbridge	1.6.88	31.3.92
Det 2 23rd HS *	H-21B	Wethersfield	11.56	58
40th ARRW	HH-43B,F	Alconbury, Lakenheath, Upper Heyford, Wethersfield, Woodbridge	3.65	10.72

* Casevac rather than rescue

Unit	Aircraft	Base	From	To
RAF Overseas				
FEAFCEF	Dragonfly HC.2	Changi	1.5.50	2.2.53
194 Sqn[1]	Dragonfly HC.4	Sembawang, Kuala Lumpur	2.2.53	4.54
	Sycamore HR.14	Kuala Lumpur	4.54	3.6.59
155 Sqn[2]	Whirlwind HAR.2,4	Kuala Lumpur	1.9.54	3.6.59
110 Sqn[3]	Whirlwind HAR.4, Sycamore HR.14	Kuala Lumpur, Butterworth	3.6.59	7.63
	Whirlwind HAR.10	Butterworth, Seletar, Changi	7.63	15.2.71
103 Sqn[2,4]	Whirlwind HAR.10	Seletar, Changi	1.8.63	1.8.75
	Wessex HC.2	Tengah		
225 Sqn[2]	Whirlwind HAR.10	Kuching	8.12.63	1.11.65

Unit	Aircraft	Base	From	To
230 Sqn[2]	Whirlwind HAR.10	Labuan	10.3.65	25.11.66
SAR Flt	Sycamore HR.14	Sylt	4.2.55	9.61
SAR Flt	Sycamore HR.14	Nicosia	5.55	15.10.56
Internal Security Flt	Sycamore HR.14	Nicosia	3.56	15.10.56
284 Sqn[2,5]	Sycamore HR.14	Nicosia	15.10.56	31.7.59
103 Sqn[6]	Sycamore HR.14	Nicosia	1.8.59	31.7.63
230 Sqn det	Whirlwind HAR.10	Nicosia	15.1.63	17.1.72
1563 Flt[7]	Sycamore HR.14, Whirlwind HAR.10	Nicosia	1.8.63	17.1.72
84 Sqn[2,8]	Whirlwind HAR.10, Wessex HC.2, HU.5	Akrotiri	17.1.72	
SF	Sycamore HR.14	El Adem	8.57	12.59
1564 Flt[6]	Sycamore HR.14 Whirlwind HAR.10	El Adem	1.8.63	2.67
1563 Flt[9]	Whirlwind HAR.10	El Adem	3.69	3.70
EACF	Sycamore HR.14	Nairobi	25.10.54	2.57
APCS	Sycamore HR.14	Khormaksar	9.7.55	31.5.57
SF[10]	Sycamore HR.14	Khormaksar	1.6.57	12.6.58
SAR Flt[11]	Sycamore HR.14	Khormaksar	13.6.58	7.64
	Whirlwind HAR.10	Khormaksar	7.64	6.67
78 Sqn[2]	Wessex HC.2	Khormaksar	6.65	12.10.67
78 Sqn[2]	Wessex HC.2	Sharjah	17.10.67	21.12.71
SARF[12]	Wessex HC.2	Muharraq	5.69	31.5.71
SAR Flt[13]	Whirlwind HAR.10	Kai Tak	67	28.2.68
28 Sqn[14]	Whirlwind HAR.10 Wessex HC.2	Kai Tak, Sek Kong	1.3.68	
1362 Flt	Whirlwind HAR.4	Maralinga	1.12.55	1.58
22 Sqn (X)	Whirlwind HAR.4	Christmas Is	3.56	31.7.57
1360 Flt[15]	Whirlwind HAR.4	Christmas Is	1.8.57	31.1.58
217 Sqn[16]	Whirlwind HAR.4	Christmas Is	1.2.58	13.11.59
202 Sqn[17]	Sea King HAR.3	Ascension	9.5.82	7.9.82
1310 Flt	Chinook HC.1	Mount Pleasant	20.8.83	21.5.86
202 Sqn[18]	Sea King HAR.3	Mount Pleasant	25.8.82	20.8.83
1564 Flt[19]	Sea King HAR.3	Mount Pleasant	22.5.86	30.4.86
78 Sqn[20]	Sea King HAR.3	Mount Pleasant	1.5.86	

NOTES

1 Ex-FEAFCEF
2 Combined trooping and casevac role
3 Ex-110 and 194 Sqns merger
4 Ex-B Flt 110 Sqn
5 Ex-SAR and IS Flts merger
6 Ex-184 Sqn
7 Ex-103 Sqn
8 Ex-1563 Flt and 230 Sqn detachment merger
9 Ex-D Flt 22 Sqn Manston
10 Ex-APCS

11 Ex-Khormaksar Station Flt
12 Detachment from 78 Sqn
13 Detachments from 103 or 110 Sqn
14 Ex-103 Sqn detachment
15 Ex-X Flt 22 Sqn
16 Ex-1360 Flt
17 Ex-D Flt 202 Sqn
18 As C Flt
19 Ex-202 Sqn C Flt
20 Ex-1310 and 1564 Flts

Between January 1956 and August 1957 a Sycamore was operated in the SAR role by the station flights at Amman, and then Habbaniya.

WESTLAND DRAGONFLY

Westland acquired manufacturing rights for the American Sikorsky S-51 in 1947 after initial military experience with the Hoverfly highlighted the potential of the helicopter. In fact the S-51 was a four-seat commercial development of the R-5 first flown in 1946. The first British-built Dragonfly Mk 1A flew on 5 October 1948, and work was put in hand to produce speculatively, by hand, a further thirty examples.

The **HR Mark 1** was ordered for the Royal Navy for assessment and trials. The first flew on 22 June 1949, and the type entered service in January 1950, soon being engaged on deck-landing trials. Several later served as plane-guards on carriers.

The **HC Mark 2** was the first version supplied to the RAF to meet an urgent need for casualty evacuation in Malaya, where Operation *Firedog* against Communist terrorists was under way. Three aircraft were built, the first being a converted civil aircraft, and like the HR.1 it had a three-bladed wood and fabric composite rotor. In service the RAF Dragonflies formed the world's first helicopter rescue unit, and the first airlift took place on 19 June 1950. After initial trials a single pannier was designed for carrying one casualty.

The **HR Mark 3** was similar to the HR.1, but with a metal three-bladed rotor and hydraulic controls to ease pilot workload. Fifty were bought for plane-guard duties on carriers and ship-to-shore communications. Range was short, but the type was more effective than the traditional destroyer escort.

The **HC Mark 4** enjoyed the same improvements as the naval HR.3, and it quickly joined the HC Mk 2 machines in Malaya. Three served in the training role, and one of these was later with the Queen's Flight. The HR Mark 5 comprised twenty-five HR.1 and HR.3 conversions, with slightly increased power and better instrumentation.

SAR units equipped – FEAFCEF, 194; 701, 705, 771

BRISTOL SYCAMORE

The Bristol Aeroplane Company had bought a stake in the A.R.III autogiro and its developer, Raoul Hafner. At the end of the war, as Bristol's chief helicopter designer, he designed the Type 171 as a single-piston-engined, four-seat aircraft, the first of which flew on 27 July 1947. This was built to Specification E.20/45 and powered by the Pratt and Whitney Wasp engine, since the intended Leonides was not ready. The first Mark 2 aircraft, powered by the Leonides, flew on 3 September 1949 to Specification 35/46. Six Mark 3 aircraft flew in military markings (one in HR Mark 14 configuration), but only one was to fly within the military designation range. The remainder were used for evaluation and tropical and Arctic trials.

The **HC Mark 10** was ordered to Specification A.9/49. It equated to the Company's Mark 3, and carried five people in a slightly redesigned shorter nose. The sole example was modified to carry casualty evacuation equipment, and undertook trials in Malaya. The **HC Mark 11** was developed for Army use to Specification A.106P. It was not ideal as an air observation type, but was used mainly for VIP transport.

The **HC Mark 13** was similar to the Mk 50 built for the Royal Australian Navy. It employed a longer-stroke undercarriage, giving better ground clearance. The **HR Mark 14** was the definitive version and was to all intents similar to the HR.13, but with four doors. It served widely in the search-and-rescue role, and latterly as a communications aircraft, in which role it was designated HC.14, but with no discernible external changes. Those operated in the VIP role by 32 Sqn had fixed external steps and an improved interior.

SAR units equipped – 22, 103, 110, 118, 194, 228, 275, 284, 1563, 1564 Flts, APCS, ASWDU, EACF, ISF, JHU

WESTLAND WHIRLWIND

The Sikorsky S-55 was a larger helicopter than its predecessor, the S-51, and it was the second type for which Westland acquired a licence in November 1950. The American prototype flew on 7 November 1949, and it entered US service in 1951. Initial deliveries to British services were of US-built machines supplied through the Mutual Defence Assistance Plan (MDAP), and they were given high mark numbers, starting with 21. This was unusual, given that at the period mark numbers from 20 were reserved for naval aircraft. Another feature of the numbering system was that odd mark numbers were applied to naval types and even numbers to RAF types.

The Whirlwind, as the S-55 became in British service, was produced in three series in the UK. Series 1 aircraft had American Wasp or Cyclone engines, Series 2 aircraft the Leonides Major and Series 3 aircraft the Gnome turbine. Although for the times a large helicopter, the Whirlwind suffered from its small payload, which was not satisfactorily addressed until the Gnome-powered aircraft came into service. It also lacked automatic flight-control systems, making night and adverse weather flying difficult. One pattern aircraft was supplied.

The **HAR Mark 21** was the first supplied under MDAP, and was powered by an R-1340-40 engine. It was similar to the USMC HRS-2, and ten were supplied, starting with WV189; they were dispatched almost immediately to Malaya, where they served within 303 Wing in the troop transport role, carrying up to ten passengers.

Transport unit equipped – 848

The **HAS Mark 22** was powered by the R-1300-3 Cyclone engine, and was equivalent to the USN HO4S-3. It was equipped with a US AN/AQS-4 dunking sonar. Fifteen were supplied, and they were used extensively for trials and SAR, attached to a range of training and fleet requirements units.

Transport units equipped – 845, 848

The first Westland-built variant was the **HAR Mark 1**, fitted with the R-1340-40. The first of ten delivered flew on 15 August 1953. The variant was mainly used for trials and then SAR duties, although it also supplemented the HAR.21 in Malaya.

SAR units equipped – 701, 705
Transport – 848

The **HAR Mark 2** was the RAF Wasp variant, and like the Navy's HAR.1 it was significantly under-powered. This was due to weight increases through the use of thicker-gauge metal and other changes in construction. The first flew on 14 January 1955; first deliveries were for air-sea rescue with 22 Sqn in February 1955.

SAR units equipped – 22, 217, 228, 284; 1360 Flt
Transport – 225; JHU

The **HAR Mark 3** was the Royal Navy's attempt to improve the disappointing performance of the Whirlwind by fitting the Cyclone R-1300-3 of the HAS.22. Unfortunately the added weight of the engine balanced any improvement, and the type still operated with limitations on payload and range. Fitted permanently with a rescue winch, the variant served mainly on plane-guard duties and trials. The prototype flew on 28 June 1955, and service entry was with 845 NAS in November 1955

SAR units equipped – 701, 737, 771, 781
Transport – 845

An attempt to improve on the performance of the HAR.2 by the installation of the R-1340-57 with more powerful supercharger was the **HAR Mark 4**. In other respects the variant was similar to the HAR.2, and the variant went first to units in Malaya.

SAR units equipped – 22, 217, 228, 275; 1362 Flt, SARF Aden
Transport – 110, 155, 225

The **HAS Mark 7** featured a Leonides Major 755 engine, and like successive variants had a drooped tailcone. It was the first British helicopter designed specifically for the anti-submarine role, and it employed a range of ASW equipment, including an anglicized AN/AQS-4 sonar, radar and provision for a single Mk 30 torpedo. It could also

While the Royal Navy first operated the Sea King (in the ASW role) the RAF was first to use it in the SAR role with 202 Sqn in 1978. XZ590 is pictured in Snowdonia. *(Crown copyright)*

In Cornwall, as in parts of western Scotland, the Royal Navy provides search and rescue services. Based at Culdrose is 771 NAS which in 1987 started operating the Sea King HAS.5 including XV666/823. *(Author's collection)*

carry a small hand winch. A combination of engine problems and weight restrictions led to later use in the commando-carrying and utility roles. The prototype flew on 17 October 1956, and first deliveries were to 820 NAS in January 1958.

ASW units equipped – 814, 815, 820, 824, 825, 829
Transport – 845, 846, 847, 848

The VIP communications **HCC Mark 8** variant was based on the cancelled HAR Mark 5, but with dual controls and sound-proofing. Given its role as a VIP transport with the Queen's Flight, external folding steps were fitted and the cabin windows enlarged. The first of three flew on 2 May 1959.

The **HAR Mark 9** comprised some HAS.7 conversions to the equivalent of the RAF HAR.10 with the Gnome turbine. This engine, in General Electric T-58 form, had first been fitted and flown in a Whirlwind on 28 February 1959, following which the RAF variant was produced, but the Royal Navy did not receive its first uprated machines until 1965; they served in the Antarctic and for SAR duties.

Utility unit equipped – 829

The RAF's **HAR Mark 10** was the major utility variant with the Gnome turbine engine, which weighed much less than the piston engines while being much more powerful. The nose was extended to accommodate the new engine. The result was much better performance and payload, and the variant was the first to be tested to carry four SS.11 ASMs. The first of sixty-eight new-build HAR.10s flew on 28 March 1961, and first deliveries were to 225 Sqn in the tactical support role from November 1961.

SAR units equipped – 22, 103, 202; 1310, 1563, 1564 Flts
Transport – 28, 84, 110, 225, 230

WESTLAND WESSEX

The Wessex started life as the piston-engined Sikorsky S-58, which in USN service was the HSS-1, HUS-1 or H-34A. Westland acquired a licence for development and production in 1956, and an HSS-1 was imported in 1957. It flew initially with the 1,525 hp R-1820-84 piston engine, but made its first flight with the less powerful, but significantly lighter, Napier Gazelle NGII turboshaft of 1,100 hp shortly afterwards, on 17 May 1957.

The Wessex design was ideal for its initial British role as an airborne anti-submarine platform. It was robust, with plenty of room for crew and equipment. The Westland-built prototype **HAS Mark 1** flew on 20 June 1958 with an uprated Gazelle and auto-stabilization. Service entry was with 815 NAS in 1961 after trials with 700H NAS. Weapons included two Mk 44 torpedoes or two Mk 11 depth charges, all carried externally; however, range was limited with armament carried. A new flight-control system relieved the pilot of much of the work involved in hovering precisely at low levels during sonar operations. Twelve of the total produced were built without ASW equipment for use as commando transports, and a number of anti-submarine variants later had their equipment removed as attrition replacements. As such they could carry up to sixteen troops plus two SS-11 missiles or rockets or GPMG.

ASW units equipped – 814, 815, 819, 820, 826, 829
SAR – 771, 772
Transport – 845

Westland developed the potential of the Wessex by installing a pair of Gnome turboshafts to meet an RAF need for a utility helicopter. The airframe was strengthened, and the first prototype, a converted HAS.1, flew on 18 January 1962. The **HC/HAR Mark 2** variant had a new nose profile and single large exhausts on each side of the forward fuselage. It carried sixteen troops or 4,000 lb underslung, and could be fitted with a range of weapons, including SS-11 anti-tank missiles. The Wessex entered RAF service with 18 Sqn in 1994. Twelve HC.2 aircraft were converted for search-and-rescue tasks by fitting a winch above the starboard door. They were used for relatively short-range tasks in the UK.

SAR units equipped – 22, 84
Communications – 21, 32
Transport – 18, 28, 60, 72, 84, 103

The next variant for the Royal Navy, the **HAS Mark 3**, was fitted with an uprated Gazelle engine and an Ekco radar on the fuselage decking behind an extended fairing behind the rotor head. A protruding pitot head supported a more advanced automatic flight-control system which enabled all phases of the anti-submarine search to be conducted automatically. To support longer flight times, air refuelling from ships without landing platforms was also developed; however, range remained a problem not resolved in Royal Navy service until the introduction of the Sea King.

ASW units equipped – 814, 819, 820, 826, 829

Two specially fitted Wessex HC.2 aircraft were acquired for the Queen's Flight for VVIP transport as the **HCC Mark 4**. Externally they were distinguished by their distinctive red and blue livery.

Experience with the HAS.1 aircraft in commando use with 845 NAS, especially in Borneo, proved the value of the type as a troop carrier, but for reliability two engines coupled with an improved transmission were considered essential. One hundred **HU Mark 5** variants were built, and they served in Aden, Borneo, Cyprus, the Falklands and Northern Ireland with distinction, having first operated with 848 NAS in 1964. Six were transferred to the RAF for use in Cyprus.

SAR units equipped – 84; 771, 772
Transport – 845, 846, 847, 848

WESTLAND SEA KING

The Sea King was the fourth of the Sikorsky designs developed and built under licence by Westland. The S-61 flew on 11 March 1959, and in US service became the H-3 series. The type featured a sealed boat hull, enabling security and recovery in the event of ditching, but not for operations from water. Four examples were shipped to the UK to act as pattern and development aircraft, and the first of these flew at Avonmouth docks on 11 October 1966, shortly after the type had entered US service.

The initial naval variant, the **HAS Mark 1**, was built to Specification HAS.261, and the first flew on 7 May 1969. The Sea King was a medium-range hunter/killer capable of flying from larger ships, although it was later cleared for use from some frigates. Search equipment included Plessey Type 195 sonar, Marconi AD580 Doppler and Ekco AW391 radar in a thimble housing on the fuselage decking. Winches were retained for rescue, and a Louis Newmark Mk 31 automatic flight-control system was fitted. Weapons included four Mk 44 torpedoes or Mk 11 depth charges or a single nuclear depth bomb. The Sea King joined 706 NAS for training in 1969, and the first operational unit was 824 NAS in February 1970.

ASW units equipped – 814, 819, 820, 824, 826

The next variant, the **HAS Mark 2**, was the result of developments for the Australian Navy, incorporating more powerful Gnome engines and a matching transmission improvement. A six-bladed tail rotor replaced the five-bladed type of the HAS.1, and various equipment changes were made, including Plessey 2069 sonar and Racal Decca 71 Doppler. Other changes included an intake guard to prevent ice ingestion, and on some aircraft provision for the Dowty SSQ904 passive sonobuoy. Twenty-one were built new, and most of the HAS.1 aircraft were converted to the standard.

ASW units equipped – 814, 819, 820, 824, 826
Utility – 825

The disastrous situation in the South Atlantic in 1982, where British ships were exposed to Argentine air attack with no airborne early warning, led to an immediate need for some form of cover. The response, managed in a remarkable eleven weeks, was to fit Sea King HAS.2A airframes with the Thorn EMI Searchwater radar in an inflatable and semi-retractable Kevlar radome attached to the starboard fuselage. The **AEW Mark 2** variant also had *Orange Crop* ESM, new IFF and a Ferranti INS.

Early warning units equipped – 824, 849

The RAF ordered the Sea King as the **HAR Mark 3** to replace and complement its Whirlwind and Wessex search-and-rescue fleet. For the purpose the rear bulkhead was moved back to accommodate up to twenty-six survivors, and extra tankage was installed. A long-reach winch was also fitted and extra observation windows provided. The radio fit was designed to enable direct communications with a range of services, and a Smiths Industries AFCS was also fitted. Six machines were given extra equipment, including the ARI 18228 RWR for use in the Falklands, where they operated in a grey finish.

In 1992 six new HAR Sea Kings were ordered to replace the remaining Wessexes in service. Externally the new HAR Mk 3A variant is distinguished only by several additional blade aerials, but the avionics fit is almost completely new, including the communications equipment, colour search radar, Smiths-Newmark FCS and Decca 91 Doppler.

SAR units equipped – 22, 78, 202; 1564 Flt

The Commando was a private venture development of the Sea King, intended typically in the utility and especially troop transport role. In due course the type was ordered for the Royal Navy as the Sea King **HC Mark 4** to replace the Wessex with the commando units. The undercarriage was changed from the retractable-into-sponsons type of other variants to a fixed unit. The radar is deleted and the extra windows of the HAR.3 retained. Night-vision goggles may be used with cockpit lighting altered accordingly, and except in the search-and-rescue role the AFCS is disabled.

The variant first flew on 26 September 1979, joining 846 NAS shortly after. Through use in a succession of war zones, including the Falklands, the Gulf, northern Iraq and Bosnia, many equipment changes have been incorporated, including armoured crew seats, GPS, jammers, chaff/flare dispensers, floodlight and Kevlar floor armour. Provision has also been made for a door-mounted FN-Herstal .50-calibre machine-gun to be fitted. Two Mark 4X aircraft were supplied to the RAE for a wide range of trials and research work, including tests of avionics and other equipment for the EH101.

SAR unit equipped – 772
Transport – 845, 846, 848

The Navy's ASW Sea Kings were subject to continuous improvement. In the **HAS Mark 5** the most significant change was the MEL Sea Searcher radar, with almost twice the range of the earlier type, housed in a larger radome. The data from a new dipping sonar and sonobuoys were processed through a GEC-Marconi AQS902 system that could, in addition, handle data from sonobuoys dropped by other vehicles, including the Nimrod. *Orange Crop* ESM was also fitted. The first was a converted HAS Mk 2, XZ916, which flew on 1 August 1980, and although some new-build helicopters were produced most were HAS Mk 2 conversions.

ASW units equipped – 810, 814, 819, 820, 824, 826

The Fleet Air Arm adopted modified HAS.5 aircraft for use in the search-and-rescue role as the **HAR.5**. The ASW avionics was removed, but the MEL radar retained, and eight aircraft were converted.

SAR unit equipped – 771

Improvements in electronics technology led to the next Navy variant, the **HAS Mark 6**. New GEC Avionics AQS-902G-DS digital sonar handled dunking to 700 ft, and a new radar display eased workload. Further changes included a better MAD system, IFF, *Orange Reaper* ESM and secure speech communications, while composite main rotors were fitted, together with emergency gearbox lubrication system. Externally the only new feature was an additional blade aerial under the forward fuselage. The first of seventy-three HAS.5 conversions flew on 15 December 1987, and in addition there were six new-build aircraft.

ASW units equipped – 810, 814, 819, 820, 824

CHAPTER SEVEN

Confrontation (2) – Territorial

Throughout the period of the Cold War there were examples of countries threatening immediate British interests or wider concerns where Britain had treaty obligations. These threats were usually made by governments at the political extremes with serious domestic difficulties which they sought to resolve in the mistaken belief that overseas expedition and expansion would result in unification at home.

Treaty obligations resulted in the UK supporting Thailand against a perceived Communist threat from Vietnam via Laos in 1962. British military interests were withdrawn before the Vietnam War (locally known as the American War, and latterly in Vietnam the Second Indo-China War) escalated.

Britain also supported ex-colonies in their formative years, typically in East Africa, where there were threats to Kenyan integrity from Somalia, and then Army mutinies in each of the former colonies of Kenya, Uganda, Tanganyika and Zanzibar. Here the ability to place troops and equipment speedily by air helped to close down problems effectively.

A much more serious threat came from Indonesia in 1962, with attacks against Brunei, which was a British protectorate. The attacks escalated, eventually extending to assaults on the Malaysian mainland, which were effectively countered. A peace treaty was signed in 1966, but at the time of writing British forces remain in Brunei at the invitation of the Sultan.

Confrontation of a different sort occurred in southern Africa in 1965, when the white minority government of Rhodesia made an illegal and unilateral declaration of independence from Britain. The UK response was to impose sanctions and enforce an oil and trade embargo that was as ineffective as it was expensive. The situation was resolved through international diplomatic pressure in 1979. While it was probably impossible to have found some short-term accommodation with the white regime, it remains a tragedy that this once prosperous country is now reduced to anarchy and poverty.

Turning to the New World, Britain has had to base military assets in or around Belize for many years to protect the colony against the very real threat of invasion from Guatemala. The latter continued to lay claim to part of what had been British Honduras until 1991. However, British forces remain in the guise of the jungle warfare training unit.

The final conflict described in the present chapter is the Falklands war. Yet again to divert attention from domestic problems, a dictator invaded a defenceless colony. Demonstrating deep divisions between branches of the Argentine military, the invasion was Navy driven, with the Army and Air Force reluctant partners.

In 1982 Britain had the political will and military power and cohesion to mount from 8,000 miles distant an invasion force to retake the islands, despite the appalling weather and size of the occupation force. While there was support from behind the scenes by France, the USA and Chile, the whole affair was singularly British, with clear objectives and sound strategy. Now Britain could never repeat the operation with her limited military resources, and since that time she has been forced to play second fiddle to the USA in a succession of militarily sound but politically bankrupt operations in the Middle East.

7.1   LAOS AND THAILAND, 1962

BACKGROUND

After the French defeat in Indo-China in 1954, the Geneva Accords left Laos neutral but with three factions ready to seek power through civil war. On one extreme was the Communist-backed Pathet Lao, at the other the military establishment and in the centre the Royalist-Neutralist government. After a right-wing coup in 1958, heavy fighting broke out in the north between Pathet Lao and government forces, the latter backed by the United States through the Central Intelligence Agency (CIA).

SEATO ACTS

On 23 March 1961 a USAF SC-47D of Project *Field Goal*, operating from Vientiane and monitoring radio frequencies at Xieng Khoung airfield on the Plaine des Jarres, was shot down. The Americans responded by bringing in fighter detachments to neighbouring Thailand. The civil war intensified until a ceasefire was declared on 10 May 1961, but by October this was broken, resulting in the USAF deploying more reconnaissance and strike aircraft to Thailand. Early in 1962 the Pathet Lao began an all-out offensive towards Vientiane, and the South-East Asia Treaty Organization (SEATO) set up a multi-national Joint Task Force (JTF) 116 in Thailand in May, ostensibly to protect Thailand against North Vietnamese or Pathet Lao incursion.

Two USAF F-100D squadrons went to Takhli, while the USMC contributed HMM-261, equipped with the UH-34D, and VMA-332, with the A-4A, to support a 3,400-strong Marine Corps contingent from the 3rd Marine Expeditionary Unit. The RAF provided support in the form of 20 Sqn with the Hunter FGA.9 (Operation *Bibber*), initially at Bangkok, and shortly moving to Chieng Mai in the north, while RAAF Sabre 32s of 79 Sqn were based at Ubon. Ground staff and supplies were transported by Beverley transports of 34 Sqn. Tactical transport was also available, including 36 Sqn RAAF and 41 Sqn RNZAF, and from June a detachment from the 777th TCS USAF with C-123B moved to Don Muang. Despite an invasion panic in June, no incursions across the Thai border occurred.

There was a further show of unity in 1963 when the Hunters of 20 Sqn were again detached to Chieng Mai in Exercise *Dhanarajata*. They were supported by Beverleys of 34 Sqn, and the exercise, which lasted only from 14 to 20 June, involved troop movements by Britannias of 99 and 511 Sqns and Hastings of 36 Sqn, all from the UK. Regionally based units involved were Canberras of 45 Sqn, Hastings of 48 Sqn and Twin Pioneers of 209 Sqn.

A further British SEATO commitment consisted of the construction of a military airfield at Leong Nok Tha in north-eastern Thailand close to the border with Laos. In Operation *Crown*, Royal Engineers built a 5,000 ft airfield with control tower, close to the US signals post at Phu Mu, between 1963 and 1966. Between February 1967 and April 1968, Sioux helicopters of the Royal Engineers Air Troop were based at Leong Nok Tha. A final British involvement in the Indo-China wars was the engagement of HMS *Albion* (R07) in late 1968. In Operation *Charlotte* the carrier, with Wessex HU.5s of 848 NAS embarked, was positioned off the Cambodian coast in an endeavour to enforce a quarantine of Soviet vessels carrying arms shipments. The detachment lasted from late November to mid-December.

SEQUEL

After talks in Geneva aimed at finding a lasting settlement, the Royalist-Neutralist government again assumed power as the Soviet Union and United States agreed to withdraw their support for the Pathet Lao and anti-Communist forces respectively. Laos was now recognized as a neutral state, and the formal position of the US State Department was one of total backing for the new government. However, as the North Vietnamese continued to back the Pathet Lao, the CIA decided to continue its covert and illegal support of the generals. Through the whole of what became known as the Vietnam War, northern Laos became the most densely bombed territory in the history of warfare until the defeat of the government by the Pathet Lao in 1975.

This was not the only British action in the region during the Vietnam War. Emergency 'flood-relief' supplies were transported to Saigon by Beverleys of 34 Sqn RAF and Bristol Freighters of 31 Sqn RNZAF in December 1961. The Beverleys flew more such supplies into Da Nang in January 1965, and again to Saigon in February 1966; in the latter exercise the aircraft also reportedly flew US mail out. Finally, no fewer than eight Beverleys of 34 Sqn were at Bangkok in March 1967 in Exercise *Fina*, the purpose of which has not been disclosed.

In respect of the Vietnam war Britain was invited to join the party but wisely declined. However, Beverleys of 34 Sqn were involved in supporting SEATO in Thailand against the prospect of attack from Laos. XM104 basks in the sun. *(Crown copyright)*

Another SEATO signatory was New Zealand which provided Bristol Freighters of 41 Sqn for intra-theatre tasks. NZ5904 is here seen at Changi. *(Crown copyright)*

SEATO JOINT TASK FORCE 116 (MAY TO DECEMBER 1962)

Unit	Aircraft	Base	From	To
RAF				
20 Sqn	Hunter FGA.9	Don Muang	25.5.62	4.6.62
		Chieng Mai	5.6.62	15.11.62
34 Sqn	Beverley C.1	Chieng Mai	5.62	5.62
RAAF				
79 Sqn	Sabre 32	Ubon	5.62	8.68
36 Sqn	C-130A	Ubon, Butterworth	5.62	10.62
RNZAF				
41 Sqn	Bristol Freighter	Chieng Mai	6.62	9.62
U S Army				
1 Av Co	C-7A	Korat AB	5.62	12.62
U S Air Force				
15 TRS[1]	RF-101C	Don Muang	5.62	11.62
510 TFS[2]	F-100D	Takhli	5.62	12.62
428 TFS[3]	F-100D	Takhli	18.5.62	2.9.62
430 TFS[3]	F-100D	Takhli	3.9.62	12.12.62
522 TFS[3]	F-100D	Takhli	13.12.62	
9 TRS[4]	WB-66D	Takhli	18.5.62	
777 TCS	C-123B	Don Muang	6.62	7.63
509 FIS[5]	F-102A	Don Muang	4.61	64
U S Marine Corps				
VMA-332	A-4A	Udorn	6.62	10.62
HMM-261[6]	UH-34D	Udorn	19.5.62	21.6.62
HMM-162	UH-34D	Udorn	21.6.62	31.7.62

NOTES
1. In theatre as Project *Able Mabel*
2. Operation *Moon Glow*
3. Ex-Cannon AFB Operation *Saw Buck*
4. Ex-George AFB
5. In theatre as Project *Bell Tone*
6. Ex-USS *Valley Forge*

7.2 CONFRONTATION OVER BORNEO, 1962–6

BACKGROUND

It was the ambition of Indonesia's President Soekarno to unite Malaysia, the Philippines and Indonesia within an Indonesian empire; a glance at the map shows how the territories are inter-related. Following the proposal in 1962 for a Malaysian Federation comprising Malaya, Singapore, Sarawak, Brunei and Sabah (North Borneo), Indonesia determined to prevent the development. One weak link in the prospective Federation was Brunei, which was autocratically ruled by a Sultan and was proportionately far richer, through oil revenues, than the other partners.

Soekarno encouraged the local North Kalimantan National Army (TNKU) to revolt. With 4,000 members, 1,000 of whom were under arms, the TNKU struck on 8 December 1962. The initial targets were the power station and Sultan's palace in Brunei Town, police posts and other administrative centres at Limbang, Bangar, Tutong and Lawas, and the oilfields and airstrip at Seria.

RECOVERING BRUNEI

Although the attacks were carried out on a Saturday, the British had some forewarning, and by midday a battalion of Gurkhas was forming up at Seletar, Singapore, while transport aircraft were readied. A prepared plan was put into action as Operation *Ale*, later changed to Operation *Borneo Territories*. From 14.00 hrs three Beverley transports of 34 Sqn and a conveniently located Britannia flew the battalion into Brunei Town and Labuan respectively, the former's runways being too short to take the Britannia; further reinforcements were flown in by a Bristol Freighter of 41 Sqn RNZAF, C-130As of 36 Sqn RAAF, Valettas of 52 Sqn, Hastings of 48 Sqn and Shackletons of 205 Sqn RAF. By late afternoon control had been restored in Brunei Town as more aircraft flew into Brunei and Labuan.

Twin Pioneers of 209 Sqn and Belvedere HC.1s of 66 Sqn were available for local transport work, and Hunter FGA.9s of 20 Sqn and Canberra B.15s of 45 Sqn were detached to Labuan for close air support if necessary. More troops arrived on 9 December, as did Auster AOP.9s and Beaver AL.1s of 14 Liaison Flight, 656 Sqn. On the 10th several Twin Pioneers landed at a grass strip at Panaga, where the police station was soon recaptured, and later in the day a Beverley took rebels by surprise when it landed at Anduki with a full load of troops of the Queen's Own Highlanders and their equipment. The airstrip was soon in British hands, and after more men were flown in the oilfield was retaken the following day.

With men of 42 Commando Royal Marines also in action, Tutong had been retaken, and Limbang and Lawas fell on the 12th. The commando carrier HMS *Albion* (R07) was now on the scene, and from the 14th Whirlwind HAS.7s of 846 NAS and Wessexes of 845 NAS were flown ashore to provide a much-needed supplement to the RAF Belvederes.

Although there were some airstrips in the region, the interior generally comprised heavy jungle with few tracks (rivers were primarily used for transport), and helicopters were essential for the rapid movement of troops. HMS *Hermes* (R12) with her air wing embarked was also in the area; as mopping-up operations continued, and by the 17th the rebellion had been squashed and most of the rebels captured.

INDONESIAN ATTACKS

On the 18th, Major-General W.C. Walker arrived as Commander British Forces Borneo Territories, and

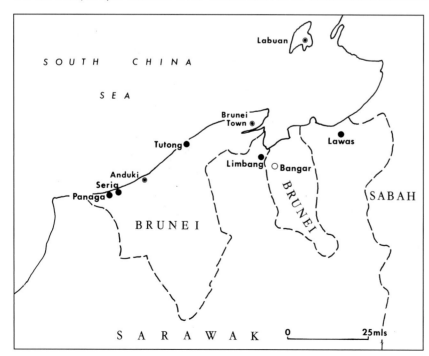

operations continued for several months to pursue the remaining rebels. Some air units returned to Singapore, but as concern grew about Indonesian intentions in Sarawak and Sabah, the ground forces were consolidated and men of 22 Regt SAS brought in to provide a much-needed intelligence resource.

The first sign of further trouble came on 12 April 1963 with an Indonesian attack on a police station at Tebedu, western Sarawak; although the attackers were dressed as guerrillas, they were believed to have been regular Indonesian soldiers. The raid was repulsed, but it set a pattern of activity for the next three years

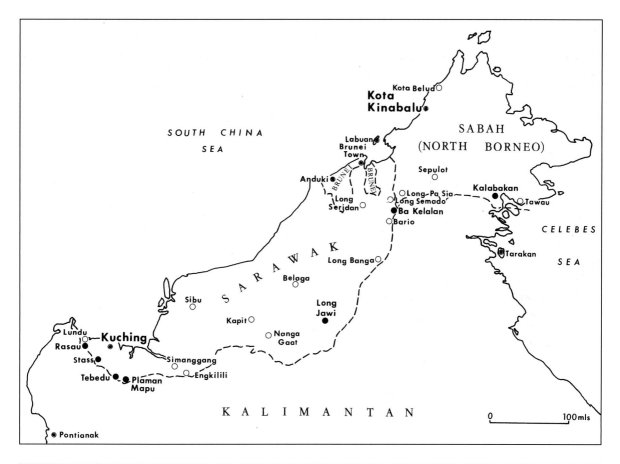

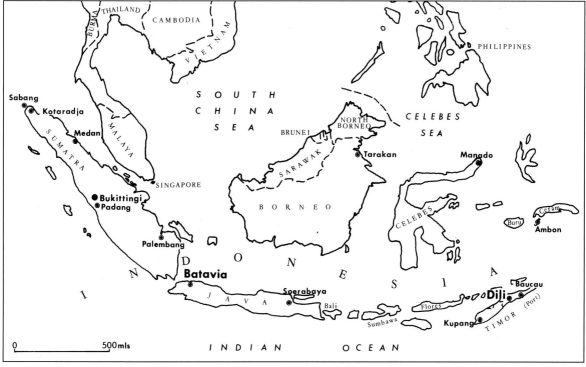

Among the based 'teeth' aircraft in the Far East at the start of the confrontation with Indonesia were the Canberras of 45 Sqn, including B.15 WH961. The B.15 was a B.6 conversion for tactical nuclear bombing. *(Author's collection)*

Also based in Malaya, at Butterworth, was 2 Sqn RAAF also with Canberra B.20s which was the Australian variant of the B.6. This B.20 - A84-201 - would go on to serve in Vietnam. *(Author's collection)*

along the difficult 970-mile-long border. More helicopters were available as Whirlwinds and Sycamores of 110 Sqn had detached from Seletar, but on 4 May a Belvedere HC.l, XG473 of 66 Sqn, crashed after taking off from Ba Kelalan, killing all eight on board, including three SAS soldiers. Two days later Sycamore XL822 of 110 Sqn was lost in an accident.

In August, preceding the proclamation of the State of Malaysia on 16 September, there was an attack on Seng. The proclamation led to riots in Djakarta, and on 19 September three Argosies of the newly formed 215 Sqn and a Hastings flew to the Indonesian capital to evacuate Britons. Indonesia had not declared war with Malaysia and Britain, and throughout the campaign all parties were careful to refer to events as a 'confrontation'.

Late in September, Indonesians attacked an outpost at Long Jawi, Sarawak, which they overran, killing five defenders, including some Gurkhas. The retreating raiders were ambushed by helicopter-borne troops and paid heavily for the raid, the largest to date. Indonesia also began overflying Sarawak with B-25s, escorted by P-51s, from Pontianak, and during November nine incursions were reported, although no attacks were made. Nevertheless, from December four Hunters of 20 Sqn and two Javelin FAW.9s of 60 Sqn were permanently detached both to Kuching and Labuan. On 18 December an Auster AOP.9 became the first aircraft lost to enemy action when it was shot down in Sarawak with the loss of the passenger, a padre. Cross-border raids increased, and on 28 December there was a concerted attack on Kalabakan in Sabah.

The Kalabakan attack resulted in more troops being airlifted into East Malaysia, and from February 1964 the Herald transports of 4 Sqn Royal Malayan Air Force (RMAF) began playing their part in the operation; RMAF Pioneers and Twin Pioneers of 1 Sqn were also detached. The extra activity put a strain on the airstrip at Tawau, which from that time had to be constantly rerolled as the surface broke up.

During January, 60 Sqn had been reinforced to counter the possibility of air strikes by Indonesia's force of Il-28 and Tu-16 bombers and MiG-17 and MiG-19 fighters: four Javelins were flown out from the UK in the markings of 23 Sqn to confuse Indonesian intelligence. On 26 February an Air Defence Intercept Zone (ADIZ) was established around Borneo, but only limited Indonesian air strikes were encountered, late in 1965. Towards the end

Not to be left out New Zealand deployed her Canberra B(I).12s of 14 Sqn to Tengah between 1964 and 1966. NZ6102 displays the distinctive Kiwi emblem on the fin. *(Author's collection)*

of June the first confirmed attack by Indonesian regulars was launched at Rasau, during which five Gurkhas were killed, and in July there were thirty-four similar attacks along the border.

AIR DEFENCE OF WESTERN MALAYSIA

There was a clue to the next significant move during June when a bomb, placed by an infiltrator, damaged a 205 Sqn Shackleton at Changi on Singapore. On 17 August 1964 Indonesia launched the first of a number of raids on West Malaysia with the landing of a hundred men at three sites on the west coast of Johore.

Army units soon mopped up the infiltrators with the help of Army Air Corps (AAC) helicopters, but on 27 August an Esso bunkering station in Singapore was attacked. The most serious threat came on 2 September, when ninety-six Indonesian paratroopers were dropped at Labis, West Malaysia, from a C-130B in Operation *Dwikova*. Two aircraft left Djakarta and refuelled at Medan, but one was forced to return. The second aircraft, which dropped the paras, was lost on the return flight to causes unknown. Fourteen Hunter sorties were flown in the day, and concentrations of Indonesian troops were wiped out in rocket attacks. As the Army again began to mop up the remnants, a state of emergency was declared on the 2nd.

The Indonesians had penetrated Malaysian airspace in a radar gap between Bukit Gombak and Butterworth, and HMS *Kent* (D12), a County Class destroyer, was stationed in the Straits of Malacca to fill the gap. From now the Gannet AEW.3s of 849 NAS flights from the carriers on station were critical to the maintenance of effective air defence, although the Type 316 radar at Bukit Gombak had been supplemented by two additional radars. On 14

Without doubt the most valuable and flexible aircraft operated by the RAF post-war was the Shackleton which served with distinction in so many campaigns. 205 Sqn with the MR.2c was based at Changi and detached to Labuan. WR952/B on patrol. *(Crown copyright)*

Shackleton MR.2 WG530/G of 205 Sqn displays the white over-fuselage and wingtop finish (over the wing tanks) designed to reduce internal temperatures in tropical climes. *(via A S Thomas)*

September a section of Bloodhound IIs of 65 Sqn was brought to readiness at Seletar, and extra 40 mm Bofors and 20 mm Oerlikon AAA cannon were transferred from Germany or brought out of naval stock.

Javelins of 64 Sqn were flown out from the UK to join those of 60 Sqn, RAAF Sabres were detached to the re-activated airfields at Alor Star and Kuantan, and Meteor F.8s of 1574 TFF at Changi were alerted for local air defence. Sea Vixens were disembarked from their carriers to Tengah. Finally, two extra Canberra squadrons were committed, 32 Sqn RAF and 14 Sqn RNZAF with the B(I).12.

On 28 November a major air defence exercise involving the RAF, RN and RAAF was held, and Gong Kedah airfield near the Thai border was reopened: Thai sympathizers of the Indonesian position were infiltrating in small numbers. During October there was another seaborne incursion, this time at Pontian, opposite Singapore, but again the insurgents were quickly rounded up with helicopter support. A further infiltration on 23 December was attacked by Hunters and Canberras, with Sycamores of 103 Sqn acting as forward air control (FAC), in Operation *Birdsong*.

CONTINUED FIGHTING IN BORNEO

Meanwhile, in Borneo, the helicopter force had been further strengthened by four Belvederes of 26 Sqn for 66 Sqn, Whirlwinds of 225 Sqn and Alouette IIIs of 5 Sqn RMAF, while 847 NAS provided Whirlwinds at Sembawang to supplement the depleted units in West Malaysia. The UH-1Bs of 5 Sqn RAAF also moved to Butterworth. In October a million leaflets were dropped over Indonesia by Argosies and Hastings, but the incursions continued. During the year British Army tactics changed, and pursuits into Kalimantan, known as *Claret* operations, were allowed on a deniable basis up to 3,000 yd, later extended to 10,000, and finally 20,000 yd.

The conflict was beginning to take a toll of the aircraft in the theatre; to the end of 1964 one Pioneer, three Twin

The Twin Pioneer light transports of 209 Sqn were based across Borneo from their home station at Seletar. XN319 is off-loading supplies at Fort Belaga. *(G A Heather via A S Thomas)*

Pioneers, two Whirlwinds, one Sycamore, one Scout, one Auster AOP.9 and a Hunter had been lost in accidents. A new form of transport entered service on 23 March 1965 with the formation of the Joint Services Hovercraft Unit equipped with the SR.N5 at Tawau in Sabah, and these vehicles were extremely valuable in negotiating the miles of river and coastline in the area.

However, still more helicopters were needed, and on 2 March the Whirlwinds of 230 Sqn arrived at Labuan, followed in April by the Wessex of 848 NAS. They were soon in action when, on 27 April, there was a serious attack on an outpost at Plaman Mapu manned by 2 Para. The attackers were held off and reinforcements were brought up by helicopter. Thirty Indonesian regulars from a company of 150 were killed for the loss of two British soldiers.

Later in the year, from 1 September, there was a series of hit-and-run attacks on isolated kampongs by Indonesian Air Force (AURI) B-25s and B-26s. These raids highlighted the inadequacy of the air defence system in East Malaysia: the Javelins could not react fast enough, and in any event would have been far too cumbersome trying to attack slower aircraft at low level. Fortunately little damage was done. Only once did the Javelins make an intercept in East Malaysia, when by chance they confronted a C-130, which turned tail and escaped. The Javelins were in their element around Singapore, however, and on 21 September an AURI Tu-16 was intercepted and escorted away from the area. The Indonesians did manage to establish a series of AAA posts along the border, and on 17 November 1965 a Whirlwind HAR.10, XR480 of 103 Sqn, was shot down near Stass. Several more Whirlwinds were lost in accidents during the year.

In West Malaysia the incursions continued unabated. To the end of March 1965, forty-one landings had been reported, with 142 Indonesians killed and the remaining 309 captured. A new threat presented itself from 29 March, when Indonesian AAA on the Riau Islands, just south of Singapore, began firing indiscriminately on aircraft approaching Kallang civilian airport. Aircraft had to be rerouted, and fortunately none was damaged. On

30 May, twenty-five regulars landed at Tanjong Pen-Gelih, East Johore, where they occupied an old Japanese fort. The following day they were dislodged by four Hunters firing armour-piercing rockets.

THE MYTH OF THE V-BOMBERS

Part of the function of Bomber Command was to demonstrate global reach in support of Britain's interests across the world. At the start of confrontation there were plans to base V-bombers in the Far East theatre both to act as a deterrent and also to attack Indonesian Air Force strike bases in the event of Indonesian attacks against Commonwealth forces. The bombers would have used Darwin or Butterworth, and then Labuan. It is understood that by 1962 nuclear bombs were already in storage at RAF Tengah.

Although committed to NATO, the UK reserved the right to deploy its strategic nuclear bombers wherever it chose (Chapter 4, Section 1). However, it was felt that the early Victor B.1s would be more easily spared from the deterrent role, given that the confrontation started so soon after the Cuban missile crisis of October 1962. These were tense and dangerous times.

In November 1963 plans were made to send four Victor B.1A bombers of 15 Sqn from Cottesmore to Tengah in Operation *Chamfrom*; the aircraft arrived in Singapore in December and in early January moved up to Butterworth. On 30 September they were replaced by four Vulcan B.2s of 12 Sqn from Coningsby, but the Vulcans did not fare well in the humid tropical climate and were withdrawn from 12 December.

In parallel with the Vulcan detachment, four Victor B.1As of 55 Sqn at Honington were detached to Butterworth from August 1964; the aircraft and crews were rotated with four from 57 Sqn, also at Honington, usually at two-monthly intervals. These detachments came to an end in September 1965, when they were replaced by Vulcans of 9 Sqn and then 35 Sqn, both from Cottesmore. Eight aircraft from 35 Sqn had detached to Tengah in April 1965 in Exercise *Spherical*. These latter detachments lasted until the end of confrontation. They were supplemented by detachments of aircraft of 44 Sqn.

It has sometime been reported that Victors dropped bombs in anger against Indonesian targets, but this is a myth. The aircraft did regularly use the bombing ranges in Western Malaysia, typically at Song Song Island, and

The rugged Pioneer, also of 209 Sqn, had a remarkable short field performance and with its sturdy undercarriage could land in the roughest of terrain. Camouflaged XK367 is here at its home base Seletar. *(Author's collection)*

XG456/A was a Belvedere of 66 Sqn, another unit already based in the Far East when the Indonesian confrontation started. The Belvedere carried eighteen fully armed troops or an underslung load of up to 5,250 lbs: in this case a Wessex fuselage. *(P H T Green via A S Thomas)*

since some of these demonstrations were conducted in front of the press it may be that this is how the rumours started.

SEQUEL

On 9 August 1965 Singapore left the Federation, and only weeks later, on 30 September, there was an attempted Communist coup in Djakarta; the military counter-coup essentially ended Soekarno's rule. Although cross-border attacks continued in East Malaysia, incursions in the peninsula soon slowed, and the prospect of peace seemed likely. At the end of the year there were 14,000 British troops in Borneo, from a peak of 17,000. They were supported by over a hundred helicopters, and the Beverleys were dropping supplies at the rate of 1,000,000 lb a month.

During 1966 the pace slowed, and peace talks began in Bangkok. Finally, on 11 August, the conflict ended with the signing of a peace treaty. Slowly forces were withdrawn, and RAAF Sabres were detached to Labuan to replace the Javelins of 60 Sqn, while a section of Bloodhound SAMs was deployed to Kuching. The confrontation in Borneo and Malaya had cost the Indonesians around 600 dead and the British 114, many of the latter Gurkhas. On 22 October a Beverley made the last airdrop of the conflict, 34 Sqn having lifted 40,000,000 lb in less than four years.

At the time of writing, some forty-two years after the end of the confrontation, British forces remain in Brunei in the form of 2 Royal Gurkha Rifles, plus 7 Flt AAC with three Bell 212 helicopters.

BRISTOL (WESTLAND) BELVEDERE

The twin-engined, twin-rotor, Type 192 Belvedere helicopter was the first in Britain to be designed from the outset as a troop carrier to meet a range of needs for Army support, including supply dropping and casualty evacuation. The design was based on that of the Type 173 which first flew in January 1952

Helicopters were much in demand in the forests of Borneo and four Naval utility squadrons were deployed with Whirlwind and Wessex aircraft. XS509/G is a Wessex HU.5 of 848 NAS. *(Author's collection)*

The Belvedere **HC Mark 1** was built to carry eighteen fully equipped troops, and both rotors were synchronized through a shaft, enabling single-engine performance through either powerplant in the event of an emergency. The first production aircraft flew on 5 July 1958, and the Belvedere joined 66 Sqn in 1961. It saw service in Europe, Africa, South Arabia and Borneo.

Transport units equipped – 26, 66, 72

Commonwealth in-theatre units at 1962

Unit	Aircraft	Base	Detached to
RAF			
20 Sqn	Hunter FGA.9	Tengah	Labuan, Kuching
28 Sqn	Hunter FGA.9	Kai Tak	Labuan, Kuching
60 Sqn	Javelin FAW.9	Tengah	Labuan, Kuching
1574 Flt	Meteor F.8	Changi	
45 Sqn	Canberra B.15	Tengah	Labuan, Kuching, Kuantan
81 Sqn	Canberra PR.7	Tengah	Labuan
205 Sqn	Shackleton MR.2C	Changi	Labuan
34 Sqn	Beverley C.1	Seletar	Labuan, Kuching
48 Sqn	Hastings C.2	Changi	Labuan, Kuching
52 Sqn	Valetta C.1	Butterworth	Labuan, Kuching
209 Sqn	Pioneer CC.1, Twin Pioneer CC.1	Seletar	Labuan, Kuching, Bayan Lepas
66 Sqn	Belvedere HC.1	Seletar	Labuan, Kuching, Brunei
110 Sqn	Sycamore HR.14	Butterworth	Brunei, Labuan, Situ
	Whirlwind HAR.10	Seletar	Labuan, Kuching

Unit	Aircraft	Base	Detached to
RAAF			
3 Sqn	Sabre 32	Butterworth	Labuan
75 Sqn	Sabre 32	Butterworth	Labuan
2 Sqn	Canberra B.20	Butterworth	
5 Sqn	UH–1B	Butterworth	
36 Sqn	C-130A	Richmond	Changi
RNZAF			
41 Sqn	Freighter Mk 31	Changi	Kuching
RMAF from December 1963			
1 Sqn	Pioneer, Twin Pioneer	Kuala Lumpur	Labuan
4 Sqn	Herald	Kuala Lumpur	Labuan
5 Sqn	Alouette III	Labuan	Tawau
8 Sqn	Caribou	Kuala Lumpur	Labuan

Commonwealth reinforcements

Unit	Aircraft	Base	From	To
RAF				
64 Sqn	Javelin FAW.9R	Tengah, Labuan, Kuching	1.4.65	15.6.67
32 Sqn	Canberra B.15	Tengah, Kuantan	10.64	1.65
16 Sqn	Canberra B.(I).8	Kuantan	2.65	5.65
103 Sqn	Whirlwind HAR.10	Seletar, Labuan, Kuching	1.8.63	post 66
225 Sqn	Whirlwind HAR.10	Seletar, Kuching	15.11.63	1.11.65
230 Sqn	Whirlwind HAR.10	Labuan, Kuching, Tawau, Sepulot	10.3.62	25.11.66
215 Sqn	Argosy C.1	Changi	31.7.63	post 66
65 Sqn	Bloodhound II	Seletar	14.9.64	post 66
RAAF				
75 Sqn	Mirage III	Darwin	65	66
76 Sqn	Sabre 32	Darwin	65	66
30 Sqn det	Bloodhound I	Darwin	65	66
RNZAF				
14 Sqn	Canberra B(I).12	Tengah	9.64	11.66
RAF Bomber Command detachments				
15 Sqn	Victor B.1A	Tengah	9.12.63	1.64
		Butterworth	1.64	2.10.64
12 Sqn	Vulcan B.2	Butterworth	2.10.64	10.12.64
55 Sqn	Victor B.1A	Butterworth	8.64	8.65
57 Sqn	Victor B.1A	Butterworth	17.10.64	8.65
9 Sqn	Vulcan B.2	Tengah	13.8.65	3.66
35 Sqn	Vulcan B.2	Tengah	3.66	24.8.66
RAF Coastal Command detachments, Operation *Hawk Moth*				
210 Sqn	Shackleton MR.2	Changi, Labuan	9.64	11.64
203 Sqn	Shackleton MR.2	Changi, Labuan	11.64	1.65

Unit	Aircraft	Base	From	To
204 Sqn	Shackleton MR.2C	Changi, Labuan	2.65	4.65
203 Sqn	Shackleton MR.2	Changi, Labuan	7.65	10.65
201 Sqn	Shackleton MR.3	Changi, Labuan	10.65	1.66
206 Sqn	Shackleton MR.3	Changi, Labuan	1.66	4.66
201 Sqn	Shackleton MR.3	Changi, Labuan	5.66	8.66

RAF and other UK-based transport support, mainly trooping

Unit	Aircraft	Base	From	To
99 Sqn	Britannia C.1	Lyneham		
511 Sqn	Britannia C.1	Lyneham		
216 Sqn	Comet C.4	Lyneham		
53 Sqn	Belfast C.1	Fairford		
British Eagle	Britannia			
British United	Britannia	Stansted		

FAA helicopter detachments

Unit	Aircraft	Base	From	To
845 NAS	Whirlwind HAS.7 Wessex HAS.1	HMS *Albion*, Semangyang Seletar, Kuching, Nanga Gaat, Labuan, Sibu, Belaga	14.12.62	4.6.64
846 NAS	Whirlwind HAS.7	HMS *Albion*, Kuching, Labuan,	15.12.62	12.10.64
847 NAS	Whirlwind HAS.7	HMS *Albion*, Sembawang	4.64	2.12.64
815 NAS	Wessex HAS.1	HMS *Albion*, Sibu	5.65	7.65
848 NAS	Whirlwind HAS.7 Wessex HU.5	HMS *Albion*, Sibu, Nanga Gaat, Bario, Labuan, Kota Balud, Sepulot	19.6.65	5.8.66

RN carrier deployments

HMS *Hermes* (R12), November 1962 to August 1963

Unit	Aircraft	Base	From	To
803 NAS	Scimitar F.1	Tengah	20.12.62	7.1.63
		Tengah	18.3.63	24.4.63
892 NAS	Sea Vixen FAW.1	Tengah	20.12.62	7.1.63
		Tengah	18.3.63	24.4.53
		Tengah	12.6.63	27.6.63
814 NAS	Wessex HAS.1	Sembawang	21.12.62	5.1.63
		Sembawang	25.2.63	20.4.63
849B Flt	Gannet AEW.3	Seletar	numerous	

HMAS *Melbourne* (R21), April 1963 to May 1963

Unit	Aircraft	Base	From	To
814 NAS	Wessex HAS.1	aboard	20.4.63	8.5.63

HMS *Ark Royal* (R09), June 1963 to October 1963

Unit	Aircraft	Base	From	To
800 NAS	Scimitar F.1	Tengah	10.7.63	29.8.63
890 NAS	Sea Vixen FAW.1	Tengah	10.7.63	25.7.63
		Tengah	6.8.63	27.8.63
815 NAS	Wessex HAS.1	Sembawang	numerous	
849C Flt	Gannet AEW.3	Seletar	numerous	

Unit	Aircraft	Base	From	To
HMS *Victorious* (R38), September 1963 to June 1965				
801 NAS	Buccaneer S.1	Tengah	25.9.63	3.1.64
		Tengah	9.3.64	3.4.64
		Tengah	19.6.64	26.8.64
		Changi	21.9.64	14.12.64
		Changi	23.12.64	6.1.65
		Changi	24.5.65	8.6.65
893 NAS	Sea Vixen FAW.1	Tengah	25.9.63	22.10.63
		Tengah	16.12.63	8.1.64
		Tengah	18.3.64	8.4.64
		Tengah	12.6.64	19.8.64
		Tengah	21.9.64	7.12.64
814 NAS*	Wessex HAS.1	Sembawang	numerous	
849A Flt	Gannet AEW.3	Tengah, Seletar	numerous	
HMS *Centaur* (R06), January 1964 to November 1964				
892 NAS	Sea Vixen FAW.1	Tengah	11.2.64	8.3.64
		Tengah	30.4.64	14.5.64
		Tengah	14.7.64	24.7.64
		Tengah	14.8.64	1.9.64
815 NAS[1]	Wessex HAS.1	Sembawang	numerous	
849B Flt	Gannet AEW.3	Seletar	numerous	
HMS *Eagle* (R05), December 1964 to April 1965				
820 NAS	Wessex HAS.1	Sembawang	numerous	
849D Flt	Gannet AEW.3	Seletar	numerous	
HMAS *Melbourne* (R21), February 1965 to June 1965				
817 NAS	Wessex HAS 1	Sembawang	3.65	4.65
HMS *Ark Royal* (R09), June 1965 to May 1966				
892 NAS	Sea Vixen FAW.1	Changi	19.7.65	4.8.65
		Changi	3.9.65	18.9.65
		Changi, Butterworth	20.10.65	7.12.65
		Changi	7.1.66	27.1.66
		Changi	15.3.66	24.3.66
849C Flt	Gannet AEW.3	Seletar, Changi	numerous	
HMS *Victorious* (R38), July 1965 to March 1966				
803 NAS	Scimitar F.1	Changi	19.7.65	7.8.65
		Changi, Butterworth	20.10.65	7.12.65
		Changi	6.1.66	27.1.66
		Changi	15.3.66	24.3.66
HMS *Eagle* (R05), August 1965 to July 1966				
800 NAS	Buccaneer S.1	Changi	11.11.65	20.11.65
		Changi	11.2.66	28.2.66
		Changi	9.5.66	2.6.66
	Buccaneer S.1, S.2	Changi	1.7.66	12.7.66
820 NAS	Wessex HAS.1	Sembawang	numerous	

Unit	Aircraft	Base	From	To
		Labis	26.9.64	31.10.64
899 NAS	Sea Vixen FAW.2	Changi	11.11.65	20.11.65
		Changi	11.2.66	28.2.66
		Changi	9.5.66	2.6.66
		Changi	1.7.66	12.7.66
849D Flt	Gannet AEW.3	Changi	numerous	

Ships flights – a number of cruisers, destroyers and frigates deployed to Malaysian waters had helicopters embarked primarily for anti-submarine warfare. They included the following.

Unit	Aircraft	Base		
SF, 829 NAS	Wessex HAS.1	Cruiser HMS *London*		
SFs	Wessex HAS.1	Destroyers HMS *Devonshire, Hampshire, Kent*		
829 NAS	Wasp HAS.1	Frigates HMS *Dido, Euryalus*		

NOTES

1 Also embarked on HMS *Albion* and RFA *Tidespring* for short periods

Army Air Corps

At the outset of the campaign the Army operated fixed-wing aircraft and helicopters in reconnaissance or liaison flights operating within 656 Sqn. From 1964 the Army Air Corps also introduced the integration scheme whereby a variety of ground forces employed their own light helicopters in air platoons or air squadrons for general tasks.

656 Sqn

Unit	Aircraft	Base	From	To
7 Recce Flt	Auster AOP.9, Scout AH.1	Brunei, Fort Belaga	24.12.62	post 66
14 Ln Flt	Auster AOP.9, Beaver AL.1, Scout AH.1	Brunei	12.62	8.66
11 Ln Flt[1]	Auster AOP.9, Beaver AL.1, Scout AH.1	Long Pa Sia	5.63	5.64
30 Flt RASC	Beaver AL.1	Kuching, Tawau, Sibu	5.64	66
10 Recce Flt	Scout AH.1	Long Pa Sia	64	12.65
16 Recce Flt[2]	Auster AOP.9		30.9.64	1.10.64
	Scout AH.1		1.10.64	66
3 Recce Flt	Scout AH.1	Kapit, Nanga Gaat	10.65	65

Infantry Regiments

Unit	Aircraft	Base	From	To
1 SG AP	Sioux AH.1	Kuching	8.3.65	8.65
		Tawau	9.65	1.66
		Kalbakan	8.3.65	post 66
2 RGJ AP	Sioux AH.1	Kuching	5.65	12.65
		Tawau, Kalabakan	1.66	7.66
1 ASH AP	Sioux AH.1	Lundu	3.65	66
1 KOSLI AP	Sioux AH.1	Lundu	66	67
1 GH AP	Sioux AH.1	Bario	1.66	2.66
1 DLI AP	Sioux AH.1	Tawau	3.66	3.66
RHR AP	Sioux AH.1	Tawau, Kalabakan	4.66	12.66
1 GR	Sioux, AH.1	Bario	8.66	11.66
		Seria	11.66	post 66
2 GR	Sioux AH.1	Kuching	7.66	9.66

Unit	Aircraft	Base	From	To
Armoured Regiments				
1 QDG AS	Auster AOP.9	Simmangang	3.65	8.65
	Sioux AH.1		8.65	2.66
4 RTR	Auster AOP.9	Seria	12.65	5.66
	Sioux AH.1			
LG AS	Sioux AH.1	Sibu, Kapit	8.66	9.66
Artillery Regiments				
45 LRRA AT	Sioux AH.1	Kuching, Batu Kitang	1.4.65	7.65
49 LRRA AT	Sioux AH.1	Kuching	12.65	4.65
6 LRRA AT	Sioux AH.1	Kuching	4.66	8.66
Other Unit				
40 RMC AT	Sioux AH.1	Seria	65	5.67
45 RNMC AT	Sioux AH.1	Lundu	65	3.66

NOTES

1   Became 30 Flt RASC (from 1965 RCT, then from 7.65 130 Flt RCT)
2   Became Air Troop 4 RTR

AURI

1 Sqn	P-51D, K, B-25D, J, B-26B	Pontianak, Taranak
21 Sqn	B-25D, J, B-26B	Pontianak
3 Sqn	P-51D, K	Kemajoram
11 Sqn	MiG-17	Iswahjudi
12 Sqn	MiG-19	Iswahjudi
14 Sqn	MiG-21	Kemajoram
10 Sqn	Il-28	Kemajoram
41 Sqn	Tu-16	Kemajoram
42 Sqn	Tu-16	Iswahjudi
2 Sqn	Il-14	Halim
31 Sqn	C-130B, An-12	Halim
5 Sqn	Mi-4, Mi-6	Various

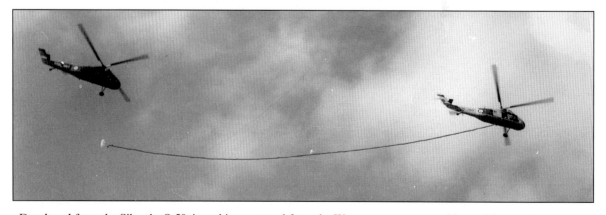

Developed from the Sikorsky S-58, in turbine-powered form the Wessex was a very capable machine whether in anti-submarine warfare, troop-carrier, gunship or in the SAR role. It also undertook air to air refuelling trials as seen here; the receiving aircraft has snagged the hose just forward of the second drogue. (*Author*)

7.3   SOMALIA AND KENYA, 1963–7

BACKGROUND

When the Italian Trust Territories and British Somaliland Protectorate achieved independence as the Somali Democratic Republic (SDR) on 1 July 1960, the new state immediately claimed rights to territory in north-east Kenya (the North Frontier District – NFD) and French Somaliland (Djibouti). Prior to independence in Kenya, a British commission was sent to the country to establish the views of Kenyans, mainly of Somali extraction, living in the north-east. Despite the people's wish to be merged into the SDR, their views were ignored, and in March 1963 diplomatic relations between SDR and Britain were broken off.

INSURGENCY

Shifta tribesmen now crossed the border, supported by the Somali government, making raids against villages and police posts. British troops and units of the King's African Rifles (KAR) were supported by Beverley transports of 30 Sqn and Twin Pioneer utility aircraft of 21 Sqn, both operating out of Eastleigh. The Beverleys typically transported fuel into the garrisons in the NFD. They were invaluable when many roads became impassable at the end of 1963 through flooding. The Twin Pioneers were equipped with bomb racks and light machine-guns to scatter raiding parties in the scrub.

Kenyan independence in December 1963 was followed by a mutiny in the fledgling army (Chapter 7, Section 4), leaving the government with no cohesive response to the continuing guerrilla war backing the SDR claims over the three provinces of Mandira, Wajir and Garissa. No. 21 Sqn remained until 1965, while an embryo air force was established with Chipmunks, seven Beavers and four Caribou. Initially, the new Kenya Air Force (KAF) was largely manned by seconded RAF officers and men, and the Beavers were soon flying out of Wajir in support of

Twin Pioneers of 21 Sqn were detached from Sharjah to Eastleigh in Kenya to support Kenyan forces against Shifta insurgents in the north of the Country. On its return to Sharjah XM960 carried five bomb markings under the quarter light. The 'Twin Pin' could carry up to 2,000 lbs of bombs on the undercarriage sponsons. *(A S Thomas)*

company-strength units of the Kenya Rifles. In the arid conditions, the Kenyan policy was to control the wells and manage small-scale operations against units wherever they could be located.

The Somali Aeronautical Corps had equipped with a few MiG-17 fighters based at Mogadishu from 1964, together with a small number of support aircraft and helicopters. However, these were not used in support of the Shifta. No Kenyan or RAF offensive sorties were flown, but the aircraft were invaluable in spotting guerrillas in the sparse scrub, which provided no cover. The Caribou flew supply missions out of Eastleigh, while the Beavers flew reconnaissance, resupply, casevac and redeployment sorties.

SEQUEL

Despite some damage caused by mined roads, the Shifta were making no progress, and following a conference at Kinshasa in October 1967 President Kenyatta offered an amnesty to any Shifta still carrying arms. The small local war ended.

Somalia and Kenya, 1963–7

RAF				
21 Sqn	Twin Pioneer CC.1	Eastleigh, Wajir	15.9.59	31.5.65
30 Sqn	Beverley C.1	Eastleigh	15.11.59	31.8.64
British Army				
8 Flt	Alouette AH.2,			
	Beaver AL.1	Eastleigh	59	66
Kenya Air Force				
	Beaver	Eastleigh, Wajir		
	Caribou	Eastleigh		
Somali Aeronautical Corps				
	MiG-17	Hargeisa		
	Il-28	Hargeisa		
	Mi-4	Mogadishu		
	An-2, An-24	Mogadishu		
	Yak-11, P.148D	Mogadishu		

7.4   EAST AFRICAN MUTINIES, 1964

INTRODUCTION

Four East African British colonies – Kenya, Uganda, Tanganyika and Zanzibar – achieved independence in the period 1961–3. Zanzibar was the last to gain independence, on 10 December 1963, but on 12 January 1964 the new government was overthrown and Britain was asked for help by the deposed ruler. This was refused, but the Rothesay Class frigate HMS *Rhyl* (F129) was dispatched from Mombasa, where it embarked a company of 1 Bn Staffordshire Regiment flown down by Beverley from Kenya to protect, and if necessary evacuate, British nationals from the island. The survey ship HMS *Owen* and the RFA *Hebe* were also on the scene. In the event, the issue was resolved without recourse to arms.

THE MUTINIES

On the mainland, trouble broke out when on 20 January men of 1 Bn Tanganyika Rifles mutinied at Colito, detaining their British officers and NCOs. They also seized Dar-es-Salaam airport and captured the British High Commissioner. Rioting in the capital left seventeen civilians dead. HMS *Rhyl* was ordered back on the 20th, and in the absence of a dedicated commando carrier in the region HMS *Centaur* (R06) sailed from Aden with 45 RM

Commando and a squadron of 16/5 Lancers. Apart from her own aircraft complement, *Centaur* embarked two Belvedere HC.1 helicopters of 26 Sqn to enable offloading of heavy equipment. The next day men of 2 Bn mutinied at Tabora.

President Julius Nyerere formally asked Britain to intervene on 24 January, by which time the British captives had been released. On the 25th Z company of 45 RM Commando was landed by four Wessex helicopters of 815 NAS and the two Belvederes by the Colito barracks, and took the mutineers by surprise after a brief display of force. This was the second heliborne landing conducted by British forces (the first was at Suez), and it was the first in which the helicopters went in without preliminary strikes or protective cover. A second assault secured the airfield. The remaining Marine companies engaged in rounding up mutineers in the neighbourhood and providing a show of force in Dar-es-Salaam, together with the Ferret scout cars of the Lancers that had been landed by lighter.

The barracks at Tabora, 400 miles inland, was the next UK objective, and men of X and Y Companies, 45 RM Commando, were airlifted by Beverley to retake the base. The aircraft were led in by the CO in a DC-4, possibly of the Royal Rhodesian Air Force; they were met by an Argosy of 105 Sqn which had flown an RAF Regiment contingent into the airfield. The Tabora base was the target for a Fleet Air Arm (FAA) strike on the afternoon of the 25th by Sea Vixens of 892 NAS, which were ten minutes from the target when the strike was aborted following the surrender of the mutineers.

The revolt was apparently a response to poor conditions and the continued employment of British officers and NCOs, and on 23 January there were further mutinies for the same reasons in Uganda and Kenya. In Uganda men of 1 and 2 Bns Uganda Rifles mutinied at Jinja, and the same day President Milton Obote asked Britain for help. In response, 450 men of 1 Bn Staffordshire Regt and 2 Bn Scots Guards were flown into Entebbe in Beverley transports of 84 Sqn from Eastleigh. The landing was preceded by a 37 Sqn Shackleton in the event that the airfield might be held by hostile troops. While the Scots Guards held the airport, the 'Staffs' drove the seventy miles to Jinja, and early on the morning of the 25th took the barracks without a fight.

In Kenya it was 250 men of 11 Bn Kenya Rifles who mutinied at Lanet. Again Britain was asked to intervene, and at Gilgil a battery of 3 RHA was ordered to the scene. The seventy-five artillerymen were unable to clear the barracks completely, and on the 24th they were joined by more gunners, some engineers and men of 1 Bn Gordon Highlanders. After negotiations the mutineers surrendered.

Two views of Sea Vixen FAW.1 XN694/463V of 893 NAS aboard HMS *Victorious*. Carriers were invaluable in bringing power to bear quickly and efficiently in local conflicts like the East African mutinies. *(Author's collection)*

A small detachment of Argosy transports of 105 Sqn was sent to Eastleigh during the Army mutinies. The squadron was based at Khormaksar where XP444 is seen. *(Crown copyright)*

As usual, the Fleet Air Arm demonstrated considerable versatility throughout. The Wessex helicopters of 815 NAS, later supplemented by those of 814 NAS, were shore-based for periods and remained in the area until mid-February, when they embarked on HMS *Albion* (R07). The Sea Vixens and Buccaneers of 893 and 801 NASs respectively were shore-based at Embakasi from 7 to 22 February.

SEQUEL

HMS *Centaur* was relieved by HMS *Victorious* (R38) on 29 January, which brought men of 41 Commando to relieve those of 45 Commando, who returned to Aden. The Belvederes, invaluable in transferring equipment and supplies from the carriers, returned to Aden aboard HMS *Albion* in mid-March. 41 Commando remained in Tanzania until April, when it was relieved by Nigerian troops. Early in April a squadron of T-28As of the Ethiopian Air Force (EAF) arrived at Dar-es-Salaam to help maintain internal stability.

On 23 April Zanzibar and Tanganyika were unified as Tanzania. The last British forces, in the form of the 1st Bn Staffordshire Regiment, left Kenya on 10 December 1964.

East African Mutinies, 1964

Unit	Aircraft	Base	From	To
RAF				
26 Sqn det	Belvedere HC.1	HMS *Centaur*	20.1.64	18.3.64
30 Sqn	Beverley C.1	Eastleigh	based	31.8.64
84 Sqn det	Beverley C.1	Eastleigh	21.1.64	
37 Sqn det	Shackleton MR.2	Eastleigh	21.1.64	
105 Sqn det	Argosy C.1	Eastleigh	21.1.64	
British Army				
8 Flt	Alouette AH.2, Beaver AL.1	Eastleigh	based	
Fleet Air Arm				
892 NAS	Sea Vixen FAW.1	HMS *Centaur*	20.1.64	4.2.64

Unit	Aircraft	Base	From	To
815 NAS	Wessex HAS.1	HMS *Centaur*	20.1.64	4.2.64
849 B Flt	Gannet AEW.3	HMS *Centaur*	20.1.64	4.2.64
893 NAS	Sea Vixen FAW.1	HMS *Victorious*	27.1.64	28.2.64
801 NAS	Buccaneer S.1	HMS *Victorious*	27.1.64	28.2.64
814 NAS	Wessex HAS.1	HMS *Victorious*	27.1.64	28.2.64
849 A Flt	Gannet AEW.3	HMS *Victorious*	27.1.64	28.2.64
Ethiopian Air Force				
16 TS	T–28D	Dar-es-Salaam	4.64	10.64

7.5   RHODESIA, 1965–80

INTRODUCTION

In 1963 the Central African Federation, comprising Northern and Southern Rhodesia and Nyasaland, broke up, and the following year Northern Rhodesia and Nyasaland achieved independence as Zambia and Malawi respectively. There were disturbances within (Southern) Rhodesia, and in September 1963 Rhodesian Special Air Service (SAS) troopers were dropped by Dakotas of 3 Sqn Royal Rhodesian Air Force (RRhAF) in the Melsetter area.

The white minority in Rhodesia had no intention of conceding black majority rule, and banned the two Nationalist parties, the Zimbabwe African People's Union (ZAPU) and the Zimbabwe African National Union (ZANU), headed respectively by Joshua Nkomo/Robert Mugabe and Ndabaningi Sithole. The principals were detained while the British Government pressed for reform. The leader of the Rhodesian Front, Ian Smith, finally made a unilateral declaration of independence (UDI) on 11 November 1965, and armed Provost T.52s of 4 Sqn were detached to Wankie and Kariba to help guard key installations against possible guerrilla attack.

First aircraft on the scene following UDI in Rhodesia were aircraft of HMS *Eagle's* air wing. First land-based fighters were the Javelins of 29 Sqn. FAW.9 XH891/R is seen with drop tanks but without the refuelling probe. RAF fighters were directed by Rhodesian air traffic controllers! *(Author's collection)*

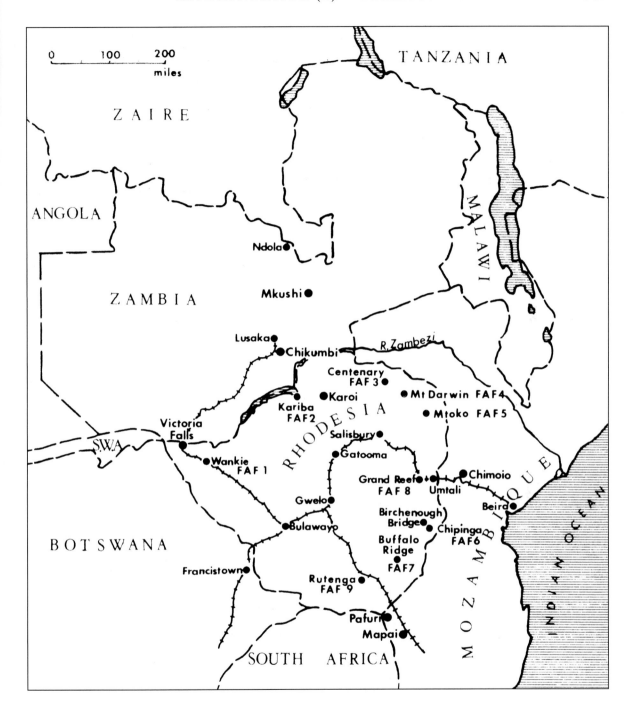

SANCTIONS AND OIL LIFTS

The British response was to impose sanctions on imports and exports, a military solution committing British troops to fight whites being considered untenable by the Government. Rhodesia is landlocked, as is her northern neighbour Zambia, but unfortunately Zambia relied on the railway link from Mozambique via Bulawayo for trade since the line to Benguela via the Congo was blocked because of the Angolan civil war. The British, with Canadian help, decided to supplement Zambia's oil stocks by airlift from Dar-es-Salaam and Leopoldville respectively.

During mid-November HMS *Eagle* (R05) arrived off the Mozambique coast to provide air defence in the event

HMS *Eagle* was relieved by *Ark Royal* in January 1966. Her air wing included the Scimitars of 803 NAS including
XD278/145R. *(Author's collection)*

of the RRhAF attempting to disrupt the airlift. Embarked were 800 Naval Air Squadron with Buccaneer S.1s and
Scimitar F.1s (for air refuelling), 820 NAS with Wessex HAS.1s, D Flt of 849 NAS with Gannet AEW.3s and 899
NAS with Sea Vixen FAW.2s which were to provide the air defence cover until relieved by ten 29 Sqn Javelins
from Akrotiri.

The Javelins were fitted with four underwing tanks, and made the flight direct to Nairobi, overflying Egypt, on
1 December. Their function was to protect the Kariba dam from attack by the RRhAF, and while the main force
was based at Ndola a section was detached to Lusaka. Air defence radars were flown in from the UK in Argosy
aircraft of 114 and 267 Sqns, but air traffic control was provided by the Rhodesians at Salisbury!

The oil lift began on 19 December, and involved Britannia C.1s of 99 and 511 Sqns, supported by Hastings C.1s
of 36 Sqn. By 31 October 1966, when the airlift ended, the Britannias had flown 1,563 sorties in more than 10,000
hours, and had carried 3.5 million gallons of oil, much of it for the Javelins. Six aircraft flew two sorties a day
carrying fifty-six 44 gal drums. The Canadian effort involved four CC-130Es of 437 Sqn RCAF operating from
Leopoldville. In addition there was US support contracted out to civilian operators.

The British Government also decided to monitor Rhodesian communications, and built a listening post/trans-
mitter at Francistown in Botswana; ostensibly run by the BBC, it was used to transmit 'black' propaganda and was
guarded by a company of 1 Bn Gloucester Regiment, which was flown in aboard Hastings of 24 Sqn.

The RRhAF was the strongest air force in the region apart from that of South Africa, and it represented a
serious threat to the integrity of neighbouring states. At UDI the RRhAF comprised 1 Sqn (Hunter FGA.9), 2 Sqn
(Vampire FB.9) and 4 Sqn (Provost T.52) at Thornhill (Gwelo) and 3 Sqn (C-47), 5 Sqn (Canberra B.2/T.4) and
7 Sqn (Alouette III) at New Sarum (Salisbury); in addition, a number of Vampires and Canberras were held in
reserve.

HMS *Eagle* departed for the Far East in December, but in January 1966 HMS *Ark Royal* (R09) and a
supporting frigate took up station off the Mozambique port of Beira. Embarked were 803 NAS (Scimitar F.1), 890
NAS (Sea Vixen FAW.1), 815 NAS (Wessex HAS.1) and C Flt of 849 NAS (Gannet AEW.3).

Relations between Britain and Portugal deteriorated, and the *Força Aerea Portuguesa* (FAP) transferred eight
F-84Cs of Esq 93 from Angola to Beira during late February. From there they flew standing patrols, and with the
resident Esq.101 equipped with the PV-2 and T-6 were prepared to counter any British intervention in
Mozambique.

On 2 March *Ark Royal* was relieved by HMS *Eagle*, which was at sea for a record seventy-one days, during which time her fixed-wing aircraft carried out 1,070 sorties observing 770 ships. The formal blockade of Beira began at this time, with the carriers supported by two frigates, or occasionally destroyers. HMS *Rhyl* (F129) and HMS *Lowestoft* (F103) were the first escorts on station. On 10 May *Ark Royal* was back on station, to be relieved by HMS *Victorious* (R38) shortly afterwards. Embarked on *Victorious* were Buccaneer S.2s (801 NAS), Sea Vixen FAW.2s (893 NAS), Wessex HAS.1s (814 NAS) and Gannet AEW.3s of A Flt 849 NAS. The carrier departed for the Far East in early August, leaving the blockade to land-based aircraft. Coincident was the departure of 29 Sqn to Cyprus.

As Rhodesia made arrangements to beat the blockade she also took the precaution of securing provision for the dispersal of the RRhAF in the event of a British military intervention. Facilities were given by the Portuguese at Lourenço Marques and by South Africa at Mpacha in the Caprivi Strip.

THE BEIRA PATROL

Early in 1966 the British Government had begun negotiating with the French for the use of Majunga airfield on Madagascar, but it was not until March that the first detachment of Shackleton MR.2s of 37 and 38 Sqns arrived from Luqa. In February 1967 it was the turn of 42 Sqn. The futile air blockade of a single port was maintained until February 1972, by which time 204, 205 and 210 Sqns had also sent detachments.

Originally under control of MEAF, the detachment became the responsibility of FEAF from 1967, although aircraft were provided by the Ballykelly wing of RAF Coastal Command. Sorties were conducted daily for between nine and eleven hours, covering 130,000 square miles. When a suspect vessel was found, it was first photographed and then details were passed on to the patrol frigate for interception. The detachment was supplied by Argosy and Britannia transports, and in turn one of its functions was to drop mail to the naval vessels on patrol.

The Royal Navy retained one frigate on station from March 1971 to August 1975, but from 1973 provision was intermittent. The patrols offered little in the way of training benefit, and by the end they had involved seventy-seven vessels at an estimated cost of £100 million. Rules of engagement were difficult and lines of communication

The Beira patrol was conducted by Royal Navy warships, including at the outset only, carriers. The blockade was supported by Shackletons based at Majunga which were detached from the UK over six years. WL785/A is very evidently from 42 Sqn. *(Author's collection)*

WL754/F is another aircraft of 42 Sqn. Apart from maritime patrol – their intended role - these aircraft were used operationally in a number of campaigns in the strike, close support, SAR, transport and latterly AEW roles.
(Author's collection)

long. Intercepting vessels were to divert tankers, and if they did not stop, orders were to open fire – in due course.

If the tanker did not stop, the frigate or destroyer was first to fire across the bow with small-arms tracers, 20 or 40 mm shells, or a 4.5 in. round; then, approaching to short range, it would give warning that it would open fire. It was then to fire practice ammunition at the ship's funnel. If these measures did not stop the tanker, the frigate was to fire a series of anti-submarine mortar bombs astern of the ship. Finally, if that failed, the ship was to open fire with 4.5 in. service ammunition at either the bridge or the engine room, or both, and continue until the ship stopped.

In total, between March 1966 and March 1971 just forty-seven tankers were intercepted and forty-two allowed to proceed. The remaining five either turned away or ignored the challenge. The problem with the blockade was that it was very high profile to start, and therefore proved very difficult to disengage from. Given the flow of oil into Rhodesia from South Africa, the whole affair was a waste of time and money, maintained only for reasons of prestige.

INSURGENCY

In April 1966 the first limited incursions by guerrillas of ZANU from Mozambique occurred, but these were quickly dealt with. Late in 1966 the RRhAF began co-operating with the Portuguese against *Frente de Libertação de Moçambique* (FRELIMO) guerrillas who were supporting ZANU in the border area. At the end of the year there were talks between the British and the Smith government, but these were fruitless, as were a second round of talks in October 1968.

The first serious incursions from the north occurred in August 1967 around the Victoria Falls, when a force of ninety ZAPU guerrillas was wiped out. From now and for twelve years the Rhodesian government mounted successive campaigns against increasingly determined and well-armed guerrillas. For several years there were limited incursions, easily met by the Rhodesian armed services; the Nationalists lost heart, and infighting resulted only in a few poorly organized raids. By 1972 the black Nationalist movements were better organized and equipped, and what amounted to civil war gradually intensified. The Rhodesians, though, had no problem securing arms from France, Israel, Italy and South Africa.

On a wider front, diplomatic attempts at a solution to the Rhodesian problem successively failed, and on 2 March 1970 Rhodesia was declared a republic, the 'Royal' prefix to the Air Force being dropped. In 1974 more than 500 guerrillas were killed for the loss of fifty-eight members of the security forces, but there was now renewed pressure for a settlement.

With Portuguese provision for independence in Angola and Mozambique and the probability of Marxist governments in both, South Africa preferred the prospect of a stable black government in Rhodesia as a buffer. As 2,000 South African paramilitary troops were withdrawn from December, a ceasefire was agreed, and the Nationalists were persuaded to form a united front under Bishop Abel Muzorewa.

By 1979 the days of the Smith government were numbered. In April 1979, after universal pressure, elections were held in which Muzorewa's United African National Council won fifty of the seventy-two seats; he was sworn in as Prime Minister in June. The banned ZANU and ZAPU parties could not participate, and in September a fresh round of talks began in London. These resulted in an agreement in December, but not before Zambia was placed on a full war footing after Rhodesian forces isolated Lusaka from the south by blowing three main bridges.

The RhAF bombed camps south of Lusaka on 25 November for the last time. Lord Soames arrived in Salisbury on 12 December as sanctions were lifted, and almost immediately a five-nation Ceasefire Monitoring Force (CMF) was established to support the disarming and potential integration of guerrillas. (The British involvement is described in Chapter 6, Section 4.)

BEATING THE EMBARGO

The Rhodesian government managed to circumvent sanctions in a number of ways, and what has been reported gives interesting insights into the arms trade. A purchasing office was set up in Geneva, and from 1967 aircraft were imported in a variety of ways. Until 1976, when the South African government responded to international pressure,

Radars and associated equipment to support the Javelin detachment were flown into Ndola by Argosies of 114 and 267 Sqns: XN856/856 is from the former unit. These aircraft could carry 69 fully equipped troops or 29,000 lbs of freight.
(Author's collection)

By 1965 the venerable Hastings was reaching the end of its service life. 24 and 36 Sqns both provided aircraft for the oil lift from Dar-es-Salaam to Ndola. WD488/488 is from 36 Sqn. *(36 Sqn)*

most arms came into Rhodesia from South Africa aboard SAAF C-130s. In addition, from about 1969, the locally based charter line Affretair (otherwise Air Trans Africa) carried exports out of Rhodesia, invariably indicating some other country of origin, and also shipped arms in, either from the supplier or from a third-party country.

After 1978 the Rhodesians secured most of their arms via the Comoro Islands, to which end-user certificates were made out by the suppliers; once landed in the Comoros, Affretair freighters delivered direct to Salisbury. Affretair also operated as Air Gabon Cargo and CargOman, with offices at Libreville and Seeb respectively. The Oman connection was useful as a focal point for the purchase of Hunter spares, and at least ten Avon engines were delivered.

As an indication of the complexity of the deals, the delivery of AB.205A helicopters is noteworthy. Thirteen AB.205s were ordered from Agusta by a customer in Kuwait. They were delivered, crated, to Beirut and off-loaded to be held in a Christian suburb. They were then handed to Israel by the Christians in exchange for arms. From Israel, eleven examples were flown to Salisbury, possibly bought by a Singapore purchaser, but on arrival the helicopters turned out to be worn ex-IDF/AF examples rather than the original order from Agusta.

The Affretair fleet comprised two CL-44s, three DC-8s and five DC-7s, at least one of which last also carried a RhAF serial. Most were registered in Gabon, and one in Oman. The aircraft also travelled the world searching for business to generate income, but they carefully avoided Britain and the USA. The main centre for European operations was Schipol, and exactly one hundred military aircraft were imported.

SEQUEL

Elections were held in March in which ZANU took 63% of the votes to form a government under Robert Mugabe. Regrettably, peace was short lived. Early in 1982 a large force of the Zimbabwe National Army (ZNA) moved into Matabeleland, where Nkomo's ZAPU received major support. Arms caches were allegedly found, and large numbers of Matabeles were reportedly massacred.

Then, on 25 July, in a series of explosions, seven Hunters, a newly delivered Hawk and a Lynx were destroyed at Gwelo (Thornhill), one Hunter and three Hawks being badly damaged. White officers of the Air Force of Zimbabwe (AFZ) were accused, but it is widely believed that South Africa was responsible in a supportive gesture to Nkomo.

Under Mugabe's rule, Zimbabwe, once secure and prosperous, has sadly declined into anarchy. At the time of writing Britain appears to have neither the will nor the capability to offer anything to the situation but words.

Rhodesia, 1965–80

Unit	Aircraft	Base	From	To
RAF				
29 Sqn	Javelin FAW.9R	Ndola	3.12.65	31.7.66
29 Sqn det	Javelin FAW.9R	Lusaka	5.12.65	24.7.66
37/38 Sqns det	Shackleton MR.2	Majunga	19.3.66	2.67
42 Sqn det	Shackleton MR.2	Majunga	2.67	4.67
Ballykelly Wing[1]	Shackleton MR.2	Majunga	4.67	10.1.71
MSU[2]	Shackleton MR.2	Majunga	11.1.71	2.72
114/267 Sqns	Argosy C.1	Benson	1.12.65	1.66
24 Sqn	Hastings C.1	Colerne	12.65	1.66
36 Sqn	Hastings C.1A, C.2	Colerne, Lusaka	12.65	1.66
99/511 Sqns	Britannia C.1	Lyneham, Eastleigh	19.12.65	72
Oil Lift				
RAF				
99/511 Sqns	Britannia C.1	Dar-es-Salaam	19.12.65	4.1.66
		Eastleigh	4.1.66	6.11.66
RCAF				
437 Sqn	CC-130E	Leopoldville	12.65	4.66
Civil				
BUA	Carvair	Dar-es-Salaam	1.66	4.66

Fleet Air Arm

HMS *Eagle* (R05) 25.11.65 to 5.12.65 and 2.3.66 to 10.5.66

800 NAS	Buccaneer S.1
800B NAS	Scimitar F.1
899 NAS	Sea Vixen FAW.1
820 NAS	Wessex HAS.1
849 D Flt	Gannet AEW.3

HMS *Ark Royal* (R09) 1.66 to 3.3.66 and 10.5.66 to 6.66

803 NAS	Scimitar F.1
890 NAS	Sea Vixen FAW.1
815 NAS	Wessex HAS.1
849 C Flt	Gannet AEW.3

HMS *Victorious* (R38) 6.66 to 8.66

801 NAS	Buccaneer S.2
893 NAS	Sea Vixen FAW.2
814 NAS	Wessex HAS.1
849 A Flt	Gannet AEW.3

Royal Rhodesian Air Force

1 Sqn	Hunter FGA.9	Thornhill
2 Sqn	Vampire FB.9, T.11	Thornhill

Unit	Aircraft	Base	From	To
5 Sqn	Canberra B.2, T.4	New Sarum		
4 Sqn	Provost T.52	Thornhill		
3 Sqn	C-47	New Sarum		
7 Sqn	Alouette II	New Sarum		

NOTES
1 204, 205 and 210 Sqn crews rotating
2 Majunga Support Unit, initially from Kinloss, then Honington

7.6   BELIZE, 1975–94

INTRODUCTION

The former colony of British Honduras has long been threatened by neighbouring Guatemala, which claims rights to the territory. In February 1948 it appeared that the Guatemalans might invade, and the cruisers HMS *Sheffield* (C24) and *Devonshire* (C39) were dispatched with 2nd Bn Gloucester Regiment; from that time, a company of infantry was deployed. In October 1961 the country was devastated by Hurricane *Hattie*, described in Chapter 6, Section 3.

Although from 1962 the People's United Party (PUP) sought independence, it was committed to freedom from Guatemalan domination, and from 1964 internal self-government was obtained. A renewed threat developed in January 1972 with a concentration of Guatemalan troops on the border. The carrier HMS *Ark Royal* (R09) was diverted from an American cruise with the frigate *Bacchante* (F69), and Buccaneer aircraft of 891 NAS demonstrated along the border. In February the carrier returned, leading a task force, and 2nd Bn Grenadier Guards reinforced the garrison. In 1973 the country was renamed Belize.

GUATEMALAN THREAT

Negotiations between Britain and Guatemala in 1975 ended in deadlock, and in October Guatemalan troops massed on the border. From 11 October, three Puma helicopters of 33 Sqn were flown into Belize Airport by Belfast transports of 53 Sqn, and the garrison was again reinforced to 1,000 men. The frigate HMS *Zulu* (F124) was also dispatched. Teeth for the Belize force were provided by six Harrier GR.1A fighters of 1 Sqn, flown out from the UK via Goose Bay and Nassau between 6 and 8 November. The aircraft were refuelled in flight by Victor tankers. During this first major investment, operational and training routines were established.

The threat was perceived to have diminished sufficiently by April 1976 for the Harriers to be dismantled and flown home in Belfasts. Further negotiations led nowhere, however, and after Guatemalan mobilization in June 1977 the garrison was again reinforced. The 3rd Bn Queen's Regiment was flown from the UK in VC-10 C.1 transports of 10 Sqn, and six Harrier GR.3s of 1 Sqn again made the Atlantic crossing, flying direct on 7 July. They were accompanied by twelve Victor K.2 tankers, each being refuelled eight times.

The frigate HMS *Achilles* (F12) took up station off the coast. The prospective invasion did not materialize, but the British Force in Belize (BRITFORBEL) remained. Four Harrier GR.3s were operated by crews from 1, 3 and 4 Sqns in rotation, under the auspices of 1417 Flt based at Belize International Airport and able to deploy to some three dozen strips. Three Puma helicopters, operated by 1563 Flt and flown by crews from 33 and 230 Sqns in rotation, were also based at Belize. One Puma, XW230, was lost on 27 August 1976, with the loss of three crew.

A second helicopter component was provided by the Army. Four Scout AH.1s were operated by 656 or 664 Sqn until 1979, when they were replaced by four Gazelles flown by 25 Flt. A Lynx HAS.1 of 815 NAS was normally available from a locally stationed West Indies guard-ship frigate. Airfield defence at Belize was provided by the RAF Regiment, with Rapier detachments from 25 or 26 Sqn and Bofors L40/70 anti-aircraft gun units from 58 or 66 Sqn. The Special Air Service (SAS) Regiment is known to have operated in Belize, possibly infiltrating Guatemala, and the Pumas were fitted for night flying in difficult terrain.

Throughout the 1970s and 1980s there was a civil war in Guatemala, with the constant threat of invasion of Belize, either as a distraction or to unify. In the event the British presence was sufficient to avoid more than posturing.

When Guatemala threatened Belize in 1975 part of the British response was the detachment of Harriers from 1 Sqn – their first operational deployment. In 1977 all of the UK based units sent aircraft to the former colony. XV759/E is from the newly formed 1417 Flt while XW923/N is in 3 Sqn markings. *(via A S Thomas)*

SEQUEL

In 1991 Guatemala recognized Belize, and a year later established formal diplomatic relations. The Harrier Flight departed in July 1993 and the Pumas followed a year later. Before the British garrison departed, the British Army Training Support Unit Belize was formed on 1 October 1994. This unit manages the British Army's jungle warfare training and is supported by a Royal Engineers squadron. No. 25 Flt remains, operating three Bell 212HP helicopters.

The Belize Defence Force was established in January 1978, and maintained two Britten-Norman BN-2B Defenders for search and rescue (SAR), medevac, liaison and anti-drug trafficking duties. In addition the US State Department operates several UH-1H helicopters and two Ayres Turbo-Thrush crop sprayers for defoliation of marijuana plantations.

WESTLAND/AÉROSPATIALE PUMA

The Puma was one of the three Anglo-French helicopters involved in a 1968 manufacturing agreement (the others were the Lynx and Gazelle). It was the largest, and was intended to fulfil a number of roles, including troop transport, casualty evacuation, freighter and even gunship. A sole French-manufactured SA.330 was supplied, and in due course it served as a trials aircraft with the RAE/DRA. The Puma has operated widely with the RAF, including Belize, Northern Ireland, the Gulf and Bosnia.

The Puma **HC Mark 1** entered service with 33 Sqn in June 1971. It carries a crew of two and up to sixteen troops or ten casualties over 390 miles at up to 174 mph. In gunship mode two 7.62 mm GPMGs are carried. A total of forty-eight were built, and of these forty-two were upgraded in 1995 under Operational Requirement SR(A)1107. The upgrade included provision for night operations and improved avionics; no new designation was applied.

Transport units equipped – 18, 33, 230; 1653 Flt

From 1980 a permanent detachment of Harriers – 1417 Flt – was based in Belize. GR.3 XV783/A over Placentia.

AÉROSPATIALE GAZELLE

The SA341 Gazelle was French designed, and came into British service as a result of the Anglo-French agreement to collaborate on helicopter development and acquisition. The original prototype flew on 7 April 1967, and the type was ordered in large numbers for all four British services (including the Royal Marines), with only very minor differences between variants. The Gazelle was significant in having a semi-rigid rotor and shrouded tail rotor (or fenestron).

The Army **AH Mark 1** variant (SA341B) carried five, including the pilot, and it was armed with TOW anti-tank missiles and the 7.62 mm GPMG. The first production aircraft, XW842, flew on 31 January 1972, and the Gazelle entered service with 660 Sqn at Soest in May 1974; in Germany it acted as reconnaissance for heavily armed Lynx helicopters. The Gazelle saw service in the Falklands, Belize and the Gulf.

Utility units equipped – 651, 652, 653, 654, 655, 656, 657, 658, 659, 661, 662, 663, 664, 669; 2, 3, 6, 7, 12, 16, 25, 29 Flts; Falkland Islands garrison; 3 CBAS

HAWKER (BAE) HARRIER

Following the success of the P.1127/Kestrel in demonstrating the viability of VTOL for a close-support combat aircraft, the type was ordered into production in mid-1966. Six development and sixty production aircraft were ordered. Whereas the Kestrel embodied about 50% of the structure of the P.1127, the Harrier was in many respects a new aircraft re-engineered around the more powerful Pegasus 101 engine.

The P.1127/7 **GR Mark 1** first flew on 31 August 1966, and the first six development-batch machines went to the manufacturer and Boscombe Down for intensive trials, development and weapons work. The first production aircraft flew on 28 December 1967, and in January 1969 the Harrier Conversion Team was formed, which in turn became the Conversion Unit at Wittering. It was there that the first VTOL squadron in the world, appropriately No. 1, was formed in July 1969. The GR.1 was fitted with four underwing and one fuselage pylons to accommodate a total of 5,000 lb of bombs or rockets. In addition a pair of Aden 30 mm cannon could be carried in detachable under-fuselage pods. Numerous GR.1 aircraft were retro-fitted with the Pegasus 102 engine of 20,500 lb thrust as the Mark 1A.

Close support units equipped – 1, 3, 4, 20

The **GR Mark 3** was developed from the GR.1. As additional aircraft were ordered to cope with attrition, the number of changes from the original was sufficient to merit a new designation. The more powerful Pegasus 103 of 21,500 lb thrust was fitted, and other differences were connected with sensors. The Ferranti LRMTS target seeker and marker was installed in a revised nose and a passive warning receiver on the fin. Forty new-build aircraft were constructed, but most were GR.1/1A aircraft upgraded as they required major servicing.

Close support units equipped – 1, 3, 4, 20; 1351, 1417, 1453 Flts

The **GR Mark 5** variant was a major redesign sufficient to justify a new name, let alone a new designation. The new type was the result of USMC pressure for a more capable aircraft, building on experience with the early Harrier (AV-8A); McDonnell Douglas was contracted to work on the new type in 1978. The RAF also required a developed aircraft, and BAe designed the machine with a larger wing to Specification ASR409. In the event, in 1981 agreement was reached for a common type to become the AV-8B/GR-5.

The GR.5 was built around the Pegasus 105 engine, with the new composite wing of much larger area and a revised forward fuselage and cockpit with much better visibility. Eight underwing and one under-fuselage hard-points allow the carriage of up to 9,200 lb of stores plus two 25 mm cannon. The avionics includes a Litton ASN 130 inertial navigation system, Hughes Angle Rate Bombing Set using both TV and laser trackers, and a Ferranti moving-map display. The prototype flew on 30 April 1985, and the new version entered service with 1 Sqn in 1988.

There were several problems in introduction into service, and in the event the GR.5 was an interim type pending the GR.7.

Close support units equipped – 1, 3, 4

Belize, 1975–94

Unit	Aircraft	Base	From	To
RAF				
1 Sqn det	Harrier GR.3	Belize	10.11.75	19.4.76
1/3/4 Sqns det	Harrier GR.3	Belize	5.7.77	3.81
1417 Flt	Harrier GR.3	Belize	1.4.80	6.7.93
33 Sqn det	Puma HC.1	Belize	15.11.75	11.83
1563 Flt	Puma HC.1	Belize	1.11.83	31.7.94
Support				
55 Sqn	Victor K.2	Marham		
57 Sqn	Victor K.2	Marham		
53 Sqn	Belfast C.1	Brize Norton		
LTW	Hercules C.1, C.3	Lyneham		
10 Sqn	VC-10 C.1	Brize Norton		
39 Sqn	Canberra PR.9	Marham		
Fleet Air Arm				
HMS *Ark Royal* (R09) 1.72 to 2.72				
809 NAS	Buccaneer S.2			
892 NAS	Phantom FG.1			
824 NAS det	Sea King HAS.2			
849 B Flt	Gannet AEW.3			
829 NAS	Wasp HAS.1	frigates	11.75	83
815 NAS	Lynx HAS.1	frigates	83	date
British Army				
656/664 Sqns	Scout AH.1	Belize	11.75	4.80
656 Sqn	Gazelle AH.1	Price Barracks	4.80	82
25 Flt	Gazelle AH.1	Price Barracks	82	94
25 Flt	Bell 212HP	Price Barracks	94	date
Belize Defence Force				
Air Wing	BN-2B Defender	Belize		
Guatemala Air Force				
Esc C-B	A-37B	Los Cipresales		
	T-33	Los Cipresales		
	CM-170 Magister	Los Cipresales		
Esc SAW	UH-1B, D, Bell 212	La Aurora		
	Alouette III	La Aurora		
Esc Transportes	C-47, C-54D	La Aurora		
	Arava	La Aurora		

7.7 FALKLAND ISLANDS/MALVINAS, 1982

INTRODUCTION

Sovereignty over the Falklands has been disputed by Argentina and the United Kingdom since 1833, when the British warships *Tyne* and *Clio* evicted Argentinian settlers and formally claimed the islands for Britain. Early in 1947 Argentina and Chile set up bases on Graham Land, and the cruiser HMS *Nigeria* (C60) was dispatched from South Africa. From then on two sloops or frigates were normally located around the Falklands during the southern summer. From time to time discussions were held, but despite a resolution at the United Nations (2065) in 1965, reminding members of a pledge to end colonialism, little progress was made.

Discussions were always likely to be fraught, given the inherent instability in Argentinian government. There was a major military coup against Juan Peron in 1955 in which elements of the military fought on both sides, and with Peron exiled a military junta was established. In 1963 naval aircraft fought on the side of rebels trying to overthrow the government; the revolt failed and many naval personnel and aircraft flew out to Uruguay. Notably, in respect of later events, there was a border dispute between Argentina and Chile in 1965.

On 28 September 1966 an *Aerolíneas Argentinas* DC-4 was hijacked by eighteen members of the New Argentina Movement and forced to land on Stanley racecourse. They surrendered after two days, and HMS *Puma* (F94) was deployed for several months. Then there was a revolt within the Air Force in 1975, during which naval aircraft flew against the Air Force.

Early in 1976 the Antarctic survey vessel *Shackleton* was fired upon by the destroyer *Almirante Storni*, and later a military government took power in Argentina. The following year the British Government sent a small naval task force to the South Atlantic comprising the nuclear submarine HMS *Dreadnought* (S101), two frigates and an oiler. This followed intelligence reports that an occupation of the South Georgia dependency seemed imminent, and after the Argentine Navy had fired on Eastern Bloc fishing vessels in the area.

With a series of right-wing military dictators with poor human rights track records, it is little wonder that the Falkland Islanders were determined to remain under British administration. In December 1981 General Galtieri

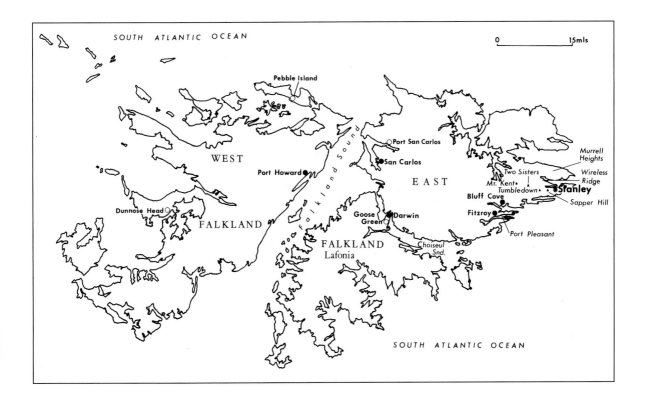

had come to power. He began planning for an early invasion of the Falklands with a view to consolidating his power base and unifying the country. From the outset the Argentine Navy was the most enthusiastic proponent of invasion, with the Air Force reluctant participants.

SOUTH GEORGIA

The invasion of South Georgia came five years later than originally feared, with the landing of demolition workers on the island from the Argentinian fleet transport *Bahia Buen Suceso* on 19 March 1982. The task of the workers was to dismantle the derelict whaling station. Four days later the polar vessel *Bahia Paraiso* was diverted from routine tasks to support the South Georgia civilians.

The first tangible British response was the landing of a small observation post on South Georgia from the ice patrol vessel HMS *Endurance* (A171) on 23 March, and the landing of a Royal Marine detachment on the 31st. From the 25th, nuclear submarines were dispatched to the South Atlantic. Meanwhile, on 23 March, the decision to invade the Falklands was taken in Buenos Aires, and five days later Argentinian Task Groups 40 (landing force) and 20 (covering force) sailed from mainland ports, bound for invasion in Operation *Rosario*.

The first Argentinian landings on the Falklands came at 04.30 hrs on 2 April as 150 men arrived to the west of Port Stanley. The British Royal Marine garrison (Naval Party 8901) comprised sixty-eight men, a number larger than usual due to the fact that the invasion coincided with a 24-hour handover period; in addition, there were twelve sailors from HMS *Endurance*.

The Falklands War was above all the Royal Navy's war. Despite the huge contribution of the RAF and Army the islands could not have been re-taken without the commitment of huge seaborne resources. The combined nature of operations is evidenced in this photograph on HMS *Hermes* with Sea Harriers of 800 and 809 NASs, Harrier GR.3s of 1 Sqn and a solitary Lynx. In the background is RFA *Fort Grange* with a Sea King of 824 NAS. (*Crown copyright*)

Detailed shot of the forward fuselage of Jaguar GR.1 XZ356/N *Mary Rose*. In addition to the slightly risqué nose art and Wing Commander's pennant the aircraft displays sixteen 4 x 1,000 lb bomb, seven CBU-87, one CVR-7 rocket and six photo reconnaissance mission markings. See Section 9.4. (*Author*)

The Buccaneer from Lossiemouth joined the party late, being sent to Muharraq to designate targets for the Tornadoes. XX885/L completed seven missions: evident on the port wing is the AN/AVQ-23E *Pave Spike* laser designator. See Section 9.4. (*Author*)

Close-up view of XX885/L *Hello Sailor: Caroline*, also named, like all Buccaneers, after a whisky, in the case the Famous Grouse. In addition to the designating sorties the aircraft also appears to have flown one bombing mission and accounted for an An-12. See Section 9.4. (*Author*)

The outer pylon on the Buccaneer's right wing held the ALQ-101(V)-10 ECM pod for protection. See Section 9.4. (*Author*)

Close-up shot of the AN/AVQ-23E *Pave Spike* laser designator. See Section 9.4. (*Author*)

The combat aircraft were not alone in sporting mission markings. Un-named Victor K.2 tanker XL161 of 55 Sqn conducted 44 war missions. See Section 9.4. (*Author*)

Close-up shot of the forward fuselage of XL161 with the tally clearly marked under the port intake. See Section 9.4. (*Author*)

Victors of 55 Sqn mostly sported nose art incorporating the squadron's spear motif from its official badge. XH671 *Sweet Sue* conducted 41 missions. See Section 9.4. (*Author*)

XH672 *Maid Marian* – 52 missions. See Section 9.4. (*Author*)

XM717 *Lucky Lou* (preserved at the RAF Museum) – 42 missions. See Section 9.4. (*Author*)

Two of 216 Sqn's Tristars were based in the Gulf and painted pink overall. ZD949 was named appropriately *Pinky*, while ZD951 seen here was *Perky*. See Section 9.4. (*Author*)

Even two of the VC-10s carried nose art including K.2 ZA142/C of 101 Sqn, *The Empire Strikes Back*. See Section 9.4. (*Author*)

Puma HC.1 XW220 of 33 Sqn is a Gulf War veteran and here displays the distinctive pink 'sand' camouflage. The RAF deployed nineteen Pumas which moved up to support troops on the offensive. See Section 9.4. (*Author*)

On its return to the UK Chinook HC.1 ZA707/V displays the night camouflage scheme applied when operating in support of special forces. The Chinook carried up to 85 men or 12 tonnes of freight at a time. See Section 9.4. (*Author*)

The British Army deployed the Gazelle and Lynx to the Gulf with three squadrons. Gazelle AH.1 XZ347/T displays the pale blue recognition stripes carried by certain types including the Gazelle, Puma and Islander. See Section 9.4. (*Author*)

Line-up of Gazelles in Gulf War camouflage. See Section 9.4. (*Westland Helicopters*)

On returning to its European style camouflage ZD747/AL of 9 Sqn retained the 29 mission markings on the nose. As *Anna Louise* the aircraft completed a number of anti-radar *ALARM* sorties. See Section 9.4. (*BAe Systems*)

The two COs were advised of the impending invasion on the 1st, and ordered to make their dispositions accordingly. They chose to defend the airfield area to the east of Port Stanley. As news came through of the size of the invasion force, the Marines regrouped around Government House, and some brisk fighting ensued. From daybreak it was clear that the position was untenable, and at 09.25 hrs, with 2,800 Argentinians ashore, the Governor, Rex Hunt, ordered the garrison to surrender.

Later in the day the first Pucaras of *Grupo 3 de Ataque* (G3A) of the *Fuerza Aérea Argentina* (FAA) landed at the airfield, and a C-130H brought in an AN/TPS-43F surveillance radar. South Georgia was captured the following day by Argentinian Task Group 60 after being stoutly defended by the small Royal Marine detachment from *Endurance*.

During the landings the first aircraft casualty of the war occurred when Puma AE-504 of *Batallón de Aviación de Combate* (CAB) *601* was hit by machine-gun fire and two Argentinian Marines were killed.

INITIAL BRITISH RESPONSE

With clear evidence of Argentinian intentions, the British decided on 31 March to assemble a task force capable of retaking the Falklands if necessary, and Operation *Corporate* was set in train. There were actually two naval task forces, TF.317 and TF.324, the latter comprising the submarine element.

On 1 April seven RAF Hercules flew into Gibraltar with essential naval supplies for ships already assembled for Exercise *Springtrain*; the aircraft also brought air traffic control staff and equipment for use on Ascension Island, which was to become a critical staging-post. Although the island is British, Wideawake airfield had been built by the United States to support its tracking station, and was managed by Pan American Airways; from its normal three movements a week, the airfield was to handle 400 movements a day at the height of the war.

Rear-Admiral John Woodward, who had been appointed task force commander, sailed from Gibraltar on board the destroyer HMS *Antrim* (D18) for Ascension on 1 April. In company were the destroyers HMS *Coventry* (D118), *Glamorgan* (D19), *Glasgow* (D88) and *Sheffield* (D80), the frigates HMS *Arrow* (F173), *Brilliant* (F20) and *Plymouth* (F126), the helicopter support ship RFA *Engadine* (K08), the stores ship RFA *Fort Austin* (A386) and fast tanker *Tidespring*. A naval party was flown into Ascension to become the basis of British Forces Support Unit Ascension Island (BFSUAI).

The Falklands campaign was at its core a naval operation. The RAF would play a supporting role, and ground forces were dependent on the Royal Navy for transport and insertion. Nearly all stores would be carried by sea over huge distances. Examination of the structure of the task force and its warships is helpful if the unfolding action is to make sense. The composition of the task force comprised two main elements.

First were the vessels needed to transport and support the troops who would eventually have to invade. This element included Ships Taken Up From Trade (STUFT) as troopships, hospital ships and transports for a vast range of equipment and supplies, including weapons, vehicles, helicopters, ammunition, fuel, food, medical stores and temporary accommodation. It also included assault and landing ships, landing craft, refuellers and smaller support vessels like tugs and minesweepers.

The second element was the prime warship component, which had no function of its own unless it could alone defeat the enemy and recapture the Islands – which it could not. At the core were the aircraft carriers embarking aircraft for defence and attack and for long-range anti-submarine warfare. The carriers were vulnerable, and so they were supported by anti-submarine, anti-surface vessel and anti-aircraft frigates and destroyers, all of which embarked their own helicopters for ASW and general duties. These warships also, of course, protected the first element. They were supported by refuellers (in turn supported by tankers), stores and ammunition ships and maintenance vessels.

The various types of ships, their performance, weapons and aircraft complement are described in the following table.

Displacement[1]	Speed[2]	Weapons[3]	Aircraft[4]
Warships			
Carrier Hermes class HMS *Hermes* (R12)			
28,700	26	2 Seacat	15 Sea Harrier, 6 Harrier, 6 Sea King, 1 Lynx
Carrier Invincible class HMS *Invincible* (R05), *Illustrious* (R06)			
19,500	30	1 Sea Dart 14 GPMG	10 Sea Harrier, 9 Sea King, 1 Lynx
Destroyer County class HMS *Antrim* (D18), *Glamorgan* (D19)			
6,200	32	2 4.5 in., 2 20 mm, 1 Seaslug, 2 Seacat, 4 Exocet	1 Wessex 3 (737)
Destroyer Type 82 HMS *Bristol* (D23)			
7,100	28	1 4.5 in., 4 20 mm, 1 Sea Dart	—
Destroyer Type 42 HMS *Cardiff* (D108), *Coventry* (D118), *Exeter* (D89), *Glasgow* (D88), *Sheffield* (D80)			
4,100	30	4.5 in., 2 20 mm, 1 Sea Dart	1 Lynx (815)
Frigate Type 12 HMS *Plymouth* (F126), *Yarmouth* (F101)			
2,800	28	2 4.5 in., 2 20 mm, 1 Seacat	1 Wasp (829)
Frigate Leander class Seacat fitted HMS *Argonaut* (F56), *Minerva* (F45), *Penelope* (F127)			
3,200	28	2 40 mm, 3 Seacat, 4 Exocet	1 Lynx (815)
Frigate Leander class Sea Wolf fitted HMS *Andromeda* (F57)			
3,100	28	2 40 mm, 1 Sea Wolf, 4 Exocet	1 Lynx (815)
Frigate Type 21 HMS *Active* (F171), *Alacrity* (F174), *Ambuscade* (F172), *Antelope* (F170), *Ardent* (F184), *Arrow* (F173), *Avenger* (F185)			
3,250	31	1 4.5 in., 2 20 mm, 1 Seacat, 4 Exocet	Lynx (815), 1 Wasp (*Active* only)
Frigate Type 22 HMS *Brilliant* (F90), *Broadsword* (F88)			
4,400	29	2 40 mm, 2 Sea Wolf, 4 Exocet	2 Lynx
Amphibious assault ship Fearless class HMS *Fearless* (L10), *Intrepid* (L11)			
12,120	21	2 40 mm, 2 20 mm, 4 Seacat	4 Sea King (845, 846)
Support ships			
Antarctic Patrol HMS *Endurance* (A171)			
3,600	14	2 20 mm	2 Wasp
Survey vessel (ambulance ships) HMS *Hecla* (A133), *Herald* (A138), *Hydra* (A144)			
2,733	14	2 20 mm	1 Wasp (829)
Fleet oiler RFA *Olmeda*, *Olna*,			
33,240	19		2 Sea King (824)
Fleet oiler RFA *Tidepool*, *Tidespring*			
25,930	17		2 Wessex (845)
Fleet Replenishment RFA *Regent*, *Resource*			
23,000	19		1 Wessex (845)
Fleet Replenishment RFA *Fort Austin*, *Fort Grange*			
22,750	20		FA – 3 Wessex (845) FG – 3 Sea King (824)
Helicopter Support Ship RFA *Engadine* (K08)			
8,960	16	14 GPMG	4 Wessex (847)
Landing Ship Logistic RFA *Sir Bedivere*, *Sir Galahad*, *Sir Geraint*, *Sir Lancelot*, *Sir Percivale*, *Sir Tristram*			
5,550	17	2 40 mm	3 Gazelle or Scout

Transports carrying helicopters included SS *Astronomer*, *Atlantic Causeway*, *Atlantic Conveyor* and *Contender Bezant*. Personnel and vehicle transports with helicopters embarked included *Baltic Ferry*, *Canberra*, *Elk*, *Europic Ferry*, *Nordic Ferry*, *Norland*, *Queen Elizabeth 2* and *St Helena*.

NOTES
1 Displacement in tons, loaded
2 Knots
3 General and AA only
4 As embarked

The main force from Gibraltar was followed by HMS *Plymouth* and the tanker *Appleleaf* on 2 April, and at the same time RFA *Brambleleaf* was directed to the South Atlantic from the Indian Ocean. Two further warships headed south on the 6th when it was decided to divert the frigates *Yarmouth* (F101) and *Broadsword* (F88) from their sailing to the Persian Gulf.

Unnoticed, the nuclear submarine HMS *Spartan* (S105) slipped out of Gibraltar on the 1st, while HMS *Splendid* (S106) departed Faslane on the same day, to be followed by HMS *Conqueror* (S48) on the 4th.

There were two main inter-related concerns in sending a task force so far from comprehensive air cover, and these were not fully addressed until after the conflict was over. First was the concern that the warships were ill equipped to combat the Exocet missiles known to be operational with the Argentine Navy, and usually launched from low level. Related was the total lack of airborne early-warning cover. The Navy had lost its AEW capability with the retirement of the Gannet AEW.3, and the RAF's Shackletons which had taken over the role had not the performance to operate at such a distance from base.

Moves were put in hand to fit the Sea King with a warning radar, but that would take time. The solution was therefore to reach an agreement with the Chilean Air Force for intelligence from long-range radars so that task force vessels and air cover could be warned and prepared for probable ship strikes. In addition, the Chileans

Emphasising the combined nature of Operation *Corporate*, and presaging the 'purple' Harrier force, is this line-up on the stern of HMS *Hermes* ready to taxi forward. Sea Harrier XZ460/26 of 800 NAS has an air defence *Sidewinder* fitted while the anonymous Harrier GR.3 of 1 Sqn is loaded with 1,000 lb bombs. Both aircraft have 100 gal drop tanks on the inboard pylons. Throughout the action the ship is being replenished by an unseen helicopter.

(Crown copyright)

probably allowed their airfields to be used by RAF intelligence-gathering aircraft. Further, there was the intention to use special forces to remove the threat on the ground by destroying the Super Etendard aircraft on their base, an operation described below.

TASK FORCE PREPARATIONS

In Britain, major elements of the task force were assembled at Portsmouth and Devonport. After a hectic weekend, during which Parliament sat on a Saturday for the first time since the Suez crisis in 1956, the task force departed from the 5th. (In fact the tug HMS *Typhoon* (A95) had departed on the 4th.) The key components were HMS *Hermes* (R12), with 800 NAS Sea Harriers, supplemented by aircraft from 899 NAS, plus 826 NAS (Sea King HAS.5), 846 NAS (Sea King HC.4) and A Coy 42 Commando; and HMS *Invincible* (R05), with 801 NAS (Sea Harrier), again supplemented by aircraft and crews from 899 NAS, and 820 NAS (Sea King HAS.5).

Accompanying the carriers were the frigates HMS *Alacrity* (F174) and *Antelope* (F170), four landing-ships (logistic), two tankers and a stores ship. The landing-ships between them had the helicopters of 3 CBAS embarked, while RFA *Olmeda* carried two Sea Kings of 824 NAS, and RFA *Resource* a Wessex of 845 NAS. HMS *Fearless* (L10) left Portsmouth on the 6th with Sea Kings of 846 NAS, and the assault platform RFA *Stromness* left on the 7th. The requisitioned liner *Canberra* sailed from Southampton on the 9th with 2,000 troops of 40 and 42 Commando and 3 Para aboard. Accompanying her with equipment was the Ro-Ro cargo ship *Elk*.

The UK contingent arrived at Ascension on the 16th, joining with the Gibraltar vessels that had arrived on the 11th. During the journey south all vessels had taken time to transfer stores and ammunition, often by helicopter, and to shake down. Every waking moment was spent in preparing for battle. As shortcomings were identified they were rectified, and the need for modification, additional stores and further equipment resulted in numerous flights into Ascension, plus the preparation of more ships in the UK. The *Stena Seaspread* was requisitioned and converted as a maintenance ship, sailing on 16 April. The cruise liner SS *Uganda* was rapidly converted to hospital ship configuration at Gibraltar, sailing for the South Atlantic on 21 April. At about the same time three survey ships *Hecla*, *Herald* and *Hydra* were converted for the casevac role.

The first RAF detachment to Ascension was made on the 6th, when two Nimrod MR.1s of 42 Sqn arrived to provide maritime reconnaissance cover for the task force. Meanwhile, in the South Atlantic, the Argentinians had established an information and control centre (ICC) at Port Stanley, and a new FAA command structure was set up to provide for integrated air defence. In anticipation of the British military response, the *Teatro de Operaciones del Atlantico Sur* (TOAS) was established, with its headquarters at Comodoro Rivadavia.

On 7 April Britain declared a 200-mile maritime exclusion zone (MEZ) around the Falklands, to become effective from 04.00 hrs GMT on the 12th. Some time shortly after the 10th it is believed that Canberra PR.9 aircraft of 39 Sqn began operating from Punta Arenas in Chile, having been given *Fuerza Aérea de Chile* (FAC) markings *en route* at Belize; it is possible that Nimrod R.1 intelligence-gathering aircraft of 51 Sqn also operated from the remote airfield at San Felix.

The UK- and Gibraltar-based ships of the task force began assembling at Ascension from the 10th. Meanwhile aircraft had been repainted in low-visibility schemes and many markings obliterated. For some ships the stay at Ascension was short. The destroyer *Antrim* (D18), the frigate *Plymouth* (F126) and the tanker RFA *Tidespring* picked up equipment and a small force comprising M Coy 42 Commando, D Sqn 22 SAS and a Special Boat Service (SBS) detachment; also embarked were a Wessex HAS.3 of 737 NAS (*Antrim*), two Wessex HU.5s of 845 NAS (*Tidespring*) and a Wasp HAS.1 of 829 NAS (*Plymouth*). As TF.317.9, they were to rendezvous with HMS *Endurance* in the South Atlantic on the 12th for Operation *Paraquet*, the retaking of South Georgia.

At Ascension, hurriedly stored supplies were reorganized on the assembling ships, and additional equipment was flown in from Britain and the United States for incorporation, VC-10 transports of 10 Sqn joining the Lyneham Wing Hercules and chartered civil aircraft in a constant airlift. The anti-submarine Sea Kings of 820 and 826 NASs performed with the HC.4s of 846 NAS, the Wessex HU.5s of 845 NAS and the ship's flights' Wasps and Lynxes of 829 and 815 NAS respectively in a continuing job of vertical replenishment (vertrep) and cross-shipping.

Vertrep tasks continued at sea after the task force had left Ascension, and on one such sortie, at night on 23 April, Sea King HC.4 ZA311 of 846 NAS ditched off *Hermes* with the loss of an air crewman. The assembly of the task force required maximum security, and on the 12th the more capable Nimrod MR.2s of 120, 201 and 206 Sqns

A Harrier GR.3 of 1 Sqn, weapons expended, landing back on HMS *Hermes*. The RAF pilots performed superbly in this first deployment aboard a carrier. *(Crown copyright)*

replaced the aircraft of 42 Sqn. Later, on the 18th, the first Victor tankers arrived, including aircraft equipped for radar reconnaissance.

ARGENTINIAN DISPOSITIONS

On the Falklands, the *Fuerza Aérea Argentina* had commissioned Port Stanley airfield as *Base Aérea Militar* (BAM) Malvinas and BAM Condor at Goose Green, and the *Commando Aviación Naval Argentina* (CANA) had established a base at Pebble Island as *Estación Aeronaval* (EAN) *Calderón*. By late April, 24 Pucaras of G3A were operating from Stanley and Goose Green, six MB.339As of *1 Escuadrilla de Ataque* (CANA) were based at Stanley and four T-43Cs of *4 Escuadrilla de Ataque* (CANA) were flying from Stanley and Pebble Island.

In addition, a search-and-rescue element of *Grupo 7 de Coin Escuadron* Helicopters (G7CEH), with two Bell 212s and two CH-47Cs, was operating from Goose Green and a range of *Ejercito* helicopters of CAB601 was headquartered at Moody Brook. Finally, two Skyvans and a Puma of the *Prefectura Naval Argentina* (PN) were based at Port Stanley. FAA and CANA transports were operating freely into Port Stanley. The two East Falklands airfields were heavily defended with 20 mm and 35 mm anti-aircraft guns and Tigercat and Roland SAMs, two companies of FAA officer cadets having been drafted on to the islands to handle airfield defence.

On the mainland bases, within striking distance of the Falklands, were the following Air Force and Navy combat units:

Unit	Equipment
BAN Trelew	
Grupo 2 de Bombardeo (G2B)	8 Canberra B.62
BAM Comodoro Rivadavia	
Grupo 8 de Caza (G8C) det	4 Mirage IIIEA
Grupo 4 de Ataque (G4A)	8 Pucara
San Julian	
Grupo 6 de Caza (G6C) Esc II	10 Dagger
Grupo 4 de Caza (G4C)	15 A-4C
BAM Rio Gallegos	
Grupo 5 de Caza (G5C)	26 A-4B
Grupo 8 de Caza (G8C)	10 Mirage IIIEA
BAN Rio Grande	
Grupo 6 de Caza (G6C] Esc III	10 Dagger
2 Escuadrilla de Caza y Ataque (2ECA)	5 Super Etendard
3 Escuadrilla de Caza y Ataque (3ECA)	8 A-4Q

Although there were limited reserve aircraft, the total number of combat machines available to the FAA was about 110, including mainland-based Pucaras. The CANA could call on just twelve, since one Super Etendard was used as a source of spares.

A pair of 656 Sqn Scouts. The nearest helicopter appears to be fitted to take an infra-red shield over the engine exhaust and also has a casualty pannier over the right skid. Army helicopters evacuated some 400 wounded soldiers.
(Crown copyright)

RETAKING SOUTH GEORGIA

In preparation for Operation *Paraquet*, Victor XL192 of 57 Sqn flew the first of three long-range maritime radar reconnaissance (MRR) sorties on the night of 20/21 April. It covered over 7,000 miles, conducting a 150-square-mile search in a record 14 hr 45 min sortie. The flight was supported by four tankers in each direction.

The first move in South Georgia was the placing of Special Forces on Fortuna Glacier by the Wessex HAS.3 of 737 NAS and two Wessex HU.5s of 845 NAS on 21 April, but weather conditions deteriorated to such an extent that the SAS called for withdrawal early the next morning. In quick succession, the two HU.5s (XT464 and XT473) were lost when they crashed in white-out conditions, fortunately without serious injury, and the troops and crews were eventually recovered by the remaining Wessex.

On the 23rd the Argentinian submarine *Santa Fe* was detected in the vicinity, and HMS *Brilliant* (F90) joined TF.317.9, bringing with her two Lynx HAS.2s. The submarine HMS *Conqueror* was also in the area. Contact with the *Santa Fe* was made by *Antrim's* Wessex, which dropped depth charges near the vessel. Damaged, she returned to Grytviken, but *en route* was subjected to a torpedo attack by *Brilliant's* Lynxes, and then to several AS.12 attacks by Wasps from *Plymouth* and *Endurance*. The now disabled submarine was beached alongside the jetty.

It was decided to launch an invasion at short notice to take advantage of the shock created by the British action, and H-Hour was set for 14.45 hrs, despite the Royal Marine component being aboard *Tidespring* some 200 miles away. A naval gunfire support (NGS) officer was flown to a suitable observation site in advance of a bombardment, and thirty SAS troopers went ashore nearby. The 235-round naval bombardment began shortly afterwards, bracketing Argentinian positions, and more troops were landed from *Endurance* and *Plymouth*. Without a fight, the Argentinian garrison surrendered at 17.15 hrs, and the small garrison at Leith surrendered the following day.

ACTION

The task force had left Ascension from the 18th, and shortly after this 5 Infantry Brigade, now comprising 2nd Scots Guards, 1st Welsh Guards and 7th Gurkha Rifles, began training in the Brecon Beacons. This follow-up force was to leave the UK early in May. The main task force was located on 21 April by an FAA Boeing 707, which was intercepted by a Sea Harrier of 800 NAS. By the 27th the fleet had reached a position north-east of the Falklands, and two days later the FAA stopped daylight transport flights into the Islands.

On the 30th, as diplomatic attempts to find an accommodation failed, the United States formally took the British position, and with seventy British ships now committed, the MEZ became a total exclusion zone (TEZ). A third operational Sea Harrier squadron, 809 NAS, had been formed at Yeovilton from development and reserve aircraft, and the first six machines made the long flight to Ascension via Banjul, involving no fewer than fourteen air refuellings each. They were to be loaded on *Atlantic Conveyor* on 5 May. The Sea Harriers of 800 and 801 NAS were by this time flying regular combat air patrols (CAPs) over the task force, which now prepared for action.

The war began in earnest early on the morning of 1 May when a Vulcan B.2 of 44 Sqn made the first *Black Buck* bombing raid from Ascension. This involved a round trip of 14 hrs 50 min, and required fifteen Victor sorties and eighteen in-flight refuellings to get the single aircraft to the target and back. Twenty-one 1,000 lb bombs were dropped from 10,000 ft across the runway of Port Stanley airfield, which was cratered by one bomb; others caused damage to aircraft and installations.

With a round trip of over 7,800 miles this attack was the longest bombing raid in history. It was a remarkable feat by crews who had little training in air-to-air refuelling using equipment which had had to be salvaged. The planning and execution worked brilliantly and there was no collateral damage on the Islands.

At 2350Z on 30 April two Vulcans (XM598 and the reserve XM607) and eleven Victors, including two reserves (for the sake of simplicity referred to below as 1 to 11) departed Ascension. The primary Vulcan had to abort, leaving XM607 to continue: Victor No. 1 also returned with problems. To gain some insight into the enormous effort which went into getting one bomber such a distance, the actual sequence of refuelling outbound follows.

Stage 1	Victor 4 refuels XM607
Stage 2	Victor 3 refuels Victor 2 and returns (nine tankers remain)

Stage 3	Victor 5 (second spare) returns. Victor 6 refuels 7, 8 refuels 9 and 10 refuels 11. 6, 8 and 10 return
Stage 4	Victor 4 (XL162) refuels XM607 and returns (now four tankers remain)
Stage 5	Victor 7 (XL512) refuels XM607
Stage 6	Victor 7 refuels Victor 9 (XL189)
Stage 7	Victor 9 refuels Victor 11 (XH669)
Stage 8	Victor 7 refuels XM607 and returns
Stage 9	Victor 2 (XL188) refuels Victor 9 and returns (now two tankers remain)
Stage 10	Victor 11 refuels XM607 twice
Stage 11	Victor 11 refuels Victor 9 and returns
Stage 12	Tanker 9 refuels XM607

The outbound tanker sorties occupied a total of 71 hrs 10 min. On the return one Nimrod and seven Victor sorties were flown to recover the Vulcan and the final Victor XL189, which had intentionally transferred some of its own fuel requirement to ensure success of the mission. The tanker time on the return sorties was 34 hrs 15 min.

Twelve Sea Harriers of 800 NAS took off from *Hermes* from 07.48 hrs to follow up the raid on Port Stanley and to attack the airfield at Goose Green. Nine aircraft bombed Port Stanley from three directions, applying a combination of toss-bombing and conventional bombing techniques and delivering 1,000 lb direct action (DA) and variable-timed (VT) bombs and BE.755 cluster-bomb units (CBUs). Little damage was done, but the airfield remained unsafe for some time. The Goose Green attack was more successful, and three Pucaras were put out of action for the duration, one pilot being killed as he waited to take off.

From midday, *Glamorgan*, *Alacrity* and *Arrow* began a naval bombardment of Argentinian positions in Port

Busy scene at Teal inlet. In the foreground is Gazelle XZ290 of 656 Sqn AAC fitted with SNEB rocket launcher while behind is Wessex HU.5 XT484/H of 845 NAS. This latter machine was later fitted with two AS.12 missiles, fired at targets in Port Stanley. *(Crown copyright)*

Stanley. Task force helicopters were also busy around the island, and it is probable that the Argentinian command saw the morning's activity as a prelude to imminent invasion. From 10.00 hrs, a series of FAA sorties was launched against the British ships, but few targets were found. The A-4 Skyhawks of *Grupos 4* and *5* and the Canberras of *Grupo 2* were provided with top cover from the Mirages and Daggers of *Grupos 8* and *6*. Later in the day *Grupo 8* lost two aircraft in quick succession to AIM-9L AAMs fired by 801 NAS Sea Harriers.

A flight of Daggers found and attacked the vessels bombarding Stanley and caused some damage. A Dagger from a separate flight was brought down by a Sea Harrier of 800 NAS, and 801 NAS completed its hat-trick by destroying a Canberra 150 miles north-west of Port Stanley. The Sea Harrier force had had a highly successful day with no loss, and the aircraft/AIM-9L missile combination was proved in combat.

The task force's helicopters had also been busy, and, in a search for the submarine *San Luis*, Sea King HAS.5 XZ577 of 826 NAS claimed a record operational sortie: with a spare crew aboard and refuelling in flight from the frigates *Brilliant* and *Yarmouth*, the aircraft remained aloft for 10 hrs 20 min. Early the next morning, the Sea King HC.4s of 846 NAS installed men of G Sqn 22 SAS on the Falklands.

On 2 May the Argentinians suffered a more serious loss with the sinking of the cruiser *General Belgrano*, torpedoed by HMS *Conqueror*; her Alouette III was lost with her. Some time in the day a CANA Lynx HAS.23 was destroyed when it collided with the destroyer *Santisima Trinidad*. The Lynxes of *Glasgow* and *Coventry* enjoyed rather more success when, early the next morning, using Sea Skua anti-ship missiles, they attacked and damaged the patrol craft *Alferez Sobel*; she had been detected by a Sea King of 826 NAS while searching for the missing Canberra crew. The Argentinians lost two aircraft on 3 May: an MB.339A of 1EA crashed on the approach to Port Stanley, where a Skyvan of the PN was destroyed by naval gunfire.

To add a dedicated ground-attack capability to the task force, the first Harrier GR.3 of 1 Sqn departed St Mawgan on 4 May for a non-stop, 4,600-mile, 9¼ hr flight to Ascension. Over the next few days more aircraft followed, and by 6 May they were embarked on *Atlantic Conveyor* with the Sea Harriers of 809 NAS; they were to join the force's carriers on 18 May. On the night of 3/4 May the second *Black Buck* raid was made by Vulcan B.2 XM607 of 50 Sqn, but on this occasion the runway was not hit.

May 4 saw the first Argentinian success, when two Super Etendards of 2ECA attacked warships on picket duty to the west of the Task Force, which for several days had been shadowed by an SP-2H of the *Escuadrilla de Exploración* (EE). Two aircraft flying from Rio Grande launched one Exocet ASM each, one missile hitting HMS *Sheffield* at 10.58 hrs. The warhead failed to explode, but in the ensuing fire twenty-one men died; the second Exocet failed to find its target. The crippled destroyer sank under tow six days later, the loss demonstrating the vulnerability of the task force, which was denied early warning of impending air attacks.

The Royal Navy was to suffer a further loss that day. Lt N. Taylor of 800 NAS was killed when his Sea Harrier XZ450 was shot down by AA fire on a raid on Goose Green airfield. At 09.00 hrs the following morning, two senior pilots of 801 NAS were lost, their aircraft XZ452 and 453 presumed to have collided in mist while searching for a contact near the hulk of *Sheffield*. On the positive side, the Argentinian carrier *25 de Mayo* returned to port, there to remain throughout the conflict, her Skyhawks transferring to Rio Grande.

Poor weather slowed activity for several days, although the Sea Harriers maintained their CAPs. To the north, *Canberra* sailed from Ascension on the 8th, and from the 11th extended MR cover for the task force was provided by the Nimrod MR.2Ps of 206 Sqn, newly adapted for in-flight refuelling. *Grupo 4* dispatched several A-4C sorties against the warships on 9 May, but suffered its first losses when two aircraft crashed *en route* in bad weather. A Puma of CAB601 was shot down by a Sea Dart fired from HMS *Coventry* over Choiseul Sound, and a UH-1H was seriously damaged at Moody Brook by naval gunfire.

The intelligence-gathering trawler *Narwal* was attacked by Sea Harriers from 800 NAS and boarded by SBS men dropped by Sea Kings. The bombardment of Port Stanley had continued, but on 12 May *Glasgow* and *Brilliant* were attacked by A-4Bs of *Grupo 5*. *Glasgow* was effectively put out of action after being hit by a 500 lb bomb which failed to explode.

The attackers paid a high price, losing two aircraft to Seawolf SAMs fired from *Brilliant*, while a third aircraft crashed into the sea and a fourth was brought down by Argentinian 35 mm AA fire. At the same time, Sea King ZA132 of 826 NAS was lost when it ditched following engine failure.

INVASION

In the UK the requisitioned liner *Queen Elizabeth 2* sailed from Southampton with 5 Brigade direct for South Georgia, where the troops would be transferred to less vulnerable ships. On 13 May *Black Buck 3* was aborted due to adverse winds. Late on the 14th, forty-four SAS troops were inserted into Pebble Island by 846 NAS Sea Kings from *Hermes*. On the night of the 11th eight members of the Boat Troop had landed across from Pebble Island to reconnoitre and set up an observation post to prepare the way for this main force. Before dawn on the 15th they attacked the airfield and destroyed six Pucaras of G3A, four Mentors of 4EA and one Skyvan. They withdrew without loss. From Ascension, Nimrod MR.2P XV232 set a new operational reconnaissance sortie record, flying 8,300 miles in 19 hrs 5 min while checking Argentinian naval dispositions.

As the time for invasion approached, the Sea Harriers attacked vessels around the Falklands coast, damaging the *Rio Carcarana* and *Bahia Buen Suceso* on the 16th. On the 18th, two Sea Kings were lost. HAS.5 XZ573 of 826 NAS ditched during a sonar search when its radio altimeter failed. More significantly HC.4 ZA290 of 846 NAS was burnt by its crew at Agua Fresca near Punta Arenas in Chile after a one-way sortie associated with the insertion of Special Forces to reconnoitre the Super Etendard base at Rio Grande. It has been alleged that this was to prepare for an aborted Operation *Mikado*, the landing of fifty-five SAS troopers and their equipment on two Hercules of 47 Sqn, flying from Ascension. As the weather continued to inhibit operations, Sea King HC.4 ZA294 of 846 NAS was lost on 19 May after a bird-strike while transferring SAS troopers from *Hermes* to *Intrepid*, and twenty-one died in the accident.

As the amphibious group joined the battle group north-west of the Falklands, the Argentinian TOAS became the *Centro de Operaciones Conjuntas* (CEOPECON). The invasion was now set for Friday 21 May at San Carlos, and in softening-up operations 1 Sqn Harriers flew their first sorties against installations at Goose Green, destroying a fuel dump.

The Navy's Wasps were kept busy and in particular those of HMSs *Endurance* and *Plymouth* which fired eight AS.12 missiles at the submarine *Santa Fe*. XT432 of HMS *Hydra* was one of three used in the ambulance role, clearly marked and fitted with blue anti-collision lights. (*Crown copyright*)

The task force entered the TEZ on the 20th, and after a redistribution of troops the first landings of Operation *Sutton* were made at San Carlos by 2 Para just before dawn on the 21st. The invasion force had moved into the protected San Carlos Water under cover of mist, but had been spotted by an FAA Canberra. A Nimrod of 206 Sqn set off from Ascension in the early hours of the 21st on yet another record-breaking sortie, covering 8,453 miles to monitor any Argentinian naval countermoves.

The invasion force comprised the following vessels:
    Antrim 3 SBS, 1 Wessex HAS.3, 1 Wessex HU.5
    Ardent 1 Lynx
First wave
    Fearless 40 Cdo, 4 Sea King HC.4
    Intrepid 3 Para 4 Sea King HC.4, 2 Wessex HU.5
    Yarmouth 1 Wasp
Second wave
    Canberra 42 Cdo, 3 Para, 2 Sea King HC.4, 1 Wessex HU.5
    Norland 2 Para, 1 Sea King HC.4
    Stromness 45 Cdo, 1 Wessex HU.5
    Plymouth 1 Wasp
    Brilliant 2 Lynx
    Fort Austin 4 Sea King HAS.5
Third wave
    Sir Tristram 3 Gazelle
    Sir Galahad 3 Gazelle
    Sir Lancelot 2 Scout
    Sir Geraint
    Sir Percivale 3 Gazelle
    Europic Ferry 2 Scout
    Broadsword 2 Lynx
    Argonaut 1 Lynx

The landings went smoothly, but there was an urgency to establish effective defensive and AAA positions ashore before the inevitable air strikes began. While the Sea Harriers flew their CAPs, the Harriers attacked a helicopter concentration on Mount Kent, from where reinforcements could have been flown to the beach-head. A Puma and a CH-47C were destroyed by gunfire at 08.00 hrs. Soon after this Flt Lt J. Glover ejected from his Harrier when it was shot down by a Blowpipe SAM while on an armed reconnaissance sortie over Port Howard.

Near the beach-head, 3 CBAS lost two Gazelles (XX411 and XX402) in quick succession in support of a Sea King sortie; both pilots were killed and the vulnerability of the type to small-arms fire was quickly apparent. The invasion fleet was spotted by a Pucara at about 10.00 hrs after one of the type had been shot down by a Stinger SAM fired by an SAS NCO. Shortly afterwards, a sole MB.339A attacked HMS *Argonaut*, causing superficial damage.

The first mainland-based attacks followed at 10.25 hrs, by A-4Bs of *Grupo 5* and Daggers of *Grupo 6*. The aircraft came in undetected, and disabled *Antrim* and *Argonaut*. One Dagger crashed into the sea after having been hit by a Seawolf from HMS *Brilliant*. The Sea Harriers had little time to spend over the landings since the carriers had withdrawn well to the east, out of range of attack. Without airborne early warning (AEW) and look-down radars, they were dependent on radar pickets for warning of raids. Around midday HMS *Ardent* was attacked by Pucaras of *Grupo 3*, one of which was destroyed over Lafonia by cannon fire from an 801 NAS Sea Harrier.

The next strike on the ships came at 13.00 hrs, by A-4s of *Grupos 4* and *5*. The carriers had increased their CAPs, and although one aircraft caused some damage to *Ardent*, two were brought down at low level by AIM-9Ls fired by 800 NAS Sea Harriers. The third mainland strike came at 14.35 hrs as Daggers of *Grupo 6* darted in at low level. One was destroyed on its run-in by a Sea Harrier of 800 NAS; another further damaged *Ardent* and wrote off her Lynx. Fifteen minutes later a second flight was bounced by 801 NAS, and all three aircraft were destroyed by AIM-9Ls.

Despite a series of attacks pressed home with determination, the FAA sorties achieved little, owing to the use of old or inadequately fused bombs, many of which did not explode. The CANA now joined the fray with a raid at 15.10 hrs by A-4Qs of 3ECA. Using retarded bombs, the aircraft again made for *Ardent*, which was fatally damaged and sank the following day. Two Skyhawks were shot down by 801 NAS pilots, who also damaged a third, which was abandoned by the pilot after an abortive attempt to land at Port Stanley.

By the end of the day the FAA and CANA had lost twelve combat aircraft and two helicopters, with four pilots killed, while British losses were one Harrier, three helicopters and two pilots. For their efforts, the Argentinians had destroyed one frigate, disabled a destroyer and damaged three more frigates. Saturday saw the Argentinians frustrated from making further attacks when the weather again favoured the British as they landed more men and supplies. Harriers again struck the airfield at Goose Green.

First blood on Sunday in the air war was drawn at 10.30 hrs when the Sea Harrier CAP spotted helicopters delivering supplies on West Falkland. In several passes, two Pumas and an A.109A were shot up by 801 NAS pilots. The first strikes on the shipping in Falklands Sound came just before 14.00 hrs. A-4s of *Grupo 5* hit HMS *Antelope*, which was subsequently destroyed when an unexploded bomb blew up while being defused. One A-4B was destroyed by a SAM, while in a later attack a Dagger was shot down by an 800 NAS Sea Harrier. Early in the evening Sea Harrier ZA192 of 800 NAS was lost when it hit the sea and exploded shortly after taking off for a toss-bombing sortie.

BREAK-OUT

By 27 May the beach-head was secure and 2 Para prepared to break out towards Goose Green. In the meantime, shipping had been subjected to further attacks. On the 24th three Daggers and an A-4C were destroyed, the former all to 800 NAS, the latter to naval gunfire. On the 25th HMS *Coventry* was attacked by *Grupos 4* and *5* while on picket duty to the west of the islands. She brought down an A-4B and an A-4C with Sea Dart SAMs before being hit and sinking shortly afterwards. A third A-4 was destroyed by naval gunfire in San Carlos Water.

The British suffered another serious loss with the destruction of *Atlantic Conveyor*, loaded with Chinook and Wessex helicopters plus many essential materials and spares. The ship was hit at 16.36 hrs by an Exocet fired by a Super Etendard. A second missile failed, leaving the CANA with just one round available. The loss of helicopters (three Chinooks and six Wessex) was critical, causing a major transport problem for the British troops.

Shortly before the breakout, troops of the *Ejercito*'s 12 Regt had been airlifted from Mount Kent to Goose Green, and the fighting from the 27th was hard, with only limited support from the Harriers. During one sortie, Sqn Ldr R. Iveson flying GR.3 XZ988 was hit over Goose Green and ejected; he hid up for three days, to be rescued by 3 CBAS Gazelle on the 30th. One A-4B (to gunfire), two Pucaras (small-arms fire) and an MB.339A (Blowpipe) were lost while attacking shipping and troop positions.

Napalm was dropped unsuccessfully by Pucaras on the 28th – the only occasion on which the weapon was used – and Scout AH.1 XT629 of 3 CBAS was shot down by a Pucara during a casevac sortie. Further afield, two Vulcans wired for firing the AGM-45 Shrike anti-radiation missile (ARM) deployed to Ascension, and *Black Buck 4* was aborted five hours into the sortie when one of the refuelling Victors' hose-drum units (HDU) failed.

On the ground, 45 Commando and 3 Para made their epic march towards Fort Stanley, initially to Teal Inlet. Air support consisted of Harrier sorties, mainly around Mount Kent, which were, however, limited by appalling weather; in addition, the depleted helicopter force was busy ferrying supplies and casualties. The Sea Harriers maintained the CAPs to protect the task force, but saw little action. One of the type was lost in an accident on the 29th (ZA174), and a second (XZ456) was shot down over Port Stanley by a Roland SAM on 1 June. The pilot ejected but spent many hours in the sea before being recovered by a Sea King of 820 NAS. A C-130E of *Grupo 1 de Transporte Aereo* (G1TA) was claimed by 801 NAS on 1 June after the aircraft had climbed out of Port Stanley to observe British shipping. In attacks on warships, a Dagger was destroyed by a Rapier on the 29th, and Sea Darts fired by HMS *Exeter* cost *Grupo 4* two A-4Cs the following day. They were supporting the last Exocet strike against HMS *Invincible*, but the missile appears to have burnt out after having been decoyed.

Argentina was searching desperately for a further source of Exocets, but despite large arms shipments from Israel in Ecuadorian, Peruvian and Uruguayan aircraft, none was forthcoming. There were no further attacks on ships until 8 June due to the continuing bad weather, which also hampered Harrier sorties. The Harriers pressed home strikes and armed reconnaissance sorties when possible, but they suffered damage from small-arms fire as a result of the heights at which they were required to fly. XZ963 was lost on the 30th when fuel-line damage necessitated the pilot ejecting short of *Hermes*. Fortunately, the forward operating base (FOB) at Port San Carlos was completed by 2 June, allowing longer time in target areas.

The first Vulcan anti-radar raid, *Black Buck 5*, on 31 May, caused little damage. *Black Buck 6*, on 3 June, was more successful, damaging a Skyguard radar, but after the refuelling probe broke the aircraft was forced to divert to Rio de Janeiro, where it was detained.

By the beginning of June, 5 Brigade was landing at San Carlos and preparations began to move elements of 2 Para to Fitzroy and Bluff Cove, just south-west of Port Stanley. With only one Chinook available, plans were made to bring up the Scots and Welsh Guards by ship, but in two sorties the Chinook lifted 156 men of 2 Para on 2 June.

The weather continued to impede air activity, but the Sea Kings maintained a constant vigil around the Task Force, while on the island a range of helicopters kept up a regular flow of supplies and casevac sorties as the Paras and Commandos pressed relentlessly on towards Port Stanley. These trips were not without risk: in the early hours of 6 June, Gazelle XX377 of 656 Sqn was shot down, reportedly by British naval fire but probably by an Argentinian missile, while delivering supplies to Mount Pleasant.

From 1 April RAF Hercules of the Lyneham Transport Wing had begun their support of *Corporate*, flying stores down to Gibraltar and latterly Ascension. Work was put in hand urgently to extend the range, as it was foreseen that the type would have to support the task force by air from the island base. Four aircraft had extra tanks fitted, while by the end of the conflict six had been fitted with in-flight refuelling probes. Work was also started on converting some to tanker configuration, but these were not completed until after the war.

REINFORCEMENT

The first longer-range Hercules flew its first successful sortie in support of the task force on 8 May, dropping equipment to HMS *Plymouth* in a 17 hr 10 min round trip. The drops to the task force were undertaken by crews from 47 Sqn, supported by some from 70 Sqn: as the Special Forces unit, 47 Sqn was trained in tactical support. Nos 24 and 30 Sqns maintained the less glamorous but equally important freight runs between the UK and Ascension. The first air-refuelled sortie was on 16 May, carrying parachutists and equipment to HMS *Antelope*, taking 24 hrs 5 min. The longest sortie was flown on 18/19 June, lasting 28 hrs 4 min.

Meanwhile additional Harriers for 1 Sqn made the long flight from Ascension direct to HMS *Hermes*. The FAA conducted several Canberra night-bombing sorties on Port San Carlos, and on 7 June a Learjet reconnaissance aircraft was brought down over Pebble Island by a Sea Dart from HMS *Exeter*.

In moving the Guards to Fitzroy by ship, the vessels were exposed without adequate air defence or natural cover, and furthermore the anchorage at Port Pleasant was within sight of Argentinian positions. The two assault ships *Fearless* and *Intrepid* were initially used, together with the LSLs *Sir Galahad* and *Sir Tristram*. Their positions were reported and, perhaps not surprisingly, they were subjected to heavy air attacks on 8 June. The weather had cleared, and on the mainland urgent plans were put in hand to mount a series of raids.

In the first strike, *Grupo 5* was to put up eight aircraft to attack the ships, supported by six Daggers of *Grupo 6* and with four Mirages of *Grupo 8* making a raid on San Carlos to distract the waiting Sea Harriers. Refuelling problems reduced the A-4B force to five aircraft, but all got through to Port Pleasant at 13.50 hrs, where they bombed the two LSLs. *Sir Galahad* was hit, and in the explosions and ensuing fire forty-three Welsh Guardsmen and seven seamen were killed, with many more suffering serious injury. *Sir Tristram* was also seriously damaged.

In subsequent rescue attempts, the Sea Kings of 825 NAS, involved in off-loading stores, played a major part. The unit had been commissioned on 7 May at Culdrose with the HAS.2 model rapidly converted to transports, and it had arrived in the Falklands only days earlier to support the overworked HC.4s of 846 NAS.

While crossing Falklands Sound, the Daggers spotted HMS *Plymouth* in an exposed position and turned to attack her, causing disabling damage. The Mirages did indeed draw the Sea Harriers in their strike on San Carlos, but they dashed off before the naval fighters could close. All the aircraft returned safely to their bases.

The second strike was planned for 16.45 hrs, this time by sending four *Grupo 5* aircraft against shipping with four *Grupo 4* machines armed with anti-personnel weapons while Mirages flew top cover. The defences were now prepared, however, and after one A-4B had attacked and destroyed a landing craft from *Fearless* between Fitzroy and Goose Green, the Sea Harriers of 800 NAS brought down three aircraft in as many minutes at Choiseul Sound. The *Grupo 4* aircraft escaped without causing damage, and the Mirages refused to be drawn into battle.

The next four days were taken up with supporting 3 Commando Brigade and 5 Brigade in reaching their positions for the final assault on Port Stanley. On the 12th, 3 Para fought a vicious battle for Mount Longdon, losing twenty-three dead and forty-seven wounded, while 2 Para moved to Wireless Ridge. The Welsh Guards and 42 Commando held Mount Harriet, with 45 Commando on Two Sisters and 22 SAS on Murrel Heights.

The Harriers were now able to fly more sorties, although there had been a minor setback on 8 June when XZ989 made a heavy landing at the FOB, putting the strip out of action for several hours. On the 10th, the first attempt at using laser-guided bombs (LGB) against strongpoints failed through target-marking problems. Early on the 12th, HMS *Glamorgan*, providing NGS, was hit and seriously damaged by a ground-launched MM.38 Exocet, losing her Wessex HAS.3. Shortly afterwards, Port Stanley shook as Vulcan XM607 made the final *Black Buck 7* raid on the airfield, using conventional airburst bombs.

Later in the day, a Wessex HU.5 of 845 NAS made a risky attack on the town hall at Port Stanley, where, it was thought, a major conference was taking place. One AS.12 ASM hit the neighbouring police station, while a second missed any target. On the 13th the FAA reciprocated with an attack on the British 3 Commando Brigade HQ on Mount Kent by A-4B Skyhawks of *Grupo 5*. No targets of significance were hit, and most of the aircraft were damaged by ground fire, although all returned to base. In the last Argentinian raid of the war, at 22.55 hrs, Canberra B.62 B-108 of *Grupo 2* was shot down over Mount Kent by a Sea Dart fired by *Exeter*. The two days 12 and 13 June saw some of the bitterest fighting on the ground as 2 Para, supported by Scouts firing SS.11 missiles, fought for Wireless Ridge.

In the aftermath of the war the services were busy with mopping-up tasks. This was the scene at Port Stanley Racecourse FOB in June with in the foreground Sea King HC.4 ZA291/VB of 846 NAS and in flight Sea King HAS.5 XZ578/21 of 826 NAS. *(Crown copyright)*

To the south, men of the Scots and Welsh Guards and Gurkhas were heli-lifted to Mount Harriet, from where they were to attack Tumbledown Mountain. At midday, Harriers made the first successful LGB attack on a company HQ on Tumbledown, marked by a forward air controller (FAC); later, in a second attack, a 105 mm gun was taken out at Moody Brook. Fighting around Tumbledown lasted into the 14th. With Port Stanley surrounded, two Harriers left *Hermes* at midday for an LGB strike on Sapper Hill. At the last minute they were advised to return: white flags were appearing in Port Stanley. By the afternoon the war was over, the surrender being signed at 23.59 hrs GMT.

SOUTH THULE

There was one last task to follow the reoccupation of the Falklands: the recovery of the base at South Thule on the South Sandwich Islands. In 1976 the Argentine military had established a weather station on this British territory, and despite diplomatic action they had refused to remove it.

On 15 June HMS *Yarmouth* (one Wasp) and RFA *Olmeda* (three Sea Kings) were sent to South Georgia to pick up Marines of 42 Commando. Further troops and a mortar crew went aboard HMS *Endurance* (two Wasps) which then joined the other vessels plus the tug *Salvageman* for the journey south. The base at South Thule was retaken without fighting on 20 June in the final act of the short war.

ANALYSIS

The outcome of the war was critically dependent upon the use of sea power, properly supported by air power, to place highly trained ground forces in the right place at the right time. The British supply lines were at all times stretched, and the sinking of a single merchantman created considerable difficulties. With the loss of two destroyers, two frigates, an LSL and a container ship, much was learned about the vulnerability of modern warships.

The carriers played a crucial role: without them the invasion could not have proceeded. The Sea Harriers offered the best protection to the task force, even without the benefit of AEW. From 1 May to 14 June they flew 1,335 sorties, of which about 1,135 were CAPs; twenty-seven AIM-9Ls were fired, scoring twenty-four hits and destroying nineteen aircraft, including eleven Daggers and Mirages. Gunfire accounted for six aircraft at the lower end of the speed spectrum.

The Harrier family proved remarkably robust, with few losses to enemy action. SAM systems were generally less effective, the ground-based variety especially so because of the difficulty of firing horizontally in close proximity to friendly shipping. The Sea Dart accounted for seven aircraft, and Seawolf three, plus possibly an incoming Exocet. Stinger, Blowpipe and Rapier brought down one aircraft apiece.

The Falklands conflict also demonstrated the full range of helicopter roles and the importance of this type of aircraft. The loss of three of the four heavy-lift Chinooks on *Atlantic Conveyor*, together with all spares, tools and manuals, placed a considerable burden on the remaining machine, which performed remarkably, and the utility Sea Kings which between them logged more than 4,600 hours. The lighter helicopters operated in a range of roles, making more than 400 casevac flights alone.

The task force was protected from submarine threat by two squadrons of Sea King HAS, plus Wessex, Lynxes and Wasps of the ships' flights. The Sea Kings undertook 2,253 sorties from 1 May, including record airborne flights.

The long distances involved in supporting a range of activity meant a heavy dependence on airborne refuelling, both between the UK and Ascension and south from Ascension. During the conflict, Vulcan bombers were refitted with probes, and Hercules and Nimrods were adapted in record time. The refuelling load fell on the Victors of 55 and 57 Sqns, who between them flew over 600 sorties in 3,000 hours, with only six missions aborted through equipment failure. By way of contrast, the FAA, operating its fighters at extreme ranges over the Falklands, lost a high proportion of sorties through lack of AAR. To supplement the Victors, work was put in hand to convert Hercules and Vulcans as tankers, but these were delivered too late to see active service.

The Hercules transports flew 13,000 hours, including, from 16 May, forty-four refuelled airdrops to the task force. The Nimrods flew 111 sorties, again including many at extreme range, while the Harriers of 1 Sqn, which relied on air refuelling to reach their 'base' on *Hermes*, flew 126 sorties in 3½ weeks.

From the time that the decision to send the task force south was taken, many developments were designed and tested, and became operational, in amazingly short periods. Apart from refuelling probes, the Nimrods were equipped to use the AIM-9 AAM and AGM-84 ASM supplied by the United States, and Harriers were fitted for the AIM-9 and with electronic support measures (ESM). Not surprisingly, however, in view of the complexity of the task, the most needed facility, AEW, could not be provided in time, although two Sea King HAS. 2s were fitted with Searchwater radars and were operational within eleven weeks, sailing south with HMS *Illustrious* in August 1982.

The Argentinian government must have weighed the decision to invade the Falklands in political rather than military terms. Given a British determination to fight, even at a distance of 8,000 miles, Argentinian equipment was no match for the range of hardware deployed by the British. Argentina's aircraft were old and generally second-hand, and spares were a major difficulty. Without modern electronic aids, they operated at extreme range, generally unable to carry defensive armament; furthermore, their weapons often failed.

Despite an appalling loss rate, the Argentinian pilots pressed home their attacks with great skill and determination, achieving considerable success against well-armed and modern ships. The military and civilian transport crews were flying into Port Stanley to the last minute, usually at night. FAA combat aircraft flew 2,782 hours, transports 7,719 hours and others, including civilian aircraft 1,953 hours. Of 505 combat sorties planned, 445 were launched, but only 280 reached their targets. The CANA mounted six Super Etendard and 34 A-4Q sorties.

There has subsequently been controversy about the benefit and cost of the *Black Buck* sorties, fuelled by inter-service rivalry and 20-20 hindsight vision. The cost was obviously phenomenal in terms of aircraft hours, aircrew stress, fuel and organization. The immediate physical benefits were relatively light and could perhaps have been achieved by Harrier or Sea Harrier sorties. The message to the Argentine command, however, was potent and compelling: if we can hit the Falklands we can hit the mainland.

There has also been considerable disinformation in respect of support to the UK from Chile and the USA. Intelligence was almost certainly supplied by both, and it seems likely, from circumstantial evidence, that some RAF reconnaissance aircraft were based in Chile. Certainly UK–Chilean relations were markedly different before and after the campaign. It is alleged that on 8 June, when the forces landing at Port Pleasant were caught unawares by FAA aircraft, the long-range radar near Punta Arenas in Chile was out of action for maintenance. No. 39 Sqn received battle honours, but there was no reported sighting of their aircraft, or those of 51 Sqn, on Ascension. The Canberras reportedly flew from Belize, which was also alleged to be the transit base for several RAF Hercules in spurious Chilean Air Force markings.

SEQUEL

Recovery of the Falklands Islands demonstrated peculiarly British qualities in abundance. Success required the strongest and unwavering political will, unambiguous rules of engagement, military experience, planning, administration, delegation, improvisation, innovation, hard work and not least huge individual courage. It was fortunate that the operation came at a time just before the UK government was about to close dockyards, de-commission warships and disband squadrons, and when there remained some manufacturing capability and capacity.

Such an operation would be inconceivable today. For that reason alone the UK maintains a small but expensive garrison on the Falklands, despite the fact that the colony has little strategic value. However, that garrison is vulnerable, and if captured and properly invested it would give the occupiers a sound base from which to prevent any recovery.

BAe SEA HARRIER

The P.1127 undertook sea trials on board HMS *Ark Royal* in 1963, but it was some time before the project reached fruition, and then only because the Navy was denied conventional carriers. A VTOL aircraft could, however, utilize the so-called 'through-deck cruiser' which had managed to escape political oversight; thus was born the Sea Harrier. Twenty-four Sea Harriers were ordered in May 1975.

The **FRS Mark 1** was closely based on the RAF's GR.3, with about 90% commonality. The naval version had Blue Fox radar, requiring a modified forward fuselage and better placed cockpit. As many as possible of the magnesium components were replaced by aluminium, tie-down lugs were fitted to an otherwise unchanged undercarriage and the brakes and V/STOL handling were improved.

There was no prototype, and the first production aircraft made its first flight on 20 August 1978. Armament comprised four AIM-9L AAMs plus twin 30 mm cannon under-fuselage pods in the fighter role or up to 8,000 lb of stores on four underwing pylons and the two fuselage mounting points. The type joined 800 NAS in March 1980 and was replaced in front-line service by the FRS.2 by 1994.

Fighter units equipped – 800, 801, 809, 899

The **F/A Mk 2** (also originally **FRS.2**) was a potent upgrade of the earlier version, incorporating Blue Vixen radar in a revised nose, improved avionics and provision for the carriage of AIM-120 AAMs. The first aircraft was a FRS.1 conversion, which flew on 19 September 1988.

Fighter units equipped – 801, 809

BOEING-VERTOL CHINOOK

The RAF had had a long-standing need for a medium-lift helicopter to replace the Belvedere when the American Boeing-Vertol 114 CH-47 Chinook was ordered in 1978. The version supplied was equivalent to an improved CH-47C with better flight-control systems and a triple cargo hook; it also operated at a higher weight limit than the basic type. Thirty-three were ordered, and the first machine flew on 23 March 1980. Four were sent to the Falklands in 1982, of which three were lost with the sinking of *Atlantic Conveyor*; replacements were ordered, together with a supplementary batch of five, and so the eventual delivery was forty-one. In addition one Argentinian CH-47C was captured and brought to the UK, where it remained in store for some time.

The Chinook **HC Mark 1** entered service with 240 OCU in January 1981, and subsequently served in the UK, Germany and the Falklands. The first fifteen aircraft had metal rotor blades and the balance composite ones. The crew of four included two pilots and two crewmen but no navigator.

Transport units equipped – 7, 18, 78; 1310 Flt

The **HC Mark 2** was a major upgrade of the HC.1 to CH-47D standards, with new dynamic parts and instruments, improved self-defence, including provision for machine-gun mountings and a long-range fuel system. All remaining HC.1 aircraft were due for conversion, and these eventually totalled thirty, of which one was written off in a crash. The first conversion flew in the UK on 20 May 1993. A further six new aircraft were ordered.

Transport units equipped – 7, 18, 78

WESTLAND WASP

The Wasp had its origins in the Westland P.531 Skeeter successor for the Army, later to be named Scout, and which flew in 1958. Trials of the new type were conducted by the Army and Navy, the latter ordering three P-531-0/N prototypes; after assessment of these the improved P.531-2 was built, by now named Sprite by the manufacturer, and with the Nimbus engine, skid undercarriage and a changed body. The Royal Navy ordered the type as the Wasp in autumn 1961; the main difference from the Scout was the fitting of four castoring wheels in place of the skid undercarriage.

The first pre-production **HAS.1** flew on 28 October 1962, and the type joined 829 NAS in March 1964. The Wasp was bought for use as an extension of the anti-submarine frigate, and was cleared for use from the small stern platforms of these warships. The first unit was to be the parent organization for the small ship flights, and as such had a large number of helicopters on charge.

The Wasp did not have any form of detection equipment, but acted as the 'killer' element of various hunter/killer combinations. The 'hunter' element might include the host ship, the larger Wessex or land-based

Shackleton. The Wasp's weapons included two Mk 44 torpedoes or two Mk 11 depth charges or the AS-12M missile. After service in Borneo and the Falklands the type was replaced by the Lynx in 1988.

ASW unit equipped – 829
Utility – 845, 848

Falkland Islands/Malvinas, 1982

Unit	Aircraft	Home Base	From	To
THE FORWARD BASE – WIDEAWAKE AIRFIELD, ASCENSION ISLAND				
RAF				
LTW[1]	Hercules C.1, C.3	Lyneham	2.4.82	19.8.83
10 Sqn	VC-10 C.1	Brize Norton	3.4.82	31.7.82
18 Sqn	Chinook HC.1	Odiham	5.5.82	31.5.82
42 Sqn	Nimrod MR.1	St Mawgan	6.4.82	5.11.82
KMPW[2] det	Nimrod MR.2	Kinloss	13.4.82	19.8.82
55 Sqn	Victor K.2	Marham	18.4.82	12.3.85
57 Sqn	Victor K.2	Marham	18.4.82	12.3.85
WBW[3] det	Vulcan B.2	Waddington	29.4.82	14.6.82
1 Sqn	Harrier GR.3	Wittering	3.5.82	24.5.82
29 Sqn	Phantom FGR.2	Coningsby	25.5.82	14.7.82
202 Sqn	Sea King HAR.3	Lossiemouth	9.5.82	7.9.82
FAA				
820 NAS[4]	Sea King HAS.5	HMS *Invincible*	5.4.82	17.4.82
845 NAS D Flt	Wessex HU.5	Yeovilton	11.4.82	10.82
CIVIL CHARTER				
British Airways	Boeing 707	Heathrow	18.4.82	18.4.82
Tradewind	Boeing 707	Stansted	18.4.82	18.4.82
Heavylift	Belfast	Stansted	4.4.82	83

NOTES
1 Lyneham Transport Wing 24, 30, 47 and 70 Sqns
2 Kinloss Maritime Patrol Wing 120, 201 and 206 Sqns
3 Waddington Bomber Wing 44, 50 and 101 Sqns
4 Aircraft of various flights passing through but aiding storing

Unit	Aircraft	Base	From	To
RAF FURTHER AFIELD – LIKELY BUT UNSUBSTANTIATED				
39 Sqn	Canberra PR.9	Belize, Punta Arenas	4.82	6.82
51 Sqn	Nimrod R.1	San Felix, Punta Arenas	4.82	22.5.82
LTW	Hercules C.1	Belize, Santiago	4.82	6.82
TASK FORCE				
FAA[1]				
Offensive				
800 NAS	Sea Harrier FRS.1	HMS *Hermes*	5.4.82	3.7.82
801 NAS	Sea Harrier FRS.1	HMS *Invincible*	5.4.82	28.8.82
809 NAS	Sea Harrier FRS.1	HMS *Hermes, Invincible, Illustrious*	18.5.82	21.10.82

Unit	Aircraft	Base	From	To
Anti-submarine				
820 NAS	Sea King HAS.5	HMS *Invincible*	5.4.82	28.8.82
826 NAS	Sea King HAS.5	HMS *Hermes*	5.4.82	26.8.82
826 NAS det	Sea King HAS.5	RFA *Fort Austin*	17.5.82	3.6.82
826 NAS det	Sea King HAS.5	San Carlos	3.6.82	23.6.82
737 NAS	Wessex HAS.3	HMS *Antrim, Glamorgan*[2]	12.4.82	29.6.82
815 NAS	Lynx HAS.2	Type 42 destroyers. Leander, Type 21, 22 frigates		
829 NAS	Wasp HAS.1	HMS *Endurance,* Type 12 frigates		
Utility				
824 NAS A Flt	Sea King HAS.2A	RFA *Olmeda*	5.4.82	27.6.82
824 NAS B Flt	Sea King HAS.2A	Gibraltar	29.3.82	7.6.82
824 NAS C Flt	Sea King HAS.2A	RFA *Fort Grange*	7.5.82	17.9.82
825 NAS[3]	Sea King HAS2, 2A	*Queen Elizabeth 2, Atlantic Causeway* Port San Carlos	12.5.82	13.7.82
846 NAS	Sea King HC.4	HMS *Hermes, Fearless,* Ascension, *Elk*	5.4.82	19.5.82
846 NAS	Sea King HC.4	*Canberra, Norland,* HMS *Intrepid, Fearless*	19.5.82	23.5.82
846 NAS	Sea King HC.4	San Carlos, Stanley Racecourse, HMS *Fearless, Intrepid, Canberra*	23.5.82	3.7.82
845 NAS A Flt	Wessex HU.5	RFA *Resource,* Teal Inlet, Stanley Racecourse	6.4.82	29.6.82
845 NAS B Flt	Wessex HU.5	RFA *Fort Austin,* various ships, Port San Carlos	8.4.82	13.7.82
845 NAS D Flt	Wessex HU.5	Ascension, HMS *Intrepid*	10.4.82	17.9.82
845 NAS C Flt	Wessex HU.5	RFA *Tidespring*	11.4.82	22.4.82
		RFA *Tidespring, Fort Grange,* Port San Carlos	14.5.82	3.7.82
845 NAS E Flt	Wessex HU.5	RFA *Tidepool,* San Carlos	5.5.82	12.7.82
847 NAS A Flt	Wessex HU.5	RFA *Engadine,* Port San Carlos	10.5.82	24.9.82
847 NAS B Flt	Wessex HU.5 Port San Carlos	*Atlantic Causeway*	13.5.82	24.9.82
848 NAS A Flt	Wessex HU.5	RFA *Regent,* HMS *Endurance*	19.4.82	24.8.82
848 NAS B Flt	Wessex HU.5	*RFA* Olna	10.5.82	21.8.82
848 NAS C Flt	Wessex HU.5	RFA *Olwen,* Navy Point, RFA *Fort Austin*	16.6.82	16.10.82
848 NAS D Flt	Wessex HU.5	*Atlantic Conveyor,* RFA *Tidepool, Astronomer*	25.4.82	3.7.82
RAF				
1 Sqn	Harrier GR.3	HMS *Hermes,* Port San Carlos	18.5.82	26.6.82

Unit	Aircraft	Base	From	To
18 Sqn	Chinook HC.1	*Atlantic Conveyor*, HMS *Hermes*, Port San Carlos	25.4.82	22.3.83
Royal Marines				
3 CBAS C Flt	Gazelle AH.1	RFA *Sir Galahad,* various shore bases	29.4.82	23.6.82
3 CBAS A Flt	Gazelle AH.1	RFA *Sir Geraint, Sir Tristram,* various shore bases	29.4.82	24.6.82
3 CBAS M Flt	Gazelle AH.1	RFA *Sir Percivale,* various shore bases	29.4.82	23.6.82
3 CBAS B Flt	Scout AH.1	RFA *Sir Lancelot, Sir Tristram,* HMS *Fearless,* RFA *Stromness,* various shore bases	29.4.82	24.6.82
3 CBAS 5 Flt	Scout AH.1	*Europic Ferry,* various shore bases	7.5.82	1.6.82
Army				
656 Sqn det	Scout AH.1	*Europic Ferry*[4]	25.4.82	7.5.82
656 Sqn det	Scout AH.1	*Baltic Ferry*	25.4.82	1.6.82
656 Sqn	Scout AH.1	various shore bases	1.6.82	2.8.82
656 Sqn	Gazelle AH.1	*Nordic Ferry,* various shore bases	9.5.82	2.8.82
	UH-1H	Stanley	16.6.82	13.7.82

NOTES

1 Date 'from' is when units first joined the ships from which they would operate
2 HMS *Glamorgan*'s Wessex destroyed 12 June
3 Ex-706 NAS aircraft with sonar, etc. removed and seats fitted
4 From 656 Sqn and returned to the unit

Unit	Aircraft	Home Base	From	To
POST 15 JUNE 1982 DEPLOYMENTS				
RAF				
29 Sqn	Phantom FGR.2	Stanley	17.10.82	30.3.83
23 Sqn	Phantom FGR.2	Stanley	30.3.83	21.4.86
		Mount Pleasant	21.4.86	31.10.88
1435 Flt	Phantom FGR.2	Mount Pleasant	1.11.88	7.92
	Tornado F.3	Mount Pleasant	7.92	date
HarDet[1]	Harrier GR.3	Stanley	6.7.82	16.8.83
1453 Flt	Harrier GR.3	Mount Pleasant	27.8.83	30.6.85
18 Sqn	Chinook HC.1	Kelly's Garden	23.3.83	20.8.83
1310 Flt	Chinook HC.1	Kelly's Garden	20.8.83	22.5.86
202 Sqn	Sea King HAR.3	Navy Point	27.8.82	20.8.83
1564 Flt	Sea King HAR.3	Navy Point	20.8.83	22.5.86
78 Sqn[2]	Sea King HAR.3, Chinook HC.1, HC.2	Mount Pleasant	1.5.86	3.12.07
1312 Flt	Hercules C.1K	Stanley, Mount Pleasant	20.8.83	31.3.96

Unit	Aircraft	Home Base	From	To
	Hercules C.1, VC-10 K.4	Mount Pleasant	1.4.96	date
FAA				
826 NAS D Flt	Sea King AEW.2A	HMS *Illustrious*	2.8.82	7.12.82
814 NAS	Sea King HAS.5	HMS *Illustrious*	2.8.82	7.12.82
845 NAS det	Wessex HU.5	HMS *Illustrious*	19.10.82	7.12.82
847 NAS	Wessex HU.5	Navy Point	25.6.82	24.9.82
845 NAS	Wessex HU.5	Navy Point	14.9.82	30.10.82
Army				
657	Scout AH.1, Gazelle AH.1	Port Stanley	2.8.82	11.86
Garrison Air Sqn	Gazelle AH.1	Port Stanley	11.86	date
Civilian				
BHL	S-61N	Stanley, Mount Pleasant	83	30.6.98
BHL	Do 228	Mount Pleasant	88	90
BIH	S-61N	Mount Pleasant	1.7.98	date

NOTES

1 Manned by 1, 3 and 4 Sqns and 233 OCU in rotation
2 Ex-1310 and 1564 Flts

7.8   PARACELS, 1988

BACKGROUND

The Paracel Islands, comprising some 130 small coral islands and reefs about a hundred miles across and seventy miles deep, sit in the South China Sea some 350 miles to the east of Vietnam and about the same distance from the Chinese island of Hainan. The islands are rich fishing grounds and are also claimed to have significant hydrocarbon deposits.

Because of their position and potential wealth they are claimed by both Chinas, Vietnam, Malaysia, the Philippines and Brunei; all but the latter have occupied one or more islands. Historically the Vietnamese probably have the most reliable claim, but in 1974 PRC forces attacked the Vietnamese garrison and killed seventy-five Vietnamese troops. Since then the Chinese have established a garrison of their own and a 2,500-metre airstrip on Woody Island.

A LOST FRIGATE?

On 23 August 1988 a Royal Navy Lynx HAS.3 helicopter of 815 NAS and the frigate HMS *Sirius* (F40) was fired on by Chinese troops on Triton Island, which is on the extreme south-west of the group. Quite what the vessel was doing in the area remains a mystery, as does the reason for the Chinese action.

Paracels, 1988

Unit	Aircraft	Base
FAA		
815 NAS	Lynx HAS3	HMS *Sirius*

CHAPTER EIGHT

Homeland Security

This shortest chapter is in some respects the most significant, since the events described paved the way for a transition in strategy and tactics. From the end of the Second World War the military shifted from a mainly conscript conventional force able to fight colonial wars in several regions simultaneously to a more limited and totally professional force. When the Cold War ended in 1990 – the end date for conflicts described in this book – British forces were primarily geared towards a major war in Europe, which might be conventional or with the employment of nuclear, chemical and biological (NCB) weapons. The Falklands campaign had been and gone, and by 1990 Britain was no longer capable of maintaining her NATO commitments *and* mounting a major independent expedition.

The conflicts over fishing rights between Britain and Iceland – NATO allies – committed a level of naval force which could not be matched by 1990, with up to nine frigates on station at a time. Even then damage through collision resulted in a high rate of attrition, but operational lessons were learned which would be put to good effect in the South Atlantic in 1982.

The 'troubles' in Northern Ireland were fuelled at an early stage by soldiers of the Parachute Regiment managing a serious demonstration with military force, resulting in the deaths of thirteen civilians. Put another way,

Several UK-based transport units were involved in transporting mail between major centres in 1955. These two Hastings, WD486/Y and WJ331/GAX are believed to be from 511 Sqn at RAF Lyneham. *(Author's collection)*

Based at Dishforth in Yorkshire was 30 Sqn with the Valetta. VW863 displays the form of transport unit markings on the fin. *(Author's collection)*

an élite fighting force was used to do police work, for which it was not trained. From that confrontational and conventional start, the forces and security services developed operational methods which were to lead to containment and eventually what appears to be peace in the Province.

This was not the first time that British forces were required to manage what has become termed asymmetric warfare. It was, though, the first time that such warfare was to be conducted at home. The characteristics of the conflict were that the enemy was not a nation; no war was declared; no true uniforms were worn; the protagonists could melt into the community with ease, even on the mainland; there were no rules of engagement; there was no Geneva convention; British military personnel were subject to civil law. Notwithstanding the constraints and peculiarities, British services gained invaluable experience and competence in covert operations, both passive and active.

Without in any way condoning, or apologizing for, the obscene barbarity of indiscriminate bombing, it must be said that the IRA campaign was both efficient and effective; the Loyalist response rather less so. To achieve major political aims very limited force was used and casualties were relatively slight; uncertainty, insecurity and disorder, on the other hand, cost the Government heavily in huge additional security, disruption to business and transport and loss of tourist income.

While it was an American who eventually brokered the Good Friday Agreement, successive US governments gave succour to the IRA 'freedom fighters', while the Irish-American communities, despite the best efforts of the Federal Bureau of Investigation (FBI), provided arms or the finances for buying them. Although several American tourists were killed in bombings in England, the impact of terrorism was not appreciated in the USA until 2001. From the bombing of the twin towers in New York national paranoia seems to have driven US policy towards the rest of the world, including the United Kingdom.

The lessons learned and systems applied in Northern Ireland were to prove of great importance in the so-called war on terrorism. In particular, and in relation to this book, the use of aircraft and helicopters for a variety of surveillance roles on a civilian population has become critical to the management of anti-terrorist warfare.

8.1   STRIKE BREAKING, 1955

From time to time the services have been required by government to handle any number of contingencies resulting from civilian industrial action, typically involving the public sector and emergency services. Aircraft have rarely been involved, but during a railway strike affecting the delivery of mail during May and June 1955, Transport Command aircraft flew more than 500 hours in Operation *Stagecoach* transporting mail between major cities.

In November 1977 in Operation *Burberry* RAF personnel covered a national fire service strike, together with personnel from other services.

In Operation *Ruddock* RAF police were deployed to several prisons following a national strike of prison officers from 10 October 1980.

8.2   SS *QUEEN ELIZABETH 2*, 1972

On 17 May 1972 the Cunard shipping line was advised that there were bombs aboard the liner SS *Queen Elizabeth 2*, then in mid-Atlantic: a $350,000 ransom was demanded. On the 18th a four-man team (an RAOC officer, one SAS trooper and two SBS men) were parachuted through low cloud next to the vessel from a Hercules C.1 of 47 Sqn from Lyneham. A communications link between the Hercules and the UK was provided by a Nimrod MR.1 of 42 Sqn from St Mawgan.

After a full search nothing was found, and in due course the US Federal Bureau of Investigation tracked down the culprit, who was gaoled. The event gives some idea of the British ability to mount small-scale but complex special operations at very short notice.

8.3   COD WARS, 1958–61, 1972–3, 1975–6

INTRODUCTION

On 28 August 1958, in an effort to protect one of her few industries, Iceland unilaterally extended her territorial waters from four to twelve miles. Five days later the Icelandic Coastguard (ICG) vessel *Thor* boarded and seized the trawler *Northern Foam* (GY490) within the new limit. Later in the day the frigate HMS *Eastbourne* (F73) counterboarded the trawler, secured the release of the fishermen and 'captured' the Icelandic boarding party, returning them in due course. NATO allies were now engaged in a conflict.

THE FIRST COD WAR

Following the boarding of *Northern Foam*, the Icelandic Coastguard tried to enforce the twelve-mile limit, and there were numerous boardings and other interventions over nearly three years. Throughout this time the Royal Navy usually had three warships and a Royal Fleet Auxiliary tanker in Icelandic waters in Operation *Whippet* in an attempt both to support British trawlers and also to ensure that they respected the legal limit. (Although the owners paid lip service to fishing limits, the crews were sometimes cavalier in their observance, given that they were paid by weight.)

While the RAF was not actively involved, the Shackletons of 18 Group maintained patrols in the area as usual, while the Icelandic Coastguard operated a Catalina flying-boat (TF-RAN) from Keflavik. The aircraft was used extensively through the dispute, and on several occasions dropped flares to warn trawlers to await boarding by ICG cutters. On 10 July 1960 the cutter *Òdinn* fired on and damaged the superstructure of the trawler *Grimsby Town*, but this was the only occasion on which shots were fired in anger.

In total, sixty-three British minelayers, frigates and destroyers were involved, in addition to ten RFA tankers. The dispute ended on 11 March 1962 when the British Government recognized the twelve-mile limit, but with special provision for fishing within the limit in restricted areas. British naval vessels remained on patrol to ensure that trawlers respected the new agreement. After the loss of four trawlers over the winter of 1967/8 the Board of Trade commissioned the trawler *Orsino* as a support vessel in Icelandic waters to provide, among other things, a meteorological service.

A NEW LIMIT AND A SECOND WAR

On 1 September 1972 Iceland again extended her fishing limit, now to fifty miles from the coast, despite the International Tribunal in the Hague ruling that it was not legal. But while the German Navy sent three tugs in support of her fishing fleet, the Royal Navy was not immediately sent into the disputed fishing grounds. However, after the ICG cutter *Ægir* cut the warps of *Peter Scott* (H103) on 5 September, the frigate HMS *Aurora* (F10) was sent on patrol, supported by RFA *Blue Rover*. During 1972 eight trawlers had their warps cut, resulting in extensive losses of equipment and time.

This new approach to deter fishing in disputed waters resulted in extremely close manoeuvring. Cutting warps was a dangerous task since it required the cutter to cut across the stern of the trawler fast and close. Inevitably there would be accidents, especially now that the ICG ships were bigger than in the 1958 dispute, three of them being around 1,000 tons. *Ægir*, *Òdinn* and *Thor* all had small helicopter decks to accommodate the Bell 47 helicopters now in service, and they each had one 47 mm and one 57 mm cannon. (*Ægir* and *Òdinn* were larger replacements for their earlier namesakes.) The smaller vessels *Albert*, *Àkavur* and *Tyr* carried cutting equipment but were lightly armed. The first accident occurred on 18 October, when *Ægir* rammed the stern of the trawler *Aldershot*. As a result a second frigate was now committed.

By now many British vessels were fitted with helicopter decks aft, and most carried a single Wasp helicopter from 829 NAS. This was fortunate when on 19 September HMS *Aurora* picked up a distress call from an Icelandic trawler and her Wasp rescued the five crew. There was a second rescue on 15 March when *Ægir* was aided by RAF Nimrods from Kinloss in searching for the crew of a lost Icelandic trawler.

Unless to engage in humanitarian tasks, the RN warships did not enter the fifty-mile zone. However, from January 1973 the British Ministry of Agriculture, Fisheries and Food deployed several civilian tugs in among the fishing fleets to come between the ICG gunboats and the trawlers. The number of warp-cutting incidents was now running at several a day. Although most of the frigates now operated helicopters, they were short-range Wasps, and a problem for the protection vessels was sound intelligence of the locations of the ICG gunboats. Therefore RAF Nimrod maritime patrol aircraft based in Scotland were used to provide information, but this resulted in a ban on British military flights using Icelandic airfields. The procedure adopted was for the patrolling aircraft to alert RN ships to the proximity of gunboats, whereupon the Wasp would be launched to help place warships in the best position to protect the fishing fleets.

In March 1973 the trawler *Brucella* (H291), which was one of three ships that had boxed in the gunboat *Arvakur*, was fired upon in a clear escalation of the dispute. The trawlers now requested direct naval support, and in view of a number of shooting incidents the decision was made to send warships into the fifty-mile limit. On 19 May 1973 Operation *Dewey* was implemented, and three frigates, HMSs *Cleopatra* (F28), *Lincoln* (F99) and *Plymouth* (F126), supported by the tugs *Statesman*, *Irishman* and *Lloydsman*, began operating within the limit.

There was further escalation on 25 May when *Ægir* fired a number of solid-shot rounds into the trawler *Everton*, which had refused to stop. HMS *Jupiter* (F60) arrived on the scene, and her Wasp transferred divers to the trawler to help repair the seriously leaking vessel.

The Nimrod patrols were stepped up to two a day, and occasionally to three, while there were now always three warships on patrol – two to the north-west and one to the south-east. Six classes of frigate and a sole destroyer were involved, of which the numerous Leander class, the Tribal class and Type 12 frigates all carried Wasp helicopters. The ships were deployed in such a way that one in each area carried a Wasp. Just as the RAF supported the RN in searching for gunboats, so the ICG operated its new F-27-200s in searching for offending trawlers.

Collisions began to occur from 7 June, when *Ægir* collided with HMS *Scylla* (F71); little damage was caused to either ship. Then on 21 June the tug *Lloydsman* cut across *Òdinn*'s bow, resulting in a collision and damage on the waterline. In July *Òdinn* retaliated by ramming HMS *Arethusa* (F38).

From 20 July the Nimrods were supplemented by Britannia transport aircraft of 99 and 511 Sqns. The latter were temporarily based at Kinloss, and carried Nimrod cockpit crew and observers; their use was to conserve airframe hours on the newly introduced Nimrods, which by now were exceeding their peacetime limits. The Britannias operated 10¼-hour sorties, transiting at height and flying around Iceland at 1,000 ft looking for rogue trawlers fishing within the twelve-mile accepted limit and searching for the ICG gunboats. From September the Wasps were also based on the larger RFA tankers, together with the more capable, radar-equipped, Wessex 3s of 737 NAS.

After a series of further collisions between gunboats and frigates, negotiations began and a truce was called. The RN and support tugs withdrew beyond the fifty-mile limit but remained until the end of November. The last RAF sortie was flown on 3 October 1973 as a NATO-driven two-year settlement was reached, and the airfield ban was lifted on 21 November.

THE THIRD WAR, 1975

On 15 October 1975, as the original two-year agreement was coming to a conclusion, Iceland yet again introduced a new limit, this time of 200 miles and pre-empting an international agreement. By now the ICG had added a further gunboat, *Tyr*, to its fleet, plus a stern trawler, the *Baldur*. Warp cutting restarted, and on 25 November Operation *Dewey* was reactivated.

In Operation *Heliotrope* the Nimrods were again soon in action patrolling around Iceland, building up a picture of the whereabouts of vessels friendly and less so. Iceland reintroduced the ban on British military aircraft using her airfields. There were plans to use Hercules and Hastings T.5 bombing trainers of 230 OCU transports to supplement the Nimrods, but in the event the Hastings were used, flying some twenty sorties out of a total of 178. Air traffic control was provided from Keflavik! Throughout the operation the aircraft undertook mail drops to naval vessels, in addition to the search tasks. Vulcan MRR.2 radar reconnaissance aircraft of 27 Sqn are also believed to have flown some sorties.

On 11 November there was an attack on British trawlers within the 200-mile limit, and by the 25th HMS *Brighton* (F106) and HMS *Falmouth* (F113) were on station. From now there could be as many as six frigates on station at any time from a total of twenty-two available, plus three support ships (from seven), nine tugs and three support vessels (*Hausa*, *Miranda*, *Othello*). The Icelandic vessels routinely cut the trawlers' warps, and there were numerous ramming incidents.

The operations continued much as in the second cod war, with the Nimrods and Hastings maintaining a wider

In the first Cod War aircraft from the Ballykelly Wing in Northern Ireland maintained a watch over the situation. Uncoded XF706 is from 203 Sqn. *(Author's collection)*

watch and the ship-based Wessex and Wasp helicopters specifically locating the gunboats from directions given by the fixed-wing aircraft. In addition, the Wasps occasionally flew very close to the gunboats, distracting them from navigation and buying precious time for the trawlers to pull in their trawls. Wherever possible the gunboats were marked by frigates in an endeavour to prevent them from warp cutting or worse. The ICG F-27s were also active keeping a watch on the location of British vessels, while both sides occasionally embarked the press aboard their aircraft in an attempt to win the media war.

On 20 January the warships were withdrawn and RAF surveillance suspended while negotiations took place, but this was short lived, and operations soon continued as before. Collisions were now commonplace, and among the more serious were those on 26 March when *Baldur* struck HMS *Diomede*, causing a twelve-foot split along the hull; on 24 April when HMS *Naiad*'s (F16) bow was damaged by *Tyr*; and on 6 May when HMS *Falmouth* (F39) was rammed in the bow by *Tyr*.

The situation deteriorated further on 11 May when *Ægir* attempted to board the trawler *Primella*, which immediately fled. The gunboat pursued and fired a number of shots around the vessel, as a result of which the Navy threatened attack from a patrolling Nimrod. A succession of Nimrod patrols was flown to shadow the *Ægir* until she disengaged. Further negotiations were held, but even then the ICG vessels continued to harass the trawlers, and further serious collisions ensued.

The damage to a significant number of frigates was so great that there was now a serious shortage, and training and trials vessels had to be deployed. Fortunately an agreement was reached, again brokered by NATO, and Operations *Dewey* and *Heliotrope* ended on 30 May 1976. This agreement limited British activity to twenty-four trawlers within the 200-mile zone at any time.

SEQUEL

The conflicts were totally economically driven, and the Icelandic position was quite understandable, given the fall in fish stocks and the fact that nearly 90% of her export earnings were derived from the fishing industry. The conflict was not one of shooting but of propaganda and seamanship, in which latter both sides displayed great competence.

Over-fishing beyond agreed limits has remained a sensitive area, and most EU countries with fishing grounds maintain extensive fisheries-protection assets, both maritime and airborne.

This was the first occasion on which helicopters had been used operationally – albeit within peacetime safety limits – in such severe weather conditions. Although the Wasps and Wessexes were restricted in the distances they could operate from vessels with helicopter decks, many valuable lessons were learned which were to prove of great value several years later in the Falklands War.

HAWKER SIDDELEY NIMROD

The maritime patrol HS 801 Nimrod was developed from the commercial Comet 4 airliner to meet Air Staff Requirement ASR381 in 1964. The prototype was built around the penultimate Comet 4C airframe, with a large, unpressurized, lower fuselage 'bubble' to accommodate the 48 ft weapons bay. Other major changes included four Spey engines and a revised fin and rudder with fin-mounted radome. First flight of the prototype was on 23 May 1967. From the outset the Nimrod was intended to be flown with the two inboard engines only while on patrol, and all systems are driven by these engines.

The Nimrod **MR Mark 1** entered service with the RAF (MOTU) in 1969. It was equipped with ASV21D radar, similar to that fitted to the Shackleton, and was capable of carrying nine Mk 44 or Mk 46 homing torpedoes, nuclear depth charges or conventional 1,000 lb bombs. Provision was made for the underwing carriage of two Martel or AS.12 missiles. The crew comprised eleven, including two pilots and a flight engineer. A range of contemporary navigation and weapons management systems was built in, including an Elliot 920 digital computer. A 70-million-candlepower searchlight was fitted in the starboard wing pod. Forty-six were built.

Maritime reconnaissance units equipped – 42, 120, 201, 203

Nimrod MR.1 XV229 of the Kinloss Wing on patrol over the North Atlantic. During the second Cod War the new Nimrods were supplemented by Britannias with additional Coastal Command observers. *(Crown copyright)*

The **MR Mark 2** was in effect a mid-life update of the MR.1. 35 airframes were converted and the first flew on 13 February 1979, although several airframes had earlier been fitted with new systems. The main external differences were the fitting of Loral ESM pods on the wingtips and an additional air intake below the fin for air cooling. Internal changes included replacement of the earlier radar with the much improved EMI Searchwater and a new twin Marconi AQS 901 acoustics system. The other major change was a new central tactical system. The new equipment increased all-up weight by 6,000 lb and the crew was increased to twelve.

The MR.2P variant was the post-Falklands fit with an in-flight refuelling probe above the cockpit. Auxiliary fins were added to the tailplanes to help improve stability during the physically tiring task of refuelling. Another recent change has been the introduction of the Harpoon anti-ship missile, carried in the weapons bay. The Nimrod was fitted with two Sidewinder AAMs during the Falklands war and this underwing fit was developed into a four-missile system from 1983.

Maritime reconnaissance units equipped – 42, 120, 201, 206

First Cod War

Unit	Type	Base
Iceland		
ICG	Catalina	Keflavik
RAF at January 1961		
203 Sqn	Shackleton MR.3	Ballykelly

Unit	Type	Base
204 Sqn	Shackleton MR.2c	Ballykelly
210 Sqn	Shackleton MR.2	Ballykelly
120 Sqn	Shackleton MR.3	Kinloss
Second Cod War		
Iceland from 1971		
ICG	F-27-200	Keflavik
ICG	Bell 47G, H	Keflavik
RAF		
120, 201, 206 Sqns	Nimrod MR.1	Kinloss
99, 511 Sqns	Britannia C.1	Kinloss temporarily from 7.73
FAA		
829 NAS	Wasp HAS.1	Type 12, Tribal and Leander frigates
737 NAS	Wessex HAS.3	RFA O and Tide class tankers
Third Cod War		
Iceland from 1975		
ICG	F-27-200	Keflavik
ICG	Bell 47G, H	Keflavik
RAF		
120, 201, 206 Sqns	Nimrod MR.1	Kinloss
230 OCU	Hastings T.5	Kinloss temporarily
27 Sqn	Vulcan MRR.2	Scampton
FAA		
829 NAS	Wasp HAS.1	Type 12, Tribal and Leander frigates
737 NAS	Wessex HAS.3	RFA O and Tide class tankers

8.4   NORTHERN IRELAND, 1969–2007

INTRODUCTION

The rifts between Catholics and Protestants, Republicans and Loyalists, in Ireland are impossible to untangle rationally. The twenty-six southern counties effectively achieved independence in 1922, leaving the six counties of Ulster an integral part of the United Kingdom. Sinn Fein insisted on a united, republican, Ireland, with its military arm, the Irish Republican Army (IRA), using terrorism to achieve political ends.

A series of incidents in the 1950s resulted in a detachment of AAC Auster AOP.6s of 1913 Flt to patrol the border with the Irish Republic. Several independent flights were also based at Aldergrove in the 1960s with the barely useful Skeeter helicopter and the Auster AOP.9. Also formed in late 1959 at

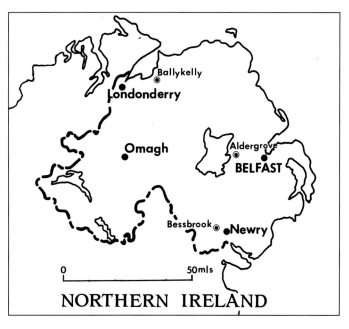

NORTHERN IRELAND

Early on the scene in Northern Ireland were the Sioux 'Clockwork Mice'; these three helicopters are from 666 Sqn.
(Museum of Army Flying)

Aldergrove was 118 Sqn with Sycamores serving in the SAR and Army support roles.

With the emergence of the Northern Ireland Civil Rights Association (NICRA) in the late 1960s, tension in the Province rose. In October 1968 there was a civil rights march in Londonderry in which seventy-seven civilians were injured in the police attempt to control the demonstrators. The August 1969 Apprentice Boys' March in Londonderry resulted in riots, and the Westminster Government was obliged to send troops to reinforce the Royal Ulster Constabulary (RUC). Operation *Banner* began.

THE 'TROUBLES' – CIVIL WAR

From 1969 there was considerable increase in the deployment of Army flying units to the Province, and from the outset these were equipped with a mix of Sioux AH.1 light helicopters and the more powerful Scout AH.1. The helicopters were based at Aldergrove, outside Belfast, Ballykelly to the east of Londonderry, Omagh, Long Kesh to the south of Belfast and for a time Sydenham in the centre of Belfast.

Most of the air units involved were rotated in from Germany or the UK on roulement typically lasting for four months, with the helicopters being flown into Northern Ireland direct via Carlisle, or in the case of the German-based units, being transported to Aldergrove on RAF Belfast and latterly Hercules transports. In addition to the bases, there were key landing sites at Bessbrook Mill, Enniskillen, Holywood and Portadown.

The conflict was three-way, involving the so-called Loyalists, whose military arms fought the IRA, the Republicans, whose military arms fought the Loyalists and the British Army, and the British services who were trying to support the police in maintaining law and order. (There is some evidence that on occasion the police and military colluded with the Loyalists in fighting the Republicans.)

Also active from the beginning of the 'troubles' was the Westland Scout which remained in the Province until supplanted by the Lynx. XW284/A shows the rugged simplicity of the design. *(Crown copyright)*

In order to pursue their battle, the Republican paramilitaries had to raise funds, mainly through criminal activities; purchase, import and then transport arms, explosives and ammunition; prepare bombs; place those bombs; set ambushes; handle casualties. In order to counter these activities, the security services needed to use helicopters for liaison between units; intelligence-gathering; pursuit; recording; placing troops; placing equipment and material; casualty evacuation; resupply of outposts.

While the Army helicopters could undertake many of the tasks, the Sioux was vulnerable, and the Scout, while more robust, was still a relatively small machine. So from the onset of the conflict the RAF based larger helicopters, detached from England, for the heavier lift functions.

The Army flying units were a mix of squadrons and decentralized air troops or platoons which operated penny numbers of Sioux, almost in the way that such units might have operated jeeps in the past. As the more capable and complex Scout came into service, it became clear that it was neither economic nor operationally effective to have small dispersed units, and so from 1969 plans were made to consolidate into full squadrons. The Army Air Corps became an independent fighting arm alongside infantry and cavalry units. The transition was slow, though, and not completed until 1979.

From the extensive table of units it will be noted that in general squadrons on roulement were based at Aldergrove and Long Kesh. From there Sioux and then Gazelle flights were detached to Ballykelly, while Scout detachments were based at Omagh. The Sioux detachments at Ballykelly were sometimes provided by the organic air squadrons. The air squadrons of armoured units operating in support of their units were based at Aldergrove, and then mainly Omagh, while the flights of 3 Commando Brigade Air Squadron (CBAS) supporting Royal Marine

Army Lynx fitted with *Helitele* realtime datalinked camera. New surveillance equipment, later of widespread application in the so-called 'war on terrorism', was pioneered in Northern Ireland. *(Crown copyright)*

deployments were mainly based at Aldergrove, Ballykelly and Sydenham. This last base operated between February 1973 and October 1977, but with gaps in basings.

Internment was introduced in 1971 and the conflict escalated. The situation worsened dramatically from 'Bloody Sunday', 30 January 1972, when thirteen civilians were killed in Londonderry by soldiers of 1 Para. The IRA responded almost immediately, placing a bomb in the Parachute Regiment officers' mess in Aldershot on 2 February, killing six civilians and a chaplain.

In March the Northern Ireland Assembly was abolished and the Province was ruled directly from Westminster. The security forces increased, to supplement the Royal Ulster Constabulary (RUC) and the locally raised Ulster Defence Regiment (UDR). In terms of death and carnage, 1972 was the worst year of the troubles, with 476 killed, including 149 servicemen and police. In that year 1,853 bombs were set and there were 10,564 shooting incidents.

Bombings and assassinations now continued to increase both within Ulster and further afield. In general, Loyalist paramilitaries targeted Catholics or Republicans, and confined their atrocities to the Province and to Eire. The Republican paramilitaries, on the other hand, were rather less discriminating, generally targeting Protestants, political opponents and the military, but with no concern for collateral damage among the civilian population. Bombing in the cities of mainland Britain now became commonplace, and continued throughout the peace process.

To provide a context for military involvement, a table of the more notable bombings is set out below.

Date	Location	Cost*	Comment
4.3.72	Belfast	2 ck 130 cw	Abercorn pub
20.3.72	Belfast	3 mk 3 ck 100 cw	City-centre car bomb
21.7.72	Belfast	2 mk 5 ck, 130 cw	22 car bombs 'Bloody Friday'
31.7.72	Claudy	9 ck	3 car bombs during Op *Motorman*

Date	Location	Cost*	Comment
17.5.73	Omagh	5 mk	Hotel bar
4.2.74	Yorkshire	9 mk 3 ck	M62 coach bomb
17.5.74	Dublin	26 ck 250 cw	UVF 3 car bombs
17.5.74	Monaghan	7 ck	UVF car bomb
17.6.74	London	11 cw	Houses of Parliament
17.7.74	London	1 ck	Tower of London
5.10.74	Guildford	4 mk 1 ck	Pub bomb
14.11.74	Coventry	1 ck	Bomber killed premature explosion
21.11.74	Birmingham	21 ck	2 pubs bombed
5.9.75	London	2 ck	Hilton Hotel
9.10.75	London	1 ck	Green Park station
18.11.75	London	2 ck	Chelsea restaurant
17.2.78	Castlereagh	12 ck	La Mon House Hotel
27.8.79	Mullaghmore	3 ck	Lord Mountbatten
27.8.79	Warrenpoint	18 mk	2 bombs
20.7.82	London	11 mk	Hyde Park, Regents Park
6.12.82	Ballykelly	11 mk 6 ck	Droppin Well pub
17.12.83	London	3 mk 3 ck	Harrods bomb
12.10.84	Brighton	5 ck	Conservative Party Conference
28.2.85	Newry	9 mk	Police station
8.11.87	Enniskillen	11 ck	Remembrance Day
22.9.89	Deal	11 mk	Marines' training base
7.2.91	London	—	10 Downing St mortar attack
10.4.92	London	3 ck	Baltic Exchange 100 lb Semtex
20.3.93	Warrington	2 ck 56 cw	2 young boys killed
24.4.93	London	-	Bishopsgate station bomb
24.4.93	London	1 ck 40 cw	Natwest Tower
9.3.94	London	-	Heathrow a/p mortar attacks 3 days
9.2.96	London	2 ck c50 cw	South Quay, Docklands
18.2.96	London	3 ck	Aldwich bus bomb: prem detonation
15.6.96	Manchester	200 cw	Arndale centre destroyed
13.8.98	Omagh	29 ck	Car bomb
22.9.00	London	-	MI6 HQ rocket attack

* m = military, including police, c = civilians, k = killed, w = wounded

In general the response to the endless rounds of shootings and bombings rested with the police, the military and the intelligence services. There were obvious limitations to the use of aircraft in the fight against a very small number of activists, who for much of the time were living anonymously within their communities.

ESCALATION

While secret meetings were being held between Government ministers and the IRA in London in June, in Londonderry and Belfast sectarian groups had barricaded areas, where police and military were denied access. Several short-lived ceasefires were offered by the IRA while the talks were progressing, but frustrated at progress they set twenty-two car bombs in Belfast city centre on 21 July 1972 – 'Bloody Friday' – which led to a speedy British response in Operation *Motorman*.

In the biggest British military operation since the Suez campaign of 1956, 12,000 troops supported by tanks and

The Lynx supplanted the Scout, first in AH.1 form and then as the AH.7. This version had shrouded exhausts and a TOW sight above the cockpit, but the missile fit itself would have been inappropriate for the counter-terrorist role. *(Author's collection)*

bulldozers cleared the barricades. The Republican response was an immediate bombing in the village of Claudy, which killed nine civilians of both persuasions.

The light helicopters were useful for monitoring activity and observation, while the heavier machines were valuable in moving troops quickly and in direct confrontation whenever the activists were caught out in the open countryside: hence the Scouts were based at Omagh, near 'bandit' country. The Army and RAF helicopters, which were unarmed, performed a range of difficult tasks: they maintained a watch on demonstrations, assisted the security forces in emergencies and, in the case of the larger types, moved heavy supplies, such as concrete for new roadblocks. Many small Army posts were supplied by air, and troops were moved to and from ambush points by air.

The first fixed-wing Beaver detachment was based at Aldergrove from March 1972, to undertake a range of utility tasks, including photo-reconnaissance. Over the years the detachment became permanent in the form of 1 Flt, with the Beavers making way for the Islander in 1989. To give some idea of the intensity of aerial activity, in 1973 some 37,000 hours were flown by Army Air Corps aircraft. The Scouts and Sioux were averaging eighty hours monthly and the Beavers just over sixty.

Violence spilled over into England on 4 February 1974 when an IRA bomb exploded on a coach carrying British soldiers and their families. Twelve were killed. Later in the year bombs were placed in popular tourist destinations, including Westminster Hall and the Tower of London, and in pubs in Guildford (five killed) and Birmingham (twenty-one killed). There were more bombings in London throughout 1975, and then a pause for several years, but there was no let-up in Ulster.

From 1976 the Sioux was gradually replaced by the more capable Gazelle, equipped in due course with powerful Nitesun lights and Iiclitclc rcal-timc datalinked television cameras. Night-vision goggles were also in use, and the Beavers were fitted with various image-intensifying and recording and infra-red detection systems. From 1979 the Lynx AH.1 began replacing the Scout, providing faster response times and better load carrying.

Troop-moving capacity was still a problem, but as mentioned Wessex HC.2s of 72 Sqn RAF had been detached from their home base at Odiham, and the unit moved into Aldergrove, with a detachment at Bessbrook, in 1981.

The Wessex operated extensively in the dangerous countryside of South Armagh in support of regular Army units and the Special Air Service Regt (SAS), and several were damaged by ground fire.

For more extensive exercises the Wessex were supplemented by Puma HC.1s detached from 33 Sqn and by naval Sea Kings. Throughout much of the conflict the Irish Air Corps maintained regular border patrols using Alouette IIIs and Cessna-Reims FR.172Hs from Baldonnel and Gormanston respectively.

Successive attempts at finding a political solution through the late 1970s and early 1980s came to little, and the violence continued with the killing of eleven soldiers in two London bombings in July 1982 at a time when the Falklands War had eclipsed the troubles. There was an attempt on the British Prime Minister's life at the Conservative Party Conference in Brighton in which five were killed.

The flying was not without risk. At least twenty-five helicopters were lost in the Province from 1970, including four Sioux, three Scouts, five Gazelles, five Lynxes, three Wessex and four Pumas. Some of these were to accidents, but at least four were brought down by paramilitary weapons. With the knowledge that the IRA had acquired some SA-7 missiles, the Army fitted exhaust suppression kits to its helicopters, while the Lynx was fitted with the ALQ-177 infra-red jamming device to counter the possible use of IRA Stinger SAMs.

NORTHERN-IRELAND-RELATED CRASHES

Date	Type	Serial	Location	Other
4.9.70	Sioux	XT502	Aldergrove	4/7 RDG
8.2.72	Puma	XW214/CL	Aldergrove	33 Sqn ran into hangar
18.4.73	Sioux	XT174	Caledon	666 Sqn hit power lines
22.5.75	Puma	XW212	Aldergrove	Gearbox cowling detached
18.12.75	Sioux	XW195	Crossmaglen	652 Sqn CO killed
7.1.76	Scout	XV133	S Armagh	652 Sqn 2k
2.1.77	Sioux	XT241	River Bann	3 Flt hit wires
10.4.78	Scout	XV132	Lough Neagh	655 Sqn 1k
2.12.78	Scout	XW614	Lough Ross	669 Sqn 2k
18.2.80	Gazelle	XZ306	Lisburn	2k
1.12.82	Gazelle	XX400	Crossmaglen	655 Sqn hit power cable
25.10.85	Wessex	XT669	Armagh	72 Sqn hit radio mast
2.1.86	Lynx 1	XZ606/E	Bessbrook	Lost lift – heavy landing
13.1.88	Wessex	XT607	Crawfordsburn	72 Sqn
23.6.88	Lynx 7	XZ664	Silverbridge	665 Sqn force landed under fire
11.2.90	Gazelle	ZB687	Clogher	655 Sqn s/d MG fire
27.4.90	Wessex	XV719	Bishops Court	72 Sqn crashed during aerobatic manoeuvre
13.2.91	Lynx 7	ZE380		S/d damaged
26.11.92	Gazelle	ZB681	Bessbrook	665 Sqn collided with Puma
26.11.92	Puma	XW233	Bessbrook	230 Sqn midair with Gazelle 4k
19.3.94	Lynx 7	ZD275	Crossmaglen	655 Sqn s/d mortar fire
2.6.94	Chinook 2	ZD576	Kintyre	7 Sqn 29k
3.02	Puma		S Armagh	
22.12.03	Gazelle		Londonderry	665 Sqn

POLITICAL MOVEMENT

On 15 November 1985 the Anglo-Irish Agreement was signed. In return for recognition of Northern Ireland the Republic was given a consultative role on the future of the Province. But progress towards a lasting solution was slow, and each time the IRA ran out of patience it found justification for more outrages.

At a Remembrance Day parade in Enniskillen in 1987 a car bomb killed eleven civilians, and then eleven Marines were killed in an attack on the barracks at Deal in 1989. In early 1991 a mortar was fired from Whitehall into 10 Downing Street, the home and work base of the British Prime Minister, but it failed to do serious damage.

From 1994 there were more talks involving Sinn Fein around the issue of de-commissioning of IRA weapons, but every time the talks stalled there were further mainland bombings to remind the Government of IRA will and capability. The security services suffered a severe setback in June 1944 when Chinook ZD576 of 7 Sqn crashed into a hillside on Kintyre. It was taking the twenty-five personnel to a conference at Fort George near Inverness, and all on board, including the four crew, were killed. No conclusive reason for the crash has been determined.

The IRA called a cessation to all 'military operations' (implying some legitimacy to its activities) on 31 August 1994, and this was followed by the combined Loyalist paramilitaries doing the same on 13 October. As talks dragged on, the IRA ceasefire was called off on 9 February 1996 with the bombing of commercial buildings at South Quay, London docklands. More mainland bombings followed, with the centre of Manchester being devastated on 15 June when a 3,500 kg fertilizer bomb exploded, injuring over 200 but miraculously killing no one.

In 1998 agreement on a way ahead was at last reached with the so-called Good Friday Agreement. The US special envoy to Northern Ireland, George Mitchell, led peace talks involving all parties from October 1995, which culminated in the agreement. There were still setbacks, but the agreement was implemented on 2 December 1999, although not until after twenty-nine had been killed in a massive car bomb explosion in Omagh in August 1998. From now British forces were steadily withdrawn. The UDR had merged with the Royal Irish Rangers into the Royal Irish Regiment as far back as 1992, and there were changes in the construct of the police force in November 2001.

SEQUEL

Operation *Banner* finally came to an end on 31 July 2007. At the time of writing it is too soon to be confident that the troubles are over. There remains tension, but the situation has improved dramatically: there remain, though,

After the Beaver utility aircraft reached the end of its service life in 1989 it was replaced by the Islander with 1 Flt. These aircraft could transport six persons, but were increasingly used for a range of surveillance roles. ZG845 is fitted with underwing pods, the purpose of which is not clear. *(Author's collection)*

Army Islander ZG846 of 1 Flt in flight. The aircraft is fitted with a variety of sensors. *(Author's collection)*

those who will never be satisfied until there is a united Ireland, free from any British influence.

The Army Air Corps experience in Northern Ireland was invaluable both to the UK and its allies in countering terrorist activity across the world. Equipment and tactics were developed which continue to have wide application, both at home and abroad. In October 2006 5 Regiment AAC, the eventual successor to all Army flying units based in Ulster, was awarded the Sir Barnes Wallis Medal by the Guild of Airline Pilots and Air Navigators for its work over thirty-seven years, during which no fewer than 700,000 hours were flown.

WESTLAND (AGUSTA-BELL) SIOUX

The intended Skeeter replacement, the Scout, was delayed entering service, and although the Alouette had been ordered in small numbers to bridge the gap, especially in hotter climates, there was an urgent need for a simple helicopter for the Unit Light Aircraft role. The intention was to provide units at battalion level with their own organic airborne observation and liaison capability, a need partly dictated by a shortage of pilots coming forward from line regiments. In 1964 the twenty-year-old Bell 47G was evaluated against the Brantly B.2A, Hiller UH-12E and Hughes 269A. Two hundred of the Bell 47G-3B1 were ordered against Specification H.240, with the first fifty being delivered from Agusta and the remainder built by Westland under licence, but in the event many more were supplied.

The **AH Mark 1** was broadly similar to the US Army OH-13S. It went first to the School of Army Aviation at Middle Wallop, and the first operational machines went to air troops in the Far East. The Sioux carried a pilot and observer, and it saw active service in Aden, Borneo and Northern Ireland. Although unarmed, it was sometimes fitted with a 7.62 mm GPMG. It was eventually replaced by the Gazelle, by which time the organic flights had been disbanded.

Utility units equipped – 652, 653, 654, 655, 656, 657, 658, 659, 660, 661, 662, 663, 664, 665, 666, 667; 1, 2, 4, 5, 6, 7, 13, 11, 16, 17, 18, 20, 23 UNFICYP Flts; LG, QDG, 5 IDG, 9/12 L, 16/5 L, 17/21 L, 10H, 4/7

RDG, RAC Air Sqns; 1, 2, 4 Eng, 14/20H, 15/19H, 17/20 L, MELF, 1, 2, 4, 5, 6, 19, 25 Fld Regts RA, 14, 40, 45, 49 Lt Regts RA, 29, 95 (Commando) Lt Regts RA, 1, 3 RHA, RAC/RA, 1, 2, 3, 4 RTR, SG, Scots Greys Air Troops; GH, 2/2 GR; 2/6 GR, 2/7 GR, 10 GR, 1 IG, KOBR, 2, 7 Para, 1, 2 RA, 40, 41, 42, 45 RMC, 1 RNF Air Platoons

WESTLAND SCOUT

Saro began design work on a successor to the Skeeter in 1957, and the prototype P-531, G-APNU, flew on 20 July 1958. The new type was powered by the Turbomeco Turmo 600 turbine engine, built under licence by Blackburn. Both the Navy and Army were interested, and an early development, the P.531-2, by now named Sprite by the manufacturer, featured the Nimbus engine, skid undercarriage and a changed body. When Westland absorbed Saro the type was renamed Scout.

The Scout **AH Mark 1** was powered by a Turmo engine, and flew on 9 August 1959. Eight pre-production aircraft were ordered, the first flying on 29 August 1960. Development of the engine caused delays with service entry, resulting in a limited Alouette purchase. The Scout carried five people including the pilot, could take a 7.62 mm GPMG, and from 1970 was equipped with four SS-11 anti-tank missiles, making it the first formally armed aircraft flown by the Army. The Scout was withdrawn from use in 1994 after more than thirty years of service in Aden, Borneo, Germany, Northern Ireland and the Falklands campaign.

Utility units equipped – 651, 652, 653, 654, 655, 656, 657, 658, 659, 660, 661, 663, 664, 665, 666; 2, 3, 6, 7, 8, 9, 10, 11, 13, 14, 15, 17, 19, 21, 26, 27, 31, 131 Flts; 3 CBAS

For rapid and secure troop movements RAF Wessex of 72 Sqn were deployed to Aldergrove from 1969. XT672/X and XT687/R display the unit marking on the tail. *(Author's collection)*

Northern Ireland, 1969–2007

Unit	Aircraft	Base	From	To
Army – leading into the conflict				
1913 Flt	Auster AOP.6	Aldergrove	14.2.57	8.57
13 Flt 651 Sqn	Auster AOP.6	Aldergrove	8.57	2.11.62
	Skeeter AOP.12		2.60	2.11.62
2 Flt	Skeeter AOP.12,	Aldergrove	60	1.11.62
	Auster AOP 9			
2 RTR Flt	Skeeter AOP.12,	Aldergrove	2.11.62	11.64
	Auster AOP.9			
QDG AS	Skeeter AOP.12,	Aldergrove	11.64	8.66
	Auster AOP.9			
	Sioux AH.1		8.66	3.69
Army – the height of the conflict and roulement 1969–79				
Aldergrove 8 Infantry Brigade				
660 Sqn	Scout AH.1		24.1.70	14.4.70
653 Sqn	Scout AH.1		21.10.70	19.2.71
664 Sqn	Sioux AH.1, Scout AH.1		19.2.71	8.6.71
665 Sqn	Sioux AH.1, Scout AH.1		7.6.71	7.10.71
666 Sqn	Sioux AH.1, Scout AH.1		6.10.71	15.12.71
663 Sqn	Sioux AH.1, Scout AH.1		14.12.71	15.4.72
651 Sqn	Scout AH.1		17.2.72	17.6.72
664 Sqn	Sioux AH.1, Scout AH.1		15.4.72	15.8.72
653 Sqn	Sioux AH.1, Scout AH.1		14.8.72	14.12.72
665 Sqn	Sioux AH.1, Scout AH.1		15.12.72	10.4.73
666 Sqn	Sioux AH.1, Scout AH.1		13.4.73	15.8.73
663 Sqn	Sioux AH.1, Scout AH.1		14.8.73	2.12.73
664 Sqn	Sioux AH.1, Scout AH.1		15.12.73	15.4.74
653 Sqn	Scout AH.1		17.4.74	15.8.74
665 Sqn	Scout AH.1		15.8.74	13.12.74
666 Sqn	Scout AH.1		14.12.74	14.4.75
663 Sqn	Sioux AH.1, Scout AH.1		15.4.75	15.8.75
664 Sqn	Sioux AH.1, Scout AH.1		15.8.75	15.12.75
653 Sqn	Scout AH.1		15.12.75	12.4.76
659 Sqn	Sioux AH.1, Scout AH.1		12.4.76	12.8.76
651 Sqn	Gazelle AH.1, Scout AH.1		12.8.76	11.12.76
665 Sqn	Sioux AH.1, Scout AH.1		11.12.76	12.4.77
659 Sqn	Gazelle AH.1		12.4.77	16.8.77
662 Sqn	Gazelle AH.1, Scout AH.1		16.8.77	12.12.77
658 Sqn	Gazelle AH.1, Scout AH.1		12.12.77	12.4.78
651 Sqn	Gazelle AH.1, Scout AH.1		12.4.78	15.8.78
663 Sqn	Gazelle AH.1, Scout AH.1		15.8.78	13.12.78
669 Sqn	Gazelle AH.1, Scout AH.1		11.12.78	11.4.79
662 Sqn	Gazelle AH.1, Scout AH.1		11.4.79	13.8.79
664 Sqn	Gazelle AH.1, Scout AH.1		12.8.79	12.12.79
654 Sqn	Scout AH.1, Lynx AH.1		12.10.79	12.2.80
655 Sqn	Scout AH.1		10.79	10.82
17/21 Lancers AS	Sioux AH.1		3.69	5.11.71

Unit	Aircraft	Base	From	To
1 RTR AS	Sioux AH.1		14.12.75	12.4.76
45 Cdo AS	Sioux AH.1		1.6.70	1.9.70
45 Cdo AS	Sioux AH.1		9.8.71	30.8.71
45 Cdo AS	Sioux AH.1		17.10.71	3.12.71
45 Cdo AS	Sioux AH.1		12.7.72	28.7.72
42 Cdo AS	Sioux AH.1		9.8.72	31.8.72
Beaver det/Flt	Beaver AL.1		3.72	10.73
655 Sqn det	Beaver AL.1		10.10.73	17.2.74
6 Flt det	Beaver AL.1		8.2.74	17.6.74
669 Sqn det	Beaver AL.1		10.6.74	10.10.74
6 Flt det	Beaver AL.1		10.10.74	9.2.75
669 Sqn det	Beaver AL.1		10.2.75	10.6.75
6 Flt det	Beaver AL.1		10.6.75	10.10.75
669 Sqn det	Beaver AL.1		10.10.75	2.76
6 Flt det	Beaver AL.1		2.76	24.3.76
Beaver Flt	Beaver AL.1		24.3.76	31.10.79

Ballykelly 39 Infantry Brigade

Unit	Aircraft	Base	From	To
1 PWO Regt AS	Sioux AH.1		28.4.69	21.8.69
8 Flt[1]	Scout AH.1		18.8.69	30.9.69
666 Sqn	Sioux AH.1 Scout AH.1		1.10.69	24.1.70

The RAF Wessex was more powerful than naval variants, using twin Gnome turbines. It was capable of carrying sixteen troops. XT674/AY of 72 Sqn showing the later style of code. *(Author's collection)*

Unit	Aircraft	Base	From	To
660 Sqn det	Scout AH.1		24.1.70	14.4.70
17/21 Lancers AS det	Sioux AH.1		12.4.70	29.6.70
665 Sqn det	Sioux AH.1		16.9.71	7.10.71
666 Sqn det	Sioux AH.1		6.10.71	15.12.71
663 Sqn det	Sioux AH.1		14.12.71	15.4.72
664 Sqn det	Sioux AH.1		15.4.72	15.8.72
653 Sqn det	Sioux AH.1		14.8.72	1.12.72
658 Sqn	Sioux AH.1		1.12.72	2.4.73
659 Sqn	Sioux AH.1		31.3.73	2.8.73
17/21 Lancers AS	Sioux AH.1		1.8.73	2.12.73
657 Sqn	Scout AH.1		1.12.73	20.3.74
661 Sqn	Sioux AH.1		25.3.74	1.8.74
14/20 RH AS	Sioux AH.1		31.7.74	29.11.74
657 Sqn det	Sioux AH.1		29.11.74	26.3.75
658 Sqn det	Sioux AH.1		27.3.75	10.6.75
664 Sqn det	Sioux AH.1		10.6.75	14.12.75
660 Sqn det	Sioux AH.1		1.7.75	31.10.75
1 RTR AS det	Sioux AH.1		14.12.75	12.4.76
659 Sqn det	Sioux AH.1		12.4.76	12.8.76
651 Sqn det	Gazelle AH.1		12.8.76	11.12.76
665 Sqn det	Sioux AH.1		11.12.76	12.4.77
659 Sqn det	Gazelle AH.1		12.4.77	16.8.77
662 Sqn det	Gazelle AH.1		16.8.77	12.12.77
658 Sqn det	Gazelle AH.1		12.12.77	12.4.78
651 Sqn det	Gazelle AH.1		12.4.78	15.8.78
653 Sqn det	Gazelle AH.1		12.6.78	13.10.78
663 Sqn det	Gazelle AH.1		13.10.78	13.10.78
669 Sqn det	Gazelle AH.1		11.12.78	11.4.79
42 Cdo AS	Sioux AH.1		1.12.71	14.2.72
42 Cdo AS	Sioux AH.1		13.6.72	18.10.72
40 Cdo AS	Gazelle AH.1		30.3.78	12.10.78
	30.3.79		13.8.79	
42 Cdo AS	Gazelle AH.1		13.8.79	30.1..79
Long Kesh 3 Infantry Brigade				
663 Sqn	Sioux AH.1, Scout AH.1		29.6.70	29.10.70
14/20 RH AS	Sioux AH.1		10.8.71	18.10.71
SDG AS	Sioux AH.1		17.10.71	17.2.72
657 Sqn	Sioux AH.1		16.2.72	17.6.72
651 Sqn det	Scout AH.1		17.2.72	17.6.72
661 Sqn	Sioux AH.1, Scout AH.1		15.6.72	15.10.72
654 Sqn	Sioux AH.1, Scout AH.1		15.10.72	15.2.73
655 Sqn	Sioux AH.1, Scout AH.1		15.2.73	15.6.73
660 Sqn	Sioux AH.1, Scout AH.1		15.6.73	15.10.73
662 Sqn	Sioux AH.1		15.10.73	15.2.74

Unit	Aircraft	Base	From	To
669 Sqn	Scout AH.1		17.10.73	15.2.74
659 Sqn	Sioux AH.1		15.2.74	21.6.74
652 Sqn	Scout AH.1		15.2.74	21.6.74
658 Sqn	Sioux AH.1		21.6.74	2.11.74
655 Sqn	Scout AH.1		21.6.74	2.11.74
651 Sqn det	Scout AH.1		28.8.74	30.6.75
662 Sqn det	Sioux AH.1		31.10.74	28.2.75
654 Sqn det	Scout AH.1		31.10.74	28.2.75
659 Sqn det	Sioux AH.1		28.2.75	30.6.75
652 Sqn det	Scout AH.1		31.10.75	2.3.76
662 Sqn det	Sioux AH.1		1.11.75	2.3.76
661 Sqn	Gazelle AH.1, Scout AH.1		1.3.76	2.7.76
654 Sqn	Gazelle AH.1, Scout AH.1		2.7.76	1.11.76
658 Sqn	Gazelle AH.1, Scout AH.1		1.11.76	12.2.77
655 Sqn	Scout AH.1		12.2.77	12.6.77
662 Sqn	Gazelle AH.1		12.6.77	12.10.77
661 Sqn	Gazelle AH.1, Scout AH.1		12.10.77	12.2.78
657 Sqn	Gazelle AH.1, Scout AH.1		12.2.78	12.6.78
653 Sqn	Gazelle AH.1, Scout AH.1		12.6.78	13.10.78
659 Sqn	Gazelle AH.1, Scout AH.1		13.10.78	14.2.79

The Pumas of 33 Sqn were detached to Northern Ireland from service delivery in 1971. Their payload was similar to that of the Wessex, but they were faster and longer-legged. XW235/CP of 33 Sqn at Aldergrove. *(Author's collection)*

Unit	Aircraft	Base	From	To
655 Sqn	Gazelle AH.1, Scout AH.1		14.2.79	13.6.79
652 Sqn	Gazelle AH.1, Scout AH.1		13.6.79	12.10.79
45 Cdo AS	Sioux AH.1		1.7.74	5.11.74
Omagh				
8 Flt det	Scout AH.1		18.8.69	30.9.69
666 Sqn det	Scout AH.1		1.10.69	24.1.70
651 Sqn	Scout AH.1		30.11.72	1.4.73
652 Sqn	Scout AH.1		31.3.73	1.8.73
651 Sqn	Scout AH.1		27.7.73	1.4.74
661 Sqn	Scout AH.1		1.4.74	2.8.74
655 Sqn	Scout AH.1		1.8.74	29.11.74
652 Sqn det	Scout AH.1		27.11.74	26.3.75
663 Sqn det	Scout AH.1		15.4.75	15.8.75
664 Sqn det	Scout AH.1		15.8.75	15.12.75
653 Sqn det	Scout AH.1		15.12.75	12.4.76
660 Sqn det	Scout AH.1		1.7.75	5.9.75
659 Sqn det	Scout AH.1		12.4.76	12.8.76
651 Sqn det	Scout AH.1		12.8.76	11.12.76
665 Sqn det	Scout AH.1		11.12.76	12.4.77
662 Sqn det	Scout AH.1		16.8.77	12.12.77
658 Sqn det	Scout AH.1		12.12.77	12.4.78
651 Sqn det	Scout AH.1		12.4.78	15.8.78
663 Sqn det	Scout AH.1		15.8.78	13.12.78
669 Sqn det	Scout AH.1		11.12.78	11.4.79
662 Sqn det	Scout AH.1		11.4.79	13.6.79
654 Sqn det	Scout AH.1		12.10.79	12.12.79
655 Sqn det	Gazelle AH.1, Scout AH.1		10.79	
17/21 Lancers AS det	Sioux AH.1		29.6.70	5.11.71
16/5 QRL AS	Sioux AH.1		3.11.71	17.5.73
14/20 RH AS	Sioux AH.1		17.9.72	17.10.72
1 RTR AS	Sioux AH.1		17.5.73	22.11.74
13/18 Hussars AS[2]	Sioux AH.1		18.11.74	21.5.76
9/12 Lancers AS	Sioux AH.1		22.5.76	25.11.76
3 Flt det	Sioux AH.1		25.11.76	11.77
	Gazelle AH.1		15.10.77	10.79
Sydenham				
42 Cdo AS	Sioux AH.1		14.2.73	14.6.73
40 Cdo AS	Sioux AH.1		14.6.73	14.10.73
664 Sqn det	Sioux AH.1		15.12.73	15.4.74
42 Cdo AS	Sioux AH.1		20.2.74	12.6.74
666 Sqn det	Sioux AH.1		14.12.74	14.4.75
663 Sqn det	Sioux AH.1		15.4.75	15.8.75
664 Sqn det	Sioux AH.1		15.8.75	15.12.75
662 Sqn det	Sioux AH.1		1.11.75	2.3.76
42 Cdo AS	Sioux AH.1		24.3.76	30.6.76

Unit	Aircraft	Base	From	To
665 Sqn det	Sioux AH.1		2.7.76	11.8.76
40 Cdo AS	Gazelle AH.1		18.8.76	16.12.76
45 Cdo AS	Gazelle AH.1		12.6.77	12.10.77

NOTES
1   Became 666 Sqn
2   13/18 Hussars Air Squadron provided service for 15/19 King's Royal Hussars

Army – Northern Ireland Regiment (from November 1979)

Unit	Aircraft	Base	From	To
654 Sqn	Gazelle AH.1, Lynx AH.1	Aldergrove	10.79	12.2.80
655 Sqn	Scout AH.1	Aldergrove	10.79	6.82
651 Sqn	Gazelle AH.1, Lynx H.1	Aldergrove	12.2.80	11.6.80
653 Sqn	Gazelle AH.1, Lynx AH.1	Aldergrove	11.6.80	23.10.80
659 Sqn	Lynx AH.1	Aldergrove	11.6.80	9.3.81
669 Sqn	Gazelle AH.1	Aldergrove	11.6.80	9.3.81
654 Sqn	Gazelle AH.1, Lynx AH.1	Aldergrove	9.80	11.81
665 Sqn	Gazelle AH.1, Lynx AH.1, AH.7	Aldergrove	86	30.9.93
655 Sqn	Lynx AH.1	Aldergrove	91	
Beaver Flt	Beaver AL.1	Aldergrove	1.11.79	30.9.88
1 Flt	Beaver AL.1	Aldergrove	1.10.88	6.89
	Islander AL.1	Aldergrove	3.89	30.9.93
655 Sqn	Scout AH.1	Aldergrove	11.79	10.82
40 Cdo AS	Gazelle AH.1	Ballykelly	1.4.80	30.7.80
42 Cdo AS	Gazelle AH.1	Ballykelly	30.7.80	30.11.80
655 Sqn	Scout AH.1	Ballykelly	6.82	86
	Gazelle AH.1, Lynx AH.1	Ballykelly	10.82	92
655 det	Scout AH.1, Gazelle AH.1	Omagh	11.79	10.82

Army – 5 Regiment (from October 1993)

Unit	Aircraft	Base	From	To
665 Sqn	Gazelle AH.1	Aldergrove	1.10.93	
655 Sqn	Lynx AH.7	Aldergrove	1.10.93	
1 Flt	Islander AL.1	Aldergrove	1.10.93	

RAF (excluding Coastal Command units)

Unit	Aircraft	Base	From	To
118 Sqn	Sycamore HR.14	Aldergrove	1.9.59	14.4.61
72 Sqn det	Wessex HC.2	Aldergrove, Bessbrook	14.7.69	81
72 Sqn	Wessex HC.2	Aldergrove	12.11.81	3.02
	Puma HC.1	Aldergrove	24.1.97	3.02
33 Sqn det	Puma HC.1	Aldergrove	6.71	5.92
230 Sqn	Puma HC.1	Aldergrove	4.5.92	
7 Sqn det	Chinook HC.2	Aldergrove	9.93	

From 1977 the Nimrods of RAF Coastal Command were responsible for Britain's maritime security. Here, Nimrod MR.1 XV244 of 120 Sqn at Kinloss overflys a Soviet intelligence gathering trawler in August 1978. *(Crown copyright)*

8.5   FISHERIES, RIG PROTECTION AND MARITIME DEFENCE

INTRODUCTION

The seas around Britain have for centuries been defended against invaders, both territorial and economic. While the last attempt to invade physically was in 1940, the important fisheries around the UK have proved attractive to poachers from far and wide. The development of the offshore oil and gas industries from the late 1960s also offered targets for terrorists and therefore the need for protection.

FISHERIES PROTECTION

Prime responsibility for off-shore fisheries protection rests with the Royal Navy, which has maintained a series of vessels dedicated to the task over centuries. Through the post-war years RAF Coastal Command had concentrated on the growing Soviet submarine threat and search and rescue, but by 1962 there was growing concern about the intensity of Soviet fishing in British grounds, especially around the Faeroes.

The RAF was tasked with the job of monitoring the concentration of trawlers in the area in Operation *Chacewater*, which involved the Shackletons of the four squadrons of 18 Group based in Northern Ireland and Scotland. Numerous sorties were made from January 1963, and at the outset it was noted that a number of trawlers were not what they seemed to be.

The Soviet Union had adapted numerous trawlers for intelligence gathering as auxiliary general intelligence (AGI) ships. These operated wherever there were likely to be British or American nuclear submarines transiting, and they were also in evidence at the margins of exercises, monitoring radio and other transmissions. While they were in international waters there was little that could be done, but they became the focus of attention for the Shackleton units, for example in Operation *Tiara* in late April 1963. Later, the Shackletons worked in concert with the Victor SR.2s of 543 Sqn to target vessels identified on the high-flying reconnaissance aircraft's radar.

POLITICAL INCURSION

There was a bizarre incident in 1976 resulting in intrusion into UK airspace of a hijacked airliner. On 10 September a Trans World Airlines (TWA) Boeing 727 flight 355 from New York to Chicago was hijacked by Croatian Nationalists. Accompanied by a TWA 707, it was diverted to Montreal, Gander and Iceland, before being intercepted by a Nimrod of 42 Sqn and escorted across London to Paris.

Over London and Paris leaflets were dropped by the 727 and 707 respectively. The five hijackers gave themselves up to the French authorities.

OPERATION TAPESTRY

In 1976 there was European Economic Community (EEC) agreement to a 200-mile exclusive economic zone (EEZ) around the UK, which was then responsible for policing it. With the developing offshore oil and gas industry, there was also growing concern about the vulnerability of rigs to terrorist attack. Therefore from 1 January 1977 Operation *Tapestry* was launched, with thrice-weekly surveillance flights combining two functions. The first was checking all oil and gas rigs both physically and by radio to ensure their continued security. The second was to monitor the fishing grounds and check the identity of trawlers against an approved list.

Four patrol areas were established, (i) to the west of Rockall, (ii) north of Shetland, (iii) the North Sea and (iv)

To support the Nimrod fleet 27 Sqn was unique in operating the Vulcan B.2(MRR) (sometimes quoted as SR.2) maritime radar reconnaissance platform equipped with LORAN radar. XM595 was one of nine conversions.
(Crown Copyright)

the Channel and Western Approaches. Poachers would be photographed and referred immediately to the Royal Navy's Fishery Protection Service (FPS). The Kinloss units covered Areas (i)–(iii), while 42 Sqn and the OCU looked after Area (iv). In 1978 a Nimrod of 42 Sqn 'arrested' a Spanish trawler which was fishing illegally by directing it to Milford Haven. The Nimrods also checked vessels illegally discharging oil and waste at sea. In respect of rig protection the Nimrods kept in touch with their charges via the VHF maritime network, using the callsign 'Watchdog', and they were backed in several ways.

When the Victor B(SR).2 radar reconnaissance aircraft of 543 Sqn were required for conversion to the tanker role, nine Vulcan B.2 bombers were adapted for maritime reconnaissance task with LORAN C radio navigation and the deletion of terrain-following radar. The aircraft equipped 27 Sqn from 1973 to 1982, and spent most of their sorties tracking Soviet vessels off the northern and eastern coasts of Britain.

In the event that there was a real threat from hostile vessels the RAF maintained two Buccaneer squadrons equipped with Martel missiles and dedicated to the maritime strike role. In addition, 809 NAS with Buccaneers was also shore based at Honington when not aboard HMS *Ark Royal*, and was available for the anti-shipping task. Finally the Royal Marines maintained specialized units for the protection of rigs, latterly the Commachio Group, which also has responsibility for protecting the RN's submarine base at Faslane.

The oil rig protection element of Operation *Tapestry* ended in August 1985, and shortly afterwards the surveillance of fishing vessels was let to civilian contract – but still with the 'Watchdog' callsign. Throughout the period covered by Operation *Tapestry* and beyond, the Nimrods have also been engaged in monitoring suspect vessels either smuggling, drug running or bringing illegal immigrants into the UK.

Fisheries, Rig Protection and Maritime Defence

Operation *Chacewater*, 1963

Unit	Type	Base		
120 Sqn	Shackleton MR.3	Kinloss		
203 Sqn	Shackleton MR.2	Ballykelly		
210 Sqn	Shackleton MR.2	Ballykelly		
204 Sqn	Shackleton MR.2C	Ballykelly		

Operation *Tapestry*, 1977–85

Unit	Type	Base	From	To
42 Sqn	Nimrod MR.1	St Mawgan		6.84
	Nimrod MR.2	St Mawgan	6.83	
236 OCU	Nimrod MR.1, MR.2	St Mawgan		
120 Sqn	Nimrod MR.1	Kinloss		2.82
	Nimrod MR.2	Kinloss	4.81	
201 Sqn	Nimrod MR.1	Kinloss		2.83
	Nimrod MR.2	Kinloss	1.82	
206 Sqn	Nimrod MR.1	Kinloss		2.81
	Nimrod MR.2	Kinloss	2.80	
27 Sqn	Vulcan B.2(MRR)	Scampton		31.3.82
12 Sqn	Buccaneer S.2B	Honington		4.8.80
		Lossiemouth		4.8.80
216 Sqn	Buccaneer S.2B	Honington	1.7.79	4.7.80
208 Sqn	Buccaneer S.2B	Lossiemouth	1.7.83	
809 NAS	Buccaneer S.2D	HMS *Ark Royal*, Honington		12.78

CHAPTER NINE

The Middle East in the 1980s

This final chapter describing British application of air power during the Cold War sets the scene for operations beyond 1990 and for the future. The actions described all occurred in the Middle East and were the precursor to the emotively described 'war on terror'. But critically they all involve the UK as a minor player hanging on the coat-strings of the United States of America.

The intervention in Lebanon was a multi-national concern, but not one derived from an extant organization. The British contribution and deployment is interesting in several respects. It was small and symbolic, but fortunately could be launched and maintained from the nearby sovereign base at Akrotiri in Cyprus. It was, perhaps, the first significant occasion when airframes and aircrew were detached and deployed regardless of unit. Thus the best aircraft and the most appropriately trained aircrew worked together without the benefit of any unit tradition or esprit de corps. From now on this was to be a feature of British involvement overseas as the small numbers of units remaining in the RAF had to adapt to roles for which they were not trained or equipped. The problem was further compounded by the high unserviceability rates of most modern combat aircraft, and the fact that they operated in environments for which they were not designed.

The United States attack on Libya was not a British affair at all, in that it did not involve British forces. It was, however, launched from British air bases, highlighting the nature of the special relationship. It also resulted, directly or indirectly, in the destruction by bombing of the Pan American 747 over Lockerbie in Scotland. Its inclusion also demonstrates the American mindset at the time, and the impact of true global reach in terms of airpower.

In the First Gulf War between Iraq and Iran (1980–88), naval units from several Western nations were engaged in patrols of the Persian Gulf to protect shipping. The war threatened oil supplies, and the presence of the Royal Navy *Armilla* patrols, in collaboration with French and American vessels, ensured the safety of many of the tankers in the Gulf.

The final section in this book covers the Second Gulf War in 1990 and 1991. In a vast coalition, including many European and Arab nations and led by the United States, the will of the United Nations was pursued against a perceived tyrant and his invasion and occupation of a neighbouring country. The British contribution was significant, and in many respects specialized, sometimes filling gaps where other Allies lacked expertise or equipment.

By now, though, the RAF was reduced to such an extent that only composite units of relevantly trained crews and serviceable aircraft could be deployed. The professionalism of personnel in all three services left no doubt as to commitment, and the conflict showed how industry and the services can innovate and introduce new equipment when necessary.

9.1   LEBANON, 1983–4

INTRODUCTION

In 1974 civil war broke out in Lebanon, mainly between Muslim and Christian militias. In 1976 Syria invaded, ostensibly to help keep the peace. Then on 11 March 1978 a Palestine Liberation Organization (PLO) group landed by sea in Israel, hijacked a coach and killed thirty-six people. The Israeli response was to launch a limited assault into Lebanon to take out the PLO camps in the south of the country.

After the Camp David Agreement (September 1978), bringing peace between Israel and Egypt, the PLO stepped up its raids on Israel, which responded with air strikes against the camps. Syria moved forces into the Bekaa

Valley, including anti-aircraft weapons, and there were numerous dogfights between Israeli and Syrian aircraft over the next few years.

On 3 June 1982 there was an assassination attempt on the Israeli ambassador in London, triggering a planned invasion of Lebanon, which began on the 4th. By 3 July Beirut was blockaded, and water and supplies cut off, resulting in the withdrawal of PLO and Syrian forces from the capital.

The Israeli assault had been ferocious, and some 15,000 deaths resulted; weapons used included phosphorus shells and Rockeye cluster-bombs containing flechettes. As international concern grew, a multi-national force (MNF) was organized in an endeavour to stabilize the situation.

THE MNF

The multi-national force comprised elements from the United States, Great Britain, France and Italy. The first contingent of French paratroopers flew from Bastia, Corsica, in Transall C-160 transports of ET-64 on 19 August 1982, and six days later the first US Marines landed. This force could

not intervene in the fighting, and shortly after its arrival Israeli Defence Force (IDF) troops stood by as Christian Militia massacred 1,000 Palestinians in the Sabra and Chatila camps.

Around Beirut fighting broke out in August, and in attacks on the airport area on the 29th two US Marines were killed. The Americans responded with artillery and AH-1T Sea Cobra gunships of HMM-169. The amphibious assault ship USS *Iwo Jima* (LPH-2), with the 24th Marine Amphibious Unit embarked, was standing off Beirut, and as fighting continued the carrier USS *Dwight D Eisenhower* (CVN-69) sailed into Lebanese waters as the core of Carrier Task Force (CTF) 60.

Israeli forces began a gradual withdrawal from 4 September, and shortly afterwards further elements of the MNF moved into Beirut. The British force in Lebanon (BRITFORLEB) was both small and relatively late on the scene. In February 1983 one squadron of the Queen's Dragoon Guards was flown into Beirut by Hercules transports via Cyprus, where Phantoms of 56 Sqn on armament practice camp (APC) were put on quick-reaction alert (QRA).

Flown in from the UK to RAF Akrotiri in Operation *Pulsator* were six Buccaneer S.2Bs of 12 and 208 Sqns and three Chinook HC.1 heavy-lift supply helicopters. The individual Buccaneers, then operated in the maritime strike role, were selected as being trouble free and with long hours before maintenance was due. Crews current were selected from both squadrons and RAF Germany from among those with overland strike experience. The Chinooks and crews came from 7 Sqn and 240 OCU, and were fitted with extra internal fuel tanks for the three-day, 16½ hr transit from the UK.

The BRITFORLEB group of just under one hundred, with twenty Ferret scout cars and ten Land Rovers, was based in a block of flats in the suburbs at Hadath, and were supported by Chinook and Sea King helicopters: by now landing large transports at the International Airport was considered too risky. BRITFORLEB could also call on the Lynx helicopters from the Royal Navy frigates standing off.

The Buccaneers made low passes over Beirut from the 11th, while Super Etendards of the French *Aéronavale* were also active. The Buccaneers, which regularly overflew the flats unarmed, were equipped with ALQ-101 ECM pods, the Pavespike designator and AIM-9 AAMs: offensive weaponry would include Paveway laser-guided bombs (LGB) and four 1,000 lb bombs internally.

The Lebanese Air Force (FAL) made its first contribution to the fighting on the 16th, when three Hunter F.70s, operating from a temporary base north of Byblos, attacked Syrian and Druze anti-aircraft positions. One Hunter subsequently crashed in the sea, while a second crash-landed on RAF Akrotiri. On 22 September 1983 eight French Navy Super Etendard fighters from the carrier *Foch*, with two more flying top cover, attacked Syrian positions at Dahr al Baidar and Ain Dara. There had been plans to base a detachment of Italian Air Force F-104S Starfighters at Akrotiri, but the Cypriot authorities would not give their blessing.

On 23 October there were bomb attacks on US and French MNF forces in Beirut, during which 239 US Marines and fifty-eight French paras were killed. The attackers were Muslim extremists supported by Iran, and on 17 November fourteen Super Etendards from *Clemenceau* bombed Iranian troops at Baalbeck in retaliation.

On 3 December the Syrians fired no fewer than ten SAMs at a pair of F-14As of VF-32 while they were flying on a reconnaissance mission; the following day twenty-eight USN attack aircraft from the carriers USS *Independence* (CV-62) and USS *John F Kennedy* (CV-67) attacked Syrian positions on the Damascus road. There is some evidence that laser-guided weapons were used against targets illuminated from the ground. One A-6E (1152915/556AC of VA-85) and an A-7E (160738/300AE of VA-15) were shot down, after which air attacks were limited, although the battleship USS *New Jersey* (BB-62) fired her 16 in. guns against Syrian targets around Beirut.

The IDF/AF had continued its reconnaissance sorties with follow-up attacks where indicated. In an attack on Bhamdoun and Sofar on 20 November a Kfir was shot down, the pilot parachuting into British positions in Beirut. These two towns and Baalbeck were to remain targets for IDF/AF attacks during early 1984, as units

Buccaneers on the ramp at Akrotiri during the Lebanon crisis in 1983. On the left is XV865/865 of 208 Sqn and on the right XV168/168 of 12 Sqn. The combination of most reliable airframes and appropriately experienced aircrew formed the basis of the composite squadrons used later in the Gulf War. *(G Pitchfork)*

A Buccaneer makes a fast and low demonstration pass over the BRITFORLEB HQ at Hadath. *(G Pitchfork)*

based there harried the Israelis in their withdrawal. In February, having achieved little, the MNF began leaving Beirut to the warring Christian and Muslim militia. The Israelis continued to attack Syrian and Shi'ite Muslim targets throughout the period of their withdrawal from Lebanon, and they also carried out reprisal raids, attacking re-established PLO camps at Tripoli on 10 July 1985 in response to car-bomb attacks at Hasbaya and Nabatiyeh.

SEQUEL

From 1986 the IDF continued to attack suspected PLO training camps, generally from the air, and undertook reprisal raids for PLO actions against Israel. The civil war continued until 1990, but the Israelis remained in southern Lebanon until May 2000. In early 2005 there were several assassinations of prominent Lebanese, as a result of which the Syrians were obliged to leave the country. There was some further fighting between Israeli and Hezbollah forces in July 2006, after which the UN brokered a ceasefire. (During this brief conflict Chinooks of 27 Sqn were engaged in evacuating British nationals from Lebanon.) There remains a small United Nations force in southern Lebanon (UNIFIL), comprising some 9,500 troops from twenty nations.

Lebanon, 1983–4

Unit	Aircraft	Base	From	To
RAF				
12, 208 Sqns	Buccaneer S.2B	Akrotiri	10.9.83	26.3.84
7, 18 Sqns, 240 OCU	Chinook HC.2	Akrotiri	9.9.83	2.84
LTW	Hercules C1, C.3	Lyneham, Akrotiri	9.82	2.84
56 Sqn det	Phantom FGR.2	Akrotiri	9.83	12.83
84 Sqn	Wessex HC.2	Akrotiri	based	

Unit	Aircraft	Base	From	To
FAA				
846 NAS det	Sea King HC.4	HMS *Fearless* (L10), RFA *Reliant* (A131), Dhekelia	20.11.83	5.4.84
815 NAS	Lynx HAS.2	HMS *Glamorgan* (D19), HMS *Brazen* (F91)	9.83	11.83
815 NAS	Lynx HAS.2	HMS *Andromeda* (F57)	11.83	2.84
829 NAS	Wasp HAS.1	HMS *Achilles* (F12)	11.83	2.84
Italian Air Force				
50° Gr	C-130H	Pisa, Larnaca	9.82	2.84
98° Gr	G.222	Pisa, Larnaca	9.82	2.84
French Air Force				
ET61, 64	Transall C.160	Bastia, Larnaca	8.82	2.84
French Navy				
Foch **Air Group**				
11F, 14F, 16F, 17F	Super Etendard		9.82	10.83
12F	F-8E		9.82	10.83
Clemenceau **Air Group**				
11F, 14F, 17F	Super Etendard		10.83	2.84
United States Navy				
USS *John F Kennedy* (CV-67) with CVW-3 embarked 7.83–2.84				
VF-11	F-14A	100 AC		
VF-31	F-14A	200 AC		
VA-85	A-6E, KA-6D	500 AC		
VAQ-137	EA-6B	600 AC		
VAW-126	E-2C			
VS-22	S-3A	700 AC		
HS-7	SH-3H			
USS *Dwight D Eisenhower* (CVN-69) with CVW-7 embarked 8.83–3.84				
VF-143	F-14A	100 AG		
VF-142	F-14A	200 AG		
VA-12	A-7E	300 AG		
VA-66	A-7E	400 AG		
VA-65	A-6E, KA-6D	500 AG		
VAQ-136	EA-6B	600 AG		
VAW-121	E-2C			
HS-5	SH-3H	610 AG		
VS-31	S-3A	700 AG		
USS *Independence* (CV-62) with CVW-6 embarked 12.83–6.84				
VF-14	F-14A	100 AE		
VF-32	F-14A	200 AE		
VA-15	A-7E	300 AE		
VA-87	A-7E	400 AE		
VA-176	A-6E, KA-6D	500 AE		

VAQ–131	EA–6B	600 AE
VAW–122	E–2C	
HS–15	SH–3H	610 AE
VS–28	S–3A	700 AE

9.2   LIBYAN STRIKES FROM UK AIRBASES, 1986

The actions described in this section are primarily American. However, they were flown from British bases and had wide political impact as well as physical impact with the loss of the Pan Am 747 over Lockerbie. The operation is therefore described in some detail, illustrating as it does the 'special relationship' between the United Kingdom and the United States of America.

BACKGROUND

Muammar al-Qadhafi assumed control of Libya in September 1969; earlier, in 1967, Britain and the USA had been asked to vacate their air bases at El Adem and Wheelus Field respectively. In 1971 links with the Soviet Union were forged, and in 1972 British oil interests nationalized. By 1973 Libya was being supplied with Soviet arms, and in October territorial waters were unilaterally extended when the 3,200 square miles of the Gulf of Sirte (Sidra) to latitude 32° 30' N were declared Libyan. Shortly afterwards a USAF C-130 was attacked by Libyan fighters in the area.

In July 1977, coincidental with the Camp David peace accords between Israel and Egypt, Libya attacked the latter, the result being a stalemate. Then in January 1980 Libyan-backed rebels attacked Gafsa in Tunisia, and the US responded by supplying immediately to the Tunisian Air Force six Bell UH-1 helicopters and a C-130, and confirming an order for twelve F-5E fighters.

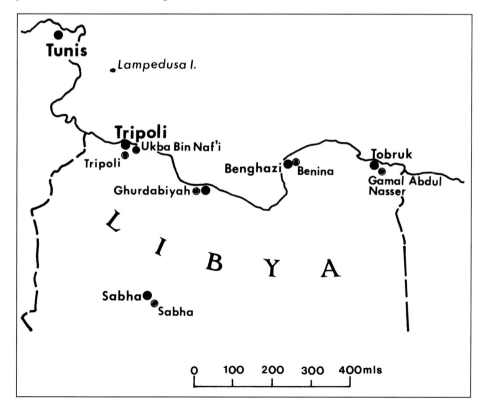

Meanwhile the US Sixth Fleet pointedly continued to exercise within the Gulf of Sirte. In one exercise on 19 August 1981, involving USS *Nimitz* and USS *Forrestal*, an E-2C of VAW-124 picked up a pair of LARAF fighters approaching the carrier group, and directed two F-14A Tomcats of VF-41 from *Nimitz*. The Libyan fighters, later identified as Su-22 'Fitter-Js', assumed aggressive attitudes, and one fired an AA-2 Atoll IR-seeking missile. This was successfully evaded by the Tomcats, the pilots of which in turn – and apparently exercising their own discretion – fired at least two AIM-9L Sidewinders. The result was the destruction of both LARAF aircraft and the loss of one pilot.

The Palestine Liberation Organization (PLO) extended its terrorist activities through the early 1980s. Perhaps frustrated by his inability to deal with the US militarily, Qadhafi had decided to increase pressure through subsidizing terrorism. In the autumn of 1985 the Italian-registered cruise liner *Achille Lauro* was hijacked and an American Jew killed.

In October the Israeli Air Force demonstrated its ability to hit the PLO by attacking its headquarters at Borj Cedria outside Tunis with a force of F-15 or F-16 fighters flying a 3,000-mile round trip from Hatzor and Tel Nof air bases. Both conventional 1,000 lb iron bombs and heavier, laser-guided munitions were used, and the building was wrecked, with many dead. Minutes before the attack the PLO leader, Yasser Arafat, had delayed his arrival at the HQ and thereby survived. The Americans also decided not to allow the PLO to go unpunished. Four of the terrorists who had taken part in the hijack were to be transferred from a military airfield outside Cairo on an Egyptair Boeing 737 to an unspecified destination.

While the present volume is about British services in action it would perhaps be incomplete without at least one photograph of a UK based US combat aircraft. On 15 April 1986 24 F-111F bombers took off from RAF Lakenheath to bomb Libyan targets. This shot, over the home base, shows off the *Pave Tack* marking system and *Paveway* guided bombs. *(USAF)*

The aircraft was picked up by a waiting E-2C of VAW-125 from the USS *Saratoga* (CV-60) and then intercepted south of Crete by two F-14As from VF-103. The F-14As subsequently handed the Boeing into the care of a second pair of Tomcats, and it was forced to land at the NATO air base at Sigonella. The terrorists were then handed over to the Italian government to stand trial. The PLO retaliated with two attacks on civilians at Rome and Vienna Airports on 27 December: nineteen people were killed, including five American citizens.

Washington declared that any PLO terrorism would be met with a 'strong US military reaction'. At the time, the Sixth Fleet comprised two carrier groups (CVW). Between Italy and Libya was CVW-13, based on the USS *Coral Sea* (CV-43), and further to the east was CVW-17, structured around *Saratoga*. Both carriers were operating two squadrons of F-14As and one of A-6Bs, together with support, but whereas *Saratoga* had two A-7E squadrons embarked, *Coral Sea* was operating the new F/A-18 in four squadrons.

The United States was not the only country targeted by Libya. The embassy in London (the Libyan People's Bureau) was a base for planning terrorist operations and was also the scene of occasional demonstrations by opponents to the regime. During one such on 17 April 1984 a gunman opened fire on the crowd from the embassy window, killing a policewoman. Controversially, after an eleven-day siege, the occupants were allowed to depart for Libya, and diplomatic relations were broken.

Through the 1980s the IRA received funding and arms shipments from Qadhafi, including automatic weapons, ammunition and Semtex explosive. In a compromised operation the small cargo-vessel *Eksund* was intercepted by French authorities in the Bay of Biscay and found to be carrying 120 tons of arms destined for the IRA, including twenty SAM-7 missiles, 1,000 AK47 automatic rifles and two tons of Semtex, all loaded at Tripoli. Progress of the vessel from the Mediterranean had been monitored by aircraft, but of what type and operator is not clear.

CONTINUED TERRORISM

Qadhafi, who was now maintaining no fewer than twenty-two terrorist training camps, responded to the US declaration by announcing a 'line of death' enclosing the Gulf of Sirte. The LARAF appeared to be one of the strongest air forces in the Mediterranean, but most aircraft were in storage in early 1986. The Soviet Union had built up large stockpiles in Libya, and the Soviet Air Force – *Voenno-Vozdushney Sily* (V-Vs) – maintained *Frontovaya Aviatsiya* (Frontal Aviation) units there to protect its interests. At least one squadron of Tu-22 'Blinder-As', one squadron of Su-20/22 'Fitter-Hs' and 'Ts' and perhaps a regiment of MiG-25 'Foxbat-As', 'Bs' and 'Rs' were operated from Ukba Bin Nafi (Wheelus) airfield.

Of the LARAF assets proper, transport and helicopter units were focused on Tripoli airport, with one or two squadrons of MiG-23 'Flogger-Fs' at Benina (Benghazi). Two squadrons of Mirage 5Ds, F.1ADs and F.1EDs operated from Gamal Abdul Nasser airfield outside Tobruk, while a small number of MiG-23 'Flogger-Es' were based at Ghurdabiyah near Sirte.

Although the air defence fighters were inadequate, the anti-aircraft equipment was formidable. For point defence there were ZSU-23-4 quad 24 mm radar-controlled cannon, M-53/59 twin cannon and Swedish 40 mm L/70 cannon. Sixty Crotale and 300 SA-2, -3 and -6 surface-to-air missiles were deployed with the recently acquired 185-mile range SA-5 Gammon radar-homing missile at several sites around the coastline.

On 24 March 1986, in Operation *Prairie Fire* aimed at provoking the Libyans, CVW-17 was exercising in the Gulf of Sirte. At 12.52 hrs GMT an SA-5 missile from a site near Sirte was fired at USN aircraft from USS *Saratoga* after two F-14As had turned away a pair of MiG-25s. The carrier group made immediate preparations to retaliate, and after two more SA-5s were launched the site was attacked by A-7E aircraft of VA-83, using AGM-88A HARM anti-radiation missiles. At least two radars were hit. USN surface units were also threatened by Libyan Navy attack vessels.

USS *America* (CV-66), with CVW-1, was on station to relieve CVW-17, and two A-6Es of VA-34 were launched to attack a French-built Combattante-II, Otomat-equipped patrol boat. It was sunk by direct hits with AGM-84 Harpoon missiles. Later in the evening several A-6Es attacked and sank a Nanuchka-II Class corvette. During the 25th there was continuing action, A-7Es again attacking SA-5 sites and causing more damage without loss, despite a further three missiles being launched in addition to at least one SA-2 from the Benghazi area. The cruiser USS *Yorktown* sank a further patrol boat, and a third was destroyed in an attack by A-6Es of VMA-533 from *Saratoga*. Action ended at 07.30 hrs GMT.

On 5 April La Belle discotheque in Berlin was blown up and a US serviceman was killed. There was evidence of Libyan complicity, and the US Government decided to act 'in exercise of the inherent right of self-defense recognized in Article 51 of the Charter of the United Nations'.

THE BRITISH CONNECTION

RAF Mildenhall was to be home to C-135C 612669 of the 4950th Test Wing (TW), USAF Systems Command, from 10 April 1986. At about the same time, several 55th SRW RC-135Ws and a sole RC-135V flew through, bound for Hellenikon AB, Greece, and the 922nd Support Squadron (SS). These aircraft, together with the EP-3Es and EA-3Bs of VQ-2 at Rota, Spain, were to pursue intelligence gathering, while the U-2Rs and TR-1As of Det. 3, 9th SRS, 99th SRW, at RAF Akrotiri on Cyprus and SR-71As of 1st SRW's Det 4 from Mildenhall were involved in the reconnaissance of possible target areas in Libya. It had been decided to mount an attack on Libyan military and terrorist targets, in Operation *El Dorado Canyon*.

Tanker aircraft also began arriving in the UK from bases and units across the United States. KC-10As of three units went to RAF Fairford (eight aircraft) and RAF Mildenhall (sixteen aircraft) between 11 and 13 April. RAF Fairford was also home to fourteen KC-135s, mainly -As, and Mildenhall hosted twenty of the type, including six -Qs. At Lakenheath, twenty-four F-111Fs of the 48th Tactical Fighter Wing (TFW) were also preparing to depart on what was to be a 5,500-mile round trip, France and Spain having denied the US the right to overfly their countries.

Included in the F-111F force, which took off from 18.36 hrs* on 15 April, were six back-up aircraft, which returned to their base after the first refuelling in the Bay of Biscay some time after 19.40 hrs. Also involved in the USAF attack force were five EF-111As of the 42nd Electronic Combat Squadron (ECS), 20th TFW, from RAF Upper Heyford. Of the five, two were standby aircraft, one of which returned to base after refuelling once, while the second apparently completed the trip.

The plan was for a joint USAF/USN attack. The specific targets for the UK-based USAF aircraft were the military side of Tripoli Airport (occupied by the Il-76 'Candids' used to transport terrorists and their equipment around the world, often under diplomatic cover), the Al Aziziyah Barracks, a command and control centre and Qadhafi's home, and Sidi Bilal, a training area which included a terrorist marine sabotage camp. The Sixth Fleet's targets in the eastern zone were the Al Jamahiriyah Barracks – an alternative to Al Azaziyah – and Benina air base.

Exact co-ordination was not of paramount importance, but it is believed that an EC-135E, possibly of the 7th Airborne Control and Command Squadron (ACCS), acted as a tactical command centre. Airborne early warning was provided for the F-111F force by an E-3A of the 960th Airborne Warning and Control Squadron (AWCS) of the 552nd AWCW, and for the naval aircraft by E-2Cs of VAW-123 (USS *America*} and VAW-127 (USS *Coral Sea*). EA-3Bs of VQ-2 from Rota are also believed to have been involved, with F-14A protection; these aircraft would have been on station by about 22.30 hrs. As the F-111F force approached Libya after a total of four air refuellings, the naval aircraft began taking off.

At 23.20 hrs USS *Coral Sea* launched six F/A-18s of VFA-132 and VMFA-323 for strike support; the ship also launched eight A-6Es of VA-196 and a single EA-6B. USS *America* launched six A-7Es of VA-46 and VA-72 equipped with AGM-88A HARM and AGM-45 Shrike anti-radiation missiles for defence suppression, six A-6Es of VA-34 and a single EA-6B of VAQ-135. The force from *Coral Sea*, with its EA-6B electronic countermeasures (ECM) support, attacked the airfield at Benina after AGM-88A HARM-equipped F/A-18s and *America*'s A-7Es had attacked air defence radars.

At least four MiG-23s were destroyed and many more damaged in the airfield strike; also destroyed were two Fokker F-27s (5A-DLP and -DLY) and two Mi-8 helicopters. Meanwhile, the A-6Es from *America* attacked Al Jamahiriyah Barracks, causing much damage. Both the airfield and barracks attacks were made at midnight, reportedly using conventional 500 lb and 750 lb bombs, although the A-6E is equipped to use both the 500 lb Snakeye

---

* Throughout this section, except where otherwise stated, the author has used British Summer Time (BST), which at the time was one hour ahead of Greenwich Mean Time (GMT), two hours behind local Libyan time and five hours ahead of US Eastern Standard Time (EST).

retarded-delivery and CBU Rockeye Mk. 20 cluster-bomb. By 00.13 hrs on the 15th, all naval aircraft reported returning, and all had recovered by 01.53 hrs. Two of the fourteen A-6Es launched aborted for unspecified reasons.

THE AIR FORCE STRIKES

Meanwhile, the F-111Fs had crossed the Libyan coast under the protection of the EF-111As to the west of Tripoli. They split into two groups, approaching their targets at 200 ft and 400 kts from the south. At midnight one group, by now comprising only eight out of an intended twelve aircraft, attacked Qadhafi's headquarters at Al Aziziyah barracks and the Sidi Bilal training camp.

The aircraft used their AN/AVQ-26 Pave Tack marking system to confirm targets and guide GBU-10 Mk 84 2,000 lb Paveway II bombs. Despite the normal efficiency of the equipment, there was considerable collateral damage south of the barracks to the embassies of Austria, Finland, France, Iran and Switzerland. The US claimed that the damage was caused by SAM boosters, but subsequently admitted a degree of responsibility.

The second group, of five aircraft, attacked the military side of Tripoli Airport with Mk 82 500 lb Snakeye retarded bombs, resulting in six Il-76s, a Boeing 727 and a G.222 being destroyed. The Soviet-controlled airfield at Ukba Bin Naf'i was carefully avoided. Shortly after the attack, at 01.00 hrs, an F-111F hit the sea twenty miles north of Tripoli. From the lack of radio transmissions it is assumed that the aircraft was not hit by anti-aircraft weapons; both crew members were killed, the only US casualties of the entire operation. At about 03.15 hrs a returning F-111F diverted to Rota AB with an overheating engine; it returned to the UK on 16 April.

After more refuellings, the F-111 bombers and their tanker support started landing at their UK home bases of Lakenheath, Upper Heyford, Fairford and Mildenhall from 05.45 hrs. Before the first aircraft touched down, however, an SR-71A departed Mildenhall for post-strike survey. On its return, the C-135C of the 4950th TW flew off to Washington with evidence of the damage. The KC-10As and KC-135s also began the return trip to the US from 15 April.

Technically, Operation *El Dorado Canyon* was a qualified success, especially with no apparent loss of aircraft to Libyan defences. However, five of the F-111F force of eighteen aborted, as did two of the A-6Es. There was, moreover, significant collateral damage within half a mile of the main Tripoli target. Significantly Qadhafi's young step-daughter was killed in the attack.

SEQUEL

Libya continued to sponsor terrorism, and the effects of one act against the USA affected the United Kingdom dramatically. On Sunday 21 December 1988 Pan American Boeing 747-121A N739PA was overflying northern England when it disintegrated at 31,000 ft. All 259 occupants were killed, plus another eleven people on the ground, at Lockerbie in southern Scotland, where much of the aircraft crashed.

Flight PA103 was from Frankfurt to Detroit via Heathrow and New York, starting with a 727 on the first sector and then transferring to the Jumbo at Heathrow. An explosive package had been loaded at Frankfurt and transferred to the 747, which eventually departed Heathrow twenty-five minutes late. Had the aircraft departed on time it would have exploded over the Atlantic, with the probability that all evidence would have been lost.

Towards the end of the First Gulf War between Iran and Iraq the United States Navy had brought down a civilian aircraft in the Gulf. On 3 July 1988 Iran Air Airbus A300 EP-IBU was shot down by Standard SAMs fired from the cruiser USS *Vincennes*, resulting in the loss of all 290 passengers and crew. Initially there was a view that the Lockerbie bombing was in retaliation.

After the most extensive criminal investigation in British history, the blame was laid at the door of Libya. After prolonged wrangling the perpetrators were eventually brought to justice and compensation paid by the Libyan government. Therefore in July 1999 diplomatic relations were resumed, and gradually Qadhafi was embraced by the West, having denounced weapons of mass destruction, accepted responsibility for the Lockerbie bombing and also having paid compensation for the death of the London policewoman in 1984. The USA opened a liaison office in Tripoli in 2004.

US Navy fighters were in action again on 4 January 1989. Two LARAF MiG-23s made a threatening approach to a pair of F-14As from the carrier USS *John F Kennedy*, then steaming eastwards, north of Tobruk. Deciding that the MiGs were intent on attack, the lead Tomcat fired an AIM-7 and an AIM-9, destroying both the LARAF fighters. The F-14As were from VF-32, and the action, which took place at midday, was over in three minutes.

There was one further international outrage, in 1989, when on 19 September a UTA DC-10-30 N54629 of Flight 772 was destroyed in mid-air over Niger. The flight was from Brazzaville to Paris via Chad, and among the 170 dead was the wife of the US ambassador to Chad. The perpetrators were confirmed as Libyan, and the motive was believed to be retaliation for French support of Chad against Libyan aggression.

Libyan Strikes from UK Airbases, 1986

United States Navy 1981

Unit	Aircraft	Code
USS *Nimitz* (CVN-68) with CVW-8 embarked 7.81–10.81		
VF-41	F-14A	100 AJ
VF-84	F-14A	200 AJ
VA-82	A-7E	300 AJ
VA-86	A-7E	400 AJ
VA-35	A-6E, KA-6D	500 AJ
VMAQ-2	EA-6B	620 AJ
VAW-124	E-2A	600 AJ
VS-24	S-3A	700 AJ
HS-9	SH-3H	610 AJ
USS *Forrestal* (CV-59) with CVW-17 embarked 3.81–9.81		
VFMA-115	F-4J	100 AA
VF-74	F-4J	200 AA
VA-83	A-7E	300 AA
VA-81	A-7E	400 AA
VA-85	A-6E, KA-6D	500 AA
VAQ-130	EA-6B	610 AA
VAW-125	E-2A	600 AA
VS-30	S-3A	700 AA
HS-3	SH-3H	730 AA

USAF 1986

Unit	Aircraft	Base	From	To
48 TFW	F-111F	Lakenheath	based	
42 ECS, 20 TFW	EF-111A	Upper Heyford	based	
9 SRS det 3	U-2R, TR-1A	Akrotiri	based	
9 SRW det 4	SR-71A	Mildenhall	based	
38 SRS 55 SRW	RC-135V, W	Hellenikon 922 SS ex-Offutt AFB	9.4.86	
4952 TS 4950 TW	C-135C	Mildenhall ex-Andrews AFB	10.4.86	16.4.86
10 ACCS	EC-135H	Offutt AFB	10.4.86	16.4.86
960 AWCS 552 AWCW	E-3A	Tinker AFB	10.4.86	16.4.86

USAF TANKER UNITS ON TDY BETWEEN 11 AND 17 APRIL 1986

Unit	Aircraft	At	Home base
68 ARG	KC-10A	Mildenhall	Seymour-Johnson AFB
5 BW	KC-135A	Mildenhall	Minot AFB
96 BW	KC-135A	Mildenhall	Dyess AFB

Unit	Aircraft	At	Home base
379 BW	KC–135A	Mildenhall	Wurtsmith AFB
416 BW	KC–135A	Mildenhall	Griffiss AFB
116 ARS	KC–135E	Mildenhall	Fairchild AFB
9 SRW	KC–135Q	Mildenhall	Beale AFB
7 BW	KC–135A	Fairford	Carswell AFB
42 BW	KC–135A	Fairford	Loring AFB
509 BW	KC–135A	Fairford	Pease AFB
19 ARW	KC–135A	Fairford	Robbins AFB
22 ARW	KC–135A	Fairford	March AFB
305 ARW	KC–135A	Fairford	Grissom AFB
2 BW	KC–10A	Mildenhall, Fairford	Barksdale AFB
22 ARW	KC–10A	Mildenhall, Fairford	March AFB
2 BW	KC–135A	Mildenhall, Fairford	Barksdale AFB
92 BW	KC–135A	Mildenhall, Fairford	Fairchild AFB
97 BW	KC–135A	Mildenhall, Fairford	Blytheville AFB
410 BW	KC–135A	Mildenhall, Fairford	Sawyer AFB
380 ARW	KC–135Q	Mildenhall, Fairford	Pittsburgh AFB

UNITED STATES NAVY 1986

Unit	Aircraft	Code
USS *Saratoga* (CV-60) with CVW-17 embarked 26.8.85–16.4.86		
VF-74	F-14A	100 AC
VF-103	F-14A	200 AC
VA-83	A-7E	300 AC
VA-81	A-7E	400 AC
VMA-533	A-6E, KA-6D	500 AC
VAQ-137	EA-6B	604 AC
VAW-125	E-2C	600 AC
VS-30	S-3A	700 AC
HS-3	SH-3H	610 AC
USS *Coral Sea* (CV-43) with CVW-13 embarked 1.10.85–19.5.86		
VFA-131	FA-18A	100 AK
VFA-132	FA-18A	200 AK
VMFA-314	FA-18A	300 AK
VMFA-323	FA-18A	400 AK
VA-55	A-6E, KA-6D	500 AK
VAQ-135	EA-6B	604 AK
VAW-127	E-2C	600 AK
HS-17	SH-3H	610 AK
USS *America* (CV-66) with CVW-1 embarked 10.3.86–10.9.86		
VF-102	F-14A	100 AB
VF-33	F-14A	200 AB
VA-46	A-7E	300 AB
VA-72	A-7E	400 AB
VA-34	A-6E, KA-6D	500 AB

Unit	Aircraft	Code
VMAQ-2	EA-6B	604 AB
VAW-123	E-2C	600 AB
HS-11	SH-3H	610 AB
VS-32	S-3A	700 AB
USN shore-based		
VAQ-2	EA-3B, EP-3E	NAS Rota, Spain

UNITED STATES NAVY 1989

Unit	Aircraft	Code
USS *John F Kennedy* (CV-67) with CVW-3 embarked 2.8.88–1.2.89		
VF-14	F-14A	100 AC
VF-32	F-14A	200 AC
VA-75	A-6E, KA-6D	500 AC
VMA(AW)-533	A-6E	540 AC
VAQ-130	EA-6B	604 AC
VAW-126	E-2A	600 AC
VS-22	S-3A	700 AC
HS-7	SH-3H	610 AC

9.3   THE FIRST GULF WAR, 1987–8

The Royal Navy's *Armilla* Patrol began in 1980 at the beginning of the Iran–Iraq war, when British warships operating in the Far East were transferred to the Persian Gulf to ensure the safety of British merchant ships operating in the region. Initially the presence was maintained by a single frigate or destroyer, but by 1986 there were usually

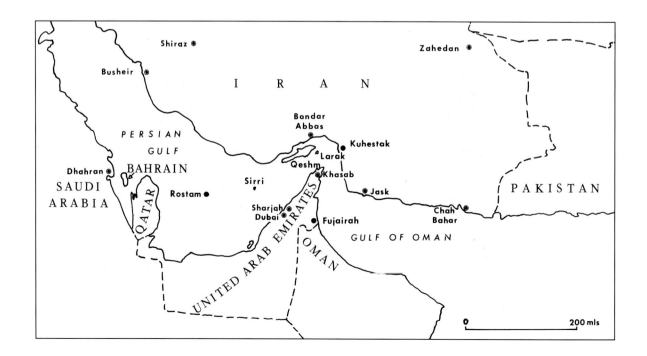

two warships involved. The position became more serious in 1987, when the Iraqis escalated attacks on shipping in the Gulf in the so-called 'tanker war'.

From March 1987 the presence was increased to typically three helicopter-equipped surface vessels and a fleet auxiliary, and these were joined by four Hunt-class minehunters in September. During 1987, 178 vessels had been hit in attacks, despite a strong US, British and French presence. The war came to a sudden end in July 1988, from which time the patrol was reduced until the Iraqi invasion of Kuwait in 1990 (Chapter 9, Section 4).

The operation succeeded in limiting the attacks on British-registered vessels, with the ship-borne helicopters serving in a range of support and humanitarian roles.

Armilla Patrol vessels, 1987–8, by class

Type 42	Type 22	Type 21	Leander	RFA	From
Nottingham			Andromeda	Orangeleaf	3.87
Cardiff	Broadsword	Active		Orangeleaf	6.87
Edinburgh	Brazen		Andromeda	Brambleleaf	8.87
York	Battleaxe		Scylla	Tidespring	1.88
Exeter				Tidespring	3.88
Manchester	Beaver			Tidespring	6.88
Southampton				Brambleleaf	9.88

NOTE
The destroyers and frigates embarked Lynx HAS.2s of 815 NAS, while the RFAs embarked Sea King HAS.5s of 824 NAS.

The British warships of the Armilla patrol in the Persian Gulf carried Lynx ASW helicopters of 815 NAS, home-based at Portland. HAS.3GM XZ228/303 of HMS *Scylla*. (*Author's collection*)

United States Navy and Marine Corps presence, 1987–8

CVW-14 (NK)	USS *Constellation*	6.87-10.87
CVW-2 (NE)	USS *Ranger*	9.87-12.87
CVW-5 (NF)	USS *Midway*	12.87-3.88
CVW-11 (NH)	USS *Enterprise*	3.88-7.88
	USS *Guadalcanal*	8.87-11.87
	USS *Okinawa*	11.87-2.88

NOTE
The assault ships carried a range of assault and attack helicopters, typically AH-1 and CH-46

9.4   THE SECOND GULF WAR, 1990–91

In common with Korea (Chapter 2, Section 4), the Gulf War was primarily an American affair. British services played an important part in the conflict as part of a broad-based Coalition, but to describe the contribution of all members would require far more space than is available in a book about British air arms. Even a full table of all Coalition air forces would run to many pages. Therefore what follows is a detailed record of the British contribution, with sufficient description of the actions of other Coalition partners to provide a context.

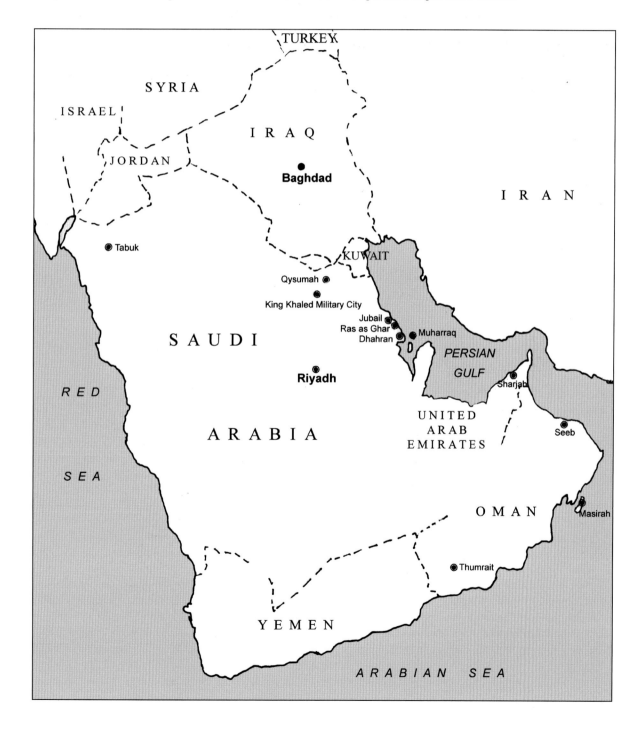

BACKGROUND

Kuwait was a tribal area at the head of the Persian Gulf that eventually became part of the Ottoman Empire. After the First World War it was declared an independent sheikhdom under British protectorate, and in 1922 its southern border with Saudi Arabia was defined with a neutral buffer zone between the two. Iraq was unhappy with the separation of Kuwait, but was itself a British protectorate.

Oil was discovered in 1930, and by 1953 Kuwait was the largest oil exporter in the Gulf, attracting foreign investors and workers. On 19 June 1961 Kuwait was granted full independence, with an agreement that Britain would support Kuwait militarily if called upon. A few days later Iraq declared Kuwait part of Iraq, and began massing troops on the border. (The resultant stand-off is described fully in Chapter 5, Section 5). Iraq formally recognized Kuwait in 1963.

In September 1980, fearful of the prospective exportation of Islamic revolution, and also in dispute of islands in the Shatt al Arab waterway at the head of the Gulf, Iraq invaded neighbouring Iran. The vicious and costly war continued until 1988, during which time it spilled over into the tanker war, described in Section 3 of this chapter. The war, which had involved extensive use of chemical and biological weapons on the part of the Iraqis, came to an abrupt end in July 1988.

In July 1990, with increasing domestic problems resulting from the inconclusive war with Iran and with a huge financial debt to Kuwait, Iraq began massing troops on the border with Kuwait. President Saddam Hussein accused Kuwait of slant drilling for oil in the Rumalia field, and also of exceeding oil quota levels set by the Organization of the Petroleum Exporting Countries (OPEC), which had the effect of forcing the price down generally.

In great secrecy some 100,000 troops were moved to the border. In the early hours of 2 August they struck, spearheaded by three divisions of the Republican Guard in heliborne and amphibious assaults, very quickly occupying Kuwait but stopping at the border with Saudi Arabia. The United Nations met and passed Resolution 660, calling for withdrawal and negotiations, and the US government froze Iraqi and Kuwaiti assets and imposed trade sanctions. On 6 August King Fahd of Saudi Arabia sought help from abroad, which resulted in President Bush launching Operation *Desert Shield* designed to protect Saudi Arabia.

UNITED NATIONS RESPONSE – A PHONEY WAR

It is remarkable that the Iraqis stopped at the border with Saudi Arabia, given the comparative military strengths of the two nations. Had Saudi Arabia been invaded, recovery would have been difficult in the extreme, if not impossible, and possession of the oilfields would have choked the West. That consideration by Western nations then influenced successive actions.

On 6 August the United Nations Security Council passed Resolution 661, imposing wide trade sanctions. On the 9th Resolution 662 was passed, which declared the occupation of Kuwait to be null and void. Saddam responded by calling for an Islamic holy war against the USA and Israel in the event of there being any attempt to recover Kuwait.

The first component of *Desert Shield* was the 82nd Airborne Division based in Fort Bragg, elements of which were immediately transferred to Saudi Arabia. Over the next two days the 1st Tactical Fighter Wing flew its F-15C Eagles direct from Langley AFB to Saudi Arabia in what was the longest fighter deployment in history, B-52s were deployed to Diego Garcia and a carrier battle group based around the USS *Dwight D Eisenhower* sailed into the Red Sea. The Iraqi government announced the annexation of Kuwait, while Britain agreed to send naval and air units into the region.

The British contribution to what was originally seen as the defence of Saudi Arabia was Operation *Granby*. The initial deployments were air and naval, and until 1 November the Air Commander British Forces Arabian Peninsula was also overall in charge of British forces. Already in the Gulf were vessels of the *Armilla* patrol, comprising HMS *York* (D98), *Battleaxe* (F89) and *Jupiter* (F60), supported by RFA *Orangeleaf* (A110) and carrying four Lynx helicopters between them. HMS *Gloucester* (D96) joined them in mid-September, bringing a further Lynx.

The first RAF move was the arrival of a Tristar at Dhahran, bringing RAF Regiment, signals and catering units into the theatre on 9 August. This was followed by a stream of Hercules, VC-10 and Tristar flights as the build-up grew. Communications and medical units plus ground crew were brought into Saudi Arabia and the Gulf states in increasing numbers. Then from October troops were ferried in by air, while their heavy equipment was generally sent by sea.

On 10 August a detachment of RAF Tornado F.3 air defence fighters arrived at Dhahran from armament practice camp on Cyprus, and they were followed on the 11th by a composite squadron of Jaguars which was first based in Oman. The initial objective was quite simply to try to prevent Saddam from continuing and attacking into Saudi Arabia. The Tornadoes were replaced from the end of August by later aircraft from 11 Sqn, with an upgraded Foxhunter radar and chaff and flare dispensers. In addition, the longer-range Skyflash 90 AAM was fitted. E-3 AWACS aircraft monitored Iraqi air movements, while the fighters maintained a constant watch, alternating with Saudi and USAF F-15s. From the outset Iraq was denied the opportunity of any appreciation of the build-up, apart from what could be read in the Western press – which was a great deal.

At this stage it may be useful to note the manner in which the 'teeth' operational units were deployed. In the case of the Tornado fighters, they were simply drawn from aircraft of 5 and 29 Squadrons already half-way to the Gulf at Cyprus. These machines were shortly replaced by aircraft in the UK or Germany selected as were all other combat types: quite simply those aircraft in the best state, most recently returned from servicing and with long airframe and engine hours. Later, aircraft were also selected for specific weapons or avionics fits. Crews were selected from among those with the most experience and/or competence in the type of operational flying considered to be most relevant.

Thus the combat deployments were not squadrons at all, but composite units of the best aircraft and the most relevantly competent crews. Presumably the lack of identity and concomitant *esprit de corps* was compensated for by the fact that the RAF was by now so small that most aircrew on a given type would already know one another, regardless of unit.

Three Nimrods from Kinloss were also among the earliest deployments in order to support naval units in the blockade of trade through Kuwait. While the Jaguars had been dispatched to counter any Iraqi ground offensive, the RAF sent a composite squadron of fifteen GR.1 Tornadoes to Bahrain at the end of August. A second unit was sent to Bahrain in mid-September, which then moved to Tabuk in western Saudi Arabia in mid-October.

With the exception of the Tornado F.3s the combat aircraft were painted overall in a shade of sand-pink Alkali Removable Temporary Finish (ARTF). In addition the various attack aircraft plus the Victor tankers and in-theatre Hercules sported nose art for the first time since the Second World War. In due course the Tornado F.3s had their fin, tail and wing leading edges painted in a black radar-absorbent paint. Later, when operations started, the helicopters and Islanders had three pale-blue or white bands painted round the rear fuselage.

COUNTDOWN TO WAR

From early August the British transport fleet was active flying mainly into Riyadh, but supporting the deployments across the region. Hercules were especially active, and in the first four weeks of the operation had completed 6,364 hours in 343 sorties.

The logistics of moving so many personnel were formidable. Most of the units sent to the region – whether Army or Air Force – had prepared for, and were equipped for, combat in quite different circumstances. The equipment and training were designed for a European war fought in a temperate climate. Given the known use of chemical weapons by the Iraqis, all personnel were inoculated as far as possible, and kitted out with nuclear, chemical and biological (NBC) kit. This was designed for use in the European theatre, not the heat of the Middle East.

On 13 August the French committed forces under Operation *Salamandre*, then *Daguet*, and Belgium and the Netherlands determined to send naval units. On the 17th Saddam announced that he would use some 3,000 Western hostages as human shields in the event of air attack on Iraq. On the 18th the Security Council passed Resolution 664, demanding the release of foreign nationals from Iraq and Kuwait, and on the 23rd the US government began calling up reservists. Iraq complied with the resolution, but just two days later yet another Resolution, 665, authorized states to use force to ensure compliance with trade sanctions.

The occupation of Kuwait had come just months after the Iron Curtain had been raised and when relations between the Soviet Union and the West were improving. Just how much the world situation had changed was evidenced when on 26 August a Soviet warship in the Gulf called on an RAF Nimrod for help in checking a suspected blockade runner.

Coalition forces suffered the first aircraft loss on 29 August. C-5A 680228 of the 433rd Airlift Wing, flown by a reserve crew and bound for the Gulf, crashed on take-off at Ramstein air base in Germany, killing thirteen of the seventeen on board. In early September Presidents Gorbachev of the Soviet Union and Bush of the USA met to discuss actions to take, and Britain committed the 7th Armoured Brigade in Germany to the forces available. The Italians announced the dispatch of a squadron of Tornadoes in Operation *Locusta*, and UN Security Council Resolution 670 prohibited air traffic into and out of Iraqi and Kuwaiti airports.

Canada sent a squadron of CF-18 Hornets to Qatar on 7 October in Operation *Scimitar*, and on the 10th the USAF suspended all flying, apart from the AWACS patrols, after a spate of flying accidents: the restriction was lifted after a thorough review of safety. The build-up of Coalition forces – especially those of the US – was such that by mid-November it was clear that force levels were far more than required for the defence of Saudi Arabia. Indeed, planning for the retaking of Kuwait had begun from the outset in the event that diplomacy failed.

The US had requested of Britain an armoured brigade with Challenger tanks to support a USMC assault, and Tornado strike aircraft with JP233, which was the only Allied type capable of taking out airfields and similar installations at the very low levels demanded by heavy anti-aircraft defences. This provision put Britain in a sound position to demand involvement in planning and tasking. At the end of October, US General Norman Schwartzkopf, in overall command, requested a further squadron of strike Tornadoes and a second armoured brigade.

Movement of troops from the UK began in earnest in October, and the RAF transport fleet was supplemented by civilian aircraft for passenger and freight movement. These included Boeing 747s (BA, Kuwait Airways), 757s (Air Europe), 767s (Britannia) and DC-10-30s (Sabena) for trooping; and for freight operations An-124s (Heavylift), CL-44s (Heavylift), Boeing 747s (Evergreen) and 707s (Skyair Cargo, Anglo Air). In addition USAF C-5A transport moved heavy equipment, including tanks and helicopters, while some time later Spanish Air Force C-130s flew British sorties from Brize Norton to the Middle East. In the course of the campaign, the civilian fleet was to fly some 21,000 passengers and 14,750 tons of freight.

During the build-up in November the process of intelligence gathering was geared up to determine the nature of the air defence and command-and-control systems operated. Probing flights were conducted by E-3, RC-135 and RAF Nimrods of 51 Sqn. While the Iraqis announced a doubling of the occupying force, Britain increased her military commitment. RAF helicopters were ferried into the theatre, while RFA *Argus* (A135), converted as a 100-bed air-conditioned primary casualty receiving ship (PCRS) with five heli-spots, brought four Sea Kings of 846 NAS. The RAF helicopters were formed into the Support Helicopter Force Middle East (SHFME) on 15 November.

The definitive resolution from the UN Security Council on 29 November was 678, which authorized 'member states co-operating with ... Kuwait unless Iraq on or before 15 January 1991 fully implements (withdrawal), ... to use all necessary means to uphold and implement Resolution 660 ... and to restore international peace and security in the area'. The wording is critical in that it left the way open to invade Iraq, not just to recover Kuwait.

On Christmas Eve Saddam declared that in the event of war Israel would be Iraq's initial target. In principle this was a clever move, since if the approach was pursued and Israel retaliated, the Coalition of Western and Arab nations would disintegrate. However, the disclosure gave the Coalition leaders time to prepare plans for supporting Israel behind the scenes.

On 2 January NATO committed fighters to Turkey in the event that Iraq might attack northwards. The RAF added a third composite Tornado strike squadron in Saudi Arabia, while the helicopter transport force was supplemented by two naval Sea King utility units, from 845 and 848 NASs. By 15 January, after failed talks between the USA and Iraq, Coalition forces were prepared for war, but on the day there was no action, giving Saddam a false sense of security. The 16th also passed without event, but it was the lull before the storm.

By now the coalition had clear military leadership in General Schwartzkopf and his key Coalition commanders, and the various military arms were reasonably co-ordinated within a plan for invasion of Kuwait as Operation *Desert Storm*. At this time there were 150 major warships on station, and the 600,000 troops on the ground with 4,000 tanks were backed by combat air assets available as described in outline in the following tables.

USAF

Sqns	Aircraft	Location	Sqns	Aircraft	Location
4	F-15C	Saudi Arabia	2	F-15C	Turkey
2	F-15E	Saudi Arabia	1	F-16C	Turkey
2	F-117	Saudi Arabia	1	F-4E	Turkey
2	F-16A	Saudi Arabia	2	F-111E	Turkey
3	F-111F	Saudi Arabia	1	EF-111A	Turkey
1	EF-111A	Saudi Arabia	1	RF-4C	Turkey
6	A-10A	Saudi Arabia	1	AC-130A	Turkey
1	OA-10A	Saudi Arabia	1	E-3B, C	Turkey
5	B-52G	Saudi Arabia	1	EC-130H	Turkey
1	AC-130H	Saudi Arabia	1	MC/HC-130	Turkey
2	TR-1A, U-2R	Saudi Arabia	1	MH-53J	Turkey
1	RC-135	Saudi Arabia	6	F-16C	UAE
2	E-3B	Saudi Arabia	1	F-4G	Bahrain
1	E-8A	Saudi Arabia	1	F-16C	Qatar
2	EC-130E	Saudi Arabia	2	B-52G	Diego Garcia
1	EC-130H	Saudi Arabia	1	B-52G	UK
2	MC/HC-130	Saudi Arabia	1	B-52G	Spain
1	MH-60G	Turkey	1	B-52G	Egypt

Supported by 36 C-130, 48 KC-135, 13 C-141, 8 C-5, 5 KC10, 2 C-21 Sqns

United States Navy squadrons (in six carrier groups): USS *America* CVW-1 (Red Sea), USS *Ranger* CVW-2 (Persian Gulf), USS *John F Kennedy* CVW-3 (Red Sea), USS *Midway* CVW-5 (Persian Gulf), USS *Theodore Roosevelt* CVW-8 (Persian Gulf), USS *Saratoga* CVW-17 (Red Sea)

Aircraft	CVW-1	CVW-2	CVW-3	CVW-5	CVW-8	CVW-17
F/A-18A				3	2	
F/A-18C	2					2
F-14A	2	2	2		2	2
A-6E, KA-6D	1	2	1	2	2	1
A-7E			2			
E-2C	1	1	1	1	1	1
EA-6B	1	1	1	1	1	1
S-3A, B	1	1	1		1	1
SH-3H	1	1	1	1	1	1

Supported by 13 P-3, 2 HH-60H, 2 MH-53E, 1 SH-3G squadrons all land-based in the Gulf. In addition there were numerous H-46D, SH-60, SH-2, SH-3, CH-53 detachments on a wide variety of ships.

United States Marine Corps (in six Marine Air Groups): MAG-1 (Bahrain), MAG-13 (Saudi Arabia), MAG-16 (Saudi Arabia), MAG-26 (Saudi Arabia), MAG-40 (USS *Nassau, Iwo Jima, Guam*), MAG-50 (USS *Tarawa, New Orleans*)

Aircraft	MAG-1	MAG-13	MAG-16	MAG-26	MAG-40	MAG-50
F/A-18A	3					
F/A-18C, D	4					
A-6E	2					
EA-6B	1					
AV-8B		4			1	
OV-10A, D		2				

Aircraft	MAG-1	MAG-13	MAG-16	MAG-26	MAG-40	MAG-50
CH-46E			3	3	2	2
H-53D, E			4	3	1	1
AH-1J, W			2	1	1	2
UH-1N				1		
KC-130	4					
UC-12B	2					

In addition there was one CH-46E squadron of 13 MEU on USS *Okinawa*

United States Army

The US Army deployed a large number of helicopters and fixed wing aircraft in Saudi Arabia. They included OH-58 observation helicopter, CH-47, UH-60 and UH-1 transports and fifteen battalions of AH-64A attack helicopters backed by several units of the AH-1S. Three battalions flew the RC-12D and OV-1D on recce tasks.

Other Coalition Air Forces

Sqns	Aircraft	Location	Sqns	Aircraft	Location
Australia[1]			**Italy**		
1	C-130E	Saudi Arabia	3	Tornado IDS	Abu Dhabi
Bahrain			0.5	F-104S	Turkey
1	F-16C	Bahrain	**Kuwait**		
1	F-5E	Bahrain	2	A-4KU	Saudi Arabia
Belgium			2	Mirage F.1CK	Saudi Arabia
1.5	Mirage VBA	Turkey	1	Gazelle	Saudi Arabia
Canada[2] **(Operation** *Friction***)**			**Qatar**		
2	CF-18	Qatar	1	Mirage F.1EDA	Qatar
0.5	CC-137	Qatar	**Saudi Arabia**		
France (Operation *Daguet***)**[3]			3	F-15C	Saudi Arabia
3	Mirage 2000C	Saudi Arabia	2	Tornado ADV	Saudi Arabia
3	Mirage F.1C	Qatar	2	Tornado IDS	Saudi Arabia
4	Jaguar A	Saudi Arabia	4	F-5E, F, RF-5E	Saudi Arabia
3	Mirage F.1CR	Saudi Arabia	2	Hawk 65	Saudi Arabia
1	Gabriel	Saudi Arabia	2	C-130E, H	Saudi Arabia
3	C.160	Saudi Arabia	1	E-3A	Saudi Arabia
1	Nord 262, Mystère XX	Saudi Arabia	1	AS565SA	Saudi Arabia
3	C-135FR	Saudi Arabia	**South Korea**		
1	DC-8F	Saudi Arabia	1	C-130H	UAE
2	Puma[3]	Saudi Arabia	**United Arab Emirates**		
1	Gazelle	Saudi Arabia	1	Mirage 2000	Abu Dhabi
Germany			1	C-130H	Abu Dhabi
1.5	Alphajet	Turkey			

NOTES

1   In addition S-70BA and AS-350BA of 723 Sqn on board destroyers

2   Plus Sea King CH-124A of 423 Sqn on board destroyers

3   Plus Lynx on board destroyers

While US forces had lost eight aircraft by mid-January, the RAF had lost three in accidents. 16 Sqn Tornado GR.1 ZA466 hit an improperly erected barrier at Tabuk; the crew ejected safely. The first casualty was the pilot of Jaguar XX754 of 54 Sqn which crashed on 13 November during a low-level training flight, while a similar sortie cost the lives of the crew of 14 Sqn Tornado ZD718 on 13 January. The first stage of the recapture of Kuwait was now the air phase, and on the eve of battle both air and ground crews were as well trained as possible.

The air assets and their related support were not the only elements of the RAF to be deployed in the Middle East. In mid-August 20 Sqn RAF Regiment with Rapier missiles was sent to Cyprus pending a decision on which airfields required air defence. Part of the unit then transferred to Muharraq to protect the air base there. The unit was replaced by 66 Sqn in November. Further units were deployed, including a number of field infantry squadrons, plus 1 Sqn with armoured cars. This unit later acted in the reconnaissance role for 1 (Br) Armoured Division, crossing into Iraq.

RAF Regiment Deployments

Unit	Equipment	Role	Base	From	To
20 Sqn	Rapier	AA	Akrotiri	11.8.90	10.90
			Muharraq	10.90	13.11.90
66 Sqn	Rapier	AA	Muharraq	14.11.90	?
34 Sqn		Field	Dhahran	8.90	?
26 Sqn	Rapier	AA	? Tabuk	28.11.90	14.2.91
1 Sqn	Scorpion, Spartan	Recce	Qysumah	16.1.91	2.91
			Front line	2.91	3.91
58 Sqn		Field	Qysumah	2.91	3.91
51 Sqn		Field	Dharan, Tabuk	11.90	3.91
66 Sqn		Field	?	?	?

Although not directly involved in the war, a Royal Navy task group had departed Portsmouth on 11 January to add protection to the USN Sixth Fleet in the eastern Mediterranean. Task Group 323.2 comprised HMS *Ark Royal* (R09) and *Sheffield* (D80), and the RFAs *Olmeda* (A124) and *Regent* (A480). HMS *Exeter* (D89) and *Manchester* (D95) were added later, supplemented by HMS *Charybdis* (F75) when *Manchester* was transferred to the Gulf. TG 323.2 was to also to provide support for Egypt and Turkey in the event of any escalation of the conflict.

COALITION OBJECTIVES AND PLANS

The initial American plan for an air campaign, *Instant Thunder*, was devised during August 1990 to support the President's four objectives. These were:

- To force unconditional Iraqi withdrawal from Kuwait
- To re-establish the legitimate Kuwaiti government
- To protect American lives
- To ensure regional stability and security

Instant Thunder was designed to destroy eighty-four strategic targets in a week. This would have involved 700 attack sorties a day. During September RAF and Royal Saudi Air Force (RSAF) planners had been drawn into preparations. By January 1991 planners had extended the original eighty-four targets to 600, of which over 300 eventually became part of the strategic target list. The commander of Air Force Central Command (CENTAF) became the Joint Forces Air Component Commander (JFACC). The Air Staff initially categorized strategic targets as follows:

- Leadership – Saddam's command facilities and telecommunications
- Key production – electricity, oil refining, refined oil products, nuclear, biological and chemical (NBC), other military production, military storage

- Infrastructure – railways, ports and bridges
- Fielded forces – air defences, naval forces, long-range combat aircraft and missiles and airfields and, in due course, the Republican Guard Forces Command (RGFC)

At the outset the Scud missiles were not seen as being of any great significance, and only the static launchers and production centres were considered as targets. Later, after Saddam had threatened attacks on Israel, JFACC refined his campaign objectives as follows, with twelve targets set:

Isolate and incapacitate the Iraqi regime:

1 Leadership command facilities
2 Crucial aspects of electricity production facilities powering military and related industrial systems
3 Telecommunications and C³

Gain and maintain air supremacy to permit unhindered air operations:

4 Strategic integrated air defence system (IADS) including radar sites, SAMS and IADS control centres
5 Air forces and airfields

Destroy NBC warfare capability

6 Known NBC research, production and storage

Eliminate Iraq's offensive military capability by destroying major parts of key military production, infrastructure and power projection capabilities:

7 Military production and storage sites
8 Scud missiles and launchers, production and storage facilities
9 Oil refining and distribution facilities, as opposed to long-term production capabilities
10 Naval forces and port facilities

Render the Iraqi Army and its mechanized equipment in Kuwait ineffective, causing its collapse:

11 Railways and bridges connecting military forces to means of support
12 Army units to include RGFC in the Kuwait Theatre of Operations

The overall military plan developed into a four-phase campaign, starting with the strategic air assault on Iraq, and then air attack on Iraqi forces in Kuwait, leading to ejection of Iraqi forces from Kuwait. In the event the first three phases were merged as the amount of airpower available increased. The planners worked to a rigid Master Attack Plan (MAP), translated daily into Air Tasking Orders (ATO). To help secure objectives the commander had at his disposal 2,430 fixed-wing aircraft, which increased to about 2,780 towards the end of the conflict. Some 60% were combat types.

THE AIR PHASE

The first task for the coalition was the neutralization of the Iraqi air defences. After that would come the task of counter-air strikes, followed by a wider range of attacks, critically including close air support. The air defences, though, were formidable and alert.

The Iraqis operated an Integrated Air Defence System (IADS) across four sectors. There were about 500 radars at a hundred sites. From the bottom up there were SAM batteries and fighters at air bases controlled by an intercept Operations Centre (IOC), directed by Sector Operations Centres (SOC) reporting to the national Air Defence Operations Centre (ADOC) at Baghdad.

The system had some problems handling multiple threats. Further, reading between the lines, the Coalition was able to hack into the computer programs and corrupt them, but this is supposition based on careful analysis of deleted elements of the United States General Accounting Office Report 1996. In terms of SAMs, the Iraqis had the following distribution of batteries by Sector:

Area/type	SA-2	SA-3	SA-6	SA-8	Roland	Total
Range (miles)	27	18	20	8	3.5	
Mosul/Kirkuk	1	12	–	1	2	16
H-2/H-3	1	–	6	–	6	13
Talil/Jalibah/Basrah	3	–	8	–	7	18
Baghdad	10	16	8	15	9	58
Total	**15**	**28**	**22**	**16**	**24**	**105**

Anti-aircraft artillery (AAA) was extensive, not radar controlled but rather fired in barrages and limited to 12,000 ft. The Iraqis had electronic jamming potential, but it appears not have been used. The combination of effective AAA and degradation of the SAMs and IADS led to most Coalition attacks being conducted from above 12,000 ft after the initial strikes on air defences and the airfields. From the outset there was limited opposition from air defence fighters. The total air defence force at the outset of the campaign probably comprised eighty Mirage F.1ECs, 200 MiG-21/F-7As, twenty MiG-25s and forty-eight MiG-29s.

The first air assaults were on Iraqi air defence radar sites made at around 02.30 on 17 January by US Army AH-64 attack helicopters using Hellfire missiles. The RAF was in action with Tornado combat air patrols, while F-117A strike fighters attacked key installations to the west of Baghdad with 2,000 lb laser-guided bombs. At the same time fifty-two Tomahawk cruise missiles were fired from US battleships at the head of the Gulf. A quite remarkable feat was a long-range attack by B-52 strategic bombers of 2 Bomb Wing based at Barksdale AFB. Seven aircraft flew a 14,000-mile non-stop return journey in thirty-five hours to release thirty-nine AGM-86C cruise missiles against power stations around Baghdad.

Numerous strike packages now joined the fray, including precision strikes with LGBs by USAF F-111Fs, and F-15Es using conventional bombs. Saudi Tornadoes hit targets, while RAF strike Tornadoes from Muharraq and Dhahran attacked Talil airfield using JP233 airfield-denial weapons, now used for the first time in anger. Each strike was supported by tankers, airborne early warning and control, covering fighters, specialized anti-radar and jamming aircraft. For aircraft carrying heavy loads the tankers were critical, allowing them to trade take-off fuel for weapons.

The JP233 airfield-denial weapon has been a controversial weapon. It comprises a 32 ft canister weighing over a ton, containing at the front thirty SG-357 anti-runway penetrators weighing 75 lb and at the rear 215 HB-876 anti-personnel mines. The munitions were ejected as the delivery aircraft made a straight low pass over the runway, and the heavier munitions dropped under small retarding parachutes. The aircraft then released the empty canisters, retrimmed and sped for home. In the light of subsequent Tornado losses, the media asserted that JP233 laydown at low level was the cause, although only one aircraft was lost during a JP233 sortie, and that was several minutes after release.

This first wave of attacks comprised 671 combat sorties for no loss. They were followed by further raids at first light, including RAF and French Air Force Jaguars against airfields in Kuwait. The first operational RAF loss came shortly after dawn, when Tornado ZD791 of 15 Sqn crashed near Shaibah airfield in southern Iraq, being one of four attacking the airfield with 1,000 lb 'dumb' bombs. The crew ejected to be taken prisoner, being released after the war: the cause has not been established. Further Tornado JP233 sorties were flown against Al Asad airfield, and in this instance they were preceded by Tornadoes armed with ALARM anti-radar missiles.

The third-wave Tornado missions in the evening of the 17th were against airfields at Shaibah, Ubaydah bin al Jarrah and al Asad. Again JP233s were dropped from very low level, and ZA392 flown by the OC 27 Sqn crashed into the ground near Shaibah, killing the crew. Four ALARM-equipped Tornadoes hit air defence radars at H-3 airfield. In the first full twenty-four hours of the air war the Tornadoes had flown sixty sorties, forty-four of which were each with two JP233s, for the loss of two aircraft. An Italian Tornado was shot down and the crew captured while attacking an airfield. In total 2,100 sorties were flown, against about twenty-four sorties by the Iraqi Air Force, which lost eight aircraft in combat in addition to scores on the ground.

On the second day the selective bombing continued, and now USAF units based in Turkey joined the attacks. The United States Air Forces Europe (USAFE) had earlier suggested basing units in Turkey in Joint Task Force

Proven Force to open a second front based on electronic warfare. The project expanded with units deployed to Turkey under various guises, and on 17 January the Turkish government gave its approval to the use of its airbases. But while operations against Iraq's air defences, control and communications and leadership targets continued without let-up, a fresh development threatened to jeopardize the prosecution of the war.

SS-1, *AL-HUSSAIN* AND THE *SCUD-HUNT*

At 02.05 local time on 18 January, seven *Scud* missiles, probably *al-Hussain* with 375-mile range, were fired at Israel. Two landed on Haifa, three on Tel Aviv and two in open land. One had been fired earlier at Dhahran, but was intercepted by *Patriot* anti-ballistic missile system (ABMS) missiles. Thus, as threatened, Iraq seemed set on bringing Israel into the war. There were significant behind-the-scenes US diplomatic moves to reassure Israel, and from the 19th additional *Patriot* ABMs were made available, with a further batch delivered on 27 January: Netherlands Air Force *Patriots* were deployed around Jerusalem later in the war.

The SS-1 was a first-generation surface-to-surface missile (SSM), with a basic but inaccurate inertial guidance system. It had been widely equated to the German V-2, but with longer range, although guidance should have been better. Range was up to 175 miles with a 4,400 lb warhead, but Iraq had improved on the original design with two upgraded versions. These were the *al-Hussain* with a 375-mile range and a smaller warhead, and the *al-Abbas*, range 530 miles, warhead 550 lb.

The launch vehicle is the MAZ-543 articulated eight-wheel prime mover, and resupply missiles are towed tail first by ZIL-157Vs. *End Tray* radar is used to track radiosonde for upper atmosphere data. Length is 37 ft, diameter 3 ft, weight 6.2 tons and range 100–175 miles. The Iraqis had organized to set up the missiles in around thirty minutes on mobile launchers at pre-surveyed sites. The mobile launchers were remarkably quick at moving, once the missile was fired – a matter of a few minutes.

The Soviet Union had sold 650 R-17 (SS-1C) missiles and thirty-six launch vehicles to Iraq, and it is thought that she had about 500 *al-Hussain* variants in 1990 and around thirty fixed missile-launch sites along the western border, with twenty mobile launchers in the area between the H-2 and H-3 pumping stations (and airfields) and ten to the south around Basrah. The Iraqis had increased the number of launchers by converting civilian heavy goods vehicles supported by tankers and supply vehicles in the guise of civilian buses.

On the night of the 18th there were nineteen F-15E *Scud*-related sorties against the western fixed sites. Through weather problems there was difficulty in securing post-attack battle-damage assessment (BDA), a problem that was to plague the Coalition forces throughout the campaign.

From the first launch against Israel on 18 January a significant proportion of Allied reconnaissance and strike assets had to be turned to locating and destroying the *Scud* missiles. Aircraft specifically tasked with the *Scud* attack mission were forward-based A-10As and F-15Es: both types flew in pairs, and in the case of the F-15Es the patrol operated at 15,000 ft. The lead F-15s were equipped with infra-red targeting (LANTIRN) and armed with GBU-10 Paveway laser-guided bombs or four 2,000 lb Mk 84 bombs, while the following wingmen were armed with six CBU-87/Bs or twelve 500 lb Mk 82 GP bombs. A-10As were fitted with AGM-65 Maverick AGMs and CBU-87s or 500 lb Mk 82 bombs. The mine dispensers were used to deter launch vehicles from straying from main highways.

The Tornado GR.1As of 2 and 13 Sqns, which had only arrived in theatre on 14 January, began operating from 19 January, generally flying at 200 ft at between 540 and 580 knots. Average duration was around three hours, with one hour spent over Iraqi territory. The hunters had no easy task. The fixed sites were in the vicinity of the oil pipeline between H-2 and H-3, and at least six were claimed destroyed by the end of Day Two. It was thought that all fixed launch sites were destroyed by the end of the first week of the war. The mobile launchers were much more problematical.

The *Scud* missiles were described as one of twelve key target types, and the location of the research and production facilities and the twenty-eight fixed launchers in western Iraq was known. Yet there was no clear plan for locating and destroying the mobile launchers, nor were they perceived as being a threat until the first missiles fell on Israel. The only previous comparable threat – to which there was no counter once launched – was that of the V-2 rockets of the Second World War a little under fifty years earlier.

The MAP was inflexible, and assumed sound intelligence for aircrew briefing. In the event, both A-10A and

F-15E crews were dispatched into western Iraq with hurriedly photocopied pictures from Jane's publications to give them an indication of what they were seeking. Stock missiles were retained in a variety of buildings, under bridges and in similar locations, and in Kuwait in hardened aircraft shelters; they were notoriously difficult to detect. RAF Tornado GR.1s attacked the *Scud* test base at Rufah Fuwad, while B-52s attacked the Sad 16 research centre near Mosul, assembly plants near Baghdad and the Rufah test range.

By Day Fifteen of the air war (31 January) some 30,000 Allied sorties had been flown in total. As a result of these strikes it was claimed that thirty-eight of forty-four airfield targets had been destroyed, as had thirty-three of sixty-six bridges, all thirty-one NBC facilities, 25% of electrical plants and 33% of Iraqi C^3. Of the total sorties, some 1,800 were on 'Scud-hunts', with little to show for the commitment.

In the early stages of the war there were *Scud* attacks on the ports of Ad-Dammam and Jubayl, where there were large concentrations of troops. In total during the war, eighty-eight missiles were believed fired, with thirty-eight against targets in Israel and fifty against Saudi Arabia. Damage was slight in general, although four Israeli civilians were killed and about 200 injured, but in one strike on 25 February, on Khobar near Dhahran, twenty-eight US soldiers were killed and eighty-nine wounded. Forty-two of the missiles launched were allegedly intercepted by *Patriot* ABMs, although the numbers and effects of interception have subsequently been challenged. A particular problem was the disintegration of the *Scuds* into several parts during the terminal phase, leaving the *Patriot* with multiple targets to intercept.

A review of the launch patterns shows over half of all missiles (forty-nine) launched in the first ten days of the forty-three-day campaign. Bad weather, which created major reconnaissance problems, started on Day Five and ended on Day Eleven. From then on launches were sporadic and, with the exception of the one on Khobar, caused little damage.

Once it was clear that SSMs were being used, there was considerable anxiety as to the effects and also about the prospective use of chemical or biological warheads. There were twenty-four *Scud*-related sites on the Coalition Basic Encyclopedia (BE) of a total of 862 targets. In the event the number of such targets increased dramatically and committed over three times the anticipated air resources to attempt to contain the threat. The problem for the Coalition in attacking the mobile *Scud* launchers was that of identification, location and tasking – all in seven minutes.

In respect of identification, the 29,000 square miles of desert in western Iraq was analysed at two extremes. The Defence Support Programme (DSP) satellites on geostationary orbit at 23,000 miles could identify a launch within about ten square miles. At the other extreme, Special Forces were inserted by MH-53J Pave Low helicopters in the two *Scud* 'boxes' in the west. The SAS operated around the H-2/al Rutbah area ('Scud Alley') from an early date, while later in the campaign Delta Force operated slightly to the north around al Qaim ('Scud Boulevard').

The precise location of launchers was to be confirmed by stand-off platforms like the E-3, E-8, RC-135 or TR-1/U-2R, or reconnaissance aircraft including Tornado GR.1As, RF-4C Phantoms or F-14A TARPS-equipped Tomcats. Tasking had to be instantaneous, and was left to attack types trailing reconnaissance aircraft or to standing patrols of A-10As (day) or F-15Es (night). The research and production facilities were planned targets for Tornado GR.1, F-15E, F-111F and A-6E strikes.

The *Scud*-hunt may be judged a limited success only. Israel was kept out of the conflict, and Coalition pressure ensured that the Iraqis were required to keep their heads down. Of the suspected 600 available missiles, only eighty-eight were fired, fortunately none with chemical or biological warheads. The exercise highlighted weaknesses in Allied planning, including inflexibility and inadequate communications between the various reconnaissance assets and Special Forces on the ground within Iraq.

THE PLAN UNFOLDS

The pattern of bombing Iraqi installations within the original plans continued for some days, during which the IAF put up some Mirage and MiG-29 sorties, losing several dozen aircraft in combat. These losses were mainly to AIM-7 missiles fired from F-15C platforms.

The attack packages were complex to organize and to fly. Air Vice-Marshal W.J. Wratten, the RAF commander, has described a notional package, which would originate from the multi-national Air Tasking Order (ATO):

A typical . . . package might include a number of Tornadoes attacking a runway while (US) Marine Corps F/A-18s struck other facilities on the airfield with direct support being provided by US Navy A-7s and A-6s in the SEAD role and USAF EF-111s acting as stand-off jammers, all operating under an umbrella of F-14s flying force protection; the whole package, which would commonly involve well over fifty aircraft, being supported by an appropriate selection of tankers and monitored by the ubiquitous AWACS. There might be three equally complex missions, 150 or more aeroplanes, to a page – and there were lots of pages.

On 20 January Tornado ZA893 of 9 Sqn was abandoned by its crew due to flying-control problems shortly after take-off from Tabuk. Later in the day ZA396 of 27 Sqn was brought down while attacking Talil airfield with 1,000 lb bombs; the crew ejected safely but were captured. From the 20th poor weather set in, reducing the number of strikes and their effectiveness; both reconnaissance and target-marking suffered through the degradation of equipment performance. On 22 January the Tornado fleet suffered yet another loss when ZA467 of 16 Sqn was shot down while attacking a radar station at a Rutbah, with the loss of the crew. From this time IAF aircraft began to fly to safety to neighbouring Iran, starting with the transport types.

On 23 January it was announced that the Coalition had achieved air superiority and that in future all strikes would be conducted from medium level. Since the bulk of the AAA had an effective ceiling of 12,000 ft this was typically the height at which Tornado strike sorties were now flown. At sea, in an example of inter-service collaboration, a Lynx from HMS *Cardiff* directed A-6 bombers to three Iraqi naval targets it had identified, and all were sunk.

A weapon blooded in the Gulf War was the British Air-Launched Anti-Radar Missile (ALARM). Still in the development stage at the outbreak of war, it was rushed into service to help clear routes through AA defences for attacking aircraft. On firing, the missile climbs to 70,000 ft, the rocket stops and it descends slowly under a parachute, searching for specific frequencies emitted by radars. (The location of radars and their frequencies would have been stored in a database assembled from data collected by ELINT aircraft like the Nimrod and RC-135.) On locating an enemy frequency the parachute is discarded, the rocket restarts and the missile guides itself onto the offending equipment. Should the radar be switched off and the lock lost, the missile continues its trajectory to explode somewhere in the vicinity. Nine Tornadoes were wired to carry ALARM, initially two per aircraft on the inner wing pylons, and later three under the fuselage. Twenty-four ALARM missions were flown, in which 121 rounds were fired in fifty-two sorties.

At this time it was estimated that all of the main Iraqi air bases were inoperable, but this was patently not the case. The airfields attacked by RAF Tornadoes with JP233s were al Asad, H-2, H-3, Jalibah South-east, Wadi al Khirr, Mudaysis, Shaibah, al Taqaddum, Tallil and Ubadayah bin al Jarrah. The emphasis of the attack now turned to ground forces and installations, starting with those in Kuwait. Coalition fighters were also on constant CAP, and during the 23rd a Saudi pilot brought down two Mirages using AIM-9 Sidewinders. The aircraft were believed to have been involved in a possible Exocet strike on Allied naval forces, and the engagement almost certainly saved a warship or two from serious damage, if not destruction.

From 25 January Iraqi forces in Kuwait began pumping oil directly into the sea to form a massive 400-million gal oil slick designed to disrupt naval operations. Two days later the pumping stations were the targets of three F-111F bombers, which put them out of action using GBU-15 LGBs. IAF combat aircraft were now fleeing to Iran in increasing numbers, but over several days seven were brought down by USAF F-15s. RAF Tornadoes attacked an oil refinery in southern Iraq on the 28th, and the following day al Taqaddum and Ubadayah bin al Jarrah airfields and fuel storage depots were the targets.

It was again the turn of the naval Lynx helicopters to join combat. Aircraft from HMS *Brazen* (F91) and HMS *Gloucester* (D96) picked up radar contacts and identified a total of seventeen Iraqi patrol boats intent on mischief. In concert with helicopters from the USMC and Royal Saudi Navy, the boats were attacked with Sea Skua missiles and five destroyed.

At this turning point in the air war, a summary of the nature of actions may be useful. In the first ten days, first air superiority, and then air supremacy was achieved. In the background the E-3 AWACS were flying routine patrols and passing on threat details to fighters in the form of USAF F-15s and F-16s, RSAF F-15s, RAF and RSAF Tornado F.3s/ADVs, USN F-14s and French Mirage 2000Cs. Intelligence gatherers like the Nimrod R.1, USAF RC-135 and TR-1 and French AF Gabriel were collecting electronic and communications data and passing it back for interpretation and application. Aircraft like the EC-130H, EF-111A and EA-6D were jamming Iraqi communications and radar. Reconnaissance types such as the Tornado GR.1A, F-14A TARPS and RF-4C identified targets from the broader picture presented by the E-3s.

The jamming enabled the strike aircraft to attack airfields, radars and communications centres. The types involved included the Tornado GR.1, USAF F-111, F-117 and F-15E, USN F/A-18 and A-6E and RSAF Tornado. Throughout, the strike aircraft were refuelled by RAF VC-10, Tristar and Victor or USAF KC-135 and KC-10 and French C-135FR tankers. At the same time as the major assault on Iraq's air force and command and control systems, lighter strike aircraft were engaged in attacking coastal and other targets in Kuwait. These included the RAF and French Jaguars, USAF A-10As and USN A-7Es, but at this stage in the war the targets were installations rather than ground forces.

Behind the scenes was a mass of activity, both in preparation for the ground war and in bringing supplies to where they were needed. Transports like the Tristar and VC-10 and USAF C-141 and C-5 were supplemented by the ubiquitous C-130 Hercules, which together with the French Transall C-160 also provided the bulk of the intra-theatre transport. The larger transport helicopters like the RAF Chinook and Puma, Royal Navy Sea Kings and the US Army CH-47 and UH-60 and USMC CH-46 and H-53 were also engaged in moving men and *matériel* more locally. In the background, communications types like the BAe 125 and Army Islander were moving senior staff around, although the latter, deployed from Northern Ireland, may have been engaged on more proactive tasks.

Helicopters were also involved in inserting Special Forces into Kuwait and Iraq, including RAF Chinooks and USAF MH-53s and MH-60s, and they were supported by Hercules C.1s of 47 Sqn and MC- and HC-130s. There was a rumour of British Special Forces being inserted into Kuwait in an Mi-8 provided by the Egyptian Air Force. The blockade of Iraqi and Kuwaiti ports was enforced by RAF Nimrods and USN P-3s, with ship-borne helicopters like the Lynx and AH-1.

With total control of the air, the Coalition air forces now turned to interdiction and attacking ground forces. However, there was a diversion when on 30 January the Iraqis made five thrusts into Saudi Arabia. They were repulsed by USMC aircraft, but one column succeeded in reaching Khafji, where it was engaged in fighting with US Marines supported by AC-130 gunships, one of which was brought down the following day. Heavy fighting continued for several days.

RN Lynx were in action again, helping to sink eight patrol boats, and sinking a landing-craft on the 31st and two further patrol boats on 7 February. Jaguars attacked a howitzer battery north of Kuwait, and later, using CRV7 rockets, sank three landing-craft. The Jaguars were initially confined to operating over Kuwait. Their offensive load was limited to two 1,000 lb bombs or two BL755 cluster-bombs by the need for self-defence measures and wing fuel tanks. The two 30 mm Aden cannon each had 150 rounds, while there were two AIM-9Ls, an AN/ALQ-101 jamming pod and a Phimat chaff pod with two AN/ALE-40 flare dispensers on the rear fuselage. The wing tanks were soon exchanged for a single centre-line tank to enable the carriage of four bombs.

Once the aircraft were operating up to medium level, the CRV7 rocket launcher was fitted in place of the cluster-bombs. This weapon was a remarkably powerful 2.75 in. rocket with 6,000 ft range and terminal velocity of Mach 4. Nineteen were carried in a LAU-5003 pod, and the rockets could be fired singly or in ripple. The standard warhead was changed, possibly for tungsten flechettes. When the Jaguars turned to medium-level attack, the low-level BL755 cluster-bomb was useless: the answer was the CBU-87 Rockeye II, of which a large number were dropped.

By now thirty-eight airfields had been attacked in 1,300 sorties, and nine were out of action, with seventy out of 597 hardened aircraft shelters destroyed through precision bombing. The airfields were especially hard targets, which by virtue of their immense size (typically twice that of London Heathrow) were easy to find but very difficult to put out of commission completely.

For the RAF Tornadoes, major installations like oil pumping stations, bridges and airfields remained key targets, while the Jaguars typically attacked gun emplacements and, where they could be found, tanks. On 5 February eight B-52Gs were detached to Fairford, from where they struck at Republican Guard positions with full loads of 51 M-117 750 lb 'dumb' bombs, joining similar aircraft based in Spain, Egypt, Saudi Arabia and Diego Garcia.

After the third night of low-level attacks against the airfields (their initial key targets) with the JP233 dispenser, the Tornadoes shifted to medium-level bombing, as recounted above. (This was after dropping 126 dispensers.)

However, this change was not without problems, since the bomb-aiming equipment was optimized for very low level, as were the engines, which did not deliver full power at height. Thus the bomb-load potential of eight 1,000 lb bombs was reduced to five, and targets assigned were those suitable for non-precision bombing, like airfields, oil installations and barracks. In summary, while losses due to flying at very low level in concentrated AAA and SAM areas decreased, so did bombing accuracy. Although various approaches were tested, including dive-bombing, it was clear that to play a full part in the interdiction phase effective target marking was required.

The solution was to deploy the venerable Buccaneers of 12 and 208 Sqns to designate for the Tornadoes. These remaining operational units were now dedicated maritime strike squadrons, but 237 OCU retained an overland designator role in the event of conflict. Aircraft and crews were rapidly prepared for detachment. The aircraft were equipped with the AN/ASQ-153 *Pave Spike* target-designating system, including an AN/AVQ-23E laser pod. An AN/ALQ-101 jamming pod, AN/ALE-40 chaff and flare dispenser and AIM-9L Sidewinder AAM were also carried, although after it was clear that there was no threat from Iraqi fighters the latter was dropped in favour of offensive weapons.

The first mission took place on 2 February against a road bridge at as Samawah, with a pair of Buccaneers marking for four Tornadoes: it was a complete success, although some later missions were aborted when weather degraded the target-marking capability. During the period 2–13 February, bridges were the main target, with some twenty-four bombs dropped. When the AIM-9 was shelved, from 21 February, the Buccaneers dropped their own LGBs after having marked for the Tornadoes. In all, the Buccaneers flew 216 sorties, in twenty-four of which they dropped bombs in addition to marking.

SOFTENING UP THE BATTLEGROUND

From 10 February the Allied air forces resumed attacking airfields, and in addition to the continuing Scud-hunts, turned their attention in more detail to targets in Kuwait and the Iraqi border area where troops were massed. The airfields were targeted simply because there was a concern that the IAF might be launched on a last-ditch attack against Coalition forces, using CB weapons once the ground fighting started.

For the RAF a further innovation was the urgent introduction of two thermal imaging and laser designating (TIALD) pods, still in the development stage. Carried by Tornadoes, they were capable of marking at night and in bad weather, and although brought into service hurriedly, they complemented the Buccaneer markers, with five aircraft fitted to carry the pod. First use of the equipment was on 10 February to mark an armament factory. From the initial precision dropping of the JP233 loads at low level, to medium-level free-fall bombing, the RAF was now back in the business of precision bombing using LGBs with some effect. Forty-nine TIALD missions were flown, usually involving two designator aircraft plus four bombers, each with three 1,000 lb LGBs.

On the 11th the RN Lynx were in action yet again against a patrol craft. The Lynx/Sea Skua represented the most powerful anti-ship weapon system available to the Coalition, and in the course of the war, with support from Nimrods, the Lynx accounted for fifteen Iraqi naval vessels, including five TNC-45 Exocet-armed patrol boats. The Lynx could be fitted with the AN/ALQ-167 *Yellow Veil* jamming pod, ESM, night-vision aids, chaff and flare dispensers and IR jammers for defence, and more offensively 7.62 mm GPMG, Sea Skua anti-ship missile, Stingray torpedo and depth charges. It could also carry up to nine Marines for boarding suspect vessels. In total the Lynx fired twenty-six Sea Skua rounds, of which eighteen hit their targets, resulting in at least ten Iraqi vessels destroyed.

Naval Sea Kings were used for shifting supplies between vessels (vertrep), mine spotting and casualty evacuation at sea, but the majority were shore based, with the RAF Pumas and Chinooks shifting troops and supplies as Support Helicopter Force Middle East. Army TOW-equipped Lynxes with Gazelles operated from just behind the front line, and with no cover in the desert conditions were hastily fitted with infra-red sighting and night-vision goggles.

And so the attacks on airfields and ground installations continued, although worsening weather meant the abandonment of an increasing number of missions. Tornadoes were now attacking targets by day, and on the 14th ZD717 of 15 Sqn was shot down with the loss of the navigator, the pilot being captured. This aircraft was the last in a package of eight Tornadoes and four Buccaneers attacking al Taqaddum airfield. From the 15th fuel-air explosive bombs, the 15,000 lb BLU-82 and smaller CBU-55B, were dropped by USAF MC-130Es and MH-53s of 1

SOW respectively to clear paths through Iraqi minefields. A total of eleven of the monster BLU-82 was dropped, each sortie being preceded by leaflet drops.

Battlefield targets and lines of communication were increasingly the priority, and anticipating the invasion the Iraqis now set about igniting oil wells in Kuwait: some 300 had been fired by the 23rd. On the eve of the ground battle it was estimated that some 1,685 tanks, 925 other armoured vehicles and 1,485 artillery pieces had been destroyed.

THE GROUND WAR

By 24 February Allied forces were in their jumping-off points ready for the advance into Kuwait and southern Iraq. Since early January all forces, with their logistics bases, had been located south of Kuwait, with a major naval and USMC force at sea in the Gulf. On the eve of what became G-Day, the units moved up to their forward assembly areas along the Saudi borders with Iraq and Kuwait.

There were six Commands involved. On the left flank was XVIII Corps, comprising the US 82nd and 101st Airborne divisions, the 24th Mechanized Infantry Division, the 3rd Armoured Cavalry Regt and the French 6th Light Armoured Division. To their east, but still on the border with Iraq, was VII Corps comprising the US 1st and 3rd Armoured Divisions, the 1st Mechanized Infantry Division, the 2nd Armoured Cavalry Regt and the British 1st Armoured Division, which consisted of 4 and 7 Brigades.

South of Kuwait were Joint Forces Command – North (JFC-N) consisting of the 9th Syrian Armoured Division, Egyptian 4th Armoured and 3rd Infantry Divisions, plus Saudi and Kuwaiti infantry. In the centre of the Kuwaiti front was US Marine Forces Central (MARCENT), comprising the 1st and 2nd USMC Divisions, plus armour provided by the 1st Armoured Brigade. On the right flank against the sea, was JFC-E, which comprised Saudi and Kuwaiti infantry. Finally, to create a major diversion and suggest an amphibious assault, was the USMC expeditionary force.

The plan was to launch XVIII and VII Corps forces north-east into Iraq as far as Nasiriyah and al Bussayah respectively, then east to contain any retreating Iraqis or confront reinforcements. By then the Arab units on the Kuwaiti border, strengthened by Marines in the centre, would invade Kuwait across the strong border defences (ditches, berms, razor wire and minefields). An important part of the plan was that Kuwaitis and other Arab units would be seen to liberate Kuwait City. Had the Arab forces made little progress, XVIII and VII Corps units would turn south and smash Iraqi units against the MARCENT anvil.

At 04.00 hrs on 24 February Coalition armoured columns advanced into Iraq and Kuwait. The US 101st Airborne Division was transported into airhead 'Cobra' fifty miles into Iraq in the largest heliborne assault in history. Around a hundred transport helicopters – UH-60 and CH-47 – carried troops and equipment, supported by up to 200 attack and observation types. Considerable progress was made, and now it was the turn of the close-support aircraft and helicopters to come into their own. These included RAF Jaguars, Army TOW-equipped Lynx, USAF A-10s and F-15Es, USMC AV-8Bs and French Jaguars. For minimal Allied losses a large number of tanks and artillery pieces were destroyed.

The following day further US plus British and French forces struck, and during the day some 270 tanks were destroyed. The retreating Iraqis were now firing Kuwaiti oil wells, and by the end of the day 517 were alight. At sea, the US battleships *Missouri* and *Wisconsin* were firing Tomahawk cruise missiles at Baghdad when two Silkworm guided missiles were fired from the shore. One landed in the water and the second was shot down by a Sea Dart fired from HMS *Gloucester*.

The invasion now turned into a rout, and by late afternoon on the 26th Kuwait City had been abandoned, but with many buildings destroyed by the retreating forces. At this stage, USAF Special Forces found a concentration of twenty-nine Scud missiles in south-west Iraq. They were attacked by A-10s over a six-hour period. It is reported that Special Forces inserted by MH-53J *Pave Low* of 20 SOS located over forty mobile Scud missiles during the campaign, which had been missed by PR, satellites and roaming F-15Es and A-10As.

The E-8 J-STARS aircraft came into its own monitoring the Iraqi retreat and directing aircraft on to strafe the huge columns of vehicles on the so-called 'Highway of Death'. By the end of the day some 1,400 vehicles had been destroyed on the road, 30,000 prisoners had been taken and twenty-one Iraqi divisions eliminated. Allied casualties included nine British soldiers killed when two USAF A-10As attacked their Warrior APCs. On the 27th there was a large tank battle north of Kuwait between US units and the Republican Guard, but by now the battle was nearing its end. Through the five-day period of the ground fighting, helicopters moved with the troops both in support and bringing up weapons and supplies. In addition, Hercules transports brought up supplies to forward strips for onward movement.

By 27 February Saddam had indicated that he had met the requirements of all UN resolutions, and at 05.00Z on the 28th the US President declared a ceasefire, which came into effect formally on 3 March. The ground war had lasted precisely one hundred hours.

THE RECKONING

The total number of coalition aircraft deployed was in excess of 2,430 fixed-wing aircraft and several thousand helicopters. In addition to aircraft involved in supply from the UK, British services deployed a total of around 244 aircraft and helicopters, as described below.

Type	Numbers	Type	Numbers
BAe 125	1	Lynx Navy	10
Buccaneer	12	Puma	19
Chinook	17	Sea King HAS	2
Gazelle	24	Sea King HC.4	20
Hercules	7	Tornado F.3	18
Islander	1	Tornado GR	48
Jaguar	12	Tristar	2
Nimrod R.1	3	VC-10 K.2, K.3	9
Nimrod MR.2	5	Victor	8
Lynx Army	24		

In terms of combat-related sorties the overall RAF total was in the region of 5,395, as set out below. This represented 4.6% of the total of 117,881 sorties recorded by all Coalition air forces excluding the British Army and Royal Navy Lynx and Sea King HAS.5. However, the figures are difficult to reconcile since they come from official US sources that include inter-theatre transport sorties. If these are excluded and the likely Army and Navy figures are added, the British contribution comes to nearer 7 or 8%.

Type	Sorties	Outputs
Tornado GR1	1,514	inc. 95 TIALD sorties, 126 JP233, 123 ALARM, 488 LGBs, 4,200 bombs
Tornado GR1A	130	
Jaguar GR.1	585	750 bombs, 385 CBU-87s, 8 BL755, 608 rockets, 9,600 rounds
Jaguar GR.1	26	recce sorties
Buccaneer S.2B	226	48 LGBs dropped
Tornado F.3	705	
Nimrod MR.2	67	
Nimrod R.1	80	
Victor K.2	277	
VC-10 K.2	359	6,800 tonnes fuel transferred
Tristar K	75	1,000 tonnes fuel transferred
Hercules C1, C.3	832	13,912 passengers, 3,356 tonnes freight
Puma HC.1 Chinook HC.1 Sea King HC.4	517	Combined total

At the outset of the war, very large casualties had been anticipated, from both conventional warfare and the prospect of Iraqi use of chemical and biological weapons. In many NHS hospitals wards were emptied and staff prepared for a great influx of wounded. Further, it has been suggested that as many as 25% of personnel deployed to the Gulf were in support of medical services. In the event, the immediate toll was mercifully small.

The UK deployed a total of 43,000 personnel, of whom twenty-four were killed, including five Tornado aircrew: a further seven were captured and held as prisoners of war. Of those killed, nine (37%) were from so-called 'friendly fire', while the United States forces lost 148 killed of 537,000 deployed, of which number 24% were lost to friendly fire. Some 85,000 Iraqi servicemen were estimated killed or wounded, and up to 80,000 civilians.

There is one residual concern as to long-term casualties from the Gulf War. In both the UK and USA there is a growing number of ex-servicemen suffering from a range of symptoms and diseases, collectively described as Gulf War syndrome. Several possible causes are ascribed, including the various (sometimes untried) vaccines and inoculations given, the possible subtle use of chemical agents, pollution from the burning oil wells and the use of depleted uranium in warheads.

RAF combat losses were confined to six Tornadoes, while the US forces lost twenty-seven aircraft in operations and other Allies lost three, including an Italian Tornado. No British Army or Royal Navy aircraft were lost. Of the Iraqi Air Force, 137 aircraft fled to Iran and 141 were claimed destroyed – forty-one in combat and one hundred on the ground.

One problem which emerged arose from the RAF use of composite squadrons made up of air- and ground-crew from a number of units. With common purpose and sound leadership, coupled with some familiarity within a small air force, the moulding of disparate parts into a cohesive unit was feasible. A problem not anticipated was that of reintegration of personnel into their original squadrons, when an 'élite' returned from the intensity and stress of operations.

For British air arms new equipment was introduced and used to significant effect, or weapons which had been available for some time were first used in action. At this juncture it might also be appropriate to refer to the significant contribution made in the UK and in the field by industry personnel who worked day and night to get weapons and equipment tested and produced in record time.

The JP233 airfield-denial weapon worked as advertised, but the numbers available were not sufficient to put all of the thirty main Iraqi airbases out of action. These main bases were vast, with parallel runways and considerable redundancy. There has been a suggestion that some weapons were released across taxiways and hardened aircraft shelters (HAS), but the photographs released show repaired cratering along and astride runways. To some extent the sandy sub-surface absorbed some of the impact of the SG-357 runway penetrators, and it appears that the craters were soon repaired.

Other successful weapons proving their worth were naval missiles. The Sea Skua/Lynx combination was the most powerful anti-surface-vessel weapon system available to the Coalition. The Sea Dart almost certainly saved a USN capital ship from a direct hit by a Silkworm missile.

TIALD was rushed into theatre for night and poor weather marking, although conditions in the region were such that marking was not always successful. It appears that TIALD performed well in the circumstances. ALARM was another weapon hurried into use, and again it seems to have performed well.

Satellites were used extensively, and some sixty were involved in this fourth dimension. Their use included communications, reconnaissance, image relay, weather observation and, through the global positioning system (GPS), navigation.

SEQUEL

The Coalition could have continued its drive north into Iraq, removed Saddam and occupied Iraq. Within the terms of UN Resolution 678, the partners could '... use *all necessary means* [author's italics] to uphold and implement Resolution 660 ... and to restore international peace and security in the area'. Indeed, there was some pressure both in the USA and in the UK for that to happen. However, not only would this have resulted in many more casualties, it would have wrecked the Coalition, since the Arab partners would have had to withdraw and distance themselves.

As the war around Kuwait ended, armed Kurds in the north of Iraq revolted in an attempt to overthrow

Saddam. Their efforts were brutally suppressed, and many militia and civilians fled to the extreme north and over the border into Turkey. At the same time – encouraged by announcements of implied US support – Shi'ite groups in the south of Iraq also revolted. Again, the revolt was suppressed by Republican Guard units with mass executions.

In the north the UK and US had responded immediately to the needs of the civilian community with the deployment of utility helicopters and transports. Two important UN resolutions then followed. No. 687 required Iraq to stop the development and manufacture of weapons of mass destruction. Resolution 688 of 5 April 1991 demanded that Iraq cease repression. On 6 April US President Bush directed US Forces Europe to set up a task force to provide relief to the Kurds in Operation *Provide Comfort*. Also providing support within the Combined Task force (CTF) were British and French transports and support.

One aspect of the US counter to Iraqi repression was the establishment of 'no-fly' zones designed to prevent the Iraqi Air Force from any flying outside central Iraq. These no-fly zones were of dubious legality, but were enforced by US and UK aircraft. The British contribution was Operation *Warden* which extended in December 1991 to provide Harrier, Jaguar and Tornado detachments to Incirlik Airbase, Turkey. From 31 December 1996 *Provide Comfort* became *Northern Watch*, as US and British aircraft continued to monitor Iraqi air activity north of the 36th Parallel. *Northern Watch* ended with the occupation of Iraq on 1 May 2003.

In the south, Joint Task Force – South-West Asia (JTF – SWA) initiated *Southern Watch* from 27 August 1992, at first insisting on an Iraqi 'no-fly' zone to the 32nd Parallel, and then to the 33rd. This time France, Saudi Arabia, the United Kingdom and United States were committed, and the RAF based both strike and air defence Tornadoes in Saudi Arabia in Operation *Jural*. On the ground, weapons inspectors from the United Nations Special Commission (UNSCOM) and the International Atomic Energy Authority (IAEA) were in Iraq, attempting to check on the removal or destruction of chemical, biological and nuclear weapons or the means of creating them.

There was action in September 1996 when the Iraqis took military action against Kurds, resulting in Operation *Desert Strike*, in which US forces fired cruise missiles against the air defence system. Then in October 1998 Saddam refused to co-operate further with the weapons inspectors unless sanctions, imposed after the 1991 war, were removed. British forces in Kuwait and Saudi Arabia were reinforced in Operation *Bolton*, and between 16 and 19 December massive air strikes were launched against a range of military targets. RAF Tornadoes of 12 Sqn launched thirty-two sorties in which sixty-one Paveway bombs were dropped within Operation *Desert Fox*. Standing off in the Gulf was HMS *Invincible* with a squadron of Harrier GR.7s on board. In June 2002 *Southern Watch* became *Southern Focus*, and the British involvement in both north and south became Operation *Resinate*.

Since 1991, in Operation *Rockingham*, British sources had been feeding the weapons inspectors with data, not all of which was necessarily accurate. There was increasing US concern about instability in the Middle East and the impact on oil supplies and therefore prices, and also a perceived need to extend the 'war on terror' in the aftermath of the bombing of the Twin Towers in 2001. In November 2002 the United Nations Security Council passed Resolution 1441 condemning Iraq for breaching the agreement on weapons of mass destruction. The USA, UK and Spain attempted to secure a further resolution sanctioning force, but this was rejected. Thus it was that on 20 March 2003 a loose coalition led by the USA, and with full UK support, illegally invaded Iraq, finally capturing the country by 1 May.

Although there appears to have been a military strategy, there was no evidence of any long-term policy, and no provision for managing the country after the invasion. The 'victors' were not universally welcomed with open arms, and at the time of writing, while British forces are desperately disengaging in the south, US forces continue to address insurgency, with no obvious way out. It seems that the imposition of Western ideas of democracy are not well received in the cradle of civilization.

PANAVIA TORNADO (FIGHTER VARIANTS)

The origins of the Tornado lie with Dr Barnes Wallis, of geodetic structures and dam-busting bomb fame. From 1944, working with Vickers at Weybridge, he had explored the feasibility of a wing which changed shape, critically by sweeping. Models were flown in the form of the *Wild Goose* and then *Swallow* on behalf of Vickers and the RAE at Predannack between 1952 and 1954. In 1963 BAC undertook a private-venture study of a military variable-geometry aircraft, and when the TSR.2 was abandoned the Government decided to pursue two collaborative programmes with France, one to become the Jaguar and the other the so-called Anglo-French variable geometry (AFVG). Intended for conflicting roles, the latter stood little chance of being built, and indeed the French pulled out in late 1966.

However, the design principles were kept alive, and after various false starts Britain, Germany and Italy agreed, in 1968, to move ahead on what was initially described as the multi-role combat aircraft (MRCA). The prototype was flown in Germany on 14 August 1974, and the first British aircraft flew on 10 October the same year. The strike versions are described in Chapter 4, Section 1.

The **F Mark 2** was very much an interim fighter version, of which only ten were built. The Tornado fighter was intended as a long-range interceptor optimized for defending against Warsaw Pact bomber attacks on the United Kingdom. Its Skyflash AAM armament enables contact at twenty-five miles range in hostile weather and ECM environments. The type was never intended as a dogfighter and it is not especially agile. The air defence variant (ADV) was not required by the other partners, and the prototype flew on 27 October 1979. Problems with the Foxhunter radar resulted in ballast being installed in the nose, but service entry with 229 OCU enabled a start to be made on training from November 1984.

The **F Mark 3** was the fully operational fighter variant of the Tornado. The engine was slightly more powerful, and fully automatic wing sweep was incorporated. Additional fuel was carried in larger (495 gal) drop-tanks and 200 gal internally. In addition there was provision for in-flight refuelling with a fully recessed probe on the port side of the fuselage. Armament comprised a single 27 mm Mauser cannon, four Skyflash and four AIM-9 Sidewinders. The first production aircraft flew on 20 November 1985. Service entry was with 29 Sqn in July 1987. Later upgrades in the light of experience in Bosnia in the 1990s include underwing Phimat chaff pods and Tracor ALE-40 chaff and flare dispensers under the rear fuselage.

Fighter units equipped – 5, 11, 23, 25, 29, 43, 111; 1435

SEPECAT JAGUAR

The Jaguar is the first warplane produced on a collaborative basis by two partners in different countries. The design of the aircraft had its distant origins in the Breguet Taon which in 1957 won a NATO light-fighter competition, in the event not progressed. The French and Royal Air Forces both had a requirement for a fast trainer, and Breguet/Dassault and the British Aircraft Corporation (BAC) collaborated in the production of both training and attack versions – in the case of the UK the fighter version was required to compensate for the cancellation of the P.1154 and the intended Anglo-French variable geometry (AFVG) aircraft, which later resurfaced as the Tornado. Agreement was reached in 1966 for joint development and manufacture, in the UK to AST362. During the course of early development the aircraft was fitted with a taller fin and larger nosewheel door. The single-seat fighter replaced the Phantom in Germany and the UK, where the latter type was an interim solution to replacement of the Canberra.

The Jaguar **GR Mark 1** first flew in French two-seat (E) form in September 1968, and the first British prototype, a single-seater, flew on 12 October 1969. The Jaguar was intended as a low-level strike aircraft capable of Mach 1.6, but operating from simple strips and carrying a powerful external weapons load of up to 10,500 lb on five hardpoints. In addition there were two fixed 30 mm Aden cannon. The RAF attack version differed from the French in having a digital inertial navigation system, and from 1974 external changes included a revised nose to accommodate the Ferranti Laser Ranger and Marked Target Seeker (LRMTS), and a radar warning receiver on the fin. The changes were retro-fitted to all surviving aircraft. Service introduction was with the Jaguar OCU in September 1973, and the first squadron was 54, from March 1974.

The **Mark 1A** was a GR Mk 1 conversion with the improved FIN 1064 INS, which gave unprecedented accuracy and was fitted from 1983. From 1978 the engines were upgraded to the Adour 104, while from 1992 a range of defensive and offensive equipment changes was incorporated, partly to meet operational requirements of the Gulf War and that in Bosnia.

Ground attack units equipped – 6, 14, 17, 20, 31, 54
Reconnaissance – 2, 41

WESTLAND LYNX

The Lynx was the third of the helicopters involved in the Anglo-French collaboration agreement of 1968 (the others were the Gazelle and Puma), and it was the only one in which Westland had the design lead. The WG.13 design was intended for civil and general naval use, and the prototype flew on 21 March 1971. The Lynx was extremely robust and was fitted with a rigid rotor driven by a pair of Gem turboshafts; its versatility soon led to British Army orders, but French interest was confined to around forty for the *Aéronavale*. The company demonstrator was developed and, in a hybrid form, with advanced rotors, secured the world helicopter speed record of 249.09 mph on 11 August 1986.

The **AH Mark 1** was built for the British Army to GSOR 3335 to fulfil a number of roles. These included troop transport (twelve troops), logistic support (2,000 lb internally, 3,000 lb externally), armed escort, anti-tank strike, casevac, search and rescue, reconnaissance and command post. The first production aircraft flew on 11 February 1977, and the Lynx joined BAOR squadrons from August 1978. From 1980 the TOW ATM was fitted (eight missiles). The **AH Mark 1GT** designation was applied to some machines taken to AH.7 standard but retaining AH.1 avionics.

Utility units equipped – 651, 652, 653, 654, 656, 657, 659, 661, 662, 663, 671

The **HAS Mark 2** was the first naval version built for the Fleet Air Arm and *Aéronavale* for the ship-borne anti-submarine-warfare role. It had a fixed castoring undercarriage, folding tail and Seaspray search radar, and it carried four Sea Skua ASMs, two Mk 46 or Stingray torpedoes or two Mk 11 depth charges. The prototype flew on 10 February 1976, and service entry was with 700L NAS in September 1976.

The **HAS Mark 3** version had the more powerful Gem 41 engine, but was otherwise similar to the HAS.2, some of which were rebuilt to HAS.3 standard. Two helicopters were downgraded for use on HMS *Endurance* as the **HAS.3ICE**. In the Gulf War eighteen aircraft were fitted with improved cooling, an IR jammer and ALQ-167 ECM system as the **HAS.3GM**.

The **HAS.3S** and **HAS.3CTS** sub-variants represented stages in the conversion of HAS.3 aircraft to HAS.8 configuration. The former included at least fifty-five airframes fitted with *Orange Crop* ESM and GEC Marconi AD 3400 radios. The CTS aircraft were in addition fitted with Racal 4000 central tactical system and flotation bags on the sponsons.

ASW units equipped – 815, 829

The **AH Mark 7** was similar to the intended Mark 5, which was very much an interim type, fitted with the Gem 41-1 engine but otherwise similar to the AH.1. However, the AH.7 was fitted with a larger tail rotor working clockwise. Like many later AH.1 aircraft, the type was fitted with a TOW sight on the cabin and a large box shroud on the exhaust. Many AH.1 machines were converted to AH.7 standard.

Utility units equipped – 651, 652, 653, 654, 655, 657, 659, 663, 664, 665, 667, 669, 671, 672; 3 CBAS; 847

The **HAS Mark 8** definitive naval variant was the first of the 'Super Lynx' variants fitted with the much improved British Experimental Rotor Programme (BERP) main rotors driven by two Gem 42-1 engines. The reverse tail rotor was employed, and improved avionics included the Racal 4000 CTS, MIR-2 ESM, together with the *Sea Owl* thermal imaging system. Sixty-five HAS.3 airframes were brought up to HAS.8 standard. Some HAS.8 helicopters optimized for attack are designated **HMA Mark 8**.

ASW unit equipped – 815

The **AH Mark 9** is, in the broadest sense, the Army equivalent of the HAS.8, incorporating BERP main rotors and the Gem 42-1 engine. But perhaps the most significant external change is the provision of a fixed tricycle undercarriage instead of skids. It is intended as an unarmed troop carrier and command post, and incorporates improved avionics.

Utility units equipped – 653, 659, 664, 672, 673

The Second Gulf War, 1990–91

Unit	Aircraft	Base	Ex	From	To
Royal Air Force – Detachments comprised *some* aircraft and crews detached from the units indicated, with the first squadron listed in each group having the lead role.					
Saudi Arabia					
29 Sqn	Tornado F.3	Dhahran	Coningsby[1]	11.8.90	30.8.90
5 Sqn	Tornado F.3		Coningsby[1]	11.8.90	30.8.90
11 Sqn	Tornado F.3	Dhahran	Leeming	30.8.90	12.90
23 Sqn	Tornado F.3		Leeming	30.8.90	12.90
25 Sqn	Tornado F.3		Leeming	30.8.90	12.90
43 Sqn	Tornado F.3	Dhahran	Leuchars	12.90	13.3.91
29 Sqn	Tornado F.3		Coningsby	12.90	13.3.91
16 Sqn	Tornado GR.1	Tabuk	Muharraq	8.10.90	9.3.91
2 Sqn	Tornado GR.1		Muharraq	8.10.90	9.3.91
9 Sqn	Tornado GR.1		Muharraq	8.10.90	9.3.91
14 Sqn	Tornado GR.1		Muharraq	8.10.90	9.3.91
20 Sqn	Tornado GR.1		Muharraq	8.10.90	9.3.91
31 Sqn	Tornado GR.1	Dhahran	Brüggen	3.1.91	13.3.91
2 Sqn	Tornado GR.1A		Laarbruch	14.1.91	13.3.91
9 Sqn	Tornado GR.1		Brüggen	3.1.91	13.3.91
13 Sqn	Tornado GR.1A		Honington	14.1.91	13.3.91
14 Sqn	Tornado GR.1		Brüggen	3.1.91	13.3.91
17 Sqn	Tornado GR.1		Brüggen	3.1.91	9.3.91
242 OCU	Hercules C.1P, C.3P	Riyadh[2]	Lyneham	9.8.90	14.4.91
24 Sqn	Hercules C.1P, C.3P		Lyneham	9.8.90	14.4.91
30 Sqn	Hercules C.1P, C.3P		Lyneham	9.8.90	14.4.91
47 Sqn	Hercules C.1P, C.3P		Lyneham	9.8.90	14.4.91
70 Sqn	Hercules C.1P, C.3P		Lyneham	9.8.90	14.4.91
40 Sqn RNZAF	C-130H Hercules		Whenuapai	23.12.90	4.91
101 Sqn	VC-10 K.2, K.3	Riyadh	Brize Norton	10.90	13.3.91
32 Sqn	BAe 125 CC.2, CC.3	Riyadh	Northolt	9.90	4.91
230 Sqn	Puma HC.1	Ras al Ghar	Gütersloh	1.11.90	22.1.91
		Riyadh	Ras al Ghar	22.1.91	17.3.91
33 Sqn	Puma HC.1	Ras al Ghar	Odiham	1.11.90	22.1.91
		Riyadh	Ras al Ghar	22.1.91	17.3.91
7 Sqn	Chinook HC.1	Ras al Ghar	Gütersloh	25.11.90	22.1.91
		Riyadh	Ras al Ghar	22.1.91	15.3.91
18 Sqn	Chinook HC.1	Ras al Ghar	Odiham	6.1.91	22.1.91
		Riyadh	Ras al Ghar	22.1.91	15.3.91
240 OCU	Chinook HC.1	Ras al Ghar	Odiham	25.11.90	22.1.91
		Riyadh	Ras al Ghar	22.1.91	15.3.91
Oman					
41 Sqn	Jaguar GR.1A	Thumrait	Coltishall	11.8.90	29.8.90
6 Sqn	Jaguar GR.1A		Coltishall	11.8.90	29.8.90
54 Sqn	Jaguar GR.1A		Coltishall	11.8.90	29.8.90
226 OCU	Jaguar GR.1A		Lossiemouth	11.8.90	29.8.90

Unit	Aircraft	Base	Ex	From	To
41 Sqn	Jaguar GR.1A	Seeb	Thumrait	29.8.90	10.10.90
6 Sqn	Jaguar GR.1A		Thumrait	29.8.90	10.10.90
54 Sqn	Jaguar GR.1A		Thumrait	29.8.90	10.10.90
226 OCU	Jaguar GR.1A		Thumrait	29.8.90	10.10.90
120 Sqn	Nimrod MR.2P	Seeb	Kinloss	12.8.90	17.4.91[3]
201 Sqn	Nimrod MR.2P		Kinloss	12.8.90	17.4.91
206 Sqn	Nimrod MR.2P		Kinloss	12.8.90	17.4.91
42 Sqn	Nimrod MR.2P		St Mawgan	12.8.90	17.4.91
51 Sqn	Nimrod R.1P	Seeb	Wyton	8.90	4.91
101 Sqn[4]	VC-10 K.2, K.3	Seeb	Brize Norton	11.8.90	15.3.91
Bahrain					
15 Sqn	Tornado GR.1	Muharraq	Laarbruch	29.8.90	5.91
9 Sqn	Tornado GR.1		Brüggen	29.8.90	5.91
17 Sqn	Tornado GR.1		Brüggen	29.8.90	5.91
27 Sqn	Tornado GR.1		Marham	29.8.90	5.91
31 Sqn	Tornado GR.1		Brüggen	29.8.90	5.91
617 Sqn	Tornado GR.1		Marham	29.8.90	5.91
16 Sqn[5]	Tornado GR.1	Muharraq	Laarbruch	19.9.90	8.10.90
2 Sqn	Tornado GR.1A		Laarbruch	19.9.90	8.10.90
9 Sqn	Tornado GR.1		Brüggen	19.9.90	8.10.90
13 Sqn	Tornado GR.1A		Honington	19.9.90	8.10.90
14 Sqn	Tornado GR.1		Brüggen	19.9.90	8.10.90
20 Sqn	Tornado GR.1		Laarbruch	19.9.90	8.10.90
208 Sqn	Buccaneer S.2B	Muharraq	Lossiemouth	26.1.91	17.3.91
12 Sqn	Buccaneer S.2B		Lossiemouth	26.1.91	17.3.91
237 OCU	Buccaneer S.2B		Lossiemouth	26.1.91	17.3.91
41 Sqn	Jaguar GR.1A	Muharraq	Coltishall	10.10.90	12.3.91
6 Sqn	Jaguar GR.1A		Coltishall	10.10.90	12.3.91
54 Sqn	Jaguar GR.1A		Coltishall	10.10.90	12.3.91
226 OCU	Jaguar GR.1A		Coltishall	10.10.90	12.3.91
55 Sqn	Victor K.2	Muharraq	Marham	14.12.90	18.3.91
101 Sqn	VC-10 K.2	Muharraq	Brize Norton	27.8.90	13.3.91
216 Sqn[6]	Tristar K.1	Muharraq	Brize Norton	1.91	2.91
United Arab Emirates					
47 Sqn	Hercules C.1P	various	Lyneham	1.91	4.91
Cyprus[7]					
19 Sqn	Phantom FGR.2	Akrotiri	Wildenrath	9.90	3.91
92 Sqn	Phantom FGR.2	Akrotiri	Wildenrath	9.90	3.91
United Kingdom					
216 Sqn	Tristar K.1, KC.1, C.2	Brize Norton	n/a	based	
Fleet Air Arm					
826D NAS	Sea King HAS.5	RFA *Olna*	Culdrose	18.8.90	10.90
		HrMs *Zuiderkruis* RFA *Olna*		10.90	13.12.90

Unit	Aircraft	Base	Ex	From	To
826C NAS	Sea King HAS.5	HrMs *Zuiderkruis*	Culdrose	14.12.90	26.1.91
		RFA *Sir Galahad* HrMs *Zuiderkruis*		26.1.91	3.91
845 NAS	Sea King HC.4	Jubail and FOBs	Yeovilton	6.1.91	4.91
846B NAS	Sea King HC.4	RFA *Fort Grange, Fort Austin*	Yeovilton	22.8.90	16.3.91
846C NAS	Sea King HC.4	RFA *Argus*	Yeovilton	11.90	4.91
846D NAS	Sea King HC.4	RFA *Argus*	Yeovilton	11.90	4.91
848 NAS	Sea King HC.4	Jubail and FOBs	Yeovilton	6.1.91	4.91
815 NAS	Lynx HAS.3GM	HMS *Cardiff Gloucester, York London, Exeter, Manchester*	Portland,	2.8.90	3.91
829 NAS	Lynx HAS.3CTS	HMS, *Brazen,* Portland *Brilliant, Jupiter, Brave*		2.8.90	3.91
Task Group 323.2 Eastern Mediterranean					
801 NAS	Sea Harrier FRS.1	HMS *Ark Royal*	Yeovilton	1.91	4.91
820 NAS	Sea King HAS.5	HMS *Ark Royal*	Culdrose	1.91	4.91
849B NAS	Sea King AEW.2	HMS *Ark Royal*	Culdrose	1.91	4.91
815 NAS	Lynx HAS.3GM	HMS *Sheffield*	Portland	1.91	3.91
829 NAS	Lynx HAS.3CTS	HMS *Charybdis*	Portland	2.91	4.91
British Army					
654 Sqn	Gazelle AH.1, Lynx AH.7	Al Jubail	Detmold	12.90	3.91
659 Sqn	Gazelle AH.1, Lynx AH.7	Al Jubail	Detmold	12.90	3.91
661 Sqn	Gazelle AH.1, Lynx AH.7 Islander AL.1	Al Jubail	Hildesheim	12.90	3.91

NOTES

1   At Armament Practice Camp, Akrotiri, at the time

2   The Hercules were active on inter-theatre tasks from the outset, but a detachment was based at King Khalid International, Riyadh, for intra-theatre tasks from 1.11.90. A main forward-operating base was at Qysumah LZ04. A residue remained at Muharraq from 14 April 1991

3   Date of departure of last aircraft

4   Detachment to support Jaguars and Nimrods, thus some moved with the Jaguars to Muharraq

5   Transferred to Tabuk

6   Intermittent detachment during January and February to supplement VC-10s and Victors

7   Six Phantoms on Cyprus for AD

Epilogue

British armed services were involved in around two dozen major conflicts during the Cold War period covered by this book. Some, like the Malayan campaign, confrontation in Borneo, and the Falklands war, were well planned and executed and achieved their objectives. Others, like the Suez affair, were poorly thought through at the political level and indifferently planned. Many were fought by national servicemen with great bravery but so often inadequately equipped for the tasks which confronted them. It seems remarkable at this distance that immediately post-war Britain could have been fighting on five fronts – Indo-China, Greece, Palestine, Netherlands East Indies and Southern Arabia – simultaneously, while retaining forces in India and Africa.

In the early years air power was used with limited precision in general support of ground forces. As time went by, and coincident with the end of national service and the emergence of a more professional military, air power was used more precisely. The development of new weapons systems enabled tasks to be undertaken with fewer aircraft and at less risk to those flying them. More specialized roles emerged.

A recurring theme in many of the actions described is the value of the aircraft carrier. These warships played a supporting role in most of the events described in this book, but were key in a number like the Suez action, the defence of Kuwait in 1961 and the recovery of the Falkland Islands. Hopefully the present government will ensure that Britain's legitimate interests may be protected in the future with the support of the two new carriers on order: at the time of writing the financial crisis threatens their completion.

Conducted without fuss has been a plethora of humanitarian relief, evacuation and peacekeeping missions. For the future these tasks will be extremely valuable both in keeping British service men and women engaged and highly competent, and also in making friends across the globe.

Experience in Northern Ireland coupled with decades of covert special forces actions in a variety of settings has given Britain a high degree of competence in addressing terrorism. Increasingly complex equipment resulting in real-time intelligence coupled with great skill and bravery have resulted in the United Kingdom leading the way and indeed training others in the black arts.

The 'multi-national' intervention in Lebanon in 1983 and then the second Gulf War pointed the way for future British involvement in overt conflicts. Conflicts outside the scope of this book – actions in former Yugoslavia, Sierra Leone and the third Gulf War – tend to confirm the future direction of British military operations. They also suggest better integration of all three services into 'purple' units.

The UK has insufficient capacity for singular engagement in anything but the smallest of wars. The UK will therefore provide specialized forces, often complementary to those of likely allies, and drawing on special equipment and training. Deployment will be of airmen and aircraft in composite units as part of a wider coalition, generally likely to be US dominated. These coalitions will include the United Nations, NATO, the European Union and others assembled for specific purposes. High on the agenda will be covert action against terrorism and the speedy deployment of specialized forces, both to fight alongside allies and to support humanitarian relief across Africa, Asia, and Europe.

APPENDIX A

Aircraft Descriptions

Aircraft are described at various relevant stages through the book. The following is an index of where details are to be found. Only significant combat types and variants are included and only their post-war use is noted.

APPENDIX B

Operations, Projects and Exercises

Operation	Section	Operation	Section
Able Mabel	7.1	Crown	7.1
Agila	6.4	Cyclone I, II	3.7
Ale	7.2	Daguet	9.4
Alfred	6.3	Damen	5.1
Antler	4.3	Dark Bottle	6.3
Anvil	3.4	Desert Fox	9.4
Ardent	6.6	Desert Shield	9.4
Armilla	9.3, 9.4	Desert Storm	9.4
Backfire	4.2	Desert Strike	9.4
Banner	8.4	Dewey	8.3
Beehive	3.7	Dhanarajata	7.1
Bell Tone	7.1	Diagram	6.1
Bibber	7.1	Dick Tracey	4.5
Birdcage	6.1	Dodge	6.1
Birdsong	7.2	Dwikova	7.2
Bison	3.7	El Dorado Canyon	9.2
Black Buck	7.7	Exodus	6.1
Black Buck	4.1	Field Goal	7.1
Blue Bat	5.4	Fina	7.1
Bobcat	1.4	Firedog	3.7, 6.6
Bold	3.7	Firework	5.1
Bold Guard	6.4	First Flute	3.4
Bolton	9.4	Fortitude	5.4
Borneo Territories	7.2	Foxhunter	3.2
Buffalo	4.3	Gopherwood	6.3
Burberry	8.1	Granby	9.4
Bushell	6.5	Grapple	4.3, 4.5
Carter Paterson	2.2	Half Cock	6.3
Castle	4.3	Hamilcar	5.3
Centipede	3.7	Hammer	3.4
Chacewater	8.5	Haystack	3.7
Chamfrom	7.2	Heliotrope	8.3
Charlotte	7.1	Helsby	3.7
Chowhound	6.1	Himaar	5.6
Constant Phoenix	4.5	Hogmanay	6.3
Cordage	5.3	Hornbeam	5.6
Corporate	7.7	Hunger I, II, III, IV	6.1
Counter Battery	5.1	Hurricane	4.3

Operation	Section	Operation	Section
Insomnia	2.4	Profiteer	3.7
Jackpot	3.7	Project I, II, III, IV	2.3
Jacobin	6.3	Provide Comfort	9.4
Jaguar	5.6	Pulsator	9.1
Jock Scott	3.4	Puma	3.7
Josstick	3.7	Quick Flight	6.2
Journeyman	6.4	Red Lion I, II	3.7
Jowar	3.5	Resinate	9.4
Ju Jitsu	4.5	Robin	4.5
Jural	9.4	Rockingham	9.4
Kadesh	5.3	Rosario	7.7
Khana Cascade	6.4	Rotor	4.4
Khana Cascade 80	6.5	Ruddock	8.1
King Canute	6.2	Saw Buck	7.1
Kingly Pile	3.7	Scimitar	9.4
Knicker	2.2	Sky Help	6.3
Legate	4.4	Snowdrop	6.2
Locust	9.4	Southern Focus	9.4
Lone Ranger	5.1	Southern Watch	9.4
Lucan	6.4	Springtrain	7.7
Lucky Alphonse	3.2	Stagecoach	8.1
Manhattan	Prologue, 4.3	Stair Step	2.6
Manna	6.0, 6.1	Strangle	2.4
Mastiff	6.1	Sunburn	1.4
Mileage	3.7	Sunray	1.5, 3.3, 5.1
Moon Glow	7.1	Sword	3.7
Moonlight Sonata	2.4	Tana Flood	6.3
Mop-up	6.3	Tapestry	8.5
Mosaic	4.3	Termite	3.7
Motorman	8.4	Tiara	8.5
Muggah	5.1	Tiger	3.7
Musgrave	3.7	Tireless	3.7
Musketeer	5.3	Titan	6.5
Niggard	5.1	Totem	4.3
Northern Watch	9.4	Trinity	4.3
Nutcracker	5.1	Valiant	3.7
Oliver	6.3	Valuable	2.3
Paraquet	7.7	Vantage	5.5
Pedal	6.3	Vittles	2.2
Pepperpot	3.2	Warbler	3.7
Plainfare	2.2	Warden	9.4
Planter's Punch	3.7	West Bard	5.1
Polly	6.1	Whippet	8.3
Polly	1.4	Wringer	4.5
Prairie Fire	9.2	Zipper	5.1
Private Eye	6.3		

Bibliography

Throughout the preparation of this book numerous references have been consulted. Some of these are very general, while others relate broadly to specific parts of the world.

CHAPTER 1, SECTION 1

Cawthorne, C. (ed), *Prisoners of ELAS Greeks*, Private, London, 1947
Kousoulas, D.G., *Revolution and Defeat*, London, 1965
Matthews, K., *Memories of a Mountain War*, London, 1972

CHAPTER 1, SECTION 2

Fall, B.B., *Street Without Joy – Insurgency in Indo-China 1946–63*, Pall Mall, London 1964
Hammer, E.J., *The Struggle for Indo-China 1940–55*, Stanford University Press, Stanford, 1966

CHAPTER 1, SECTION 3

Lee, D., *Eastward: A History of the Royal Air Force in the Far East 1946–1972*, HMSO, London, 1984
Wehl, D., *The Birth of Indonesia*, Allen & Unwin, London, 1948

CHAPTER 1, SECTION 4

Azcarate, P. de, *Mission in Palestine, 1948–1952*, Middle East Institute, Washington, 1966
Kurzman, D., *Genesis 1948: The First Arab-Israeli War*, Vallentine Mitchell, London, 1972
Lorch, N., *The Edge of the Sword: Israel's War of Independence 1947–1949*, Putnam, London, 1961
O'Ballance, E., *The Arab-Israeli War 1948*, Faber & Faber, London, 1956

CHAPTER 2, SECTION 2

— *Berlin Airlift*, HMSO, London, 1949
Charles, M., *Berlin Blockade*, Allan Wingate, London, 1959
Cole, C., *But Not in Anger*, Ian Allan, Shepperton, 1979
Collier, R., *Bridge Across the Sky*, Macmillan, London, 1978
Donovan, F., *Bridge in the Sky*, David McKay, New York, 1986
Giangreco, D.M. and Griffin, R.E., *Airbridge to Berlin*, Presidio, Novato, 1988
Jackson, R., *The Berlin Airlift*, Patrick Stephens, Wellingborough, 1988
Morris, E., *Blockade: Berlin and the Cold War*, Hamish Hamilton, London, 1973
Phillips Davison, W., *The Human Side of the Berlin Airlift*, Rand Corp, Washington, 1957
Rodrigo, R., *Berlin Airlift*, Cassell, London, 1960
Tusa, A. and J., *The Berlin Airlift*, Hodder and Stoughton, London, 1988

CHAPTER 2, SECTION 3

Bethell, N., *The Great Betrayal*, Hodder and Stoughton, London, 1984
Dorrill, S., *MI6: Fifty Years of Special Operations*, HarperCollins, London, 2000

CHAPTER 2, SECTION 4

Bruning, J.R., *Crimson Sky: The Air Battle for Korea*, Brassey's, Dulles, 2000
Davis, L., *Air War Over Korea*, Squadron/Signal, Carrollton, 1982
Davis, L., *MiG Alley*, Squadron/Signal, Carrollton, 1978
Doll, T.E., *USN/USMC Over Korea*, Squadron/Signal, Carrollton, 1988
Halliday, J. and Cumongs, B., *Korea: The Unknown War*, Penguin, London, 1990
Hallion, R.P., *The Naval Air War in Korea*, NAPC, Baltimore, 1986
Hastings, M., *The Korean War*, Michael Joseph, London, 1987
Lansdown, J.R.P., *With the Carriers in Korea*, Crécy, Manchester, 1997
Scutts, J., *Air War Over Korea*, Arms and Armour Press, London, 1982
Thompson, W., *Korea: The Air War* (Vols 1 and 2), Osprey, London, 1992

CHAPTER 2, SECTION 7

Cate, C., *The Ides of August: The Berlin Wall Crisis of 1961*, Weidenfeld and Nicolson, London, 1978
Grathwol, R.P. and Moorhus, D.M., *American Forces in Berlin: Cold War Outpost*, DoD, Washington, 1994

CHAPTER 2, SECTION 8

Geraghty, A., *BRIXMIS*, HarperCollins, London, 1996

CHAPTER 3, SECTION 4

Lee, D., *Flight From the Middle East*, HMSO, London, 1980
Corfield, F.D., *The Origins and Growth of Mau Mau*, Kenya Government, Nairobi, 1960

CHAPTER 3, SECTION 7

— *Conduct of Anti-Terrorist Operations in Malaya*, HQ Malaya, Kuala Lumpur, 1952
Barber, N., *The War of the Running Dogs: The Malayan Emergency 1948–1960*, Collins, London, 1971
Clutterbuck, R., *The Long, Long War*, Cassell, London, 1967
Henniker, M.C., *A Red Shadow over Malaya*, Blackwood, London, 1955
Majdalaney, F., *State of Emergency*, Longman Green, London, 1962
Miers, R., *Shoot to Kill*, Faber & Faber, London, 1959
Miller, R., *The Story of Malaya*, Faber & Faber, London, 1965
O'Ballance, E., *Malaya: The Communist Insurgent War*, Faber & Faber, London, 1966
Paget, J., *Counter-insurgency Campaigning*, Faber & Faber, London, 1967
Postgate, M.R., *Operation Firedog: Air Support in the Malayan Emergency, 1948–1960*, HMSO, London, 1992
Scurr, J., *The Malayan Campaign 1948–60*, Osprey, London, 1982
Short, A., *The Communist Insurrection in Malaya, 1948–1960*, Frederick Muller, London, 1975
Taber, P., *The War of the Flea*, Paladin, London, 1966

CHAPTER 4

Wynn, H., *RAF Nuclear Deterrent Forces*, HMSO, London, 1994

CHAPTER 4, SECTION 1

Allward, M., *Buccaneer*, Ian Allan, Shepperton, 1981
Brookes, A., *V-Force*, Jane's, London, 1982
Darling, K., *Avro Vulcan*, Hall Park, Milton Keynes, 1995
Chesneau, R., *Tornado IDS*, Linewrights, Ongar, 1988
Clemons, J., Delve, K. and Green, P., *English Electric Canberra*, Midland Counties, Earl Shilton, 1992
Fopp, M.A., *The Washington File*, Air Britain, Tonbridge, 1983
Foster, P. and Jackson, P., *Blackburn Buccaneer*, Hall Park, Milton Keynes, 1992
Foster, P.R., *RAF Phantom*, Ian Allan, Shepperton, 1989
Garbett, M. and Goulding, B., *Lincoln at War 1944–1966*, Ian Allan, Shepperton, 1979
Hazell, S., *Mcdonnell Douglas F-4K and F-4M*, Hall Park, Milton Keynes, 1995
Hazell, S., *Handley Page Victor*, Hall Park, Milton Keynes, 1997
Horseman, M. (ed), *Tornado in Service*, Ian Allan, Shepperton, 1984
Lake, J. (ed), *McDonnell F-4 Phantom*, Aerospace Publishing, London, 1992
Laming, T., *V-Bombers*, Patrick Stephens, Yeovil, 1997
Laming, T., *The Vulcan Story*, Silverdale Books, Enderby, 2002
Morgan, E.B., *Vickers Valiant*, Aerofax, Hinckley, 2002
Price, A., *Panavia Tornado*, Ian Allan, Shepperton, 1988
Ward, R.L., *Phantom Squadrons of the Royal Air Force and Fleet Air Arm*, Linewrights, Ongar, 1988
Wynn, H., *RAF Nuclear Deterrent Forces*, HMSO, London, 1994

CHAPTER 4, SECTION 2

— 'The RAF and Nuclear Weapons 1960–1998', in *Royal Air Force Historical Society Journal 26*, RAFHS, 2001
— 'Air Power – Anglo-American Perspectives', in *Royal Air Force Historical Society Journal 32*, RAFHS, 2004
Brookes, A., *V-Force: The History of Britain's Airborne Deterrent*, Jane's, London, 1982
Gunston, W., *Rockets and Missiles*, Salamander, London, 1979
Lamb, R., *The Macmillan Years 1957–1963*, John Murray, London, 1995
Neustadt, R.E., *Report to JFK: The Skybolt Crisis in Perspective*, Ithaca, New York, 1999
Wynn, H., *RAF Nuclear Deterrent Forces*, HMSO, London, 1994

CHAPTER 4, SECTION 3

— *Proceedings, RAFHS Seminar on the RAF and Nuclear Weapons 1960–68*, RAFHS, 2001
Arnold, L., *Britain and the H-Bomb*, MoD, London, 2001
Cathcart, B., *Test of Greatness: Britain's Struggle for the Atom Bomb*, John Murray, London, 1994
Gaddis, J.L., Gordon, P.H., May, E.R. and Rosenberg, J., *Cold War Statesmen Confront the Bomb*, OUP, Oxford, 1999
Gibson, J.N., *Nuclear Weapons of the United States*, Schiffer, Atglen, 1996
Hansen, C., *US Nuclear Weapons: The Secret History*, Orion, New York, 1988
Rhodes, R., *The Making of the Atomic Bomb*, Simon and Schuster, New York, 1986
Thomas, G. and Witts, M.M., *Ruin from the Air: The Atomic Mission to Hiroshima*, Hamish Hamilton, London, 1977
Zaloga, S.J., *Target America: The Soviet Union and the Strategic Arms Race 1945–1964*, Presidio, Novato, 1993
Zaloga, S.J., *The Kremlin's Nuclear Sword*, Smithsonian, Washington, 2002

CHAPTER 4, SECTION 4

Franks, N., *RAF Fighter Command 1936–1968*, PSL, Yeovil, 1992
Gough, J., *Watching the Skies*, HMSO, London, 1993
Rawlings, J.D.R., *Fighter Squadrons of the RAF and their Aircraft*, Macdonald, London, 1969

CHAPTER 4, SECTION 5

— *Proceedings, RAFHS Seminar on Electronic Warfare*, RAFHS, 2003
Aldrich, R.J., *The Hidden Hand: Britain, America and Cold War Secret Intelligence*, John Murray, London, 2001
Burrows, W.E., *By Any Means Necessary*, Hutchinson, London, 2002
Hardy, M.J., *The de Havilland Mosquito*, David and Charles, Newton Abbot, 1977
Jackson, R., *High Cold War: Strategic Air Reconnaissance and the Electronic Intelligence War*, PSL, Yeovil, 1998
Lashmar, P., *Spy Flights of the Cold War*, Sutton, Stroud, 1996
Miller, R.G. (ed), *Seeing Off the Bear: Anglo-American Air Power Co-operation During the Cold War*, Air Force History Program, Washington, 1995
Peebles, C., *Shadow Flights: America's Secret Air War Against the Soviet Union*, Presidio, Novato, 2000

CHAPTER 5, SECTION 1

Paget, J., *Last Post: Aden 1963–67*, Faber & Faber, London, 1969
Shagland, P., 'The Dhala Road', in *Royal Engineers' Journal*, London, 1969
Stevens, T., 'Operations in the Radfan', in *RUSI Journal*, London, 1965
Trevaskis, H., *Shades of Amber*, Hutchinson, London, 1968

CHAPTER 5, SECTION 2

Allfree, P.S., *War Lords of Oman*, Robert Hale, London, 1967
Geraghty, A., *Who Dares Wins*, Arms & Armour Press, London, 1980
Townsend, J., *Oman: The Making of the Modern State*, Croom Helm, London, 1977

CHAPTER 5, SECTION 3

Barker, A.J., *Suez, the Seven-Day War*, Weidenfeld & Nicolson, London, 1967
Beaufre, A., *The Suez Expedition 1956*, Faber & Faber, London, 1969
Bromberger, M. and S., *Secrets of Suez*, Pan Books, London, 1957
Browne, H., *Suez and Sinai*, Longman, Harlow, 1971
Cavenagh, S., *Airborne to Suez*, William Kimber, London, 1965
Childers, E., *The Road to Suez*, Macgibbon &. Kee, London, 1962
Cull, B., Nicolle, D. and Aloni, S., *Wings Over Suez*, Grub Street, London, 1996
Dayan, M., *Diary of the Sinai Campaign*, Weidenfeld & Nicolson, London, 1966
Eden, Sir A., *Full Circle: The Memoirs of Anthony Eden*, Cassell, London, 1960
Eisenhower, D.D., *Waging Peace, 1956–1961*, Heinemann, London,1966
Finer, H., *Dulles over Suez*, Heinemann, London, 1964
Fullick, R. and Powell, G., *Suez, the Double War*, Hamish Hamilton, London, 1979
Gaujac, P., *Suez 1956*, Charles-Lavauzelle, Paris, 1986
Golani, M., *Israel in Search of a War*, Sussex Academic Press, Brighton, 1998
Gorst, A. and Johnman, L., *The Suez Crisis*, Routledge, London, 1997
Henriques, R.A., *A Hundred Hours to Suez*, Collins London 1957
Jackson, R., *Suez 1956: Operation Musketeer*, Ian Allan, London, 1980
Kyle, K., *Suez*, Weidenfeld & Nicolson, London, 1991
Lloyd, S., *Suez, 1956*, Jonathan Cape, London, 1978
Lucas, W.S., *Divided we Stand: Britain, the US and the Suez Crisis*, Hodder and Stoughton, London, 1991
Mansfield, P., *Nasser*, Methuen, London, 1969
Marshall, S., *Sinai Victory: Israel's Hundred-Hour Conquest of Egypt*, Morrow, New York, 1958
Nutting, A., *No End of a Lesson: The Story of Suez*, Constable, London, 1967
O'Ballance, E., *The Sinai Campaign 1956*, Faber & Faber, London, 1959
Overndale, R., *The Origins of the Arab-Israeli Wars*, Longman, London, 1984
Robertson, T., *Crisis: The Inside Story of the Suez Conspiracy*, Hutchinson, London, 1965
Thomas, H., *The Suez Affair*, Weidenfeld & Nicolson, London, 1966

Watt, D., *Documents on the Suez Crisis, 26 July to 6 November 1956*, Royal Institute for International Affairs, London, 1957
— Parliamentary Debates, *Hansard, Vol. 558*, HMSO, London, 1956
— *Proceedings 3, Royal Air Force Historical Society*, RAFHS, London, 1988

CHAPTER 5, SECTION 4

Akehurst, J., *We Won a War: The Campaign in Dhofar 1965–1975*, Michael Russell, Salisbury, 1982
Clements, F., *Oman, the Reborn Land*, Longman, London, 1980
Jeapes, T., *SAS: Operation Oman*, William Kimber, London, 1982

CHAPTER 7, SECTION 2

Blaxland, G., *The Regiments Depart*, William Kimber, London, 1971
Dickens, P., *SAS: The Jungle Frontier*, Arms and Armour Press, London, 1983
James, Halsbury D. and Sheil-Samll, D., *The Undeclared War: The Story of the Indonesian Confrontation 1962–1966*, Leo
     Cooper, London, 1971
Mackie, J.A.C., *Konfrontasi*, Oxford University Press, Oxford, 1974

CHAPTER 7, SECTION 4

Parson, T.H., *The 1964 Army Mutinies and the Making of Modern East Africa*, Greenwood Press, London, 2003
Percox, D.A., *Britain, Kenya and the Cold War*, I.B. Tauris, London, 2004

CHAPTER 7, SECTION 5

Brent, W.A., *Rhodesian Air Force: A Brief History 1947–1980*, Freeworld Publications, Kwambonambi, 1987
Henriksen, T. and Gann, L., *The Struggle for Zimbabwe*, Praeger, New York, 1981
Hudson, M., *Triumph or Tragedy: Rhodesia to Zimbabwe*, Hamilton, London, 1981
Johnson, P. and Martin, D., *The Struggle for Zimbabwe*, Faber & Faber, London, 1981
McLaughlin, P. and Moorcraft, P., *Chimurenga! The War in Rhodesia 1965–1980*, Sygma, Marshaltown, 1982
Nesbit, R., Cowderoy, D. and Thomas, A.S., *Britain's Rebel Air Force*, Grub Street, London, 1998
Stoneman, C., *Zimbabwe's Inheritance*, St. Martin's Press, New York, 1982
Thomas, A., 'Rhodesian Air Force', *Scale Aircraft Modelling, Vol. 4/11*, Berkhamsted, 1982

CHAPTER 7, SECTION 7

Braybrook, R., *The Falklands, 1982. Battle for the Falklands (3): Air Forces*, Osprey, London, 1982
Brown, D., *The Royal Navy and the Falklands War*, Leo Cooper, London, 1987
Burden, R.A., Draper, M.I., Rough, D.A., Smith, C.R. and Wilton, D., *Falklands – The Air War*, BARG, Middlesex, 1986
Critchley, M., *Falklands: Task Force Portfolio (Pts 1 and 2)*, Maritime Books, Cornwall, 1982
English, A. and Watts, A., *Battle for the Falklands (2): Naval Forces*, Osprey, London, 1982
Ethell, J. and Price, A., *Air War South Atlantic*, Sidgwick & Jackson, London, 1983
Fowler, W., *Battle for the Falklands (1): Land Forces*, Osprey, London, 1982
Fox, R., *Eyewitness Falklands*, Methuen, London, 1982
Franks, Lord, *Falkland Islands Review (Cmnd 8787)*, HMSO, London, 1983
Frost, I., *2 Para Falklands*, Buchan & Enright, London, 1983
Godden, J., *Harrier: Ski-jump to Victory*, Brassey's, Oxford, 1983
Hastings, M. and Jenkins, S., *The Battle for the Falklands*, Pan, London, 1983
Hooper, A., *The Military and the Media*, Gower, Aldershot, 1982
Huertas, S.M., and Briasco, J.R., *Argentine Air Forces in the Falklands Conflict (Warbirds Illustrated No. 45)*, Arms and Armour
     Press, London, 1987
Middlebrook, M., *The Fight for the Malvinas*, Viking, London, 1989
Morgan, D., *Hostile Skies*, Weidenfeld & Nicolson, London, 2006
Oakley, D., *The Falklands Military Machine*, Spellmount, Tunbridge Wells, 1989
Sunday Times Insight Team, *The Falklands War*, Sphere, London, 1982

Tinker, D., *A Message from the Falklands*, Junction Books, London, 1982
Ward, N.D., *Sea Harrier over the Falklands: A Maverick at War*, Pen and Sword, London, 1992
West, N., *The Secret War for the Falklands*, Little, Brown, London, 1997
White, R., *Vulcan 607*, Bantam Press, London, 2006
Witherow, I., *The Winter War*, Quartet, London, 1982
Woodward, S., *One Hundred Days*, HarperCollins, London, 1982
— *The Falkland Islands: The Facts*, HMSO, London, 1982

CHAPTER 8, SECTION 4

Coogan, T.P., *The IRA*, Fontana, London, 1980
Darby, J., *Conflict in Northern Ireland*, London, 1976
Kelly, K., *The Longest War: Northern Ireland and the IRA*, Zed Books, London, 1982
O'Ballance, E., *Terror in Ireland*, Presidio, London, 1981
O'Brien, C.C., *State of Ireland*, Dublin, 1972
Utley, T.E., *Lessons of Ulster*, J.M. Dent & Sons, London, 1976
Warner, G., *Army Aviation in Ulster*, Colourpoint, Newtonards, 2004

CHAPTER 9, SECTION 4

— *Statement on the Defence Estimates: Britain's Defence for the 90s*, HMSO, London, 1991
Allen, C., *Thunder and Lightning: The RAF in the Gulf*, HMSO, London, 1991
Atkinson, R., *Crusade: The Untold Story of the Persian Gulf War*, Houghton Mifflin, New York, 1993
Bailey, R., *Support-Save-Supply: Hercules Operations in the Gulf War*, Airlife, Shrewsbury, 1992
de la Billière, P., *Storm Command*, HarperCollins, London, 1992
Black, I., *Desert Fist*, Airlife, Shrewsbury, 1991
Black, I., *Desert Air Force*, Osprey, London, 1992
Blackwell, J., *Thunder in the Desert: The Strategy and Tactics of the Persian Gulf War*, Bantam, New York, 1992
Boswell, R., *Weapons Free: The Story of a Gulf War Helicopter Pilot*, Crécy, Manchester, 1998
Braybrook, R., *Air Power: The Coalition and Iraqi Air Forces (Desert Storm Special 2)*, Osprey, London, 1991
Drendel, L., *Air War Desert Storm*, Squadron/Signal Publications, Carrollton, 1991
Foster, E. and Hollis, R., *War in the Gulf: Sovereignty, Oil and Security*, RUSI, London, 1991
Gunston, W., Hogg, I. and Richardson, D., *High Tech Weapons of the Gulf War*, Salamander, London, 1991
Jefford, C.G. (ed), Journal 32 Royal Air Force Historical Society, Northmoor, 2004
LaBarge, W.H., *Desert Voices: Personal Testimony from Gulf War Heroes*, Harper, New York, 1991
March, P.R., *Desert Warpaint*, Osprey, London, 1992
March, P.R. (ed), *Air War in the Gulf (RAF Yearbook Special)*, IAT Publishing, Fairford, 1991
Mason, P., *Pablo's War*, Bloomsbury, London, 1992
Micheletti, E., *Air War over the Gulf (Europa Militaria No. 8)*, Windrow and Greene, London, 1991
Morse, S. (ed), *Gulf War Debrief*, Aerospace Publishing, London, 1991
Peters, J. and Nichol, J., *Tornado Down*, Michael Joseph, London, 1992
Rentoul, I. and Wakeford, T., *Gulf War British Air Arms*, Concord, Hong Kong, 1991
Rosenkranz, K., *Vipers in the Storm*, McGraw Hill, New York, 1991
Smallwood, W.L., *Warthog: Flying the A-10 in the Gulf War*, Brassey's, Dulles, 1993
Smallwood, W.L., *Strike Eagle: Flying the F-15E in the Gulf War*, Brassey's, Dulles, 1994
Timmerman, K.R., *The Death Lobby: How the West Armed Iraq*, Bantam, London, 1992
Trevan, T., *Saddam's Secrets: The Hunt for Iraq's Hidden Weapons*, HarperCollins, London, 1999

GENERAL

Armitage, M., *The Royal Air Force*, Arms and Armour Press, London, 1993

Ashworth, C., *RAF Coastal Command 1936–1969*, PSL, Yeovil, 1992

Ashworth, C., *RAF Bomber Command 1936–1968*, PSL, Yeovil, 1995

Beaver, P., *Encyclopaedia of the Fleet Air Arm*, PSL, Wellingborough, 1987

Bedford, R.G., *RAF Rotors*, SFB Publications, Huntingdon, 1996

Congdon, P., *Per Ardua ad Astra: A Handbook of the Royal Air Force*, Airlife, Shrewsbury, 1987

Critchley, M., *British Warships and Auxiliaries*, Maritime Books, Liskeard, 1983

Delve, K., *The Source Book of the RAF*, Airlife, Shrewsbury, 1994

Farrar-Hockley, A., *The Army in the Air: The History of the Army Air Corps*, Alan Sutton Publishing, Stroud, 1994

Flintham, V., *Air Wars and Aircraft: A Detailed Record of Air Combat, 1945 to the Present*, Arms and Armour Press, London, 1989

Flintham, V., *Aircraft in British Military Service*, Airlife, Shrewsbury, 1998

Flintham, V. and Thomas, A., *Combat Codes*, Pen and Sword, Barnsley, 2008

Franks, N., *RAF Fighter Command 1936–1968*, PSL, Yeovil, 1992

Gardner, R. and Longstaff, R., *British Service Helicopters: A Pictorial History*, Hale, London, 1985

Halley, J.J., *Squadrons of the Royal Air Force*, Air-Britain, Tonbridge, 1988

Jefford, C.G., *RAF Squadrons*, Airlife, Shrewsbury, 1988, 2001

Lee, D., *Eastward: A History of the Royal Air Force in the Far East 1945–1972*, HMSO, London, 1984

Lee, D., *Wings in the Sun: A History of the Royal Air Force in the Mediterranean 1945–1986*, HMSO, London, 1989

March, P.R., *Military Aircraft Markings*, Ian Allan, London, published annually

Marriot, L., *Royal Navy Aircraft Carriers 1945–1990*, Ian Allan, Shepperton, 1985

Mason, F.K., *The British Bomber*, Putnam, London, 1994

Mason, F.K., *The British Fighter*, Putnam, London, 1992

Moyes, P., *Bomber Squadrons of the RAF*, Macdonald, London, 1964

Pearcey, A., *Lend-Lease Aircraft in World War II*, Airlife, Shrewsbury, 1996

Rawlings, J.D.R., *Fighter Squadrons of the RAF*, Macdonald, London, 1969

Rawlings, J.D.R., *Coastal, Support and Special squadrons of the RAF*, Jane's, London, 1982

Sturtivant, R., *Squadrons of the Fleet Air Arm*, Air-Britain, Tonbridge, 1984, 1996

Sturtivant, R., Hamlin, J. and Halley, J.J., *Royal Air Force Flying Training and Support Units Since 1912*, Air-Britain, Tonbridge, 1997, 2007

Thetford, O., *Aircraft of the Royal Air Force since 1918*, Putnam, London, 1957, 1958, 1962, 1968, 1971, 1976, 1979, 1988, 1995

Thetford, O., *British Naval Aircraft 1912–1958*, Putnam, London, 1958

various authors *Action Stations* (Vols 1–10 and Overseas), PSL, Cambridge

various compilers *RAF Aircraft* (Volumes in serial ranges), Air-Britain, Tonbridge

Wansborough-White, G., *Names With Wings*, Airlife, Shrewsbury, 1995

The Putnam series on specific aircraft manufacturers is also strongly recommended. It includes detailed volumes on the following: Airspeed, Armstrong Whitworth, Avro, Blackburn, Bristol, de Havilland, English Electric, Fairey, General Dynamics, Gloster, Handley Page, Hawker, Lockheed, McDonnell Douglas, Miles, Saunders and Saro, Shorts, Supermarine, Vickers and Westland.